REMEMBERING
THE UNIVERSITY OF CHICAGO

1891-1991

A CENTENNIAL PUBLICATION OF
The University of Chicago Press

Remembering
THE
UNIVERSITY
OF
CHICAGO

Teachers, Scientists, and Scholars

EDITED BY EDWARD SHILS

THE
UNIVERSITY
OF
CHICAGO
PRESS

Chicago and London

The University of Chicago Press, Chicago 60637
The University of Chicago Press, Ltd., London
© 1991 by The University of Chicago
All rights reserved. Published 1991
Printed in the United States of America
00 99 98 97 96 95 94 93 92 91   5 4 3 2 1

ISBN (cloth): 0-226-75335-2

Publication of this book was assisted by a subvention from Near North
Insurance Brokerage, Inc., in recognition of the influence of great
teachers at the University of Chicago and in celebration of the institution's
centennial. The University of Chicago Press gratefully acknowledges
Near North's generosity.

Library of Congress Cataloging-in-Publication Data

Remembering the University of Chicago : teachers, scientists, and
scholars / edited by Edward Shils.
p.   cm.
1. University of Chicago—Faculty—Biography.   2. University of
Chicago—History.   I. Shils, Edward Albert, 1911–
LD920.R46   1991
378.773'11—dc20   91-16741

∞ The paper used in this publication meets
the minimum requirements of the American National
Standard for Information Sciences—Permanence of
Paper for Printed Library Materials, ANSI Z39.48-1984.

CONTENTS

v

FOREWORD

E D W A R D   S H I L S

*"Let us now praise famous men . . . leaders
of their people by their counsels, and by their
knowledge of learning . . . for the people, wise and
eloquent in their instruction," said Jesus,
son of Sirach.*
(Eccles. 44)

· I ·

REMEMBERING THE UNIVERSITY OF CHICAGO is intended to recall from memory the second and third generation of teachers of this University. These two generations extended roughly from about the end of the First World War into the 1970s; some of them were still active in the 1980s. This should not be interpreted as a failure to appreciate the merits of the first generation who taught in the University from its beginning up to the First World War. That generation comprised numerous great scientists and scholars. Those men and women—very few of the latter—of the first generation were the figures who, already by the turn of the century, were in process of bringing renown to the University of Chicago. William James wrote in 1902, "Chicago University has during the past six months given birth to the fruit of its ten years gestation under John Dewey. The result is wonderful—a *real school* and *real thought.* Important thought, too! Did you ever hear of such a city or such a university? Here we have thought, but no school. At Yale, a school, but no thought. Chicago has both." (*Letters of William James,* edited by Henry James, [London: Longmans, Green, 1926,] 2: 201, 202.) Thus, it was very early that "Chicago schools" began to be spoken about in the land. This was evidence of powerful didactic and exemplary achievements in teaching and research. They were a great generation: in addition to John Dewey, there were George E. Hale, James H. Breasted, George Herbert Mead, T. C. Chamberlain, Paul Shorey, Albert

Michelson, Eliakim Hastings Moore, Gilbert Bliss, William I. Thomas, Thorstein Veblen, Carl D. Buck, Jacques Loeb, Leonard Bloomfield, et al.

Harper's first recruits did not have an easy time of it. Harper was an extraordinary individual with great talents and virtues but he was also an enthusiast and, in the style of American university and college presidents of the nineteenth and early twentieth centuries, quite capable of making appointments without consulting the future colleagues of the newly appointed persons. The University, conceived by Harper on a grand scale, never had enough money to pay for all the things Harper wanted the University to do. These pioneers were living the life of frontiersmen, uncertain about the durability of their academic settlement. They were also isolated from the rest of the country in a venture which had no past. They had nothing to look back on to give them assurance for the future. They were also working in isolation from each other. Departments were very small and not all the members of a department were of the first class. Persons of the first class were very rare throughout the country; many of those whom Harper tried to win for the University did not wish to leave a settled institution for an alien and uncouth part of the country to join an institution without a secure future. Furthermore, Harper had a great gift for the selection of geniuses but below that level he was rather fallible. There were some queer ducks appointed by Harper to work with the small number of already or imminently distinguished persons.

Nevertheless, it was in the quarter of a century from the foundation of the University that it made its great name. This was done against obstacles. Financial resources were always short and Harper's death, in 1906, was followed by selection of a new president from within the existing staff. For nearly seventeen years the University was under Harry Pratt Judson, a hard master, unsympathetic and frugal, whose chief concern was to keep the University in a state of solvency. Despite these discouraging conditions, the University made its way.

By the beginning of the 1920s, the atmosphere was more propitious. The new president, Ernest Burton, was a gentle scholar of the New Testament but he was one who knew enough to give men of great talent a free hand to exercise those talents. Burton has not often been credited with a major role in the transformation of the University of Chicago, but it was in his brief presidency that the University grew from an institution with a small number of persons of great intellectual gifts to a university in which the leading scholars and scientists had an encouraging environment in which to work. The generation which came to the fore in the 1920s could carry on in an institution of proven excellence. The first generation, under difficult circumstances, had created an institution of which its new members could be proud; departments acquired intellectual traditions which fortified those who joined them. There were also enough outstanding men and women to set a standard and to compel exertion to live up to it.

· II ·

The University of Chicago from its first decade took a place in the forefront of the institutions which produced the new generation of university teachers who were also outstanding scientists and scholars. This was partly because it originally set out to do exactly that, while the other, older universities came to such objectives relatively slowly. The last decade of the nineteenth and the first two decades of the twentieth centuries were decades of expansion and with an attendant increase in the demand for university teaching and scientists. This was a most happy condition for the University of Chicago.

By the end of the First World War, the University of Chicago had many competitors for its foremost position. This was the time when American universities really came into their own. They were no longer so dependent on the German universities—although their separateness from their Germanic lineage should not be overstated. This could not have happened without an enhanced degree of intellectual self-reliance. This self-reliance was a product of acknowledged achievement over the past quarter of a century.

The excellent graduate students who were finding and refining their own talents through their studies in the main universities were contributing to the creation of an atmosphere of intense intellectual concentration and exertion. Their efforts gave pleasure to their teachers and stimulated them. The University of Chicago in the approximately six decades in which the persons written about in this book were active was a wonderfully exhilarating place. Many who were here at the University in those years and who then went to other universities have recalled it as a place of high intellectual intensity. It was a place where the world, and the intellectual activities which focused on it, were taken with extraordinary seriousness. There was no lightheartedness, no frivolity about it. Christopher Driver, a British journalist, who visited the University of Chicago towards the end of the period dealt with in this book—he came with the intention of writing a book on *The University Explosion*—called the University of Chicago "a very German place." What he meant was that intellectual *gravitas* was the distinctive mark of the University of Chicago. He meant that, at the University of Chicago, scholarly and scientific work was thought of by students and teachers alike not simply as a means of gaining a livelihood or as an agreeable setting for a life of ease and pleasure, but as a matter of the gravest moment. Even now, when frivolous and antinomian attitudes towards learning and discovery have become common in universities in the United States and where students often look on their studies and research as no more than a means of becoming certified for a lucrative or comfortable professional career, that is not the way it is in the University of Chicago. Clough's opening line of his unnamed poem: "Say not the struggle naught availeth, the labour and the wounds are vain" (*The Poems of Arthur Hugh Clough,* [Oxford: The Clarendon Press, 1951], p 63), could as well have served as the motto of the teachers of the University of Chicago and their students. They all thought that the struggle to acquire better knowledge than they already possessed was worth the labor and the wounds. They all accepted that thinking, investigation, teaching, and study were a struggle, a struggle for the achievement of an invaluable objective.

As will be evident from the memoirs which follow, the professors of the University of Chicago were a very various lot, in temperament, in politics, religion, and ethnic origin. Some—very few—came from wealthy families, some—a larger number—came from families of very modest standing; most of them came from hard-working families in the learned professions and the mercantile lower middle class, some came from farmers' families. But whatever their origins, tempers, and affections, they all cared for their subjects. They were not above spending seven days a week on their work, week in week out, year in year out. They were not working for promotions, although they usually welcomed them when they came. Permanence of tenure was rarely a consideration for them. They did not fear that if they did not publish they would perish. They investigated what appeared to them to be of the utmost importance; they published because that is what scholars and scientists did when they discovered what they thought was true and important. They wanted to know what their colleagues thought about their ideas. They wanted to persuade their colleagues on the basis of careful observations, made as rigorously as they could be, and as their reason compelled.

I think that it is fair to say that the teachers of the University of Chicago would not have been as good and as devoted to their teaching and research as most of them were in the more than half a century covered by these memoirs if the students whom they taught were not as good as they were. By "good" I do not mean being uniformly brilliant and original. What I mean is their capacity for hard and persistent work.

Several decades ago, Denis Brogan in a conversation with me and several friends about British and American university students said that British undergraduates were better than American undergraduates because they were better educated in their secondary schools. But at the level of the graduate students, the Americans were better than their British coevals because they worked harder and because graduate training was better organized in the United States. I think that there was much sense in what he said but he omitted an important element; he failed to observe that the American graduate students were better served by their teachers and supervisors in the American universities because the students themselves were more demanding towards their teachers. When students are more demanding intellectually, teachers are more responsive intellectually to the expectations of their students. Those matters are not explicitly discussed in any of the memoirs that follow because such things are not spoken of much, if at all, among the teachers of the University of Chicago. From my own observation I have concluded that in at least the fields I know about, departing from the University of Chicago for some other American university, in a large fraction of the cases known to me, was followed by a decline in the quality of intellectual achievement of the person in question. I attribute this decline to the absence of our particular type of serious graduate students. (I am not sure that this applies to the effect of undergraduate students on their teachers, although it certainly was the case when I knew undergraduates at the University of Chicago in the 1930s and 1940s.)

· III ·

Persons who have taught at the University of Chicago and then gone to teach elsewhere have frequently spoken of the high esprit de corps of the University as one of the features which they have missed most in the other institutions where they took up appointments on their departure from the University of Chicago.

Very few of the persons told about in this book ever seemed to concern themselves about the University as a whole. When they tell or told of their satisfaction with the University, it was usually as having done something pleasing or beneficial to themselves. They practically never express concern for the intellectual well-being or the reputation of the University. They seldom express any interest in other departments except when they refer to their gratifying collaboration with one or more of the members of an adjacent department. Yet, I remember that in 1968, when a small number of students in a state of emotional possession, interrupted the working of the University, the teachers of the University rallied nearly unanimously to affirm their appreciation of the University and their devotion to it.

Now it might well be that this topic was not written about because I did not ask the authors to write about it. Nevertheless, if their subjects had spoken about it often, they might have noticed it and mentioned it.

This has caused me some reflection. Am I to conclude that the scholars and scientists who are remembered in this volume were not really good citizens of the University and did not think about the University except as a setting of their own work? There can be no doubt about their preoccupation with their own research and their teaching and training of young persons. This is shown by the fact that many of the memoirs are largely accounts in summary and in simplified form of the scientific achievements of their subjects; that is the way in which their students and colleagues saw them and that is the way in which they presumably thought about themselves and their colleagues. It has been their research and their teaching of their own fields that they have thought about and that is the way in which they are portrayed by their colleagues or pupils who write about them here.

When the administration is spoken about, it is usually adversarially, about contending with it to get something: pleased when granted, dissatisfied when refused.

Yet, it is hard to think about these persons as being quite indifferent to the rest of the University, uninterested in its quality, unmoved by its embrace of their being. It is, of course, possible that their attachment was so deep that it seldom came to the level of consciousness. Can it be that academic work has now become so specialized that interest is concentrated entirely on one's own field of work and the department in which it mainly falls?

It is possible that the German system of the nineteenth and early twentieth centuries was better than the present American system. In Germany all professors in a faculty, i.e., a major division of the university very roughly like the divisions of the University of Chicago, had a voice in the proposal that any particular scientist or scholar be appointed, even though that candidate was not in the same discipline. Thus, a professor of modern European history would have had a voice in the appointment of a professor whose field was Central Asian languages, and so on. A professor was thus forced to take some responsibility for decisions outside his own discipline. There were complaints about this arrangement because, so its critics charged, it permitted persons who were not qualified to participate in decisions of academic appointments. Yet, the German system worked pretty well. It could however work only when the faculties were small and professors made up most of the teaching staff. Once the number of *ausserplanmäßige* professorships increased, ditto the number of *Privatdozenten* and *Assistenten,* the old practice could no longer be effective. In the United States, where many departments have as many teachers as whole faculties had in German universities a century ago, it is utterly impracticable to practice the old German system. What has been lost is a strong sense of responsibility for the whole university. Yet, under these unfavorable conditions of specialization and of departmental size, professors at the University of Chicago do think about their University. Perhaps this is because of the system of university government designed by Laird Bell nearly a half century ago. The Council of the Senate, meeting monthly, and the Committee of the Council of the Senate, meeting biweekly, with detailed minutes circulated to all persons with an academic appointment in the University, fortifies the esprit de corps against the erosions of specialization and size.

· IV ·

Another factor of the intellectual vitality of the University of Chicago in those decades, in addition to the native talent of its carefully selected teachers and the deadly seriousness of both teachers and students about the importance of thinking and discovering, was the animation which the consciousness of freedom brought with it. In the period just after the First World War, there was a flurry of hostility to radicalism; there was another in the first half of the 1930s. The latter subsided and then came to life again in the late 1940s and early 1950s. These were times when rude politicians, silly journalists, and demagogic priests were seeking to advance their respective interests at the cost of universities; businessmen sometimes joined them. The University of Chicago was as safe from storms as a sheltered inland sea.

The University of Chicago was fortunate in its strong-willed teaching staff, in its devoted trustees, and not least in its brave and unswervingly determined presidents, to allow no truckling to vulgar opinion. The University of Chicago was also freer than most American universities from the simpleminded fellow-travelers who began to affect the academic world from the late 1920s onward. The University of Chicago had nothing to hide, no convictions which cowardly academics thought they must disguise or deny. It had a good conscience because it was not politicized.

This consciousness of being free and of being protected in that freedom by one's elders and those in authority helped to maintain the University in a state of serenity.

It is not that teachers at the University of Chicago were indifferent to their civil obligations. They did have political views but their politics did not affect the honesty of their teaching or their research. It will be noticed that in the forty-odd memoirs which follow, very few of their authors refer, and then only marginally, to the political concerns of their subjects. These few exceptions were also great scientists; two of them were acknowledged by the award of the Nobel Prize. It surely cannot be said that their political views had any effect on their concentration of their mind on scientific problems or in any way influenced the substance and scale of their discoveries.

If there were any relationship between political attitudes and their scholarly studies, it was usually the other way around. Let me cite an example.

Not many months ago, I entertained some distinguished economists at dinner in my house at Cambridge. One of them had been awarded a Nobel Prize in economics about a decade ago, the other was a leading American historian of technological innovation. For some reason, the outlook of the "Chicago school" came into the discussion. The wife of one of the economists, herself a highly intelligent person and well abreast of the situation in economics, remonstrated with me when I said that Milton Friedman, whom I have known since 1933, was one of the most rational, least prejudiced men I had ever known. This did not satisfy her. The American economic historian, himself rather a collectivistic sort of liberal, said, "Milton Friedman does have a strong political standpoint and above all strong views about economic policy but it is a standpoint rigorously drawn from his economic analysis. It is not the other way around." I do no more than paraphrase this bit of our discussion but my guest's formulation told a great deal about the atmosphere of the University of Chicago in the decades when many universities were highly politicized, just as many still are. It also shows that this intellectual integrity is appreciated outside the University.

That was a great boon. It has continued to be a boon to the University of Chicago at a time when such a situation is not as common in American universities as it used to be. Still, it is better here in this regard than it is nearly everywhere else on the American academic scene. The mind has been left free for study and research, for scrupulous teaching and thinking. This freedom has always been here at the University of Chicago and it has been used, not for political agitation—although we have had a handful of political agitators and politicians—but for the pursuit of knowledge with full fervor and with only the limitations of our own intellectual powers.

· V ·

The memoirs of which this book is made up are about teachers of the period of about a half century, between, roughly, 1920 and the 1970s. It is confined to the time between those two very approximate terminal dates not because before 1920 the University of Chicago did not have on its staff great scientists and scholars who were among the greatest of their time. There were numerous such figures in the first quarter of a century of the life of the University; it is indeed those great figures who laid down the tradition which was reproduced and amplified by those who are written about here. They are unfortunately not remembered in this volume. Nor has the closing date, which is very approximate, been decided on because there are no distinguished scholars now alive in the University of Chicago. I cite, for example, only Stephen Stigler, Richard Posner, Gary Becker, James Coleman, A. K. Ramanujan, Robert Lucas, Richard Epstein, and Erica Reiner among others who are well known to me. These persons are excluded because, happily, they are very much alive and at the height of their powers. There are other persons whose research and teaching at this University added greatly to its quality and who are now active at other universities. They too have to be excluded on the same grounds. I mention only illustratively Thorkild Jacobsen and Stanley Tambiah.

It is for other reasons that this book is confined to those who flourished between 1920 and the 1970s. The reason for the absences of figures of the great generation which dominated the intellectual life of the University before 1920 is simply that I could not find any persons now alive who knew them well even as students, and there is probably none left who knew them as colleagues. The memoirs of which this book is made are the recollections of persons by students or colleagues who knew them personally. It was in fact very difficult to find persons who knew personally and could write well about those whose careers at the University of Chicago were largely in the 1920s and early 1930s. I have not been able to find authors who could write from personal experience about George Sherburn, John Manley, Edith Rickert, Archer Taylor, Edward Sapir, Anton Carlson, J. A. O.

Larsen, Edith and Grace Abbott, Sophonisba Breckinridge, and others no less worthy of being remembered. The closing terminal date is perhaps less rigorously observed and for different reasons.

The closing date falls well short of 1991. That was necessary in order to avoid slighting those whom I might have excluded, when some of their coeval colleagues were included. I did not wish, either, to give rise to a chorus of suggestions about candidates for inclusion made by chagrined admirers. No present or recent members of the University have been included with one class of exception. I have included among the persons still living only those who had been awarded the Nobel Prize for their work in scientific research and in economic analysis and whose merits are therefore incontrovertible. I have also included Mr. Edward Levi whose importance in the history of the University of Chicago for more than half of the period in question cannot be disputed by anyone at all familiar with this University.

But even within the limits which I have set for myself in the determination of who among the dead should be included, it has been impossible to bring all the desired members of the University into the purview of this book. It will be readily observed that there are notable omissions, even of persons about whose merits there can be no doubt and whom I wished to include in the volume. Those omissions do not result from my ignorance or indifference or my lack of appreciation of their high distinction. In at least two cases I could not find anyone at all who was willing to write; in one case, the person was awarded the Nobel Prize only a few days before I sent this book to the publisher; another Nobel laureate had to be omitted because I could find no one able and willing to write about him. There are at least a dozen persons—and not only among the Nobel laureates— whom I would have liked very much to have among those remembered here. But the readers of this book will surely know what university professors are like when it comes to accepting responsibilities outside their teaching and research. Some whom I have invited were unwilling to contribute. Others have promised but for one reason or another failed to produce their promised memoirs. Some referred me to others who were, they said, better qualified than themselves. In some cases, I was passed from one invited author to another and in the end nothing came of the invitations.

The person who was invited to write about Harry Johnson was sent four letters and replied to none. In the end I had to adapt a memoir which I wrote of him on the occasion of his death. In another case, a very distinguished member of the University who was asked to write his recollections of another great figure in the history of his department—one of the most outstanding in the University—rudely refused and then was angry that I did not persist in trying to coax him. Eager acceptance of my invitation turned out in several cases to produce no memoirs.

One major cause of regrettable omissions from this volume is my own limited knowledge. Although I have been a member of the University of Chicago for nearly sixty years and have known personally many of its best scholars and scientists, I have not known them all. I have tried to do justice to the eminences of the divisions of the biological and physical sciences but my knowledge of their members was scantier by far than it was of persons in the divisions of the social sciences and of the humanities, in the law and divinity schools and the School of Social Service Administration. To find contributors who could write satisfactorily about members of the divisions of biological and physical sciences of the University was difficult for me, and those to whom I turned for advice about subjects and authors of the memoirs tried to help me but sometimes their suggestions ran up against replies to my invitations which told me that they had not known the persons in question, or had seen them once and never exchanged a word with them, etc.

Whereas all the contributors of memoirs of persons from the divisions of the social sciences and the humanities are known to me personally, as were the subjects of their memoirs, the same is not true of those from the other parts of the University. There I have had to rely on accident and advice and neither of these has been sufficient to overcome the handicap of my deficient knowledge at firsthand. I hope that readers who are disappointed by the absence from the book of teachers and colleagues to whom they feel intellectually indebted and whom they recall with pleasure will bear in mind that willing writers of memoirs cannot be created by an editor's wish and that even where they exist and give assurances of the will to recall their teachers or colleagues, their will is not always strong enough to carry through to completion. And even among those with a strong enough will to fulfil their promise the results are not always what they were invited to write about. In my letter of invitation I requested that ". . . it should be a brief appreciation of the intellectual distinction of the person and above all, it should give a personal portrait, preferably in the form of reminiscences of conversations with that person or observations of the person in the classroom or seminar, in the laboratory and in the library. . . ." The results were in some cases admirable summaries of the scientific achievements, replete with precise footnotes and long bibliographies.

A final word of self-exculpation for my authorship of four memoirs in the total of forty-seven. That is too many. It was originally my intention to write only about Robert Park since I am probably the only person still living who knew him at firsthand, who also has studied his works and who was willing to write about him. In the end I have also written about Robert Hutchins, Harry Johnson, and Ernest Burgess. In the case of Hutchins, the person who in all the world was the best qualified to write about him, decided, despite my repeated requests, that he had been too close to him to write a memoir. Since I could not omit Hutchins, whom I knew slightly but probably a little better than anyone else still alive and ready to write, I had to assume that task myself. (I should add that in two cases members of this University asserted that they were "too close" or "owed too much" to the person whom they were invited to write about. In one case, I was fortunate to be able to avoid the consequences of ingratitude and could find a very good replacement. In the other case, I could find no substitute and so an extremely distinguished scholar has had to be omitted.) I have already explained the reason for my presence as the author of the memoir on Harry Johnson. My authorship of the memoir on Ernest Burgess was likewise *faute de mieux*. Four memoirs by one author are too many but there was no alternative except to omit persons who very clearly had to be included.

These are some of the obstacles which I have encountered in preparing this volume. I relate them here for readers who are sorry that one of their favorite teachers or colleagues has not been included, in the hope that they will understand why this had happened.

· VI ·

I undertook to prepare this book as a labor of love for the University of Chicago and out of admiration for some of its great scientists and scholars from whom I have learned and whose presence in the University made it, in my time, into one of the closest approximations to the idea of the university as propounded by Wilhelm von Humboldt in the first decade of the nineteenth century. For the reasons given above, and others, the volume is not all that I would have liked it to be.

Nevertheless, when I reread all the memoirs at least for the third time in most cases, in others for the fourth or fifth time, each of the memoirs separately, and all of them together and consecutively for a final editorial recension, I experienced once more the marvelous sensation of being a member of a great university. I think that in nearly all of the memoirs in this book, the reader will come into the presence of the pursuit of truth in teaching and research. Some of the memoirs dwell more on teaching, some dwell more on research, some dwell on both, some do little more than summarize in chronological sequence the main results of the research which the subjects did. With all these insufficiencies, however, I think that readers of this book will find themselves in the presence of a great period in the history of the University of Chicago, a great spiritual corporation encompassing many diverse ends and functions, the product of many diverse and striking individualities but all of them bound together into a single intellectual society in which the value of truth and the virtue of its pursuit and possession have been at the very center.

May its second century live up to the standard set by its first!

1 January 1991

Remembering

The University of Chicago

1

ERNEST W. BURGESS

1 8 8 6 – 1 9 6 6

E D W A R D   S H I L S

CYNTHIA COHEN was an undergraduate in sociology in the first half of the 1930s. She was a very good young woman, a little on the fleshy side, very eager to learn sociology, and she had something like a crush on Professor Burgess, who at that time was under fifty but who, when we were in our early twenties, seemed, like any person over thirty-five, rather old. One day in a course on the family, to which undergraduates as well as graduate students were admitted, Miss Cohen asked Professor Burgess how one would define "love." Professor Burgess, small, somewhat pale, already silver-haired, very gentle in bearing, and not given to excesses in speech, tried to answer. He spoke in a soft, low voice, almost bell-like—he sounded a bit like the bells of the sunken cathedral; when his voice became louder, it sounded as if it contained a sob. He wished to answer Miss Cohen's question but it was difficult. He said, "Love is . . . ," then he gulped and began again, after a moment of silence, "Love is . . . ," and he gulped again. This went on for several more beginnings of "Love is . . ." with several more gulps and several more moments of silence. Finally, the smile of a besieged person who hears the drums of a relief column came on his face and he answered the question by saying, "Herbert Spencer said, 'Love is . . .'," whatever it was that Herbert Spencer said it was. Professor Burgess was not a man to evade responsibility but love was a bit beyond his depth. He always gave the impression of being an aged, very well brought up boy. He was extremely reticent, deferential to this elders, considerate to his coevals, and remotely kind to his juniors. If Miss Cohen had a crush on him, he was undoubtedly quite unaware of it. He was certainly the last man in the world to encourage a young woman to have a crush on him. He was not that sort of a man at all.

3

· I ·

The only entanglement Ernest Burgess sought was entanglement with sociology. There were probably only two persons in the world to whom he was unqualifiedly devoted, his sister Roberta, a good, quiet spinster who was as gentle as he was and who looked after him, and Robert Park, in whom he found a complementary spirit. He did not have to seek his sister; she was always present to him. He did not have to seek Park; once they were housed in the same office, Park could not be avoided. Park was as nosy as a bear, he looked into everything, was never timid, loved to prowl the streets of big cities all over the world and then to talk about it to Burgess. Although Park read a very great deal, he was constantly impelled to stand up, to walk about, to start a conversation with anyone at hand, to ask questions, to find out what that person was doing; he was just as ready to say what was on his mind. Burgess was almost the opposite; he could sit still for hours on end. Burgess, like Park, was indefatigable. But whereas Park did not find it easy to sit still, Burgess was capable of working steadily in his room at the University throughout the day and into the night. Once, when his assistant towards the end of the 1930s, after a long morning's work, urged him, in the early afternoon, to take off time for lunch and was disregarded, the young man remonstrated by saying, "You must eat something." Burgess replied with characteristic simplicity, "No. I don't have to."

Park and Burgess were coupled with each other not just in the minds of sociologists of several decades as the co-authors of what was for many years the best textbook and the main theoretical treatise of sociology in the United States. The book was begun by Burgess as the syllabus of an introductory course he had been requested to teach when he first was appointed to a junior post at the University of Chicago. Since Park and Burgess shared a room in the east tower of Harper Memorial Library, whatever Burgess did attracted Park's interest; whatever Park did or thought he compelled Burgess to listen to it. Burgess's original syllabus became the famous "green Bible," the *Introduction to the Science of Sociology.*

· II ·

Burgess was a Canadian by origin but he was raised in the United States with the good manners and dutifulness which were imprinted on him by life in a small town and by a closely knit family and the respectability which was common in the United States at that time. He was an undergraduate in a small, Midwest college and came to the University of Chicago to study for the doctorate in sociology. He received it in 1913 and then taught in several

ERNEST W. BURGESS, about 1950

Midwest universities until 1919, when he was appointed to the department of sociology at the University of Chicago.

Park, in contrast with Burgess, came to the University of Chicago with a very different set of experiences behind him. Unlike Burgess, whose entire adult life was spent in teaching and studying in universities, who had not traveled widely, who knew only small towns in Ontario and university towns in the Midwest of the United States, and whose entire experience of a metropolis was confined to Chicago, Park had been a journalist in a number of large cities in the United States, had lived in Germany for about four years, had studied under John Dewey, William James, Georg Simmel, and Wilhelm Windelband at Harvard and the Universities of Michigan, Berlin, Heidelberg, and Strasburg, had lived in the "deep South," and had occupied himself with conditions in the Belgian Congo.

The two men were also very different in temperament and culture. Park, who was at ease with everyone, had no place for small talk when the world around him was so stimulating to his imagination; his literary and philosophical culture was immense. "The world was his oyster." Burgess was probably at ease only with his sister and with Park. Even with students, who were timidly deferential to him, he was as ill at ease as they were. But with Park it was a different matter. He knew how to cope with Park's outbursts and sallies, with Park's sternly held and strongly expressed opinions. He often smiled at Park's animadversions.

· III ·

Although they were very different in character and ultimately in the kinds of research which they did and encouraged, they got on extraordinarily well. Burgess was much more interested in the traditional subjects of American and European social reformers: the strains on family life in large cities, desertion, divorce, drunkenness, poverty, juvenile delinquency, and adult criminality. Burgess associated closely with social workers and reformers of the courts who dealt with families and adolescents, and he shared their views. Burgess continued the tradition established in the department of sociology by Charles Henderson, a clergyman who was appointed dean of the University of Chicago Chapel but who accepted the deanship only on condition that he be allowed to teach sociology—a subject almost unknown to him. He thought that sociology was necessary for social reform. Henderson was intensely interested in the "social problems" of the working classes of the great cities. Burgess had many of Henderson's interests and moral beliefs but he was more exigent and imaginative as a sociologist and had greater intellectual power.

Chicago was full of the problems of any large city at the end of the nine-teenth century; being one of the largest, its problems were more severe. It was full of immigrants, mainly from rural societies. Its condition was aggra-vated by the fact that its immigrants were not natives; they came almost entirely from Europe, mainly Eastern and Southern Europe. To all the diffi-culties of countrymen settling in cities, they added ignorance of the domi-nant language, and remoteness from its customs. Xenophobia from the native population and towards each other added to their difficulties. They were mostly semi-skilled and unskilled industrial workers. They came to the United States with little or no savings and their earnings were low. To this, many of them added improvidence. They were accordingly nearly all impoverished, they lived in neglected buildings. They had difficulties with their children, their children had many difficulties with them and often ran afoul of the law. Max Weber, when he visited Chicago in 1904, described it as resembling a human body with the skin removed.

These were the facts which sociologists like Henderson and Burgess, in his early years, wanted to learn about and to describe with meticulous at-tention to detail and with the use of what published or unpublished statis-tical information was already available. Henderson never did any fieldwork, i.e., direct observation. He depended on published reports and what infor-mation could be obtained from others. He and his pupils gathered from social workers, magistrates, residents in settlement houses, probation offi-cers, judges, physicians and psychiatrists, municipal officials, housing in-spectors, and others what they could offer from their own experience. Burgess continued along these lines but went further by adding to his sources the compilation of new statistics and the material gathered by his students through interviews and participant observation.

Burgess did not roam the streets like Park, he did not have the strong desire to see, question, or interview the persons whose conduct he stud-ied. He preferred to work on these subjects in his study from reports of persons who did interview them; he knew, however, that ultimately he was dependent on direct observation and interviews of particular "cases," al-though for the first part of his career he did not gather his data at firsthand. (This changed in the middle of the 1930s, when he engaged directly in in-terviewing on his own.) In addition to this, Burgess to a far greater extent than Park believed in the necessity of statistics.

Park did not like the simplifications of statistics; he liked concreteness and particularity within a wide perspective, spatial, historical, and theoreti-cal. He had little confidence in statistical data, neither the data gathered and summarized statistically by governmental bodies nor the statistics worked up by sociologists and social workers. He wanted to be able to see in his mind's eye particular individuals and particular types of individuals. Statistics, Park thought, could never satisfy that desire. Park had the powerful support of the tradition of the techniques of the life history precipitated by W. I. Thomas.

Burgess differed from Park in this respect. Although he was not at all a sophisticated statistician as the term is now understood—for most of his career as a sociologist averages and percentages were as far as he went in his use of statistical measures—nevertheless, his statistical bent brought about an important development in sociology and particularly in the development of sociology at the University of Chicago. It is likely that it was his preference which determined the decision that resulted in the appointment of William Ogburn to the department of sociology in the University of Chicago in 1926. Ogburn was in his time the leading proponent of the use of quantitative methods in sociology and he was the research director of the President's Committee on Recent Social Trends from which the great survey of *Recent Social Trends* came into existence.

· IV ·

Burgess was a peaceable man. He did not wish to break away from the technique of sociological research which had been elaborated at the University of Chicago. Burgess wanted to continue to use the written life-history which had become an important constituent of sociological research at Chicago. It had been first used by W. I. Thomas in *The Polish Peasant in Europe and America* in which "the autobiography of an immigrant" took up one thick volume of the original five volumes; his method was also very sympathetically viewed by Park, who found in it concreteness of the sort which he preferred. Burgess contributed greatly to the further progress of this technique through the work of his pupil Clifford Shaw. Under the auspices of the Institute of Juvenile Research, of which Burgess was one of the prime movers, and under Burgess's inspiration, Shaw produced *The Natural History of a Delinquent Career* and *The Jack Roller.* Skillfully executed by Shaw, those life-histories were conceived and guided by Burgess. They were the high points in the history of this technique.

The "life-history" was an autobiography written to order, according to some guiding themes set by the sociologist. Some of them were very long. They were mostly written by the subjects themselves; the subjects were selected because it was thought by sociologists that they were more or less typical. Each one of them certainly described many situations, and the life-history itself offered a concrete account of how each stage of the life of the individual in question was affected by his dispositions and beliefs acquired in the past and the kinds of situations in which he was located. The life-history also took the form of elaborate answers, recorded by the sociologist, to questions put by the sociologist. The author of the life-history was often paid for his work by the sociologist, although the payments were very small indeed.

Life-histories had the great merit of vividness in representation. They had the disadvantage that it was difficult to collect a large number of them in any single investigation and that it was difficult to classify their contents systematically and to deal quantitatively with them.

Nevertheless, the technique of the "life-history" in its time was a mark of the progress of sociological observation and it was widely used. Even where it was not used, it served as a standard. It raised the level of aspiration of young sociologists in their fieldwork. This technique, together with what came to be called the technique of "participant observation" and the "ecological technique," were hallmarks of "Chicago sociology."

Participant observation was an amalgam of the methods used in collecting data which went into records produced by missionaries who had resided for a long time in small societies in Africa or Asia, by consular officials and merchants long resident and active in a particular place, by travelers and explorers who dwelt in the same place for an extended period. The technique, which ever since Malinowski has been a standard practice, was in the 1920s still not common in anthropology except among Malinowski's pupils; it was practically unknown in sociology before Park began to require it of his students. There had been approximations to it by other sociologists who made studies of small communities around the turn of the century before Park became an academic sociologist. (W. E. B. Du Bois in his study of the Negro in Philadelphia and James Mickel Williams and Newell Sims in the research which they did for their doctoral dissertations at Columbia University were among these pioneers.)

The technique was, in retrospect, dictated by common sense. If the sociologist wishes to understand a small, local society, the best way to do it is to live among its members, observe them every day, ask them questions to encourage them to explain their actions which the sociologist has observed and to describe actions which the sociologist has not observed and the motives for those actions. It entailed living in the community or being there frequently and for very extended periods so that the sociologist ceased to be regarded as wholly an "outsider." It entailed becoming accepted, at least in part, as in some respects a member of the community, reasonably well liked, and worthy of confidences. This was the ideal which Park and Burgess held before their students. Although neither of them had done that kind of research themselves in any concentrated way, they were remarkably successful in teaching some of their students how to do it.

The ecological technique which was another major "Chicago specialty" was to a very large extent the outcome of Burgess's efforts to give a quantitative form to Park's brilliant imaginings about human ecology. As a walker in the city and as a student of human life everywhere, Park had attributed particular importance to urban centers. He also saw that the urban centers were in themselves differentiated into centers and subcenters. Every city, in this view, was differentiated into zones. Park had always been interested in the specialization of functions in various areas of a city; his own direct observation as a newspaper reporter in the eighties and nineties of the last century, his interest in local and occupational traditions and collective consciousness, and his reading of books on plant and animal ecology, particularly *Animal Ecology,* by the Danish zoologist Eugenius Warming, had confirmed him in his belief in the universality of ecological processes in society. He had also been interested in the phenomenon of industrial location, or why particular industries and particular cities were where they were, why certain occupations were located in one section of a city or on a certain street and others were in other sections and on other streets. He had read enough economic theory and human geography to catch a glimpse of why this occurred. All these ideas, put into some sort of order, had already appeared in the *Introduction to the Science of Sociology* in the four major processes of competition, conflict, accommodation, and assimilation.

There they would have remained had Burgess not undertaken to subject them to quantitative and cartographic descriptive measures. The ecological method and the theory of urban zones, which rested on it, for which Chicago sociology became famous, were in that period the result of Burgess's methodical work on the products of Park's far-reaching imagination. The five zones into which the activities of cities were differentiated were the results of Park's impressionistic observations and Burgess's ingenious adaptation of data gathered for the United States census.

The data of the census of population of a large city, published in summary form for an entire city, could be redistributed, by specially commissioned "runs" by the Census Bureau, into small zones, called "census tracts," of which there were 935 (in 1930). In this way, the social characteristics of many small areas could be calculated and other data, gathered by sociologists, could be calculated for each of these small areas. The several series could then be correlated with each other. (Durkheim had used a similar technique in his study of suicide in France in the 1890s but he had to use very large territorial units—*départements*—and the small number of such units made his measures much cruder than could be used when there were many more units each relatively homogeneous within itself.) Numerous "spot-maps" could be overlaid on each other, visually and by statistical calculations—usually the latter. This was the "ecological method." The use of this method added to our knowledge of urban society. By the use of these techniques, a considerable number of vivid monographs—based on doctoral dissertations done under Park and Burgess—were published in the University of Chicago Sociological Series.

It was this series which gave a basis to the notion of a "Chicago school of sociology." But by the end of the decade of the 1920s, in which the fame of the "school" was at its height, the technical devices of sociology were changing. The causes of these changes were internal to Chicago and external.

The three techniques which had been developed in Chicago largely by Burgess, under the stimulus of Park and by Burgess's own intellectual resourcefulness, began to lose their ascendancy by the end of the 1930s. The increased sophistication of sample surveys rendered the calculation of the associations of separate series of traits much more subtle and much more capable of a wider and richer application than the ecological method. The use of questionnaires, administered as parts of the sample surveys, replaced the life-history and participant observation, the results of which could not easily be treated quantitatively. The ecological method, which was quantitative, was also much cruder than the methods which came into operation through the use of sample surveys of opinion and action.

· V ·

Up to this point of his intellectual career, Burgess was very much a running mate—not simply a subordinate—to Park. Yet even during the period when they were so close to each other in their interest in urban sociological studies, Burgess moved further into the use of quantitative methods. The most notable study in which he used these methods was the predictive study of success and failure in the parole system. This was a characteristic piece of Burgessian sociology; a practical problem, namely which inmates of prisons should be released on parole and which should be retained in confinement, was approached through a combination of the techniques of case studies, i.e., studies of the characteristics of individuals, with the technique of statistical correlation, which demonstrated relationships between the characteristics of individuals prior to their imprisonment and their behavior after their release on parole from imprisonment. Thus, a parole board could refer to Burgess's prediction of probable law-abidingness after release to decide whether to grant parole to a prisoner or to deny it.

Burgess's contribution to the establishment of a policy for release on parole was perhaps the nearest approximation to a closely articulated application of sociological knowledge to the handling of a practical problem. This would not have been possible without Burgess's long association with persons active in dealing with practical problems. What is now called "policy research" has not exceeded Burgess's achievement nearly two-thirds of a century ago. That achievement and Burgess's other work in the 1930s inaugurated a new phase in sociological research. Despite Burgess's effort to combine the old tradition with new methods, the old order passed.

· VI ·

Burgess had never had a driving interest in large sociological perspectives. As long as Park was near him, he could not escape them. When Park retired from the University of Chicago and went on his travels over many countries—he returned only for a few years in the mid-1930s, prior to leaving Chicago permanently—Burgess moved in the direction which fitted his disposition; he proceeded cautiously and worked with data which appeared to be free from ambiguity and which lent themselves to precise classification, correlation, and assessment.

But unlike the eminent empirical sociologists who came after him, he regarded it as desirable to collect by himself as many of the observations as possible. In the second half of the 1930s, he initiated a long-term project in the prediction of success and failure in marriage. The basis of the study was a series of intensive and prolonged interviews with engaged couples. This was the first stage of the study. The second was to follow-up those couples, by re-interviewing them, some years later, with the aim of discovering whether their marriages had been "successful" or had "failed." Unlike in many projects, most of the interviews were conducted jointly by the "principal investigator" with his assistant. The assistant was not a surrogate for the principal investigator, as he is usually misleadingly called nowadays. Burgess did as much of the interviewing himself as did his assistant.

In the period after the Second World War, the current of sociological research in which Burgess was moving became the predominant one, but it also moved much beyond Burgess's accomplishments. The department of sociology at Chicago ceased to be the department of Park and Burgess. Under Burgess's leadership and chairmanship the department became much more heterogeneous, and other centers of academic sociology became established elsewhere. This did not disturb Burgess. He had little sense of rivalry or competitiveness towards sociologists in other universities any more than he had towards other sociologists within his own department.

At the same time, it must be said that considerate and kindly though he was to individual members of his own department, he did not have much inclination to think of the department as a whole. His own attention was concentrated on his research. His chairmanship of the department occurred in the years when the national preeminence of the department of sociology at Chicago was slipping away. He had been a pioneer, perhaps the chief pioneer, of the new type of research which combined uniform and schematic interviews with individuals with quantitative treatment of the protocols of the interviews, but he fell away from the center of attention of the new generation. His own pupils proved unequal to the new tasks which were being accepted by sociologists in other universities.

He was out of touch with the new developments in American sociology. Because of that, he could not single-handedly reorient the department of sociology into the new paths in which he had moved; he could not keep alive and adapt the old tradition which he had received from Thomas and Park and he could not find young persons capable of taking over that task. It was probably too large.

He had gone so far in this early collaboration with Park that he wanted after that to be independent and to follow paths of his own choosing. He wanted to do his own research. He was not interested in bringing the department along with him. It is, of course, possible that he wished to do so but found that the conflicts between the two parties which had developed within the department—between the advocates of quantitative methods and those who in various ways adhered to the older tradition—could not be assuaged. It was not that the new and old traditions were incompatible; it was rather that their respective proponents were.

Ernest Burgess was certainly intellectually courageous in following his own bent in research and that bent showed one way in which the conflicting traditions could be reconciled. But he was unable to reconcile their conflicting exponents. He was patient and generous with those who disagreed with him but he was too shy to attempt to impose himself or to argue forcefully for his own syntheses of techniques of research. In consequence, when the time came for him to become the leader in the department to resolve conflicts and to lay a map of the path along which sociology should be developed, the shy, gentle Burgess could not do it. The appointment of Everett Hughes would have appeared to have done what was necessary, but excellent sociologist though Hughes was, he too could not give guidance to the department.

As Ernest Burgess became a really old man, he began to study aged persons. He helped to found a new field of sociology. He still worked incessantly, conducting interviews himself, counseling younger collaborators in his newly defined field. He remained practically as active after retirement as he had been while on active duty. He yielded to no distraction; he still worked incessantly.

· VII ·

Ernest Burgess never became a man of the great world like his contemporaries and elders of the University of Chicago. Sophisticated ways and deep philosophies meant little to him. He did not seek honors, and when he received them he did not vaunt them. He never "threw his weight around." Painstaking, assiduous work was what he loved; it was the mark of his life. More than anything else, he wished to be left alone to pursue his own aims as a sociologist.

Alongside his shyness, there was always the streak of boyishness. One of the last times I saw him—it must have been when he was already well into his seventies—was late in the afternoon on 59th Street. It was in the summer quarter, when the campus was practically empty. There was no one else about to see him and he was unaware that I was looking at him. He was walking on the south edge of 59th Street, carefully balancing himself on the curbstone, putting one foot in front of the other, his arms stretched out from the shoulders to balance himself, seeing how far he could go without losing his balance and being forced to step to either side of the curbstone. It was the kind of thing he must have done when he was a boy.

It was only another expression of that shy boyishness so long disciplined by the strictness of his conscience which had been given courage by his intelletual conviction. It seemed of a piece with the modesty, gravity, and unworldliness which I saw in him when I attended his course on the "green Bible" in 1932.

2

PAUL R. CANNON

1 8 9 2 – 1 9 8 6

D O N A L D A . R O W L E Y

PATHOLOGISTS traditionally studied disease by correlating change in structure with abnormal function. The autopsy provided the material and the instruments were those of the anatomists. Pathology evolved to use the tools of other basic and clinical sciences, and materials for study now include tissues, cells, and secretions obtained from the living as well as the dead. But the study of disease by controlled experiment using animal models was largely outside the domain of traditional pathology in Cannon's time.

Paul Cannon as a young M.D. with a doctorate in bacteriology joined the department of pathology at the University of Chicago in 1925. He became an experimental immunologist as well as a trained pathologist and was appointed chairman of the department in 1940. Cannon retired seventeen years later, having made major contributions to the science of nutrition. The forces and logic for the change in direction of his research were straightforward, consistent, and dominated by experiment. Cannon helped transform traditional academic pathology to include experimental pathology, so that an apt definition for today might be: Pathology is the study of disease by any scientific means at the disposal of pathologists. This was Cannon's accomplishment.

· I ·

After graduating from college in 1915 and spending two years in the army as a lieutenant in the Sanitary Corps, Paul Cannon entered the graduate program in bacteriology at the University of Chicago and received a Ph.D. in 1921. He was professor of bacteriology and pathology at the University of Mississippi until 1923, when he returned to enter Rush Medical College, then affiliated with the University of Chicago. Cannon received his

M.D. in 1926 and was a member of the department of pathology of the University of Chicago from 1925 until he retired in 1957. H. Gideon Wells, Cannon's mentor and chairman of the department, was an accomplished experimental immunologist and pioneer in using chemistry to study pathologic processes; he was also director of the Otho Sprague Memorial Institute, which was located in the department of pathology. The Institute provided departmental members with unique resources before the era of governmental and private support for medical research, and these resources helped make the department preeminent in experimental pathology.

Cannon developed very early an approach to research and reporting which he used throughout his career. He invariably worked with collaborators: occasionally colleagues, but usually graduate students. Most of the students were working on an M.S. or Ph.D. degree in the department and all of them had received their medical degree or were in some stage of progress toward it. Only toward the end of his career were his collaborators research associates, supported by grants. Each area of Cannon's research is marked by a series of related papers: initial short papers with Cannon as first author followed by longer definitive reports usually with Cannon as last author or written only by the graduate students, culminating in a summary and generalization of the findings by Cannon in reviews, published addresses, or editorials.

When Cannon began doing research, almost all of the general public health measures we are familiar with were already being practiced or were understood in principle. With vaccination, immunization and antiserum therapy, diseases such as smallpox, typhoid fever, rabies, diphtheria, and whooping cough were preventable or treatable. Salversan (or 606) was reasonably effective for treating syphilis, but it was the only example of a chemotherapeutic agent given systemically for an infectious disease. No specific preventive or therapeutic measures existed for tuberculosis, pneumococcal and streptococcal infections, poliomyelitis and many other infectious diseases, which together were the major cause of morbidity and mortality. Probably most medical scientists anticipated that the important advances in public health lay in better understanding of the biology of the immune system in order to develop new ways for preventing or treating infectious diseases.

Cannon was concerned with two related problems in his early research: the role of phagocytic cells in immunity and the mechanisms of local immunity. While it was known that the cell-free portion of blood contained

PAUL R. CANNON

antibodies which accounted for specific immunity following infection or vaccination, it was not until the 1930s that antibodies were characterized as globulins, a form of protein. Infectious organisms or other foreign particles are rapidly engulfed by large cells called phagocytes, or macrophages, which are present in blood and all tissues. It was generally assumed until the 1950s that the organisms (antigen) engulfed in macrophages formed a template on which complementary protein molecules or antibodies were synthesized. To test this idea, ablation of all macrophages was not feasible but tissues rich in macrophages such as the spleen could be removed, or macrophages could be "overfed" with inert material to determine if antibody production was hampered. These tactics were used by Cannon to study a severe infectious anemia which occurred in normal-appearing rats following splenectomy. Cannon confirmed that the anemia was caused by a parasite and he established that the causative organism could be transmitted in blood by lice in a manner analogous to the transmission of malaria by mosquitoes. Injection of infected nonsplenectomized rats with large quantities of inert carbon particles (about the size of many infectious organisms and obtained from India ink) caused the anemia to occur and suppressed antibody responses to immunizations. Concurrently, Cannon was collaborating with Professor William Taliaferro of the department of bacteriology in studies on canaries and monkeys experimentally infected with malaria. The course of disease was followed by quantitating numbers and distribution of organisms as affected by the dose of organisms, splenectomy, and prior infection as a form of immunization. From these studies Cannon and his collaborators confirmed the importance of macrophages to immunity.

In separate studies Cannon was working on a concept of tissue immunity based on the idea that sessile macrophages in tissues produced antibody locally. They worked with diverse infectious organisms which characteristically entered the body by different routes, e.g., the respiratory or gastrointestinal tract, and caused different kinds of lesions. Some findings were consistent with the idea of local antibody formation; local prior infection or immunization increased phagocytosis of organisms by macrophages and helped decrease spread and growth of organisms, often at the expense of increased local injury to tissue. Cannon's early research in immunology was extended and elaborated by his first graduate students, John Fox, George Hartley, and Clarence Lushbaugh. Fox and Hartley worked on different aspects of local or tissue immunity and Lushbaugh studied the adverse effect of alcohol intoxication on pneumococcal infection in rabbits. Also, in the late 1930s, Cannon encouraged another graduate student, Howard Hopps, to explore the adverse effects some immune responses had on the host's reaction to injury, studies which anticipated by more than ten years related concepts of auto-immunity.

· II ·

Cannon became chairman of the department of pathology in 1940. The new duties and war did not stop the flow of Cannon's research. His stature as an experimental immunologist was marked by election to the presidency of the American Association of Immunologists in 1942 and election to the National Academy of Science in 1944. But a turn in direction of his research was signaled in his presidential address to the immunologists, "Antibodies and the Protein Reserves." Cannon argued that since antibodies are a form of protein, antibody production must be a part of the basic process of synthesis of body proteins. He referred to current work by others who measured the repletion of plasma protein in dogs whose protein reserves had been reduced by low protein diet and plasmaphoresis (a process requiring repeated bleeding, the blood then being separated into a fluid fraction which contains the blood proteins and a cellular fraction containing red and white blood cells; the blood cells are returned to the circulation, the proteins are discarded). Cannon alluded to work begun in his laboratory to test the effect of low protein reserves on antibody responses.

The global implications of the simple relationship between protein nutrition, antibodies, and disease was presented in a brilliant essay entitled "War, Famine, and Pestilence." Cannon paraphrased Lincoln, "man must love disease because he makes so much of it," and then described some of the many ways we intentionally and inadvertently injure ourselves. He reviewed historic examples of rampant disease and death which followed great famines caused by natural and man-made disasters and then expanded on his earlier argument. Amino acids are the building blocks of proteins; therefore, the essential amino acids which cannot be synthesized by the body must be absolutely limiting for constructing new proteins, including antibodies. Sufficient protein intake, in addition to adequate carbohydrate, fats, vitamins, and minerals, must be essential for preventing pestilence. Cannon recalled the effectiveness of the blockade of Germany in World War I and the war slogan: "Food Will Win the War," a theme he expanded on in a separate essay, "Will Food Win the War and Write the Peace?"

Cannon reported in 1943 that rabbits fed a diet low in protein but adequate for all other components failed to gain weight, had reduced total serum proteins, and responded to immunization with lower serum antibody titers than control rabbits; results were similar for rabbits treated with prolonged plasmaphoresis.

The world was at war and mass destruction and relocations of populations were occurring. Famine and pestilence would follow unless a minimum adequate diet could be provided to the populations at risk. From this time until retirement in 1957, Cannon systematically and progressively worked to determine: (1) how protein deprivation affected the response to injury, (2) the minimum requirements for protein or essential amino acids for growth, rehabilitation, and maintenance, and (3) the relationship of the separate needs for protein or essential amino acids and the needs for other dietary components, particularly calories and potassium.

· III ·

From 1944 on, Cannon's studies acquired an added clarity and incisiveness based on a new experimental model he developed. Rats are immunologically more comparable to man than rabbits or most other laboratory animals, and rats, like man, are omnivorous. Reasonably healthy, genetically similar though not identical, albino rats were commercially available, cost less, and could be housed in much less space than was required for rabbits. In Cannon's new model, adult rats were fed a completely adequate diet except for protein. Plasmaphoresis was not used. Rats were ready for assay when they had lost 20 to 30 percent of their body weight. With this weight loss, serum protein concentrations were reduced comparably. Supplementing the diet with adequate protein for seven to ten days completely restored body weight and serum proteins; recovery was linear and measurable as soon as 24 to 48 hours after repletion was started. Over time, the model was modified for reaching different objectives, but for each purpose the protein-depleted rat was always acutely responsive to nutritional rehabilitation; the time required for the assay was short and results were reproducible.

Cannon had a compact laboratory complex of about 1,800 square feet which included a large, central animal room opening at one end into a diet kitchen and at the other end into a laboratory, which in turn opened into his working office (in contrast to the larger chairman's office two floors above). The animal room had cages and support facilities for more than 1,000 rats and was the first room in the University of Chicago's Billings Hospital to be air-conditioned. The diet kitchen had industrial food-mixers, an autoclave, and storage facilities. The laboratory was well equipped for small-animal surgery and manipulations such as bleeding and for analyzing serum proteins and antibody levels. The office was large enough for Cannon's research group to crowd together for weekly planning sessions. In addition, the department had a large, well-equipped chemistry laboratory where many kinds of analyses critical for the nutritional studies were done.

By 1946 Cannon had six full-time staff: two animal caretakers, an overseer of the diet kitchen and animal room; Mr. Randolf Hughes, a laboratory technician; Mr. Robert Woolridge, a bacteriologist and serologist, and Mr. Lawrence Frazier, in charge of the chemistry laboratory and responsible for the analyses done there.

Collaborators included Cannon's peer, Eleanor M. Humphreys, a gifted anatomical pathologist with keen scientific intuition, and young teachers, residents, and graduate students in different stages of training. Robert Wissler was key to successful organization of many of the activities; Earl Benditt brought experience in micromethods in chemistry and an appreciation and understanding of biostatistics. Wissler, Harold Steffee, and Olaf Skinsnes interrupted medical-school training to work with Cannon, and all received Ph.D. degrees before completing medical school. In 1946 the group expanded to include Robert Stepto, Matthew Kobak, and M. Asirvadham, all M.D.'s who came to the department for experience in research, and myself, a dropped-out medical student who needed help. The more experienced of the entourage had or shared additional laboratories for their independent research so that the group grew exponentially as Wissler, Benditt, and Lushbaugh attracted their own trainees, including Lamont Jennings and John Green, who had medical degrees, and Ernst Jaffé, Frank Fitch, and Benjamin Spargo, who were medical students. But Cannon's laboratory remained the focus for the "protein project." Virtually all of the funds for the "protein project" until the early 1950s came to Cannon from grants and contracts from the Office of Naval Research and the Army Quartermaster Corps.

· IV ·

Cannon and his colleagues reported in 1944 that the protein-depleted rat immunized with sheep red blood cells had four- to six-fold lower antibody titers than control rats or protein-depleted rats rehabilitated with adequate diet. Rats on the protein depletion diet had a progressive linear loss of hemoglobin, serum, liver, and total carcass proteins; the antibody response fell more rapidly than the loss of protein in the other compartments. Feeding a mixture of amino acids was as effective as protein for restoring the antibody responses of protein-depleted rats. Wissler showed that the findings were relevant to resistance to infection since protein-depleted rats (or rabbits) had more severe disease and decreased survival following experimental infections with pneumococci. The response to infection includes an increase in the number of white blood cells, which derive from the bone marrow; protein depletion decreased both the rate and magnitude of the bone marrow response to infection. Penicillin could save protein-depleted animals from fatal infection, but infectious organisms persisted and tissue damage was more severe in the protein-depleted animals. These findings by Skinsnes emphasized the importance of continuing antibiotics after infections were apparently eliminated so that host defense mechanisms in concert with antibiotics could eliminate all infection. The rapidity and quality of healing of noninfected wounds were decreased in poorly nourished rats; susceptibility to lethal irradiation was increased, and natural resistance was reduced. Rats on low-protein and high-fat diets developed liver damage. Transplantable tumors grew more slowly in protein-depleted rats, the only benefit attributable to protein depletion.

Cannon's views and findings on the relationship between protein nutrition and infection were not universally accepted, and in 1950 he analyzed in a critical review both the experimental and epidemiological studies which purportedly failed to support or contradicted the results of the Chicago group. He could identify critical flaws in design of experiments or in interpretations of data in most laboratory studies, either in the formulation of diets or the method for testing decreased resistance to infection. Cannon acknowledged that disruption of public health and social services during war and famine might be important factors contributing to the epidemiology of disease, but he presented a persuasive case for the correlation between morbidity and mortality for tuberculosis and malnutrition; he acknowledged the case was weakest for some viral diseases but certainly suggestive for most kinds of infections.

Basic questions about immunity and the host response to injury continued to be investigated in Cannon's laboratory and the laboratories of his young collaborators, but Cannon's own scientific contributions from about 1947 on were in the field of protein metabolism and nutrition. By this time Cannon's laboratory had all of the capacities necessary for detailed metabolic studies. Dietary intake could be precisely prescribed, if necessary by forced, i.e. tube, feeding. Repeated injections of drugs or other agents could be given intravenously or by other routes. Animals could be bled repeatedly. Microanalyses, not only on what was ingested or excreted, but also for blood, whole carcass and body compartments, were possible for proteins, fats, and minerals.

The precise dietary requirements for maintaining healthy rats and for rehabilitating protein-depleted rats were determined for a "standard protein" of high quality and for mixtures of amino acids. The minimum daily requirement for each of the nine essential amino acids was established. The ratio of essential amino acids which was optimal for maintenance or rehabilitation was the same ratio as was present in the "standard protein," but four to five times more of either the mixture of amino acids or of the standard protein was required for optimal rehabilitation than for maintenance.

All of the essential amino acids had to be available together for protein synthesis; the effect of eliminating a single essential amino acid from the diet (or the restoration of an amino acid to a diet deficient in it) could be detected in one to two days, using the rat repletion model. In fact, protein synthesis did not occur when rats received optimal amounts of all nine essential amino acids if five were given in the morning and four in the evening, a finding confirmed through the use of tube feeding to eliminate any effect on appetite that different amino acid mixtures might have. These studies taken together laid to rest the idea that the body could draw on stored resources of protein or amino acids for synthesizing new proteins.

The rat repletion model became a powerful instrument for analyzing an important clinical problem concerning the separate roles of carbohydrate and protein in maintenance and rehabilitation. During the Second World War, at the University of Minnesota, a group of conscientious objectors were voluntarily severely starved and then refed under controlled conditions. The Minnesota investigators concluded that calories were overwhelmingly important for nutritional rehabilitation; according to them, within reasonable limits every increase in calories was associated with an increased rate of recovery.

The implications of this conclusion were important not only for rehabilitation following famine but also because, after the war, use of sulfa drugs and the new antibiotics made radical surgery on the gastrointestinal tract more feasible. Often surgery was for lesions which obstructed the tract and caused severe malnutrition. Nutritional rehabilitation before and immediately after surgery was critical for helping to control infection and to promote wound healing. Feeding had to be by vein and therefore as efficacious as possible. Human plasma was useful but supplies were limited and complications from use of plasma were frequent. Stimulated by this need, the amino acid requirements in optimal ratio for man had been determined by other investigators, and the requirements were remarkably similar to those for the rat; however, the separate needs for amino acids versus carbohydrates or calories were in dispute because of the earlier studies on conscientious objectors. Using the rat repletion model, Cannon's group established the precise relationships between proteins and caloric needs for protein synthesis. With adequate caloric intake, the rate of utilization of dietary proteins or essential amino acids was a direct function of the level of intake. Restricting caloric intake below a critical level restricted the utilization of dietary proteins for fabricating tissue protein, but increasing the caloric intake above that critical level did not augment utilization of a given quantity of protein. The critical level was calculated to be 1,240 calories/sq. meter body surface/day. Increasing the caloric intake above this critical level resulted in increased deposition of fat. Finally, the requirements for protein and energy were found to be the same for fabricating tissue during growth as for rehabilitation following protein depletion.

The relevant data from the Minnesota study were recalculated and presented in the same manner as data for the rat. Man and rat were remarkably similar in their needs. An adequate intake for rehabilitation for man was calculated at 1,460 calories/sq. meter/day. As for the rat, the rate of protein utilization was independent of caloric intake above this level. This finding seemed reasonable since, as they pointed out, the basal energy requirements of animals varying in size from mouse to elephant are directly proportional to a function of the body mass which approximates mathematically the surface area. Thus, the Chicago group proposed that the role of caloric intake in problems of human nutrition had been vastly overdrawn. Of course caloric intake must be adequate to cover needs, but protein of high quality (or the essential amino acids in appropriate ratio) should be provided in amounts in excess of that needed for equilibrium and be provided with adequate other dietary needs such as vitamins and minerals. It was customary to compute human diets on the basis of total caloric content, including the caloric equivalent of proteins in the diet. It was far more rational, they argued, to feed protein as a source of building material and provide the energy needs separately in the form of carbohydrates.

With the essential amino acid and caloric requirements defined, the tools were in hand to test the quality of different proteins, to define the specific amino acid deficiencies of low quality proteins and to demonstrate that fortifying low quality proteins with the appropriate amino acids raised the quality to high standard. The effects of storage and processing on protein quality were tested with immediate practical implications. For example, a solution of amino acids for intravenous feeding could be sterilized by autoclaving providing the pH was controlled; otherwise, almost all nutritional value was lost. In another case, wheat containing high quality protein prepared in a dough with sugar and toasted for 30 minutes at 375° lost almost all value as a protein source, a finding which caused Cannon to quip: the cardboard box containing a popular cereal said to be favored by champions contains as much protein nutrition as the contents of the box. And in fact, protein-depleted rats fed that brand of cereal as the source of protein, all other constituents being adequate, continued to lose weight.

While the interrelations between protein and other dietary components, e.g., fats and fat emulsions, were examined, Cannon's studies on potassium intake and adrenal cortical steroid hormones probably had more important scientific and clinical impact. Cortisone, a steroid hormone derived from the adrenal, and the hormone from the pituitary, ACTH, which stimulates release of the adrenal hormones, were introduced into clinical practice for the treatment of rheumatoid arthritis in the late 1940s. The hormones suppressed inflammation and often gave spectacular relief from pain; when they became more readily available, they were used empirically for many different unrelated conditions. Side effects were common, sometimes severe and usually related directly or indirectly to sodium retention and increased potassium excretion. Many patients receiving the hormones were in poor nutritional status and side effects involving the heart were particularly severe in these individuals.

Again Cannon had the ideal laboratory to attack the problem. Cortisone did not affect appetite, i.e., food intake by rats. In the protein-depleted rat, cortisone acted catabolically to increase the urinary loss of potassium and nitrogen which is derived from protein. This effect of the hormones was not altered by increased intake of carbohydrates, vitamins, or by varying the intake of sodium or potassium. The protein-depleted rat had to receive both protein (or all of the essential amino acids) and potassium to synthesize new protein. Elimination of a single amino acid or potassium prevented rehabilitation. In fact, depleted rats fed a complete diet missing only potassium developed severe, often fatal, injury to the heart in several weeks. The inference was that cardiac and muscular abnormalities observed in malnourished humans receiving cortisone/ACTH were caused by loss of potassium. The common practice of giving potassium-glucose solutions to patients with clinical evidence of low potassium levels would exacerbate the condition in protein-undernourished patients by causing diuresis and additional excretion of potassium. Complications could be prevented only by increasing intake of both protein and potassium.

As the Protein Project evolved, Cannon had marked each stage of development with papers or addresses which placed the findings of his group in perspective with scientific, clinical, or social problems.

· V ·

Cannon's studies were restricted to the laboratory; others extended and applied his findings to the field and hospital. Certainly Cannon's essential findings were validated on a large scale by the successful use of food provided by the United States during and after the war to prevent famine and to rehabilitate those who were starved. Soy bean flour, a condensed source of high quality protein, was used extensively by the armed forces and relief agencies for fortifying foods given to large populations. I think this is Cannon's most important legacy.

The number and quality of Cannon's trainees are another measure of his scientific legacy. These trainees generated important research independent of the immediate objectives of Cannon's laboratory, and often these studies marked new directions they would take later in their own careers. Cannon was ultimately responsible for evaluating the pathology of radiation damage to tissues found in studies done for the Manhattan Project at the University of Chicago; he delegated the immediate responsibility to Lushbaugh, who expanded these beginnings to become the authority in the country on radiation pathology, first at Los Alamos and then at Oak Ridge. Wissler, working with members of the department of medicine, produced atheromatous lesions in rats. Rowley described conditions in which the spleen played an absolutely critical role for the production of antibody in rat and man. Wissler and Fitch together with Leon Jacobson, then director of Argonne Cancer Research Hospital, found that shielding the spleen from x-irradiation prevented the almost complete loss of antibody formation in heavily irradiated animals. Ernst Jaffé, working with Wissler and Benditt, showed the importance of methionine and choline for preventing dietary-induced injury to the liver. Benditt, in the process of studying the effects of cortisone on inflammation, discovered that mast cells contain (in addition to histamine) 5-hydroxytryptamine and a chymotrypsin-like enzyme which mediate acute inflammation in tissue injury. Cannon encouraged Spargo to study the rest of the carcass of protein/potassium-depleted rats after he had removed the hearts for his own studies. Spargo discovered severe renal lesions specific to potassium deficiency. All told, Cannon had twenty pre- or post-doctoral fellows; all became professors, seven became chairmen and five directors of research institutes.

Cannon ceased laboratory research when he became editor of the *Archives of Pathology* in 1955, but thirty-five years later the two dominant research groups in the department of pathology at the University of Chicago trace direct lineage to him: basic immunology, with seven members of the department, and lipid metabolism/cardiovascular pathology, with six members; and both groups have members who began with Cannon. Wissler succeeded Cannon as chairman in 1957 and Benditt moved in the same year to the University of Washington at Seattle to become chairman of the department there. The United States now had two preeminent academic departments of pathology.

Clearly, Cannon's personal commitment to medicine was through public health: how to devise ways which would improve the health of large populations. He wrote how vaccination against smallpox "changed the face of the world"; how chemotherapy and antibiotics changed the pattern of disease; and how the next great public health problems facing the world would be secondary to changes in the environment and growth of population. Cannon expressed these views in 1949 when as a senior medical student I met him to discuss my future. I told him I wanted to become an immunologist. He thought for a moment, looked me in the eye, and said, "No young man with aspirations for becoming a scientist should stake his future in immunology; all of the important questions in immunology have been answered." Taken out of context, the advice seems careless or irresponsible, but he articulated exactly what he meant and why. Even if the immunologists could prevent or cure cancer and cardiovascular disease, the immunologist could never have the impact on public health that immunization and antibiotics had already had. The next great problems would be man-made and the young future scientist should prepare accordingly. Of course he was right, though I think none of his disciples had the courage to risk their future as he advised; thus, possible additional achievements based on his legacy were lost.

· VI ·

Probably most medical students find their first real excitement in medicine when they take courses in pathology. Finally anatomy, biochemistry, physiology, and the other basic sciences bear on an understanding of actual patients, though admittedly dead ones. The student learns through case studies to correlate the patient's history, physical and laboratory findings, treatment, and clinical course with the structural, biochemical, and microbiological changes found at autopsy. The pathologist is the arbiter, and as an astute observer-analyst can help shape medical care. Cannon played this role in two dramas, one involving nose drops and the other a new sulfa drug preparation.

Oil accidentally aspirated or experimentally instilled in the trachea causes an indolent irreversible cellular filling of air spaces in the parts of the lungs where the oil settles. This process referred to as "lipid pneumonia" was found in children usually dying of other causes, but the occurrence of the pneumonia was traced to use of nose drops containing a vasoconstricting agent suspended in oil to prolong decongestion of the nasal passages. Similar oil produced lipid pneumonia experimentally; ever since, agents for inhalation therapy have been in aqueous suspension or solution. In the second instance an outbreak of acute, usually fatal, renal failure occurred in patients without known previous kidney disease. The renal pathology was recognized as characteristic for changes caused by diethylene glycol. Through effective detective work the affected patients were all found to have been treated with a new "elixir" of sulfanilamide solubilized in diethylene glycol. The incident was a turning point for establishing new criteria for verifying the safety of drugs for human use.

The postmortem examination was the core of hospital pathology in Cannon's time and the number of autopsies per number of deaths was, and still is, an important indicator of institutional quality. But the autopsy is continuously under attack for being an antiquated, ineffective, and costly luxury no longer affordable. One such public attack made in the 1950s by an influential clinician from another institution was effectively answered for the pathologists by Cannon in an article, "Lessons Learned in the Morgue." (Though Cannon espoused the case for the autopsy, he stopped working in the morgue in 1943, and it is fair to point out that he visited so infrequently that my only encounter with him there concerned a boat. Over a weekend Benditt and I used the tools of the department workshop to assemble a dinghy in the morgue. Before we could remove it on Monday morning, someone objected. Cannon inspected and he was amused but firm: get the dinghy out. We did not hear of the matter again.)

Cannon and his departmental colleagues brought the genuine intellectual challenge of pathology to medical students and physicians most effectively, but many departments of pathology were still dominated by men trained in Germany and Austria—autocrats who considered pathology synonymous with anatomical pathology. Cannon, probably by nature but reinforced by a background in experimental biology, brought to pathology an understanding of the limitations as well as the strength of traditional pathology. He understood the importance of experiment and the range of procedures that could be used to study disease. Thus, he built a department begun by Wells that was remarkable for the time. Just after the war, Cannon became the first chairman of the National Institutes of Health study section on pathology, the first federal arrangement for providing financial support for experimental pathology. As an author and editor, Cannon gained the respect of most conventional pathologists and became an important spokesman and leader for American pathology. In this capacity, Cannon recruited to the department two young, already-trained pathologists who developed research interests independently: Werner H. Kirsten, a viral oncologist, who succeeded Wissler as chairman in 1977, and Seymour Glagov, who became an authority on cardiovascular pathology and has remained at the University.

Cannon's leadership in American pathology contrasts interestingly with Howard Florey's leadership in Great Britain. The department at Chicago and the Sir William Dunn School of Pathology, University of Oxford, were probably the only two comparable university pathology organizations then extant. Cannon and Florey, both M.D.'s with similar backgrounds in basic science, were pioneers in academic medical research in that each was the first in his country to orchestrate reasonably large and focused research enterprises involving multiple independent scientists from different disciplines. The Dunn school, like the department in Chicago, was responsible for teaching pathology to medical students, but the Dunn school, unlike the Chicago department, had no responsibilities for human or any other anatomical pathology and taught no postdoctoral anatomical pathology; the faculty were entirely experimental pathologists. Florey built the group which brought penicillin to clinical use, shared the Nobel Prize for this achievement; initiated important research in immunology, inflammation, and vascular disease; edited an internationally used textbook of pathology, and was president of the Royal Society. But relations between Florey and organized pathology in Britain were very cold. Florey and the Dunn school had virtually no influence on the development of academic pathology in Great Britain so that to this day most experimental pathology there is conducted outside of academic departments of pathology. Both Cannon and Florey recognized long before most that increased population due to control of infectious disease would create the next major global problems. Cannon's concern became how to feed the growing population; Florey's concern became how to control man's numbers by birth control.

· VII ·

Our recollections of Cannon are of the mature and successful chairman who was balding, gray, fair-skinned, blue-eyed—almost cherubic. He had the vigor and agility of a former athlete and was usually in excellent humor; he was self-assured and not pompous. Cannon was straightforward, simple in speech, writing, and action; he smoked self-consciously and sometimes furtively as he was continuously quitting or cutting down. Assessments of his special qualities are remarkably similar: an uncomplicated man; a mentor who was fatherly, supportive, and permissive—but not too permissive. Cannon had an uncanny ability to assess the quality of his young colleagues and to instill in them self-reliance, independence, and a strong sense of responsibility. He delegated real responsibility in teaching service, and in laboratory investigation. This was very good for developing young investigators and accounts in part for the great productivity of his department. Cannon was a sought-after leader possibly because he threatened no one and was not seeking advantages for himself.

Cannon was a staunch political conservative, and some of us in our youth had difficulty reconciling this "defect" with his obvious fairness and lack of bias. He became animated over baseball and "politics," which usually meant the Democrats but sometimes the dean's office and the central administration. He obviously enjoyed the excitement and surprises of the laboratory, but he was very critical and believed in reconfirming findings in several different ways before he concluded that the findings were acceptable.

Cannon's laboratory conveyed a feeling of frugality and sufficiency, of enthusiasm and efficiency, and most of all a sense of the importance of the work. Except for Cannon at the top, there was no rank or echelon. We assumed our responsibilities for teaching in the classroom and for service in the morgue, but we knew without being told that our laboratory work took precedence over all else. Laboratory notebooks were open; discussions were unconstrained and most of us were advised at least once to the effect: you have read too much; get out of the library and into the laboratory, and do the experiment. As a career, Cannon suggested to Frank Fitch that experimental pathology gave the opportunity for intellectual pursuit without diversion of clinical responsibility; the financial rewards would be small but sufficient for shabby gentility. There were no laboratory celebrations, but each fall Cannon invited the entire department to a picnic on his farm.

Cannon was an excellent and frequent public speaker but he revealed to us that he was always nervous and fearful before audiences. He persistently encouraged us to speak and to publish our research. He advised us, however, not to write reviews, chapters, or textbooks; he said: let your competitors have that pleasure. Cannon did not follow his own advice scrupulously; he was joint author of a textbook on nutrition just before he retired. His earlier advice gave me an excuse some years later when I declined to write reviews for Cannon when he was an editor.

Cannon unconsciously dramatized for us the adage that we are only as old as we think we are. We, in our twenties and early thirties, had gathered one Saturday morning for the weekly meeting at the laboratory. Cannon had just returned from Washington and was regaling us with his views of the silly extravagances of the Democrats. Then he became serious and warned of a new problem the country would face. The population was going to age substantially; new ways had to be found to feed, treat, and house all of these old people. The study of the aged was called gerontology, a word we probably had not heard before but a word we must become accustomed to. As he talked, the sunlight was streaming through the window and reflecting off his bald head ringed by white hair. Probably most of us thought we knew already who the old people were, but forty-plus years later I suspect most of us are no more willing than Cannon was then to think of ourselves as old and needing the concern of young scientists.

For at least two years before retirement, Cannon deliberately refused to make decisions which might encumber the next chairman. Most of us were dismayed and too inexperienced to appreciate the wisdom of this inaction. And about this time Cannon informed Dean Coggeshall that retirement, like any serious activity, would require experience and experience meant spending longer weekends on the small farm he and his wife had built near Aurora, Illinois, where he could also be near his son's family. Cannon remained editor of the *Archives of Pathology* for five years after retirement; he had a small office provided by the department for his editorial work and in this way he maintained contact with the University. On his seventieth birthday a *Festschrift,* an entire issue of the journal *Archives of Pathology,* was presented to him. It included nineteen original papers by twenty-two former students and colleagues; it was a unique expression of admiration from the entire profession of American pathology. Thus Cannon left the University and science most gracefully.

3

RUDOLF CARNAP

1 8 9 1 – 1 9 7 0

A B R A H A M   K A P L A N

THE UNIVERSITY OF CHICAGO initially attracted me as a place to pursue scientific studies. In 1934 I visited the Century of Progress Exposition in Chicago, where it was the science pavilion that compelled my imagination. I returned to my sophomore year at Duluth Junior College with a change in my major from pre-law to chemistry. The attraction of Chicago was strengthened by the circumstance that the University offered a tuition scholarship to transfer students on the basis of a competitive examination, which the local professor administering it had encouraged me to take as a freshman, for practice. Somewhat to his embarrassment and mine, my ineligibility was disclosed when my paper was awarded a scholarship. Lack of personal finances, however, prevented me from accepting it.

I first heard of Rudolf Carnap from my boyhood companion and lifelong friend, Irving Copi, now a distinguished logician. Copi was then a student of mathematics at the University of Michigan, while I was studying chemistry at the College of St. Thomas. We spent our summers pursuing a common interest in philosophy, for instance by an intensive though amateurish reading of Kant's *Critique of Pure Reason*. Carnap had come to the University of Chicago a year or two earlier. An English translation of his *Logical Syntax of Language* had just appeared, though it was too technical for me to make much of, as I had also found true of Wittgenstein's *Tractatus Logico-Philosophicus* the year before, though Copi, having a mathematical background, was able to help considerably. Carnap was becoming more and more widely known as having been the leading figure of the intriguing Vienna Circle and of the logical positivism it espoused.

That kind of philosophy appealed to me not only because of its explicit concern with science and mathematics as subjects for philosophical reflec-

RUDOLF CARNAP

tion but even more because of the scientific outlook it appeared to be bringing to bear on philosophy. Moreover, the glamorous disciplines of logic and semantics which it cultivated in order to bridge science and philosophy were fascinating in themselves. Accordingly, when, through the efforts of Copi's father, private funds were made available to me to enter graduate school, I decided on the University of Chicago. There I found not only Carnap but also, as my advisor, Charles W. Morris, Carnap's colleague and friend—the only one Carnap had in the department of philosophy, so far as I could tell. Morris was combining logical positivism with American pragmatism and arousing wide interest in semiotic, which comprised Carnap's syntax and semantics as well as the pragmatics of Charles Peirce and George Herbert Mead.

Intellectual excitement at the University was even greater than I had hoped for when I left the small parochial college of my undergraduate days. The University at that time was often stereotyped as a place where Protestant students were taught Roman Catholic philosophy by Jewish professors. As for the students, most of my acquaintance were either Jews, like Saul Bellow, Isaac Rosenfeld, and Irving Janis, or else not Protestants but secular, anticlerical Marxists, as many of the Jewish students were. Roman Catholic philosophy was extolled by Mortimer Adler, President Hutchins's associate, and applauded by the president himself, but not by the department of philosophy, which was Aristotelian rather than Thomist. Nor was I aware of any Jewish professors in the department until the following year, when Morris R. Cohen, having retired at the City College of New York, came to the University as a visiting professor.

The air was full of ideas and doctrinal controversies about religion, politics, education, and especially philosophy. Verbal skirmishes were fought every evening in student taverns and coffee shops, and pitched battles almost daily in formal debates, panels, and what a later generation was to call "teach-ins." The battlelines, most broadly defined, divided the Ancients and the Moderns. The former were championed by the paladins of the "Great Books" and such reputable scholars as Richard McKeon, professor of philosophy and dean of the division of the humanities. The Moderns were represented most notably by Carnap, some professors of scientific subjects, and, when he came the next year, by Bertrand Russell. There was also a neutral "third world," viewed by the two camps of the Ancients and the Moderns as retrograde, not changing with the times, yet clinging to tradition from inertia rather than as a matter of principle.

The fellow student who shortly thereafter became my wife once invited me to visit a course she was taking in the history of music. The course was being taught, as called for in the stereotyped image of the University of Chicago, by a converted Jew who left the University the next year to become a monk. As he entered the classroom, he glanced at the back row where I and one or two friends were sitting, and remarked quite audibly, "Aha! Spies!" as well we might have been, I suppose. His lecture was on Mozart, whose music he was subjecting to an Aristotelian analysis. Mozart's compositions, he explained, all satisfied the requirements laid down in Aristotle's *Poetics,* that a work of art must have a beginning, a middle, and an end. Whether such philosophical musicology contributed to driving the lady of my heart into my arms I cannot say—in those days she was playing Chopin as Sunday dinner music in Hutchinson Commons.

My nephew, Abe Krash, who came to the University of Chicago a decade or so later (and eventually edited the *Daily Maroon*), swears that before his departure from his home in Cheyenne, Wyoming, I drew him aside to warn him of the perils awaiting him at the University—not, as he was expecting, of the sins of the big city, but of quite other temptations. "Beware!" he claims I warned, "and again I say, Beware! Beware of the Aristotelians!" Perhaps his memory is more reliable than my own.

What I do remember well is the disparity in the strength of the two sides, at least in the department of philosophy. Though Carnap was increasingly being recognized as a logician and philosopher of world fame, at the University he had very few serious students. There were only a handful, even, of visitors, whom Carnap never saw as "spies" or even as tourists, but as students motivated only by intellectual interests. Apart from Milton Singer, who before long turned to anthropology (perhaps in part as a practical matter), there were only myself, my roommate Norman Dalkey, and, during Russell's year at the University, Irving Copi, as well as two or three others. Departmental fellowships were correspondingly rare for the Moderns—my own appointment to a fellowship, according to the grapevine, was attributable to a rare display by Carnap of an unyielding insistence. For a time, Carnap had the assistance of Olaf Helmer and Carl G. Hempel, who later became a distinguished philosopher of science in his own right; they had worked with Carnap in Europe but were at the University, I believe, without formal appointments.

Carnap often used the expression "My friends and I" to refer to what others identified as "the logical positivists," but he did not see himself as the leader of a school. That was not in his nature. He was simply at the forefront, looking neither ahead to find enemies, nor behind to make sure of followers. He was not a man with a mission but an explorer, matter-of-factly sharing his findings with anyone who might be interested in them.

An outstanding quality of his character was humility, a trait today as rare among philosophers as among political leaders. Neither was he afflicted by false modesty—self-disparagement to win the approval of others. He did have a great deal of pride in the power of the human mind, but not a trace of personal vanity. He admired the power in individuals like Kurt Gödel and Bertrand Russell, but it never occurred to him to lay claim to recognition of it in himself. At most he might have applied to his own work what Wittgenstein claimed for the *Tractatus,* that, in it, the problems with which it dealt were definitively solved, but this was only to show how little had been achieved when those problems were solved.

Other positivists were more royalist than the king. This is not uncommon, I suppose, in movements of thought. (At Chicago, I was struck by the stridency and dogmatism of some of the Ancients as contrasted with the intellectual openness and flexibility of the Jesuits who introduced me to philosophy at St. Thomas.) Positivists in those days often wielded their version of Occam's razor, the verifiability theory of meaning, as if it were an axe with which to chop to bits their nonsensical adversaries. Not so Carnap, for whom it was an instrument to use in trying to understand what others were saying. To students who occasionally visited his seminar and asked questions in the idiom of the Ancients he was unfailingly as gentle and earnest as he was to everyone else: "Perhaps what you mean is . . ." and some technical logico-linguistic formula would follow; "or is it perhaps . . . ?" These were not rhetorical devices. He genuinely did not know and was trying to find out.

Years later when Carnap had gone on to the University of California in Los Angeles, I lunched with him and a well-known polemicist of positivism just before leaving on an extended trip to the Orient to study Asian philosophies at firsthand. It was all a waste of time, said the other, while Carnap tried to draw me out as to my expectations and conjectures, prepared to weigh seriously and without prejudice any eventual findings. Still later, with the complete dominance of logico-linguistic philosophy in Anglo-American thought, I had occasion to confide to Carnap that, remembering the old days in Chicago, I sometimes felt like a Trotskyite: once a dedicated band of revolutionaries, we lived to see the triumphant revolution institute an orthodoxy more authoritarian than the one we had hoped to eradicate.

Those who know Carnap only through his publications might find this portrait surprising, for his written style had a good deal of Q.E.D. about it.

Indeed, the chief failing in his philosophy, in my opinion, lies in this gap between the philosophy he professed and what was embodied in his own life and character. The difference between these is marked in a sharp contrast between Carnap and Hans Reichenbach, the major figure of the Berlin school of logical positivism, or "scientific empiricism," as he preferred to call it. Reichenbach was a thoroughgoing probabilist in his professed philosophy, while Carnap believed that certain presuppositions of scientific method were beyond question. But Reichenbach maintained his probabilism with uncompromising certitude, while Carnap unceasingly searched for more secure foundations for his thought.

There is a story that Russell once challenged Reichenbach's probabilism with the remark that a lunar eclipse had been predicted for that very evening—in a few minutes, in fact. "It is quite probable," said Reichenbach. They went out and saw the eclipse. "What do you say now?" asked Russell. "Much more probable," was the reply. Carnap would not have said anything at all until he had reflected on the matter more fully.

For a time I shared an office with Reichenbach, and once had to cut short a conversation to go to my class. "What course are you giving now?" he asked. "Philosophy of Art," I replied. "Is there such a subject?" said he. Carnap would have tried instead to formulate exactly what the aims and methods of such a subject might be, and he would have invited my help in the enterprise. On the other hand, I do not recall any particular interest in the arts by Carnap, while Reichenbach was a music-lover and enthusiastic photographer. As might be expected of a "scientific empiricist," however, it was the acoustic and optical processes underlying these arts that most interested Reichenbach.

Carnap had a childlike simplicity and innocence, the curiosity and naïveté of genius. Russell, with typical irony, once said of Carnap that he was a promising young man—Carnap was then forty-seven and Russell not quite twenty years older. Carnap was certainly young in his ideas, wholly undeterred by received opinion. His naïveté was sometimes his undoing. Visiting him once during his stay at the Institute for Advanced Study in Princeton, I was saddened to hear him tell of his loneliness. "Nobody ever comes to see me," he complained. "Perhaps they're afraid that you have no time for visitors," I said. "But I once told them they could come!" he countered. He had set down the postulates; it was for them to deduce the theorems.

Often such apparent insensitivity to the feelings of others is a result of self-centeredness. With Carnap it was decidedly not so, but rather that he simply did not appreciate that others did not order their lives with the same rationality as he did. Carnap was very far from uncaring of others. Nor was it only for his intimates that he showed concern. Early in my association with him he asked me, as a prospective student and assistant, whether I was getting enough to eat, which I suppose was doubtful at the time though not all that obviously. Years later, teaching in India, I had occasion more than once to ask the same question of students there, who thereupon looked on me as their guru for taking such a personal interest in their welfare. Carnap could have been venerated as a saint, and perhaps not only in that part of the world.

Of the prophet who became a byword for modesty it was said that his face shone and he knew it not. That attribute of a prophet, at any rate, Carnap shared. He was extraordinarily lacking in self-consciousness. At the first meeting of the department of philosophy at the University of California in Los Angeles after he had joined it, he ingenuously confided in me, then chairman of the department, "I used to look on you as a son; now, see—you are my father!" Such feelings came to him as a discovery, and a self-revelation.

He was certainly aware of and concerned about the larger world—he was, after all, *Mitteleuropäisch,* educated in Germany and having taught in Vienna and Prague. The International Congress for the Unity of Science, a meeting of positivists and empiricists from all over the world for which Milton Singer and I were reporteurs, was held at Harvard in 1939. The opening session took place on September 1, only hours after the Nazis marched into Poland and ignited the Second World War. Carnap shared fully the anxieties of friends and colleagues from Poland, Holland, and elsewhere, like the mathematician Alfred Tarski. Reichenbach, fortunately, had left Berlin some years earlier, sojourning in Istanbul before coming to Los Angeles (as a result of which Turkish grammar was able to contribute to the logical analysis of the European languages).

Carnap's responses to world events were wholly dissociated from doctrinaire ideologies, party lines, or political "positions." This was all the more remarkable because at the University of Chicago such commitments were pandemic then. It was a time on the campus when socialists of the Third International did not talk to those of the Second International, Stalinists did not talk to Trotskyites, and no one talked to fascists, who were universally held in contempt as troglodytes incapable of rational discourse. Some, like myself, had sold what books we could spare to help the Spanish Loyalists; others were preoccupied with the murders being perpetrated by some of the loyalist forces on other parties of the left. Carnap was somehow above all such differences without being indifferent to them, aware of their existence and importance but without knowing any details about them.

A political standpoint which Carnap did express from time to time was anticlericalism, brought to a focus by the assassination in Austria a few years earlier of an influential positivist, Moritz Schlick, by a possibly deranged student who saw Schlick as a monstrous enemy of religion.

Carnap also had a strong strain of egalitarianism, involuntarily brought to the fore by the adulation accorded "Lord" Russell in Chicago. For Russell himself, Carnap had boundless regard, because of Russell's qualities of character as well as of intellect. During the inflation in Europe which followed the First World War, Carnap had written to Russell asking whether Russell knew of a used copy of *Principia Mathematica* Carnap might obtain, since no one in Austria could afford to buy a new copy of the three-volume work. Russell, Carnap recounted with appreciation even years afterward, thereupon wrote out by hand all the important propositions (designated as such in the printing) in all three volumes, and sent them to Carnap. Carnap once showed me these papers as one of his most precious possessions.

It was only in such contexts that Carnap ever spoke—in my hearing—of Vienna. The place was only the scene of earlier intellectual pursuits, in what was called the Vienna Circle—the Wiener Kreis; Carnap had nothing about him of the *Fledermaus* Viennese. Prague he hardly mentioned at all. Russell once wrote that the beginning of wisdom is to emancipate oneself from slavery to time; Carnap seemed to have emancipated himself from space. During one academic year, however, it was hard to avoid making geographical identifications of the members of the department of philosophy of the University of Chicago, because of the distinctive accents of Russell, Carnap, Morris R. Cohen, and the Texan Charner Perry; only Charles Morris seemed to be speaking standard American English.

In a way, Carnap even seemed to be dissociated from the body. He was a huge man, not obese but tall, broad-shouldered and muscular. His warm bear-hugs whenever we met later in life were bone-crushers. In my student days, Charles Morris was much taken with Sheldon's classification of body types, which was then in vogue. On that typology, Carnap was a mesomorph, like a football player, not an ectomorph, a thin, small-boned intellectual, like Russell. But come to think of it, Plato had been a wrestler, and was known as "Broad-Shoulders." A golden intellect is where you find it.

Carnap's intellect was the pure metal. For one thing, the integrity of his thought was uncompromising. A story about him current at the time concerned the assignment of his teaching duties. "Would you like to teach a course on the British empiricists?" he was asked. "No," said Carnap. "On Kant's theory of knowledge?" "No." "On Comte's positivism?" "No." "Well, Professor Carnap, then what would you like to teach?" "I?" was the reply, "I would like to teach the truth!" If he did say it, and he very well might have, he would have been in dead earnest.

Asked for his opinion of the views of some specific philosopher, or in a specific book or article, he would want first a clear statement of the views he was being asked to respond to. Often, his attempt to understand just what the view was conveyed a fuller and more reasoned response than the questioner had expected. The usual practice in philosophy, then as now, was rather to judge first—negatively, or course—and only later to try to understand.

I once asked Carnap with which philosopher of the past he felt a close kinship. His reply was Leibnitz—not surprisingly, given Leibnitz's devotion to logic and mathematics, his aspiration to a universal symbolism in which philosophical questions might be formulated so as to be solvable by "calculation," and his penchant for dealing with such questions by considering possible universes. Carnap, like his mentor Russell, was an empiricist in his professed philosophy, but in the style of his life and thought he was a thoroughgoing rationalist.

The peak experience of my studies—as I think it must have been for everyone present on the same occasions—was a seminar on semantics conducted jointly by Russell and Carnap. The contrast between the styles of the two philosophers was even more exciting and instructive than the content of the seminar. Russell wielded a rapier—thrust, cut, and parry, with flashing wit and insight. Carnap was a whole panzer division all by himself, a *Star Wars* fighting machine clanking inexorably with heavy tread and crushing all in its path.

The style of thought lies in its details, to which the thought owes its force as well as its character. Carnap had a passion for detail, even in his personal life. He once told me about the vacation trip he was about to take; the trip had been planned not just to the day, but even almost to the hour.

Because of his devotion to exactitude, Carnap's courses had a deceptive simplicity, occasionally to the point of boredom. But as detail was piled on detail, a quite unexpectedly rich and complex structure began to emerge. He might say, "We will use small letters in the second half of the alphabet for propositions, thus: p, q, r, s, [and so on and so on] and capital letters from the beginning of the alphabet for the sentences in which propositions are asserted, as: A, B, C, [and so forth, for some time]." The spelling out seemed endless, but one never forgot the essential distinction between symbols and what they signified. This distinction and others like it were then explored like the flora and fauna of a new domain.

Degas is supposed to have said to his friend, the poet Mallarmé, that he himself should have been a poet, because every day he had a hundred ideas for poems. The story goes that to this Mallarmé replied, "Poems, my friend, are not made of ideas but of words." The poem does not exist until it is put into words. Carnap might have said that philosophies are not made of words but of symbols; until they are put into symbols they are only hints and suggestions for philosophical views, not philosophies themselves. Symbols must be handled with care; Carnap was a very careful man.

"Bliss was it in that dawn to be alive," said a romantic poet about another era, "But to be young was very heaven!" So it was with me at the University of Chicago in Carnap's day. The bliss lay in more than the play of ideas which people like Carnap expressed, and evoked in their students. What mattered most to us, as I suppose it always does to the young, is that he and others like him were providing us with models for the life of the mind and, indeed, for the life of the heart.

Carnap was both mind and heart. Hindus might have called him "Mahatma," Great Soul. In my mother tongue he would have been called a "kosher soul," an Adam before the Fall giving names to the animals. In speaking of the honored dead, both in Yiddish and Hebrew a certain expression is conventionally added; for me in this remembrance the expression is more than a matter of convention. It is: *Zichrono l'vrachah,* May his memory be a blessing.

4

Subrahmanyan Chandrasekhar

1 9 1 0 –

K A M E S H W A R   C.   W A L I

> *I have always been proud that I had a*
> *part in bringing you to the University of Chicago.*
> Robert M. Hutchins, 22 September 1971

· I ·

BEGINNING IN 1937, Williams Bay, Wisconsin, became the home of Chandra and his wife, Lalitha, for twenty-seven years. This marked the beginning of a new era at Yerkes and also in American astronomy, which then was still dominated purely by observational studies. As Martin Schwarzschild says, "It was quite novel to have a pure theorist like Chandra in an observatory devoted to pure observations." European born and trained, Strömgren and Kuiper brought the prevalent strength of Europe, that of mixing theory with observations and placing theoretical considerations in the context of observations. Chandra's Cambridge training made him more of a mathematical astronomer, but unlike his mentors Milne and Eddington, Schwarzschild says, "Chandra had no snobbishness in regard to his mathematical work. He did not shy away from numerical, computational solutions. He mixed rigorous analysis with numerical calculations, as the problem required."

Chandra's principal assignment when he joined Yerkes was to develop a graduate program in astronomy and astrophysics. Along with Kuiper, Chandra devised a sequence of eighteen courses spread over two years; courses in solar and stellar atmospheres and interiors, stellar dynamics, solar and stellar spectroscopy, solar systems, and atomic physics. During

This account, condensed from chapters 9, 10, and 11 of *Chandra: A Biography of S. Chandrasekhar,* by Kameshwar C. Wali (University of Chicago Press, 1991), describes Chandra's association with the University of Chicago and his editorship of the *Astrophysical Journal.*

SUBRAHMANYAN CHANDRASEKHAR, 1984

the years that followed, he taught twelve and thirteen of the eighteen courses, teaching at least one, sometimes two, courses each quarter. He was put in charge of the library (ordering books and journals), of advising students, and of arranging the weekly colloquia. Soon "with Struve, Kuiper, Chandrasekhar, Morgan, and Hiltner, Yerkes became a leading institution in every respect," says Schwarzschild, "including the development of one of the most outstanding, if not *the* outstanding graduate school in astronomy and astrophysics in the country. . . . Chandra was by far the most active member of the group. He just loved to give lectures and was very demanding of his students, many of whom felt enormous loyalty to him."

Schwarzschild recalls his own experience when he first met Chandra in 1937. Schwarzschild was a guest of the Kuipers, who had invited him to spend the Christmas holidays, and he met Chandrasekhar at a small party at Kuiper's house. "I remember that evening vividly," says Schwarzschild. "It was the first time I was in personal contact with a dark-skinned person, and I am embarrassed to say, I recall feeling an instinctive aversion throughout the evening. Then and there I made up my mind that this was something I had to overcome extremely strongly. When we met again a few days later, whatever the aversion was, it had completely disappeared. Even though I was a guest of the Kuipers, I spent most of each day with Chandra. We had terribly important things to discuss about stellar structure. . . . We very fast found our way to each other, he soon, jokingly, gave me home assignments to read at night. One evening the Kuipers decided it would be fun to go to a movie, but I said, 'I cannot. I have Chandra's homework to do.' Mrs. Kuiper insisted, and we went to the movie when she offered to sign a letter of excuse of why I couldn't do my work. I presented that letter to Chandra the following morning."

Chandra's reputation as a teacher, and his youth and enthusiasm for research, soon began to attract students from all parts of the world: Paul Ledoux from Belgium; Mario Schönberg, Jorge Sahade, and Corlos Cesco from Argentina; Gordon W. Wares, Ralph E. Williamson, Wasley S. Krogdahl, Margaret Kiess Krogdahl, and Louis R. Henrich from the United States. These were some of Chandra's students and associates during his early years at Yerkes. Later on, after the Second World War, Guido Münch, Arthur Dodd Code, Donald E. Osterbrock, Esther Conwell, Jeremiah P. Ostriker, and many others were to follow. Chandra's own research and writing continued, unabated by the teaching, the advising, and the weekly colloquia he instituted. For instance, during his first year at Yerkes, in addition to writing half a dozen research papers, he completed the manuscript of his first monograph, *An Introduction to the Study of Stellar Structure.*

This pattern of teaching, research, and writing was to persist from 1938 to 1944, a period in which his researches encompassed work on stellar dynamics, dynamical friction, stochastic problems in physics and astronomy, and the negative hydrogen ion. From 1944 to 1949, Chandra's preoccupation was with radiative transfer and, as he often says, it was the happiest period of his scientific life. "My research on radiative transfer gave me the most satisfaction," says Chandra. "I worked on it for five years, and the subject, I felt, developed on its own initiative and momentum. Problems arose one by one, each more complex and difficult than the previous one, and they were solved. The whole subject attained an elegance and a beauty which I do not find to the same degree in any of my other work. And when I finally wrote the book *Radiative Transfer,* I left the area entirely. Although I could think of several problems, I did not want to spoil the coherence and beauty of the subject [by further additions]. Furthermore, as the subject had developed, I also had developed. It gave me for the first time a degree of self-assurance and confidence in my scientific work because here was a situation where I was not looking for problems. The subject, not easy by any standards, seemed to evolve on its own."

· II ·

The onset of the Second World War, and his anguish and concern for India and the world at large, dampened Chandra's exuberance for science. "With the War dispersing all values," he wrote to his father on 26 December 1940, "the pursuit of science and of study and scholarship seems almost futile and unimportant."

He was impatient with America prior to the Pearl Harbor disaster. Finally, when America did enter the war, Chandra wrote in a jubilant mood on 11 December 1941: "America has entered the war with unity and determination and though the final round may not come for a long time, no one doubts that the eventual outcome will be [a total] victory for the United States and Great Britain."

Lalitha and Chandra spent October to December 1941 at the Institute for Advanced Study in Princeton. Chandra had maintained contact with John von Neumann, his friend from Cambridge days. Von Neumann had often expressed the hope that Chandra would make an extended visit to Princeton. After some effort, and with the help of Henry Norris Russell and H. D. Smyth (heads of the astronomy and physics departments), he was able to gather a sum of $1,000 for Chandra's visit. Chandra wrote to his father on their arrival at Princeton on 3 October, "To be in the same Institute as Einstein, Weyl, Pauli, and others, it is a privilege! But terrifying all the same. I have an office at the Institute with a marvelous view. I have to give two lectures a week and am planning to attend a fair number of lectures by others. Three months will pass before we even notice them."

On 7 December 1941, while Chandra and Lalitha were still at Princeton, the Japanese struck at Pearl Harbor and America entered the war. Chandra decided to take the initiative and join the rest of the scientific community, which was unanimously behind the war effort. However, because he was not a citizen of the United States, he could not enter into classified work.

Von Neumann was engaged in war-related work. He was a consultant for the Ballistic Research Laboratory at the Aberdeen Proving Grounds (APG) in Maryland, and he thought Chandra's service could be useful there. He had written to Chandra earlier, on 18 October 1940, "There is great interest at the Ballistic Laboratory at Aberdeen and among men working there on interior ballistics in general, in the theory of gases, and especially in questions of the equations of state of very dense gases. In spite of the dissimilarity of the interior of a white dwarf and of the explosion chamber of a gun, it is probable that your past experience in this field would be very valuable. If you feel like following up such a subject, will you let me know, or write directly to Mr. R. H. Kent."

Robert H. Kent was the leader of a group of mathematicians, astronomers, and physicists assembled at the Aberdeen Proving Grounds in Maryland to study and solve the ballistics problems. "APG was a very large encampment with thousands of troops in various stages of training in the handling and maintenance of weapons," says Robert G. Sachs. It had isolated test areas sticking out at the northern end of Chesapeake Bay, known as Abbey Point. Apparently, according to Sachs, the Ballistic Research Laboratory was established during the First World War with a small group of scientists whose task was to study the ballistics of artillery missiles and prepare firing tables to be used in the battlefields to set the elevation of the artillery piece so that the missile could be fired at a certain predetermined range and then hit the target.

Chandra wrote to Kent after returning to Yerkes in the early part of 1942, but it took more than a year before he got the necessary clearance to work at the APG. He was a British subject; the clearance has to go through British intelligence channels. The appointment, after considerable bureaucratic delay, was finally authorized by the Secretary of War on 27 January

1943, and Chandra started his work at the APG in early February of that year. The work carried a remuneration of $30 per day with travel allowance. From February 1943 until the end of the war, Chandra commuted between Yerkes and APG—three weeks at Yerkes, three weeks at APG. "It was pretty strenuous," recalls Chandra. "But the entire scientific community was behind the war effort. No two opinions as in the case of Vietnam. I was part of that effort. I didn't mind the strain."

Lalitha recalls: "when he returned to Yerkes, he was busier than ever. He would double his teaching to make up for the three weeks, plus his research. . . . I used to marvel at him though, how he could switch from one type of work to another."

At APG, Chandra became a part of an outstanding group of scientists which included John von Neumann, Ronald Gurney, Joseph Meyer, I. H. Thomas, Martin Schwarzschild, Edwin Hubble, Robert Sachs, and many others. Chandra shared an office with Sachs and worked on ballistic tests, the theory of shock waves, the so-called Mach effect, and transport problems related to neutron diffusion. He felt stimulated by the novelty of the applied, war-related work, the companionship of scientists from diverse fields, and the feeling of service and sacrifice in the cause of humanity.

At the same time, he was exposed to ugly incidents of harassment and humiliation because of the color of his skin. Scarred by earlier incidents of discrimination, Chandra totally avoided bringing Lalitha to Aberdeen, a rural community that, although not in the South, shared southern attitudes when it came to segregation. On the proving grounds he was given accommodations in the officer's annex. After an embarrassing first incident, when he was refused service at the officers' mess, things were straightened out. "Kent went to the commanding general," recalls Sachs, "and laid it on the line."

In the United States, meanwhile, von Neumann attempted to enlist Chandra for the Manhattan Project in 1944. Chandra knew about the A-bomb project vaguely, since he used to talk to Eugene Wigner, Edward Teller, Enrico Fermi, and others at Chicago. Their indirect questions regarding his work on radiative transfer and neutron diffusion gave him some hints. In any case, on 9 March 1944, in a letter marked confidential, von Neumann wrote:

> They are convinced, and I am in full agreement with them, that the project would gain very much if it could acquire your collaboration. A number of their problems are such, that you are the one logical man to deal with them considering your astrophysical work—others [some

other problems] would be quite logical continuation of your present work on shocks. Your joining the project would certainly further several essential phases in a way in which nothing else could. I have no doubt that it will be successfully completed in a very finite time, and that the possession of its results by one country or the other and the manner of its use will greatly influence and, with a not inconsiderable probability, decide the future of the world. . . . The scientific problems of the project are very interesting, the group which dealt with it is first rate. I would only say that I have never lived before and never expect to live hereafter in a better intellectual atmosphere.

Hans Bethe, the man in charge of negotiations, followed up von Neumann's letter and wrote on 20 March 1944 how happy Teller, Weisskopf, Oppenheimer, and he would be if Chandra joined them. "We are in great need of your help," Bethe urged, "and we believe that you would be the best man to ask to take charge of certain calculations which have some loose connection with work you have been doing in Aberdeen. We have no other person who understands this type of problem with the exception of Johnny [von Neumann], who is here only a fraction of the time, and is then very busy with certain other problems. Apart from taking charge of this work, we would also like to have you here in general because there never seem to be enough intelligent people to do all the theoretical work that is necessary."

Chandra agreed to join them, although he had considerable reservations regarding leaving Yerkes and living at Los Alamos. Clearance procedures were set in motion and in September 1944, Chandra was informed that he was cleared; an apartment had been reserved for him, and Oppenheimer would do everything to make the work and surrounding circumstances as attractive as possible. However, by then Chandra had changed his mind. He felt that the war was coming to an end. He had strong obligations to Yerkes. Moving to Los Alamos would also mean a total disruption of his work. "You are certainly right," wrote Bethe on 27 September 1944, "that it looks as if the European War would be over in a short time and that is quite a decision to go full time into war work just at this time." Nonetheless, von Neumann continued to exhort Chandra to go to Los Alamos. In the end the idea was dropped and Chandra did not go to Los Alamos.

In spite of the disruptions caused by the war and commuting between Yerkes and Aberdeen, Chandra's research continued, and he produced a steady stream of papers and books. He was promoted to an associate professorship in 1942, followed by a promotion to full professorship in 1943. A letter from Milne in 1941 gave indirect hints that he was going to be nominated as a Fellow of the Royal Society of England, with a warning, however, not to be unduly disappointed if the honor was delayed.

· III ·

As the war ended, the process of rebuilding the universities began everywhere. Scientists involved with war work began to return slowly to their home institutions. Hutchins was on the move to rebuild the University of Chicago. "He made several new 'distinguished service professor' appointments," Chandra recalls, "though the convention at the University had always been that the title of a distinguished service professor was given someone who has in fact served the university for a number of years. But people like Enrico Fermi, Harold Urey, Carl Rosby, Marshall Stone, and James Franck, who did not fit this category, were appointed as distinguished service professors." On the other hand, Struve, who *had* served the University for a number of years, was not offered one. Chandra was responsible for reminding Hutchins of the oversight, and Hutchins went on to give Struve the appointment.

Chandra received an offer of a research professorship from Princeton to succeed Henry Norris Russell in August 1946. When Hutchins learned of the Princeton offer, however, he called Chandra to his office in the presence of Struve and Dean Bartky and offered him a distinguished service professorship and matched the Princeton salary. Chandra was in an awkward position. Hutchins approached him again and asked to see him alone. Chandra recalls that meeting with Hutchins vividly. "If you feel that your work is going to be enhanced by going to Princeton, I wouldn't stop you," Hutchins said, "because what is in your interest and in the interest of your future scientific work, is also my interest; and I do not gain anything by pressuring you, by asking you to be here, offering you higher salary, and so on. I do not want to do that. You have to make up your own mind whether there is something scientifically which we lack in the way of support. If there is nothing lacking then you ought to stay."

After this meeting, Chandra decided against going to Princeton and wrote tactfully to decline. "I am sorry to inform you," wrote Chandra to Russell on 15 October 1946, "that in consequence of my discussions [with Hutchins], I have reversed my earlier decision and [have decided] to continue my association with the Yerkes Observatory and the University of Chicago. . . . I would, however, like to say that the two factors which have weighed most heavily are first my increasing conviction that I could not do justice to the great tradition you have built at Princeton and second, that having already built to some extent theoretical astrophysics at the Yerkes Observatory during the past ten years, I did not want to start all over again."

Russell accepted Chandra's decision graciously.

That was the last time Chandra ever considered leaving the University of Chicago, even though offers began to come from other institutions in the States and Cambridge, England.

This particularly happy phase in Chandra's life ended in the early 1950s. In 1952 he became the managing editor of the *Astrophysical Journal;* while the editorship constituted a distinctive service of the highest merit to the scientific community at large, it tempered the pure joy of doing science, since the position imposed serious demands on his time and made him vulnerable to criticism by others on whose work he had to make judgment.

Other events intervened. Acting as chairman of the department in 1952, in place of Bengt Strömgren, who was spending the summer months in Copenhagen, Chandra came into an administrative conflict with his colleague, who had been a friend since Chandra's stay in Copenhagen in 1932–33. Strömgren, though an able astronomer, proved to be an inefficient administrator. And Chandra thought that it was "a frank, straightforward matter" to say to Strömgren, whom he considered a close friend, "Bengt, things are so disorganized, How can you continue to do that? In the best interests of the observatory, you should resign. Let Kuiper be the director." Apparently, Strömgren did not take the criticism well. He talked to other members of the faculty. A deputation went to President Kimpton, who reappointed Strömgren as the director with a letter to the department expressing his and Kuiper's full confidence in him.

Furthermore, during the same year (1952), Strömgren named a committee entrusted with the task of revising the curriculum that Chandra had designed and taught for the preceeding fifteen years. It became apparent that in the committee's revised curriculum Chandra had no place. At a faculty meeting where the new curriculum was on the agenda, Chandra had to leave before this item came up for discussion. As he was about to leave, Strömgren asked him for comments on the revised curriculum. Chandra recalls having said, "If you have a committee and you want to revise the curriculum, and if the department votes positively on it, of course, you have the right to go ahead, and I shall have no objection. But there ought to be one thing about which there is no misunderstanding. To the extent that I have had no role in revising the curriculum nor been consulted, I retain for myself the right to find a place in the University outside the astronomy department if I so choose." Notwithstanding the clear warning from Chandra, the faculty went ahead and voted to adopt the new curriculum.

As Peter Vandervoort says, "If you look at the graduate catalog of the astronomy department during the years 1938–52, you will see that Chandra did an enormous amount of teaching during those years, giving six or more courses a year. Basic courses: a three quarter sequence on stellar interiors, a three quarter sequence on stellar dynamics and galactic structure. He followed that up the following year with a three quarter sequence on stellar atmospheres, a three quarter sequence on interstellar matter, and so on. After 1952, you see an abrupt change in the program."

By coincidence, not long after this incident, Enrico Fermi invited him to become a member of the Research Institute (now the Enrico Fermi Institute) and the physics department of the University of Chicago. And fortuitously, Marvin Goldberger in the physics department wanted to take a leave of absence but could not do so unless he found a substitute to teach his course on mathematical physics. Chandra offered to teach this course. To no one's surprise, students liked Chandra's lectures. When the chairman of the department (Andrew Lawson) asked Chandra whether he would like to continue teaching in the physics deparement, Chandra readily agreed. Since 1952, although he did not officially resign, Chandra has rarely taught a course in the astronomy department.

"I think on the whole, this experience in the early 1950s did as much for my science if not more than my earlier episode with Eddington, because it made me associate with people like Fermi and Gregor Wentzel, whom I would not have had close contact with if I had stayed at Yerkes. I set up an experimental laboratory in hydromagnetism with Sam Allison. I taught all the standard courses in physics, quantum mechanics, electrodynamics, etc. I was the first one to teach relativity at the University of Chicago, which of course led me to research in relativity."

This turn of events, however, was not without an effect on his attitude towards his colleagues. It ruffled his inner self. It marked an end to a period of blissful naiveté, a period in which he was totally oblivious to all matters other than his science. He had continued his research, which brought steadily increasing recognition and stature in the scientific world. Thus, he was elected to the Royal Society in 1944, was awarded the Bruce

Medal in 1952, and the Gold Medal of the Royal Astronomical Society in 1953. With the exception of Eddington, no other astronomer had received both of these medals by the age of forty-two.

Chandra's thoughts also wandered to his early years at Yerkes, to the discrepancies and discrimination in Struve's treatment of him relative to his colleagues Strömgren, Kuiper, and Morgan. They had all been appointed as assistant professors in the first year, whereas Chandra was designated a "research associate." The following year, they were promoted with tenure. Chandra was reappointed as an assistant professor with no change in salary and remained an assistant professor for four years, until 1942. When they joined Yerkes, Kuiper and Strömgren were reimbursed for their travel expenses. Struve made no such offer to Chandra, who had in fact borrowed money from his father to pay for Lalitha's passage from India. They all had secretaries of their own, while Chandra had no secretary until 1944, after he was elected to the Royal Society; even then he had only a part-time secretary, Frances Herman. Manuscripts for his scientific papers, books, and his correspondence were all handwritten during his first seven years at Yerkes.

· IV ·

However, remembering these incidents did not in the least interfere with his work. "I became aware," he said, "but not affected. They had no real impact on my daily life. The incredible fact is that in earlier years I was not even aware that something impolite, something improper had been done to me."

The years that followed as managing editor of the *Astrophysical Journal* only worsened matters. No longer wrapped in pure science, his mood of optimism and innocence gave way to one of pessimism and frustration.

Chandra was managing editor of the *Astrophysical Journal* from 1952 to 1971. When he began, *ApJ* was essentially a private journal of the University of Chicago. Chandra played a decisive role in transforming it into the national journal of the American Astronomical Society. When circumstances thrust upon him the editorship, he became, by his own admission, "autocratic, the complete master, and totally responsible for the journal."

During the first twelve years of his tenure, the journal staff consisted only of Chandra and a part-time secretary with an office in Yerkes Observatory. "Between us we took care of all the routine work," says Chandra. We took care of the scientific correspondence. We prepared the budget, advertisements, and page charges. We made out the reprint orders and sent out the bills." In the final stages of the publication of a paper, Chandra personally transcribed the author's corrections on the galleys to the printer's copy. "This task would appear to be needless," observes Chandra, "but I am sorry to say that the corrections made by the authors are often in the form of hieroglyphics, which only a person who has some understanding of what is being written can understand."

In his first year as editor, six issues of the journal totaling 950 pages were published. Every year, the journal grew. In 1968, it became twelve annual issues, and starting in July 1970 it became twenty-four issues, totaling over 12,000 pages a year. In addition to the regular *Astrophysical Journal,* Chandra was also responsible for the Supplement series of the journal, and, as though this was not enough, in 1967 he started a separate Letters section of the *Astrophysical Journal* to be able to publish short accounts of important discoveries faster. At the end of his tenure, he left behind a reserve fund of $500,000 for the journal.

The journal, according to all those I talked with, improved in quality under Chandra's leadership to become the leading astrophysics journal in the world. "It was a kind of Golden Age for all of us," says Eugene Parker. "Many of us, at times, had difficulties publishing papers in the *Astrophysical Journal,* but it was the Golden Age compared to other times and other journals." Chandra selected referees, sought their advice if needed, and communicated the relevant, edited version of the referees' remarks to the authors. He handled controversial issues deftly and diplomatically, but never relaxed his high standards regarding scientific substance and presentation. The final decision to publish a paper or not was entirely his. He was not immodest, but only truthful, when he wrote to Herman Bondi, "The policies of the *Astrophysical Journal* are my policies." This authoritarian rule did not go unopposed. Threats of impeachment ensued, but by and large there was universal acclaim of his stewardship, to which he responds:

> A journal is what the authors write. The editor doesn't solicit articles; the articles come to him. If the editor has in some way encouraged publication of good papers, promptly, efficiently, and fairly, he has done a little service, but the credit for the quality is not the editor's. It belongs to the astronomical community.

This may be true; however, few would disagree that the journal required an enormous investment of time and energy on Chandra's part. With strict self-discipline, apportioning his time meticulously between the two roles, he maintained his usual level of research activity. He sought no reduction in his teaching load or other responsibilities. For nineteen years he remained tied to the job without sabbaticals or periods of leisure. He imposed upon himself an isolation from the astronomical community in order to be fair and without prejudice for or against particular individuals.

"Why? Why do you do this?" asked Enrico Fermi once, seeing Chandra carrying a stack of manuscripts to the Press. Chandra had no answer then nor does he have one now. "In retrospect, it was a mistake," he says, "a distortion of my personal life. I had no idea I would keep it for so long when I took it. I had no choice then."

Nonetheless, it is amazing that Chandra did not let this interfere in any way with his own scientific work. When he took on the editorship, he had made up his mind to that effect, and indeed, when one looks at the record of his scientific work, which continued essentially undiminished in quantity and untarnished in quality, it is difficult for anyone to believe that he was also the editor of the *Astrophysical Journal* for nineteen years.

Furthermore, he did not let the journal affect his teaching responsibilities, nor did he seek in any way to reduce them. "In those years, I integrated my research with my teaching, which I have always felt to be an essential component of my scientific efforts." How did he manage? "By being extremely strict about apportioning the time." The journal office, although located in the same building, was separate from his usual office and had strictly prescribed hours. Outside those hours his mind was firmly closed to journal business.

Chandra likes to tell a story about his "extremely good relations" with the Press. In February of 1963, Maarten Schmidt called him from Pasadena and told that he had found an enormous redshift—a redshift of 0.2, the biggest at that time—showing that the quasars were at cosomological distances. Would Chandra publish his findings in the journal?

Chandra said to him, "Well, today is Wednesday. If you send the manuscript by airmail, I will get it on Friday morning. The next issue of the journal is going to press on Friday. I will hold it, and I will have your paper typeset. And I will read the proofs over the weekend. Your article will come in the next issue." He told the Press about it, and they agreed not to print the journal until Monday.

The six-page paper arrived on Friday, not by the morning mail, however, but by the afternoon mail. When Chandra took it to the typesetter at two in the afternoon instead of ten in the morning, as he had anticipated, the foreman said, "Mr. Chandra, we can't do anything about it because we are not supposed to work on Saturdays. So how are we to do that?" When Chandra looked sad and disappointed, the foreman said, "Wait, let me see what my men tell me." He returned after talking to them for a few minutes and said to Chandra, "Well, Mr. Chandra, nobody need know that we worked on Saturday. Right? But one condition: on Monday, at lunch time, you will have to tell us what this is all about." The paper was typeset and proofread on Saturday, and the journal rolled off the press on Monday. And on Monday, at lunch time, the compositors and the proofreaders of the Press were the first in the whole world to learn about quasars! "I don't know whether they understood it," says Chandra, "but a few months later, when Maarten Schmidt appeared on the cover of *Time,* copies of it were plastered all over the place. From that time on, anything I said went. They were extraordinarily nice."

· V ·

Beginning in 1952, Chandra became more closely associated with the physics department on the main campus of the University of Chicago. He began to teach regular physics courses instead of only the astronomy and astrophysics courses he had taught in the years before and after the war. Furthermore, physics began to dominate Chandra's research, beginning in the early 1950s with his work in magnetohydrodynamics, stability of rotating fluids, plasma physics, and ellipsoidal figures of equilibrium. Eventually, beginning in the early 1960s, he became more and more interested in Einstein's general theory of relativity and the mathematical study of black holes and of colliding waves, which he has continued to explore.

Since the curriculum change introduced in the astronomy department at Yerkes had oriented it towards observational astronomy rather than the theoretical problems in astrophysics, Chandra's research students after 1952 came almost exclusively from the physics department. The formal relations between Chandra and his colleagues at Yerkes after this had little or no effect on him or on the students and visitors at the observatory. Life went on as before. Chandra continued to be in charge of the weekly colloquium he had instituted. Every time these serially numbered colloquia reached a new hundredth mark, Chandra would give a special colloquium. Lalitha would provide a "birthday" cake. If there was a popular film in one of the neighboring larger towns, Lalitha and Chandra were always ready to take a car full of visitors or students. Their home was frequently open for afternoon teas. "I remember Lalitha's homemade crumpets," says Margaret Burbidge. "They were baked in a special ring on a griddle in front of your eyes and then served with butter. Since my husband and I were from England, we perhaps had a better chance than some people of meeting Chandra on a more informal basis. Chandra loved to gossip about what was going on in Cambridge and in England in general. Another special thing I remember is the annual autumnal leaf-raking parties to which all his graduate students, research associates, and visitors were invited—those wonderful teas to follow an afternoon spent raking the leaves on Chandra's lawn."

In the early 1960s, long after he had ceased to be the university's president, in a lecture widely reprinted in the newspapers, Hutchins asserted that the chairman of a science department had opposed the appointment of a leading theoretical astronomer to its faculty "because he was an Indian, and black." and when the *New York Times* called Chandra to ask what he thought of Hutchins's remark he said, "The University of Chicago was thirty years ahead of the times."

Williams Bay continued to be their home of Chandra and Lalitha until 1964. During the years 1946–52, Chandra used to drive to Chicago to teach every Thursday, occasionally staying overnight at the International House at 59th and Dorchester. From 1952 onwards, however, overnight stay became a regular feature because of editing the *Astrophysical Journal* and teaching on the main campus. "I used to give two lectures," Chandra recalls, "one on Thursday and the other on Friday. I used to come early on Thursday morning to the campus. During the time I worked with Fermi, I spent Thursday mornings largely with him, and whatever time I had left over I used to spend at the journal office and/or attending colloquia. Fridays I would mostly attend to the journal work. I preferred direct meetings to correspondence with the people with whom I worked for the journal. The stay at the International House used to cost $3.00 a night, which was all that I could afford at the time." It also turned out that for many of his students it was a splendid opportunity to talk to him while waiting in the cafeteria line.

· VI ·

During those years of commuting between Williams Bay and Chicago, especially after Chandra started teaching regularly on the main campus in 1952, Chandra and Lalitha had often considered moving to Chicago. As an initial step in this direction, in 1959 they had rented a one-bedroom apartment near the University (5550 Dorchester Avenue) so that they could stay overnight during their weekly Thursday-Friday visits to Chicago. "But we had some misgivings about moving permanently to Chicago," they now say.

In Williams Bay, people were accustomed from the beginning to our way of entertaining friends and guests with only vegetarian food and nonalcoholic drinks. In Chicago, especially after the war, people had taken to giving cocktail parties. And during our stays in Chicago over the weekends and other visits, we were often invited to such parties and also to dinner parties with the Mayers, Ureys, Fermis, and Andersons. We used to be invited at 7 PM, but sometimes the drinks went on for hours. We thought we would of course have to reciprocate such hospitality but we couldn't imagine ourselves being able to reciprocate in the same manner, in the proper style. Gradually we realized that we didn't have to. And one day in 1964, as we were driving past the newly constructed highrise building at 4800 Lake Shore Drive on our way back to Williams Bay, Lalitha suggested that we go and look at the model apartment and find out if any apartments were available. A two-bedroom apartment on the twenty-fifth floor was available, and we signed a lease. After staying there for three years, we moved to our present location on Dorchester Avenue.

Chandra's closer association with the main campus also brought about his closer association with the university administrators and his participation in university affairs. Besides Hutchins, who played such a significant role in getting Chandra to the University of Chicago and retaining him, Chandra had extremely friendly relations with two other presidents of the University, namely, Edward Levi and John Wilson. "Chandra always symbolized, to me at least," says Levi, "a kind of humanistic scientist, a person of enormously high standards, determined, idealistic, brilliant, and one who never seemed to deviate from his own ideals, ideals for a great scholar. I always thought of him as the kind of person for whom and through whom the university existed."

"In the low period that followed Fermi's death," says James Cronin, "Chandra's loyalty to the University of Chicago and his remaining in Chicago while many well-known scientists left has been an enormous contribution to this University. With his monumental stature, he has served as the conscience of the department, acting strongly whenever needed in preventing bad appointments, bad scholarships, etc." However, opinions differ in regard to his having exerted strong influence within the department. As Valentine Telegdi, a great admirer and friend of Chandra, says, "In the early fifties, there was this unbelievable constellation of people. There was Fermi, there was Edward Teller, Gregor Wentzel, Joe and Maria Mayer, Harold Urey, Willard Libby, and a good number of other people whom I may have overlooked. Then came Murray Gell-Mann, Richard Garwin. . . . After Fermi's death, a sort of decay began, and Chandra and Wentzel, who had such unique positions and universal respect in the university and in the department, did not do enough to stem the decay. Of course, Chandra's reserved nature and character, his resolve not to say anything unless he felt he was absolutely correct, were responsible for his reticence in speaking out."

When Chandra speaks of his singular association of more than fifty years with the University of Chicago, he has only good things to say. "I have been through the administrations of six presidents," he says, "and I had extremely cordial relations with all of them; more than what a faculty member is likely to have with the chief administrator of the university. I have never felt that any other university could have or would have done anything more than what the University of Chicago has done for me."

Age seems to have little or no impact on Chandra's fervor for science and the pursuit of the life of the mind. Since his classic work on the mathematical theory of black holes, published in 1983, he has pursued the study of colliding waves and the Newtonian two-center problem in the framework of the general theory of relativity. These studies are again, as one has come to expect from Chandra, not in the mainstream of contemporary activity in the study of general relativity. And it may take some time to appreciate some of the startling results that have emerged from his studies. But that does not perturb Chandra in the least.

The year 1987 marked the 300th anniversary of the publication of Newton's *Principia.* Responding to lecture invitations in Cambridge, England, and other places, Chandra began to delve deeply, not only into the origins and circumstances of the writing of the *Principia,* but also into the very heart of the *Principia* itself, as few people have done. After three centuries, Newton comes to life again, as Chandra describes his experience in studying some of Newton's well-known propositions. "I first constructed proofs for myself," he writes. "Then I compared my proofs with those of Newton. The experience was a sobering one. Each time, I was left in sheer wonder at the elegance, the careful arrangement, the imperial style, the incredible originality, and above all the astonishing lightness of Newton's proofs; and each time, I felt like a schoolboy admonished by his master."

5

LOWELL T. COGGESHALL

1 9 0 1 – 1 9 8 7

L E O N   O.   J A C O B S O N

LOWELL COGGESHALL was born in Saratoga, Indiana, May 17, 1901, the son of William E. and F. Anne (Warren) Coggeshall. In the unpublished memoirs that he wrote (and that are used here with the permission of Mrs. Becky Coggeshall), he said: "The Coggeshall and Warren families were early immigrants to North America who fled England because of religious persecution. The first Coggeshall (John) arrived in the American colony in 1620 along with Roger Williams, Ann Hutchinson, John Winthrop and other pilgrim fathers and settled in the newly formed Massachusetts Bay Colony. This was the first organized government in the New World. Because of the arbitrary rules of the Church of England many of these original immigrants moved to other parts of the east coast. John Coggeshall moved to Rhode Island in 1636 and became its first president 150 years before it became a state of the new nation." Additional Coggeshall families followed John's migration in those early years and settled on the East Coast.

As the west opened and free land was made available, many Coggeshalls along the East Coast migrated westward. Lowell's father moved in the early 1800s and with other families homesteaded in Indiana. Lowell Coggeshall's grandfather William Rufus Coggeshall studied medicine under the apprentice system and practiced medicine in Farmland City, Indiana, and its surrounding territory. He was a typical country doctor who made house calls using the only means of transportation then available, horseback, carriage, or sleigh; Lowell looked to him for advice and inspiration. Lowell's father and mother were farmers and shopkeepers. They had three children all of whom attended the then typical one-room grade school and a consolidated high school.

· I ·

After graduation from high school in 1918, Lowell T. Coggeshall enrolled at the University of Indiana (Bloomington) and graduated in three years (1921) with a bachelor's degree and a major in zoology. He was an honors student. During his years at Indiana he decided to seek a master's degree and then a doctorate in zoology. In 1921 he was accepted by the department of zoology. His assigned mentor was Professor William Scott. In discussions with Professor Scott on various areas of research Coggeshall finally chose a study of the productivity of the common blue gill (Lepomis paledus). He asked his mentor how he should proceed with such a study and received a sharp reply. Professor Scott said, "Start the project and if you find you cannot solve some of the real difficulties come back and tell me and I'll try to help you. Otherwise I suggest you might as well forget about becoming an investigator." Lowell told me that he had never forgotten that statement. In fact he then proceeded with his own ideas, which he described as follows "This research effort involved counting the number of blue gill nests in Winona Lake, the circumference of which was 20 miles."

In his account of this project he wrote, "The first part was easy since each nest was seen from a rowboat as a clear spot on the lake bottom 10 to 15 feet below the water surface. How to count the larvae was the problem. I solved the counting problem in a rather simple way. I would descend to the nest with a diver's helmet, holding one end of an empty rubber tube tightly closed with my fingers and the other end of the tube projecting above the water. When I released my finger tip from the end of the tube over the nest, the larvae were neatly swept quite cleanly into the tube. The larvae were transferred to a pickling solution for later counting. In view of my mentor's remarks I had completed my project before I reported my results to him." Coggeshall presented his finding at a departmental meeting and it was accepted as qualifying for a master's degree and publication was recommended. "I was thus off and running, to work on a doctorate in freshwater biology with my first publication."

This work attracted the attention of Professor E. A. Riggs, an international authority on limnology (the study of freshwater lakes) at the University of Wisconsin. He was seeking an assistant to aid him in the intensive study of the flora and fauna and chemical components of the water of Green Lake in Wisconsin near Madison.

Coggeshall accepted the offer for the summer months of that year. He

Lowell T. Coggeshall

arrived with his diving bell at the University of Wisconsin in late spring to join Professor Riggs and Professor Juday. "The procedure was to take samples from one square meter plots on the lake bottom at depths of from one to twenty feet. Air was pumped down to me and I recall having heavy lead weights on my waist and ankles. The water was very cold and I could tolerate only about five minutes per dive."

At the end of summer Coggeshall returned to the University of Indiana eager to start on research for his doctorate. "I was soon discouraged. The project assigned to me was to attempt to breed the blue gill in an old discarded lead tank. The small fingerlings collected and placed in the tank not only would not breed, they would not even eat. However, I struggled along until luck turned in my favor again. I was invited to join a Rockefeller Foundation research team in Georgia which was under the direction of S. T. Darling who formerly was the chief pathologist at the Panama Canal Hospital during the construction of the canal."

"I joined the Rockefeller field team for the summer quarter and began collecting water samples and adult larvae to be identified back in the laboratory. Before the end of the summer I had found that the malaria-carrying mosquito larvae could breed proliferatively in fresh water and standing water where there was an abundance of microscopic organisms and algae, whereas they would not breed but would subsist in other water." These results were published and widely quoted. Dr. Darling invited Coggeshall to return the following summer to continue the studies by making a chemical analysis of the different kinds of water in which larvae would survive and thus try to determine why the larvae would be found in some waters and not in others. Unfortunately Dr. Darling was killed in a car accident in Yugoslavia, where he had gone as the U.S. representative of the newly established World Health Organization.

· II ·

It was after this experience that Coggeshall made the decision to study medicine. His physician friends in Indiana and those he had met in the Georgia experience convinced him that if he wished to continue studies on disease-transmitting insects he would be handicapped if he did not have a medical degree, for the reason that a Ph.D. would encounter problems working on the definitive host, man.

Coggeshall told me that some members of the department of zoology were not happy with his decision but among those who encouraged his decision was Professor Alfred Kinsey, who was a professor of entomology in the zoology department. He convinced Coggeshall not to be unduly concerned with the critical remarks of the zoologists toward his decision to pursue the study of medicine. Kinsey went on to say, "the reasons you have given me are valid ones but life and one's work sometimes lead one from one direction to another." As a matter of fact, Kinsey added, "I am going to change from the study of insects to pursue some elemental aspects of human reproduction." Professor Kinsey did indeed change his direction, the change producing the famous Kinsey report on *Sexual Behavior in the Human Male,* which we all remember as a best seller and which caused a number of raised eyebrows. Cogg received his master's degree in 1923 in zoology.

Coggeshall next applied, was accepted and enrolled at the Medical School of Indiana University. He graduated in the spring of 1928. It was during his medical school years that he met and fell in love with an art student, Miss Jackie Holland, who came to the medical school in order to take a course in anatomy which was required of art students. Dr. Coggeshall was her teacher. After her anatomy studies were completed, she moved on to San Francisco for additional study in her field. Coggeshall, in the meantime, had applied to the new medical school at the University of Chicago, where he became one of its first interns in the hospital complex built to teach medical students and the more advanced house officers. Here Cogg served as intern (1928–29), resident (1929–30), instructor (1930–31), and assistant professor (1932–35). Soon after his arrival at the University of Chicago he became interested in the infectious disease unit under Oswald Robertson and with him published a number of papers on the pathogenesis of pneumococcal pneumonia and attempts to produce a specific antiserum for its treatment. There were no antibiotics available at that time.

In Cogg's memoirs he states, "One wonderful day I received a letter from Miss Jackie Holland, my first love during my Indiana med school days, saying she planned to come through Chicago on her way to Indiana and would like to stop and say hello. We met, much to my joy, had dinner at the Black Hawk Restaurant in Chicago where I proposed to her. She accepted and we were married in Chicago on May 15, 1930." They had three children, Richard, who is now a physician practicing in Texas, and Diane and Carol, who are married and have children of their own.

· III ·

In 1936 he was offered the opportunity to join the staff of the Rockefeller Institute as an investigative staff member. His research there involved studying the biology of several species of malarial parasites as well as directing some of his attention to antimalaria therapy. In 1941 he accepted an offer from the University of Michigan in Ann Arbor as professor of epidemiology and chairman of tropical diseases in the school of public health.

With the outbreak of the Second World War, the Naval Medical Corp found him, or he found the navy. His interest and broad expertise in medicine and tropical disease in general was needed to solve major health problems of the armed forces and those of the allies that were preparing for encounters in Africa and the Far East. In 1942 Coggeshall took a leave of absence from the University of Michigan and with others established the medical services for the military air routes in Africa, the Middle East, India, and China. The central problem was medical services in general with a major emphasis on prevention of malaria and other tropical diseases.

In 1944, he was commissioned captain in the United States Navy and became the senior medical officer of the 5,000-bed rehabilitation center and hospital in Klamath Falls, Oregon. This hospital received troops from the battle fields of the war zones and was devoted exclusively to the care and treatment of naval and marine personnel suffering from tropical diseases, especially malaria. Under Coggeshall's direction this hospital was a center for the testing of new antimalarial drugs being developed by various drug companies and medical schools, including a large project under Professor Alf Alving, which was carried out at the University of Chicago and at Stateville Prison in Illinois.

For this naval service he received the Gorgas Medal, named after the Panama-Canal builder, from the Association of Military Surgeons as well as a letter of commendation and medal from the United States Navy.

· IV ·

After his enormous contribution to his country and its allies he returned to the University of Michigan. Soon thereafter, however, in 1946, he was persuaded by Chancellor Robert Hutchins to become professor and chairman of medicine at the University of Chicago. At that time I was serving as an associate dean of the biological sciences medical division under Wendell Harrison. During my contact with Coggeshall at that juncture I quickly learned of his genius in leadership as well as his enthusiasm for the Chicago plan that included the medical school and hospitals within the division of the biological sciences.

Coggeshall's previous experience at the University of Chicago from 1925 to 1934 had provided him with a thorough understanding of our unique medical school, which had a medical staff of full-time salaried physicians who were equally trained in patient care, teaching, and research. To my knowledge the Chicago medical school was the only one in the world so organized. Coggeshall did not profess to be a master clinician but he had broad experience as a research worker, special teaching assistantships, and his assistant professorship earlier in his career at the University of Chicago as preparation for his new duties.

As a chairman of medicine, he did not establish a general medical service under his personal direction, as is found in most medical schools, but he participated by seeing outpatients and would, without warning, join various speciality services on "grand rounds" with the chief of a given service and medical students, house officers, and younger teachers. He continued his research, again joining the infectious disease group with which he had been associated in the late 1920s and early 1930s.

As chairman of medicine he was a very effective and active leader. It was during this short period of three years that he had great success in enriching the division with a larger endowment and better facilities. He changed the general attitude of the teaching staff from its steady state to one of enthusiastic participation in patient care, teaching, and research. No doubt his past experience and his immediate success as a leader convinced Chancellor Hutchins in 1950 that he needed Coggeshall as dean of the entire division of biological sciences and the medical school.

As dean of the division, a position he held for sixteen years, he had many connections with Presidents Eisenhower and Nixon, the American Cancer Society, the National Institutes of Health, the National Academy of Sciences, and numerous other research and educational organizations and business leaders in the Midwest and on the East Coast. Coggeshall more than doubled the endowment of the division of biological sciences, improved the quality of the teaching staff, and increased the research activities of the members of the biological and medical divisions.

· V ·

During his regime as dean, I served as associate dean or was an assistant dean for a relatively brief period. I had assumed the position of the director of the medical and biological program of the Argonne Cancer Research Hospital, and the Metallurgical Laboratory on campus, which was part of the Manhattan Project. One day I walked into his office across the hall and after a brief exchange on other matters, I said, "Cogg, with our experience of the Met Lab and biological medicine and our enormous efforts studying the biological effects and localization in tissues of thousands of radioactive isotopes, I think we should seek government support to build a modern research hospital on campus in an effort we could call Atoms for Peace."

We discussed this for perhaps half an hour. Coggeshall thought it was a great idea. While I was in the office he started the ball rolling by picking up the phone and calling Leonard Scheele, the director of the National Institutes of Health. The conversation lasted only four minutes. Coggeshall outlined to Scheele our interest and Scheele explained that at the present time the only monies that were available were for studies on heart disease and cancer and were essentially committed. However, he told Cogg that recently two United States senators, Brian McMahon and Arthur Vandenberg, former chairman of the Atomic Energy Committee, had died of cancer and that 25 million had been appropriated by Congress to the Atomic Energy Commission for research in this field. He suggested that Cogg apply to the Atomic Energy Commission. Cogg then called the atomic energy commissioner in Washington. His response was that Cogg should make a formal application to the commission at once. Within two days, Cogg had the approval of the board of trustees and the central administration of the university for the first hospital devoted to treatment and research using atomic energy. He asked me to prepare the application for the cancer hospital to be located on an open area on Ellis Avenue between 58th and 59th Streets. In short order, I had a rough draft of the requirements of such a building, which would include two floors for patients, two floors for basic biological research, one floor for animal studies, and three below-ground-level floors for work involving high-energy therapy machines, high-energy source machines, a cyclotron, a betatron, and related facilities. After approval by the board, Cogg and William Harrell went to Washington with the plans. Within six weeks of his original call to the Atomic Energy Commission, an OK to go ahead was given. Then a problem developed; the commission had a mandate that no medical-biological installation could be located outside of a National Laboratory Compound. Cogg contacted Walter Zinn, who was the director of the Argonne National Laboratories in Lemont, Illinois. Zinn told Cogg that the last thing he wanted at the Argonne labs was a cancer hospital. This was quickly resolved by a meeting of Cogg, Harrell, and Professor Zinn in Washington at the offices of the Atomic Energy Commission; the cancer hospital would be located on campus providing it was made part of and had to report to the Argonne National Laboratory. This was agreed to by the chancellor of the University of Chicago and the board of trustees. The rest is history. The Argonne Cancer Research Hospital was built on campus and became a vital part of the medical school and biological sciences division.

The establishment of the Argonne Cancer Research Hospital inaugurated a revolution in biological research. It was a national commitment to the use of radioactive isotopes from high-energy radiation sources for the diagnosis and treatment of diseases and for continuing study of isotopes in the body, revealing the intricacy and widespread relationships of different parts of the body to each other in their normal and abnormal functions. This episode illustrated Cogg's insight into the developing nuclear revolution in medicine and biology. Above all, it illustrated the respect the federal government had for his innovative mind and abilities. The Argonne Research Hospital was built with the financial support of the Atomic Energy Commission, which not only paid for the construction of this unique hospital but for more than twenty years fully supported its operation and staff, including the professional staff.

After serving as dean for sixteen years, Coggeshall was persuaded by President Kimpton to join the central administration as vice-president; he continued in that capacity under the presidency of George Beadle. His first year as vice-president he was elected to the board of trustees of the University of Chicago. To my knowledge he was the first vice-president to be elected to the university's board of trustees.

After six years as vice-president of the University of Chicago he resigned in 1966, and he and his wife, Jackie, moved to Foley, Alabama, to join other University of Chicago friends, including Mr. and Mrs. Wendell Harrison and Mr. and Mrs. Wright Adams in a beautiful area partially surrounded by a river which flows southward to the sea and provides fish for the fisherman and alligators for the sightseers.

· VI ·

Coggeshall published more than ninety papers, most of them in prestigious journals. These published papers related to his research on the cause and treatment of infectious diseases including malaria and other so-called tropical diseases and well as pneumococcal and streptococcal infections which were common and often fatal before the era of antibiotic drugs. As significant as these scientific contributions were, a single publication became one of the most widely known of its time; more than two million copies reached every part of the world. This publication entitled *Planning for Medical Progress Through Education* was published in 1965, sponsored by the American Association of Medical Colleges. A distinguished group of physicians and medical scientists were appointed to a committee with Lowell T. Coggeshall as chairman, to study medical education. Their task was to review all aspects of medical education at that time and suggest the paths medical education should follow in the future.

In the journal *Modern Medicine,* in the issue of March 28, 1966, the editor, Irving N. Page, a physician and scientist of international reputation, wrote a two-page article which extolled Coggeshall's great contribution as chairman of the group. Dr. Page wrote: "Colleagues describe Lowell T. Coggeshall as a soft sell telephone diplomat who asks rather than directs and usually gets what he wants. They point out that his talents are multi-dimensional but that he is, above all else, a medical statesman."

During the years in Foley, Alabama, Coggeshall continued to serve on many boards of directors for businesses and educational institutions throughout the nation and regularly attended meetings of the board of trustees at the University of Chicago. It was in Chicago that his first wife, Jackie, passed away after a long, incapacitating illness. About two years later Coggeshall married a lovely lady named Becky who had lost her husband some years previously.

Lowell T. Coggeshall died almost instantly in 1987 of a massive coronary. We all lost a friend and colleague as well as one of the great figures of American medicine. He had been elected a member of the National Academy of Sciences, which is one of the highest honors one can achieve in the world of medicine. He was a member of the American Association of Physicians. I cannot help but wonder why Coggeshall accepted membership on so many boards and committees, but I feel confident that to each of these he offered the help of his talents as a leader.

· VII ·

As I write this brief history of the life and times of Cogg, I look upon him as one who served his country, the world, and the University of Chicago well. In decades to come, his work and the example of his service will continue to bring a message to others. I agree with what Page wrote about him. Having lived for more than forty years as a close associate of Cogg, I can state that he guided me all those years, but that would be only partly correct. I have never known a mentor who gave advice so freely and so graciously and who wasted so few words. He had many talents and characteristics that led him toward the more important and relevant problems of the moment or the future. He was a modest man who took his accolades with pleasure but in stride and treated his family, friends, and peers, of which he had many, as equals. Those fortunate friends who knew him and who had the opportunity to benefit by his wisdom will always remember him and the University of Chicago which he served and enriched.

6

ARTHUR HOLLY COMPTON

1 8 9 2 – 1 9 6 2

J O H N   A.   S I M P S O N

ON A CRISP autumn afternoon in 1928, a father and his son, who had just graduated from high school, wandered into the Ryerson Physical Laboratory on the University of Chicago campus. Although it was Saturday, in one of the research rooms they noticed a man setting up a new instrument and soon found themselves in a lively discussion with physicist Arthur Compton about his plans for work on X rays.

Compton, at the age of thirty-five, had only ten months earlier received the Nobel Prize for physics for his experiment called the "Compton effect." Later he made important discoveries concerning cosmic rays and during the Second World War organized the scientific research that led to the controlled release of nuclear energy.

The young man he encouraged was Luis Alvarez, who joined him in the work on cosmic rays and himself became a Nobel Prize winner. Alvarez later wrote that he could not think "of a more appropriate way for a freshman inclined to science to spend his first day on campus than in conversation with a Nobel Laureate." (1)

Alvarez's recollection calls attention to Compton's wonderfully friendly and helpful attitude towards young scientists. This characteristic pervaded his whole career. It was evident even in the occasional personal encounters I had with him and was vivid in the minds of his colleagues still alive who recalled their memories for me.

He was a charismatic personality. George E. Boyd, who worked as a chemist with Compton during the Second World War, noted that he was: "Handsome, tall, and strongly built, and endowed with a piercing gaze. Possessed with an extremely high IQ, [he was] exceptionally modest and tactful towards others. Unquestionably, he was extremely creative, but he kept this always as a highly personal secret."

Volney Wilson, a close associate of Compton for many years, told me: "As far as my career was concerned, the greatest thing I did was to arrange to do my Ph.D. work with A. H. Compton. No one could have been more supportive of his graduate students. He was considerate, generous in his praise, and treated his graduate students as he would sons."

Volney Wilson came to me in 1942 while I was in my second year of studies for a Ph.D. in physics at New York University and eager to finish my graduate work in order to assist in the war effort. Wilson indicated that there was "a project" at Chicago which would benefit from the invention and development of a super-fast detector for counting particles from radioactive sources. The department of physics of New York University agreed that this problem could be part of my doctoral thesis, and further conversation with Wilson led to my being asked by Compton to come to Chicago. At first I demurred, because I had been offered a position at the Radiation Laboratory in Cambridge with an assurance of housing. This reluctance was overcome when I was told that Compton had offered me a room on the top floor of his own house on Woodlawn Avenue. Soon thereafter I found myself the scientific group leader of the instrumentation section for the project on the third floor of Ryerson Physical Laboratory.

During the war and after, I had only fleeting moments when I talked with Compton, and never on the subject of the origin of cosmic rays. It was not until recently that I fully realized where his personal charm, high goals, and exceptional abilities had their roots.

· I ·

Arthur Compton, the youngest of three sons, was born in 1892 in Wooster, Ohio, to a family which was to become known for its distinguished educators and scientists. Compton's mother was a Mennonite who was devoted to the College of Wooster and its ideals. His father was an ordained Presbyterian minister and professor of philosophy at the College of Wooster. The first son, Karl, became the president of Massachusetts Institute of Technology; the second, Wilson, was president of Washington State University. Their sister, Mary, was a missionary in India. As Compton's colleague Samuel K. Allison said: "The family tradition of teaching was in his blood." (2) It was also a family tradition and part of Compton's credo that a person should keep himself physically and mentally fit to serve at his highest efficiency.

From an early age Compton displayed an interest in mechanical devices and collected rocks and butterflies. At twelve his enthusiasm shifted to as-

Arthur Holly Compton, about 1940

tronomy aided by a telescope purchased from Sears Roebuck with money earned doing chores. The years around the turn of the century must have been exciting for a boy attracted to science and inventions. Popular science magazines told of the discovery of X rays, the electron, and radioactivity, and of the fabulous biplane flights of the Wright brothers. By Compton's sixteenth year, he had begun experimenting with model airplanes and gliders. In a letter to his father, who was in England at the time, he presented a persuasive case for letting him design, build, and fly a glider with a 27-foot wing span. As a result of this enterprise he invented a glider-balancing mechanism with financial help from his brother Karl and patented it. These experiments "were done entirely with my own hands and with a minimum of contact with others. . . ." (3) A year later he published three articles on air flight.

Compton entered the College of Wooster in 1909 and encountered X rays for the first time in the laboratory where his brother Karl was working on his master's thesis. Following Karl to Princeton, he began graduate studies with the distinguished British physicist O. W. Richardson as his advisor. Richardson had built up a fine laboratory with modern X-ray equipment during his stay at Princeton. So impressed was he with his first-year graduate student that when he returned to Great Britain at the outbreak of war in 1914, he passed the laboratory on to him with his "blessing and some advice." In later years Richardson observed, "This turned out to be a very good thing to have done as it is very unlikely that I could have done as much good with it as he did." (4)

Compton and Richardson were again in contact when Compton was at the Cavendish Laboratory in Cambridge during 1919–20 and Richardson was at King's College, London. Both were attempting, unsuccessfully, to use the classical electromagnetic theory of the nineteenth century to explain Compton's X-ray results obtained at Washington University in St. Louis in 1921. Compton was faced with a basic conflict as old as Newton: Was light a wave or a particle phenomenon, or both?

· II ·

The early years of the twentieth century brought a rethinking of the classical theories of mechanics, electricity, magnetism, and light which had been so fruitful for science and engineering in the nineteenth century. However, there were many difficulties in explaining new experimental evidence, such as the absorption and emission of light and heat by material bodies. These difficulties could be removed, said Max Planck in 1900, if we assume that light, as radiant energy, exists only in the form of discrete packages or "light quanta," rather than as continuous electromagnetic waves.

Five years later Einstein was able to apply this idea to explain the ejection of electrons from the surface of a metal when it was irradiated by light of sufficiently short wavelength, i.e., of sufficiently high energy, a phenomenon called the photoelectric effect. This concept of the quantization of energy enabled Niels Bohr in 1913 to develop a powerful theory for atoms in which radiation was absorbed and emitted in discrete quanta of energy corresponding precisely to the discrete spectral lines of different colors that had been observed for many years but were unexplained by classical theory.

By the early 1920s, physicists were faced with the dichotomy of the continuity of energy flow versus quantization of energy. Great resistance remained to the acceptance of quantum mechanics and to Einstein's theory of relativity as applied to atoms. It was in this period that Compton's experiments on the scattering of X rays by electrons in atoms began to have a decisive influence in understanding how light quanta interact with electrons in an atom.

The basic idea in Compton's experiment—in which an incident light quantum collides with an electron at rest—is easily understood by analogy to the collision between two billiard balls on a table. Before the collision, the ball driven by the cue has all the energy (light quantum), whereas the second ball is at rest. After the collision, the two balls share the energy; clearly the cue ball (equivalent to the light quantum) now has less energy than it had before the collision.

To prove that light radiation was quantized, Compton employed X rays, whose light quanta carry large amounts of energy compared with visible light quanta. Since the energy with which the target electron is bound in an atom is very much smaller than that of an X-ray quantum, the electron behaves as a free particle in a collision with the X-ray quantum.

Compton found that the measured energy (vibration frequency) of the scattered X ray (after collision) was less than the energy before scattering (colliding). Classical theory predicted that the energy (vibration frequency) would have remained unchanged.

Compton's experiments were in agreement with the conservation of energy and momentum, provided light radiation was quantized. This was the Compton effect, for which Compton received the Nobel Prize in 1927, sharing it with C. T. R. Wilson, who produced further evidence in 1923 for Compton's discovery by his invention and use of the cloud chamber.

In spite of Einstein's enthusiasm for Compton's discovery, which confirmed his own photon hypothesis, many criticisms and attacks on Compton's experimental results persisted. In rereading some of the literature from that period I found an apparent consensus that Compton—although he utilized the photon concept of localized energy and momentum and the special theory of relativity in his theoretical work—concentrated on extending classical physics with modifications to accommodate quantum phenomena. Even his Nobel Prize lecture was entitled "X rays as a Branch of Optics."

The Compton effect forced physicists to take account of the dualism of the corpuscular versus wave nature of the photon—indeed, of all radiation. This dualism was not destined to converge into a unifying theory until the emergence of the work of P. A. M. Dirac in the late 1920s, which included the theory of relativity. Today, important high-energy interactions of photons and electrons in our galaxy are being investigated and explained by the Compton effect.

In 1923 Compton had moved to the department of physics at the University of Chicago, taking up the professorship formerly held by Robert A. Millikan, who had resigned to become president of the California Institute of Technology. Compton continued his X-ray experiments and built up a large and eager group of graduate students, many of whom became distinguished scientists. He was joined in his researches by a younger colleague, Samuel K. Allison. The collaboration led to the famous textbook *X-Rays in Theory and Experiment,* published in 1935, and a close association that continued through the Second World War.

· III ·

In 1911 Victor Hess discovered in manned balloon flights to high altitudes a mysterious ionizing radiation that increased in intensity with altitude and, therefore, had to be of extraterrestrial origin. Many years of experimentation elapsed before there was significant progress in understanding the physical characteristics of this penetrating radiation found everywhere in the world.

Two interactions roused Compton's interest in cosmic rays. The first, in 1930, involved the publications and public speeches of Robert Millikan, who proclaimed that cosmic rays were gamma rays from the "birth cry" of atoms in the cosmos. As gamma rays, they would not be electrically charged and would enter the earth's magnetic field undeflected, with the same intensity anywhere in the world. By 1931, Compton, with others, had published a note on the constancy of this cosmic radiation. The second encounter was at a conference in Rome in December 1931 where the twenty-six-year-old Bruno Rossi presented what he thought were "irrefutable arguments" against Millikan's hypothesis. (5) Rossi told me that Compton gave him credit for further motivation to develop a research program in cosmic rays at the University of Chicago.

A key experiment, which would decide whether the incoming radiation was electrically charged or uncharged, was the measurement of the dependence of cosmic ray intensity on geomagnetic latitude. If the radiation was electrically neutral, such as gamma rays, there would be no dependence on the strength of the magnetic field. On the other hand, if the cosmic rays were electrically charged particles, say electrons or protons, their deflection in the earth's magnetic field would cut off access of all but the highest-energy particles at the equator, but admit all particles at the highest latitudes. Thus, the cosmic ray intensity would be less at the equator than at high latitudes.

In carrying out latitude surveys, Millikan and his junior colleague from the California Institute of Technology, H. V. Neher, had not detected latitude effects. This reinforced Millikan's claim about gamma rays. In 1927 the Dutch physicist Clay did find a latitude effect, but his work—mostly unpublished in notebooks—was not immediately recognized.

With the question of a latitude effect in dispute, Compton organized a worldwide survey in 1931. With all investigators using identical ionization chambers, the earth was divided into nine zones and approximately 100 physicists were assigned to undertake the task. (3) One team was composed of his wife, Betty, their fourteen-year-old son, Arthur Alan, and himself, traveling over 40,000 miles and crossing the equator five times. By September 1932, he announced that there was a latitude effect and that cosmic rays were charged particles: Robert Millikan was wrong!

At about this time, Millikan had sent Neher on another latitude survey to South America. Unknown to the survey party, their electroscope had malfunctioned on the way down and they reported no latitude effect. This was triumphantly proclaimed by Millikan, who attacked Compton in a debate at the Christmas meeting of the American Association for the Advancement of Science in 1932, reminding the *New York Times* correspondent of the alleged disputes of the Middle Ages about the number of angels that could dance on the point of a needle. (6)

The electroscope did not fail on the Millikan party's return northward across the equator. The dispute ended in February 1933 when Millikan admitted that there was a latitude effect and that the cosmic rays must be charged particles.

But what was the sign—plus or minus—of these cosmic-ray particles?

Bruno Rossi and Manuel Vallarta both recognized that oppositely charged particles should be deflected by the earth's magnetic field in opposite directions. If most of the particles came from a westerly direction they would be positively charged, but if more came from the east they would be negatively charged.

The race was on to decide the question. Vallarta invited Compton at Chicago and Thomas Johnson at Swarthmore to come to the lower latitude and higher altitude of his native Mexico City where, he calculated, the "east-west" effect would be large. In Italy Rossi prepared instruments for an expedition to Eritrea with the same objective.

Compton turned to his graduate student, Luis Alvarez, who had been building instrumentation readily adapted to the problem. Alvarez recalled working around the clock preparing equipment. At Compton's suggestion, they set up their apparatus in Jackson Park and operated it for a few days as a test before going to Mexico.

In Mexico City, the Compton and Johnson groups carried out measurements which displayed more cosmic rays coming from the west than the east. The radiation was composed of positively charged particles. Compton gave much of the credit to Alvarez for their joint work. A few months later Rossi also found the east-west effect in Eritrea. (5)

· IV ·

In the early 1930s, Auguste and Jean Picard received much publicity for their manned balloon flights in the stratosphere that claimed to study the origin of cosmic rays. In 1933 the promoters of the Chicago "Century of Progress" World's Fair engaged them to make such a flight, with Compton agreeing to arrange all the scientific instrumentation to be carried in the manned gondola. Compton seized on this opportunity to seek a collaboration with Millikan. "It would seem too bad to let an expensive flight of this kind occur without making use of it for some high altitude measurements," he wrote. (7) He invited Millikan to supply his automatic recording electroscope to be flown with the Chicago instruments in order to reconcile differences in their performance. Millikan, who had claimed his instrument was superior, agreed to meet Compton's challenge.

The manned flight was from Soldier Field in Chicago with thousands of excited onlookers waiting over seven hours to see the launch at 3:00 A.M. (7) Once the balloon was released, the lone pilot had to avoid the Sky Ride cables and the 186-meter tower of the exposition. As the balloon rose, its vent control system malfunctioned and the balloon and gondola ignobly descended into a nearby railroad yard.

This and a later, more successful, flight must have convinced Compton and the scientific community of the value of unmanned balloon flights with automatic instruments. The intense concentration on human survival and the high cost of the supporting technology necessary in manned flights left little time or funds to support the science.

The Compton-Millikan venture appeared to have no impact on the advancement of cosmic ray physics. However, the development of the Compton-Bennett model-C ionization chamber became in the long run the standard adopted by the Carnegie Institution when a worldwide network of stations to search for cosmic ray variations with time was set up with the Chicago-built instruments at sites at the Institution's Department of Terrestrial Magnetism. The work of Scott E. Forbush, who was responsible for one of the stations, led to the proof that the observed intensity of cosmic rays in the atmosphere varied with time. (5)

· V ·

When war came, Compton took on an important leadership role in the development by the United States of the nuclear bomb. He was responsible in establishing the University of Chicago as the secret center both for the achievement of man's first nuclear chain reaction and for the production of plutonium, essential for the making of a bomb and the development of nuclear power.

In his book *Atomic Quest,* Compton wrote that it was in the spring of 1940, as he talked with Ernest O. Lawrence, inventor of the cyclotron, "that the atom's energy first began to take on for me a vital, personal significance." (8) As the war in Europe expanded and it became evident that the United States would soon be faced with decisions regarding its participation, Compton's conscience and religious beliefs were troubling him. In 1940, his forty-eighth year, as he noted in his reminiscences,

> I began to feel strongly my responsibility as a citizen for taking my proper part in the war that was then about to engulf my country. . . . I talked, among others, with my minister in Chicago. He wondered why I was not supporting his appeal to the young people of our church to take a stand as pacifists. I replied in this manner: "As long as I am convinced, as I am, that there are values worth more to me than my own life, I cannot in sincerity argue that it is wrong to run the risk of death or to inflict death if necessary in the defense of those values." (3)

Events moved swiftly. At the request of the president of the National Academy of Sciences, Compton accepted the chairmanship of a committee to "assess the possible military value of energy from atomic nuclei." The committee report mainly focused on uranium and the need to secure a chain reaction. Later, plutonium entered the discussion when Emilio Segrè and Glenn Seaborg determined that plutonium-239 was fissionable with slow neutrons. Lawrence convinced Compton of the importance of this effort. James Conant of Harvard was unconvinced, and for a short time took an adversarial position in Washington regarding making a very costly commitment to a major effort for an atomic bomb. Lawrence and Compton prevailed.

Compton soon became the general director of current work at Columbia, Princeton, and Chicago. He decided to combine these various laboratory activities into a few centers, which included the Clinton Laboratory at Oak Ridge, Tennessee, and the Metallurgical Laboratory at the University of Chicago. (8) Enrico Fermi, Herbert Anderson, and Leo Szilard, among others, came to Chicago from Columbia University where they had carried out critical experiments providing convincing evidence that a chain reaction could be achieved. Compton's enthusiasm contributed to his leadership in bringing together the crucial groups for the enterprise. (9)

Edward Creutz, who had an important role at the Metallurgical Laboratory in the fabrication of uranium metal, recalled to me that Compton

> was always offering encouragement, even in the dark moments of tough perceived difficulties. The great respect we all had for him as a scientist, and his thorough understanding of what we were trying to do, even if he did not always agree fully with the way we were doing it, made him a truly inspirational leader.

The entire United States effort, at first called the "S-1 Project," became the "Manhattan Engineer District," under the command of General Leslie Groves. Although Compton understood General Groves's dedication to service as "a classic example of the patriot," he remarked that "on several certain rather fundamental matters the General and I could never come to a complete understanding."

As the project developed, Compton found himself "an intermediary between those on the one hand who were schooled to self-reliance and to the questioning of all authority and, on the other hand, the military and industrial men to whom dependence on orders was second nature." This problem was continually to beset the effort at Chicago and led to a lack of appreciation among many of the scientists for the difficult position in which Compton found himself with respect to security and scientific and engineering decisions.

By February 1942 the Metallurgical Laboratory was established on the University of Chicago campus, with the United States Corps of Engineers in charge from June of that year. General Groves approached the Du Pont de Nemours Company to send teams of their best engineers under Crawford Greenewalt to build the plant for processing plutonium. During 1942, rapid progress was made in designing and acquiring materials for an experimental nuclear reactor. In August the first pure sample of plutonium was isolated in Jones Chemical Laboratory at the University of Chicago.

Although a site in Argonne Forest Preserve outside Chicago had been chosen for building the experimental chain reactor, Fermi told Compton that he believed it could be made to work safely right on the campus. Compton did not inform President Hutchins of the decision to build the first pile in the squash court under the west stands of Stagg Athletic Field.

"On December 2, 1942, man achieved here the first self-sustaining chain reaction and thereby the controlled release of nuclear energy." This is the description on the site where the nuclear age was born.

Compton called James Conant at Harvard: " . . . you will be interested to know that the Italian navigator has just landed in the new world."

"Is that so," replied Conant. "Were the natives friendly?"

"Everyone landed safe and happy," was Compton's response.

It was now clear that plutonium was a major competitor as the fissionable material for the atomic bomb, provided it could be successfully separated from uranium and its fission products by chemical processes on a vast scale. The pilot plant where these major problems had to be solved was to be located in Tennessee—the "Clinton Engineering Works" at Oak Ridge. When Compton approached Conant about the management of this daunting industrial enterprise, Conant replied that he wouldn't touch it with a ten-foot pole. E. T. Filbey, vice-president of the University of Chicago, countered that the fact that Harvard would not touch it did not mean that the University of Chicago should not do so. "Isn't this a war for the survival of freedom . . . ?" was his attitude. Compton was assured that Chicago would take on the operation of the Oak Ridge Clinton Laboratory's pilot plant along with the new Hanford, Washington, reactors as part of the Metallurgical Project.

Soon thereafter, President Hutchins received a somewhat cryptic letter marked SECRET from General Groves, in which the War Department asked the University of Chicago to undertake the development of "a new product" in a project "of the utmost importance in the war effort." With the assurance that the Du Pont Company would assist in the operations, Compton persuaded Hutchins to reply that "the University would be glad to undertake the work to which you refer." (10)

· VI ·

Under great secrecy, the vast Hanford, Washington, project for the production of plutonium was set up during 1943, with engineers and scientists from Du Pont and Chicago coming and going. Groves insisted that many individuals who were known in nuclear physics be assigned pseudonyms so that the purpose of the facility would remain secret. Compton was Mr. Comas, Fermi was Mr. Farmer, and so on.

I remember being amused on one of the trips out on the Portland Rose train—which made a special stop at Pendleton, Oregon, to let off a very unlikely-looking group for a cowboy town—to see how many there were on the train from Chicago, all trying to behave like tourists. As we waited to go into the restaurant car, a sailor somewhat the worse for a few drinks slung his arm around Groves's civilian-clad shoulders and bemoaned the hardships of wartime service. With Groves sputtering, Compton urged their would-be companion, "Tell him, sailor!"

Hanford was a miracle of industrial technology and management. After some anxious periods when it appeared that the first pile would not achieve its goal, Hanford came through in time for the fabrication of the bomb at Los Alamos.

· VII ·

With many of the Metallurgical Laboratory's staff moving to Los Alamos for the development and testing of the bomb, major activities at Chicago by 1944 were focused on the plutonium project, instrumentation, and the solving of critical practical problems. Consequently, many of the Chicago scientists began to have time to think about the questions which had been raised in their minds by the development of nuclear energy and the use of the bomb—if it worked.

A small group of senior scientists under the chairmanship of James Franck participated in a report which presented mainly arguments against the use of the bomb on Japan. The report recommended a demonstration on a barren island. Compton thought that the major fears expressed in the Franck Report and in a petition, initiated by Szilard and signed by sixty-seven Chicago scientists, "were considerably exaggerated." (8) He emphasized the counterargument of saving American lives by the quick termination of the war with Japan.

While these matters were being secretly discussed by a small group of senior scientists, several of the younger scientists became increasingly concerned and agitated that there was an apparent lack of attention within the laboratory to the implications of nuclear energy. In March 1945 I asked permission to conduct a series of seminars for a group to meet weekly under security in Ryerson Laboratory. Our purpose was to discuss not only the use of the bomb but also its international control and the impending need for education of the public for the coming nuclear age. Both the Franck committee and the younger scientists' group independently informed Compton about their views, in spite of General Groves's efforts to suppress discussion at Chicago.

In his book *Atomic Quest,* (8) Compton devoted great attention to defending his point of view regarding the use of the bomb. Writing of a debate among a small group of senior scientists in 1945, he declared: "My vote is with the majority. It seems to me that as the War stands, the bomb should be used, but no more drastically than needed to bring surrender." Two weeks later the atomic bomb was used on Hiroshima.

· VIII ·

The end of the war with Japan led to the establishment of the Atomic Scientists of Chicago and subsequently to the growth of a scientists' movement at the other Manhattan District laboratories. (11) The May-Johnson bill, which was sponsored by the War Department and which would have given control over the development and use of nuclear energy to the military, was about to come before Congress. The scientists at Chicago were opposed to this bill and argued that international control was essential. As chairman of the Atomic Scientists of Chicago, I wrote to Compton, who was then chancellor of Washington University in St. Louis, about our views and those of our colleagues at the Clinton Laboratories. He responded 22 October 1945, stating on the one hand, "your prompt action has undoubtedly had an effect on preventing hasty action at Washington along a line that, in my opinion, would have been detrimental." On the other hand, he went on to note that his position was one of accepting the bill provided it was revised so that "the interests of science were adequately protected." He disagreed with our recommendation for a delay until a civilian bill on atomic energy could be prepared. He emphasized in his letter that our statements should be those of citizens and not scientists. (10)

The efforts of the scientists, however, led to the drafting of a prototype civilian bill in the office of Edward Levi in the law school at the University.

By December—with some rewriting—it was formally submitted to the Senate by Senator Bryan McMahon. (11)

· IX ·

"I cannot refrain from expressing my pleasure at speaking again from this pulpit [in Rockefeller Chapel]. Here nineteen years ago (1928), as chairman of the University's Committee on Social Service and Religion, I had the honor to accept this beautiful chapel as the gift of Mr. John D. Rockefeller Jr." (10) With these introductory remarks Arthur Compton addressed the University of Chicago class of March 1947 in the Baccalaureate oration. Throughout his life, Compton clearly revealed his strong religious convictions and his Christian ethics in many ways. Indeed, while he was professor of physics at Chicago he taught Sunday school. In his later years his religious outlook permeated his writings and public lectures. For example, from a book of collected essays from a conference entitled *Christianity Takes a Stand* he discussed "the moral meaning of the atomic bomb" (3) and concluded:

(a) The good world which the Christian should seek is that in which everyone can share in making the life of all worthwhile. This is the world of greatest freedom, freedom for people to become the children of God.

(b) War, while itself an evil thing, must be accepted and waged with determination when the alternative is the loss of values which one considers more important than the lives that will be lost. The Christian has always recognized the existence of such supreme values. Prominent among these is the right of all men to freedom as described above.

(c) The enormous destructiveness of the atomic bomb makes it doubtful whether an occasion will again arise in which even a defensive war will promote rather than retard the growth of human values. This gives greatly increased incentive to find a way by which war cannot again occur.

In looking over Compton's papers in his archive at the University of Chicago I found what appeared to be an unpublished manuscript, "Immortality From the Point of View of Science," in which he argues—not as a scientist—for faith in a future life. (10)

This dualism of the brilliant scientist versus the devout man of the church with his public religiousness was a mystery to many of his contemporaries in the sciences in spite of his statement that "a large majority of

the scientists with whom I was in contact had a high respect for religion."
(3) To some scholars of his generation he was widely viewed as a human-
ist. The dualism, which appeared from time to time in his role as director
of the Metallurgical Project, prompted some of the scientists to question
his leadership. Nevertheless, he was able to sustain his leadership role in
seeing the project through to a successful conclusion.

Throughout his life as scientist and administrator, Compton was encouraged by his wife, Betty. He felt so strongly about the importance of
discussing all issues with her that General Groves agreed to give her secret
clearance for the Manhattan Project. She was probably the only wife outside of Los Alamos who had such clearance.

Her clearance explained for me the surprise I experienced on arriving
at the Compton home from New York in 1943. While I was unpacking in
what was the room of the Comptons' son Arthur, Betty Compton came in to
talk, indicating that she knew of the critical nature of the project and its
dependence on nuclear physics. In subsequent months I would often return from the Ryerson Laboratory very late at night and find a plate of
cookies on the top step of the staircase. Her attention to the needs of incoming families was a legend in Chicago.

When the Comptons returned from a mountain trip to Northern India
in 1926 on which they had taken turns reading a cosmic ray meter at high
altitude, their host, Nazir Ahmad, said, "Compton, you don't know how
lucky you are . . . to have a wife who understands what it is that you are
doing." (3)

In the Compton home there was a photograph of the family gathered
around a piano with Compton playing the banjo. Their home was a center for graduate students, out-of-town visitors, and friends. I learned that
Sunday evenings were special and that a longtime Baptist friend, John W.
Watzek, a Chicago industrialist, would regularly come for dinner in the
1930s. In 1974, Mr. Watzek's will revealed a bequest to the University of
Chicago to honor the memory of Compton. The University established the
Arthur H. Compton Distinguished Professorship and supporting research
funds for a teacher in the University. With additional funds, I instituted the
Arthur H. Compton Saturday Lectures in Science for the University and
the residents of the Hyde Park community, a series in its fourteenth year at
the time of writing this account.

It is my opinion that Compton's receiving of the Nobel Prize at the exceptional age of thirty-five gave him most of a lifetime of privileged access
and entry into many sectors of society and government. He seized this op-

portunity on behalf of science and his philosophy of life, an opportunity accorded very few scientists in this century. My encounters with him over many years and numerous exchanges of letters also impressed me with his fundamental gift for helping others, especially young scientists who were moving ahead with their post-war careers.

Vannevar Bush, who had close relations with Compton and Presidents Roosevelt and Truman on behalf of scientific activities connected with the Second World War and afterwards, summed up Compton's characteristics well in his foreword to *The Cosmos of Arthur Holly Compton:*

> To those who did not know him it would be impossible to convey his human qualities of charm, simplicity, friendship, modesty. Let me just say that knowing him furnishes me with one of the most cherished of my memories, and that his friendship gave me an enhanced optimism as to the ultimate destiny of the human race.

REFERENCES

1. Alvarez, Louis A. *Adventures of a Physicist.* New York: Basic Books, 1987.
2. Allison, Samuel K. "Arthur Holly Compton, 1892–1962." In the Biographical Memoirs series, vol. 38, pp. 81–110. Washington, D.C.: National Academy of Sciences, 1965.
3. Johnston, Marjorie, ed. *The Cosmos of Arthur Holly Compton.* New York: Knopf, 1967.
4. Shankland, Robert S., ed. *Scientific Papers of Arthur Holly Compton: X-Ray and Other Studies.* Chicago: University of Chicago Press, 1973.
5. Sekido, Y., and H. Elliot, eds. *Early History of Cosmic Ray Studies.* Dordrecht: D. Reidel, 1985.
6. Kevles, Daniel. *The Physicist.* New York: Knopf, 1978.
7. DeVorkin, David H. *Race to the Stratosphere—Manned Scientific Ballooning in America.* New York: Springer-Verlag, 1989.
8. Compton, Arthur Holly. *Atomic Quest: A Personal Narrative.* New York: Oxford University Press, 1956.
9. Rhodes, Richard. *The Making of the Atomic Bomb.* New York: Simon and Schuster, 1986.
10. The University of Chicago Archives for A. H. Compton, R. M. Hutchins, J. A. Simpson. Department of Special Collections, Regenstein Library, University of Chicago.
11. Smith, Alice Kimball. *A Peril and A Hope.* Chicago: University of Chicago Press, 1965.

7

R. S. CRANE

1 8 8 6 – 1 9 6 7

E L D E R   O L S O N

ONE AFTERNOON in 1933 I sat with some thirty other students in a classroom of the classics building at the University of Chicago, awaiting the arrival of a professor named Ronald Salmon Crane. The course was English 303, a survey of English literature from 1660 to 1800. All of us had taken some survey courses and knew what to expect. There would be names, dates, bibliographies, short biographies of the major figures, assessments of their work, occasional excerpts for illustration. It would be the sort of thing one could get—minus a human presence, some bursts of eloquence, and perhaps some mild academic humor—from a college outline; the sort of thing that would permit a student who had digested the matter and done the required reading to say afterward, "I've got that period cold." In short, it would be not too unlike Kant's definition of a lecture as a process by which the notes of the professor become the notes of the student without passing through the head of either.

Precisely at 3:30 a man entered the room. He was in his late forties, a little under medium height, and dressed in a neat gray suit. He walked rapidly to the professorial table, glanced at the class through his spectacles, nodded, and sat down. There was nothing in his modest bearing and mild manner to suggest that, for some of us at least, this might be one of the more important moments of our lives. Nor was there any such suggestion in his opening words about the bare mechanics of the course: it was to be a lecture course; there were to be three short papers, each typed, single-spaced, on both sides of one and one sheet only (this, he explained, to

An earlier version of this essay appeared in *The American Scholar* (Spring 1984), pp. 232–38, and is used with permission.

ensure concision); there would be a final examination. Then the lecture proper began.

I can still see him very clearly, sitting in a shaft of that long-ago sun, and suddenly the man himself is vividly present to me. And I realize the difficulty, perhaps the impossibility, of the task I have undertaken. For I do not wish to offer one more eulogy, but to state the facts—to make a just portrait ("just" was one of his favorite words)—although the mere facts may indeed constitute a eulogy. Yet is it possible to see, unclouded by emotion, the facts about someone who was my revered professor, eventually one of my three closest friends, my colleague, and, at his wish, my office mate until his retirement?

· I ·

There were several extremely able, even very eminent, scholars in the department of English at the University of Chicago at that time; but Crane stood in sharp contrast to all of them. He presented, not a mass of facts in topical or chronological succession, but a narrative—and more important, not mere narrative but inquiry into the construction of his narrative, questioning explicitly or implicitly as he proceeded. What was a "fact"? When did a fact become evidence? What were the demands of evidence? What were the kinds of evidence? What determined relevance? What were the assumptions underlying the account? Could the same fact be used to prove opposite positions, and, if so, how? What was required of a historical statement or narrative? How many kinds of history were there? How many kinds of historical statements? What was probability as opposed to certainty, and how did one evaluate probability? What was a hypothesis? How could it be tested? How could one evaluate alternative hypotheses? What were legitimate and illicit uses of hypotheses? To cut this list almost brutally short, we were given not merely the results of scholarship but insights into what underlay it, into the sophisticated mechanisms at its foundation, so that we were first forced to worry about it and then subtly and gradually equipped to do it. In all this, he must have resembled somewhat his professor in medieval history at the University of Michigan, Earle Wilbur Dow, whom he mentions with such respect in his preface to *The Language of Criticism and the Structure of Poetry*. Crane did these things in English 303 on a simple level—but simple only as compared with what he did in his more advanced courses.

This is not to suggest that English 303 consisted chiefly of such suggestions as I have enumerated. On the contrary, they were a mere accompani-

R. S. CRANE

ment to a vast history of British and international politics and diplomacy, court intrigues, the rise of certain sciences, the history of the Royal Society, and the attitudes toward them, the current philosophies and the fortunes of others, contemporary religions, religious disputes, religious figures, and much besides—all, of course, as reflected in or as affecting the whole literature of the period. Everyone was pleased with the course, except the teacher. He told me later that he was dissatisfied with it because he thought it dealt with externals, not internals (by which he meant that it did not really deal with literary forms as opposed to conventions, and thus he was not truly offering a history of any of the literary arts *per se*). His feeling may in part explain the transformation of a literary historian into a formal critic—a transformation that astounded many and caused some historians to mutter about "treason."

My first seminar with him was on William Collins and Thomas Gray. The concept behind all his seminars was the same: he thought of a seminar as a course in which the questions pursued were ones to which the professor himself did not know the answers. Other than guiding discussion, he took the role only of a more experienced and skillful collaborator. His earlier seminars, however, differed in format from his later ones. The Collins-Gray seminar, after a preliminary lecture in which he laid out what we were to do and what he would do, consisted entirely of class discussion. We were to write the one-sheet papers, write a term paper that substituted for a final examination, and, of course, read a lot; he was to be concerned with the poems in themselves. The phrase "poems in themselves" has meant many things in our time, chiefly the ignoring of, or even being ignorant of, historical, bibliographical, and other matters. The student who supposed Crane to mean *that* was courting disaster.

What Crane meant was that he had observed a tremendous gap in humanistic education, which was evident in the inability of students to discuss "an imaginative work in terms appropriate to its nature," as he says in "History Versus Criticism in the Study of Literature," an essay that he was writing during that very quarter. That gap he proposed to fill; what is more, he proposed to reform humanistic education itself. Exactly how to do this, he was by no means sure; admittedly, he was groping and searching. Crane has sometimes been accused of being doctrinaire, but anyone who had seen the diffidence with which he felt his way through an unknown terrain—looking for a firm foothold, trying and testing at every step—would have been compelled to the opposite view.

He was willing to consider any opinion, so long as it was not one of the outworn formulae. In my case alone, there were many instances in which almost any other professor would have seen to it that I was suppressed at once, like the guinea pig in *Alice;* but Crane heard me out. For example, I criticized two sacred cows—"Ode to Evening" and "Elegy Written in a Country Churchyard"—arguing that both went beyond their proper limits in that both shifted the object of emotion without due cause. I argued that the former should have ended with "The gradual dusky veil" and the latter with "the noiseless tenor of their way." As they stood, the one degenerated into abstraction and nonsense, the other into abstraction, clichés, faulty syntax, and maudlin self-pity. Knowing Crane's formidable reputation and his admiration for Johnson (who had most esteemed the lines I had just cut from the "Elegy"), I fully expected to have my head torn off—at least that had been my usual fortune with other professors. Crane, on the contrary, listened very carefully, even when I went on to say that the remainder of both poems badly damaged the intended effect; he asked a question or two; then he sat back and said thoughtfully, "You know, I believe you're right." His breadth of mind was reflected in the latitude he allowed us in our written work; our papers could be on anything we chose, provided that they were relevant to the poetic problems under consideration in the course. Thus my own term paper was on neither Collins nor Gray, but on the prosody of the anonymous *The Taming of a Shrew.*

I was greatly attracted to Crane. To explain why, I must intrude upon his portrait. For some years before I encountered him, I had realized that whatever other ambitions I had, I was compelled to be a poet. I had left the University of Chicago after my second year because, despite the many and strong attractions it had for me, I felt that little if anything of what I was offered had really to do with the essence of the art or, rather, arts that I was doomed to practice. That essence I had to understand. I knew from my musical training that however overwhelming the performance of a great musician, the effects were those of certain things done, as surely as I knew that in some chromatic passages of Chopin a very delicate portamento could be achieved by trailing the fifth finger. Technique, though only an instrument, always underlay every performance. I was convinced that this was true of poetry as well. I knew from my own experience in composition that there were many kinds of lyric poetry, each presenting its specific problems as well as problems unique to each poem—problems that had to have practical solutions if a poem was to ensue. But where was there any treatment of such matters?

I ransacked literary criticism without much success. I knew personally by this time a good number of poets and critics, but these, almost without exception, were either mystical about or indifferent to such questions; some were frankly superstitious about them, even fearful of or hostile to an inquiry into them. And I was not to be put off by such professorial evasions as "Ah, but that is precisely the genius of Shelley!" or "Ah, but that is the *magic* of Shakespeare!" *Magic,* indeed! Unless you believe in the supernatural, all magic is worked by human beings doing certain things that then have their natural effects. To such responses I found it hard, more frequently impossible, to be polite. I fear that some of my professors found me more difficult than I found their courses.

I had reentered the University of Chicago after a four-year absence, partly at the urging of Bernard Weinberg, partly at the even more persuasive urging of Thornton Wilder. Wilder, who knew my poems and foresaw my fate even better than I did, argued that, since no poet nowadays can support himself by his poetry alone, and since teaching was the occupation which might permit the most leisure, I should obtain my bachelor's and master's degrees and find a post in some small college. I went back and took some courses with no other idea in mind than to carry out the rest of the plan. But even in the courses I took with Wilder, who was then teaching at Chicago, I found little that pertained to what I wanted most to know.

And then I encountered Crane.

Here was a man of immense erudition—an erudition that was not the mere passive effect of extensive reading but the result of intense study coupled with a constantly active critical intelligence. In my very first course under him, I found someone who strained my capacities. Here also, as I was to discover, was a man who was worrying about the same problems that were worrying me and who felt, as I did, that there were serious omissions in education; that criticism should be made into and recognized as an academic discipline; that with the exception of some monographs, literary history was not really history; that the theory of both literary history and history in general must be more closely looked into; and that the present condition of critical theory was deplorable—a situation in which most of what was pressed upon us as riches was either counterfeit or the currency of some inaccessible, perhaps mythical, foreign realm: witches' money, apparent gold that changed to dead leaves in our wallets.

We shared, too, certain objects of distrust or contempt: *Geistesgeschichte,* the "spirit of the age"; spurious, if conventionally accepted formulae; such nonsensical classifications as "Classical" or "Romantic" (after all, Goethe, who had invented the distinction simply to differentiate his own poetry from Schiller's, had in later years complained that he no longer understood what such terms had come to mean); merely thematic studies such as "The Sailor in Eighteenth Century Literature"; pseudocriteria like "sincerity" as applied to a lyric; the idea of a work as "definitive" (Crane thought scholarship, as I did, a perpetually ongoing process); the confusion of historical with artistic importance; and the citation of unexamined authority. "There is no authority but evidence," he said. To show our closeness of thought, I had long maintained that authority was not a man but a proof.

His later seminars, as I have said, differed from the earlier in format. In the opening session Crane would assign each student the writing of a paper that was to be read before the class on a given day and to take no less than a half hour in the reading. Another student was designated a critic of the paper. Each paper had to be typed with two carbons, one of which was to be delivered to Crane, the other to the critic one week in advance of the reading. After author and critic had spoken and had been given a chance at counterargument, the class would discuss both. Finally, Crane would criticize the entire proceeding and, as one student put it, "clean up on all of us." Crane called this the "French system." Such a system would work, obviously, only wth superior students, but these were never lacking. The format may sound innocuous enough, but discussion, with every student on his mettle, sometimes became very vehement.

Crane's *Tom Jones* seminar, the first of many on that work, employed the French system, and here discussion often reached white heat. One incident may show that I do not exaggerate. To a student's question Crane had replied that the Man of the Hill episode in *Tom Jones* was simply another interpolated tale in imitation of Cervantes. I took exception to this, contending that, on the contrary, it was a crucial point in the plot—in fact, a turning point in Tom's career. It may have been that my manner was unintentionally offensive, but Crane became extremely irritated, quite uncharacteristically, and made a remark about me to the class that I could take only as an uncalled-for and unforgivable insult. I was so furious that it was difficult for me to remain in the room.

Sensing my anger, Crane waited for me after class and asked me to walk home with him. I complied, and when, after walking several blocks in dead (and deadly) silence, I could finally bring myself to speak, I told him curtly that I was dropping the course and would work with him no longer. Crane did not apologize, but somehow calmed my wrath by questioning me about my view, until he had persuaded me to continue and to write my term paper on the subject. I did just that, and although, in contrast to his custom, he said nothing about it other than it was accepted, I have noted that he adopted my view. I still have the paper in my files. I have not told anyone about this incident before; perhaps it reveals more than I am aware about both of us. But this was only the first of many stormy clashes, none of which ever had the faintest effect upon our relationship.

· II ·

The "Neo-Aristotelian movement," or the "Chicago School," as it has also been called, has been primarily associated with Crane, and justly so. Whether Crane was, in fact, its founder is difficult to say; but there is no question that he was a leader in it and that it would not have existed without him. The difficulty is that in the first place it was neither a movement nor a school in the sense of a number of people holding uniform doctrines or even identical views about Aristotle, and that in the second place it was—whatever else it was—the consequence of many converging influences, without which it would not have existed. At the same time of the Collins-Gray seminar, for instance, Crane was much impressed with Mortimer Adler. Adler was a strong advocate of Aristotle—I suspect in the Jesuitic tradition of interpretation, or at least with a heavy flavoring of Aquinas, Maritain, and Josephus Gredt—and he held that, whatever errors of fact or conjecture might be found in Aristotle, the Aristotelian method remained unassailable and permanently useful. I do not know whether it was Adler who suggested to Crane the possible use of the *Poetics* as an instrument in literary criticism, particularly formal criticism; but Crane told me that he had set up a discussion group at his home with Adler and other faculty members, with the purpose of studying that work, and that Richard McKeon had astounded them all with a brilliant analysis of the opening paragraph. At any rate, the influence of McKeon superseded any that Adler may have had upon Crane.

All of us were influenced by McKeon, Rea Keast and I especially, since we were his students—I most of all, I think, for I took more courses under him and may even have conversed with him more often, on technical matters at least, for we formed the habit of taking long, late nocturnal walks together. It is impossible that any who recognized his prodigious learning, his greatness as a teacher and lecturer, and his profound philosophic genius should not have been influenced by him. You do not walk away unimpressed after being struck by lightning, and we were all struck repeatedly. Yet influence must not be taken to mean producing similarity. I never studied the *Poetics* with him, though I read a great deal of Aristotle under his tuition, and to this day I have only a general conception of how he might analyze the work and no idea at all whether he would approve or disapprove of my own analysis of it. In conversation about it he would offer only somewhat cryptic hints.

I am sure that Richard McKeon approved of some of our efforts, and I am equally sure that he disapproved of others. But there was no such unanimity of the Chicago School as its critics and commentators have supposed. For example, I am told that McKeon has repeatedly denied my distinction between mimetic and didactic poetry—a distinction absolutely fundamental to some of my later theories—and certainly there must have been many other points on which he would have disagreed with me. While Crane accepted that distinction, I doubt that the terms meant for him what they meant for me. I, in turn, sharply disagreed with Crane's interpretation of mythos or plot. I do not think that any of us should be held responsible for the views of the others, however much we may have influenced each other. We were no more unanimous in our views than we were exclusively Aristotelian, for we were unanimous only in our view that Aristotle—in our interpretation of him—had certainly offered one of many possible methods of criticism. In truth, in our discussions I often wondered whether—to borrow Saintsbury's borrowing of Langland— there was any other such "fair field of *fighting* folk."

Nor could it have been otherwise. Friends though we were, we were all strongly individual, markedly different in temperament, talent, and—except for certain areas—interests. What we had in common, besides friendship, was a concern with certain problems and a general agreement about methods we might use to solve them. But if there was any other unity of the Chicago school, it was the unity of a log fire in which, by their proximity, the logs stimulate and inflame one another, while each burns with its individual fires.

Robert Maynard Hutchins, too, had a great influence on Crane, though Crane, always his own man, adopted only such ideas of Hutchins as he deemed useful. Hutchins's main interest was in general education; Crane's in humanistic studies. The extent of their agreement and disagreement may be seen by comparing Hutchins's proposals for education with the program of the department of English that Crane established when he became chairman. Crane's program was based on the four disciplines of linguistics, history (both, however, as ancillary to literary study), intellectual analysis (the analysis of argument in philosophical, rhetorical, and other texts), and criticism (the study of "imaginative literature" as such). Hutchins always thought in terms of educating a chiefly nonacademic public; I think Crane saw general education as preparation for graduate study, for the training of scholars and teachers. Hutchins's Great Books program, as opposed to Crane's English program, should clearly mark the difference between them. Besides Hutchins, there were many others who influenced Crane, as he freely acknowledged; for instance, his colleagues, the economist Jacob Viner, and the political scientist and international lawyer Quincy Wright.

As a man—and the man always underlies the teacher—Crane was a warm, tolerant, solicitous, and steadfast friend and a genial and stimulating companion. He more than compensated for any small faults he may have had by an abundance of important virtues. Like Socrates, he was "willing to take the truth from oak or rock" but he always examined it carefully to be sure that it was the truth. If his interests were limited, it was no doubt because of his intense and constant passion for his real concerns. He seemed to have no great interest in music or in any of the arts beyond the literary, although he was well versed in the fine arts of the eighteenth century. He did not often go to concerts or art galleries; when I played records of dazzling performances for him, he would listen politely and patiently, appearing to sympathize with, rather than to share, my enthusiasm. Beyond literature and university affairs, his great interests were in national politics and international developments. Naturally, as an historian, he watched with particular anxiety the events before, during, and immediately following the Second World War. His own political beliefs were judiciously tempered; he had a horror of both fascism and communism as extreme and oppressive.

· III ·

As a teacher, Ronald Crane was extremely demanding—demanding because he felt that scholarship was demanding. He made no effort to entertain his students with jokes, personal anecdotes, and similar devices. If his erudition was, as I said, awesome, it was not used for display. Like his eloquence (and he could be very eloquent), it was manifest only when it was required. This refusal to display for the sake of display was common among the more distinguished professors at the University of Chicago, but I first noticed it in Crane. He cared only about what students might be taught, not about how he could impress them. He did not put on professorial dignity, for dignity was natural to him. His presentations were so precise and compact that it was perhaps impossible to summarize them or to put them in other words. One came away from his classes invariably with a sense of the terrific labors that he must have put into them.

"Occupation likely to afford most leisure," indeed! Most of the *waking* hours of a true professor are *working* hours—something that nonacademics can hardly comprehend. Why Wilder should have said such a thing I cannot imagine, for he himself was a fine scholar and excellent teacher and, writer though he was, never permitted his writing to interfere with his academic duties.

Crane's classroom manner was brisk, businesslike, and composed. Such was his composure that I was surprised, after he had invited me to share his office, to discover that he was often tense, impatient, even somewhat agitated before a class. It was not stage fright; it was partly the revving up that is natural before any performance, but chiefly anxiety lest he should fail to present his subject fully and clearly. In class, he treated all students alike; while undoubtedly he must have had favorite students, he never exhibited any kind of favoritism. If there was any sign of his favor, it was that, as he told me, he tended to be most exacting with the best. I never saw him (nor did I ever see any good professor) come out of a class glowing with self-satisfaction; however enthusiastic the response, he was always more or less unhappy with what he had done. In class lectures he used notes typed on 8½-by-11-inch paper, folded in half and arranged into little booklets, but he hardly glanced at them. In seminars he made careful notes on the discussion. His public lectures were from complete texts and could have been printed as they stood.

His published works were, for the most part, addressed to serious students and were in no case intended for any who read as they run. Very hard work went into them, and it is sometimes hard work to comprehend them fully, for they require close and alert attention. In consequence, they have been often gravely misinterpreted. A muddle-minded or wrong-headed interpretation of them disturbed him, chiefly because he feared that he had failed in the expression of his thought. "What did I say that could possibly be taken to mean that?" he could ask. The difficulty was that he had assumed his readers had erudition and intelligence equal to his own. I used to remind him that while an author may use every device to make himself clear, there are no devices to prevent his being *misread.*

Although his courses offered much for the development of critical and scholarly skills, their principal attractions probably were the ideas that he disseminated, for Crane was preeminently a man of ideas. I do not think I can justly claim for him that he was a great originator of ideas. Original he was, and greatly so; but his genius lay rather in finding new uses for ideas, arranging ideas into new significances, and keenly seeing consequences, objections, and further problems. In such matters few could match him. Those who could appreciate him found new areas opened up, new interests cultivated, new capacities developed, new equipment provided. The least any student could carry away from him was a sense of the enormous, endless responsibilities of scholarship and teaching. A good teacher teaches knowledge and skills. An excellent teacher does this superbly. A great teacher does this and more: he changes lives for the better. Ronald Crane changed my life so, and the lives of innumerable others.

8

FRED EGGAN

1906 – 1991

T R I L O K I   N .   P A N D E Y

· I ·

FREDERICK RUSSELL EGGAN came to the University of Chicago in 1923 as an undergraduate and remained there until 1974, when he retired as the Harold H. Swift Distinguished Service Professor of Anthropology. Even after his retirement he continued to live in Hyde Park, and it was only during the last decade of his life that he and his wife moved to Santa Fe, New Mexico. The Eggans acquired a beautiful adobe home in that lovely city, but Fred found it hard to sever his connection with the University of Chicago. During his half-century of association with the University, he had become too attached to it. Belonging to Chicago was very important to him. Even though he had invitations to professorships in other universities he never considered them seriously.

I came to the University of Chicago in 1963 as a graduate student from Lucknow University in India, where I had studied a version of British social anthropology. While a student at Lucknow, I had come across a copy of *Social Anthropology of North American Tribes* which Fred Eggan had edited, and I was familiar with some of his writings. Just a few days after my arrival, my advisor, McKim Marriott, took me to meet Professor Eggan, who was chairman of the department of anthropology at that time. Even though our first meeting took place some twenty-eight years ago, I still remember his warm and friendly greeting. On my way to his office, I saw Manisha Roy, an Indian lady anthropologist, who was waiting to see Professor Eggan. As I entered his office, I saw him getting up from his chair in order to shake my hand. He said, "Welcome to Chicago! When you applied, you were single. I am glad you got married and have brought your wife along." I was startled, and my instant reaction was, "Where is my wife? I am not married." Whereupon I saw a shy man, who was visibly embarrassed; he was relieved when I changed the subject and gave him greetings from Professor Evans-Pritchard, whom I had met in Oxford while I was on my way to Chicago. Evans-Pritchard had told me how lucky I was to be going to Chicago, which had "a vigorous department under Fred Eggan." He had also said that he respected only two American anthropologists—Kroeber and Eggan.

During the first year of my course work, I had concentrated on the Hopi Indians of Arizona and wrote my term papers on their culture and social structure. My tutor, Lloyd Fallers, had encouraged me to consult Eggan, "the leading expert on the Hopi." It was during my consultations with Eggan that I had decided to do my doctoral fieldwork either with the Zuni or among the Hopi, if I managed to survive my first year of graduate work. Eggan was very supportive of the idea of "a Hindu scholar working among the pacifist Hopis," but with the publication of Frank Waters' *Book of the Hopi* (1963), there was so much turmoil on the Hopi Reservation that I was advised to go elsewhere for my fieldwork. (I have described this in my paper " 'India Man' among American Indians," which I published in 1975.)

I took Fred Eggan's course in "Kinship and Social Organization," was a member of his seminar on the southwest, and did several reading courses with him. This gave me an opportunity to learn firsthand what he had to say on various topics and also to read closely his own works, such as *Social Organization of the Western Pueblos* (1950) and *The American Indian: Perspectives for the Study of Social Change* (1966). Since Eggan wrote an autobiographical essay, "Among the Anthropologists," for the *Annual Review of Anthropology* (1974), and Raymond D. Fogelson, one of his close Chicago colleagues, has written a judicious assessment of Eggan's contributions in the *International Encyclopedia of Social Sciences: Biographical Supplement,* (vol. 18, 1979), and more recently he was interviewed by Ernest Schusky, "Fred Eggan: Anthropologist Full Circle" in *American Ethnologist* (1989), I will confine myself to a personal account of Fred Eggan, relying on my voluminous correspondence with him and on my visits with him that took place over a quarter of a century in Chicago, in Zuni, in the Hopi country, in Cambridge, England, in New York, in Salt Lake City, in New Delhi, in Santa Fe, and in Santa Cruz.

· II ·

Eggan was born in 1906 in Seattle, where his parents had moved from Vancouver. His father was an engineer and his mother a schoolteacher. He once told me that both of his parents were born in Minnesota, and if it had

FRED EGGAN

not been for the disruptions of the First World War, he would very probably have gone to the University of Minnesota. When he was twelve, his parents moved to Lake Forest, near Chicago, and he grew up on the North
Shore. He attended the local public schools, where he became interested
in physics and chemistry. He enrolled in the College of the University of
Chicago in 1923 and majored in psychology. He took several courses in
anthropology with Fay-Cooper Cole and Edward Sapir. He was dazzled by
the brilliance of Sapir, but he was not confident enough of his own "native
skills in language" to continue his studies in linguistics. He was fond of
saying that "archaeology was his first love," and in this pursuit he was encouraged by Cole. He spent several summers excavating Indian mounds
and village sites in Illinois. He was also good in mathematics. After his
graduation, he continued at the University for another year and produced
an M.A. thesis, "An Experimental Study of Attitudes Toward Race and Na-
tionality" (1928), that combined his anthropological and psychological interests. He wanted to continue at the University but paucity of funds made
him take up a teaching position at Wentworth Junior College and Military
Academy in Missouri. He spent two years there, teaching history at the
academy and psychology and sociology at the college. Earle Reynolds, who
had taken several of Eggan's courses there, once told me that "Fred was
quite isolated in Missouri. He was a good teacher and well liked by his
students, but his expectations were too high to make him stay there." He
continued spending the summers working on Cole's archaeological field
projects and was relieved when Cole suggested that he come back to
Chicago.

Eggan returned to the University in the summer of 1930 as a full-time
graduate student in anthropology. He recalled in his presidential address
on "Social Anthropology and the Method of Controlled Comparison," for
the American Anthropological Association, that "My early anthropological
education was in the Boas tradition as interpreted by Cole, Sapir, and
Spier—with additions from Redfield. But before the mold had hardened
too far I came under the influence also of Radcliffe-Brown." He became
Radcliffe-Brown's first research assistant in 1931–32. Radcliffe-Brown had
come to the University in the autumn of 1931 to replace Sapir, who had
departed for Yale University. Eggan took Radcliffe-Brown's courses on Africa and Australia "somewhat reluctantly," as he used to say, and was much
impressed by his "methodological and theoretical sophistication," as well
as by his lecturing style. As his research assistant, Eggan pored through the
vast ethnographic and historical literature on Native American kinship and

social organization, especially on the tribes of the plains, southeast, and southwestern regions. He prepared summaries on various tribes for Radcliffe-Brown, who wanted to re-analyze the social systems and social structures of Native Americans along the lines that he had developed in his *Social Organization of Australian Tribes* (1931).

In 1932, he got a field-training fellowship from the Laboratory of Anthropology to join a field party under the leadership of Professor Leslie A. White of the University of Michigan, with Edward Kennard (Columbia), Mischa Titiev (Harvard), Jess Spirer (Yale), and George Devereux (Paris), as fellow students. Edward Kennard, who was my colleague at the University of Pittsburgh, once told me that there was a real division of labor among them. "I was working on the Hopi language, Mischa was studying Hopi politics and religion, and that left Fred to figure out their kinship system," said Kennard. He also added, "Fred did not have to work too hard; with the help of Radcliffe-Brown, he had already figured that out. I don't know why he had to come there, in the first place." Eggan collected sufficient material on the Hopi to complete his doctoral dissertation on the "Social Organization of the Western Pueblos" in 1933. He used part of the material he had collected while doing documentary research for Radcliffe-Brown on different Pueblo groups to provide a comparative perspective.

Eggan used to say that with his thesis done he was destined to be a social anthropologist, but during the Depression there were few teaching positions available. He remained at the University as a postdoctoral research associate. Radcliffe-Brown had arranged for him to do fieldwork in northwestern Australia, but the devaluation of the dollar reduced the value of his grant by about half. So instead of Australia, he ended up in the northern Philippines for a year, to investigate "what had happened to the Tinguian culture as a result of American and other influences." Some twenty years earlier, the Coles had worked in this region, and Redfield also encouraged Eggan to see whether "some of the general processes of change that he had recently discerned in Yucatan could be replicated in another area of Spanish contact." Eggan developed good rapport with the people, wrote several papers on their religion, and maintained a life-long research interest in the Philippines.

On his return to the University, he was made an instructor in anthropology in 1935. He continued his fieldwork with various American Indian groups—the Hopi, the Choctaw, the Cheyenne, and the Arapaho. The accounts of these researches began to appear in various professional journals. On October 27, 1936, he presented a lecture before the Division of

Social Sciences at the University on "Culture History Derived from the Study of Living Peoples." After presenting a brilliant critique of Boasian anthropology, he made a case for a closer relationship between history, archaeology, and social anthropology—the agenda for the new approach to the study of anthropology he had undertaken. This must have impressed the luminaries in social sciences at the University of Chicago because Eggan told me that he had to go to see President Hutchins, as he was the only one proposed for a rise in salary in the entire division that year. These must have been very happy years for Eggan. He wrote several papers and edited a volume, *Social Anthropology of North American Tribes,* which he presented to Professor Radcliffe-Brown in 1937 when he left for a chair in social anthropology at Oxford University.

· III ·

In 1938, Fred married Dorothy Way, and together they visited the Hopi Reservation quite frequently. In 1940, they began a project on social and cultural change at New Oraibi, but that was interrupted by the Second World War. Eggan seldom mentioned his wartime positions and experiences to me, just as he rarely said much about his contribution to applied anthropology. I learned much about them from talking with his friends, such as E. D. Hester, G. P. Murdock, Milton Singer, and Alexander Spoehr. Similarly, he did not discuss with me his Philippines research, as he did the works on American Indians that bound us together. It seems to me that, as he had two separate studies for his American Indians and his Philippines research, he also had two different sets of students and colleagues.

He once told me that he was never sure whether he was taken that seriously before the appearance of his *Social Organization of the Western Pueblos* in 1950, seventeen years after he had completed it as a Ph.D. dissertation, one that was regarded by Radcliffe-Brown as "the best thesis he had ever examined," as Max Gluckman told me in 1971. The book was warmly received and was claimed to be the American counterpart to the classic studies of lineage-based societies that the British social anthropologists had been doing in Africa. It is unquestionably the theoretically most sophisticated book on the Western Pueblos. Its value lies in its unique integration of Radcliffe-Brownian theory of social systems and social structure with Boasian concerns with culture process and sound comparisons.

Eggan was acclaimed as a "creative innovator" by Murdock, a "master theorist" by Lévi-Strauss, and various honors were heaped upon him. In quick succession, he was elected to the presidency of the American Anthropological Association, to the American Academy of Arts and Sciences, the National Academy of Sciences, and the American Philosophical Society. His colleagues in Great Britain bestowed upon him an honorary fellowship in the Royal Anthropological Institute of Great Britain and Ireland and foreign fellowship in the British Academy. In recognition of his impressive scholarship and achievement in anthropology, he was awarded the Viking Fund Medal—the highest honor in the discipline—by the Wenner-Gren Foundation for Anthropological Research.

By 1963, when I first met him, clearly he had become a senior statesman in anthropology. Earlier that year, he had been to Cambridge, England, to attend the first decennial meeting of the Association of Social Anthropologists of the British Commonwealth, where he played an important role. Eggan himself presented his views in a paper, "Social Anthropology: Models, Political Systems, Religion, and Urbanization." In 1964, he gave the Lewis Henry Morgan Lectures at the University of Rochester; these were published in 1966 under the title *The American Indian: Perspectives For the Study of Social Change*. Here, relying on the method of controlled comparison so admirably used in his earlier works, and against a historical background provided by Morgan's studies, Eggan assessed the changes which had taken place among various American Indian groups such as the Choctaw and their neighbors in the southeast, the Cheyenne and the Arapaho in the plains, the Ojibwa and their neighbors in the northeast, and the Hopi and the Tewa groups in the southwest. In another important survey, "One Hundred Years of Ethnology and Social Anthropology," presented as the 1966 centennial celebration of the Peabody Museum of Archaeology and Ethnology at Harvard University, Eggan examined the major developments in these fields and pointed out the new trends which were emerging during the 1960s.

Clearly, this was a very busy period in Eggan's life. His wife, Dorothy, was in poor health, and he had to be away frequently from Chicago, attending various meetings and conferences. Yet, he never missed a class, or ever came late or unprepared for the courses he offered. He once told me that he did not enjoy teaching, but that once he agreed to teach a course, he tried to do a good job.

Eggan felt that he was not a good lecturer, like his teachers Radcliffe-Brown and Sapir, but he was fully prepared to give even undergraduate courses, which he considered "time-consuming." During my time at Chicago he would occasionally ask me or Alfonso Ortiz to give lectures in the graduate and undergraduate courses he was teaching, but he would read the students' papers himself and write comments in the margins. He was very good in reading courses I took with him. I fondly remember many a time when there was a twinkle in his eyes, if I said something new about the Zuni or the Hopi ethnography we were discussing. Later on, when I came to know some of his Hopi friends, I could see that in many ways Eggan was like a Hopi elder. He enriched the life around him not only by what he taught but even more, perhaps, by being what he was.

· IV ·

Eggan was a shy and modest person, quite serene and self-confident. I never saw him laugh loudly, but his eyes laughed constantly. He was a kind and generous person. In 1976, while he was a visiting professor at Santa Cruz, I bought a house near the University. Whatever money I had saved went into buying some furniture for the new house. I was touched by Fred's generosity when I found a letter in my mailbox with a check for $1,000 along with a note: "You need it more these days than I do. Return it when you can."

During the period I was at Chicago I went to Eggan's apartment only twice, but I have heard from his older students that earlier the Eggans had been very friendly and hospitable. He was seen as somewhat aloof by many students during my time, but his genial appearance was quite visible at his Monday afternoon seminars. He was at his best when he was receiving overseas visitors who had come to give papers at these departmental seminars. I still remember his jovial relations with Evans-Pritchard, Raymond Firth, Meyer Fortes, Lévi-Strauss, Audrey Richards, M. N. Srinivas, and Monica Wilson, all of whom visited Chicago while I was a student there.

Later I came to know that Eggan was having a hard time those days in connection with Dorothy's poor health. While I was in the field, Dorothy Eggan died in October 1965. The letter from Eggan that gave me the sad news of his wife's sudden death also had this advice: "Be friendly with everybody—take the role of a student who wants to learn—learn as much as you can and tell them about customs in India in exchange." This was the teacher in Eggan, always willing to instruct his student, despite his personal tragedy. I came to know the human side of him when he visited Zuni later that year and spent a week with me. After that visit, I stopped calling him "Mr. Eggan"; he had become just "Fred" to me, a friend. It was largely because of him that during my four years' stay I had become very fond of Chicago, and before leaving for Pittsburgh when I went to say goodbye to him my eyes were full of tears, as were, I noticed, Eggan's.

During my stay at Pittsburgh, I began reading George Santayana and other philosophers. When I sent him a copy of *The Last Puritan,* he wrote back saying, "Santayana is one of my favorite philosophers—as far as I understand philosophy." I remember him discussing Santayana's views in one of his lectures, and he was always encouraging me to read outside of anthropology. His letters were full of news about his department and its activities. He never ever mentioned anything about the politics of the department, just as he seldom gave me much news about himself. Therefore, I was happy for him when he announced in one of his letters, "I am going to get married this summer to Joan Rosenfels, whom I think you met at the Singers'."

The marriage took place while I was back in India, and his cards and letters from Europe, where the Eggans had gone on their honeymoon, were full of news about the places they had visited, the people they had seen, and the events they had attended, including the Schneider-Dumont conference on kinship held at the Wenner-Gren conference center in Burg Wartenstein, Austria. Eggan was "impressed by Dumont's view of Indian civilization," and he was quite enthusiastic about the new approaches to the study of kinship developed by Schneider and Dumont. They were different from his own and Radcliffe-Brown's approaches, but he saw them as complementary, and not a challenge.

While I was on my way to India, he had suggested that I should visit Evans-Pritchard at Oxford and Meyer Fortes at Cambridge. It was from Evans-Pritchard that I learned that Eggan would be visiting Oxford for six months. Evans-Pritchard was wondering whether he was going to bring his "bride," since All Souls College had to make arrangement for their accommodation. The Eggans developed "a real affection for Oxford and the countryside," as he wrote me from there. He was quite taken by the rituals and pomp of Oxford life, and he wrote to me about the installation of "Sir Edward's bronze head" at his retirement ceremony. His regard for Evans-Pritchard was very genuine.

· V ·

In December 1970 I came to Cambridge as a fellow of St. John's College. While there, I came to know that Eggan had had a hand in my election to the fellowship. He never said anything about it to me. Next year I had an opportunity to welcome the Eggans when Fred was invited to deliver the Frazer Lecture at Cambridge. Eggan was attached to King's College, but we saw a great deal of each other during November 1971. Together we went to London to hear Murdock give his Huxley Memorial Lecture on "Anthropology's Mythology," in which he was very complimentary to Eggan. I attended parties which were given in honor of Murdock and Eggan. Fortes had persuaded Edmund Leach to give a dinner party at the provost's lodge at King's. The Eggans, the Forteses, Murdock, Caroline Humphrey, and I were the guests. Just before the dinner, John Barnes and Esther and Jack Goody came for drinks. The whole evening was dominated by conversations about various approaches to the study of kinship, focused around three recent unsigned *T.L.S.* reviews of Fortes's *Kinship and Social Order,* Goody's *Comparative Studies in Kinship,* and Barnes's *Three Styles in the Study of Kinship.* From the tone of the reviews, it was widely suspected that Rodney Needham was the anonymous reviewer. This made Fortes very upset because, he said, whatever Dr. Needham knew about the subject he had learned from him while he was teaching at Oxford.

These conversations must have affected Eggan because, when he was invited by Fortes to address the Friday afternoon seminar, he presented a paper on kinship. It was a brief version of his later paper, "Lewis Henry Morgan's Systems: A Reevaluation," which was published in 1972 in *Kinship Studies in the Morgan Centennial Year.* He was quite critical of Fortes's and Leach's formulations on kinship, and pointed out some ways to get out of the rut. This generated a lot of discussion in which Fortes, Leach, Goody, Barnes, and other Cambridge anthropologists took part. Eggan was at his best, and I do not remember a more lively public performance ever given by him.

After this seminar, he was quite nervous about his forthcoming public lecture. I lent him a copy of Leach's paper, "The Nature of War," which he had not seen. He liked the paper and used it in his Frazer Lecture on "Headhunting," which was a brilliant demonstration of the value of his method of controlled comparison in making some sense of this activity practiced by tribal communities in Borneo, India, and the Philippines. I wish he had published that paper. Fortes had asked the Cambridge University Press to publish it and Eggan had promised the manuscript. Whenever I reminded him, he said that only after making a careful study of Renato Rosaldo's *Ilongot Headhunting, 1883–1974: A Study in Society and History,* which appeared in 1980, would he be able to do it. Evidently he got busy with other projects and never found time to return to it.

Another such project that was shelved was a book on Radcliffe-Brown to appear in the Leaders of Modern Anthropology series published by the Columbia University Press. The book was announced, but he never came to do it. After reading his defense of Radcliffe-Brown in his review article,

"Aboriginal Sins," against a personal attack by Needham, I thought he should complete the project. I mentioned this to him a few times. After reading Leach's Radcliffe-Brown Lecture for the British Academy on "Social Anthropology: A Natural Science of Society?" Eggan was encouraged to continue working on the project. He wrote to me that he found some of Leach's remarks "puzzling in many respects." But he moved to respond to other challenges. One of them was a request from the Zuni Tribal Council to help the tribe get back the land they had lost since the establishment of their reservation in 1877. He called me on the telephone seeking my advice. Since I had also received a similar request, I was all too happy to have him as a member of the team. While he was in Santa Cruz as a visiting professor in the winter of 1976, we had organized jointly a panel on "Land Problems in the Pueblo Southwest" for the annual meeting of the American Anthropological Association to be held in Washington, D.C., later that year, with David Aberle, John Bodene, Eggan, Kennard, Charles Lange, and myself as participants. We had a lively discussion at the meeting. We continued our collaboration through correspondence before getting together again in December 1978 in New Delhi, where we had gone to participate in the Tenth International Congress of Anthropological and Ethnological Sciences. With T. N. Madan, Eggan was co-chair of a symposium on kinship, where he presented his paper on "Shoshone Kinship Structures and Their Significance for Anthropological Theory."

· VI ·

On our return from India, we became busy with the Zuni land-claims case. During the next three years, we met several times in Zuni with the Tribal Council, its team of attorneys, and the tribal archaeologist and historians in order to prepare the case. I helped the attorneys in taking depositions from the tribal elders. Eggan and I wrote papers on the aboriginal land-use patterns of the Zuni people, we prepared rebuttal documents, and we met in Salt Lake City with other members of the team to review some eight thousand pieces of evidence before filing the case in the federal land-claims court. In March 1982, we appeared in the court and gave oral testimony as expert anthropological witnesses. Eggan's testimony was remarkable in demonstrating for the court his vast and intimate knowledge of the Apache, the Navajo, the Hopi, the Acoma, and the Zuni cultural and historical experiences. Without him it would have been hard for me to make the case for the Zuni in the court alone. Our collaboration was successful; last December we received news of the settlement of the case for

$25,000,000. This made Eggan very happy. He had helped the Hopi win a similar, albeit smaller, settlement almost three decades ago. He came to be known as a friend and a champion of the southwest Indians, seeking justice for them in a "white man's court."

During the period of our collaboration I came to learn a great deal about him. Eggan had a very inquisitive mind. While we were together in Zuni or in Hopi pueblos, I would see him take notice of everything. He would greet everyone he met with an effortless and ready smile and would say something which made them feel at ease. Once we had been to see one of his old Hopi friends. When we arrived, his friend was listening to a tape of the Kachina songs and we saw tears rolling down his smooth face. We were at a loss for words to greet him, when he broke the ice and said, "Listen closely, Fred! The Kachina says, 'Look at me, and look at yourself. See how much you have changed, and how we have remained the same.'" We were moved, and I told Eggan that I thought the song summed up the Hopi philosophy. He said, "You know, like the Zuni, the Hopi conceive of their society as in a steady state, unfolding according to a preordained plan and continuing in a timeless existence." When I gave him some details about the Zuni historical experience, he said, "The Hopi situation is simpler because of greater isolation and smaller communities, but the problems are similar, as is the trend."

"The Hopi traditionalists are right," he had stated in an unpublished paper on "Progress and Conservatism Among the Hopi Indians of Arizona." He continued, "It is not possible to maintain Hopi culture and society as it was and still participate fully in American economic life. The social problems which afflict our communities—disorder, drunkenness, violence, homicide, etc.—are beginning to appear in Hopi communities where they were once almost completely absent. The Hopi who have survived on austerity for a thousand years may not be able to stand prosperity." I think perhaps it was because of this feeling that it was on their vision of life in which their society was at the center that he would dwell mostly in his lectures as well as in his writings.

During the past few years, Eggan had contemplated doing what he called a "biography of the Hopi," tracing how they evolved from their Shoshoni hunting and gathering past into a farming and horticultural community. How he would have gone about doing it can be seen in several essays he had recently written. I have already mentioned the paper he presented in the kinship symposium in New Delhi. The other paper I have in mind is on "Great Basin Models for Hopi Institutions," presented at the symposium on "Models of Pueblo Prehistory," at the Eleventh International Congress of Anthropological and Ethnological Sciences, held in Vancouver in 1983. He once told me that if he succeeded in doing this book, "that would be the ultimate in controlled comparison."

I think Eggan continued to be deeply committed to the Radcliffe-Brownian vision of social anthropology as a science. He thought that there was insufficient support for this vision to become a reality, and he became, it seems to me, somewhat unsympathetic to the current developments in what he called "the use of history and literary analysis of texts" in anthropology. But in his last letter to me, written just two months before his sudden heart attack on May 7, 1991, he had stated that he had "no regrets" in life. He was quite at peace with himself. When I called him on the telephone four days before his death and made inquiries about his health, since he had fallen down and broken a hip bone, he responded in his usual cheerful voice, "Well, now I have graduated to walking with a cane. With my cane, I am going to look my age now. That's fine with me. I really don't mind it." That was typical of Fred Eggan!

9

ENRICO FERMI

1 9 0 1 – 1 9 5 4

V. L. TELEGDI

· I ·

THROUGHOUT ITS long and glorious history, the University of Chicago has been particularly successful in attracting great men in one particular area, namely in the Physical Sciences. In this field, an almost uninterrupted chain of Nobel Laureates graced the University practically from its foundation on: Michelson, Millikan, Compton, Franck, Fermi, Libby, Maria Mayer, Mulliken, and Urey in the past, and Chandrasekhar as well as Cronin at present. The University was a place of excellence in physics well before the forced emigration of European scientists and the war effort raised the United States to the level of preeminence which we take today for granted. Michelson was the first American to be awarded (in 1907) the Nobel Prize in physics. These great scientists, to a lesser or greater extent determined by their personal characters and the periods in which they were working, attracted and trained a multitude of brilliant students who in turn through their own academic work and their scientific contributions (frequently again recognized by that famous award) spread the fame of the University further.

None of the great scientists who worked at Chicago ever had a greater impact, on his surroundings and world-wide, than did Enrico Fermi. Nobody in the history of modern physics possessed greater versatility than he; he had as great achievements in pure theory as in concrete experimental work; he could with equal ease solve abstract problems or design and build, with his own hands, astonishingly useful experimental tools. He was, as one of his best Chicago students, M. L. Goldberger put it, *the* "Compleat Physicist." To these qualities he added those of an exceptionally lucid lecturer and expositor, as well as of an active and patient thesis supervisor. It is imaginable—hypothetical situations are by definition hard to evaluate objectively—that some other physicist (or group of physicists) might have obtained the research results that Fermi achieved while in Chicago (including the realization of the first nuclear chain reaction), but it defies the bounds of human imagination to speculate that any other man or woman might have played Fermi's role as a teacher (in the broadest sense of this term). Through the influence of his students, Fermi effectively revolutionized the training of physicists in the United States and, one hopes, in the whole Western world.

When asked to prepare this essay, the present writer was reminded of what an eminent French physicist, Prince Louis de Broglie, wrote in his short biography of A.-M. Ampère:

> When one examines as great and as complex a figure [as Ampère], one can adopt one of two points of view: One may contemplate him as a human being, examining the details of his life and his career, the peculiarities of his character or the external manifestations of his intelligence, features which undoubtedly did contribute to transform such a man into an exceptional personality, though still living within the framework of his historical period, immersed in all the contingencies of everyday life from which none of us can subtract ourselves. One thus achieves a live picture in which the sadnesses and weaknesses inherent in the human condition necessarily take their places, whatever the beauty of the man's character and the greatness of his accomplishments.
>
> But one may also, in order to evaluate such a champion of intellect, adopt a somewhat more abstract point of view, neglecting particular physical or moral features of the individual, fading out the details of accidental events of his existence as well as the conditions of his historical period and of the atmosphere into which the evolution of History and the randomness of human destiny had placed him, so as to see in him only the splendor of his accomplishments and the greatness of the example he set. The great man then appears to stand out as a symbol illuminated by the clear light of History. He shows us what talent can accomplish in the short span of one human existence when sustained by conscience and hard work.
>
> There has been no genius, however complete he might have been, who could produce great achievements without long and painful effort. (From *Continu et Discontinu en Physique Moderne* [Paris, Albin Michel, 1941]; translated by the present writer)

Ampère (1775–1836) was, like Fermi, a universal genius, but there the analogy stops. He was, to use de Broglie's own words, a "tormented genius," much influenced by the vicissitudes of his personal life and much given to philosophical, yea even metaphysical speculations. Fermi was as well-balanced and dispassionate a person as one can imagine, little interested in matters outside (all of) physics. For this reason, we shall follow de Broglie's second approach to biography, concentrating on Fermi's professional activities, i.e. his research (Section II) and his teaching (Section III). In discussing these, we shall furthermore confine ourselves to his two Chicago periods, thus omitting some of Fermi's greatest glories, e.g. Fermi (-Dirac) statistics, the theory of β-decay, and his initial work on neutron-induced reactions (that led to his Nobel Prize), which were achieved in Rome. The reader is referred to the booklet *E. Fermi, Physicist* by E. Segrè (University of Chicago Press, 1972) for a more balanced picture.

Notwithstanding our (and Fermi's!) preference for physics over psychology and sociology, we offer a short section (no. IV) about Fermi's human personality and his style of work. To those who do not have the good fortune of having known Fermi personally, the few anecdotes reported in that Section may convey a better feeling for his nature than any literary effort on this writer's part could. In this context the reader is advised to peruse the charming but objective book *Atoms in the Family* (University of Chicago Press, 1954) by Laura, Fermi's wife. Note that that account was written in Fermi's lifetime. Fermi joined the Chicago faculty in January 1946, and died at Billings Hospital in November of 1954, six weeks after being admitted. He was felled by a multiply metastasized cancer that had escaped early detection. He was a physically strong man and only fifty-three years old.

· II ·

Enrico Fermi spent two distinct periods at the University of Chicago. During the first of these, from spring 1942 until September 1944, he was the key figure of the "Metallurgical Laboratory," the top-secret wartime project aimed at developing nuclear reactors and, ultimately, the atomic bomb. This work culminated on December 2, 1942, in the start-up of the first reactor or "pile," a graphite-uranium assembly erected under the West Stands of Stagg Field (this reactor was soon removed to the wartime site of Argonne National Laboratory, and Stagg Field yielded its terrain to the Regenstein Library). Today, the approximate location of that first reactor is marked by an abstract sculpture created by Henry Moore. It is safe to speculate that if the city of Chicago should ever be destroyed (possibly as an ultimate tragic consequence of the work done in the Metallurgical Labo-

Enrico Fermi

ratory), a new monument would be erected on the same spot to commemorate forever the place where Man first unleashed nuclear energy.

The work headed by Fermi in the Metallurgical Laboratory is described in over sixty declassified reports. These were preceded by some seventeen analogous reports, all already directed towards the goal of achieving a self-sustaining chain reaction, which Fermi and his collaborators wrote at Columbia University from the fall of 1940 on. Although Fermi's style, about which we shall say more later, emerges unmistakably from any report that carries his name, there is a marked difference between these two series. At Columbia, Fermi directed a small group of physicists and participated personally in even the most menial experimental tasks. The experiments were on a small scale, and the theory was in a field where Fermi, through his pioneer work in Rome, was already the accomplished master. In Chicago the project assembled a large group of scientists and engineers from various fields. Fermi had to assign the execution of experiments to various subgroups (he called this doing "physics by telephone"), but he generally evaluated the data himself, mostly in his office in Eckart Hall, because he preferred his knowledge to be firsthand. His efficient leadership was greatly enhanced by his marvelous powers as a lecturer; he instituted a series of lectures on Neutron Physics. Later, at Los Alamos, he gave a more extensive course, complete with homework problems. The transcripts of all these lectures, available in his collected papers, are good introductions well worth reading even today.

On the tenth anniversary of the first chain reaction, i.e. after returning to the University of Chicago, Fermi published an extensive paper on the construction and start-up of the first pile. Nothing in that paper reveals anything about the dramatic nature of the event. In fact, on about December 15, 1942, Fermi wrote tersely in a progress report: "The activity of the Physics Division [of the Metallurgical Laboratory] in the past month has been devoted primarily to the experimental production of a divergent chain reaction. The chain reacting structure was completed on December 2 and has been in operation since then in a satisfactory way."

A personal account of Fermi's matter-of-fact attitude at the critical moment has been given by his closest associate, H. L. Anderson:

> The next morning, December 2, I came bright and early to tell Fermi that all was ready. He took charge then. Fermi had prepared a routine for the approach to criticality. The last cadmium rod [control element] was pulled out step by step. At each step a measurement was made of the increase in the neutron activity, and Fermi checked the result with

his prediction, based on the previous step. That day his little six-inch slide rule was busy for this purpose. At each step he was able to improve his prediction for the following. The process converged rapidly, and he could make predictions with increased confidence for the following step. So it was that when he arrived at the last step. Fermi was quite sure that criticality would be attained then. In fact, once the cadmium rod was pulled out entirely, the pile went critical, and the first self-sustaining reaction took place. (From *The Collected Papers of Enrico Fermi,* ed. Segrè [Chicago: University of Chicago Press, 1965], comments on reports 180 and 181)

In September 1944, after witnessing the start-up of the first plutonium producing pile (at Hanford, Washington), Fermi left Chicago for Los Alamos, a laboratory he had frequently visited previously. Since this essay is devoted to Fermi at Chicago, we need not say much about his activities there, mentioning merely a few facts. Fermi witnessed the explosion of the first atomic bomb on July 16, 1945. Characteristically he had foreseen a simple way to estimate the power of the bomb: At the appropriate moment, he dropped a few slips of paper and measured the distance to which the blast blew them. His estimate agreed closely with that obtained by the sophisticated "official" methods. At the laboratory, he was in charge of a division (quite aptly called F-Division) that concerned itself with special projects. E. Teller worked in that division on the "Super," i.e. the hydrogen bomb. It is conceivable that Fermi's postwar opposition to the actual building of such a device was based on technical knowledge gained during that period and subsequent summer visits to Los Alamos. (In the summer of 1950, Fermi investigated, in collaboration with the mathematician S. Ulam, the thermonuclear reaction in a mass of deuterium. They concluded that ignition would not propagate. To the writer's knowledge, their report [LA-1158] is still classified.)

After V-J day, the original mission of Los Alamos had been fulfilled and the unprecedented galaxy of scientists assembled there began to disperse. They were anxious to return to their customary academic habitat, but with a new attitude: the wartime effort had ushered in "Big Physics," the use of large-scale equipment and the availability of massive financial support. Fermi, together with a group of other brilliant senior scientists, (e.g., Willard Libby, Cyril Smith, Leo Szilard, Edward Teller, Harold Urey) and their junior wartime associates (e.g., the physicists Herbert Anderson, Bob Christy, John Marshall, Leona Marshall, Darragh Nagle, and the chemists Nathan Sugarman and Anthony Turkevitch) accepted offers from the University of Chicago. Some kind of "package deal" was involved (it is rumored that the same "package" had proposed themselves earlier to the University of Washington, but that that deal fell through). President Hutchins, by inclination a philosopher and personally not particularly drawn to the exact sciences, realized the immense potential of this "package." He found the means to launch three new research institutes: one for Nuclear Studies (today named after E. Fermi), one for the Study of Metals (now the James Franck Institute) and one for Biophysics. All three were meant to be interdisciplinary, and their scientific members to serve on the faculties of their respective fields. Fermi was expected to run the Institute for Nuclear Studies, but he gratefully left the formal directorship to S. K. Allison, a distinguished native American physicist who had served the University already before the war.

Fermi came back to Chicago on January 2, 1946 (exactly seven years after reaching the United States). He immediately took up his teaching—both in the classroom and by sponsoring graduate students—and research. The experimental facilities in the Physics Department being minimal at that time ("the shelves were empty"), Fermi realized his interest, conceived in 1943, to exploit the intense flux from a reactor for experiments in neutron physics. The CP-3 reactor, at the original Argonne site, was well suited for this purpose (Argonne was then still a section of the Metallurgical Laboratory, and became a National Laboratory only in July 1946). Nine remarkable papers, all but one produced in collaboration with Leona Marshall (née Woods), came out of this research over a period of two years.

All of these papers have the hallmark of Fermi's style: extreme economy of technical means, efficiency of execution, and self-contained theoretical discussion, formulated in the most elementary terms. The most interesting of the investigations was a search for an interaction between the neutron and the electron, i.e. in modern terms a possible determination of the charge radius of the neutron (this particle being only overall electrically neutral). That experiment was unfortunately not sensitive enough to give a positive result—it yielded only an upper bound for the quantity sought. On this rare occasion, Fermi was "scooped" twice: on the one hand, Rabi and his collaborators Havens and Rainwater succeeded in obtaining, almost simultaneously, a concrete result using a different technique, while on the other L. Foldy could prove by a simple theoretical argument that the known magnetic properties of the neutron lead without any specific model to the existence of the sought electron-neutron interaction.

After these neutron physics investigations, Fermi's personal participation in experiments came temporarily to an end. He returned to what he considered to be his main vocation, theoretical physics, focusing his interests on entirely novel topics. In the years 1946 and 1947 some of the most exciting results came from cosmic-ray physics, primarily from experiments done in Europe. A group of young physicists in Rome reported an extraordinary anomaly: the negative "mesotrons" (the old name for mesons) when brought to rest in carbon did not appreciably get absorbed by the carbon nuclei as they were expected to do—*if* they were indeed (as their mass had suggested and as had universally been believed since their discovery in 1937) the mesons postulated by Yukawa as the quanta of the nuclear force field (i.e. the carriers of the strong nuclear interaction, to use modern parlance)—but decayed in about 10^{-6} seconds. Fermi and Teller, and independently V. Weisskopf at MIT, gave convincing arguments that this could not be explained in terms of some anomaly in the slowing-down process, as had been conjectured by some very eminent physicists, and estimated that process to be ten million times faster, i.e. to last but 10^{-13} seconds. The three authors published a joint Letter, followed by an extensive article by Fermi and Teller. Shortly thereafter, Occhialini, Powell, and their collaborators discovered—examining, in Bristol, tracks produced by cosmic rays in photographic emulsion—that the cosmic-ray "mesotron" (now called "muon") was but the decay product of a heavier particle (now called "pion") which indeed exhibited the properties of the particle postulated by Yukawa. (Incidentally, the terms "pion" and "muon" were coined by Fermi. These particles were previously called "π meson" and "μ meson" respectively.)

Thus two new fields opened up: "pion physics," the study of the interactions of the Yukawa particle, and "muon physics," the study of the heavy electron (which the muon turned out to be). The Bristol discovery was quickly followed by the production of "artificial" pions (positive, negative, and neutral) at the Berkeley accelerators. The era of High Energy Physics had begun. It was decided to equip the new Institute for Nuclear Studies with a 450 MeV synchrocyclotron; its construction was directed by H. L. Anderson (Fermi's closest associate since Anderson's graduate student days at Columbia) and John Marshall (also a wartime associate). This accelerator, with its experimental area specifically laid out for experiments with external meson beams, started operating in the spring of 1951. It was, for a few years, the highest energy accelerator in the world! Fermi contributed in many ways to the cyclotron project. He calculated the orbits of the pions from the production point ("target") to the experimental area using the MANIAC electronic computer at Los Alamos (Fermi immediately realized the potential of electronic computing and became fluent in writing programs in machine language). He also designed and built a small electrical cart with which one could readily move the target around the periphery of the cyclotron, in a region of high magnetic field; the latter served as the stator for the cart's motor. Fermi was quite proud of this device, universally called the "Fermi trolley." He also devised a simple way to measure the intensity of the internal beam through the energy deposited in, i.e. the temperature increase of, the target (generally a piece of beryllium metal).

As was implied above, Fermi's prime research from 1947 to 1951 was theoretical. The first major paper was on the origin and acceleration of cosmic rays, where Fermi advanced the idea that a galactic magnetic field played the key role in the acceleration mechanism. This paper was stimulated by E. Teller (often Fermi's favorite intellectual sparring partner) who has argued, together with H. Alfven, that cosmic rays originated in the solar system. Fermi presented this work at the Basel/Como conference in September 1947, and returned to the subject in later years. Another remarkable paper was one that Fermi wrote in collaboration with C. N. Yang (formally a student of E. Teller's), entitled "Are Mesons Elementary Particles?" Conventionally, it had consistently been assumed that pions and nucleons had the same mutual relationship as photons (light quanta) and electrons, i.e. that of a field and its source. Fermi and Yang advanced the bold hypothesis that the pion is a *bound state* of a nucleon-antinucleon pair. This hypothesis, neither readily verifiable nor very useful in itself, subsequently paved the way for several radical ideas in the theory of elementary particles, e.g. "Sakata model," "bootstrap," etc. Today, we picture the pion indeed as a bound state of a quark-antiquark pair! The next theoretical problem that Fermi attacked was to provide simple estimates as to what would happen if, say, a proton hit a nucleus at extremely high energies (such as were available then only in cosmic-ray-induced events), e.g. with what probability a given number of pions would be produced in a single collision. In doing this, Fermi discarded dynamical consideration entirely and based his deductions solely on statistical arguments. (It is little known, and it was certainly unknown to Fermi, who at that stage of his life hardly ever read the journals, that the key idea of his approach had been anticipated by a young German theorist, H. Koppe [Zs. f. Naturforschung *3a*, 251 (1948)]). Incidentally, although Fermi's versatility was and is legendary, it is probably fair to assert that he had a deeper feeling for statistical methods than for any other subject (indeed, the "Fermi statistics" constitutes probably his most lasting theoretical contribution). As always, Fermi was fully aware of the limitations of his simplified model and meant it to serve only as a guideline. He hence resented it when experimental departures from his predictions were raised as serious objections.

During the summers, Fermi liked to return to Los Alamos, where he served as a consultant. There he worked on a radically different class of problems (we can obviously discuss only what has been declassified). One of these concerned the famous "Taylor instability," a subtle problem in hydrodynamics. With his characteristic gift for simplicity, Fermi first discussed this phenomenon in terms of a glass of water turned upside down. Subsequently, partly in collaboration with John von Neumann, he wrote a very technical paper on the subject, extending it to the case of two incompressible liquids. What a wrestling of titans that collaboration must have been! An anecdote, told by the late Herbert Anderson to the present writer, can give us a hint: One day, after spending a whole afternoon at the blackboard with von Neumann, and being thereby completely exhausted, Fermi met Anderson and said to him, "Herb, that guy Johnny knows more about differential equations and all sorts of mathematics than I do, and I know more than you do. . . ." (Recall that Anderson was a pure experimentalist.)

Once the Institute's large synchrocyclotron began operating routinely, Fermi returned to experimentation. Before we discuss this important phase of his work, let us pause to mention the outstanding textbooks he produced while at Chicago. The first of these was *Nuclear Physics,* an extensive set of lecture notes compiled by his students Orear, Rosenfeld, and Schluter. It is a classic, a compendium of simple (or at least seemingly elementary!) solutions of all the relevant nuclear problems of its time. It is still of value today. The second was *Elementary Particles,* the written version of his 1950 Silliman Lectures at Yale University. Because of the explosive development of our factual knowledge of "elementary" particles, this work is today primarily of historical interest. Fermi also planned to produce an American version of a high school physics textbook that he had published much earlier in Italy. Because of frequent disagreements with an "educational expert" appointed by the publisher (who, for instance, refused the use of a vector notation), Fermi, who was extremely punctilious about the text of his publications, abandoned this project (I am indebted for this information to Prof. R. A. Schluter of Northwestern University). What a boon to U.S. education this book would have been, especially after Sputnik, when the country suddenly realized the low level of its high school science education!

We now turn to Fermi's experimental work with the cyclotron. This concerned almost exclusively the interaction of pions (both positive and negative, designated at π^+, π^-) with protons, i.e. with transmission of pions through, and the scattering by, liquid hydrogen. Some measurements of this kind had been done slightly earlier, at lower energies, at the Nevis (Columbia) cyclotron, and D. E. Nagle (as mentioned, already associated in wartime with Fermi) was the first to propose such measurements at Chicago. Fermi undertook the pion experiments in close collaboration with Nagle and H. L. Anderson; in the earliest stages of work Dr. E. A. Long, of the sister Institute for the Study of Metals, contributed his expertise in the construction of cryogenic targets. Occasional collaborators were a visitor from Norway, Arne Lundby, and G. B. Yodh, R. Martin, and M. Glicksman, three good graduate students.

The work, described in a series of nine experimental papers, lead Fermi and collaborators to two outstanding discoveries: (a) the nucleon (i.e. both the proton and the neutron) had an *excited state,* with an excitation energy of some 180 MeV; (b) the pion-nucleon interaction obeyed a symmetry principle, "charge independence" (already sketchily known from nuclear physics), which is characterized by a new conserved quantity, "isotopic spin." The excited state manifests itself as a peak or "resonance" when the probability of interaction (cross section) is plotted vs. the energy of the incident pion beam. An explanation in these terms by K. A. Brueckner (Phys. Rev. *86,* 106[1952]) had anticipated some of the most striking data of Fermi's group by several days.

> In fact, Fermi could (and did) read the preprint of Brueckner's paper the very day he found the [astonishingly] high $[\pi^+P]$ cross section. Brueckner had seized upon isotopic spin as being an essential element in the pion-nucleon $[\pi^-\mathcal{N}]$ interaction. Arguing that the dominant state was one with total angular momentum 3/2 and isotopic spin 3/2, all the features of the experiments could be understood at once. It took hardly more than a glance at Brueckner's paper for Fermi to grasp the idea. Twenty minutes after he left the experimental room to work through the idea by himself in his office, he emerged with this happy conclusion. "The cross sections will be in the ration 9 : 2 : 1," he announced. He referred to the π^+ elastic, π^- charge exchange, and π^- elastic processes, in that order. (From H. L. Anderson's comments in Fermi's collected papers; parts in [ ] added by the present writer.)

As seductive as the resonance hypothesis was, Fermi could not consider it proven until he had completed the detailed analysis of the angular distributions in terms of certain parameters (called "phase shifts"). He performed the requisite numerical analysis, in collaboration with N. Metropolis and E. F. Alfei, on the MANIAC electronic computer at Los Alamos. Unfortunately, at least two possible fits emerged; the one favored by Fermi did *not* correspond to the proposed resonance. The delicate matter of the "correct" solution was settled, including data from other laboratories, only after Fermi's death (confirming the excited state).

Fermi looked for possible additional *experiments* that could distinguish between the various solutions alluded to above. He realized that the polarization of the recoil proton in the scattering experiments, i.e. the orientation of the proton's intrinsic angular momentum (spin) with respect to the normal to the scattering plane, would have a high discriminating power. In a short theoretical paper, one of his last, he showed that this was indeed the case and that large effects were to be expected.

Even in the midst of the excitement of his experiments on pions, Fermi took time to further his theoretical interests in other areas of physics (in the broadest sense!). Thus during the fall of 1952 and in the winter and spring of 1953, Fermi met with S. Chandrasekhar once a week for two hours to discuss a variety of astrophysical problems related to hydromagnetics and the origin of cosmic radiation. Two major joint papers came out of these discussions, one on "Magnetic Fields in Spiral [Galaxy] Arms," the other on "Problems of Gravitational Stability in the Presence of a Magnetic Field." The first of these bears the stamp of Fermi's power to obtain estimates by simple means, the second of Chandrasekhar's analytic virtuosity. What a fertile meeting place the Institute for Nuclear Studies was! Fermi returned to these topics in August 1953 in his invited H. N. Russell Lecture to the American Astronomical Society. He was the first (and probably the only) non-astronomer to be so honored, and was quite pleased by this appreciation coming from outside his field.

We have already mentioned Fermi's particularly deep feeling for statistics, or more precisely for the theoretical study of the behavior of systems composed of a large number of identical objects, e.g. molecules or mass points ("statistical mechanics"). In the summer of 1953, Fermi, in collaboration with J. Pasta and S. Ulam, decided to check by a "computer experiment" whether the standard conjecture that in such a system the energy would be shared, after some time, equally among the degrees of freedom was indeed fulfilled ("trend towards equipartition"). Surprisingly, the result was negative. This calculation was completed and published only after Fermi's death.

Fermi's interests and contributions during his postwar Chicago period ranged even further than can be deduced from his publications. Maria Goeppert Mayer, who received (together with J. H. D. Jensen) the Nobel Prize for proposing the correct shell model of nuclear structure, acknowledges that she was put on the right track by a single crucial question raised by Fermi (who, characteristically, does not refer to this fact in his own published discussion of that model!). Not reading the literature, Fermi sometimes invited experts to bring him up to date on some topic of current interest. One of these experts was V. Weisskopf, who lectured for several afternoons to Fermi and a select group of physicists on the "Collective Model" of nuclei. During these lectures, Fermi would occasionally extract from his coat pocket a very large sheet of paper, covered with notations and multiply folded, and compare it silently with Weisskopf's writings on the blackboard. At the end of the lecture series, he simply said: "Well, this all agrees with what I already know. . . ." Another lecturer invited by Fermi was Richard Feynman (well known to him from their Los Alamos days), who gave several talks on liquid helium. Last but not least let us mention Fermi's interest in superconductors, both theoretical and technical. It was he who got Berndt Matthias (then on the Chicago faculty) interested in high-temperature superconductors, by raising at lunch the question: "Would it not be enormously important to have superconductors at, say, liquid hydrogen temperature?"

No single individual in this century has contributed so much to physics, through theory as well as experiment, as did Enrico Fermi. Still, in this writer's opinion, his greatest contribution in the Chicago period lay in his teaching. Through his students and their teaching, the Fermi spirit is still alive today.

· III ·

It is perhaps useful to reproduce the impressive record of the courses taught by Fermi in the Physics Department:

Quarter taught	Title	Number
Winter '46	Nuclear Structure	328
Spring '46	Electrodynamics I	310
Autumn '46	General Physics I	105
	Special Problems in Physics	371
Winter '47	General Physics II	106
	Special Problems in Physics	372
Spring '47	General Physics III	107
	Special Problems in Physics	373
	Research in Physics	403

Autumn '47	Quantum Mechanics and Atomic Structure I	241
Winter '47	Quantum Mechanics and Atomic Structure II	242
Winter '49	Nuclear Physics I	262
Spring '49	Nuclear Physics II	263
Summer '49	Mathematical Physics II	202
	Quantum Mechanics and Atomic Structure II	242
	Nuclear Structure	262
Winter '50	Quantum Mechanics and Atomic Structure II	242
Autumn '50	Nuclear Physics	463
Winter '51	Physics of Solids	411
Spring '51	Nuclear Particles	464
Autumn '51	Thermodynamics and Statistical Physics I	251
Spring '52	Thermodynamics and Statistical Physics II	252
Winter '53	Nuclear Physics II	463
Spring '53	Nuclear Particles	464

What is remarkable about this list is the variety of subjects taught by Fermi and the fact that he generally carried more than his share, as was his custom in any undertaking he joined. Note that Chicago operated under the "3Q System," i.e. that a faculty member was expected to give service for (and was only paid for!) three quarters out of each year. As we mentioned earlier, Fermi generally spent his summers as a consultant at Los Alamos. In the summer of 1949, he taught *three* courses, presumably to compensate for—exceptionally—not teaching in some other quarter. The fact that "Research in Physics" (403) is listed only for Spring '47 is an amusing quirk of departmental bookkeeping—of course he did and supervised research at all times! He once taught the big sequence of general (i.e. introductory) physics courses, although (or, because) he abhorred the humanistic approach to science teaching that prevailed then in the College ("they want to discuss how Galileo thought, but not teach what he thought about").

We have already mentioned Fermi's legendary talent for classroom teaching. His simplified exposition of any subject was no accident; it was the fruit of careful preparation. Many a time one could see him, well in advance of the appointed hour, going up and down in front of the classroom, consulting a sheet covered with formulae. Fermi seemed to derive pleasure from the *act* of teaching, without regard for the result. He never showed annoyance at a student's failure to grasp for the first time (or even the second!) what Fermi was trying to teach. On the contrary, if Fermi had to repeat an explanation he seemed to derive twice the pleasure. An apparent corollary was for Fermi's disinclination generally to evaluate students.

One of his former students has conjectured that all of the students at Chicago were so inferior to Fermi in talent that he could not (or did not think it useful to) recognize differences between them.

Fermi's style of lecturing was not entirely above criticism, and differed radically from his private approach to working problems. In class, he often chose to discuss general problems in terms of specific examples, with all factors carefully adjusted to be "of order unity" (and hence rapidly dropped). In his own calculations, generally performed on $2' \times 3'$ drafting sheets—far from the proverbial back of an envelope—all factors were carefully kept, even those which by convention are often put equal to 1. He delighted in giving simple derivations of results which on the part of others required elaborate calculations, but he occasionally sidestepped certain topics for which he too did not have a very elementary argument (e.g. the Thomas precession in atomic physics). His lucid lectures had an almost hypnotic effect; in class, the student felt that he had understood everything, but subsequently often felt empty-handed. The present writer found those of Fermi's lectures most fascinating that covered familiar notions. It was like "the view of a landscape as seen by an eagle—all remarkable points stood out clearly."

In several of his courses Fermi handed out mimeographed notes before each lecture. These contained mostly formulae and little text. Fermi said that he did this because he personally was unable to listen and take notes at the same time. For this reason he had hardly ever taken any notes during his student years at the University of Pisa. Some of these mimeographed notes (e.g. Quantum Mechanics) were subsequently published by the University of Chicago Press in book form. In our opinion, they do Fermi's memory a disservice: they present the formulae, but not Fermi's comments. It is like showing a skeleton instead of a full-length portrait.

Fermi's way of thinking about, and teaching of, Quantum Mechanics deserves a special mention. His attitude was an entirely pragmatic one: Quantum Mechanics is acceptable *because* its predictions agree with experiment (he once said "the Schrödinger equation has no business agreeing so well. . ."). Nothing else counted. He devoted no time to such topics as "The Quantum Theory of Measurement." He was immune to the "Copenhagen spirit," both by temperament and by educational background. He was completely self-taught in quantum mechanics, an outsider to the Göttingen-Zürich-Copenhagen circle of its founders. It may be supposed that Fermi always needed to draw a firm line between physics and "philosophy." Although endowed with remarkable analytic powers, Fermi often affected an aversion to abstract mathematics. Two anecdotes may serve to illustrate his attitude: (1) Once a notice appeared on the bulletin board announcing a course on the Fundamentals of Quantum Mechanics. This notice read "Students should be familiar with the mathematics of Hilbert spaces and Banach spaces." Fermi commented "Unfortunately I cannot learn about the fundamentals of quantum mechanics; I know about Hilbert spaces but not about Banach spaces." (2) Even when a mathematical argument had played a role in his initial thinking about a problem, he was careful to erase all of its traces from his final account. Chandrasekhar once was to talk in a seminar; when he expressed doubts as to what he should talk about, Fermi advised: "If I were you, I would not be technical." And Chandrasekhar asked: "Do you mean, if I were you or you were me?" This baffled Fermi: it was the only time Chandra got the better of him.

We now turn our attention to Fermi's doctoral students. No other physicist has ever trained such a score of eminent pupils (in Rome *and* Chicago); one might object to this statement by mentioning Rutherford and Sommerfeld, but the first of these trained only experimentalists and the second only theoreticians, while Fermi trained both categories.

Here is the list of Fermi's graduate students at Chicago:

Name	*Ph.D. awarded*
George Farwell	Spring '48
Geoffrey Chew	Summer '48
Marvin Goldberger	Summer '48
Lincoln Wolfenstein**	Winter '49
Jack Steinberger*	Spring '49
Owen Chamberlain*	Autumn '49
Richard Garwin	Autumn '49
Tsung Dao Lee*	Spring '50
Uri Haber-Schaim	Summer '51
Jay Orear	Summer '53
John Rayne	Spring '54
Robert Schluter	Spring '54
Arthur Rosenfeld	Autumn '54
Horace Taft[†]	Autumn '55
Jerome Friedman*	Spring '56
	(awarded after Fermi's death)

*Nobel Laureate
**To the writer's knowledge, Wolfenstein was a student of Teller's. The above table, provided by the Department of Physics at the University of Chicago, lists him under Fermi.

Fermi not only attracted outstanding graduate students, but brilliant junior faculty—"the Young Turks"—as well. At the celebration of T. D. Lee's sixtieth birthday, held at Columbia University, S. Chandrasekhar has movingly described the atmosphere created by these young people as the "Russian Spring."

· IV ·

Fermi was completely devoted to physics and his whole existence centered around it. He appeared to have very few outside interests, such as literature or the fine arts. He engaged in sports, e.g. in mountaineering and tennis, but one often got the impession that it was all for "mens sana in corpore sano"—i.e. to be in the best physical condition for doing physics; it must be added that in sports as well as in parlor games (which he occasionally organized in his home) he liked to win, being fiercely competitive. His salient features as a scientist were absolute integrity, total dedication to the task, and an incredible gift for efficiency. He was a very clear thinker, but not an exceptionally quick one (compared, say, to Landau or Teller). He solved simple and difficult problems at the same steady pace. In his dealings with others he displayed much reserve and great modesty, the latter in the sense that he "did not like to throw his weight around." A characteristic incident may serve to illustrate this: One day he needed an oscilloscope owned by somebody outside his own group. He asked one of his associates to go and fetch it—but added: "Don't tell him that it is for me."

Fermi liked to pass as an ordinary man, a "man of the street," simply a good artisan who happened to specialize in physics. He liked to do what "ordinary people" (as opposed to highbrows) do: when American intellectuals, in the early fifties, ridiculed the possession of a television set, Fermi promptly bought himself one (and fell asleep in front of it by 10 P.M.). Fermi had very regular working habits and a frugal life-style. He usually came to work before 8:30 A.M., in good weather, either walking or biking. He had worked for several hours before.

Totally secure in his own physics talent, Fermi almost never displayed jealousy of another. The only exception, as one of his students recalls, was Einstein. More than once Fermi expressed annoyance at the attention Einstein received from the press. He also disliked "high-class mannerisms"; once he commented about Robert Oppenheimer, "He was born with a golden spoon in his mouth. . . ." The day the Oppenheimer case broke, we were having lunch with Fermi at the Quadrangle Club. He said: "What a pity that they took him and not some nice guy, like Bethe. Now we all have to be on Oppenheimer's side!" Fermi's testimony at the hearings (Grey report) were, as expected, sober and not damaging.

Fermi hardly ever made disparaging comments about the scientific work of others. In the same vein, he refrained from laudatory remarks and rarely provided the encouragement that would have meant so much to the young people around him (curiously, during his first stay abroad, in Göttingen at age 23, he missed receiving encouragement from Born).

He did not have an exceptional memory, and in fact claimed to have a very poor one. He created for himself an "Artificial Memory," an encyclopedic collection of notes, summaries, calculations, numerical data, etc., classified according to a decimal system invented by him. This "Memory" is conserved (in twenty boxes) at the University of Chicago.

Fermi displayed hardly any of the behavior patterns that one (rightly or wrongly) often attributes to Italians: loud speech, vivacious gestures, gregariousness, fondness for wine, food, and song, concern for a well-tailored appearance, assertion of authority ("Lei non sa chi sono io" = you don't know whom you are speaking to, etc.). He possessed, however, one Italian quality, one that many American intellectuals lack: a total absence of psychological complexes (prewar Italy was the country with the smallest number of psychoanalysts per capita).

Perfectly well integrated into American life, he preferred to be "Enrico" rather than "Egregio professor" or "Herr Geheimrat." He participated in the students' social life, going to their modest parties and inviting them to his home for square dancing (the girls were provided by his wife, Laura). Although he never lost his Italian accent (e.g. he would always say "veertual"), his English was excellent; he delighted in using vernacular expressions and typically Anglo-Saxon constructions, such as "It is—is it not?"

Friendly with everybody, always helpful, Fermi seemed to eschew close personal relations. In my opinion, he felt that these would interfere with his quest for efficiency. His ability to provide order-of-magnitude estimates on the spot was phenomenal, and he would sometimes exercise it under surprising circumstances. An authenticated anecdote will illustrate this: William Zachariasen, a distinguished crystallographer and close colleague, was in the hospital recovering from a heart attack. Fermi decided to pay him a visit there. Zachariasen complained bitterly that he was given too little to eat, only 1,500 calories' worth. Fermi asked him "Willy, you are a great reader of detective stories, are you not?" Zachariasen replied "Yes, I am." Fermi then asked, "Willy, how long does it take a corpse to cool?" to which Zachariasen replied "4 to 5 hours." After some thought about heat losses, Fermi concluded "Then you cannot possibly survive on 1,500 calories!"

Fermi did not lack a sense of humor, even at his own expense. At the yearly Christmas parties, the physics students would compete with the faculty in various tests (always loaded in favor of the students!) and put on theatrical sketches. In some of these an electronic computer able to provide instant order-of-magnitude estimates, aptly named the ENRIAC, was displayed. This computer consisted of a large box, complete with blinking lights, and contained a junior faculty member who could imitate Fermi's voice and accent. The ENRIAC was asked: "Yesterday a corpse was found inside the cyclotron tank. What should we do?" to which the computer, in Fermi's voice, replied "An average adult weighs 60 kilos, 40% of which are water. The pumping speed of our cyclotron is so-and-so many liters per hour. The corpse is well desiccated by now and there is hence no point in opening the tank. . . ." Fermi shared in the general laughter.

Fermi's sense of humor and gift for irony show in two anecdotes. Once somebody presented a talk about the H (read eta) Theorem; his argument seemed unconvincing to Fermi. So he asked, "Are you talking about a theorem or simply about an H?" In Los Alamos, one of the most favored pastimes was fishing. Emilio Segrè enjoyed it, and tried to convince Fermi to come along with him. Fermi did not seem to show any interest in doing so. Segrè then tried to convince him of the intellectual merits of fishing: "You see Enrico, it's not so simple. The fish are not stupid, they know how to hide. One has to learn their tricks." Fermi replied "I see, matching wits!"

Another example of Fermi's humor is told by T. D. Lee. At some point, Fermi decided to teach his private seminar Group Theory. He took out his index cards on that subject, and started to discuss, first *Abelian* groups, then *B*urnside's theorem, then the *c*enter of the group, and only much later he got to the concept of group itself. Some of the students were a bit confused by this unorthodox approach. The Master said, "Group theory is merely a compilation of definitions." Therefore he simply followed the *index* at the end of Weyl's book.

Fermi looked at his surroundings mostly with a physicist's eyes. Once, answering a question of Bill Libby's (in the Institute Seminar) about mixing in the ocean, he derived instantly an equation describing that phenomenon. There was only one parameter in it, λ, the wave-length of surface waves. For this, Fermi promptly inserted a numerical value of 200 meters. Somebody in the audience asked: "Enrico, is it not rather 600 meters?" to which Fermi replied "Maybe so. But it was certainly 200 meters when I last crossed the Atlantic." During a trip to Brazil, one of the things that impressed him most was that there "the moon increases on the opposite side from what it does here."

One of Fermi's greatest assets was his wife, Laura. She was a beautiful person, in every sense of the word, of considerable intellect and great charm. During the frequent parties in their home, she managed to make the younger crowd, especially the Europeans overawed by the presence of the Master, feel perfectly relaxed. No picture of Fermi would be complete without her: Behind every great man there is a great woman.

10

JAMES FRANCK

1 8 8 2 – 1 9 6 4

E D W A R D   T E L L E R

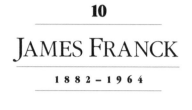 IN 1931, WHEN I arrived in Göttingen with my almost brand-new Ph.D., the famous James Franck called me. I was, of course, most eager to meet him. Together with Gustav Ludwig Hertz, Franck had provided the first experimental verification of quantum jumps, one of the strange and definite ideas of Niels Bohr about the nature of the atom. Franck and Hertz won a Nobel prize for that work.

For more than two thousand years, people had accepted Democritus' claim that atoms were indivisible. Yet an atom contained a heavy, positively charged nucleus and an appropriate number of negatively charged electrons compensating the positive charge. Bohr claimed that atoms, instead of being indivisible, could be divided into parts and that, while atoms were stable, they could exist in more than one stable state. But changes from one state to another in the atomic world, Bohr said, did not occur in the gradual, continuous manner described by classical mechanics: changes in the atomic world should be described in quantum leaps. (While the words "quantum leap" have become part of everyday language, the appreciation of the revolutionary nature of their meaning seems to be mostly restricted to professional physicists.)

As a result of his call, Papa Franck took me out for a ride "to show off my new car and to inspect the environs of Göttingen." (I quickly got into the habit, like everybody else, of calling him Papa Franck, although in 1931 he was barely middle-aged.) The car and tour were, of course, just an excuse to meet and talk physics.

I believe I asked him on that very first occasion about the Franck and Hertz experiment. Franck's response was, "Of course, Bohr's ideas were completely crazy, but he was such a nice man that Hertz and I thought we must give his suggestions a try." They had bombarded various atoms with

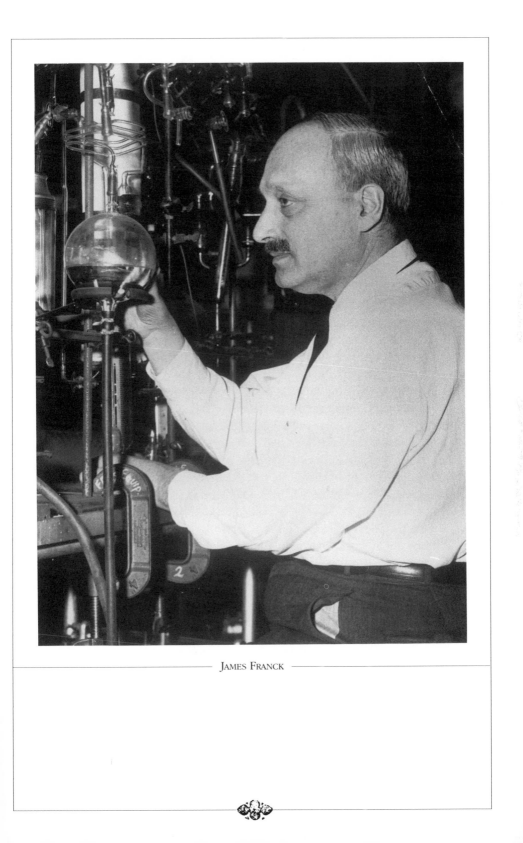

JAMES FRANCK

electrons of well-defined energies. Most of the collisions proved to be precisely elastic, with no loss of energy. But when the bombarding electron carried energy in excess of a particular amount (which varied for atoms of different types), then the electron was apt to lose just that energy and carry away the excess. Thus Franck and Hertz demonstrated that, indeed, Bohr was just as crazy as the atoms. Atoms were willing to accept their quantum of energy—nothing more, nothing less.

In that way, Franck became one of the originators of the great revolution of ideas that created atomic physics, called quantum mechanics, and unified the two sciences of chemistry and physics. To my mind, those ideas were a historic development as great, revolutionary, and isolated in time and even in location as was the development of Greek philosophy, Renaissance painting, or Baroque music.

During our little excursion, Franck wanted to discuss his latest elaborations of the new synthesis of physics and chemistry. He did not talk in formulae; he talked in the concepts of classical physics. That was indeed appropriate, because according to Bohr's correspondence principle, each new statement about the behavior of quantum states corresponds to a law already known in classical physics.

Franck had a distant (and perhaps limited) respect for mathematical formulae, which he liked to call the "integral salad." As it turned out, my culinary talents as a prospective salad chef were being assessed that day as he drove me around Göttingen. Franck's special interest was in the applications of what is now known as the Franck-Condon principle. The ideas were those of Franck, the formulae had been worked out for simple cases by E. U. Condon.

Franck's idea was that, when the electronic structure suffers a quantum jump by emitting or absorbing light, the sluggish nuclei cannot follow the rapid change of the light electrons. The nuclei will retain their position and their momentum, but their mutual attraction and repulsion is suddenly changed when the electrons are moved from one quantum state to another. The consequence is that the original vibration in the initial electronic state will change into one of several new vibrational states for the final electronic configuration.

By 1931, the behavior of diatomic molecules—a straightforward case—was well understood. But what would happen in a polyatomic molecule? There the several nuclei have several ways in which they can vibrate in each electronic state. What would be the influence of the symmetry of the molecule? That was the core of the problems on which Franck's laboratory was working and for which I was destined to provide the appropriate mathematics.

My work was rigorously supervised by Franck's assistant, Herta Sponer. I always considered her as a truly acceptable model of a Prussian general. She introduced me to the practice of numbering the pages of my manuscripts with such firmness that this bit of orderliness became a permanent habit, which thereby has rendered my efforts slightly more understandable. Many years later, in Chicago, after Mrs. Franck died, Papa Franck married Herta.

Those two years I spent in Göttingen were the last of the heroic period of physics. The theory of atoms, molecules, solids, metals took their accepted shape. While contributions came from all over the world, the original impetus came from central Europe. Members of Franck's Institut at Göttingen, collaborators, and students were often invited to parties at James Franck's house. Such a gathering took place on January 30, 1933. When I arrived, Franck met me at the door. "Do you know who your new chancellor is?" he asked. "Adolf Hitler." I thought I knew what that meant, but, of course, I didn't.

By March, a first consequence was becoming clearer: the remarkable golden age of atomic physics in Germany was over. Franck was one of the first to work actively on rescuing the Jewish scientists. Two outstanding British visitors came in succession to stay at Franck's home: the well-known physical chemist Frederick Lindemann and the noted biochemist F. G. Donnan. They were there as part of the Academic Assistance Council, a combined effort of the British scientific community and the Imperial Chemical Industries to rescue the scientists at risk in Hitler's Germany. They were conducting interviews and issuing invitations to come and work in England.

Franck made sure that I talked with both men. Lindemann later became Churchill's wartime scientific advisor and, still later, became Lord Cherwell (the name of the little river next to Oxford). I was familiar with Lindemann's work, but our conversation did not amount to much. Lindemann spent most of the time criticizing some recent fanciful papers peripheral to our common interests and then issued a general invitation to come to Oxford. Donnan, on the other hand, did not offer me a job but asked that I come and visit London as soon as possible. During that visit he discovered that I had an unpardonable shortcoming: I had not read *Alice In Wonderland*. His invitation to me to join London City College was conditional on my correcting that omission.

Thus I escaped the personal tragedy that, in so many individual cases, was caused by the Nazi dictatorship, anti-Semitism, and war. The generosity of the British together with the close-knit structure of the scientific community saved almost all of the physicists from such suffering, and, of course, James Franck was one of the prime movers who guided that remarkable operation. In high school in Budapest, I had three close friends: two of them died in concentration camps, the third escaped only by going over to the Soviets through the disorganized fighting lines.

After Göttingen, I never again had the opportunity to work closely with Franck, but our personal relationship grew even stronger. In the early fall of 1933, I saw him at an informal physics meeting in Copenhagen and told him my big news: I was going to marry at Christmas. As it turned out, Papa Franck played an amusing and fortunate role in that marriage.

After having to pull up stakes in Göttingen, I got relocated in London, but I then promptly went off on a Rockefeller Fellowship to Copenhagen. Unfortunately that fellowship was accompanied by a peculiar prohibition: I was not supposed to get married because a honeymoon was considered to be bad for research. By the time the Rockefeller Foundation had instructed me about the ill-effects of marriage on science, Franck had arrived in the United States. I wrote to tell him how I was doing and, having earlier mentioned my forthcoming marriage, I added (without complaining) that on the Rockefellers' command, I had postponed my marriage.

Franck promptly stormed into the Rockefeller office in New York and enlightened the bureaucrats about their objectionable behavior. In light of their embarrassment at having to back down, he then wrote to me suggesting a compromise to save all the involved faces: I should write a mild letter complaining about being separated and explaining how that unhappy state interfered with my research.

I wrote such a letter promptly and with considerable enthusiasm. But I then made the near-fatal mistake of showing it to Bohr, since, after all, my fellowship specified that I was to work with him. Niels Bohr, who gladly suffered the paradoxes in physics, would not put up with the paradox of my complaining that pining for my beloved had lowered the effectiveness of my work. He claimed he could detect no such thing.

"Why don't you just write to New York and tell them that Franck told you to do so?" "Because Franck explicitly asked me not to do that." Bohr replied: "That does not matter; after all, Franck is our friend." Eventually, with some help from Harald Bohr, I sent the letter. I did get married on February 26, 1934, with only a two-month delay. Franck's practical advice had finally overcome Bohr's theoretical objections (and without any noticeable damage to physics). For me, the story illustrates some aspects of the characters of Bohr and of Franck and of their mutual relation.

A couple of years later, I was teaching theoretical physics at the George Washington University in Washington, D.C., only an hour's drive from the Johns Hopkins University, which had become Franck's headquarters. He had a seminar on molecular spectra every second week, and I attended it religiously. It was the center of friends, new and old. Among the latter, Herta Sponer and Lothar Nordheim had resettled at Duke University. They too came to the seminar fairly often. A lot of the old spirit was being transplanted.

Franck in turn visited our home in Washington several times, and I am indebted to him for another one of his nonscientific interventions. In the early years of our marriage, my wife, Mici, criticized me somewhat severely for my undignified interest in detective stories. During one visit Franck borrowed one of my favorites. Mici's criticism stopped. (I must confess, however, that more recently my interest has shifted to history books. Not only does history offer more surprises, but the inventive imagination shown by authors of detective stories pales by comparison with the reports of historians.)

The Second World War and the advent of the atomic energy project produced additional changes in our work and our locations. I wound up in Los Alamos working on the atomic bomb; Franck moved to Chicago to work with the group that, with the help of nuclear reactors, was supposed to produce plutonium, the raw material for our atomic stockpile.

The plutonium work in Chicago was completed at the same time that Hitler's suicide provided the final note for the defeat of the Nazis. It became clear that, if the atomic bomb was to be used, the target would be Japan. Leo Szilard, my Hungarian friend who had directed my interest toward atomic energy even before the Manhattan Project started, had also been working in Chicago. About this time, Franck and Szilard began discussing the question of what should be done with the atomic bomb.

They drew up a petition which pointed out that nuclear explosives would have a deep and terrible influence on events after the war and that threatening the Japanese with the use of the bomb would be incomparably better than the actual use. Many people in the Chicago project signed the petition. I suspect that the contributions that Szilard and Franck made to that petition may have differed. Szilard, I think, would have been likely to emphasize matters of principle and morality; Franck, I think, would have put more emphasis on the practical issue of how to build a better world after the war was ended.

Unfortunately, the memorandum never had any effect, in part because Oppenheimer opposed it. If Truman had acted on the petition (which he probably never saw), the war might possibly have ended with the demonstration of the power of science and without the sacrifice of a single additional human life. A demonstration high over Tokyo Bay would have been seen and heard by ten million Japanese including Emperor Hirohito. The Emperor might then have acted to end the war as he did after Hiroshima. Under those circumstances, the hysterical development of antinuclear and antitechnological movements might never have gotten started. It is a terrible pity that the potential benefits of Szilard's ingenuity and Franck's wisdom were not more fully realized.

After the war, I moved to Chicago and had the pleasure of seeing Franck and Szilard in their state of amicable coexistence at the University of Chicago's Quadrangle Club. Franck enjoyed recounting one of their disagreements, which, while friendly, remained completely insoluble. Franck attempted to put an end to the discussion by saying to Szilard, "It seems to me that both you and I are crazy." Szilard's reply was, "Sir, with the deepest respect, I agree with half of your statement." I must say that whenever Franck disagreed with the people I most admired, like Bohr or Szilard, my sympathies were always with Franck.

In Chicago, during his later years, Franck started to work on a new fundamental problem in biochemistry: photosynthesis. Some people who regretted his abandonment of the details of spectroscopy said, without due respect, that now Franck is only working on spinach. But that particular spinach indeed represents a turning point in the development of life on earth. I like to call photosynthesis the first great technological innovation on our planet.

According to early work done by Harold Urey, life, or at least the substances on which life was feeding, started in the stratosphere. There ultraviolet light from the sun, which delivers large quanta of energy, could bring about chemical changes that stored energy. This manna from heaven rained out into the oceans, which thereby became a soup rich in nutrients that could be easily assimilated by any form of life, wherever it may have originated.

However, the main characteristic of life is to multiply. Four billion years ago, the spirit of Malthus would have predicted that overpopulation would bring about an early extinction of life. But then, as Franck saw it, history took a decisive turn: life discovered that food produced by the sun need not be produced in one big quantum jump. Franck stated that useless carbon dioxide can be changed, through photosynthesis, into sugar or starch by four quantum jumps. After the absorption of each of these smaller quanta, the intermediate products would have a life that was long enough to wait for the next quantum.

The point, of course, is that ultraviolet light carrying large quanta penetrates only the uppermost parts of our atmosphere where it finds relatively little material to work on. The bulk of the energy carried by sunlight reaches the earth in the form of small quanta that can be used only by the artifice evolved in the complex molecules of primitive plants.

Until the end of his life, Franck retained his flair for asking the decisive questions and for knowing the direction to turn for an answer. In his last years, he was troubled by angina and he finally died of heart disease. Had medical science introduced the bypass operation sooner, Franck might have lived long enough to earn a second Nobel Prize for his important work on "spinach."

11

MILTON FRIEDMAN

1 9 1 2 –

G A R Y   S .   B E C K E R

MILTON FRIEDMAN came to Chicago's department of economics in 1946 and remained there until 1977, when he moved to the West Coast. During this thirty-year period, he was clearly the dominant influence in a department that may well have been the most innovative and lively one in the profession.

Friedman was thirty-four years old when he came back to Chicago. Nowadays, up-and-coming economists have many publications and are already well known by that age. Friedman was not widely known, and his publication record did not foretell the major impact he was to have on the economics profession.

Economists who received their training during the great depression of the 1930s advanced much more slowly than do those trained in recent decades. Little fellowship money was available and jobs were scarce. Before completing his studies in 1935, Friedman had to take a job in Washington with the National Resources Commission. In 1937 he moved to the National Bureau of Economic Research, then in 1941 to the Treasury. In 1943 he began working on military problems at Columbia's Statistical Research Group, which was headed by his friend and fellow student at Chicago, W. Allen Wallis. He completed his studies at Columbia and was awarded his doctoral degree there in 1946.

Prior to *Income from Independent Professional Practices* in 1945 (jointly written with Simon Kuznets), Friedman's publications record was not extensive. Little wonder that when Chicago's economics department looked to replace the departing Jacob Viner—who had exerted a major influence on Friedman—its first choice was George Stigler, who already had an impressive publication record. But in an interview, Stigler alienated the central administration, and they refused to approve his appointment.

MILTON FRIEDMAN

Only then did Friedman receive the offer. Fortunately for Chicago, Stigler also returned a decade later, when in 1957 he became Walgreen Professor in both the department of economics and the graduate school of business. Like the famed West Point duo of Blanchard and Davis, who were known as Mr. Inside and Mr. Outside, Stigler and Friedman became Mr. Micro and Mr. Macro of Chicago.

Dwight Yntema, who reviewed *Income from Independent Professional Practices* in the *American Economic Review* of 1946, did not appreciate the book's significance: "This reviewer [has] definite reservations regarding . . . the sheer length of a volume that is spun from so limited a subject."

He was dead wrong, for the book provides insights on practically all pages. The preface indicates that Friedman's contributions include: the distinction between permanent and transitory income, calculation of the present values of gains from entering various professions, and estimates of the monopoly power of the American Medical Association. These have enormously influenced discussions of the consumption function, labor economics, and human capital analysis. Yet publication of this book was delayed for five years because a member of the National Bureau of Economic Research's board of directors did not like the conclusion that doctors are overpaid and had restricted entry into medicine. Eventually a compromise was reached, whereby a largely irrelevant comment by the director was included at the end of the book.

Friedman produced a remarkable collection of articles and books during his first decade at Chicago. These include famous papers on choice under risk (with L. J. Savage), methodology of economics, the school voucher system, and flexible exchange rates, as well as two highly influential books: *A Theory of the Consumption Function* (1957) and *Capitalism and Freedom* (1962). These publications established his reputation as one of the premier economists of his generation.

Friedman's rise to the top was not smooth and was filled with controversy. The obstacles were personally painful, but they renewed his dedication to research and accustomed him to being unpopular. The obstacles also made all the sweeter the adoption of many of his ideas by professional economists and the introduction by governments the world over of many of his programs—such as flexible exchange rates, flatter tax schedules, and privatization of many government activities.

His enormous research output after the return to Chicago clearly greatly contributed to his becoming the dominant member of the so-called Chicago school of economics. Yet he would have had tremendous influence at Chicago even if he had published much less. I will try to explain why.

During most of his Chicago career, he gave one section of a two-quarter sequence on price theory taken by all graduate students in economics. Friedman was at his best in this course. He developed the theory in a clear, systematic, logically consistent fashion. He also gave numerous illustrations and applications, which included why companies often sell several products tied together in a package, as when movie distributors sell movies in blocks rather than separately; how trade unions affect wages and employment; why people buy lottery tickets; the determinants of parental demand for children; and on and on in endless variety. These applications helped students absorb Friedman's vision of economics as a tool for understanding the real world, not as a game played by clever academics.

Friedman encouraged give-and-take with students. He welcomed questions, restated them much more clearly than struggling students were able to, and then usually showed why they revealed confused thinking. Some students found the intensity of the course, the high standards demanded, and the bluntness of Friedman's comments on questions and written work too difficult to absorb psychologically. They found excuses to take the alternative sequence although it was demonstrably inferior to Friedman's. Most students, however, found Friedman's approach an eye-opener, and were willing to put up with pressures and low grades to be exposed to his brilliant insights about price theory.

I had taken several graduate courses in economics and mathematics while an undergraduate at Princeton, and I was preparing two articles for publication when I entered the University of Chicago. In a meeting with the advisor to graduate students, D. Gale Johnson, just after I came to study at Chicago, Johnson said that it probably was not necessary for me to take the theory course that was a prerequisite for Friedman's sequence. I was annoyed by the mere suggestion that I might have to take that prerequisite, and replied that I doubted whether even Friedman's sequence was necessary. After all, I already had graduate price-theory courses at a top university. Gale handled the ignorance of a twenty-year-old gently, and suggested that I might learn a little from Friedman's course.

I went to his first lecture in a skeptical mood. After fifteen or twenty minutes he asked a question, my hand shot up, he called on me, and I gave an answer. Forty years later I remember his response: "That was not an answer but merely restated the question in different words." I felt humiliated, but I knew he was right, and I was much impressed by his quick and correct evaluation of my answer. I remained silent the rest of the class while Friedman gave an excellent lecture.

I am still grateful to Friedman for knocking me down when I deserved it. Going back to my room that day, I told myself that I must forget for a while about writing more articles—I had been working on a third one. It had already become evident that I had an enormous amount to learn about real economics, and that I should spend the next few years investing in new knowledge and disinvesting misperceptions. I kept to this resolution, for I did not publish anything between 1952 and 1957. Then, among other things, I published a paper written jointly with Friedman in the *Journal of Political Economy.*

The emphasis in his course on applications of theory to the real world set the tone for the department. It was considered necessary to have a strong working command of basic price theory, especially so-called partial-equilibrium supply and demand analysis. Yet the theory was not an end in itself or a way to display pyrotechnics. Rather, the theory became worthwhile only insofar as it helped explain different aspects of the real world.

The Chicago approach also emphasized that the relevance of theory could not be determined only by illustrations, introspection, and "casual empiricism." Nor could doing theory be separated from doing quantitative testing. A good theorist had to do some of his own empirical work. Lewis, Schultz, Stigler, and others were not only good theorists but conducted systematic and insightful tests of theoretical implications. Friedman himself was a superb statistician and a careful empirical worker. His paper in 1937 on the use of ranks in statistical analysis became a classic. He and Allen Wallis saw the potential of sequential analysis and posed the problem for Abraham Wald. The book on income from the professions, mentioned earlier, surely ranks among the best empirical studies in economics, with a remarkable combination of theory, statistical techniques, and careful analysis of data.

This approach to economics was not common then at other major departments; for that matter, it still is not common. Elsewhere, the basic theory course usually contained few applications and little mention of empirical testing. And the emphasis in the profession is increasingly on rigor; economics has become more rigorous than physics and chemistry!

I am not claiming that theory is usually taught for its own sake or as a branch of mathematics—although some theorists look at it that way. Rather, the problem is that many economists teaching theory are not confident that it is very helpful in understanding behavior. And their lack of confidence in its relevance is absorbed by students.

Students at Chicago were aware that what they were learning from Friedman and others differed from what was being taught elsewhere. It was not only particular ideas, the views of the so-called "Chicago school," but the basic approach to economics that differed. Some students found this conflict with most of the profession difficult to handle, but others developed a chip on their shoulder and became aggressively proud of being Chicagoans. Indeed, the aggressiveness of Chicago graduates was notorious; for this and other reasons, many prominent economics departments refused to appoint any Chicago graduates.

As an undergraduate and graduate student, I had many fine courses, especially from Jacob Viner at Princeton, and from Gregg Lewis and Jimmie Savage at Chicago. But no course had anywhere near the influence that Friedman's did. I looked forward with excitement to every lecture. Friends wondered how I could be so excited about the prospect of going to a class. But it was a marvelous intellectual experience, and I was quite sad when the last lecture was finished.

In retrospect, my only complaint about the course is that more attention should have been paid to general equilibrium analysis and to the potential of mathematical economics. Friedman always did stress, correctly in my opinion, that there is no basic conflict between partial and general equilibrium analysis; he did not hesitate to use the mathematical tools at his command, and no course can do everything. Still, the impression was conveyed that most mathematical economics was sterile, and that models of general equilibrium tend to be untestable (see, for example, his excellent reviews of "Lange on Price Flexibility and Employment" and "Walrus and His Economic System" in the *American Economic Review* in 1945 and 1955). Although his criticisms were relevant, and still apply to some of this literature, I now believe he was excessively negative on the prospects for developments in these areas.

Friedman exerted a profound influence on students and on other faculty not only through this course, but also from his comments on their research, especially on dissertations. He was very busy, and it took a while before he returned a paper he been asked to read. But it was evident from the many written questions, criticisms, and suggestions, that he read very carefully. His comments usually showed deep insight into the problem being discussed, often in a much better way than that in the paper. He did not overdo negative comments, for he also gave many helpful suggestions on how to improve the research. He emphasized, as in his course, careful formulation of the problem, concern about empirical implications, and testing these, when possible, with real data.

I remember vividly waiting impatiently in 1953 for his reaction to an initial statement of my analysis of racial discrimination. Friedman was spending the year in Cambridge, England, and it took a couple of months before his reply arrived in the mail. I eagerly tore open the letter, only to be dismayed by what I found. He blasted me for a presentation that was more notes to myself than a discussion readable by others. He also attacked ambiguities, imperfectly stated ideas, and other defects. He did add that he thought the ideas were promising and well worth developing.

I was crushed and did not return to the topic for a few weeks. By that time I fully realized that, as usual, his criticisms were right on the mark. I gained a little solace from his belief that the ideas were interesting. I went back to the research, but the experience taught me an important lesson. Even in early stages of research, it is necessary to state the main ideas in a form that can be understood by readers who are not engrossed in the subject and cannot determine what is in the writer's mind.

Many students worked with Friedman, perhaps more than with any other faculty member. But I was struck by how many of the best ones did not. Partly, this was because their interests lay elsewhere, and excellent faculty were available to supervise dissertations on industrial organization, labor, agriculture, trade, and other subjects. Still, I believed at the time that some top students shied away from working with Friedman because they could not take the heat: they could not handle psychologically his sharp and blunt criticisms, and his quick insights. In essence, they feared being overwhelmed intellectually. I also had these fears but managed to control them enough to recognize how much I could learn from him. This was well worth the effort, no matter how inferior intellectually one felt.

Eventually, Friedman influenced research at Chicago mainly through the Money and Banking Workshop. This was the first workshop at any economics department, and it was begun in 1953 with support from the Rockefeller Foundation. Initially, it met twice a week and required an intense commitment. Practically all students who attended regularly were writing dissertations on money. Although mine was on discrimination, I joined it from the beginning and was a regular participant. When I became an assistant professor in the department in 1954, I spent half my time assisting Friedman in running the workshop. So I was closely involved with it during the early days. I still remember going with Friedman to a downtown Chicago store to buy a half dozen used Marchant and Monroe calculating machines for the graduate students in the workshop, who had a room in the basement of the Social Science Research Building.

I have often been asked what distinguishes workshops from seminars.

The Money and Banking Workshop rather immediately established the policy of distributing the speakers' papers in advance to all participants. The papers were to be read carefully before the meetings. This has become the tradition of the Chicago workshop system that helps distinguish it from workshops and seminars at most other universities. Elsewhere, papers usually are not distributed in advance; even when they are, few faculty or students more than glance at them. Since Friedman assumed that papers were read beforehand, speakers had only a few minutes to introduce their topics and approach, and then discussion took over.

Workshops are also usually oriented toward students writing their dissertations in particular areas, although the Industrial Organization Workshop and some other successful ones have not had this orientation. Chicago workshops do generally involve an intense commitment by regular participants and by several faculty—at least three and sometimes up to a dozen. And workshops concentrate much more on discussion than on presentation of papers.

Despite the frequency of the meetings of the Money and Banking Workshop in its early days, I looked forward to each one. The discussion was exciting even when the papers were mediocre. To me and others the main purpose of a meeting was to hear Friedman's comments on different subjects. Papers were often just a catalyst for the general discussion, and this is still the case at several Chicago workshops. Frequently, the most interesting exchanges were between Friedman and other faculty participants, and speakers were at times gently told not to butt in too much.

No matter how many faculty were present, Friedman was the leader and did most of the talking. He could be unsparing in his attacks, but he also gave valuable suggestions on how to correct weaknesses and redirect the research in more fruitful directions. This was no lion's den where the sport was to destroy hapless victims, although it sometimes appeared that way to speakers. Instead, it was tough intellectual brainstorming, where the goal was to learn more about the role of money and macroeconomics, and to provide suggestions on how to improve the speaker's research.

Of course, nobody likes to see defects in one's research exposed, especially in front of others. I do not remember Friedman ever attacking a speaker personally or making fun of his work. Yet he definitely did attack deeply and persistently, and often would not stop until speakers cried the equivalent of "Uncle." Although his comments were not cruel, I believe it would have been better if he permitted more face-saving after it became clear that some research was worthless or had serious flaws. But Friedman has a missionary's zeal in the worship of truth. He tried first to find the truth and then to convert others. This zeal left no room for posturing, and embarrassment and psychological wounds were to him a small price to pay for the pursuit of the holy grail.

Chicago's workshop system was a major innovation in conducting economic research and in apprenticing students in research. It has been copied by many other economics departments—often at the instigation of Chicago graduates—and also by business schools and law schools. Although often successful, workshops elsewhere usually do not achieve the intensity of those at Chicago. This is attributable to the faculty commitment at Chicago to the workshop system, and to the extensive discussion of papers read prior to meetings.

The department of economics' workshops also inspired the recommendation of the commission on graduate education, of which Keith Baker was chairman, to develop interdisciplinary workshops throughout the humanities and social science divisions at Chicago. I was a member of the commission and was skeptical whether workshops would flourish when they did not develop spontaneously. But by encouraging a more general workshop system and by providing small amounts for expenses, the University of Chicago did develop valuable workshops in other departments as well.

I believe that Milton Friedman will rank among the two or three most influential economists of the twentieth century. That judgment is controversial, but there is no doubt that he was the dominant economist at Chicago for thirty years. He solidified and expanded the reputation of the Chicago school, as the economics department increasingly reflected his approach and interests. These included deep commitment to the truth, appreciation of markets and free enterprise, frank and blunt discussion, and enormous zeal to convince the heathen. But most important was the commitment to economic analysis as a powerful instrument for interpreting economic and social life.

Practically every student who passed through the economics department from 1948 to 1977 remains in Friedman's debt. Along with Stigler, Schultz, Lewis, Harry Johnson, Gale Johnson, Harberger, and others, he made the department, through his teaching, research, and personality, an enormously stimulating and unusual place to learn economics. I doubt if many other departments, regardless of field or university, have provided such an attractive atmosphere. I continue to be grateful that I was wise enough—and lucky enough—to come to Chicago and to spend six years studying at Friedman's feet.

12

E. M. K. GEILING

1 8 9 1 – 1 9 7 1

P H I L I P   C .   H O F F M A N N   A N D

A L F R E D   H E L L E R

 PHARMACOLOGY, as a scientific discipline, is first mentioned in the *Annual Register* of the University of Chicago in its 1900–1901 edition. On page 292 of the *Register* there appears the entry:

XXIV. THE DEPARTMENT OF PHYSIOLOGY
(Including Physiological Chemistry and Pharmacology)

The future Nobel Prize winner Jacques Loeb headed the department, and the name of Waldemar Koch, Ph.D. was entered among the officers of instruction as an assistant in pharmacology.

In 1917, the subordinated disciplines of physiological chemistry and pharmacology were formed into a new department independent of the department of physiology. The study and teaching of pharmacology remained in this hybrid department for the next nineteen years.

· I ·

In 1936, Dr. Eugene Maximilian Karl Geiling became the first professor and chairman of a separate department of pharmacology at the University of Chicago. In the year prior to Geiling's arrival in Chicago, the *Announcements* of the University listed as officers of instruction in pharmacology within the department of physiological chemistry and pharmacology Edward William Wallace, Ph.D., instructor in pharmacology, and Bert John Vos, Jr., Ph.D., assistant in pharmacology. The officers of instruction in Geiling's first year included himself as chairman of the independent department of pharmacology, Vos as an instructor in pharmacology, and Frances K. Oldham, M.Sc., as a research assistant in pharmacology. The department also included Clarence Weinert Muehlberger, Ph.D., as a professorial lecturer in toxicology.

Within the first year of his chairmanship, Geiling recruited five new scientists to his staff, including Carl C. Pfeiffer and Julius M. Coon, both of whom later became distinguished scientists in their own right.

Geiling remained at the University of Chicago for twenty years, retiring in December 1956. At the time of his retirement, the *University Announcements* listed 21 officers of instruction in his department; he had begun with three about twenty years earlier! Included in this list was Geiling's first graduate student, Frances Oldham Kelsey, Ph.D., M.D.

Geiling became the Frank P. Hixon Distinguished Service Professor in 1941, succeeding in that chair the noted physiologist Anton (Ajax) T. Carlson, who was one of the best-known biomedical scientists of his time. Geiling's research interests fell into three major categories: characterization of hormones; important toxicological investigations; and pioneering attempts to label chemically complex drugs with radioisotopic carbon atoms, so as to be able to study the drugs' sojourn throughout the body.

· II ·

Geiling was born in 1891 in the town of Branford in the Orange Free State in South Africa. He received the degree of bachelor of arts from the University of South Africa in 1911 and came to the United States in 1914 as an overseas fellow from the Union of South Africa to study in the department of animal husbandry and nutrition at the University of Illinois. He received his doctorate in physiological chemistry from that institution in 1917, whereupon he returned to South Africa to teach agricultural chemistry and nutrition at the Potchefstroom Agricultural College. Shortly thereafter he was appointed a senior lecturer in physiological chemistry at Cape Town Medical School. Dr. Geiling was awarded a Seesel research fellowship at Yale University in the autumn of 1920, and he spent the year studying and doing research with the physiological chemist Dr. Lafayette Mendel.

In 1921 Dr. Geiling made the decision to move to The Johns Hopkins University in Baltimore, Maryland, to work in pharmacology with Professor John Jacob Abel in that institution's school of medicine. Abel was the most famous pharmacologist of his era, and indeed, has been called by many the "father" of American pharmacology. Abel's program of studies was typical of the American scholars in the rapidly advancing biomedical disciplines in the late nineteenth century. He spent the seven years from 1884 to 1891 in intensive study in Europe, attending the Universities of Leipzig, Strassburg, Heidelberg, Bern, and Vienna, studying with great European scientists as Ludwig, Schmiedeberg, Hoppe-Seyler, Drechsel, von Nencki,

E. M. K. Geiling

and Wislicenus in the fields of physiology, pharmacology, biochemistry and chemistry. Abel took his examination for the medical degree at Strassburg in 1888, and was called two years later to his *alma mater,* the University of Michigan, as a full-time professor of materia medica and therapeutics (this title was equivalent to that of professor of pharmacology). Two years later, he was called to the chair of pharmacology at Johns Hopkins.

Abel's early scientific research was focused mainly on the newly emerging discipline of endocrinology, the study of hormones. He had isolated a derivative of the hormone of the adrenal medulla, epinephrine, performed extensive research concerning the purification and chemical properties of hormones of the posterior pituitary gland, and was the first to crystallize the important pancreatic hormone, insulin, in collaboration with Geiling.

It was in Abel's laboratory with its intellectual ferment that the thirty-year-old Geiling began his pharmacological career under the tutelage of his sixty-four-year-old mentor. His tenure at Hopkins was very productive in research, with the publication of almost fifty papers; perhaps the most famous of these was "Crystalline Insulin," by Abel, Geiling, Rouiller, Bell, and Wintersteiner, which appeared in the *Journal of Pharmacology and Experimental Therapeutics* in May 1927. He became increasingly independent of Abel, and the publication concerning "Crystalline Insulin" is the last one by Geiling on which Abel appeared as co-author.

· III ·

At this stage of his career, Geiling became increasingly interested in the hormones of the posterior pituitary gland. These could be pharmacologically detected by their ability to raise blood pressure (pressor effect); by the stimulant effect on uterine smooth muscle and the milk ejection response from the mammary glands (oxcytocic effect); and inhibition of urine formation (anti-diuretic effect). There was controversy at the time as to the site of formation of these hormonal principles within the pituitary gland. This gland in many species consists of three lobes; the anterior, the intermediate, and the posterior. Geiling set out to resolve the controversy by applying the strategy of comparative anatomy to this endocrinological problem. Specifically, he sought out species of animals in which the intermediate lobe was missing, and hence only the anterior and the posterior aspects of the gland developed—each enveloped by its own membrane.

Among animals having the desired anatomy were five species of whales. Shortly before coming to Chicago in 1936, Geiling began to spend his summers at the whaling station at Rose Harbor on Queen Charlotte Island, 450 miles northwest of Vancouver in Canada. Geiling was able to confirm that the pituitary of the whale possesses no intermediate lobe. Furthermore, his pharmacological analysis of extracts of the posterior lobe demonstrated conclusively that the pressor, oxcytocic, and anti-diuretic effects were produced by substances contained within the posterior lobe. He described in some detail the surgical procedure involved in obtaining pituitary glands from the whale carcasses, saying that "the delicate instruments of the neurosurgeon must be laid aside and an axe and saw used in their place."

· IV ·

Upon moving to the University of Chicago in 1936, Geiling organized the department as an academic unit devoted to teaching and graduate research. The department at that time consisted of himself as professor, Dr. B. J. Vos as an instructor, and Frances K. Oldham as a research assistant. His laboratory was located on the fifth floor of what was called the Biochemistry Building at 947 East 58th Street. The building was renamed Abbott Memorial Hall in 1939. Frances Oldham was the first graduate student in the department who went on to receive the doctorate in pharmacology. Her dissertation dealt with the site of formation of posterior lobe hormones.

Her teacher, Geiling, also played a crucial role in promoting drug safety in the United States. During the months of September and October in 1937 at least seventy-six persons in various localities in the United States died as a result of poisoning by the drug formulation elixir of sulfanilamide made by Massengill. The synthetic chemical sulfanilamide—one of the "sulfa" drugs—had been shown just a few years previously to be among the first synthetic anti-bacterial substances. In the absence of effective regulation of drug manufacturers, chemical companies, like Massengill in Tennessee, could simply prepare solutions of sulfanilamide for distribution to the unwary public. Sulfanilamide is nearly insoluble in water but readily soluble in a number of organic solvents, including diethyleneglycol. This firm prepared a 10 percent solution of sulfanilamide in about 72 percent diethyleneglycol as a solvent, together with some coloring and flavoring agents. As the number of deaths associated with this elixir continued to mount, the chemical laboratory of the American Medical Association requested Geiling and his colleague at the University of Chicago, the pathologist Paul R. Cannon, to determine what was responsible for the toxic effects of elixir of sulfanilamide-Massengill. The makers of the product had distributed it freely without having tested it adequately on animals. There was widespread fear among physicians using other formulations of sulfanilamide for the treatment of their patients, and the American Medical Association received hundreds of inquiries concerning it and possible antidotes. Geiling and Cannon rapidly demonstrated that the toxicity was associated with the solvent, diethyleneglycol, and not the anti-bacterial substance, sulfanilamide. These findings were very rapidly communicated to the *Journal of the American Medical Association* in a report entitled "Preliminary Report of Toxicity Studies on Rabbits and Dogs," dated November 6, 1937. This was followed by a final, more complete report, which appeared about one year later. At the conclusion of the report Geiling and Cannon recommended eight safeguards regarding the preclinical testing of therapeutic agents in animals that should be fulfilled prior to their being available for therapeutic use in humans. These recommendations were the basis of the Pure Food and Drug Act of 1938, which gave the power to the Food and Drug Administration to promulgate rules and regulations for the preclinical testing of drugs destined for use in humans.

By this time, Geiling was a recognized leader in the disciplines of pharmacology and toxicology in the United States. The American Society for Pharmacology and Experimental Therapeutics (ASPET) had been founded by John Jacob Abel in 1909. Geiling was elected to membership in this society in 1925. He also was elected to membership in two sister societies, the American Society for Biological Chemistry (also founded by Abel) in 1927 and the American Physiological Society in 1933. He served as vice-president of the American Society for Pharmacology and Experimental Therapeutics from 1937 to 1939 and was elected president for the years 1940–41. In 1940, he also served as chairman of the executive committee of the Federation of American Societies for Experimental Biology, which is the organization that unites the various disciplines in experimental biology.

Dr. Geiling's preeminence as an investigator had been firmly established by this time. His incumbency of the various important posts in the community of biological scientists testified to this. It is possible that this eminence contributed to the decision of the University of Chicago to appoint Geiling to the Frank P. Hixon Distinguished Professorship in 1941 on the retirement of Anton Carlson.

The outbreak of the Second World War changed Dr. Geiling's research directions, as it indeed did for the research of many of the teachers at the University of Chicago. Just prior to the entry of the United States into the war, the University had been asked by the National Defense Research Committee to develop a laboratory facility for the evaluation of the toxicity of chemical agents, in order to attempt to avoid the horrible injuries suffered by individuals exposed to chemical warfare during the First World War. A number of one-story buildings were erected between 57th and 58th Streets, and between Ellis and Drexel Avenues to house the laboratories; the facility was known as the Toxicity Laboratory. Dr. Geiling was the principal investigator, working along with Dr. Franklin McLean as director of the laboratory. These buildings were demolished in 1985, and the site now is the center of the new Science Quadrangle, on which the John Crerar Library faces. Geiling directed a staff of almost sixty investigators in screening over 2,000 potential chemical warfare agents for their cytotoxic properties. Among the agents screened were the so-called nitrogen mustards, the cytotoxic properties of which were taken advantage of by Dr. Leon Jacobson following the war, in developing them as some of the very first chemotherapeutic agents against cancers, such as Hodgkin's disease.

Another research program carried out in connection with the war in the department of pharmacology under Geiling's direction was initiated by the critical shortage of two main-line antimalarial agents—quinine and atabrine—resulting from the occupation by the Japanese armed forces of the Southeast Asian areas where these agents were produced. Because of the widespread incidence of malaria in the Pacific war zone, substitute drugs were urgently needed by the United States military forces. Hundreds of compounds were studied for antimalarial activity and their acute and chronic toxicity evaluated under the aegis of this research program; a new and valuable antimalarial drug, chloroquine, emerged from this search.

At the end of the war twelve scientists at the University of Chicago were cited for their important contributions in the war effort. Four of the scientists who received certificates of appreciation were cited for their work in the Toxicity Laboratory. They were: Dr. Franklin B. McLean, professor of pathological physiology and first director of the Toxicity Laboratory; Dr. William B. Bloom, professor of anatomy and member of the Institute of Radiobiology and Biophysics; William L. Doyle, associate professor of anatomy and second director of the Toxicity Laboratory; and Dr. Eugene M. K. Geiling, Distinguished Service Professor and chairman of the department of pharmacology.

· V ·

After the war, Geiling's research interests shifted yet again, undoubtedly in part as a consequence of the presence of the Metallurgy Project on the University of Chicago campus. Geiling now sought to utilize the newly emerging nuclear technology to label chemically complex drugs obtained from plants, so as to be able to follow their disposition within the body. Some of mankind's oldest and most valuable drugs come from plants; e.g., digitoxin for the treatment of congestive heart failure is obtained from the foxglove plant; morphine for the alleviation of pain can be isolated from the poppy plant. These substances are generally active in minute doses, and therefore are undetectable by ordinary chemical analysis. Geiling saw that if he could label these compounds with radioactive atoms, it should be possible to detect the radioactivity being emitted from the drugs and their metabolic breakdown products with much higher sensitivity than that afforded by ordinary chemical analysis. However, the chemical structures of these "plant" drugs were far too complex for laboratory synthesis with the chemical methods available at the time.

To avoid this problem, Geiling chose to adopt the strategy of growing the requisite plants in an atmosphere containing radioactive carbon dioxide ($C^{14}O_2$, hoping that the plants would incorporate the radioactive carbon atoms into the drug molecules which they were synthesizing.

William Bloom, the Charles H. Swift Distinguished Service professor of anatomy, wrote shortly after Geiling's retirement that "In this field" (the biosynthesis of radioactively labeled drugs of plant origin), "he was the real pioneer. Despite all the handicaps of red tape and frequent difficulties in obtaining the necessary apparatus, and, above all, against the discouraging advice of many scientists, he was determined to get his 'radioactive farm' going. In the face of certain pessimistic calculations which led some to prophesy that Geiling could not get enough C^{14} into the drugs by exposing the growing plants to $C^{14}O_2$, he persisted, and, as you know, he and his colleagues succeeded magnificently in his endeavor." Indeed by 1948, Geiling and his collaborators were able to report that radioactive digitoxin and nicotine had been successfully produced by his technique. Moreover, the level of radioactivity was sufficiently high for him to investigate the disposition of these drugs, not only in laboratory animals, but in human volunteers.

These investigations occupied Geiling until the time of his retirement in December 1956. He was succeeded as chairman by Dr. Lloyd J. Roth, the chemist who had been encouraged by Geiling to collaborate with him on the projects involving the biosynthesis of radioactively labeled drugs. Roth had been a nuclear chemist at the Los Alamos nuclear facility during the war. Geiling had encouraged Roth to obtain his medical degree at Chicago at the relatively ripe age of thirty-five, not unlike Geiling, who himself completed the requirements for the M.D. at Johns Hopkins while doing research with Abel.

· V ·

Geiling was devoted to his academic life. He never married and he had only three domiciles in the twenty years that he lived in Chicago: first at 1413 East 57th Street, moving in 1940 to 1366 East 57th Street, and finally in 1950 moving across the Midway to the new Faculty Apartment Building at 6011 South Ingleside Avenue. He once listed his major avocations as gardening and listening to music.

It was customary during Geiling's tenure in the department for "The Professor" to give most of the lectures on pharmacology to second-year medical students. This he is reputed to have done with an excellence similar to that of his research. In fact, as he reached the conclusion of his last lecture to a class of such students in the year of his retirement, it is said that the students were preparing to give him a round of applause for his achievement; this was not a very common event in those days. Unfortunately during the slight pause that followed Geiling's concluding words, a junior colleague arose from his seat and announced to the class in a loud voice: "Don't forget to come to lab this afternoon." This interruption apparently broke the spell, and the students' tribute to Geiling was never rendered. It is not known whether Geiling regretted not having heard this public accolade for his teaching efforts, but it is likely that his inner satisfaction with a job well-done was enough for him.

At the 1956 reunion of the Medical Alumni Association, Geiling received the Gold Key Award, and shortly thereafter accepted an appointment as a visiting professor of pharmacology at the University of Rochester. He had received a Guggenheim Fellowship to write the biography of his eminent teacher, John Jacob Abel. Shortly thereafter he moved to Washington, D.C., to accept an appointment as a professor of pharmacology at Howard University. This was his last academic appointment. The chairman of the department at Howard, Walter M. Booker, an alumnus of the University of Chicago, who received the doctorate in physiology in 1942, later stated that Geiling "played a very significant role in our teaching of medical students" during his years at Howard.

In 1961–62, Dr. Frances Oldham Kelsey, Geiling's first graduate student at Chicago, was employed by the Food and Drug Administration. She was in charge of reviewing an application by a drug company to market a new sleeping medication called thalidomide. She became suspicious that the testing of this agent in animals might be misleading as to its effects in humans when she noted that the drug did not induce sleep in animals. She insisted on additional information concerning the effects of thalidomide.

As a result, the drug was never cleared by the Food and Drug Administration for general distribution in the United States before the realization that thalidomide was a teratogenic agent, a substance that induces birth defects. In many countries, but primarily the Federal Republic of Germany and Great Britain, the widespread use of thalidomide led to the birth of over 10,000 malformed babies with defective or absent upper limbs. In August of 1962, Dr. Kelsey received the President's Award for Distinguished Civilian Service from President John F. Kennedy. Shortly thereafter the Pure Food and Drug Administration Act was further amended to provide even more stringent testing of drugs prior to their use on humans. Dr. Geiling is not known to have recorded his response to his student's achievement, but its similarity to his own achievement in the episode of the elixir of sulfanilamide-Massengill and the subsequent Pure Food and Drug Act of 1938 might well have occurred to him.

Dr. Geiling returned to the University of Chicago campus for the last time in June of 1964 to deliver the opening lecture at an International Conference on the Uses of Isotopically Labeled Drugs in Experimental Pharmacology sponsored by the United States Atomic Energy Commission, the International Atomic Energy Agency, and the Rockefeller Foundation. In the course of the lecture he reviewed his own "very modest" contributions to the field, concluding that advances reported at the "conference can be expected to sustain our faith in the power of 'the atom' in advancing our knowledge."

For reasons which are not apparent, Dr. Geiling never completed his biography of John Jacob Abel, and he died on January 12, 1971, in Washington, D.C., at the age of eighty. *The Medical Alumni magazine* in its issue of Spring 1971 noted his death. The last sentence in the obituary read "Dr. Geiling had no immediate survivors." This obituary elicited a letter from two alumni of the University of Chicago's division of biological sciences which appeared in the next issue of the *Medical Alumni Magazine*. Both alumni were associated with Howard University, and in their letter they wrote, "a rather bleak feeling was communicated when your obituary ended with the standard phrase, 'Dr. Geiling had no immediate survivors.' Certainly, all of us who were touched by him were changed by him. Who has ever taught more memorably than did Dr. Geiling, as he stressed the need for prudence and sound judgment in employing elements of the 'therapeutic armamentarium' upon one's fellow human beings? In one sense, then, much of the best in American medicine must be regarded as Dr. Geiling's 'immediate survivor'."

13

CHARLES JUDSON HERRICK

1 8 6 8 – 1 9 6 0

L O U I S E   H.   M A R S H A L L

WHEN WILLIAM RAINEY HARPER set out to establish the University of Chicago, his first appointment in science was Clarence Luther Herrick, at that time the most outstanding comparative neurologist in the United States. The appointment failed because of broken commitments on Harper's part. In 1907, Harper's successor appointed Clarence's younger brother, Charles Judson Herrick, professor of neurology. The appointment was supported by the head of the department of anatomy, to which the position was attached, and brought distinction to the University beyond all expectations. The younger Herrick in later life wrote that his brother Clarence was "my exemplar in childhood, my teacher in youth, and my inspiration and guide of all my subsequent endeavors." Clarence did indeed play a substantial role in the development of Charles Judson. It is not an exaggeration to claim that the Herricks, especially the younger, longer-lived brother, were key figures in what later became known as neuroscience, briefly defined as the interaction of brain and behavior. The background of European ideas was well known to them, not only the comparative neurology exemplified in Edinger's embryological studies but also the behavioral approach of Wundt and his school. Anecdotal field studies of animal behavior had been replaced by controlled experiments yielding reliable data, and it was a natural attraction to view behavior in terms of brain anatomy and function.

After his brother's premature death, Charles Judson Herrick's work progressed toward his later recognition as the patriarch of the American school of comparative neurology. His career passed untouched through an era when neurology was losing ground to neurosurgeons and psychiatrists who were encroaching on the domain of neurology in their practices. Herrick's steadfastness in teasing apart the biological components of the evolutionary history of lower vertebrate brains and their relation to behavior, his capacity to extrapolate those facts to the human condition, and his success in propounding his ideas in the classroom and in print placed him at the wellspring of American neuroscience.

· I ·

The four Herrick brothers were reared near Minneapolis on a frontier farm that provided the major subsistence for a Baptist minister's family. Their mother had been a schoolteacher and created a home in which a Christian attitude, love of nature, and intellectual expectations abounded.

Charles Judson followed his brother to Denison University in Ohio for the first two years of college, then to the University of Cincinnati to finish his work for the bachelor of science in biology in 1891. A year of teaching in Kansas exposed him to the educational attitudes of that period. The new teacher of natural sciences attempted to move towards his goal of inter-relating study of the brain with that of psychology by proposing to the school's president, who also taught the course in psychology, that he present an accompanying, interrelated course on the brain. The irate president exclaimed, "Young man, the brain has no more to do with the operations of the mind than have the cabbage heads in my garden!"

Herrick returned to Denison to study for the master's degree under his brother's supervision. His thesis, "Cranial nerves of *Amblystoma punctatum*," was hastily completed and published in the *Journal of Comparative Neurology* in 1894. The circumstances were related by Herrick many years later. When his brother became ill in 1893 and Charles Judson assumed sole responsibility for the pioneering journal his brother had launched, there were no manuscripts or funds for the fourth volume. With his wife's encouragement and some ingenuity, the theses of students for a master's degree in the Neurology Laboratory of Denison University were gathered together and the journal was saved. Herrick was twenty-five years old at the time and for more than sixty years the journal was one of his major interests as he progressed from editorial associate, to managing editor, and finally to chairman of the board of editors.

For advanced study, Herrick chose Columbia University, where the only significant work on the vertebrate brain stem was being done. Working under the direct tutelage of Oliver S. Strong, he patiently prepared and described a complete series of sections of the whole head of a bony fish, *Menidia*. Elizabeth Crosby, a long-time collaborator, wrote that he "was already acquiring some of the later skill in reading microscopic sections as

CHARLES JUDSON HERRICK, about 1955

others read simple print." She could have added that he was also perfecting his drawing ability, for he prepared his own illustrations for his many publications.

His doctoral dissertation, like his master's thesis, had an unusual publication history: it not only won the Cartwright prize at Columbia but was published three times, in the *Journal of Comparative Neurology,* then in the *Archives of Neurology and Psychopathology,* and finally as a monograph. Such lavish dissemination of a doctoral thesis was possible because the director of the Pathological Institute of the New York state hospitals was so impressed by the completeness of the analysis that he had enough copies of the large lithographs printed for all three publications. Through this study of origins and terminations of cranial nerves and later work after he returned to Denison as profess. of zoology, Herrick consolidated in higher fishes the concept that impulses from various sense organs entering the brain by the cranial nerves were correlated in the brain stem according to a specified pattern that met the survival needs of the organism. Herrick later elaborated that theme in *Brains of Rats and Men.* "Some particular sense organ may be very highly developed—eyes in the trout, nose in the shark, taste buds in the carp—and the entire action system is built up around this dominant sense. In each . . . a different cerebral reflex center—optic, olfactory, gustatory—is greatly enlarged and correlation fibers from other sensory centers converge into it, so that this particular center, . . . becomes the center of highest physiological dominance." Herrick called on phylogeny to show that control of behavior had moved during evolution to progressively more rostral parts of the brain. He considered that the "rapid elaboration of the neopallium within the single class of mammalia is one of the most dramatic cases of evolutionary transformations known to comparative anatomy." To quote Crosby again: "It is hard to over-estimate the amount of confusion with regard to brain stem organization that these papers on the fish medulla helped to dispel."

· II ·

More important, however, than the organizational details of the vertebrate brain stem that Herrick helped to unravel was the emergence of psychobiology as a theme which permeated his research and writing thereafter. Based on ideas held by his brother and by their friend, the embryologist George Ellett Coghill, Herrick was impelled to seek answers to the mind-body problem through the coordination of evidence from all relevant disciplines dealing with brain and behavior. "Our fragments of knowledge must be united into a coherent and consistent unitary system in which all factors take their appropriate places in the cosmic order," he wrote in 1956. He defined psychobiology as "the scientific study of the experience of living bodies, its method of operation, the apparatus employed, and its significance as vital process, all from the standpoint of the individual having the experience."

Years earlier Herrick had written in a letter to his great friend at Washington University, neurophysiologist George Bishop: "Our difficulties in understanding the 'behavior' of the brain stem from the fact that the conscious component of this 'behavior' is incommensurable by any existing metric with the physiological components. It is not a question merely of greater complexity. No amount of complexity on the physiological level can generate a thought. The brain generates the thought, it is true, but only when working at a higher integrative level than those physiological processes that we can observe perceptually. The laws of the higher level, as known to us introspectively, cannot be *reduced* to those of the lower level." He went on to brand as "nonsense" any attempt at making a computing machine that could think. Herrick was confident that knowledge of the mind could come only from understanding the human brain as it had evolved, and he set about to convey that confidence through teaching and writing.

· III ·

Soon after arrival at the University of Chicago in 1907, Herrick demonstrated his unusual teaching ability in a series of lectures for graduate students on comparative neurology. In the words of a former student and later biographer: "To those of us whose knowledge of the nervous system was confined to its gross anatomy, the course was a revelation and an inspiration." As described by Elizabeth Crosby, "Dr. Herrick was an entirely adequate teacher of medical students, but he was a truly inspired teacher in the small graduate class or seminar as, tilting back in his chair, with his legs crossed, his pipe lighted, and his face aglow with interest and enthusiasm, he discussed his favorite subjects—the evolution of the nervous system as exhibited in the structure of the brains of various vertebrates, the relations between the structural and functional activity of animals, including man, as evidenced by their behavior, and the philosophical significance of the anatomical and the physiological patterns of the nervous system. His profound scholarship, his great knowledge of the detailed structure of the nervous system in various forms, and his intense interest in the discussions held his listeners enthralled. This was graduate teaching at its best."

By his own estimate, the course in which Herrick did "[p]erhaps the best" teaching, in response to a request from the department of psychology, was for students who lacked the prerequisites for the medical course in neuroanatomy. There were no prerequisites, and it "was immediately filled . . . from all quarters of the campus—psychology, physiology, zoology, education, sociology, philosophy, divinity. . . . Here was a group of mature and competent students who presented a fantastic pedagogical problem. . . . This was a pedagogical adventure for all of us. . . . and, because I felt free to experiment as I liked, I got more fun out of this course than from any other teaching in my forty years of experience." There were no examinations or quizzes but term papers that critically surveyed the literature on the student's chosen topic were required with a brief statement of what the student had found pertinent to his own program. Thus this master teacher contributed to "the sheer genius of intellectual exhilaration, the passionate electricity of spirit" experienced by a student at the University in the 1940s.

Early in 1909, Herrick sent a copy of his syllabus for the course in neurology to Adolf Meyer, a Swiss émigré and then professor of psychiatry at Cornell Medical College, thus initiating an exchange of thoughtful letters which defended each writer's approach to an integrated neurology and psychobiology. The two young teachers (they were both in their early thirties at that time) in the end agreed that they were aiming at the same goals regarding a more rational and interesting presentation of what medical students should know but proceeding toward it by different pathways.

Meyer acknowledged that Herrick's plan brought in more comparative material, whereas he himself preferred embryological material, and pointed out an additional difference: "I feel rather strongly that your plan appeals too much to the anthropocentric conception of the receptive-conscious function. . . . I prefer . . . to put the emphasis on the motor outfit, as the pragmatic and morphological expression of the essentials of the normal; while the sense organs are perhaps more essential from a psychologizing view-point and from that of evolution, they are far less open to accurate experimentation. I can see that both sides deserve being pushed. But for the beginner the motor side has the easier foundation." Meyer's comments reflect the state of physiological experimentation of the time, when the nerve-muscle preparation was in widespread use for precise measurements, whereas behavioral studies of sensation and perception were less "scientific." Meyer promised to send a copy of his own syllabus, which he hoped "to be able to test on some unspoiled material before long." That may have been a veiled reference to his prospects at Johns Hopkins, where he was appointed the next year.

After receiving Meyer's syllabus, Herrick responded with his customary helpful critique but then ended his letter on a rather despondent chord: "Your course I suppose is complete in itself; mine is one of three related courses, for it is followed by a course on the physiology of the nervous system by Dr. [Anton J.] Carlson and later by a clinical course. . . . The absurd organization of departments in this university makes an effective correlation of these three courses a practical impossibility, which of course weakens the whole greatly. If I could have my own way I would have given a brief general course, partly anatomical and partly physiological, followed by a series of elective courses in which different phases of the nervous system would be worked up each with a small group of students. . . . I think it would be worth more to the student to be independent in his thinking than to cram the whole field of neurology into his mouth at once." Apparently the legacy of Harper, which left many positive elements for later presidents of the University of Chicago, did not include flexible departmental borders; they did not permit the realization of Herrick's integrated course.

When he commenced teaching medical students, Herrick perceived the need of a textbook based on a functional approach to study of the nervous system. The first of five editions of *An Introduction to Neurology* was published in 1915. The later editions overlapped the appearance of another text written by Stephen Walter Ranson, a younger neurologist whose mentor for his master's degree had been Donaldson, Herrick's predecessor. Ranson was at the opposite end of the city, at Northwestern University Medical School. The appeal of his *The Anatomy of the Nervous System from the Standpoint of Development and Function* (1920) was immediately recognized and was said to have been smuggled into Herrick's classes by the students at Chicago.

From the rich collection of more than 25,000 letters preserved at the Kenneth Spencer Research Library on the Lawrence campus of the University of Kansas we may reconstruct the interaction between these two dedicated investigators of the human brain whose careers developed along such divergent lines. Herrick wrote a favorable review of Ranson's *Anatomy* but questioned the pedagogical method of making things so easy for the student by its "symmetry and completeness." He believed it more "ad-

vantageous" to force the students to go to the original literature and atlases
to round out their information. That criticism was made from the perspective of a teacher of advanced graduate students; Ranson seems to have
been more realisitc about the reading habits of medical students. In a subsequent letter Herrick expressed himself philosophically. "There are really
only a few things that the medical student needs to get in a first course and
it is better to get these thoroughly than to skim over a larger pan of milk."
The choice of metaphor reflects the farm youth whose letters contain
many such rustic allusions. Another example is in his advice to a former
student who had become disillusioned about a future in teaching in a
small college. "I cannot but feel that times for us will improve within a few
years. In the meantime (however mean that may be), one can best go on
sawing wood. But something depends on the woodpile one selects."

Herrick's sustained loyalty to his ideas regarding a unified psychobiology led him to participate in designing a graduate course that crossed
departmental lines. The episode is described in a letter to James O'Leary,
Washington University neurologist, who had asked Herrick to comment on
the draft of a report on the status of the neurological sciences. In his reply
Herrick recalled an experience that occurred shortly before his retirement
in 1937: "As a first step toward encouragement of interdepartmental research programs and training . . . a half-dozen professors from as many
departments planned an elective . . . graduate course on the general principles of neurology. We agreed to contribute our services to this cooperative teaching program. . . , so that no additional expense was involved. For
several years we got no encouragement. Then we outlined the proposed
content of the course, submitted it to the chairmen of the departments
concerned, and got their verbal approval. . . . Approval of the faculty of the
Division . . . we thought would be only a formality, but . . . a few senior
professors opposed it . . . because it was an invasion of the sacrosanct independence and autonomy of the departments. . . . [T]he project was
abandoned, although we knew that the university administration [then
headed by Robert Maynard Hutchins] was giving strong support and encouragement to such interdepartmental cooperation."

The episode was initiated by Percival Bailey, head of the department of
neurology in the medical school. The plan stemmed from an earlier attempt by Bailey, made shortly after his appointment in 1927 to the newly
organized department, to create a small neurological clinic to serve as a
magnet to students in neurology, who were in short supply at the time.
Herrick's cooperation (and the recognition of his influential status at high

administrative levels) had been sought not only by Bailey but also by Ralph W. Gerard, then a rising young neurophysiologist from the department of physiology. Herrick's position may be deduced from the report to his departmental chief titled "Neuro-anatomy at the University of Chicago," forwarded in late 1929 and conceivably a reaction to the turmoil at the time over full-time status of the clinical faculty. Herrick defended vigorously the nearly forty-year "unique" policy (from Donaldson in 1882) of maintaining a professor of neurology who had no clinical responsibilities. He pointed to the fruits of the policy: more than twenty-five doctoral degrees conferred, and subsequent to 1907, publication of forty-four volumes of *Journal of Comparative Neurology,* six books, and sixty-two scientific articles.

Failed in that early plan, Bailey's interdisciplinary scheme had been embodied in a proposal made in 1936 for coordination of neurological interests in teaching and research. Seven eminent university professors, including Herrick, endorsed the new plan. It was undoubtedly influenced by their discussions at an informal neurology club, a fertile milieu for nurturing novel ideas concerning the interaction of brain and behavior. The proposal described the club as having met monthly since 1929. Whether initiated by Bailey or Herrick, the sheer mass of preeminence among the Chicago faculty available to participate attests to the university's high status in that field. A partial listing includes Bartelmez, Bucy, Carlson, Gerard, Grinker, Halsted, Kleitman, Klüver, Ralph Lillie, Lashley, Luckhardt, Polyak, Sperry, and Weiss. That group, in addition to the members of Ranson's Institute of Neurology at Northwestern University Medical School and from the basement Laboratory of Neurophysiology at the Illinois Neuropsychiatric Institute headed by Warren Sturgis McCulloch, constituted a powerhouse of talent in American neuroscience not matched elsewhere during the 1930s and 1940s.

Although some of its members were conversant with the labors of the electrophysiologists on the nerve action current, the neurology club had broader interests focused on the central nervous system and related behavior. The proposal of 1936 stated: "partly stimulated by these conferences, several investigations have been prosecuted jointly with happy results," and listed eight examples, including a study by Herrick and Lashley with Tsang, "The influence of brain lesions on learning by rats."

A few years before his retirement, two issues of the *Journal of Comparative Neurology* (1932) were designated "Charles Judson Herrick Anniversary Volumes." The anonymous dedications to Herrick as "Elder, Teacher, and Scientist" uniformly praised him as "elder statesman," "Magister," and as having played "a major role in the establishment of the 'American School' of Neurology." The unusual feature of that praise was its implication that Herrick's work was done. In fact, Herrick's major work, *The Brain of the Tiger Salamander,* was only in press and his future retirement was to yield other influential publications.

· IV ·

Before accepting appointment to the University of Chicago, Herrick had hesitated for several reasons, among them being apprehension about the pressure engendered by the exchange of quiet Denison University for the busy life of a professor in a large, urban university. His wife's question, "Would you rather go to Chicago and burn out or stay here and rust out?" had settled the matter. To counter "burn-out," there was a retreat on the Indiana Dunes, where the isolation was conducive to quiet reading and writing. Professor Herrick was once encountered there by a young neuro-anatomist and his family taking a day's respite from an apartment in Hyde Park. When a sudden shower intruded on their picnic, they approached the elderly man reading under a canopy and asked to share his cover until the rain passed. They were made welcome, and in the conversation discovered the identity of their host. Herrick's innate cordiality is still remembered by Horace W. Magoun, who was then carrying out fundamental experiments on the brain-stem reticular formation at Northwestern University.

The release from his beloved teaching in 1934 provided Herrick with time to tidy up the loose ends of his scientific studies. Three years later and in full retirement, he became immersed in organizing his data, convinced that he now had new opportunities for thinking and writing. His earlier publications, *The Thinking Machine* (1929) and *Brains of Rats and Men* (1926), had been well received. (Their author pointed out mischievously that although the rat and human male brains were the most studied of the mammalia, a book about the brains of cats and women would prove to be even more popular.)

Herrick wrote two lengthy biographies. One, published in 1949, was of George Ellett Coghill, whose discoveries of patterns of embryonic and fetal behavior in salamanders similar to those in humans had greatly influenced both Herricks. The other biography was of his brother Clarence, published in 1955, in which the details of Clarence's resignation from his appointment at the University of Chicago were fully investigated. In both biographies, references were made to the tragedy of creative academic scientists hampered by administrative forces, but the author did not apply such a melancholy estimate to his own academic life, in spite of the disappointments already noted. The maturity of his own personal creed shines forth from his letters and manuscripts. Work soon commenced in earnest on *The Evolution of Human Nature,* published in 1956, which he characterized as "a combination of the Evolution of Behavior and the Evolution of Brains in one volume." As drafts of chapters were ready they were sent to colleagues for comment. (The comments are a rich primary resource of correspondence on early neuroscience.)

Especially notable is the exchange of long, letters—typed by Herrick himself—with George Holman Bishop, one of the "axonologists" at Washington University. As indicated earlier, *Human Nature* embodied Herrick's struggle with "the hoary mind-body problem." He wrote that conscious thought could not be measured by "any existing metric." Their jaunty but serious exchange of criticism was around what they had dubbed "fairy stories," or guesses as to perception and thought mechanisms. Herrick chided his friend for writing that "' . . . the visual system is presumably all one modality.' Luminosity and color vision seem to me as different as touch and pain.

"Your theoretic excursions may get you into hot water but like G. K. Chesterton 'I believe in getting into hot water. I think it keeps you clean.'" Herrick had been reading reviews of *Human Nature:* "Almost every page . . . deals with controversial matter and I had expected to be roasted by the critics, especially by the objective psychologists and sociologists. I am pleasantly surprised to find most of the reviews highly complimentary and the few adverse criticisms are courteous and invariably accompanied by commendation of the excellence of the book as a whole. This comforts me."

The high esteem for Herrick's work held by Bishop and others was demonstrated at an international symposium in Detroit on the reticular formation of the brain. In a joint paper, Herrick and Bishop clarified the morphology (and nomenclature) of six spinal tracts in an amphibian and a mammalian brain. Herrick was too frail to attend, however, and on March 15, 1957, Bishop sent a telegram to his friend saying "The spirit of the tiger salamander broods over this conference reminding us of your fundamental analysis of the vertebrate nervous system and its afferent paths." When Bishop's paper, "The place of cortex in a reticular system," was published, it had an addendum: "I think I should have designated as co-author of the following paper, C. J. Herrick, whose consultation and the information contributed towards its preparation is the greater part of the result. As I have listened to the papers presented . . . I have been repeatedly reminded of his remarkable analysis of the nervous systems of *Amblystoma* extended and extrapolated to man—an analysis in relation to which current work can only be an elaboration of details. Dr. Herrick, over eighty-nine years old and still active . . . is present at this conference in as real a sense as if he were sitting here in person."

Charles Judson Herrick applied imagination in assigning meaning to the facts he saw in the thousands of sections that passed under his microscope. Perhaps his focus on anatomical revelations shielded him from the electronic era of investigation, which he chose to leave to younger experimentalists. In contrast to his brother, who "was born a naturalist," Herrick thought of himself as a "naturalist by acculturation." "I could endure plodding methodically and persistently toward an objective and endure the tedious but necessary drudgery of fact-finding in minute detail, adequate verification, and the preparation of reports that were carefully edited with due attention to orderly arrangements, accurate documentation and scrupulous proofreading." He crossed several disciplinary boundaries in attempting to understand what he saw. He established a solid foundation of facts, then pushed on to imagine how mind and consciousness might have evolved. Here his philosophical and religious beliefs received expression in writings on social issues. Herrick could envision the interrelatedness of society at large, the behaving individual, and the cerebral mind. I think he would have enjoyed being called a "pure" neuroscientist in the original broad sense of that term.

14

CHARLES BRENTON HUGGINS

1 9 0 1 –

P A U L   T A L A L A Y

 IN 1927 CHARLES HUGGINS made the fateful decision to accept the invitation of Dallas B. Phemister, chairman of the department of surgery, to join the original faculty of the University of Chicago School of Medicine, instead of entering the private practice of surgery in Kalamazoo, Michigan. It was a fateful decision not only for Huggins but also for the University. Charles Huggins was not quite twenty-six years old. He had graduated from Harvard Medical School and had just completed advanced training in surgery at the University of Michigan under another great American surgeon, Frederick A. Coller. He was also recently married to his beloved Margaret Wellman. Few could have predicted that Huggins would become one of the giants of the Chicago medical faculty, still serving his University at the laboratory bench each day, more than sixty years later. During these extraordinarily fruitful and exciting years, he was not only the leading urologist of his day but also received the Nobel Prize for discovering a new principle for the treatment of advanced cancer. He founded a renowned cancer research laboratory, and he trained and inspired the lives of numerous prominent medical scientists.

· I ·

The opening in 1927 of the Albert Merritt Billings Hospital, the site of the new medical school at the University of Chicago, heralded a bold and unique experiment in the training of physicians for research and medical care. All its academic members were to receive salaries only and to devote their energies full-time to scholarly work. Training in medicine was to be accomplished on a scholarly plane not previously available in other schools of medicine. In fact there was no formal "school of medicine" at the University of Chicago. Rather, the academic departments concerned with medical subjects were all components of the division of biological sciences of the University; completion of specified courses offered by these departments fulfilled the requirements for the degree of doctor of medicine. These revolutionary innovations, designed to elevate the level of academic scholarship in medicine, were regarded with suspicion by members of the conservative medical profession in Chicago and elsewhere, who felt intellectually and financially threatened. Charles Huggins was to play a central role in assuring the success of this iconoclastic University of Chicago venture.

Although initially uncertain how his career would develop, Huggins was deeply influenced by Phemister's insistence that a spirit of inquiry in medicine was fundamental to excellence in clinical care. Unable to find a urologist who met these criteria, Phemister asked Huggins to organize the urology service at Billings. Huggins was attracted by the opportunity, but not the image, of urology as a specialty. He and Reed M. Nesbit, his lifelong friend and fellow intern in surgery at Michigan, had already decided that general surgery was the only worthy career; after all, the general surgeon was the "general among surgeons." By coincidence, Nesbit in time became the chief of urology at the University of Michigan, a position he occupied for the remainder of his career. But some considerable time passed before Huggins and Nesbit admitted their "downfall" to each other, and then only on condition that their friends would not be so informed.

Huggins was largely self-taught in urology. He developed and delivered a series of succinct lectures on urology to twenty-five successive classes of medical students. The lectures were models of clarity and compactness. Few who heard them could ever forget "the five causes of hematuria," and some students have in fact claimed quite seriously that the lectures in urology were the only memorable part of their didactic education as medical students. Everyone knew that there were many more causes of hematuria, presence of blood in the urine, but it was Huggins's view that it would be more useful to remember the important ones than to be overburdened with trivial ones and forget them all. His aphorism "we travel light" provided the impetus for the incisive lectures that left an indelible impression on his students.

Phemister, who had a lifelong interest in bone pathology, directed Huggins's interest to earlier reports that transplantation of epithelial cells evoked bone formation. The analysis of this phenomenon provided highly important information on osteogenesis that will be described below. But

CHARLES BRENTON HUGGINS, 1987

Huggins—undoubtedly because of his experiences in clinical urology—soon focused on the prostate gland. He wondered why virtually nothing was known of the functions of this enigmatic organ, which was commonly the site of distressing diseases, especially in older men. In the course of studies on the prostate he adhered to his long-standing conviction that appropriate animal models susceptible to quantitative analysis were the key to the solution of problems of many human diseases. He developed such a model for the study of the hormonal control of growth and secretion of the prostate gland. The findings led to his major discovery: that the growth of some prostatic cancer cells is not autonomous but can be controlled by steroid hormones.

From that point on Charles Huggins was smitten by the excitement of scientific discovery. For him, urology became "the queen of the sciences." Dedication to "discovery is our business," work at the laboratory bench, and simplicity of concepts, were the dominant themes of his philosophy. This dedication to the art of discovery was so intense that in his Nobel address Huggins, who was profoundly devoted to his Margaret, avowed: "It is possible that the wife of a lab worker is never quite sure whether she or science comes first in her husband's affection."

· II ·

In summarizing his own contributions to understanding the role of hormones in the control of human cancer, Charles Huggins wrote:

> The control of cancers by hormonal means rests on two principles. (1) Cancer is not necessarily autonomous and intrinsically self-perpetuating. Some neoplasms, perhaps all, retain biochemical characteristics of the normal cells from which they arose. When the original cells are dependent upon hormonal subvention for metabolic activity at a high rate, its cancers can be similarly dependent, and these cancer cells atrophy when hormonal support is withdrawn. *Be the causes of the cancers what they may, removal of supporting hormones causes the death or atrophy of hormone-dependent cancer cells. Therefore in cancers of this class, the hormones are a component of critical importance.* (2) Cancer can be sustained and propagated by hormonal function that is not abnormal in kind or exaggerated in rate.

On December 10, 1966, Professor George Klein of the Royal Caroline Medico-Surgical Institute in Stockholm presented Charles Huggins to His Majesty the King of Sweden for conferral of the Nobel Prize in Medicine and Physiology, with the following citation:

Your fundamental discoveries concerning the hormone dependence of normal and neoplastic cells in experimental animals and their immediate practical application to the treatment of human prostatic and breast cancer have already given many years of an active and useful life to patients with advanced cancer over the entire civilized world;—patients who would have been lost to all other forms of therapy.

The Nobel Prize for 1966 was awarded jointly to Huggins and Peyton Rous of the Rockefeller University. It was a felicitous and congenial combination of laureates, and a long-awaited recognition of two profound contributions to our understanding of the nature of human cancers and their treatment. For Rous, discoverer of the first virus (the Rous chicken sarcoma) that induced solid tumors in animals, and originator of the field of tumor virology, was not only Charles Huggins's "hero in medicine" but also one of the first to recognize the importance of Huggins's discovery. Thus, Rous wrote about the work of Huggins: "the importance of this discovery far transcends its practical implications; for it means that thought and endeavor in cancer research have been misdirected in consequence of the belief that tumor cells are anarchic."

How, then, was the discovery made that some prostate cancer cells, even after they have become disseminated and have produced massive disease, still remain under the control of hormonal regulatory influences that prevail in the body, and can be caused to shrivel by manipulating the hormonal balance of the body?

The development of the concept of hormonal dependence of human prostatic cancers arose from studies of the hormonal control of prostatic secretion in the dog. These discoveries are perhaps most vividly and succinctly recounted in the words of their originator, thereby also conveying some of the excitement generated by these discoveries, the logic of Huggins's scientific strategy, and the economy of his expository style. In his Nobel lecture delivered on December 13, 1966, Huggins wrote:

> a simple technique was devised to collect the prostatic secretion of dogs quantitatively at frequent intervals for years. Often the prostatic fluid of normal adult dogs is secreted for many months with little variation in its quantity or chemical characteristics. . . .
>
> Following orchiectomy, the prostate shrinks . . . and secretion stops. Testosterone corrects these defects. The cycle of growth and atrophy created by alternately providing and then withholding testosterone was induced repeatedly in the course of the life of the castrate

dog. The prostatic cell does not die in the absence of testosterone, it merely shrivels. But the hormone-dependent cancer cell is entirely different. It grows in the presence of supporting hormones but it dies in their absence and for this reason it cannot participate in growth cycles. . . .

It was good fortune that some of our metabolic experiments had been carried out on dogs since this is the only species of laboratory animal in which tumors of the prostate occur. As in man, it is very common to find spontaneous neoplasms of prostate in aged dogs. . . .

At first it was vexatious to encounter a dog with a prostatic tumor during a metabolic study but before long such dogs were sought.* It was soon observed that orchiectomy or the administration of restricted amounts of phenolic estrogens caused a rapid shrinkage of canine prostatic tumors.

The experiments on canine neoplasia proved relevant to human prostate cancer; there had been no earlier reports indicating any relationship of hormones to this malignant growth.

Measurement of phosphatases in blood serum furnished proof that cancer of the prostate in man is hormone responsive. . . . acid phosphatase is rich in concentration in the prostate of adult human males. Gutman and Gutman found that many patients with metastatic prostate cancer have significant increases of acid phosphatase in their blood serum. Cancer of the prostate frequently metastasizes to bone where it flourishes and usually evokes proliferation of osteoblasts. In the school of Robert Robison, Kay found that brisk osteoblastic activity gives rise to increased alkaline phosphatase levels in serum.

Human prostate cancer which had metastasized to bone was studied at first. The activities of acid and alkaline phosphatases in the blood were measured concurrently at frequent intervals. . . . The level of acid phosphatase indicated activity of the disseminated cancer cells

* Those students involved with procuring the animals with prostatic tumors will recall the Sunday morning excursions to the Chicago Municipal Dog Pound, which was operated by the police department and located on the West Side. The back seat of the Huggins family Ford was removed and newspapers were carefully spread over the floor to guard against failures of house training. One wore old clothes and entered with trepidation the enormous cages housing perhaps twenty unkempt and ferocious-looking dogs, and tried to identify the best candidates for prostatic tumors—those with cataracts and worn teeth: signs of old age. The dogs were transported in the back-seat compartment where they would express their displeasure at confinement by barking at a time which usually coincided with the end of Sunday church services in the ethnic communities along the route, and caused a certain amount of consternation and commotion. Once arrived at Billings Hospital, the not inconsiderable task of cleaning up the back seat was undertaken. Mrs. Huggins was never aware of these clandestine operations, and could provide no plausible explanation to her friends for the residual odor that persisted in the Ford during the remainder of the week.

in all metastatic loci. The titer of alkaline phosphatase revealed the function of osteoblasts as influenced by the presence of the prostatic cancer cells that were their neighbors. By periodic measurements of the two enzymes one obtains a view of overall activity of the cancer and the reaction of non-malignant cells of the host to the presence of that cancer. Thereby the great but opposing influences of, respectively, the administration or deprival of androgenic hormones upon prostate cancer cells were revealed with precision and simplicity. Orchiectomy or the administration of phenolic estrogens resulted in regression of cancer of the human prostate whereas, in untreated cases, testosterone enhanced the rate of growth of the neoplasm. . . .

The control of activity of cancer by excision of endocrine glands is physiologic surgery wherein removal of a normal structure can cause healing of distant disease. . . .

The first series of patients with prostatic cancer treated by orchiectomy comprised 21 patients with far advanced metastases; only 4 of them survived for more than 12 years. Despite regression of great magnitude, it is obvious that there were many failures of endocrine therapy to control the disease but, on the whole, the life span had been extended by the novel treatments and there had been a decrease of man-pain hours.

These restrained statements did not convey to the world that in 1941 a medical revolution had occurred: our understanding of the neoplastic process and the prospects for its successful treatment were immeasurably brightened. The pioneering contributions of Charles Huggins were an immense stimulus to studies on the hormonal control of certain cancers and prolonged the lives of many men who had previously been considered as beyond hope.

In 1950 Charles Huggins made the decision to attack the problem of advanced breast cancer, at that time the most prevalent cancer of women. Several considerations led him to suggest that endocrine secretions, including those of the adrenal cortex, might play a role in supporting the growth of at least some mammary cancers. Huggins's earlier work on prostatic cancer had established that the adrenal cortex was responsible for the secretion of substantial quantities of steroids in orchiectomized men. He first performed bilateral adrenalectomy in such men in 1944, and observed some amelioration of their prostatic cancers. In a logical extension of these observations, Huggins reported in 1951 that bilateral adrenalectomy with cortisone replacement therapy could be performed safely and, in conjunction with removal of the ovaries, resulted in substantial regression of the disease in 30 to 40 percent of patients with advanced breast cancer. The results were dramatic not only in terms of relief of pain but also in the objective criteria of reduction in size of the primary lesion and of metastases, healing of bone fractures, and other beneficial effects. In some cases adrenalectomy and oophorectomy induced remissions of advanced mammary cancer that were of considerable magnitude and prolonged duration. The therapeutic effects of adrenalectomy on advanced mammary cancer were soon confirmed in many clinics all over the world.

Combined andrenalectomy and oophorectomy is no longer widely used in the treatment of advanced cancer of the breast. Nevertheless, the dramatic therapeutic effects of deprivation of estrogenic hormones and their precursors originating from the adrenal cortex provided the impetus for the identification by Huggins's colleague E. V. Jensen of the estrogen receptor, a protein essential for the hormonal action of estrogens, and the classification of breast cancers into those that are receptor positive or negative, thereby providing an important prognostic criterion and therapeutic guide. The results of the adrenalectomy operation also stimulated the search for estrogen antagonists, which have become important therapeutic and prophylactic tools in the contemporary treatment of breast cancer.

· III ·

In the annals of medicine the name of Charles Huggins will be rightly associated with his pioneering contributions to the hormonal treatment of human cancer of the prostate and breast. But this should not be permitted to overshadow a number of other original and quite separate scientific discoveries, which were by no means secondary in their importance.

During the early days of Billings Hospital, when patients were few and far between, more time was available for scientific discussion. It was at this time that his chief, Dallas B. Phemister, drew Huggins's attention to the experiments of Harold Neuhof in 1917. In the course of studies on the repair of surgical defects in various organs (as models of war wounds), Neuhof had observed that when a defect in the bladder of a dog was repaired with a piece of connective tissue fascia, the latter was converted remarkably rapidly into well-differentiated bone. Huggins extended these experiments and showed that bone formation occurred even when the course of urine was diverted from the bladder, thereby eliminating the possibility that high concentrations of urinary salts were responsible for the genesis of bone. Although these findings did not augur well for developing bladder replacements, the experiments had a far broader scientific significance and even potential clinical importance. Huggins concluded that the (transitional) epithelial lining of the bladder produced factors capable of irreversibly transforming a variety of types of connective tissue to bone—a permanent change in cell types. Similar osteogenesis (as well as dentine and enamel formation) was observed when the epithelium surrounding the base of the permanent cuspid teeth in young dogs was transplanted to the abdominal wall fascia.

Although Charles Huggins wrote the *Physiological Review* in 1937 on "The Composition of Bone and Function of Bone Cell," he had already decided to abandon work on ectopic bone formation and did not return to this problem until the 1970s. The reasons for this change in course were undoubtedly complex, but on several occasions he mentioned that he had difficulty in convincing others—and presumably in the final analysis himself—of the importance of this problem and its relevance to human disease. But his own belief in the significance of his observations never completely faded, and in a series of papers published from 1972 to 1975, he provided new and important insights into this cell "transformation" phenomenon. He studied powders of acid-treated (demineralized) dried bone matrix, developed by Marshall Urist, as the source of the osteogenic stimulus. He injected these osteogenic preparations subcutaneously in the rat, and described the time sequence of bone formation, demonstrating that the development of bone under these conditions recapitulated the normal stages of endochondrial bone formation, including the development of marrow that elaborated the elements of blood. He recognized that charge and particle size of the matrix were important determinants of the rate of bone formation, and standardized this system to achieve a high degree of reproducibility. It seemed only natural that he proposed the measurement of alkaline phosphatases—familiar to him from his experience with osteoblastic prostate cancer metastases—as a quantitative index of bone formation. This standard assay system was used by others to monitor the isolation of a family of acid-stable and extremely potent proteins that induce bone formation. Some of these morphogenetic proteins have been cloned and their structures are similar to certain transforming growth factors. The potential usefulness of proteins that stimulate bone formation is beginning to be explored in orthopedics, in plastic and reconstructive jaw and face surgery, and in periodontal surgery.

These experiments illustrate cogently how important fundamental observations often lead to totally unanticipated and potentially very fruitful practical applications.

As already mentioned, the objective assessment of the effects of hormonal manipulations on the status of metastatic cancer of the prostate relied on monitoring serum levels of acid and alkaline phosphatases. In the 1940s, when most of this classic work was being done, methods for measuring phosphatases were cumbersome. In an effort to simplify such assays, Huggins conceived the idea of synthesizing substrates that were in themselves colorless but gave rise to colored products upon enzymatic cleavage. The first example was phenolphthalein phosphate. Appreciating the potentially more general importance of this principle, Huggins coined the term "chromogenic substrates," and provided three analytical encores: phenolphthalein mono-β-glucuronide for the measurement of β-glucuronidase activity, p-nitrophenyl sulfate for sulfatase, and various p-nitrophenyl esters for esterases. Chromogenic substrates are now in widespread use in biochemistry and molecular biology, but few who search their Petri dishes for colorless, rather than blue, bacterial colonies (as evidence for DNA insertions that interrupt the β-galactosidase gene), are aware that they are observing the splitting of a chromogenic substrate of the type conceived by Charles Huggins, and that we owe to him the designation "chromogenic substrates."

The development by Charles Huggins of the DMBA (7,12-dimethylbenz [a]anthracene)-induced rat mammary tumor is probably one of the most successful validations of his fervent conviction that an appropriate animal model was the critical requirement for understanding and devising treatment of human diseases.

Mammary tumors are among the most common neoplasms of humans and of rodents. When Charles Huggins undertook to develop a relevant experimental mammary tumor model, much was already known about this process in mice; but the growth rate of the majority of such established murine mammary tumors was not influenced by hormones, unlike their human counterparts.

Soon after he had shown that deprivation of both adrenal and ovarian secretions could markedly benefit some cases of far-advanced human mammary cancer, Huggins commented on this state of affairs as follows:

> Whereas advances of considerable magnitude have been made in the clinical treatment of far-advanced mammary cancer, these arose at the bedside exclusively through clinical investigation. The laboratory had contributed nothing for the therapy of disseminated cancer of the breast. Until the present studies were undertaken, no hormone-dependent mammary cancers were available in laboratory animals. Moreover, the earlier methods of induction of mammary cancer were

slow. . . . An additional vexation was that the incidence of mammary cancer rarely occurred in 100 percent of the creatures. These disadvantages were overcome in the work now to be described. A method was devised for the invariable production of mammary cancer in a few weeks rather than in months or years. In addition, a considerable proportion of the cancers so induced were hormone-dependent and underwent atrophy after appropriate hormonal manifestations to be discussed.

In the period from 1959 to 1964 Huggins and colleagues systematically explored the conditions necessary for the induction of mammary cancer by polycyclic aromatic hydrocarbons in female Sprague-Dawley rats. Under carefully defined conditions, a single feeding of DMBA to female Sprague-Dawley rats resulted in the appearance of multiple mammary tumors in 100 percent of these animals in less than two months. This method of tumor production proved so useful and became so widely adopted that it is now universally referred to as the "Huggins tumor." In an encyclopedic review, made in 1985, of the studies carried out with this tumor and factors influencing its growth, Clifford Welsch cites no less than 741 references and concludes that the Huggins tumor "today represents the most intensely investigated laboratory animal model of human breast cancer." Apart from the rapidity and invariability of induction resulting in 100 percent incidence, many of the tumors bear histological resemblance to mammary cancer of man and are subject to endocrine control, thus permitting elucidation of hormonal factors controlling growth. The development of this tumor model was therefore a contribution of signal importance for cancer research in general, and mammary cancer, in particular.

· IV ·

Those who have been privileged to work closely with Charles Huggins have fallen under the spell of his powerful personality. Few, if any, have emerged without undergoing profound changes in personal philosophy or objectives. How is it that he has not only made a series of highly important and original discoveries in biomedical science, but that he has also trained so many distinguished leaders in diverse fields of medical science? Charles Huggins's pupils have assumed roles of academic leadership in all parts of the world and in diverse disciplines, including surgery, urology, biochemistry, pharmacology, endocrinology, cancer research, pathology, and others. Most outstanding scientists can provide little real insight into the mystery of their own success. Undoubtedly the ingredients of intellectual genius are not the same for all creative scientists, nor are the methods of transmitting dedication to scientific scholarship. Charles Huggins recognized this enigma of creativity.

> What are the rules for discovery? I suspect that there are none. I guess that Einstein and Mozart and Michelangelo themselves did not understand the process of creativity or what mystique possessed them during their sublime creative moments. There are no rules but there are guidelines.

In the preface to his monograph *Experimental Leukemia and Mammary Cancer. Induction, Prevention, Cure,* published in 1979, Huggins gave us a glimpse, behind-the-scenes, of his leitmotif:

> One works along at the lab bench without haste and without rest. Time has no meaning; every day something will be done, something will be found out. It is total commitment to the task at hand. It requires Spartan self-discipline. These are happy days, one follows another, hopefully without end, so great is the delight of discovery.
> Always the students are here—not many of them because, with Paul Ehrlich, I believe the great creative things do not emerge with too many pigeons flying about the room. The students are necessary and a joy. Discussion is helpful in originating new ideas and in bringing out the strength and weakness of the protocol. Both the eye and the ear are useful in the design of the great plan and, at the end of the experiment, in admiration of elegant results. The student provides the zing; he has great self-confidence and the energy of youth and, for him, always there is the carrot, never the stick.
> In the biological sciences research is the "quiet art," a cottage industry done in the *stoa,* where one can work with the students in serenity ten or more hours a day with an abiding faith that the most vexatious medical problems here can be solved and very soon.
> Science is not cold and unfeeling. In scientific investigation one becomes emotionally contained in his problem. Head, heart, and hand, the three *H's* of experimentation, all are involved in innovation in the medical sciences and the combination enables us to recognize a good problem that can be solved. Science is ruled by idea and technique, which are welded to form a wheel that revolves and gains momentum. Activity arouses idea, which in turn begets method. With blood on my hands I can discover, seated at my desk I have no chance. This is the philosophy of activism, which governs science.
> In science one always strives for simplicity, which is the elegance of proof: *Simplex sigillium veri.*

He was often heard to say—more than half seriously—that if the principles employed by nature were not basically simple, much more would be going wrong with the human body all the time. He was also enthralled by the beauty of science: *Pulchritudo splendor veritatis.* While simplicity is the sign of truth, beauty is its splendor.

For him science was the art of the twentieth century, and he often spoke of the "nobility" of a scientific problem, especially when its solution impinges upon the relief of human suffering. He was much given to quoting Ralph Waldo Emerson: "In silence, in steadiness, in severe abstraction, let him hold by himself; add observation to observation, patient of neglect, patient of reproach, and bide his own time—happy enough if he can satisfy himself alone this day he has seen something truly."

But these statements provide little insight into how these scientific principles were transmitted so effectively to his disciples, and how it was that Charles Huggins trained such a large number of scientific leaders. What was the nature of his Midas touch? Of course, no one really knows, but some of his unique personal qualities and interactions with his students were summarized by one of his students as follows:

> Exposure to Charles Huggins is a mutational event. Few have come under the stamp of his influence without discovering in themselves unrecognized abilities and intellectual powers, without gaining a deeper awareness of their scholarly responsibilities and capabilities— for Charles Huggins directs not by directing but by example. The ability to elevate the sights of his pupils, to awaken their dormant talents, to encourage, to infuse his youthful enthusiasm in others—these are his commanding qualities. His basically simple view of complex scientific problems and his search for profoundly important and simple solutions have created an environment that encourages the development of self-direction and nurtures success in others as well as himself.

The cult of discovery, joy in the beauty of an elegant solution, and the pursuit of a medically important problem: these were all part and parcel of his personal philosophy. Success in science implied learning how to experiment economically. His deep dedication and singularity of purpose were supported by an optimism and sense of wonder about the prospects for discovery. He was always personally involved in his experiments and frequently demonstrated his remarkable powers of observation by detecting clues from nature that others had not seen.

Charles Huggins advised his students and colleagues to think in simple concepts, to keep their laboratories small, and never to work on more than a single problem at a time. Although Huggins was a highly effective and efficient administrator, he admonished his pupils to stay clear of administration, which he claimed "attracts mediocre minds."

· V ·

In 1927 Charles Huggins married Margaret Wellman, a neurosurgical operating-room nurse at the University of Michigan. They lived in Hyde Park—in the "shadow of the University"—for fifty-six years, where they became familiar figures in the community. They were utterly devoted to one another. Margaret Huggins was in charge at home. She managed the finances and the household affairs, and created the atmosphere that allowed her husband to devote himself without distraction to his highly disciplined professional life. He depended on her for strength, encouragement, and inspiration. But she was also a surrogate mother to his young colleagues in the laboratory, taking great interest in their families and children. She was a woman of grace, good sense, and good judgment, and created the serenity of the Huggins home. Mrs. Huggins died in 1983, leaving an enormous void in her husband's life.

Dr. and Mrs. Huggins frequently entertained distinguished scientific visitors at dinners in their home. These were memorable evenings and nearly always included younger colleagues and students. The wide-ranging conversations encompassed classical music, travel, memories of other scientists, and of course the latest scientific discoveries. On one occasion, their daughter Emily, then sixteen, wrote nostalgically from boarding school in the East: "You know, I really miss those dinner parties at home and all that fascinating talk about cancer."

The Hugginses went to bed early. After several invitations to dinner, specially designated students learned to rise at nine o'clock, announce that it was their bedtime, and offer to escort the visitors home.

Among the many honors that Charles Huggins received, his election to be chancellor of his alma mater, Acadia University, was very precious to him; he served in this post from 1972 to 1979. By lending the weight of his prestige to the chancellorship, he wished to repay in some small measure the gratitude he felt for the excellence of his undergraduate education. No doubt he often surprised and amused his audience at convocations, for Charles Huggins has a keen sense of humor and by his own admission could be a "bit of a brat," sometimes to the discomfiture of others, although rarely with malicious intent. It was sometimes hard to tell whether or not he was serious about some of his more outrageous statements; but on reflection, his listeners usually realized that his wit often concealed advice and wisdom, and relieved the tensions of life and work. He served on committees only rarely. "I can sleep better in my office than in committee meetings," he maintained. Nevertheless, he was briefly a member of a National Institutes of Health peer-review group. A research grant for Harvard was being considered and various budget categories such as "personnel and equipment" were being discussed by the group. When it came to the request for travel funds, Huggins simply asked: "Why should they travel when they are already there?"

On another occasion, Huggins was very busy in the midst of an experiment. An imposing-looking physician, who did not know Huggins personally, was attending the American Medical Association meeting in Chicago and wanted to meet Huggins. He finally found his way to the laboratory and asked Huggins whether he had seen Dr. Huggins. "Not recently," came back the immediate response.

Huggins maintained long-term personal and scientific friendships with many prominent individuals all over the world; these relationships were characterized by mutual admiration and respect. We have already dwelt on the profound role played by his chief, Dallas Phemister, in molding Huggins's career and directing him towards medical investigation. In 1930, when Huggins spent a year of training and travel in Europe, he occupied a laboratory bench at a Hamburg clinic opposite the distinguished biochemist Hans A. Krebs, with whom he maintained a lifelong friendship. He also visited Otto Warburg at the Kaiser-Wilhelm Institut in Berlin-Dahlem. Warburg, who in his day was the towering figure in the world of biochemistry, reputedly declined Huggins's application to work in his laboratory, on the basis that surgical training was incompatible with a serious scientific career. Nevertheless, there was an affinity between them, which finally developed into a friendship when Warburg visited Huggins in Chicago after the Second World War, and was enormously impressed with the work on cancer of the prostate. They continued to meet regularly after Huggins was elected to the order "Pour le Mérite."

A few final words about his habits and personality. Charles Huggins leads an enormously disciplined, simple, and organized life. He is and expects others to be punctual; he answers letters by return mail; he is never too busy to see friends and colleagues but keeps his meetings short, convinced that nothing useful is accomplished by extended discussion. He regards wasting time as evil, and strongly holds to the view that those who waste time only rob themselves of their most precious and irreplaceable gift. He has until recently worked a seventy-hour week. But he has no briefcase. Although no formal work appears to be done at home, where he reads the classics and listens to Mozart and Bach, undoubtedly he rarely stops thinking about his experiments.

15

ROBERT MAYNARD HUTCHINS

1 8 9 9 – 1 9 7 7

E D W A R D   S H I L S

THE YEARS IN WHICH Robert Hutchins was the president and then chancellor of the University of Chicago, from 1929 to 1951, were among the greatest in the century-long history of our University. They saw a reawakening of the sense of participation in a great collective intellectual and moral effort such as William Rainey Harper had borne within himself and instilled into the leading members of his academic staff in the first decade. Harper embodied in himself and called forth in this University a profound and exhilarated vision of what a university in the United States should be. After his death, there occurred what observers of the history of the University of Chicago call a period of consolidation. The term is a misnomer. It was a period of steady progress of the University as a site of great research and inspiring teaching. In a relatively short time, the University of Chicago became one of the major centers of advanced education and research in the United States; it trained a disproportionately large percentage of the university teachers, scholars, and scientists of this remarkable period when American universities began the endogenous expansion of the traditions which they had inherited from the European universities of the nineteenth century.

It was at the end of this consolidation that Robert Hutchins was chosen to be the president of this young university—then less than forty years old. The University was less than a decade older than its new president.

· I ·

Let me say that I have only two qualifications for writing about Robert Hutchins here. The one person who knew him best in the great years of his presidency, who was as intimate with him as anyone except Thornton Wilder, who was very closely related to him in the business of the University, and who is therefore the person best qualified to write decided that it

185

was not possible for him for those very reasons to write this essay for this volume on the persons who made this University what it was and is. He was so overpowered by his admiration and affection for Robert Hutchins that he thought that he could not attain a state of sufficient detachment to write an assessment of a man who was so replete with distinctive and great qualities. I am a poor substitute. The only qualification is that I observed him, from a distance, with admiration and in a critical but affectionate way for about two decades, that I was dazzled by him although I did not agree with all that he thought desirable. This disagreement has scarcely qualified my affection for him and my gratitude for what he gave to this University. In addition, I am one of the few members of our present teaching staff who knew him at all. That is why I am rushing in where angels fear to tread.

I should say at the outset that although I came to the University of Chicago only three years after Robert Hutchins began his presidency, I never exchanged a word with him until 1945. This does not mean that I did not know him. He was very much a presence to me. That was not only because his office was on the ground floor of the west end of the Harper Memorial Library while my own room was at the west end of the Social Science Research Building and later in the east tower of Harper but because, in those days, I used to go into the stacks of the library practically every day. The entrance to the stacks of the library was adjacent to the quarters of the president so it happened that I did see him rather frequently as he was entering and leaving his office. I never spoke to him but the sight of him was tremendously impressive. He was very tall and handsome beyond my descriptive powers. Later when I became somewhat acquainted with him personally, I said that he was a reverse-Pygmalion. Pygmalion was the man who fell in love with a statue. I said that his qualities and his bearing which expressed those qualities were such that a statue would have fallen in love with him.

One of the reasons why he was such a presence to me, aside from the accidental but not infrequent glimpses of him, was his writings, which as stylistic performances were perfect in their own way. Each of his writings always had one main point—frequently it was the same point—set forth with almost geometrical rigor and exactitude. Although I was a social scientist, and it was clear to me that Hutchins cared little for the social sciences, that did not affect my view of him. I was not all that impressed by the then state of the social sciences—nor am I so impressed now—so that was no barrier between him and myself on that ground.

Quite apart from my study of his writings, which were mainly speeches,

ROBERT MAYNARD HUTCHINS

I was research assistant to Louis Wirth and an admiring pupil of Frank Wright and John Nef. I also knew Harry Gideonse, who was at that time chairman of the social sciences in the College and of whom I was not a great admirer. Wirth, Gideonse, and Knight were very antagonistic to Hutchins or at least to his educational ideas; Wirth and Gideonse were very defensive on behalf of the social sciences; Knight, who was not at all protective of the social sciences, was a man of extraordinary penetration and subtlety of mind as well as very dogged; he thought that Hutchins believed in easy solutions, a thought utterly abhorrent to Knight. Knight was just as critical of John Dewey as he was of Hutchins but for opposite reasons. Dewey thought that empirical and scientific knowledge provided the ultimate criteria of the valuable and the good; Knight criticized Hutchins for what he thought was moral absolutism derived by metaphysical reasoning. These three gentleman were frequently exchanging memoranda, scrutinizing and bitterly censuring Hutchins's latest pronouncement. I could not be indifferent to what they were saying and writing. I had no sympathy for the views of Wirth and Gideonse. I was impressed by Knight's arguments although later I concluded that he was unnecessarily riled by Hutchins.

I organized a small lunch-society of other research assistants in the social science division—most of the others were political scientists—and we used to meet from time to time in a small private dining room in Hutchinson Commons to discuss Hutchins's educational ideas. It was evident to me that my friends, Victor Jones, John Vieg, William Fox, and a few others were rather unsophisticated defenders of the social sciences. They were not on Hutchins's side. I was rather more so. But whether we disagreed or agreed with Hutchins it was clear that they too felt that it was a great thing to be members of a university of which such a man was president.

I doubt whether the minds of the teachers and students at the University of Chicago were deepened by the disputes and discussions about the nature and tasks of university education. I am not doubtful however about the sense which was aroused in them of the importance of universities in general and of the pride of being at the University of Chicago. More important they became aware that the classical works of political philosophy from Plato onward were works to be studied because they had a permanent intellectual value, not just as documents in the history of thought but because they were still pertinent to our understanding of the world. Such notions made those who participated in them think that they were in the presence of great ideas, even though they did not quite know what to make of them.

· II ·

Towards the end of the 1930s, I had two experiences of Hutchins—one direct, the other indirect. The former was my attendance at one of the Great Books classes for undergraduates given jointly by Hutchins and Mortimer Adler. Hutchins would have been a wonderful teacher had he followed such a career. He had a Socratic gift for raising questions which made students aware that what was visible on the surface of their minds was insufficient. He could question without causing discomfiture, he would persist in his questions without causing embarrassment. He also had the marvelous gift, which I was to witness later, of reformulating a reply to one of his questions with a clarity and generosity which enabled a student to see more clearly what he, the student, had said poorly. It was not a matter of just learning the right answers but of being shown the way to better answers. I think that there was nothing in Hutchins's comments in that class which bore any resemblance to the schematic statements in his public addresses or to the metaphysical absolutism of which he was accused by his critics, or of the dogmatism with which his detractors within the University and outside charged him.

The indirect contact with Hutchins came through my appointment as an instructor in social sciences in the College at the University of Chicago. I did not have a very high opinion of social science I and social science II—I taught the latter. It was extremely miscellaneous and except for a work of Frank Knight's, the required readings were undistinguished and the staff was little different. The students were, however, enthusiastic. I learned that their enthusiasm was very general. Insofar as it had a focus, it was on three teachers, Louis Wirth, Joseph Schwab, and David Grene. Louis Wirth was a fluent and persuasive lecturer who gave his audience a new sense of life in a great city. Schwab and Grene were great teachers and supporters of Hutchins. A broader focus was the survey course in humanities. I think that there was near unanimity among my students, to whom I spoke about their studies, about the courses in the humanities. Neither Hutchins—nor Adler, whose name was always coupled with Hutchins's but who was an altogether different sort of person—had any direct contact with these survey courses in the College. Hutchins, as far as I know, never suggested any books which were to be studied, he never suggested any interpretations, but the teachers in those survey courses in the humanities and in Schwab's part of the biological sciences were deeply affected by the awareness that the president of their University shared their views about the greatness of the works and ideas for the teaching of which they were responsible. That added to their sense of responsibility to the works and the students.

In the second-year social sciences survey course, I, without being officially charged with it, took over the course and introduced into it the best authors who could be found, given the task set by the title of the course, which was "Freedom and Order." Locke, Hobbes, Simmel, Weber, Tawney, Dicey, MacIlwain, John Dickinson, Frank Knight were among them. The students saw the seriousness of the effort to give them the best education obtainable within the limits of my knowledge and capacity and they responded appropriately. Hutchins never said a word to me, either directly or indirectly, about the course although I learned later that he knew about it and approved of it. Nevertheless, I too was aware that I was participating in a great intellectual undertaking which owed much to the spirit which emanated from Hutchins.

· III ·

My first closer contact with Robert Hutchins came about in August and September immediately after the end of the war with Japan. It was a consequence of the use of the atomic bombs. I had immediately become interested in the development of a system of international control and began to work out a scheme to that end. Leo Szilard heard about it and came to see me. I believe that he thought that my scheme was not ingenious enough— he was a genius of ingenuity. What emerged from our first discussions was a plan for a conference to consider the problems raised by the atomic bomb. Szilard went to see Hutchins—Robert Redfield was our mediator in this—and Hutchins agreed immediately with our proposal. Of course, it was very difficult for anyone except General Groves and Enrico Fermi—so I was later told—to resist Szilard's melancholy and cheerful earnestness, his patent imaginativeness and his prestige as the progenitor of the Manhattan Project. Hutchins responded at once. He agreed that we should hold such a conference; he provided the funds. Szilard and I set to work. He provided the names of the scientists—Urey, Franck, Wigner, Langmuir, Stearns, Rabinovich, and others. I provided the names of the social scientists and men of affairs—Jacob Viner, Jakob Marschak, Chester Barnard, David Lilienthal—I am not sure of this, perhaps Szilard suggested Lilienthal—Beardsley Ruml, Adolf Löwe, and a few others. Hutchins suggested that we invite Charles Lindbergh which we did; none of his friends, with whom his name was associated in the polemics in the university, were suggested by him. The conference was held in the last week of September

1945. The meetings were held in Room 302 of the Social Science Research Building. Hutchins was in the chair at all sessions. I presented my scheme, which was shot down at once by, among others, Hutchins, who declared it utopian. In later years, after Hutchins had created a Committee to Frame a World Constitution, I recalled from time to time Hutchins's conviction of my utopianism. It was indeed a utopian scheme. Some parts of it were, however, taken in the scheme later put forward, first by Lilienthal, then by Robert Oppenheimer and Dean Acheson and adapted by Bernard Baruch for the United States proposal to the United Nations commission on the international control of atomic energy. One of the points of my scheme was the "internationalization of scientific research" and, particularly, the close collaboration of scientists from the United States, France, Great Britain, and the Soviet Union so that there could no longer be any secrecy within the world scientific community. Forty years later, the desirability of such free collaboration became obvious. In any case, the Soviet Union would have nothing to do with Baruch's proposal and it disappeared from sight. Now it appears to be a very obvious thing.

Hutchins was a masterful chairman. He listened with perfect attentiveness and courtesy to everyone—except myself, whom he interrupted. I was too young and shy at that time to disregard his interruption but I took no umbrage at it. I knew that my scheme was utopian and he declared it to be such with such frankness and good will that I did not have any sense of having been treated disrespectfully.

He showed the same extraordinary gift as a chairman when the policy committee of the College met him to discuss a certain matter. Again he was a master of the art of reformulation, always improving and clarifying what had been mumbled and, even when not mumbled, said inchoately and often in a not very sensible way. Each time that he replied to what had been said rather poorly, it was much improved and more sensible.

Not long after that I left the University of Chicago for London and returned for only one term a year. I presumed on his good nature during those summers to call on him—I acted as secretary of the Committee on Social Thought in those terms when I was present at the University—to discuss Committee business. Since the powers of the chairman, John Nef, were in my hands when Nef was absent—as he always was during the summer quarter—I went once to propose the appointment of Michael Polanyi, who was willing to leave the University of Manchester to join the Committee on Social Thought. Hutchins listened to my presentation of Polanyi's merits, asked a few questions about him, and then said, "Yes, let's have him." Whereupon an invitation went out to Polanyi, which he gladly accepted but which the stupidity of the Department of State prevented him from taking up. On another occasion, the matter was more complicated. It had to do with an appointment in political philosophy, necessitated by the retirement of Charles Merriam who had taught the history of political theory for many years, decently but very nebulously and probably not very inspiringly.

There were three persons proposed: Alexander d'Entreves, then professor of Italian at Oxford, Alfred Cobban, then professor of French history at University College London, and Leo Strauss of the Graduate Faculty of the New School of Social Research in New York. Strauss was an exile from Germany who after a difficult life in Great Britain came to the United States towards the end of the 1930s to take up a very arduous existence as teacher, working simultaneously at several small colleges in the northeastern part of the country before he obtained the more satisfactory appointment at the Graduate Faculty. A small committee, consisting of Theodore Schultz, Hans Morgenthau, and myself was constituted, how I do not know, to consider the alternatives. Theodore Schultz with his characteristic modesty did not take an active part in our discussion because he thought it was beyond his ability to assess the merits of the candidate in a field in which he was not a master such as he was in economics. Morgenthau agreed with me that Strauss was, by all odds, the best of the three; he was however reluctant to take an active part in making the proposal. Although he was acting chairman of the department of political science in the absence during the summer quarter of Leonard White, who was chairman of the department, he told me that he was fearful of arousing the dissatisfaction of Leonard White, who might not approve of Strauss. It was therefore left to me to handle the business. John Nef favored d'Entreves, who was a most charming person, and after that Cobban; I think he knew nothing of Strauss, although Strauss had benefited from the patronage of R. H. Tawney whom Nef greatly admired. I proceeded without consulting Nef; I wrote a long cautious memorandum to Hutchins, reviewing the merits of all three candidates but making it clear that Strauss was my preference. I did not want to ride roughshod over Nef's desire but I did not wish to be subservient to it either. The memorandum went to Hutchins and I called on him shortly afterward in order to speak more freely than I had written. Hutchins had obviously read my long-winded memorandum very closely and he saw my preference. He said simply something like, "Who is the best of them?" I replied that Strauss was very much the best. He then replied, "All right, let's have Strauss." That settled the matter.

On still another matter, I took an opportunity to speak with Hutchins. In those days, I began a practice which I continued up to the time of Edward Levi's presidency of visiting the president of the University about once a year to give him my impression of "the state of the University." In the summer of 1949, I went to Hutchins to tell him in the course of my review that the University of Chicago was coming into difficult times because of the deterioration of the neighborhood and because Harvard and the University of California at Berkeley were rising in prestige and attractive power, relative to the University of Chicago, and that it would become increasingly difficult for the University to appoint the kinds of scholars and scientists whom we needed to keep the University in the forefront of the world of learning. After listening to me for some time, Hutchins said that he had to go to the center of Chicago to attend a meeting but he invited me to accompany him in the car on the journey downtown so that we could continue our discussion. I went on in the new setting for a few more minutes. Then he said, "You are wrong. Don't you know that the greatness of the University of Chicago has always rested on the fact that the city of Chicago is so boring that the professors having nothing else to do but to work?" I think I turned out to be right, at least for some years.

About three years after that Hutchins resigned from the presidency of the University—he was then called chancellor. The University did decline for some years after that. The neighborhood did continue to go down, great men like Fermi died, Urey left the University to go to the California Institute of Technology, James Franck retired, Ronald Crane retired, Frank Knight retired. Jacob Viner went off to Princeton, Paul Weiss left the University, and so on. The University began to recover under the presidency of George Beadle who wisely appointed Edward Levi to be the provost with most beneficial effects. In that decade of doldrums, not all was neglected. Julian Levi with the support of Lawrence Kimpton began a titanic effort to reclaim the neighborhood and they succeeded in doing so against the most difficult obstacles. Then came the presidency of Edward Levi, who had been appreciated by Hutchins from the very beginning of their connection. Under the presidency of Edward Levi, the University reentered its greatness. That was to a large extent Levi's own doing, but he was able to draw on the somewhat subsided but still living tradition of the University. The recovery of the University may be attributed, not least, to Edward Levi's determination to carry on in his own distinguished way, the inspiration and inheritance of Hutchins.

After Hutchins left the University of Chicago, he went to the Ford Foundation where he tried to do notable things but was not successful. He then created the Fund for the Republic with the support of the Ford Foundation. There too he tried to do what he could for the protection of academic freedom and civil liberties at a time when Senator McCarthy was creating a large and noisy public disturbance. In the end Hutchins created the Center for the Study of Democratic Institutions. There I think he was a failure, partly because it got off the wrong foot and partly because Hutchins could not find the colleagues, collaborators, and staff which such an institution needed to make a mark on its self-assigned task. In those years he was a prince in exile.

· IV ·

While he was president and chancellor of the University of Chicago, Hutchins attempted to do many things in accordance with his convictions. His proposals for institutional changes were either rejected or carried through against much resistance from a block of teachers who were determined to have nothing to do with Hutchins's proposed innovations. I think that some of the innovations might have benefited the University but institutional changes are in fact less important than spiritual changes, which are not usually the product of any one person's intentions. Yet it was in that aspect of academic life that Hutchins left his most enduring mark. Hutchins was one of the very few university presidents of his time—perhaps the only one—who believed in the value of intellectual life as an intrinsic good, who believed that intellectual achievement in teaching and research was the only worthwhile objective for a university to pursue. This gave the University of Chicago its distinctive tone. The teachers of the University of Chicago appreciated this, even those who opposed Hutchins's attempts to change certain institutional arrangements at the University. He helped to keep the University alive as a university devoted to intellectual things and not just as an institution to handle the administrative and financial burdens of self-enclosed departments and to enable strong-willed, gifted and mediocre individuals to get on with their specialized research and teaching. Of course, a university needs strong-willed and gifted teachers and it cannot entirely avoid being saddled with mediocre ones. But it also needs at its head a person of great devotion to intellectual matters and a deep solicitude for the university as a whole. In Hutchins the University of Chicago had exactly the right man.

Before ending these scanty reminiscences of Robert Hutchins, I should also like to say something about his uprightness of character and his determination to do the right thing. I need not say much about his concern about academic freedom. He was unparalleled among university presidents in the United States where populistic and demagogic turbulence and the silliness of academics from time to time menace academic freedom. He never allowed popular prejudices to stand in the way of his determination to secure the intellectual quality of the University. I will cite a few instances. First the appointment of Edward Levi as dean of the Law School, which was a momentous event in the history of that part of the University. When he proposed it to the board of trustees, a body which has always been unique in its devotion to the University but not always perfectly so, one or several of the trustees demurred on the ground that it was untoward to have a Jew as dean of the Law School. Hutchins threatened to resign over that issue and he had his way, to the great benefit of the Law School, the University, and the United States.

Another instance has to do with the appointment to the University of Subrahmanyan Chandrasekhar, the great astrophysicist. Professor Chandrasekhar was still a very young man and he had not yet made the resounding name for himself which he later acquired by his scientific achievements. He was proposed to Hutchins by Otto Struve, then the head of the department of astronomy and astrophysics and director of the Yerkes Observatory. Hutchins accepted Struve's recommendation. A professor of the University then wrote a letter to Hutchins asking whether it was right to have "a colored man lecture to students of the University of Chicago." Hutchins, who was a master of epistolary brevity, did not attempt to dissuade the man who complained. He simply replied in an extremely succinct note: which read something like: "Dear . . . From [such and such date], Dr. S. Chandrasekhar will be associate professor of astrophysics at the University of Chicago. Yours sincerely, Robert M. Hutchins." The result of this refusal to be moved by prejudice is there for all to see.

Finally, sometime in the 1930s, Hutchins had the idea of bringing William I. Thomas back to the University of Chicago from which he had been harshly dismissed in 1919 for having committed an act of adultery which was reported in the press. Thomas was at the time of his dismissal at the height of his intellectual powers. He was then with Robert Park the most outstanding sociologist in the United States and one of the most outstanding in the world. He still remains in that category despite the passage of years and the multitudes of busy sociologists. Not many others match his originality of mind and his great energy and fertility as a research worker. In the mid-1930s, Hutchins proposed that he be reappointed to the University. He was dissuaded by Harold Swift, one of the best trustees the University has ever had. It might not have worked out; Thomas was already around seventy years of age and he had declined considerably in his intellectual powers after the traumatic experience of his dismissal. Nevertheless, the suggestion showed what a man Robert Hutchins was. Many other instances could be cited in evidence of the view that in Robert Hutchins the University of Chicago had at its head a man of great moral qualities and of rarely equalled consecration to things of the mind.

All of us who served under him and after him are deeply in his debt.

16

HARRY G. JOHNSON

1 9 2 3 – 1 9 7 7

E D W A R D   S H I L S

· I ·

ONCE ON A WALK in the Cotswolds during the war, R. H. Taw-ney suddenly said to me: "Shils, have you ever pressed a mole in your hand?" I said that I had never done so. He told me that if I were to do so I would be surprised by its strength. "It is all muscle."

I recalled Tawney's words not so long after I first met Harry Johnson. He seemed to be intellectually "all muscle." Physically too he gave the impression of tremendous power, under easy self-control. He was about five feet ten inches tall, broad, thick-chested, inclined towards a solid plumpness. He had the most remarkable, large sparkling brown eyes, darkly ruddy cheeks, shining black hair. A matter-of-fact, a dry Canadian melodiousness of speech without flourishes or dramatic emphases, was characteristic of his conversation as it was of his writings. He did not pause when he spoke. There were no hems and haws. He spoke as he wrote, steadily, in long sentences, always grammatically correct and coherent, reaching out through numerous sub-ordinate clauses to bring in relevant but not usually perceived aspects of the subject and to reveal connections which are seldom noticed, while never losing sight of his main theme.

He always gave the impression of possessing a serene and powerful in-tellectual and physical vitality which permeated everything he did or said. There were no empty sentences in what he wrote. There was also none of that excess of energy which is wasted in twisting paper clips, moving things around pointlessly, speaking without saying anything. All his energy

This essay first appeared in the *University of Chicago Record*, vol. 11, no. 7, and is used with permission.

was mastered and applied to the production of something tangible, whether it was the sharpening of a pupil's dissertation, commenting on a seminar paper, assessing a paper submitted to a journal, delivering a lecture, writing a paper, or carving wooden figurines at seminars and conferences and during conversations in which his attention was never diverted from the issue under discussion. In conversation or in discussion, he noticed all that others said and responded justly and in sequence to every significant point. Even in the time of his plumpness, which for a period passed into stoutness, there was never anything sluggish or pulpy about him. When for a time his figure was at its maximum, he evoked my recollection of Babe Ruth, the great baseball player, whose large girth never impeded his speed, grace, or power in batting, running, or fielding.

There was no contentless conviviality or small talk in Harry Johnson's conversation. He never spoke for the pleasure of speaking or to fill in the blank moments of a conversation. It is not that he was given to withdrawal into silence; on the contrary, he could talk for hours. All that he said, however, had a point and it was not an isolated point; it was also part of an elaborate analysis resounding with overtones of new perspectives. He was not a Benthamite calculator of a felicific optimum, but when he considered any problem he had a way of tracing out ramifications of costs and benefits which no one else I have ever met possessed to such a degree.

It is not that he spent all his extraordinary energy and intelligence in discussing economics and university affairs. He would sometimes talk or write about some of the things which make up the substance of the gossip of others, but when he spoke about such things, often very vividly, they were discussed entirely without malice, or *Schadenfreude,* or prediction of disaster, but always in a way which traced out causes and consequences and which saw implications. When in a series of articles in *Encounter* and in a paper entitled "The Shadow of Keynes: Cambridge in the 1950s" which I published in *Minerva,* he wrote about the teaching and study of economics at Cambridge, or when he touched, in passing, on the same activities at Yale and Chicago, he was not gossiping. He was trying to understand and explain why distinguished talents went astray in pursuit of economic truths. As he wrote me in his last note in the last year of his life, about the paper on economics in Cambridge in the 1950s, "I am really after something complex—what causes the decay of academic excellence." When he discussed the "Keynesian revolution" and the "monetarist counter-revolution," his aim was to understand and explain the zigzagging course of the growth of economic knowledge, and the significance of external social conditions and

HARRY G. JOHNSON, about 1975

internal professional relationships in the improvements and retardation of
economic analysis.

Matter-of-factness and evenness were the characteristic of his voice and
written style but it was a matter-of-factness which exhibited the simulta-
neity and interconnectedness of events which only a person with a subtle
and sympathetic intelligence could discern.

Harry Johnson seemed to work under the principle which his much
older fellow-Kingsman, E. M. Forster, had put into the maxim: "Only con-
nect!" But in Harry Johnson's application of the rule the connections he
made were those which linked scattered events together, in all sorts of remote, roundabout, self-annulling, and self-accentuating ways. He brought
together these intricate connections with speed and rigor; he articulated
evidence and assertion at a speedy and even pace. The consecutiveness of
his thoughts was as marked in his spoken discourse as it was in his writings. He did it all unceasingly.

· II ·

Like many distinguished teachers at the University of Chicago, Harry
Johnson was a Canadian by origin. He graduated from the University of
Toronto in 1943, and thereafter served in the Canadian armed forces in the
Second World War; he took a second bachelor's degree at Cambridge. Between these two bachelor's degrees and after his military service, he taught
for a year at a small Canadian university. After the second B.A., he proceeded to take in rapid sequence two master's degrees, both in economics.
The first was at the University of Toronto, the second at Harvard. He then
returned to England as a graduate student in economics at Cambridge University, then as a fellow of King's College, Cambridge, and as lecturer in the
faculty of economics and politics at that university. In 1956, he became professor of economics at Manchester, and in 1959, he became professor of
economics at the University of Chicago. He was awarded the doctorate in
economics at Harvard in 1958. With all this studying and teaching, he began
his extraordinary career as an author. By the time he became a Ph.D., he had
already published fifty articles in economics. He worked unceasingly. He
did not confine himself to working out his own ideas; he believed in the
collaborative nature of intellectual progress and he took seriously the
work of all other writers in his field, young and old, past and contemporary. He read the literature of economics omnivorously and remembered
it in all its elaborate detail. He knew its history as well as its current state.
In everything he wrote as an economist, he regarded himself as a con-

tinuator and improver of the works of other economists and above all as their colleague. He not only read extraordinarily widely, attentively, and retentively in economic theory; he also covered the relevant statistical literature and sources. He was as empirical as he was theoretical. He was sensitive to minute analytical differences but saw them in the perspective of the larger field of economics. That is why he was ideally fitted to write a history of economic thought. As far as I know he did not intend to do so; but many of his writings, by their meticulous appreciation of the steps by which economic analysis has progressed, are fragments of such a history.

Harry Johnson was not an antiquarian. He was not like Piero Sraffa, a person to whom the history of economic thought was a subject to be savoured for its own capacity to give intellectual pleasure. He was not in the least inclined towards piety towards the past because of its pastness. He wanted economics to be a science, and in order for it to become such it was necessary to appreciate what had already been accomplished and to work forward from it.

He accepted that economics had to progress by improving on what had been done previously. That required unremitting study of the entire literature of economics, but it was not enough. It also required the study of the evidence. Fortunately the strength, speed, and capaciousness of his mind allowed him to do this. This was not enough for him either. He wanted those around him to write and publish and to discuss what they were doing straightforwardly but without acrimony. His colleagues and pupils at Chicago were prolific in their production of papers and books, and intense and forthcoming in discussion. This was one of the grounds of his satisfaction in his last decade and a half at the University of Chicago.

As one of the Chicago economists in what he called the "theoretical missionary movement," which extended economic analysis to race relations, family life, and education, Harry Johnson reached into the consideration of universities and the organization of learning. He did not study the literature of these subjects as he studied the literature of economics where he seemed to have read everything, old and new, and to remember the details of the most intricate arguments and of out-of-the-way statistics. But without reading so much of the disordered literature on the history of universities, and the history and administration of scientific research, he went to the heart of the matter, tracing preconditions and ramifications at many removes from the topic first considered and then bringing them back again to the main topic.

The result of his belief in the rightness of the task which he had accepted—to improve economics and to spread its light—was a list of writings unequalled by his contemporaries and by few economists of the past. He wrote about 525 articles and about twenty books, and every one of them was as tough and solid as he himself was.

Harry Johnson was a "missionary" in another, somewhat traditional sense. The goal of the progress of economics in academic study, and suppression of pride and prejudice in economic policy, laid upon him the obligation to travel to innumerable conferences and to teach in many universities. He did not go to conferences in Pakistan or Japan, or wherever else, in order to have his fare paid so that he could go sight-seeing. He went to conferences to learn from the best and the youngest of his colleagues, to question them about what they had written and to correct their errors, and to bring them into the procession of economists who were contributing to the progress of their subject. After he was well settled in Chicago, he accepted a concurrent professorship at the London School of Economics so that the light of economics as he understood it could shine over larger areas. After he left the School and after his first stroke, in Venice, he accepted a second concurrent professorship at the Institut des hautes études internationales of the University of Geneva. He accepted visiting professorships at various universities, he conducted summer schools so that he could shepherd the flock of economists onto the right path.

In addition to his assiduity in teaching, research, writing, delivering of lectures in many universities and many countries, Harry Johnson also made time for being an editor. He first began that role as one of the editors of the *Review of Economic Studies* and later as chief editor of *The Manchester School*. His real career as an editor began shortly after his arrival in Chicago, when he became editor of the *Journal of Political Economy*. That journal already enjoyed a high reputation; the reputation grew markedly when Harry Johnson became editor. His work as editor of the *Journal of Political Economy* has been said to have been the best of any editor of any economic journal since John Maynard Keynes was in charge of the *Economic Journal*. Again, the speed and thoroughness with which he dealt with articles submitted to the journal, the precision and profusion of his suggestions to the authors for the improvement of their papers, and his steady discrimination of judgment of the quality of what was sent in was no different from what he did in his seminars and in his own writings.

· III ·

My own relations with Harry Johnson were at the margin of his labors in economics. I first met him not long after he came to the University of Chicago towards the end of the 1950s. He had come from Manchester where, although we had not overlapped in time, we had both taught and had many common acquaintances. We also had a common connection with England. We had both been fellows at King's College, Cambridge, although, again, not at the same time. He was at first not entirely home at the University of Chicago, where the rough and tumble of discussion in the economics department, inherited from the time of Frank Knight and Jacob Viner and carried on more courteously and relentlessly by Milton Friedman and with sardonic joviality by George Stigler, was not quite what he liked. He was thinking of throwing up his post at the University of Chicago and accepting a very attractive invitation to the Johns Hopkins University. He wanted my advice; I tried to persuade him to stand his ground and to give as good as he got. He soon demonstrated his mastery of that kind of intense give-and-take and enjoyed it thoroughly. So much so that he came to regard it as one of the merits of the department where "economics is really taken seriously."

At the University of Chicago, my connections with him were mainly through his participation in the committee for the comparative study of new nations, his advice and written contributions to *Minerva,* and his activity as a member of the committee on the criteria of academic appointment which had been appointed by President Levi and of which I was chairman. In all these settings, he was a patient expositor of the principles of the "theoretical missionary movement" of economic analysis and a self-confident, scornful exponent of the view that a university department in which everyone was not hard at work in rigorous research and intensive teaching was contemptible.

Harry Johnson's contact with the Committee on New Nations came about in the following way. A little after my first conversation with Harry, Lloyd Fallers, who was one of the co-founders of the committee and who seemed to know everyone in the University, suggested that Harry would be a valuable member of the committee. I responded at once and very positively because I appreciated Harry's unsentimental attitude towards the problems of the new states and his censure of self-defeating "planning" and because I thought the benign atmosphere which had been generated in the submarine-like rooms of the committee at the bottom of Foster Hall would compensate him for the sometimes excessively sharp debates in the department of economics and make the University of Chicago more pleasing to him.

I was right. He accepted with eagerness and that was a wonderful thing for all of us. Year after year he came regularly to our weekly seminars. He would come in quietly, sliding his substantial bulk through the crowded reading room where we usually had coffee before settling down to business; he sometimes stood with us for a while, not speaking but looking on gravely. Sometimes he went directly into the seminar room and began to carve while waiting for the proceedings to begin.

In the seminar, he extended his ideas about the consequences of protective tariffs for the relationships between trade, economic growth, and development, and about economic nationalism. He reported on his study of the historical origins of nationalistic and collectivistic economic policies in the poor—mainly recently colonial—countries. The economic nationalism which he censured in his native Canada, he censured no less stringently when it was practiced in poorer countries. He was no less severe in his criticism of the "economic planning" in these countries. As he wrote in *Encounter* in his appreciation of Professor Peter Bauer and as he said in his lecture at the University of Ghana, the price of these policies was paid by the poor, i.e., the peasantry, and the beneficiaries of these policies were university graduates in the civil service and the universities. This was an underlying theme of his thought and he made it repeatedly in his visits to poor countries and in his discourses to academic social scientists in the United States and Great Britain.

He taught the members of the committee much that they had not known before; above all, he straightened out the minds of some of the members of the committee who took the then-common uncritically protective attitude towards the new states. Above all, he exemplified, week in and week out, his talent for tracing interconnections. He organized the seminar during one term and from it produced a book which at that time was unusual in its sympathetic realism and in its application of the powerful techniques of economic analysis to a field which was then dominated by social scientists and by economists who thought that compassion required that they set aside the hardheadedness on which they prided themselves.

· IV ·

Very soon after I founded *Minerva* in 1961 I discovered that Harry Johnson's "missionary" work had also reached into its territory. He had written a very trenchant, almost too tough-minded memorandum for the Committee on Science and Astronautics of the United States House of Representatives which I reprinted in the Reports and Documents section of *Minerva*. I used thereafter to send him papers which I had decided to publish, asking him to write a comment in the form of a letter to the editor. He did this about a half dozen times, and each of his comments, which came back to me almost at once, was just as painstaking, in its exposition of where the author had gone wrong and of what the right solution was, as a paper for a major conference or a leading learned journal. Even his briefest note bore his distinctive intellectual signature. He was so helpful that I invited him to join the board of advisory editors of *Minerva* and he soon became one of my most active, faithful, and solicitous associates. His generosity toward younger, less well-known colleagues and his loyalty to *Minerva* brought me into contact with a number of excellent scholars of whose work I would otherwise have been ignorant and who subsequently helped me to develop one of the distinctive features of *Minerva* of which I have been most pleased—namely, the analysis of certain aspects of the support of science and of higher education in the light of economic theory.

His economic analysis of the "brain drain" and of scientific research, of graduate education and of the functions of universities were all works of much originality. The discussion of the "brain drain" was transformed by his cool, matter-of-fact dissipation of the mixture of resentment, nationalism, and sentimentality which had prevailed until he went into the matter. His writings on science policy and research, on the organization of graduate studies in economics, and on universities more generally, were of the same very high standard. They showed what is gained when a great logical power and the fundamental theorems of economic analysis are combined with a dispassionate and ample knowledge of facts and are applied to the study of a particular topic. Just before he died, he sent me a paper on the study of economics at Cambridge in the 1950s. It was a superb sociological and economic analysis of intellectual fertility and decline. He wished to present it to an audience at the University of Chicago and I began to make preparations for its presentation at a seminar, to be followed by a dinner and then a long evening's discussion on the causes of decline from excellence and how to avoid it. This was increasingly on his mind, as a result of his experiences and reflections on Cambridge and Chicago. Unfortunately, that seminar was never held because of his death, but the paper was published in *Minerva*. It is more than a monument to his clarifying presence in its pages; it testifies to his intellectual courage in facing difficult problems and his concern to maintain universities at a high level.

With all his travels, his illness, and his torrential outpouring of papers and books on monetary policy and international economic relations, he always had an indulgent moment for *Minerva*. He even tolerated my rejection of some of his offerings and my thorough rewriting of others which I accepted. I sometimes thought his sentences too long and I cut them into two or three. I also used to eliminate the touches of asperity which sometimes entered when Harry castigated inexcusable or self-serving errors. I recall once when I saw him at the foot of the staircase which joined the fourth and fifth floors of the Social Science Research Building at the University of Chicago. He was standing with his secretary and I had just given him back, for his inspection, one of his excellent papers which I had rewritten in the margins and between the lines of every page. He looked at his secretary with an amused smile, which suggested that he thought it just that he, the critic who swept through the manuscripts of others with an iron broom, should have the same thing done to his own manuscripts. He said to his secretary: "If I am to be published in *Minerva,* I have to allow my papers to be rewritten."

By the time the committee on the criteria of academic appointment was brought together in 1971, it was clear to me that Harry Johnson was one of the relatively small group of scholars and scientists who knew what a university should be and who was not afraid to say what he knew. This was a time when minds, even serious and able and otherwise mature minds, were still addled by the events of the last half decade. I do not remember now whether it was president Edward Levi or I who suggested that Harry Johnson should be a member. Whoever it was, the choice was an important one for the committee and the University of Chicago.

There was a lot of work involved in membership in it since it met nearly every week, and Harry Johnson never missed a meeting when he was in Chicago. Universities were still shaking from the troublesome events of the past few years, although the University of Chicago had kept a cooler head than any other. My committee began with a few uncertainties. Harry Johnson did not share these; he patiently and irresistibly argued down every suggestion which would contradict the idea that the University must not be diverted from its obligation to the most stringent intellectual training, and the most exigent application to the tasks of reliable and fundamental discovery. After we got under way, I submitted a new draft of our report almost every week. Harry Johnson's copies were always the first to come back to me with copious remarks, critical and unfailingly alert to slovenly formulations and oversights, and very suggestive of better reformulations. Even when he was in London, his annotations invariably came back by return of post, which was not so long in those days as it is now. Once, when his comments were put in terms which I would not accept, I reprimanded him sharply, and once again was given the indulgence granted to an incorrigible favorite. By this time, he had become a member of the University of Chicago family. Even though he was away for about half of each year, the University of Chicago and of course the department of economics held him by an unbreakable bond of almost organic firmness.

· V ·

My meetings with Harry Johnson were almost always on occasions provided by our common academic concerns. Sometimes we met for dinner at his home or mine. In the course of them I was able to see both those things which were constant and those which were growing in him.

What was constant was the flawless lucidity of his mind, his extraordinary rapidity of thought, and the justice of his comprehension, the austere and elevated conception which he had of the university teacher's obligations and the economist's calling, his capacity to pursue complex chains of reasoning, and his incomparable industry, assiduity, and efficiency. He disliked pomposity and pretence; he disliked the claims of educated civil servants and academic social scientists that a society which they dominated would be made better by the very fact of their determination of its policies. He took the responsibility of a teacher of economics as unqualified. One never put a question or a task to him to which one did not receive a written reply in a very short time, very cogent and succinct and as brief as the problem permitted and as long as it required.

What grew in him was the indomitability of his will. When he had been in good health, there was no journey which he would not undertake to deliver a paper or to participate in a seminar and to leave behind a few home truths about economic theory and economic policy.

As he acquired more students he became even more devoted to them than he had been before. Increasing fame and widely dispersed obligations did not divert his attention from his students. He spent more time with them when he had less of it to spend. He required from his students that they be as serious about economics as he was and as willing to work as hard at it. In terms when he was away from the University of Chicago, he might sometimes pass through Chicago for a day on a flight from London to Pakistan with a stop at Singapore or some other far-off corner of the earth; he would gather his students around him for most of that day to review and criticize their work and to give them new directions and stimuli. When Harry Johnson and his pupils went to the faculty club for a drink before dinner, there still was no aimless camaraderie. It was all about some fine points of international economics or monetary policy. Then he would be off.

After his stroke it was hardly any different, except that he no longer drank alcohol. He had in the past been capable of drinking large quantities of wine and whiskey and practically never showed any ill effects in his thought or speech. When, not so long before his first stroke, he was ordered to stop drinking alcohol, he stopped at once and totally, just as earlier he had stopped smoking cigarettes and had taken to wood carving.

Whatever he did, he did unremittingly and thoroughly. Life must have been more difficult for him after his first stroke since he had to walk with a stick, and he never fully recovered the use of his left hand. But the stroke could not stop him. Even his carving did not stop; his left hand not being quite strong enough for him to hold the wood with it while he carved with his right hand, he had a small vise attached to his desk so he could get on with his carving while speaking with his students and colleagues.

Within a week of the stroke which befell him in Venice in October 1973, when he lay in bed in the Opesdale Civile Reuniti in the Campo SS. Giovanni e Paolo, with his left side paralyzed, scarcely able to speak but still able to smile, he was already back at economics. There was a pile of new books on economics by his bedside and a writing pad and a pencil at his right hand. He said, with a difficult smile, as if craving my understanding, and speaking with difficulty, "I still have to work." Within a few weeks, although still very handicapped in his movements, he was again writing articles and comments. In a fairly short time, the flow of papers and books took up where it left off. Not much later, his travels began again. When he resigned from the London School of Economics, although I regretted the atmosphere in which it occurred, I thought to myself: "Now Harry will take life a little more easily and he won't dash about so much." That was a wrong prediction. He was soon off to Japan, the Fiji islands, Pakistan, etc., etc. He seemed to be traveling as much as ever and he smiled wanly but proudly when I chided him for it.

Why did he do it? Of course, he was proud of his reputation as an economist of great intellectual powers and voluminous bibliography. He was delighted when his accomplishments were recognized; he took pleasure in the honors which he had received and he liked the attention given to him in all those places of the world which he visited. He was especially pleased by the reverent—and uncomfortable—attention which he was accorded in his native Canada.

It was certainly not vanity which caused him to put in so many hours, days, weeks, and years in teaching so many students so thoroughly and patiently and in working so painstakingly over such masses of economic literature, reports, and documents in order to write those numerous papers and books which could not have been written without hard and unrelentingly thorough work. Harry Johnson believed that some men might be persuaded to behave more reasonably in the conduct of their economic affairs. That is why he believed in economic analysis. He did not, however, think that economic development should be the be-all and end-all of human existence. Insofar, however, as it is sought, serious economic analysis is an indispensable condition of effective action. He thought that intellectual integrity in the discussion of public policy would be impossible without the mastery and advancement of economic analysis. He thought economics was a science with exigent claims of its own as an intellectual discipline and with no less strong claims on the conduct of politicians, civil servants, businessmen, and journalists. He himself heeded those claims and he thought that other academics should do so too. He gave his life to their service.

17

ARCADIUS KAHAN

1920-1982

RICHARD HELLIE

· I ·

ARCADIUS KAHAN played a role in my life as a teacher, colleague, native informant, wise adviser, and friend. I knew him personally between 1959 and 5 P.M. on Friday, February 20, 1982, when he danced out of the Economic History Workshop as usual, went home, and died of a heart attack five hours later. Since then I have had many occasions to remember him, whether it was assembling and editing for publication by the University of Chicago Press his *The Plow, the Hammer, and the Knout: The Economic History of Russia in the Eighteenth Century,* arranging my own perspective on current events based partly on his fascinating stories about life in Eastern Europe, or managing a large study on the seventeenth-century Russian economy in which I am currently engaged.

I can no longer remember my first encounters with Arcadius Kahan, although I do recall that I heard about him from his colleague, and my mentor, Leopold H. Haimson, who moved to Columbia University in 1963. I had always been interested in being a student of Russian history. When I was in the College of the University of Chicago from 1954 to 1958, the academic pickings were so slim that my harvest was limited to three years of Russian. They improved greatly in 1958, however, when I entered the graduate program in history. When Kahan arrived at the University of Chicago in 1955 after having been granted the Ph.D. in economics from Rutgers, he worked as a research assistant for D. Gale Johnson and thus was not available as a Russian-area "public utility." When he began to make himself available, however, I soon made his acquaintance.

Professor Haimson was often on leave directing his project on the history of Menshevism, so graduate history students interested in things Rus-

ARCADIUS KAHAN

sian had to meet their course requirements away from his tutelage. I got what I needed by taking or auditing a dozen courses with Professor Hugh McLean of the department of Slavic languages and literatures and by taking the courses Arcadius Kahan offered. The first course, in autumn 1960, was on the history of the Soviet economy, his "bread and butter" course in the department of economics. I never knew what Kahan thought of that course, but I assume he must have had a good time. On the other side of the desk since 1965, I have often wished I had such a responsive class. It worked as follows: Kahan would lecture a bit, and then one of the half dozen students would interrupt with a question. Politically, the class was about as diverse as possible: an Egyptian student represented the far right "King Farouk" line, I represented the state interventionist-centralization ("Stalinist") line, and an Indian student every so often interjected something about Nehru's "New Way." Employing the tools of economics with its sundry graphs and tables, Kahan tried to lecture, but the three of us would hardly let him, and I assume he probably got through only a third of his material. Subsequently I wished that Kahan had dominated the discussion more, but his personality at the time did not allow it. I also think he had a good time letting the students argue.

The most instructive class I took with Kahan, also in the autumn of 1960, was "Economic History of Russia." This one covered the period from the tenth through the eighteenth centuries. Like most of his classes, it met first thing in the morning, an excellent arrangement for covering up the fact that initially he was not a very popular teacher, and later, when he became popular, for keeeping the enrollment down. I was the sole student registered for the class. Twice a week Kahan came in and sat down at the end of the big oval table by the window; I sat at the other end, by the door. He lectured and I took voluminous notes. While he was lecturing, he played with his matches or dismantled a cigarette package. That course was one of the most solid I took in the University, and taught me the possible utility— expensive, to be sure—of "each one teach one." I do not recall that there was much, if any discussion, in that course.

For that course I wrote a paper, "The Economics of the *Ulozhenie* (Law Code) of 1649," that served as part of the background to my doctoral dissertation and to much of the work I have done since. I recall that he took me to the Harper Library stacks, practically running all the way, and introduced me to many of the books I would be using, including the two-volume set of documents on the great Boris Morozov estates, published between 1940 and 1945; one of the volumes had been catalogued under

DK (history), the other under HD (economics). As was his wont in those years, while he was still unsure of his English, Kahan wrote nothing on my term paper. Several months later, when I wanted it back (those were the days before Xeroxing and computers), he told me that he had left it in the office of the department of history, where I found it on a radiator.

A while later, it was time to select a topic for my dissertation. Leopold Haimson was an intellectual historian, but Kahan pointed out to me that no first-rate Russian intellectuals or philosophers had ever existed, that those "thinkers" American scholars were at the time—it was the spring of 1962—writing about were third-rate by any standard, and that it would be wise for me to pick a dissertation topic in a field in which the returns would be higher. That was excellent advice, for which I have been forever grateful. I have repeated Kahan's observation about the intellectual merit of the Russian radical intelligentsia to generations of students.

I prepared part of one of my fields for the oral examination for the doctorate—comparative economic development of the United States and Russia from 1850 to 1913—under Kahan's direction. He sent me to his older colleague Professor Earl J. Hamilton, a specialist on the Spanish price revolution of the seventeenth century, for the part having to do with the United States. Kahan had hardly begun to work on nineteenth-century Russian economic history at that point, but he knew the bibliography well. For me, the most fascinating thing I learned was that the business cycles of the two countries were contradictory; when it was boom time in Russia, it was bust in the United States and vice-versa. The comparative approach advocated by Kahan has been one that has informed much of my work ever since.

About this time one of the many tragedies of Kahan's life occurred. I knew that he had been working during the years from 1960 to 1962 on the development of the Russian iron industry in the eighteenth century, and especially the role of the Demidov family. Yet he never published anything on this, and the section on the iron industry in *The Plow, the Hammer, and the Knout* is skimpy indeed. Only years later did I learn what had happened. He was preparing to go on leave for a year and clearing out his office for its next occupant. That professor came in prematurely and told the janitor to dispose of what was left there. When Kahan came back to remove his papers, he found them gone; he tried to get them back, but discovered that they had already been thrown into the University incinerator. For someone who had known many persons who had gone into Nazi incinerators, this was more than Kahan could bear. He told me once that it took him two years to recover from that disaster.

Leopold Haimson was the major reader of my doctoral dissertation (in 1965), and Arcadius Kahan played some role, but I can no longer remember what it was. My first university job was at Rutgers. I was appointed from there to teach at the University of Chicago on the recommendation of Professor William H. McNeill in 1966, and have no knowledge of what role, if any, Kahan played in that process. After I arrived, however, we began to work more and more closely together. I took over the Russian civilization course which had been begun by Thomas Riha, for whom I had served in 1961–62 as a Carnegie intern in the course on non-Western civilization. I recall that Kahan had given a guest lecture for Riha in that course; the problem was then that his English was still so indistinct that the students could barely understand him. Half a decade later, however, his English was much improved, and I made as much use as I could of Kahan in the Russian civilization course. Nearly every time the year-long sequence was taught, he gave one lecture in the winter term on the eighteenth-century economy, another in the spring term on the Soviet economy. My own idea was that the guest lectures were opportunities for teachers to demonstrate their wares to about a hundred students every time the course was taught. Kahan always took the assignment seriously, prepared well, and gave a good lecture. The students almost uniformly appreciated his lectures and found them informative and intellectually stimulating. Some of them told me that they deliberately took Kahan's other courses because they had found his presentation in the course on Russian civilization worthwhile.

· II ·

Kahan took on a three-year term as master of the social sciences collegiate division in 1968, at a time of considerable turmoil on American campuses because of the Vietnam War. As master, he was my immediate "boss" in my work on the course in Russian civilization. Years later another colleague, declining the mastership, observed that this was the only place he knew of where a slave was called a master. Kahan was only the second master of that division—Donald Levine was his predecessor—and the functions of the office were not yet well defined and its relations with the dean of the division of social sciences were strictly ad hoc and informal. This latter fact made the job difficult, Kahan said. I used to observe him during staff meetings, trying to get things done, something that is difficult in an environment in which each professor is ordinarily almost totally autonomous. Kahan often complained that the use of the telephone meant that there was no paper trail of anything, that there was no way to know who had decided what, when, how, or why. In these meetings and in his individual encounters with colleagues, Kahan was invariably quiet and mild-mannered. It was in those years that I began to realize that he was not only extraordinarily intelligent and well informed but that he was wise. He always seemed to have the wise solution to problems. Wisdom seemed to be a major part of his character in a way that it has been for few other persons I have ever met.

During Kahan's years as master, students were more assertive than they ever had been before, or have been since. That was the time when the word "demand" in an unconditional sense became an acceptable word in the student lexicon. As far as I know, Kahan was able to meet or defuse every student demand that came his way. One major demand by a perceptible part of the student body was for a Jewish studies program, or at least for a handful of courses on modern Jewish subjects. In the mid-1950s at least half of the students at the University of Chicago were Jewish in some way or another, e.g., in religion, ethnicity, or culture. This had declined somewhat by the end of the 1960s, but the movements for civil rights in this country and for national liberation throughout the world had heightened ethnic and religious consciousness, and it is not surprising that a number of Jewish students at Chicago were wondering about their origins. Just as there was a disdain for "Black studies" at Chicago, however, so there was similar disdain for "Jewish studies," in spite of the large number of Jewish members of the teaching staff. In that environment, a number of Jewish students went to Kahan in his role as master of the social sciences collegiate division and requested that he do something about Jewish studies, which at Chicago went no further than the end of the biblical era. Knowing that he could not coerce others to offer courses in modern Jewish subjects, Kahan undertook to offer a course himself on the modern economic and social history of the Jews. This stimulated his work on Jewish economic and social history, some of which was published posthumously in the volume collected and edited by Roger Weiss. That work was also stimulated by his personal plan to reestablish the YIVO Institute studies on Jewish social history. During this period he served as YIVO research director—at a distance—and read papers to various conferences.

Kahan's Judaism was strictly secular. As far as I know, he never went to a synagogue and he never expressed any need for religion, of any kind. On the other hand, he was intensely Jewish. He did not teach on the High Holidays, and instead of playing tennis or continuing his research, he studiously read poetry or some other matter worthy of the solemnity of the day. He never missed a Hanukkah celebration, and expressed respect for Hasidism. He was very well versed in Jewish secular culture, which was a part of him. His native languages were Russian and Yiddish. Once we both were addressing a Jewish group in downtown Chicago on various aspects of nineteenth-century Jewish culture. While awaiting his turn, Kahan was making notes in Yiddish, writing from right to left.

The humanitarian side of Arcadius Kahan was revealed in the years he was master of the social sciences collegiate division. In 1968 one General Mieczyslaw Moczar became the de facto leader of Poland, and he resolved to eliminate all Jews from Poland. Kahan told me how he had known Moczar in 1945, when Polish nationalists under Moczar's command were hunting down the few Jews Hitler had missed. Kahan went in to see Moczar as part of a partisan group to demand that the murderers cease their activity. At the end of the 1960s, Moczar was persecuting the Jews again, and one of his intended victims was Benjamin Nadel, the sole graduate of Kahan's high school class, besides Kahan himself, to survive the Holocaust. Nadel, a world-famous specialist on the history of the Jews in the Greco-Roman world, happened to be in Paris when he was called into the Polish embassy, his passport was confiscated, and he was told that he was stateless. Kahan sponsored the immigration to the United states of Nadel, his wife, and two children, got him miscellaneous jobs and lectureships, and helped him survive the transition to life in the United States.

· III ·

The years of Kahan's mastership of the social sciences collegiate division were a disaster for his scholarship. I vividly remember going into his office on the fourth floor of the Social Sciences Building and looking at his table; it was piled about a foot high or more with books and other materials he had been using at the time he had been appointed master. All was just as he had left it about three years earlier, covered with a deep layer of dust. It was one of the most depressing sights I have ever seen in my life.

Kahan got his scholarly work under way again after leaving the mastership, but was then informed of another disaster: he had glaucoma. He was told that there was a 2 percent chance he would go blind from the glaucoma, but he expected to live a long time and feared losing his sight. Thereupon he ceased writing completely and embarked on a full-time reading program. He had a near-perfect photographic memory, and calculated that he could still write when totally blind if he had the materials stored up in his brain. (On another occasion, he told me the following about his memory: When he was about eleven, his father once came to him and said: "Arcadius, you can remember everything you ever read. Unfortunately, you did not understand anything you read. Go back and read it all over again.") So, Kahan did nothing but read for a few years. It turned out, however, to have been a false alarm: he had been misdiagnosed. He had "false glaucoma," not the real thing.

Roger Weiss put together and edited a collection of Kahan's essays entitled *Russian Economic History: The Nineteenth Century*. Historiographically, these were extraordinarily interesting. Fundamentally, the positions are those of "the Soviets" and that identified with the name of the late Alexander Gerschenkron of Harvard. The Soviets had advanced two positions, which in fact might seem somewhat contradictory: on the one hand, the economy of the Russian Empire was developing at such a pace and in such a way that the October Revolution was inevitable; but on the other hand Tsarist Russia was so incredibly backward that Soviet power can claim credit for the advancements in education and health that their propagandists like to boast about. Kahan adhered rigorously and predictably to the "Gerschenkron position" on the noninevitability of the Bolshevik triumph in 1917, trying to show that the Emancipation of 1861 was not as adverse economically to the peasants as had been previously thought, and spending considerable effort trying to show that Lenin's thesis about the impoverishment of the peasantry in the later nineteenth century was based on a mistaken count of horses. He also worked to demonstrate that the alleged early Soviet achievements in education and medical care in fact were illusory, being mere continuations of pre-1914 trends. Much of this work aroused considerable controversy among auditors and readers.

I began to teach with Kahan around the end of the 1960s. Staffing the College semi-required courses has always been a problem, one that has been especially burdensome since the 1970s as the student body of the College has grown while the administration has tried to shrink the size of the teaching staff. Meanwhile the teachers had aged, and the older ones were less willing to teach in the College. (I once had the impudence to ask the then dean of the College, Charles Oxnard, what the meaning of the College was. He responded: "The College is that unit of the University which can raise a million dollars when no other unit can.") For the course in Russian civilization, this has caused particular difficulties as the number of teachers of Russian subjects has shrunk through death, retirement, dismissal, and resignation, with few replacements. Kahan had been a stalwart in the old Social Sciences 3 and the Social Sciences 1 courses (of which he was chairman after Marvin Meyers and before Roger Weiss) and then master of the social sciences collegiate division. He was also pressed into teaching the required European Economic History survey in the department of economics. Regardless, I had the temerity to ask him to teach in the course on Russian civilization, and he agreed to teach during the Spring quarter, when the Soviet experience was dealt with. He was very popular with the students. Solzhenitsyn's volumes on the Gulag had just been published, and we were using volume 2 as one of the books in the course.

That book by Solzhenitsyn brought back horrible memories to Kahan. His friends always said he never talked about himself, but that just was not true. In connection with the volume on the Gulag, Arcadius told me about his life on the left in Vilnius before the war, where he had followed in his father's political footsteps. (His father had been a leader in the Jewish Bund before the 1917 Revolution and once abroad had been the roommate of Felix Dzerzhinskii, who after 1917 became head of the Soviet secret police, the Cheka.) In Vilnius the Communists had threatened to have young Arcadius, a Bundist-Menshevik, hanged when they got to Palestine. Instead, they got their chance to harass him after the Soviets invaded the Baltic states in 1940. He was arrested almost immediately, and held for four days in solitary confinement, in *karzer,* a wooden box covered on the bottom with excrement, in which it was impossible to stand up or sit down. When he was released, the Russian NKVD guard told him: "Ordinary people are kept in a cell, but you, you son-of-a-bitch, are in karzer!" Arcadius observed: "Where in the world but the Soviet Union would anyone say that 'ordinary people are kept in a cell'? In most countries, ordinary people are free!" From *karzer* in Vilnius, Kahan was sent by ship to the White Sea, and then walked 100 miles to the coal mines of Vorkuta, where most convicts soon died of hypertension (because of the intense cold). Kahan filed charges against his Vilnius prosecutor. The Soviets, in an inexplicable concern for "socialist legality," returned him from Vorkuta to press the charges, at which moment the Nazis attacked the Soviet Union.

Kahan never once said a word to me about what happened between the time he was returned from Vorkuta and his confrontation with Moczar, i.e., the period of the Second World War. There were all kinds of rumors which were untrue; one was that he had been in Auschwitz. He once told me, as he was about to go to Munich, that he had eschewed going there for years out of fear that he would recognize one of his old camp guards on the street; this led to speculation that he had been in Belsen, a Nazi camp near Munich. In fact, however, he spent much of the war in a Soviet prison, and, upon release, joined a detachment of Polish troops in the Soviet Union commanded by General Sigmund Berling. As Alexander Erlich, professor of Soviet economics at Columbia, mentioned at Kahan's memorial service, these had been among the troops to liberate Berlin. In the Berling army, he attained the rank of major. Years later, he was very apprehensive that the Soviets might find out who he was. Thus when visiting delegations from the Soviet Union arrived, Kahan made it very clear that no one was to tell any of the visitors who he was. He loved to talk with the visitors in Russian, and then refuse to tell them his origins. As he once put it to me, "They might then put 2 and 2 together." For that reason Kahan never visited either the Soviet Union or any of the other "socialist countries."

·   IV   ·

Kahan remained a "socialist" of some stripe to his dying day. His disdain for "Soviet socialism," on the other hand, was unrelenting, and his frequent comments about its inefficiencies have only recently become commonplaces. Over the years I came to know with great precision how he would respond to events or persons of any particular political color. When someone of a leftish persuasion was holding forth in his presence, I always looked at him to see what his reaction would be—and the same reaction was always there. He would fidget, look at his knees or feet, put a hand on a leg, sit slowly more upright, and then look around in absolute wonderment over the inanity being uttered.

As the years progressed, more graduate students came to have greater respect, esteem, and admiration for Arcadius Kahan. One thing he came to insist upon was that there was no point in any student's trying to get into the intricacies of Russian economic history without some grounding in economics. His favorite method for "enforcing" this was to have the students get an M.A. in economics, in addition to the "regular" work in history. He supported vigorously the applications of students for IREX disciplinary training grants to study economics. During the later 1970s, Kahan's attempts to raise standards met considerable resistance on the part of some students. I believe that he felt that the only way to break into the very depressed market for graduate students in Russian history was to offer a product of extraordinarily high quality. Some of the students, on the other hand, believed that it was irrational to work so hard for jobs that seemed, in all probability, nonexistent. In sum, about eighteen students got Ph.D.'s under Kahan's direction, The number certainly would have been greater had the academic market not collapsed in 1972.

Students were as distressed by Kahan's death as any of his mourners.

One young man, employed in the United States Department of State, talked with him briefly on the evening of Kahan's death, had been told to call back on the next morning for further discussion of his doctoral dissertation, and nearly fainted when he called again on Saturday morning and was told that his mentor was dead. He called me immediately in a state of shock and incredulity. Many students attended the huge funeral at the KAM Synagogue on Monday, and a number accompanied the cortege to the cemetery. I have never before or since at the University of Chicago witnessed such an outpouring of grief as there was over the unexpected death of Arcadius Kahan.

Kahan has continued to live through his writings. I spent a year editing his *The Plow, the Hammer, and the Knout*. Simultaneously I typed the text and the necessary codes for computer typesetting to keep the costs down so that the University of Chicago Press could afford to publish the 250,000-word work. In it his personality, his work habits, and his fine intellect can still be found. The volume has 333 tables, almost all of which Kahan found in various sources and presented with relatively little alteration. He accumulated little primary data himself. Unfortunately he did not worry much about recording whence he took the data, and the origin of much of the information remains unknown. Perhaps some tables he reconstructed from memory but could not remember where they came from. He also did not worry about historiography. As someone said around 1960, "Kahan never reads secondary works." While not totally correct, that was fundamentally true. The exercise of intellectual history was not for him. He also therefore did not worry about bibliography; I compiled the bibliography in *The Plow* primarily from my own library, which explains why there are few books in Western languages in it: I did not have them, so they were not included. A number of reviewers attributed this bibliographic shortcoming to Kahan, but one may be fairly certain that he had not read the works. What interested him most was making his own microeconomic interpretation of what he hoped were reliable data series, which led him in *The Plow* to the conclusion that the indivdual consumer in the market, not the state, was the crucial factor in the economy. His own microeconomic interpretation of phenomena, in the last analysis, is what Arcadius Kahan's career at the University of Chicago was primarily all about. He was a remarkable citizen, a superb and solicitous friend, a wise adviser, a conscientious administrator, but primarily he wanted to be a solid microeconomic historian. In that he succeeded.

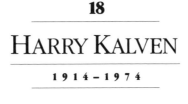

18

HARRY KALVEN

1914–1974

VINCENT BLASI

 THE FIRST WEEK of law school is for most students an intimidating experience. Everyone is so *serious*. My first week was leavened considerably by Harry Kalven. A group of students and Kalven were watching the seventh game of the 1964 World Series in the Burton-Judson Lounge. The broadcast was interrupted by a news bulletin: Nikita Khrushchev had just been deposed. Viewers were treated to several minutes of news analysis, with correspondents around the globe speculating on what this might mean for East-West relations. One of my classmates, an amateur Kremlinologist not doubt, expressed surprise: "I can't understand why they would do this now." Kalven agreed: "Yeah, in the seventh inning. This is an outrage."

Though well liked and greatly respected, Harry Kalven was not the most popular teacher in the Law School during my time as a student. Some classmates thought his classes moved too slowly, that he belabored and repeated points. Everyone warmed to his wit, his imagination, and his generous spirit, but not everyone found in Kalven's classes the crackling intellectual tension, the rigor, the sense of analytic closure that some other teachers provided. By any measure Kalven was a good, effective teacher— but was he a great one?

For me, he was more than a great teacher; he was a unique force in my education. He remains a continuing force. Other former students—practicing lawyers, law teachers, law school graduates who have made careers outside of law—tell me the same thing. His ideas stick in the mind; his personal example continues to lead. His teaching has stood the test of time. He seems a better teacher now than he did at the time. That is, in my opinion, the test by which teachers should be judged.

All the more remarkable is Kalven's staying power when one considers that he was quintessentially a man of his times, an observer, a writer and teacher at his best when responding. He wrote mostly about recent cases and issues of current public controversy. His thought seemed always in progress, seeking but never quite reaching resolution. He was interested in theories and produced a number of theoretical insights, but neither in the classroom nor in his writings did he offer anything like a systematic, well-elaborated personal perspective. He was the most creative legal thinker I have known, but his scholarship was patently, proudly, derivative. He was not, and did not try to be, a definitive thinker. Nor was he a forceful personality. He was the antithesis of a self-promoter. And yet he left his mark on his field and on his students in a way that few professors ever do.

The word that best describes Harry Kalven is "inquisitive." To him learning was a joyous, almost playful activity—not a chore, not a source of power or distinction, more an experience than a quest. His inquisitive mind observed no boundaries; he never became a prisoner of his own expertise. His work as a scholar was unforced.

Kalven wrote and taught on a diverse range of legal subjects. His first major scholarly achievement was in the field of civil procedure. In 1941, he was the co-author of an article on the class-action lawsuit that is considered by modern proceduralists to have been a breakthrough in thinking about that increasingly important subject. Early in his career he examined with Walter Blum the "uneasy case" for progressive taxation. Again with Blum, he produced a provocative, skeptical critique of the modern reform proposals for compensating victims of automobile accidents and conducted some spirited debates with various proponents of "no-fault" insurance. He wrote extensively on the subject of tort theory and edited, with Charles Gregory, one of the most thoughtful and widely used casebooks on torts. With Hans Zeisel and others Kalven conducted an ambitious empirical study of jury behavior. A valuable by-product of the jury study was a series of reflections by Kalven on the use of social science methods in the study of legal problems and institutions. Toward the end of his life, he taught a seminar on slavery. He was never superficial and he was frequently penetrating. But he liked to move on, to explore fresh terrain.

One legal subject, however, engaged him more completely and more continuously than any other. Harry Kalven never tired of thinking about the freedom of speech and he never ran out of fresh, important things to say about the subject. Seventeen years after his death, in some cases thirty years after initial publication, his writings on obscenity, legislative investigations into political beliefs, street demonstrations, and libel remain the

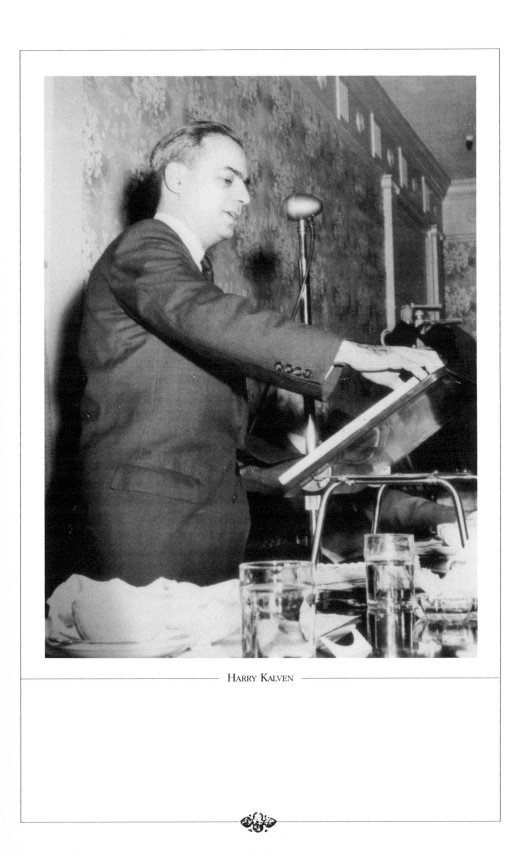

HARRY KALVEN

classic texts from which almost all subsequent work takes off. It is a fitting tribute both to the devotion he could inspire and to his significance as a scholar that his major work on the First Amendment, left unfinished at his death in 1974, was painstakingly and perceptively brought to completion by his son Jamie and published just three years ago. Astonishingly, as several reviewers have observed, the book suffers hardly at all from the circumstances of its authorship. It is a contemporary book, one that challenges and inspires today's students of the First Amendment.

What explains Harry Kalven's striking capacity to live on in the minds of his students and readers? I believe he remains so alive because he had an uncanny ability to engender creativity in others—in his students, in his readers, even I would guess in his collaborators. Driven by a genuine curiosity, he tried to enlist those around him in the search. To sit in a Kalven classroom was to be a participant, not an auditor. I was called on to recite only a handful of times, but in my mind I formulated hundreds of answers—and hundreds of questions as well—as I observed him conversing with other students. Similarly, reading a Kalven article or book is a participatory experience. One is constantly "revising" the analysis, adding new applications or refinements, imagining objections and responding to them. I suppose most teachers and authors seek this effect; few actually aspire to have the last word. But Kalven was extraordinary in his capacity to converse about law productively with persons far less knowledgeable and far less gifted than himself, and in the process to raise them toward his level. That, I believe, is why his influence persists and why his thought is not dated. He started conversations that are continuing today.

Exactly how does a gifted teacher induce his students to probe and create on their own? Is it simply by force of personal example? Or are there techniques? Can someone not blessed with a mind so fertile as Kalven's nonetheless have the pedagogic impact that he had? As a teacher who would love to do for my students what he did for me, I have pondered these questions for years.

Certainly one secret to Kalven's success was his utter lack of intellectual pretense or arrogance. He wore his considerable erudition lightly. In matters of the mind he did not seek to separate himself from others. Just the reverse. He was an intellectual populist. He did not believe that all ideas or traditions or minds were equal—he had high standards, deep commitments, and heroes—but he did believe that ordinary people could often contribute to his understanding, and not just to his understanding of them. In his writing and teaching he lavished attention on the reasoning of judges whose talents were modest and whose opinions he could easily have savaged. I doubt whether any modern legal scholar has been so generous as he was in discussing judicial opinions. And I do not think his intellectual generosity was a product of personal kindness, deference to authority, or an aversion to confrontation. He was generous with the thought of others because he believed he could learn best by appreciating and building upon the ideas that moved ordinary people.

In fact, Harry Kalven's distinctive understanding of the First Amendment may be traced to his unusual respect for the thought processes not only of ordinary persons but also of persons at the margins of the social and political culture. Kalven did not argue that dissenters ought to be tolerated; he argued that they ought to be heard. He fought tirelessly in the law journals against those who would require that acts of expression satisfy minimal standards of rationality and civility in order to qualify for First Amendment protection. He believed that the freedom of speech belongs to the inarticulate and the angry as well as to the loyal and respectful opposition. His writings abound with sympathetic translations distilling messages of social and cultural protest from expressive endeavors that others would dismiss as self-indulgent or coercive rantings. He did not think that "crackpots" and "subversives" and "extremists" deserve First Amendment protection because they are harmless. He thought they deserve protection because they have something to say that ought to be heard in a democratic society. Kalven's passion for free speech was a product of his curiosity and his humility, not of any sense of noblesse oblige.

Strong proponents of free speech are often somewhat disengaged from the struggles of their time, or sympathetic to the messages the dominant forces seek to suppress, or so rigid in their embrace of principle that they become more or less heedless of consequences. Kalven was none of the above. He wanted to hear the voices of protesters, even the voices of fanatics, precisely because he was an engaged, moderate, perceptive, and practical participant in the controversies of his day. He thought that vigorous, fundamental challenge contributes to understanding and effective adaptation.

He conducted his classroom in accordance with this belief. I have never seen a teacher work so hard to elicit the "counter-argument" to whatever idea he was proposing. He wanted the counter-arguments stated persuasively and developed with imagination and respect. Seldom have I heard the arguments for censorship presented so well as they were in his class.

His genuine interest in uncongenial ideas, his openness to challenge at the most elementary level, proved to be a pedagogic boon. He could introduce a subject more sincerely, and more spontaneously, than any teacher I have known. One classmate said of his teaching: "He begins each hour doing algebra and ends each hour doing calculus." The key point here, however, is that he found the algebra fascinating.

I took detailed notes in his torts class and uncharacteristically managed not to lose the notebook. Twenty years later I found myself teaching torts. On rereading the notes a few years after I started teaching the subject, I was struck by how simple and straightforward were Kalven's initial questions for each class period. My teaching of the subject had been more elliptical; I had truncated the introductions and jumped quickly to the hard questions and elaborate theories. One year I attempted to do it Kalven's way. I started each hour with simple, basic questions—sometimes taken straight from his notes. It didn't work. In my hands the technique was artificial; I learned that I can only teach spontaneously by moving as quickly as possible to the levels of analysis that most excite me. To my students' detriment, I did not have the patience, the fascination with basic formulations, or the curiosity about the legal culture that he possessed. The experience made me realize that Kalven's ability to think freshly—and, yes, excitedly—about some of the most familiar features of the legal landscape was one of his greatest attributes, both as a teacher and a scholar. His calculus was so sophisticated, so subtle, so original in large part because he loved his algebra so much.

One expression of his fascination with basics was his penchant for schematic exposition. A Kalven blackboard was certain to be covered with diagrams, matrices, even hand-drawn maps and pictures illustrating how an accident occurred. The practice was contagious. It became a game among my classmates to concoct new, ever more elaborate matrices, sometimes to the point of silliness. But he had the last laugh. In our lighthearted efforts to caricature Kalven's teaching style we wound up noticing relationships and making connections on our own. I had assumed that his ability to induce us to think originally through graphic emulation was an unintended by-product of his schematizing impulse. But when he sent me off to begin my own teaching career, his parting advice was: "Use visual aids." From this conversation I learned that he was, after all, a self-aware and calculating pedagogue. He employed visual aids to challenge students, not to comfort them. He simplified in order to investigate complexities and he wanted his students to do the same.

This commerce between the simple and the complex, between the beginning student and the scholar at the forefront of his specialty, was central to Harry Kalven's view of knowledge and the process of discovery. He allocated his time accordingly. One day he appeared in our First Amendment class seeming exasperated and exhausted: "Don't ever," he said "try to teach proximate cause and obscenity in the same week." An accident of scheduling had caused him to be covering the most philosophically challenging and doctrinally confusing topic in the torts course at the same time he was tackling perhaps the most perplexing segment of the First Amendment course. But he had been teaching those subjects, and writing renowned articles on them, for years. The comment revealed how hard he prepared for class each time he taught a subject, not just by considering strategies of presentation but by rethinking his views on the merits seriously enough to be tired and frustrated and confused. He may have spent his time this way out of a sense of responsibility to his students, but I think more was involved. I am convinced that to an unusual degree his writing grew out of his teaching; that he knew of no better way to grapple with a subject than to think about it with a group of students—and to do so without holding back.

People often behave in a manner that reflects the expectations others have of them. Kalven treated his students as fellow explorers. His classes were open-ended conversations. That is why some students found the class sessions insufficiently structured, the points that emerged insufficiently conclusive. But open-ended conversations have a way of continuing. And students who are treated like original thinkers tend to keep thinking for themselves. And so, Harry Kalven's teaching endures.

19

HEINRICH KLÜVER

1897–1979

SIDNEY SCHULMAN

ON AN AFTERNOON in the fall of 1950, as first-year resident in neurology at Billings Hospital, I was going over some microscopic sections from autopsied brains with my teacher and "chief," Dr. Richard Richter.

"Ah, Heinrich, come in, come in!" was Richter's greeting to the smiling, bespectacled man with arched eyebrows accenting a broad Slavic face, who appeared in the doorway of the laboratory carrying a wooden box of slides under his arm. He was about fifty, a little less than medium height, with a physical sturdiness about him which seemed somehow to defy concealment by his loose-fitting suit.

As he entered, I rose and moved to a workbench on the other side of the laboratory to wait out this interruption. Klüver, taking my seat at the table, passed his slides to Richter, who began to examine them under the microscope, exclaiming with pleased excitement about the greater precision of the staining in these than in the last batch.

Klüver fished out one of the slides himself and squinted at it as he held it up to window light, saying, "And the outer line of Baillarger—do you ordinarily see it this well?" (A century earlier, Baillarger, a French anatomist, saw for the first time two faint white lines in the gray matter as he looked with a hand-lens at a bit of unstained brain tissue pressed between two pieces of glass and held up to the light.)

"Baillarger"—the first and last syllables, stressed and rhyming, filled the room like a plucked tenor string, while the rest of what he said was barely audible. It was the first time I had heard the lilting speech of people born and raised in Schleswig-Holstein. It was beguiling, but hard to understand without some practice in it.

I was not introduced to him during that interrupted slide session, but I

HEINRICH KLÜVER

knew who he was. People who had been at the University for any length of time were likely to know of him. It was generally understood that he was a scientist who worked alone in the "old way," and whose research was unusually diverse, spreading into areas beyond what seemed to be his central interest, which was primate psychology. When pressed, however, there were few who could say much more than that.

But there was something more in our collective consciousness than this vague familiarity with Heinrich Klüver. By the end of the first decade of his forty-five years at the University, an aura of legend had come to surround him. The most apparent of the reasons for this was his immovable nonconformity. This was something that could never mar his essential dignity, nor was it just that he was odd in ways that were endearing to his friends. It was a nonconformity which shaped the whole of his unusual career, and there was a certain attractive, teasingly mysterious quality about it. For it seemed to point in the direction of its own origins without revealing them.

It was on an evening a few months later that I learned more about him, and about the new staining method he had been tinkering with. Together with a dozen or so other residents, I attended a symposium held in the private dining room of the Quadrangle Club. The participants were Stephen Rothman, professor of dermatology at the University, Warren McCulloch, a neurophysiologist at the University of Illinois, and Heinrich Klüver. The subject was "The Porphyrins"—a group of natural pigments sharing a common ring structure with a metal atom at its center. When the metal is iron, the porphyrin is either part of the hemoglobin molecule or a respiratory enzyme, depending on variations in the details of the ring. When the metal is magnesium, the porphyrin is part of the chlorophyll molecule.

Because skin lesions characterize the most common of the disorders of porphyrin metabolism, and Rothman was an authority on the biochemistry of the skin, he seemed appropriate enough, but I wondered about the credentials of the other two. It turned out that McCulloch, an old friend of Klüver's, had "come to learn," as he himself said. He acted as interlocutor for the first ten minutes, after which he was dispensable. The give-and-take between Rothman and Klüver quickly became spontaneous and lively, its direction altered occasionally by questions from the audience. Rothman had a certain proprietary tone—justified and not disagreeable. But Klüver often introduced what he said with a disclaimer about not being "a porphyrin chemist, but. . . ." What followed would be a fluent discourse on, for example, how to set up a spectrometer so as to get an accurate fluorescence emission spectrum from the porphyrin in an extract of the root nodules of a soybean plant.

That an animal psychologist might work out a new staining technique for brain tissue was all right, but what was he doing with porphyrins and soybean root nodules? It turned out that these were connected in a round-about way. For years, Klüver had been interested in hallucinations and eidetic imagery as a category of perception—perception of things not present to the senses. He had published experimental observations as monographs on each topic in the 1920s, both classics to this day. The one on hallucinations was based on his own, induced by a dose of mescal. It was later, when he began to study the pharmacology and behavioral effects of hallucinogens in monkeys, that he ran into the porphyrins. Using the only technique then available for detecting minute quantities of such drugs in tissues—absorption and fluorescence spectroscopy—he noticed incidentally that whenever he happened to focus a light beam of short wave-length on the white matter of the brain, the tissue responded with a red fluorescence. Following this up, though it had nothing to do with the drugs he was studying, he found that the spectrum of this emission was characteristic of free porphyrins, substances not previously known to be present in the nervous system.

This set in motion an enterprise which extended over ten years. Before he was done, he had examined sixty vertebrate species, including man, for free porphyrins in white matter, to say nothing of the root nodules of leguminous plants, which he studied because they were known to contain hemoglobin. But the meaning of the myriad facts turned up by all of that work remains obscure to this day.

In any case, by coincidence, while Klüver was exploring these esoterica, industrial chemists had been developing synthetic porphyrin compounds for use as dyes. With the possibility of a stain for white matter in mind, he tested the commercial products for a property he had discovered in their natural analogues—affinity for white matter. It turned out that they had it, and moreover some of them stained myelin sheaths selectively. Combined with the pale violet of a standard stain for nerve cells applied to the same tissue, the deep blue of the myelin sheaths in "Klüver preparations" makes them the most beautiful of the routine stains for nervous tissue now in use, almost half a century later—an elegant memorandum to a long study of what may turn out in the end to have been an unsurprising "leftover" of metabolism, a kind of biochemical dust.

I was formally introduced to Heinrich Klüver in 1954. The symptoms of a patient with an unusual neurological disorder had led me to think that certain behavioral observations on monkeys might help clarify a long-disputed question about the cognitive functions of a particular part of the brain. Because I had no experience in behavior research, Richter arranged for me to consult with Klüver for advice.

Receiving me at his door on the third floor of Culver Hall, he invited me in. We walked past roomy cages containing monkeys of various species, with whom he stopped to banter; areas for behavior tests partitioned off by his own carpentry; through chemistry and histology laboratories; then a large room with a conference table in the middle, loaded with stacks of books, and walls lined with shelves and oak cabinets bulging with test equipment, notebooks, and reprints; and finally a smaller room, housing together the following: a secretary at a typewriter, two noisy, brilliantly colored parrots in a cage on the top of a filing cabinet, and, in a large cage on a low table, a family of bright-eyed squirrel monkeys. There were no cartons of commercial feed for the animals, but instead, fresh produce in gunny sacks and bushel baskets. There were plants everywhere. The universal clutter, controlled, warm, cheerful, was of an earlier time, and it was not to change in the course of the next twenty-five years.

We entered his office, a small room at the northeast corner of the building, crowded with books—on the floor, on shelves, and on a central table. He moved to his desk, motioning me to the chair beside it. The desk was in a corner up against the wall so that he sat with the east window at his left, which I recognized as the solitary lighted one that I had seen for years at 10 or 11 in the evening from Hull Court below. We spoke for about an hour. He listened attentively, asking questions now and then, as I described my proposed research. When I finished, he said that it all seemed very interesting, and then changed the subject, or so it seemed at first. He spoke of the superficial character of "all that passes for research these days in biological psychology." I listened for what he thought would constitute good research, but his remarks were all negative and very general. They could be summed up by another sweeping statement I recall word for word: "Nobody seems to know what is involved in a real analysis of behavior." Clearly, this was intended to apply to me as well as everyone else.

Eventually, he said quietly, "Now as for your plan, I doubt that you will find anything." Then, gazing steadily at me, he added, "But I think you should do it. You should go ahead and do it. For now, the only advice I can give you is to keep your eyes open. If you run into problems along the way, let me know."

So I proceeded to "do it." I never did ask for specific advice, but on his frequent visits to Richter over the years (who, I came to learn, was his closest friend), he would sometimes drop in to visit me also. Contrary to his prediction, I did find some things, and he was genuinely pleased when I could show him some positive results. But I knew that they concerned nothing that he would consider fundamental; and merely from chatting with him— he was never explicitly didactic—I was coming to understand why.

The first time he visited my animal quarters, he strode up to a cage, opened the latch, raised the sliding door and thrust his arm inside, asking brusquely, "Did somebody sell you these for cages?" The large aggressive male within dashed wildly about and slapped Klüver's arm repeatedly, barking in that peculiarly formidable staccato that rhesus monkeys have. I covered my mouth to stifle a novice's "Careful, they bite!" Casually elbow- ing the animal aside, Klüver explored the interior of the cage, running his hand over the steel meshwork floor and the horizontal perch-bars at the rear. As he withdrew his arm and closed the door, he urged me to replace the flooring and perch-bars with smoothly sanded wooden boards for the animals' comfort.

He had uncanny intuition for the moods of primates. On one occasion, he asked Ted Rasmussen, head of the department of neurosurgery, and me to accompany him as "clinicians" to the Lincoln Park Zoo. Marlin Perkins, the director, had asked Klüver to look at an orangutan with symptoms of weight loss and anorexia. When we arrived, someone in Perkins's office conducted us to the basement of the primate house, where he pointed to a door, saying "Dr. Perkins and the patient are in there; go right in." Open- ing the door, we entered a large open area, where some thirty feet away, a female orang, looking quite healthy and as if she weighed at least 150 pounds, sat placidly on the floor. Perkins and an animal keeper, squatting beside her, were trying to persuade her to eat the vegetables that were scattered around. As we approached, she sprang up without warning and charged us furiously. Rasmussen and I shrank aside. I looked toward Klüver. He was standing fast, eyes narrowed to slits and fixed on the animal making directly for him. When she was within ten feet from him, he sud- denly opened his arms wide. She leaped on his chest, and as he closed his arms about her, she hugged him contentedly, arms and legs clasped about him. With the huge animal in his arms, nuzzling his neck, he turned to us, smiling, and said, "And we have not met before!"

It was the experimental psychologist, Karl Lashley, who introduced Klüver to animal research when both were at the University of Minnesota in the middle of the 1920s. In 1928 they both took positions as research psy- chologists at the Institute for Juvenile Research in Chicago. There, during a period of five years, Klüver continued an investigation he had begun at

Minnesota, which was to form the basis of his monograph *Behavior Mechanisms in Monkeys,* published in 1933 by the University of Chicago Press. In that year, both moved to the University of Chicago, Lashley, seven years Klüver's senior, as professor of psychology, Klüver as fellow in the Otho Sprague Memorial Institute. A few years later, Lashley moved to Harvard—alone, having failed in his effort to persuade Klüver to accompany him.

A problem arose after Lashley's departure. Klüver was made associate professor, but he refused to become a member of the department of psychology. This was not altogether as outrageous as it might seem. What one historian of psychology called "the great schism" between experimental psychology and the mental testing movement had not yet healed, and it was then being manifested locally. Soon after Lashley left Chicago, the psychology department came under the stewardship of L. L. Thurstone, the distinguished contributor to the mathematical theory of factor analysis, the elaboration of intelligence testing which had been introduced around 1910 by Spearman. The rest of the department consisted of three younger men, all with the same interests as Thurstone's. Thurstone, cordially and repeatedly, invited Klüver to join the department, but his overtures were expressed in terms which Klüver interpreted an envisaging Heinrich Klüver doing mental testing research. In charitable moods Klüver would grant some usefulness, even interest, to mental testing, but not that it was the proper business of biological psychology. His real view, which he generally did not hide, was that the very terms "tasks," "achievement," "scores," "abilities," and "deficits," and the whole notion of "factors" in intelligence, derived from the tests which measured them, and that all of this was "paper-and-pencil psychology," irrelevant to biology.

Eventually, the dean of the division of biological sciences, William Taliaferro, recognized, as he wrote in a note to Robert Hutchins in 1939, that placing Klüver in psychology would be impossible. It was not a personal matter, he explained, "but a fundamental difference in . . . viewpoint which involves the entire concept of psychology and of biological science." The matter was settled by making him professor of experimental psychology in the division of biological sciences. In addition to his research he was expected to give at least one seminar course for graduate students in the division. Whether he would wish to take on candidates for the doctorate was left up to him.

As far as I know, Heinrich Klüver never did supervise a doctoral candidate, but for many years he gave a seminar course limited to six graduate students. Twice weekly they gathered around a table in his laboratory. He would speak for about an hour on some topic in psychology, anatomy, or physiology—announced, together with suggested readings, at the preceding session—and then conduct an informal discussion for another hour. The last few weeks were reserved for oral presentations by the students on topics of their own choosing. There were no time limits on these, but he warned the students that he would question them for as long as they took to speak.

Intimidated at first by premonitions of harshness, the students were surprised by his gentleness. He took a personal interest in them, which lasted long after the course was over. Tension did creep into the sessions devoted to the student papers, which were expected to be thoughtful and fresh. The greater the verbiage covering over a mere catalogue of information, the more unnerving were his questions, and a very occasional student who thought to conserve energy by presenting a warmed-over paper from another course would be recognized forthwith and reduced to a pitiable state.

I did not take that course myself. My account is from the reminiscences of others who did. I would guess that all of them heard him say things from time to time which they did not comprehend, but that few would make any special point of this. For it would be natural to attribute it reverentially to the breadth of the professor's scholarship. He seemed to have read everything on any subject that happened to come up. When he suggested a book or paper to a student because of its relation to the student's interest, he would give a masterly summary of its content on the spot.

But there were some exceptions. A few of his students, more self-assured and independent-minded than usual, have told me such things as, "Klüver was somebody I just didn't get," and "I tried to read his *Behavior Mechanisms* book, but I couldn't see what he was getting at."

If speaking of that kind of experience was rare among students, it was not altogether unusual among his contemporaries. "Heinrich is not always easy to understand, and it's not just his accent," was a familiar remark. But the "not always" is important. He did not go around perversely speaking in riddles. A cryptic quality did crop up now and then at meetings and seminars in which he participated as an extemporaneous discussant, but not tiresomely. On the contrary, he was sought after in that role for his gift for fresh associations, and for touches of an almost zany, yet dignified and pointed, whimsy.

There is really only one place where "what is he getting at?" is likely to come up more than a few times, where Klüver's originality is at its most relentless: the monograph on *Behavoir Mechanisms in Monkeys.* True, he made other contributions in experimental psychology which were landmarks in the usual sense. The studies already mentioned on toxic visual hallucinations and eidetic imagery became "ur-texts" for the renewed legitimacy of talking and theorizing about, and experimenting on, imagery. A later work on the monkey occipital lobes settled an issue about the cortical visual area which dated back to the nineteenth century. His most famous discovery was made in 1938; this was the "Klüver-Bucy syndrome" in monkeys following removal of the temporal lobes (Paul Bucy, his friend and a neurosurgeon at the University, did all the animal surgery for him in this research). His analysis of the behavior of those animals revealed for the first time the nature of the cognitive functions dependent on the temporal lobes, and it formed the groundwork for a vast amount of research by several succeeding generations of anatomists and physiologists.

But behind these efforts there was something quite different from them but which made them possible, certainly insofar as they were to be accomplished by Heinrich Klüver—and, it is arguable, by anyone else; for the Klüver-Bucy syndrome, for one—visual agnosia in monkeys—had already been seen in 1888 by two British investigators who disposed of it with a single sentence: "It was a condition resembling idiocy." To characterize that special ground in the most general way: it was a viewpoint that was unique, and it is embodied in the monograph on *Behavior Mechanisms.*

The greater part of the book, some 290 pages, is a meticulously detailed account of his observations over a period of five years on fourteen monkeys of five species, and a lemur. They were his subjects in a vast number of behavior tests of his own design. This core of observations is preceded by an introductory chapter of 15 pages, and followed by a concluding chapter of 55 pages, entitled, respectively, "The General Problem of Behavior Mechanisms" and "Discussion of the Results in the Light of Various Problems." Neither of these is quite what one expects, no matter how vague one's expectations may be. The most striking things about them at first are the arresting remarks that spice the text, and the strangeness of some of the issues raised, considering that this is a book about monkeys. Here are a few examples.

We are not interested in the fact that there is such a thing as behavior.

Many investigators have raised that question as to . . . whether a given animal . . . is capable of abstracting "triangularity *per se*" or "form *per se.*" Such a thing as a response to "form *per se*" cannot be discovered anywhere; it has no psychological existence.

If an animal responds differentially to stimuli which are identical in all respects except one, it is wrong to consider the stimulus difference the only factor which, on the objective side, is operating in bringing about the consistency of response.

The smaller-than relation in the objective sense exists not only when we deal with rectangles or circles of decreasing size but also when the size series contains objects as different as a dog and a cloud.

It is of fundamental importance to recognize, first of all, that there must be some properties capable of rendering similar or equivalent such different stimuli as the face of a woman, a melody, a rhythm, a "nonsensical" configuration of lines, a word, and a landscape.

It is of course nonsensical to say on the one hand that what counts in determining our response to a number of "red" stimuli is an "objective" property and to say on the other hand that what counts in determining our response to the stimuli we have termed "aggressive" or "energetic" are "subjective impressions."

Some of these remarks reflect the polemical tone which runs through the whole text—and in a peculiarly pitiless way, because there is no bother about the identity of its targets. These, it turns out, are all of the traditions of the psychology of the time—behaviorism, functionalism, structuralism, Gestalt psychology, and the rest. They are scarcely mentioned, but none escapes. It was not just a way of talking when he spoke to me of the triviality of "everything that passes for research in psychology," and the universal ignorance of what is involved in a "real analysis of behavior."

"A real analysis of behavior"—what he meant by this, and what was to be gained by it—is the soul of the book, but there is no single place where it is spelled out, and doing this for oneself is not a straightforward business. The text moves freely and unpredictably between the abstract and concrete, with the relation between them not always obvious. Moreover, what I take to be the truly ultimate goal of a "real analysis of behavior" is merely hinted at.

The point of departure is simple enough—starkly simple: a stage swept clean. What was so casually and completely rejected is replaced by an enormous number and variety of experimental observations on perception and tool-use, all carried out according to a single method. He called it the "method of equivalent and non-equivalent stimuli." The bare, noncommittal notion of "equivalent stimuli" is applied without exception to what everyone else called "generalization." For Klüver, contrary to everyone from Ivan Pavlov to the Gestalt psychologist Wolfgang Köhler and, later, to the builders of learning machines, to call one kind of behavior "differentiation" or "discrimination," and another "generalization" or "abstraction," tells us nothing.

The already old observation and others like it, that an animal who has learned to select the larger of two rectangles will reject it in favor of one still larger, were the focus of a proud enlightenment in the psychology of perception which began around the turn of the century. The stimuli—so the prevailing doctrine ran—constitute a series arranged according to a single ordering principle, which determines the organism's response.

For Klüver, such behavioral facts tell us little, least of all that the stimuli constitute such a series. It is always possible to alter the situation so that the larger-than relation, for example, though still present, no longer determines the response. Only certain things, not all things, larger than something else are selectively responded to. So a "generalization" is always at the same time a "differentiation," and we cannot say that what determines the response to the larger is a single ordering principle. What must be looked for is not what happens in the presence of a conveniently limited set of stimuli differing along a single dimension, but what continues to happen in "the presence of hundreds of other stimuli," varying along multiple dimensions. Only then would we have "a *typical* response," and hence "a matter of systematic interest." What is important is not that an animal "abstracts" and "generalizes," but that it does so in certain directions and not others.

The practical import of this was that the work involved would have to be prodigious, especially with Klüver's daemonic inventiveness in concocting stimulus variations. This reached a pinnacle when, in studying responses to weight relata by having a monkey pull in, by means of an attached string, one of two boxes differing in weight, he placed live rats of different color and markings in little cages attached to the boxes, switching the rats randomly between the boxes from trial to trial.

From the title of his concluding chapter, "Discussion of the Results in the Light of Various Problems," one expects some discussion of the significance of some of his findings. But his observations, he says, are preliminary, not systematic enough to justify discussing them individually. In effect, he announces at the beginning that he will leave it to the reader to decide what some of them might mean in relation to "various problems," which he proceeds to expound independently.

At things stand, there are some connections to be made. To take just one of them: he trained his animals to pull in a box all the way if the illumination of the opal glass geometrical figure on its front side remained steady, and to stop pulling it in if the figure suddenly began to flicker as they pulled. The animals consistently quit pulling whenever the flickering began, regardless of variations in size, form, brightness, color, and in the flicker-frequency of the figure. But when, not the figure, but the light-bulb illuminating the entire room began to flicker, though they noticed this and were startled by it, they did not stop pulling in the box. Here was a series of stimulus situations objectively ordered according to a "single principle." But more than a single principle was at work in the animals' responses. The sensory manifold was organized in such a way that a luminous figure was one thing, and the light-bulb illuminating the room was another, each with its own properties.

The real point of this—to which the objection to the single-ordering-principle thesis is a corollary—is that the ordering of sense impressions is not given along with them, or in some way by them. It is a function of an active process in the perceiving subject. The "field theory" of the Gestalt psychologists was wrong in requiring nothing but a passive sensibility. Klüver says picturesquely, "the perceptual world does not inflict itself upon us as a series of ever-changing pictures." It has an "organization which cannot be understood without reference to some form of autonomous activity in the reacting organism."

There is another side to this, which, to me, is a marvel of suppleness. With all of his positivist stringency in barring the logical presuppositions of "generalization" and "abstraction" from the psychology of perception, Klüver without warning turns around and takes certain aspects of behavior entirely at their face value. The change in attitude is so extreme that it hinders taking what he seems to be saying as what he means. But here the language—at least in places—is quite direct, and it concerns a fundamental aspect of his views. He thought it was nonsense to disallow, even methodologically, subjective experience in animals, certainly when it comes to monkeys. He speaks insistently about the "phenomenal properties" of things, by which he means simply what things look like to a monkey. It is these, not the "objective properties," to which a monkey responds. An interest in monkey behavior, then, implies an interest in something inaccessible, the monkey's phenomenal world. That this problem is not the psychologist's fault does not exempt him from facing it as squarely as he can. Neither is it his fault that all he can do is "juggle objective properties and observe responses," and proceed to make reasonable judgments. Klüver extended this viewpoint to the whole general character of the monkey world. A few minutes spent in watching a monkey explore things are enough for the observer to know that it is a world of spatio-temporal objects.

So the phenomenal world of a monkey is a world of objects—objects in space and time, distinct from the subject perceiving them. The same statement for humans is, from any ordinary standpoint, a banality—and in regard to monkeys, not really startling either. But for Klüver—in regard to both organisms—it was something quite strange, not understood, something to be inquired into. This is what I take to be the hinted at, Klüverian ultimate problem of biological psychology, or perhaps better, its ideal problem, with a solution to be approached, and in the nature of things never quite achieved. But in the approach to it, questions never otherwise asked come to the fore, questions which are relevant also, and indispensably, to problems not that close to the most elementary borders of inquiry.

The experimental observations in *Behavior Mechanisms* did not yield discoveries. They were instead validations of a point of view about the nature of the problems in a peculiar domain of the biological sciences. It is peculiar because its subject-matter is not merely the physiology of the nervous system, but the relation of that to awareness of a world of objects in space and time. It is a domain in which science cannot turn its back on subjective experience.

I came to understand about this enough to wonder how it was that one experimental psychologist thought about behavior in such ways. No doubt, there were people among his contemporaries who could answer that question, but I did not know them. Richter, his friend of many years, could not. Nor could any of the neuropsychologists I knew who were better acquainted personally with Heinrich Klüver than I was.

Richter died in 1971, a very sad event for Klüver and for me—the loss of a dear friend for him, and a friend and teacher for me, a teacher for twenty years, an impossible duration unless the teacher never acts like one. For Heinrich, I became a poor substitute for Richter. Heinrich, whose wife had died in 1967, was by that time quite alone. They did not have children, and they had no family in the United States. From time to time, he would invite me to lunch at the Quadrangle Club, which he always otherwise had in his office alone.

Our conversations on those occasions were rarely about himself and not often about monkeys or behavior. He preferred to talk about people. This notoriously reclusive man knew personally an astonishing number of anatomists, physiologists, neuropsychologists, and neurological clinicians all over the world. He knew their personal characteristics, their interests, and the course of their careers. He was fond of many of them, and I was struck by how much more their human qualities counted for him than their achievements. He relished telling occasional gossipy stories, always frustratingly withholding the names of the characters.

I learned only a little from him about his own past. After surviving the unspeakable experience of three years as a German soldier on the western front in the First World War, he went to graduate school, first at the University of Hamburg, then Berlin, and finally Stanford University, where he received his doctorate in experimental psychology. He did not speak much about his teachers in psychology, the most famous of whom were William Stern at Hamburg and Lewis Terman at Stanford. Ironically, both, but primarily Terman, had strong interests in mental testing. He greatly admired Karl Lashley, his colleague of the early years. There was one man, however, to whom he referred regularly whenever our talk bordered on the topic of early influences on him. He was the philosopher Ernst Cassirer. "Those wonderful lectures of Cassirer's at Hamburg on the philosophy of science" were clearly a treasured memory for him.

For me, his speaking of them turned out to be the key. In his book *Substance and Function*—which preceded his later works in the philosophy of culture, symbolism, and linguistics—Cassirer traced the changes in classical logic that were required for a natural science which had to go beyond biological taxonomy. In the process, he soon landed in the realm of the sensory and intellectual processes involved in perception—the factors involved in the relation between "knowing and being," or "subject and object." From a thousand angles he discussed the error of applying the "logical theory of abstraction" to perception, the inadequacy of a merely passive receptivity, and the necessity of ordering processes within the knowing subject, without which the cognition of an objective world— objects as distinct from the sense data which constitute their raw material—would be incomprehensible. The "object" and "objectivity" have no meaning apart from these conditions of their cognition.

These were Kantian ideas translated into modern idiom by a distinguished Kant scholar. If at lunch the thought of speaking to me of Immanuel Kant ever occurred to Heinrich Klüver, no doubt he rightfully dismissed it as futile. But he did not always keep such matters to himself. In a letter to Klüver in 1951, Karl Lashley, then at the height of his fame as the leading American comparative neuropsychologist, relates the difficulties he was having in trying to write a neurological theory of the experience of time intervals, difficulties which made him remember Klüver's comments of long ago on the "helpfulness of training in philosophy" and which made him "bewail" his own lack of "philosophical background." He also bewailed his separation from Klüver: "I was always astounded at the scope of your reading and your phenomenal grasp of it," he wrote. "I may have stimulated your interest in physiological psychology, but you did more to educate me in the field than did anyone else, and I regret the untimely termination of that education before it was completed."

There are not many such explicit evidences of the attraction which philosophy had for Klüver. A few others—all of them expressing or referring to Kant's philosophy of cognition—turn up in his own numerous informal comments at ten transcribed meetings of the Cybernetics Society, where he was a kind of gadfly. In one of them, during an informal discussion on ideas experienced during dreams, he related one of his own in which a dreamed event evoked as a further content of the dream itself the Kantian idea of "the synthetic unity of the manifold." The dream occurred, he said, "at a time when I worked every day with Java monkeys and in spare moments thought about the principles of Kantian philosophy."

Another, more directly functional in a verbal exchange, and unmistakably Kantian though Kant is not mentioned, was evoked by a talk by a physicist on the design of a proposed machine capable of forming concepts from its "experience." The principles of its function involved statistical analysis of the signals it received. Klüver—I imagine him quite provoked—rose to say, "I wish to get one thing clear. Do you imply that what you have described is really involved and occurs in human thinking?" When the speaker, with some hedging, replied in the affirmative, Klüver continued, "Does the concept of 'chair' come down to a sort of statistical consideration of its components? Experience enters only because we can catch it by means of schemata. What are these schemata? And are we to say that the very schemata by means of which we catch experience in turn are influenced by experience?"

Setting aside the uncharacteristic ellipsis and infelicity of wording, which I take to reflect his exasperation over something he considered preposterous, it would be impossible to consider this as coming from anyone who had not been immersed in Kant's first Critique. First there is Kant's difficult concept of "the schematism of the understanding" brought to bear here—in right-on-the-button fashion—and then the indignant reference to the speaker's violation of the logic of the Kantian "condition of experience," which cannot itself be influenced by experience

I am no more an expert on present-day kinds of artificial intelligence than on those of 1951, when that exchange occurred, nor on the "cognitive psychology" of the present era. But things have changed considerably since then. Both movements now refer to Donald Hebb's *Organization of Behavior* of 1949 as the general model for brain mechanisms of cognition and thinking, and Hebb was one of the few neuropsychologists whose theories Klüver admired. To make the connections specific: in the pages of Hebb's book, we get what amounts to the spelling out in nerve networks of Kant's insistence on the fundamental distinction between sensation and thought (thought = Klüver's "autonomous suprasensory factors"), and on the absolute necessity of a working partnership of both, to account for any awareness of an objective world.

This is really a notion with an ancient history, as the grand sweep of Cassirer's account tells us—announced by Plato, diluted by Aristotle, discarded by the empiricists of the Enlightenment, and finally in roundabout, stepwise fashion, revived and reinstated, so that, as Cassirer says, psychology will start at the beginning again.

Being face-to-face with someone whose ideas he thought were wrong never stopped Heinrich Klüver from being candidly critical then and there, usually playfully, sometimes caustically. But for his friends, no one could have been more kind or genuinely caring. When one of them, Stephen Polyak, the great student of the anatomy of the vertebrate visual system, died in 1955, leaving unfinished the manuscript of his 1400-page book on the subject, Klüver, fulfilling a voluntary promise in an act of immense selflessness, shelved his own work for more than two years to finish Polyak's.

For the few people who worked for him over the years as secretary and technician, he was warmly considerate. "Sweet" was the word they used of him. It was comfortable yet zestful to be in his company. He was guileless and unaffected, his humor was lively and imaginative, his talk widely informed but plain, not stiltedly elevated.

It is hard for scientists to concede that there are questions about nature which science cannot answer. Those who do are prone to depreciate the status of such questions—to call them "nonscientific," "metaphysical," or "meaningless." But for Heinrich Klüver, it was the primitive, elementary questions that counted most, among them those which he knew could not be answered. He was one of that special strain of scientists who are explicitly aware of the heuristic character of such questions, of the way they broaden the vision of science and extend the possibilities of explanation.

That view of science is likely to lead to a lonely existence. Heinrich Klüver was a warm and deeply human man who yet, in his work, lived in that cold and barren place at the edge of the known, unsheltered by anything taken for granted. It was an existence that he chose and loved.

20

FRANK H. KNIGHT

1 8 8 5 – 1 9 7 2

J A M E S   M.   B U C H A N A N

FOR THOSE WHO swelled the ranks of graduate economics at the University of Chicago immediately after the Second World War, as well as for many who came before us, Frank Knight dominated the intellectual atmosphere. Other professors instructed us, but it was Frank Knight who captured our interest and who seemed, to most of us, to epitomize the spirit of the university. We were stamped with a different logo: One that we display in the small imitative gestures and attitudes that we carry with us, even after almost a half century.

· I ·

What was there about Frank Knight that made him so different from his peers, at Chicago or anywhere else, and at any time or place? David Hume, whose challenges to established ideas guaranteed his own exclusion from academic employment in eighteenth-century Scotland, was the person whom Frank Knight most closely resembled. The two shared a willingness to question any authority, whether scientific, moral, aesthetic, or institutional. It is perhaps not surprising that Knight proved too persistent a querent for the philosophers at Cornell, who actively orchestrated his initial transfer into economics.

To Frank Knight nothing was sacrosanct, not the dogmas of religion, not the laws and institutions of social order, not the prevailing moral norms, not the accepted interpretations of sacred or profane texts. Anything and everything was a potential subject for critical scrutiny, with an evaluative judgment to be informed by, but ultimately made independently of, external influence. The Knightian stance before gods, men, and history embodies a courage and self-confidence that upsets the self-satisfied propounders of all the little orthodoxies, then and now.

FRANK H. KNIGHT

If there are no exemptions from critical inquiry, if there are no absolutes, in science, morals, religion, politics, how, then, does the skeptic
keep his bearings? Frank Knight resolved this central question for himself,
for me, and for many others by resort to three words. The principle of the
"relatively absolute absolutes," which was repeatedly invoked by Knight,
can be almost magical in its ability to keep the skeptic from the abyss. This
principle stakes out a position between that of epistemological, moral, and
cultural relativism at the one extreme and the related absolutisms at the
other. To those who raise the relativist accusation, the relatively absolute
absolutist can respond: "I acknowledge that there may exist relatively absolute absolutes. By this I mean that there may exist certain precepts, rules,
codes, laws, interpretations, explanations, etc. that, for the purposes of getting on with the business of ordinary living, including that of inquiry in the
academy, we may want to accept as if they are absolute. But this is emphatically not the same stance as that which exempts some of these ideas
from our ultimate critical scrutiny."

Critical intelligence matched by the courage to challenge authority—
these are the human faculties that are most desperately needed, and these
are the faculties that seem so scarce in the observed discourse that ultimately guides our action. Most of us, most of the time, are fools, in the
literal meaning of the term, and the greatest of these are to be found in
positions of intellectual and academic leadership. Our aim is to expose
error more than to discover and propound new truths, and the precaution-
ary warning must be: Beware of the gospel, no matter when and by whom
proclaimed. Frank Knight was a radical critic, who exhibited little respect
for the "classical," whether in Greek philosophy or in British political
economy. We should, indeed, pay attention to those whose ideas have
been influential, but our objective is to learn from their errors, not to cele-
brate their final achievement of truth.

How did this critical spirit come to be located in time and place?

· II ·

Frank H. Knight was a product of middle America, of the agricultural
economy of Illinois, of the late nineteenth century, of evangelical Christianity. His teenage escape from the large family of McLean County Knights
was an extension of "education" in a fledgling "American University" in
East Tennessee. By the time this institution failed two years later, Knight
had become its star student, an assistant instructor in mathematics and a
part-time administrator. He was then forced to seek employment in the
real world for some time before returning to the academy, this time to en-

roll in a church-related college, Milligan, still located in East Tennessee, where he joined his earlier mentor, Frederick Kershner, who exerted considerable influence on the development of Knight's early ideas. As he had done before, during his years at Milligan (1908–11), Knight assumed several roles—student, teacher, and administrator. His interests covered the whole limited curriculum, but with some emphasis on chemistry and German. Poverty joined proximity to keep him in Appalachia as the academy still beckoned, and he next commenced graduate work at the University of Tennessee where he worked in German literature. (Precisely thirty-six years later, in 1948, I met an ancient emeritus professor of history while walking on the Knoxville campus. He recalled Frank Knight in these words: "A brilliant young man, but too pessimistic, too much influenced by Schopenhauer.")

After Tennessee, he entered Cornell University as a graduate student to study graduate philosophy, only to be shunted off into economics, where he was more than welcome in a discipline that was just achieving its American independence. Frank Knight once told me, personally, that the only economist from whom he learned much was Allyn Young, with whom he worked at Cornell. Knight's dissertation, which, as revised, became *Risk, Uncertainty, and Profit* (1921) is, even now, accorded status as a seminal study.

In one sense, however, this initial work is Knight's only book. The later books, which really indicate his abiding critical interests more adequately by some of their very titles—*The Ethics of Competition* (1935), *The Economic Order and Religion* (1945), *Freedom and Reform* (1947), *Intelligence and Democratic Action* (1960)—are collections of essays or lectures. But the early book, *Risk, Uncertainty, and Profit,* established Knight as an economist in the intellectually stimulating times of the 1920s and early 1930s. There were two early years at Chicago, 1917–19, followed by a stint at the University of Iowa, where he wrote some of his most provocative critical essays. As a final move in a strictly academic career, Frank Knight shifted again to the University of Chicago in 1927. He remained a part of the Chicago academic community until his death in 1972.

· III ·

There seems relatively little in this biographical account to suggest the origins of the intense critical spirit. To return to my original question: "Why was Knight so different from his peers?" my hypothesis is that he can be explained, phenomenologically, only through recalling his roots in evangelical Christianity. Only through an early experience of having wrestled with God, the source of the ultimate putative authority, and having at least held his own in the encounter, Frank Knight had no difficulty at all in taking on any or all of the lesser gods, as variously represented in the many small dogmas of science, art, politics, and history. His fascination with theological issues throughout his life can, I think, be explained by his implied acknowledgment that God had proved, indeed, to be the most difficult adversary to be faced. If man can use his own critical intelligence in wrestling God to a draw, why should he cower before any other claim to authority?

Why were the representatives of the several monastic orders so attracted to Knight's classroom lectures? Surely they considered attendance a test of faith. If they could return with their faith unshaken after listening to Frank Knight's railleries, they would indeed have measured up.

If I interpret Frank Knight correctly, he was driven by his own intellectual embarrassment at having at one time in his life been ensconced in a faith that no longer seemed remotely plausible. (Professor Donald Dewey, who has worked extensively with the source materials relevant to Knight's early years, and notably his years in church-related schools in Tennessee, differs from my interpretation here. Dewey concludes that Knight was a skeptic from the start.) He was, in any case, sufficiently self-confident to predict that his own lapses were by no means idiosyncratic. He criticized others by way of celebrating his own achievement of intellectual freedom while, at the same time, warning the unwary of the pitfalls of authority. No function of the academy could be more important than the exposure of error, and all who knew Frank Knight recall his frequent reference to Josh Billings' comment to the effect that "it isn't ignorance that does the most damage, but knowin' so derned much that ain't so."

The problems of social order were those that emerge from failures to apply and use our critical intelligence; they are emphatically not amenable to the solutions of science. The continuing task is defined as coming to agreement on the set of rules that constrain our behavior toward one another, and the ethical norm is best described by analogy to sportsmanship in games, playing by the rules, again with the rules in existence accepted as relatively absolute absolutes. Rule-making was to be distinguished from play within the rules. Frank Knight was not a "game theorist," as such, nor was he a "constitutional economist," as these terms apply to research programs too recent for his active participation. But he would surely have applauded both the positive search for solutions to varying game-like interactions and the analysis of alternative sets of rules for social organization.

· IV ·

Frank Knight was perhaps at the zenith of his influence around the time of the University of Chicago's semicentennial. For a period of a quarter century, his intellectual presence helped to shape the spirit of the quadrangle and his influence extended, selectively, to the far corners of the academic world. (His works were required reading at the London School of Economics, where he was, I am sure, much better known than at Harvard.) But Knight was very much a man of the academic cloth; he did not succumb to the temptations that destroy the minds of so many of his peers in the social sciences, especially in economics. He remained within the ivory tower; he did not provide consulting services, to private or public agencies.

Aside from his lifelong struggle to keep romantic nonsense from taking precedence over the truth that only emerges from hard thinking, Knight was not a crusader for this or that cause. He resisted taking on the arrogance of academic office that converted "others" into the clay that was to be molded on one's own potter's wheel, even in the realm of discourse. Frank Knight could never have joined those of the self-selected elite who, in idea or practice, seek to plan, steer, or direct the lives of those who are excluded. He was a classical liberal, not because he predicted that only with widespread individual liberty would desired results be generated, but because the liberal order is required to allow individuals, all individuals, to define their own objectives. It is not surprising that Frank Knight opposed Roosevelt's New Deal, Keynesian-inspired macromanagement of the national economy and any and all proposals for socialist planning.

We should note, however, that these were the prevailing orthodoxies that described the 1930s, 1940s, and 1950s, the three decades that spanned Frank Knight's middle years. During these times his critical focus was necessarily on arguments advanced in defense of politicization, of extension of coercive powers of government. In this context, it is useful to recall that, in the 1920s, Knight aimed some of his most acute critical barbs at those who, blindly, defended market capitalism or free enterprise without recognizing the ethical dimension. Had Frank Knight lived to observe the collapse of socialism, in idea and in reality, his critical fire would surely have been once again redirected, and he would have centered his attacks on those latter-day pundits who would deny the very existence of the moral-ethical elements of market capitalism, elements which, at least in part, made the socialist century possible.

Knight earned his credentials as an economist. His early book clarified the understanding of the competitive model of economic process, including the identification of profit as the distributional return to those who bear uncertainty. He wrote a seminal paper that proved precursory to the much later emergence of the economics of property rights. He also advanced the understanding of the Ricardian model, and he participated in an inconclusive, if heated, controversy with the Austrians over capital theory. But the embroidered nuances on the edges of economic theory were much less challenging to him than the larger issues in moral and social philosophy, upon which the economist could, indeed, say something of relevance. Especially during his Chicago years, Frank Knight's important essays are to be classified, in subject matter, as well outside economics, even of that time. And it was during those years, and especially later, that economics, as a discipline, was to become less rather than more philosophical. As economists came to be captured both by the fascination of mathematical manipulation and by the technology of computational possibilities, they had less time for serious consideration of the issues addressed by Knight, who objected, and strenuously, to the "scientification" of his disciplinary base. Analytical rigor was not to be equated with conversion into symbolic language, and the reality of human interaction was far too complex for much to be learned from the empirical testing of hypotheses analogous to the procedures that describe the activities of the physical scientists.

· V ·

Unfortunately, the philosophical economics of Frank Knight was not to be kept alive by his rearguard criticisms of the developing orthodoxies. As a result, his penetrating critical essays found increasingly smaller numbers of readers, both at Chicago and elsewhere. Knight's sort of analysis, interesting as it might be, simply did not fit into any research program. It is an intellectual tragedy that modern economists, always busy students, and research scholars know little or nothing of this great man's work.

Although approached always from the perspective of the economist, Knight's subjects were within a broadly defined moral philosophy, and his influence might have been expected to be great among those who professed specialized competence in this ancient inquiry. Again, however, the time was out of joint. Professional philosophy, during Knight's most productive years, was itself passing through its empty phase, only to escape partially in the 1970s, when Rawls and Nozick sparked a rebirth of interest in substantive issues. Frank Knight's essays of the early mid-century would have surely found more receptive readers among the philosophers of today than during the years in which they were published.

I noted earlier that Frank Knight stamped us with a different logo. Let me clarify what I mean here. We accepted Knight as a model of sorts; we sought to be like him in that we sought to achieve a competence to criticize anything and everything, including the ideas of Frank Knight himself. This relationship is totally different from that which describes the student's attitude toward a master, from whom he has learned the gospel and to whom all authority is granted. Discipleship, which describes the student-master relationship, was entirely absent from our linkage to Frank Knight. I could not imagine a Knight student looking for answers to questions by consulting the text as written by Knight, or defending a proposition, in argument, by reference to the word, as spoken by the master. (Indeed, Knight had little or no respect for his own prior statements. He refused to go back and read anything he had previously published, and he commenced each new essay from scratch, as it were. This explains, in part, the appearance of considerable redundancy in the arguments of the separate essays.) The heritage that Frank Knight gave to those of us who would, and could, take it was a critical attitude; it was not a set of propositions, whether these be scientific or ideological.

· VI ·

I have classified Frank Knight as "Chicago's critical spirit"; I have said little about the man himself. But the qualities that made such a spirit possible also allow some predictions to be made about the person who possessed it. Frank Knight was, at base, a pessimist. He observed the behavior of fools, and he expected relatively little by way of improvement or reform. But he tempered his pessimistic predictions with hope that the application of only a modicum of shared intelligence could put most things right. The apparent emotional tranquillity that could be observed alongside the pessimistic perspective stemmed from the absence of any sense of personal responsibility for the behavior of others than himself. He found no cause for the despair about the course of world events that destroyed the balance of so many of his academic peers. The world was not there waiting to be "saved" by his own efforts, and he would have steadfastly refused to give advice to a reforming despot. Frank Knight was happy in his role; he had found his niche. His self-assigned task was to expose the absurdities of others and nothing more. Would that other academicians could be so humble!

I knew Frank Knight first as a graduate student, but as one a bit more equal than others. An affinity was established based on our shared rural upbringings, along with a Tennessee connection. As a result, I was a one-way beneficiary of many hours of good conversation that ranged from ships and sealing wax through the off-color stories that he enjoyed immensely. He also enjoyed his sherry spiked with peach brandy, and we shared an admiration for the sometimes gloomy poetry of Thomas Hardy. There was always a hint of righteous anger mixed with the bemusement of the cynic in Frank Knight, but there was also an earthiness that removed any sense of social distance. And, yes indeed, Frank Knight did sell off his reprints at varying prices, determined by relative supply and demand. Years later, at the University of Virginia, when I was a host departmental chairman for an extended Knight visiting stint, there was no discernible shift in our relationship. To Frank Knight, there were no members and nonmembers to be treated differently by rank or status.

I shall end this piece with a story that, to me, illustrates Chicago's critical spirit better than almost anything else. "And lo! Ben Adhem's name led all the rest." For most of us who recall this line at all, it would invoke high school memories of some early Victorian poetry. But Frank Knight could not turn off his persistent critical mind, which was always accompanied by a twinkle in his eye and with a bit of the jester about him. So his entry into class one day commenced with the statement: "Abou Ben Adhem, his name led all the rest. Why shouldn't it, it begins with 'Ab'?"

21

TJALLING C. KOOPMANS

M A R T I N   J.   B E C K M A N N

· I ·

 TJALLING C. KOOPMANS (Tjalling to his friends, TCK to his subordinates) would have chuckled or frowned at the idea of this essay. He eschewed publicity, he did not want to be fussed about. He also intimated that on occasions he felt like an outsider in the department of economics at the University of Chicago. In the 1950s he had become increasingly unhappy with life in Chicago. It was he who carefully arranged the departure of the Cowles Commission from Chicago to Yale in 1955. But when all is said, it was in Chicago that he did the work for which he received the Nobel Prize in 1975. While productive throughout his academic life, it was during the years from 1944 to 1955 in Chicago that he achieved his most innovative and path-breaking contributions to economic analysis and statistical methodology. Scientifically—not financially—these were the golden years of his life.

I will focus on TCK in Chicago. It was my good fortune to be a fellow member of the Cowles Commission for Research in Economics from 1951 to 1955 and of the Cowles Foundation at Yale from 1956 to 1959, and to work directly under TCK from 1951 to 1954. This means that I have known TCK mainly from the "frog's perspective."

Tjalling C. Koopmans was born in 's Graveland, the Netherlands, a small village in the Friesian part of Holland (near Hilversum) on August 10, 1910, TCK was the very image of a Friesian Dutchman: tall, lean, forthright and deliberate in speech, manner, and action.

His father was principal of the local Protestant school. TCK has described his early years and his intellectual development in an essay for the Nobel Prize volume of 1975, copies of which he gave to his friends. I am taking the liberty of quoting from this.

When the oldest son was already receiving a university education while the second sought training in engineering, the family in general, and I in particular, were fortunate indeed when at the age of 14 I was awarded a study stipend by the St. Geertruidsleen of Wijmbritseradeel in the Dutch province of Friesland from where my parents originated. . . . The Geertruidsleen has supported my studies up to my 26th birthday. I shall be forever grateful for its support, which gave me financial and therefore intellectual independence and the opportunity to explore various fields of knowledge before settling down to the particular combination of fields to which my efforts have been devoted since.

I went to the University of Utrecht at age 17. In the first three years my principal emphasis was on mathematics, in particular analysis and geometry, which were taught in a precise but traditional style. Much of my time in Utrecht went directly into the studies I had undertaken. However, some of the long vacations in 's Graveland were devoted to broader reading. Ernst Mach, *Geschichte der Waermelehre,* and various expositions of the theory of relativity, taught me how a whole field of science can at various junctures be on the wrong track, and how entirely new concepts may then be needed to make further progress. . . .

In 1930, I switched my emphasis to theoretical physics—a timid compromise between my desire for a subject matter closer to real life and the obvious argument in favor of a field in which my mathematical training could be put to use. My teacher and shining example of what a scientist should be like was Hans Kramers, after the death of Ehrenfest the leading theorist in Holland in that period, and a very humane and inspiring person with a gentle wit. His attitude and style in the application of mathematics to a substantive field have exerted a pervasive influence on all my later work. . . .

The early thirties brought what liberal economists called the great depression and Marxist economics described as the great crisis of capitalism. It dawned on me that the economic world order was unreliable, unstable, and, most of all, iniquitous. I sought intellectual contacts and friendship with a group of socialist students and also with a small handful of communist-oriented students and unemployed workers. Thus Karl Marx, *Das Kapital,* vol. I, came to be the first book in economics that I studied. While never accepting the labor theory of value, I was stirred by the famous chapter on the state of the English workers during the Industrial Revolution. . . .

From my explorations of Marxist thinking in my student years I have retained a lifelong interest in the prior formulation of that fundamental part of economic theory that does not require specifying the

TJALLING C. KOOPMANS, 1975

institutional form of society, to be used as a framework for the description and comparison of different economic systems.

Still in Utrecht, a physicist friend had mentioned to me that a new field called mathematical economics was being developed, and that Jan Tinbergen, a former student of Ehrenfest, was the leader in this field in the Netherlands. This information opened the way for me to apply my mathematical training to a subject still closer to human concerns. Probably in mid-1933, Tinbergen received me cordially and included me among the small number of young people who had already gravitated toward him. In January 1934 I moved to Amsterdam where Tinbergen was then lecturing once a week. In the first half of that year I had the privilege of almost weekly private tutoring from him over lunch after his lecture. I have been deeply impressed by his selflessness, his abiding concern for economic well-being and greater equality among all of mankind, his unerring priority at any time for problems then most crucial to these concerns, his ingenuity in economic modeling and his sense of realism and wide empirical knowledge of economic behavior relations.

On Tinbergen's advice I now read Cassel, and, with a group of friends, Wicksell. I also studied the econometric and statistical literature. For my doctoral dissertation I chose, staying close to my training, a subject in mathematical statistics aimed at application in econometrics. In the fall of 1935 I spent four months in Oslo with Ragnar Frisch, this giant of mathematical economics whose finest work tended to remain hidden for long periods in mimeographed lecture notes. At his request I gave some lectures on the new ideas in statistics then being developed in England by R. A. Fisher, J. Neyman and others. However, I did not succeed in persuading him that probability models were useful in assessing the significance and accuracy of econometric estimates. I in turn departed impressed, but not persuaded by his econometric approach either.

Since my dissertation was to be presented to the faculty of mathematical and physical sciences, Kramers, who had moved to the University of Leiden, agreed to be the thesis supervisor, consulting with Tinbergen about the economic aspects. The degree was granted in November 1936 by the University of Leiden.

This thesis, *Linear Regression Analysis of Economic Time Series* (Haarlem: Bohn, 1939), showed how to measure relationships and test hypotheses from data arising as time-series. It pursued TCK for another twenty years. It was also the bridge that led TCK from mathematics and physics to economics. TCK had become a bona fide physicist. He did some original work in quantum mechanics, and his article "Uber die Zuordnung von Wellenfunktionen und Eigenwerten zu den Einzelnen Elektronen eines Atoms," *Physica,* vol. 1, 1933–34, pp. 104–113, was a thorough piece of professional work and drew considerable attention. According to Tinbergen, an entire group of young Dutch physicists was making that move in the thirties of the great depression. They included J. B. D. Derksen, G. Goudswaard, A. Bijl, and Jan Tinbergen. Mathematical economists used to come from other areas of applied mathematics, although that is no longer true today. Today it is understood that the average student of economics must know some mathematics, and that economic theorists should, in fact, have a good working knowledge of it. But until the 1960s those economists who called themselves "mathematical economists" or "econometricians" were considered part of the lunatic fringe and outside the main stream of economics. A university of the caliber of Chicago or the up-and-coming Massachusetts Institute of Technology could afford to have them, but no decent department of economics elsewhere.

Of course, it has been said that "a person who knows only economics is not even a good economist" but that was meant to refer to knowledge of such subjects as history, law, and politics, not exactly mathematics or physics.

There is a maxim, well known among economists, "if it is worth doing, it is even worth doing badly." That would not sit with TCK. He was a perfectionist, whether that was economical or not. As a boss, a research director, a project leader or senior co-author, he was extremely demanding. But he did this in a gentle way, so that one would gladly rise to the challenge.

In Amsterdam TCK met his future wife, Truus Wanningen, "among a small group of students of economics whom I tutored in mathematics. Among our shared interests were economics, music, nature, love, and independence from the views and lifestyles of our parents. We married in October 1936."

· II ·

By 1936 TCK's academic interests and career had definitely shifted to economics. From 1936 to 1938 he was lecturer at the Netherlands School of Economics in Amsterdam where he taught Tinbergen's mathematical economics course, while Jan Tinbergen was on leave to do his famous study of the causes of the depression which became the world's first macroeconomic model. (Keynes's views of this work were somewhat mixed.) TCK was doing business-cycle research at that time for the Netherlands Eco-

nomics Institute. It was more modest in scope but allowed deeper understanding of the problem at hand, tanker freight rates and tankship building
(published by Erwin F. Bohn, Haarlem, 1939). TCK was able to show how
the gestation period that lies between ordering a ship built and its completion gives rise to lasting cycles in the manner of the well-known hog cycle.
It was a thorough piece of work that together with TCK's thesis launched
him as one of the up-and-coming econometricians. His reputation among
theoretical physicists had already been made by the earlier article on
quantum mechanics that appeared in the newly started *Dutch Journal of
Physics.*

Jan Tinbergen, only a few years older than TCK, once more became influential on the course of Koopmans' life when he recommended that TCK
continue Tinbergen's own pioneering work on macroeconomic models at
the League of Nations. The model of the American economy having been
completed, TCK was to make a model of the British economy. This was
interrupted in 1939 by the outbreak of war, which brought the activities of
the League to a standstill.

In June 1940 the Netherlands were invaded. TCK, in Geneva, decided to
bring his young family—his wife and a six-week-old daughter—to the
safety of the United States and to return himself to defend his country. (He
mentioned this to his associates "for the record.") The first part he managed to do against wild odds. When the Koopmans arrived in the United
States, the Netherlands, Belgium, and France had fallen. TCK had to join
the war effort in some other way. From 1942 through 1944 he worked for
the British Shipping Mission and the Combined Shipping Adjustment
Board in Washington the task of which was to organize merchant shipping for the war effort. The scientific fallout from TCK's work for this
agency was nothing less than the famous transportation problem of linear
programming:

> My direct assignment was to help fit information about losses, deliv-
> eries from new construction, and employment of British-controlled
> and U.S.-controlled ships into a unified statement. Even in this humble
> role, I learned a great deal about the difficulties of organizing a large-
> scale effort under dual control—or rather in this case four-way con-
> trol, military and civilian cutting across U.S. and U.K. controls. I did my
> study of optimal routing and the associated shadow costs of transpor-
> tation on the various routes, expressed in ship days, in August 1942
> when an impending redrawing of the lines of administrative control
> left me temporarily without urgent duties. My memorandum (on the

transportation problem) was well received in a meeting of the Combined Shipping Adjustment Board (that I did not attend) as an explanation of the "paradoxes of shipping" which were always difficult to explain to higher authority. However, I have no knowledge of any systematic use of my ideas in the combined U.K.-U.S. shipping problems thereafter.

Between 1940 and 1942, before TCK could get going in Washington, he had to find other employment. He was able to obtain a small research job at Princeton and to teach a course on statistical methods at New York University. In 1941, he found employment as an economist for the Penn Mutual Life Insurance Company in Philadelphia where he worked on an investigation of investment methods.

Getting a foothold in the academic world in the United States proved difficult: the universities were still feeling the effects of the great depression. With America's entry into the war they were also losing students.

· III ·

In the 1930s, at a conference in Cambridge, England, of the newly founded Econometric Society, TCK had met Jacob Marschak, an already famous mathematical economist and econometrician some ten years older than TCK. Marschak, a Russian refugee, had studied in Berlin and Heidelberg, and had been *Privat dozent* in Heidelberg. Dismissed by the Nazi regime, he fled to England. At Oxford he founded an econometric research project which soon became internationally famous. Marschak came to the United States just prior to the Second World War. After some time at the Graduate Faculty of the New School for Social Research, he was appointed to the economics department of the University of Chicago.

In mid-1944 my work at the Merchant Shipping Mission fizzled out due to another reshuffling of responsibilities, this time between the Ministry of War Transport in London and its representation in Washington. I corresponded with Jacob Marschak with whom I had had many discussions in Oxford in 1939 and in New York in 1940–41. He invited me to join the staff of the Cowles Commission for Research in Economics, affiliated with the University of Chicago. This was the beginning of a long period of close interaction, collaboration, and personal friendship with Marschak, a gentle, wise, and witty scholar who sees through pretense and timidity alike. In Chicago, Marschak created a rare kind of research environment, by shrewd selection of staff members and by a truly open style of work and discussion.

The Cowles Commission, whose fame as the cradle of Nobel prize-winning economists would grow some twenty-five years later, was famous then only among the small band of econometricians and mathematical economists, of whom there were but a few dozen in the entire world. The Cowles Commission had been founded by Alfred Cowles, stockbroker and later minority stockholder of the *Chicago Tribune* but also a serious student of economics. His paper in *Econometrica,* "Can Stockbrokers Predict the Stock Market?"—the answer was no—had made his reputation overnight. But heading a research organization, even a small one, was something else. Finding a professional for that had proved difficult while the Cowles Commission was still in Colorado Springs, where Alfred Cowles resided for reasons of health. When he moved to Chicago in 1940 and took the Cowles Commission with him, he was able to get Jacob Marschak for this job. And Marschak lost no time converting a small research team of advisers to a brokerage firm into an active, lively, and extremely productive research organization that blossomed in the midst of the economics department of the University of Chicago. Under Marschak, and later under Koopmans, this unique institution was unrivaled as the most successful small economic research organization of its time and the center of the universe for mathematical economists.

From 1944 to 1946 TCK was just a research associate, not a regular teaching member of the faculty and he was on a short-term appointment. His work was focused on the estimation of simultaneous equations, a deeply rooted problem that was basic to all applied economic research and had emerged from Tinbergen's attempt to estimate large macro-economic models for business-cycle analysis, models that require several (at first dozens and later hundreds of) equations. This was a team effort involving among others T. Haavelmo, L. Hurwicz, H. Rubin, and H. Chernoff contributing their various talents. Eventually it was TCK who as project leader also headed the effort of writing it all up in orderly and sequential fashion in the celebrated monograph 10 of the Cowles Commission, *Estimation of Simultaneous Equations.* His own contributions had appeared earlier in three journal articles between 1945 and 1949. TCK's best-known contribution was to the "identification" problem. In the simplest terms this means how can we distinguish statistically between a supply curve and a demand curve?

TCK had not given up trying to develop the ideas conceived in his grappling with the ship-routing problem. His first publication on what became known as the transportation problem of linear programming appeared as

"Optimum Utilization of the Transportation System" in an appendix to *Econometrica* in 1949. This was actually part of the proceedings of a conference held in Washington in 1947.

My work on the transportation model broadened out into the study of activity analysis at the Cowles Commission as a result of a brief but important conversation with George Dantzig probably in early 1947. It was followed by regular contacts and discussions extending over several years thereafter. Some of these discussions included Albert W. Tucker of Princeton who added greatly to my understanding of the mathematical structure of duality.

To make this new approach known and enlist the support of the mathematical economists elsewhere, TCK organized a conference at the Cowles Commission, held in the fall of 1949, the theme of which was linear economic models. For the linear allocation model, TCK coined the term "activity analysis." This conference brought together the leading research workers on production economics including, among others, Paul Samuelson, Oscar Morgenstern, Herbert Simon, and a number of mathematicians who had become attracted to this new branch of "linear algebra"—Gerschenkrone, Gale, and Motzkin. The proceedings of this conference, Monograph 13, *Activity Analysis of Allocation and Production,* containing the article by T. C. Koopmans on "Production as an Efficient Combination of Activities," became the bible for students of the new science of linear programming. It was typical Koopmans; though hard to read, it was precise, explicit, thorough, and totally new. Besides this fundamental exposition by TCK the book also contained the first published version of Dantzig's "Simplex Method"—to this day the most commonly used algorithm for calculating numerical solutions to linear programs.

In 1948, TCK succeeded Jacob Marschak as director of research and was promoted to a full professorship at the University of Chicago.

In addition to his responsibilities as research director, TCK taught an average of two courses per year and supervised several Ph.D. theses. In order to have time for his own research, he insisted that an assistant director be appointed to handle the administrative side of the Cowles Commission.

The postwar era brought an innovation to the academic world: grants by government agencies such as the Office of Naval Research for particular research projects or subcontracted by newly created independent research institutes, such as the RAND Corporation.

To pursue the study of linear economic models, TCK was able to enlist RAND support. The project was named "Allocation of Resources" and this general title permitted a wide range of topics. What TCK had in mind were applications of activity analysis to what is now called spatial economics, namely to the economics of transportation and location.

The project on the allocation of resources got under way in 1951, after a sabbatical leave in 1950 that TCK spent in Western Europe. Research efforts went in several directions but were focused first on models of railroad transportation. The routing of empty box cars was a natural analog to the reallocation of empty ships. It fell to Marc Nerlove, as a research assistant, to work this out. TCK and his research associates Martin Beckmann, Charles B. McGuire, and Christopher B. Winsten looked into freight transportation and discovered an interesting (though nonlinear) allocation problem in how sorting work is divided among freight yards along the route traversed by a freight train. At the point of origin one might put together a train of cars to only one destination, but that would incur a long "accumulation delay." Mixed trains can depart more frequently, but they require sorting work further along the line. Railroad officials to whom this was presented at a meeting in Chicago of the Railroad Systems and Procedures Association and at an early meeting of the Operations Research Society in Cleveland in 1953 were skeptical. But the methods developed by TCK and his co-workers to optimize switchyard work are now being used by Japan Railways to speed up freight movements.

A friendlier reception was given to the work on the optimal utilization of capacities in a congested road network. This became the main content of *Studies in the Economics of Transportation* (Yale University Press, 1956) by Martin Beckmann, C. B. McGuire and C. B. Winsten, under the editorship of, and with an introduction by, T. C. Koopmans. Although TCK did not think highly enough of this to publish it as a Cowles Commission monograph, it did have a lasting impact on the traffic engineering profession and sold as many copies as any Cowles Commission monograph. The fifties and sixties saw a vast expansion in roads and highways, both intraurban and interurban. The required cost-benefit studies were based on forecasts of how traffic would respond to the expansion of capacity. The idea of a "traffic equilibrium" and the methods of calculating such equilibrium-flows which were presented in this book proved to be essential to such forecasting work. Another significant idea was the distinction between individual and social or systems optima and the need for "road pricing" to bridge the gap between private and social costs of transportation in the presence of congestion. For traffic equilibrium proved to be an important example of an economic equilibrium that is not by itself optimal. Road pricing and second-best methods to control traffic congestion continue to be discussed professionally, as traffic conditions in many places deteriorate with disastrous consequences for the quality of urban life—here and elsewhere.

A third problem that emerged in research on the allocation of resources concerned the "assignment problem," originally formulated for military personnel and jobs but modified by Koopmans and Beckmann to deal with the assignment of industrial plants to locations. When transportation costs for the exchange of intermediate goods among the plants are significant, then there exists an optimum, but it cannot be discovered or sustained as an equilibrium through location rents and firms' prices. Only the presence of high moving-costs prevents the situation from becoming a game of musical chairs. To an economic theorist, this type of "market failure" is a deeply disturbing result.

For the research project it meant the end of hopes to penetrate the deeper issues of location theory with linear activity analysis—or its direct descendants, quadratic and convex programming models.

RAND was willing to continue the project, but in the direction of work which was applied to military problems. TCK, after consulting his associates, declined and the team was disbanded in 1954. Winsten returned to England and Beckmann and McGuire were assigned to Marschak's projects, "Decision Making Under Uncertainty" and "Organized Decision Making."

· IV ·

In 1954 TCK wanted to be released from the directorship, and the search began for a successor. James Tobin was invited, visited the Cowles Commission, but in the end declined the offer, preferring to stay at Yale. As James Tobin has told it, TCK did not appear too disheartened and inquired whether he himself might spend his imminent sabbatical leave in 1954–55 at Yale University. This was gladly arranged. In the course of his year at Yale, TCK undertook the arrangements that brought about the removal of the Cowles Commission to Yale in the fall of 1955. More exactly, the Cowles Commission was terminated and the Cowles Foundation established at Yale University, where Alfred Cowles had been an undergraduate. Five members of the staff moved to Yale. James Tobin became director of research.

TCK became professor of economics at Yale University. He moved his family into a large comfortable house on Ridge Road in Hamden, Connecticut, a leafy suburb of New Haven. This was a distinct improvement over his apartment in Chicago in a deteriorating area north of the campus.

At Yale University TCK's research interests shifted to economic growth and subsequently to the newly emerging economics of energy. Throughout his life he remained involved in issues of economic methodology.

In 1961, when James Tobin joined the Council of Economic Advisors, TCK took over the directorship of the Cowles Foundation once more and held it until 1967. He thereupon became Alfred Cowles Professor of Economics at Yale University.

His sixtieth birthday in 1970 saw the publication of his collected articles as *Scientific Papers of Tjalling C. Koopmans,* New York, Springer-Verlag, 1970. This publication was a joint effort of Truus Koopmans, Marc Nerlove, Carl Christ, and Martin Beckmann. TCK was visibly pleased. Later he said in private conversation that he thought this might have helped him to be awarded the Nobel Prize.

In 1975 TCK and Leonid Kantorovich shared the Nobel Prize in economics for their discovery of linear programming. To TCK's consternation, George Dantzig, who in his opinion—and that of others—was equally deserving, had been left out. It is said that TCK proposed to Kantorovich that they decline the prize, but was persuaded not to do this. TCK then donated one-third of the Nobel award (that part of his share which should have gone to Dantzig) to the International Institute for Applied Systems Analysis.

In 1978 TCK became president of the American Economic Association following the unexpected death of his great friend, Jacob Marschak. In his presidential address "Economics Among the Sciences" he advocated interdisciplinary collaboration while also pointing out its difficulties.

TCK retired in 1980. He still attended seminars and regularly came to his office on 30 Hillhouse Avenue, the Cowles Foundation's castle. But he was somewhat of a recluse then. His health had deteriorated and his hearing was troubling him. Escaping to a better climate in the winter by visiting Stanford and Irvine did not improve matters. Tjalling C. Koopmans died on February 26, 1985.

· V ·

TCK was a very reticent person. Even professionally his circle was small. This may not always have been his own choice. There was tension between TCK and one other member of the department of economics at the University of Chicago whose star was just rising and who later won a Nobel Prize too. When TCK's student, Harry Markowitz, submitted his thesis on "Optimal Selection of Portfolios," it was originally rejected by the department as "not economics." (Ironically it was for work along the same lines that James Tobin later received the Nobel Prize.) The work of some other members of the Cowles Commission, notably Gerard Debreu—now also a Nobel laureate—and Edmond Malinvaud was similarly criticized as being mathematics rather than economics. Jealousy over space may have contributed to the somewhat unsympathetic attitude that the department of economics occasionally displayed toward the Cowles Commission. For his own part TCK, being rather sensitive, did not feel truly accepted by his colleagues in the department of economics at the University of Chicago.

Koopmans was a conscientious and methodical teacher. His lectures were clear but demanded constant attention. As a result his classes tended to be small, but they attracted good students. In the fifties TCK taught two courses which he had created: "Econometrics," which focused on the newly developed estimation of simultaneous equations, and "Allocation of Resources," which presented the new activity analysis. Between 1950 and 1955, TCK had as doctoral students Harry Markowitz, George Borts, Stanley Reiter, Charles Holt, and Robert Strotz. They all became professors and distinguished economists; Strotz also became the president of Northwestern University.

TCK's reserved and seemingly forbidding manner may have discouraged others from becoming his students. His courses were tough, he was known to be as demanding of his students as he was of himself. Once accepted as a Ph.D. student, one could be sure, however, of close attention. TCK took his teaching and administrative responsibilities seriously. He would read papers pencil in hand and mark them with exclamations like "obtuse," "cryptic," or put capital letters in the margin with detailed comments under each letter on separate sheets. In the case of our joint paper, "Assignment Problems and the Location of Economic Utilities," it started out as a Cowles Commission discussion paper under my name, reporting the results of discussions between TCK, the mathematician Y. Herstein, and myself. It then went through at least five revisions with much contributed by TCK which substantiated, lengthened, and clarified it.

Although TCK was an exacting director and team-leader, he managed to create a very relaxed working climate. Before any important decision (e.g., whom to appoint as an associate or as a secretary) he would consult his associates. Working hours were not fixed and times set for meetings were at very convenient hours. Cowles Commission staff meetings were held regularly on Fridays, often both mornings and afternoons. Gerard Debreu complained there were too many. Seminars that addressed a wider audience were on Wednesday nights. They were followed by informal gatherings of the junior staff for beer and pizza at "Jimmy's" on 55th Street. The Cowles Commission also held staff luncheons at the Quadrangle Club. Debreu did not think that eating and professional conversation mixed well.

TCK was accessible at short notice to have any new ideas tried out on him. He often scheduled meetings on his own initiative to mull over new problems. When research entered the stage of being written up, regular "progress sessions" were held, and this provided the necessary motivation.

TCK, in his later years became fond of travel. He liked good food, courteous and efficient service, and fine accommodations. But his style of life on the whole was modest, perhaps even austere.

In a set of brief portraits of economists by *Fortune* magazine in the fifties, TCK was referred to as an "austere Dutchman." There was that side to TCK, to the point where he turned off the heat in his office, did not drink alcohol, and used coffee but sparingly. But he was also a warm-hearted person, ready to laugh or chuckle, and concerned with the personal welfare of those working under him. His most intimate friend was also his senior colleague at Cowles, Jacob Marschak.

Throughout his life, Koopmans never acted rashly and came as close to being a rational decision-maker as is humanly possible. (His advice to me, when we separated after nine years of professional association, was to control my impatience.)

TCK played the violin and the piano. He composed music; according to his own description, its mood was somewhat like that of Charles Ives's. TCK also liked chess and according to Herbert Scarf played chess rather aggressively. He invented a type of chess to be played on a hexagonally tesselated board, but apparently the rules were too complicated and it did not catch on.

Those who have known TCK will never forget him. We all have learned from him. Economic science owes to him as his most lasting contributions the solution of the "identification problem" in estimating simultaneous equations and the "activity analysis of allocation and production," which has laid new foundations to the economic theory of production.

The University of Chicago was fortunate to have him from 1944 through 1955. But the converse is also true. The University of Chicago provided the environment where the best efforts of Tjalling C. Koopmans could flourish.

22

BENNO LANDSBERGER

1 8 9 0 – 1 9 6 8

H A N S   G.   G Ü T E R B O C K

BENNO LANDSBERGER was considered the best of all Assyriologists. This reputation was fully justified by the width of
his knowledge and the depth of his penetration.

· I ·

Landsberger was born in Friedek, a city in what was then called Austrian
Silesia—now northeastern Czechoslovakia. He studied Semitics and especially Assyriology at the University of Leipzig which already then was
known as a major center of Near Eastern studies, a reputation which Landsberger was greatly to enhance in later years. His principal teachers were
the Arabist August Fischer and the Assyriologist Heinrich Zimmern. He received his doctorate in 1913 with a dissertation on *Der kultische Kalender
der Babylonier und Assyrer* (Erste Hälfte) (Leipzig, 1915; the second part
was not published). It is a fundamental study of lasting value. During the
First World War, he served in the Austro-Hungarian Army on the eastern
front, was wounded and decorated. At the end of the war he successfully
led his unit back to the German border and safety.

After his return to Leipzig, he became *Dozent* in 1920, while Zimmern
still held the chair. In 1926 he was promoted to the rank of *ausseror-
dentlicher Professor*. In 1928 he accepted the professorship of Assyriology
at the University of Marburg vacated by the retirement of Peter Jensen. One
year later Zimmern retired from his chair in Leipzig and Landsberger received the call to the chair which he held until 1935. At the time of the Nazi
seizure of power, Landsberger, as an ex-combatant, was exempt from immediate dismissal in accordance with the Nazi policy of dismissing all Jews
except those who had served at the front in the First World War. He was
nevertheless dismissed by the authorities in 1935.

At that time, the Turkish government was making plans for a new institution of higher learning which should be devoted especially to those languages and civilizations that were considered important for the early history of Turkey. It was at first only a single faculty—or division; in 1946, after other faculties or divisions were added, it became a part of Ankara University; its name was "Faculty of Languages, History and Geography" (*Dil ve Tarih-Coğrafya Fakültesi*). Landsberger became professor of Assyriology or, as the Turks preferred to call it, *Sümeroloji*. In accepting the appointment, he set as a condition that the institution should purchase the library of the late Professor Zimmern. This was done. He thus laid the foundation for a usable Near Eastern library. I was appointed as a Hittitologist. With the exception of the foreign-language teachers, the teaching staff of the faculty was made up of Germans, refugees as well as others, and Turks. Among the Germans, Landsberger was by far the most distinguished. In consultation with the Turkish Ministry of Education, he and the classicist Georg Rohde were influential in organizing the new school along German lines.

· II ·

In 1948, Landsberger was invited to become professor at the Oriental Institute of the University of Chicago. On reaching the age of sixty-five in 1955, he retired from his professorship, but in 1963–64 he taught Sumerian, filling the vacancy caused by the departure of Thorkild Jacobsen. He continued his own research and remained on the editorial board of the *Assyrian Dictionary* until his death in 1968.

Landsberger became an honorary member of the American Oriental Society in 1941 and a member of the American Philosophical Society in 1956; in 1958, Dropsie College awarded him the honorary degree of Doctor of Law. In the same year, the Academy of Sciences at Leipzig, East Germany, made him a corresponding member. In 1959, he became an honorary member of the Deutsche Morgenländische Gesellschaft. He was also honorary member of the Société Asiatique of Paris and corresponding member of the British Academy, the Danish and the Finnish Academies.

On his seventieth birthday an issue of the *Journal of Near Eastern Studies* was dedicated to him (vol. 19 [1960], no. 2), and on his seventy-fifth birthday he was presented with a major *Festschrift* (Güterbock, H. G., and Jacobsen, Th., eds. *Studies in Honor of Benno Landsberger on His Seventy-Fifth Birthday,* Chicago, 1965 [Assyriological Studies 16]).

BENNO LANDSBERGER, 1965

· III ·

Benno Landsberger was a scholar of a stature rarely encountered. His reputation as the leading Assyriologist of his time was fully justified. He had a great gift for languages and a phenomenal memory which enabled him to write his many lexicographical studies without the help of files; he remembered where a given word occurred in other texts. He was familiar with all fields of Assyriological studies, and there was no category of text which he had not studied. He was also well versed in the other Semitic languages. He said that "language was the only tangible determinant of a national culture." Grammar, syntax, the structural difference between, e.g., Akkadian and Sumerian or between Akkadian and the other Semitic languages were regarded by him as means for understanding the essence of the culture of the various Ancient Near Eastern peoples. He developed these ideas in his programmatic inaugural address of 1926, entitled, "Die Eigenbegrifflichkeit der babylonischen Welt" (*Islamica* 2 [1926–27], 355–72; an English translation was prepared during his later years but published only posthumously: *The Conceptual Autonomy of the Babylonian World,* translated by Foster, B., Jacobsen, Th., and von Siebenthal, H., Undena Publications [Materials of the Ancient Near East, 1–4], Malibu, 1976). In it he tried to grasp the characteristic traits of Babylonian culture by a heuristic method without applying to it extraneous concepts, taking language as the decisive concept of a culture. But language was not the only means he used to characterize the autonomy of Babylonian thought. Starting from an analysis of the verbal system, he progressed to other grammatical features, to poetry, "encyclopedic" word lists, law, and institutions. He rejected the theory of a general "Babylonian worldview" which had been advocated by scholars of an earlier generation. On the contrary, he favored the diachronic view which rendered change intelligible. To describe every period of Babylonian history and of the different parts of Mesopotamia using only their own sources was always one of the aims of his work. Economic and political systems, legal and religious practices—to name just the most obvious fields—were studied for each period separately. Linguistic change, such as the loss of old and the introduction of new terms, or the change in meaning of a word over a long time formed a feature of his diachronic study. The observation of these changes was one of Landsberger's contributions to lexicographical method.

Landsberger's interest was not limited to ancient Mesopotamia: he was familiar with the history and institutions of Israel and often drew upon them for comparison or contrast. He was, at the same time, opposed to a narrow, one-sided "biblical" history. His reasons were the breadth of his own scholarship and his personal ties to the Jewish tradition which rejected all apologetics.

His interests also took Landsberger beyond the borders of Mesopotamia. He was the first to recognize that the Old Assyrian tablets coming from a mound called Kültepe near Kayseri did not, as another scholar had claimed, attest the existence of an early Assyrian empire but rather belonged to the archives of Assyrian merchants settled in Anatolian countries. ("Assyrische Handelskolonien in Kleinasien," *Der alte Orient,* 24,4, Leipzig [1925]). He also recognized that among the personal names occurring in the Kültepe texts those that were not Assyrian belonged to local individuals. ("Über die Völker Vorderasiens im 3. Jahrtausend'," *Zeitschrift für Assyriologie* 35 [1924], 213–28, esp. 221–28]). During his Ankara years, his interest in this special branch of Assyriology was naturally intensified; the results are some articles of his own and especially the works of his pupils, inspired and guided by him. To the so-called Late Hittite period he devoted the monograph *Sam'al* (*Sam'al: Studien zur Entdeckung der Ruinenstätte Karatepe,* Ankara, Türkische Historische Gesellschaft, 1948), in which he contributed to the clarification of the history of the Aramaic and—as we now say—Luwian small kingdoms of the first millennium; he also made some good observations about the art of the period.

Landsberger always stressed the importance of collaboration with specialists in those fields in which the philologist could not be fully competent. Wherever possible, he acted in accordance with this principle. One result of such collaboration is the book *Die Fauna des alten Mesopotamien* (Abh. d. Sächs. Akad. 42.6, Leipzig, 1934), written together with the Leipzig zoologist I. Krumbiegel.

In Ankara, he took advantage of the opportunities to confer, on agricultural technology, with O. Gerngross, and, on grain cultivation, with F. Christiansen-Weniger; for a short time also with the zoologist Bodenheimer. Although none of these discussions led directly to a publication, Landsberger gained valuable insights from them. He also studied the literature on the fauna and flora of Mesopotamia which by then had become available. From his period at the University of Chicago, I do not remember any such specific collaboration, although in writing his study of the date palm he must have had some advice. (*The Date Palm and Its By-products according to the Cuneiform Sources, Archiv für Orientforschung,* Beiheft 17, Graz, 1967).

The best known and most fruitful collaboration was that of Landsberger with the legal historian Paul Koschaker, in Leipzig. As a participant in the joint seminar conducted by the two professors, I vividly remember how the jurisprudential interpretation of the one inspired the other to refine his philological analysis of a sentence or the definition of a word, and how this, in turn, sometimes led to a more exact understanding of the legal contents of a document. Both scholars were deeply hurt by Landsberger's dismissal in 1935, and it was a tragic coincidence that Koschaker was appointed to teach at the law faculty at Ankara just when Landsberger was leaving Turkey in 1948.

· IV ·

Landsberger's connection with the Oriental Institute of the University of Chicago had already begun during his Leipzig years. The planners of the *Assyrian Dictionary* had introduced the policy of asking Assyriologists from all over the world to contribute editions of certain groups of texts which were to serve as the basis for lexicographical files. Landsberger was assigned the so-called "vocabularies," i.e., lists of signs and words, mostly, but not exclusively, bilingual—Sumerian and Akkadian. Landsberger fulfilled his task with the technical help of his pupil, H. S. Schuster, and sent the manuscripts to Chicago. He defined the various kinds of lists according to their purpose as manifest in the arrangement of words and signs, using ancient titles of the individual series as preserved on colophons. These manuscripts served as a basis for the "lexical section" with which the treatment of every word in the dictionary begins. His emigration interrupted this work, but after his arrival in Chicago he began to revise his own manuscripts for publication in the series *Materialien zum Sumerischen Lexikon (MSL)*, which was published by the Pontifical Biblical Institute in Rome but was very much the work of the Oriental Institute. He himself edited volumes 2–9 (Landsberger et al., 1951–67); the rest is being completed by his colleagues. (Reiner, Civil, et al., *Materials for the Sumerian Lexicon,* 1970–).

He was on the editorial board of the Chicago *Assyrian Dictionary* until his death. His knowledge was drawn upon by all who worked on the dictionary, the local staff as well as the foreign Assyriologists who came to Chicago to work on the project. He was regularly consulted on individual words, especially the more problematic ones, and wrote his comments on the yellow legal foolscap pads that became associated with him.

Landsberger was not a writer of general books. He believed that thorough and comprehensive studies of individual problems were still needed. To such problems he devoted articles or monographs. Some dealt with such basic concepts as the terms for colors ("Über Farben im Sumerisch-

Akkadischen," *Journal of Cuneiform Studies,* 21 [1967], 139–73]), or the names for the seasons ("Jahreszeiten im Sumerisch-Akkadischen," *Journal of Near Eastern Studies,* 8 [1949] 248–97).

His lexicographical articles are numerous. A "Bibliography of Benno Landsberger's Works" was published by Anne Kilmer and Johannes Renger in the *Journal of Cuneiform Studies,* 26 (1974), 183–92. Most of his definitions are still valid. Anne Kilmer together with Daniel A. Foxvog also published a glossary under the title "Benno Landsberger's Lexicographical Contributions," in the same journal (27 [1975], 3–129). Such monographs as his study of the fauna and the cultivation of the date palm and the use of its products, are also largely lexicographical; both grew out of his studies of the vocabularies.

· V ·

As a teacher Landsberger had a great influence. Some of the best Assyriologists were his pupils. From his years in Germany the following come to mind: Theo Bauer, Adam Falkenstein, Wolfram von Soden, Wilhelm Eilers, Lubor Matouš, Fritz Rudolf Kraus, and Hans-Siegfried Schuster.

In Turkey, the Assyriologists Kemal Balkan, Emin Bilgiç, Melbrure Tosun, and Kadriye Tansuğ were his main students, but he also helped Furuzan Kinal to use cuneiform sources for a degree in ancient history; and he counseled the archaeologist Tahsin Özgüç on his dissertation on Anatolian burial systems. Hatice Kizilyay and Muazzez Çiğ, who, as curators of the tablet collection of the Istanbul museum performed invaluable services for Assyriology, received their basic training from Landsberger. For several years, during the war, he devoted all his time to his students.

In supervising dissertations, he shared his ideas freely with the candidates. Many of these dissertations reflect—in various degrees—Landsberger's own ideas. I would mention only my own experience. My dissertation owes its very title, "Die historische Tradition und ihre literarische Gestaltung" and its printed form in *Zeitschrift für Assyriologie,* 42 (1932), 1–91, to a thorough revision carried out under his guidance.

Another instance of Landsberger's ideas being represented in the work of one of his pupils is the following: Landsberger developed his system of Akkadian grammar in his classes, but—apart from the programmatic article mentioned above—it was not given systematic form in print. It is no secret that W. von Soden's *Grundzüge der akkadischen Grammatik* (*Analecta Orientalia,* 33, Rome [1952]) is to a large extent based on the teachings of Landsberger. It is no exaggeration to say that Landsberger has placed the understanding of the Akkadian language on a new level.

In Chicago, Landsberger did not supervise dissertations. One reason was the short duration of his tenure here; he was professor at the University of Chicago only for seven years, from 1948 to 1955. Another reason was that students were afraid of the great man and what he might demand. Most students attended his classes and some of them consulted him for their own work but they were fearful of doing their dissertations under him. On the other hand, several younger scholars came to do post-doctoral work with him. Two of his former pupils, Kemal Balkan and Mebrure Tosun, came from Turkey to enjoy his guidance again; for them his departure from Ankara had occurred too early. Others were Moshe Held (Semitics and Akkadian for his own work on Ugaritic), Hayim Rosén (Comparative Semitics), and others, also the foreign co-workers on the *Dictionary* already mentioned. Anne Draffkorn Kilmer worked for Landsberger as research assistant under a Guggenheim grant during his last few years. Erica Reiner, who received her doctorate under the sponsorship of Leo Oppenheim, tells me she considers herself Landsberger's pupil. Closest to him among his colleagues was Thorkild Jacobsen, who as dean of the division of the humanities and director of the Oriental Institute, had been influential in bringing Landsberger to the University.

All in all, Landsberger's influence on the work of the "third floor" of the Oriental Institute is immeasurable.

· VI ·

I would like to add a few lines about the man Benno Landsberger. He was a big man, rather heavy except for his last years when he lost weight. He suffered from flat feet, and this gave him a peculiar gait. He loved to go out without an overcoat. Once in Ankara, he was stopped in the street by the minister of education, who admonished him not to expose himself to the cold weather. He was impeccably dressed in public, but at home, when he worked until late in the night, he used to shed several layers of clothing.

He was a human being in the full sense of the word. He brought his whole self to everything he did. He loved good food, drink, and women. He favored hearty dishes like pig's feet and veal hocks. In Leipzig, he ate his noon meal in the restaurant "Die Feuerkugel" in its backroom with bare wooden tables, while Kraus and I sat in the front room at tables covered with white tablecloths—the price was the same. In Ankara, there was at first only one delicatessen shop from which he could obtain the pork products he wanted for his cold supper. He preferably ate it directly from the refrigerator, while walking around and working. For some years, he and I shared apartments. He could not stand it that I set the table and asked him to sit down for our cold supper. He soon asked me not to include him any longer in these meals.

In Chicago he did, of course, adjust to the American meal schedule, but he usually skipped lunch. In his later years a routine developed, according to which he ate dinner three times a week at the house of his physician, Dr. I. I. Ritter; twice a week his black maid Catharine cooked for him; Thursdays he ate at Binyon's restaurant in the Loop before the symphony concert, and on Sunday nights he ate at the Güterbocks. Mrs. Ritter studied Hebrew and Akkadian with him. The classes took place after dinner. At our house he would often play piano four hands with my wife. All this was duly kept in flux with many bottles of Heineken beer. He had a remarkable knowledge and understanding of music. He would write letters to the newspapers with his criticism of some performances of the Chicago Symphony Orchestra.

He was proud of his United States citizenship which he acquired in the minimum prescribed time. He took a lively interest in political life and on occasion even sent a telegram to the president of the United States. He loved to be a gadfly. He enjoyed telling the story how he once, at a German Orientalists' convention proposed that the planners should think of ways to make it possible that such gatherings should also have scholarly results (*auch wissenschaftliche Resultate*).

Landsberger enjoyed an occasional card game, mostly the German game *Skat*. In Germany he also loved to bet on horses. He often boasted that he used to read the pink racing papers openly during faculty meetings. Neither in Ankara nor in Chicago did he find the races interesting.

He liked children and was especially fond of our two boys. During their high school years, they went to him regularly for "German lessons," but much more than the language teaching they enjoyed the food he served and long conversations with him about all kinds of problems.

His determination to explore a problem to the last was an expression of the wholeness of his approach to life. A vivid example is his monograph *Brief des Bischofs von Esagila an König Asarhaddou* (Royal Dutch Academy, Amsterdam, 1965). It started with a simple question of one of his former students about an Assyrian letter discovered in the Tokapi Sarayi. It grew into a monograph on the politics surrounding the rebuilding of the main sanctuary in Babylon.

It was this personality that attracted students and colleagues and made him such a challenging and inspiring teacher.

23

HAROLD D. LASSWELL

1 9 0 2 – 1 9 7 8

L E O   R O S T E N

· I ·

I MET HIM IN 1927. I was a grubby sophomore; he was an assistant professor who had only recently begun to teach a course in political science which he had invented: "Non-Rational Factors in Political Behavior." He had written a spectacular thesis for his doctorate, based on archival research in Washington, London, Paris, and Berlin: *Propaganda Techniques in the First World War.* It was, and remains, a remarkable wholly original analysis of the psychological symbols and emotional appeals used in the propaganda strategies of the contending powers.

Harold Dwight Lasswell was his name. He was only twenty-five. There were nine or ten students in the class. He lectured us frantically (that is the only word I can think of to describe his desperate loquacity), with a glazed stare into space, unaware of whether we understood a word of what he was saying, and entirely indifferent to our bewilderment. He talked so fast, tumbling idea upon idea in such a torrent of excitement, that his monologues became a blur from which only occasional words, or startling phrases, or academic jargon (encased within new and discombobulating contexts) emerged to aggravate our dumbfoundedness: "psychosomatic . . . frame of reference . . . libido . . . Sherrington, time-space continuum . . . anxiety . . . the Marxist theology . . . systematic . . . ambivalent . . . super-ego . . . quantify . . . dichotomy . . mobilization of discontent . . . Freud . . . authoritarian manipulations . . . preferential delusions . . . Bukharin . . . infantile yearnings for omnipotence . . . Pareto . . . the Id . . . methodology . . . narcissistic . . . cyclical inflation . . . projection . . . Adler . . . neuroses . . . introject . . . Jung . . . insecurity . . . configurative . . .

Harold D. Lasswell

Rorschach . . . participant-observer . . . the equilibrium analyses of economics . . . world revolution of our time. . . ."

Remember: the year was 1927.

Our mentor seemed unable to leave a moment of time unoccupied by language—or vatic sounds designed to maintain control of the listener: "um . . . er . . . well . . . um . . . the . . . uh. . . ." I wondered if he suffered from some strange psychological impediment which he was trying to drown in a flood of words or hide within an avalanche of unrelated monologues. I thought him dazzling, brilliant, baffling—and a freak.

I was not helped, of course, by the fact that Lasswell blithely scrambled together technical jargon from a dozen disciplines. In each of these he appeared to be entirely at home: history, philosophy, sociology, political science, neurology, psychology, economics, physiology, international law, anthropology, quantum physics (!), statistics, psychiatry, psycho-analysis. He seemed to be in the demonic grip of a compulsion to be absolutely "systematic" and entirely "objective." The goal struck me as inhuman, his method inhumane.

I shall never forget my first private meeting with him. I was considerably miffed because, apart from not understanding what this antiseptic pastor was talking about, I was groaning under the burden of a bizarre assignment he had given each member of the class: to subscribe to two daily newspapers and to measure precisely each story in them, in column inches, classifying the figures in categories that ranged from city-hall shenanigans to astrological advice. He had named two papers in Arizona for me to subscribe to and dissect.

After three weeks of this unorthodox work, which had not yet been elevated to the status of "content analysis," I mobilized my indignation and marched to Dr. Lasswell's office, where I poured out my heartfelt complaints. He listened, steely-eyed and silent. Thrown off-base by his steady, clinical stare, which made me feel like a case-study, I managed to quaver that I did not understand what on earth he had been talking about for over a month.

To my anguished protestations, Lasswell finally sniffed icily: "Communication, after all, comes down to a fortuitous parallelism of bio-psychic variables."

I staggered out. I could not repress my reluctant admiration over the beauty and precision of that ad-lib.

· II ·

Lasswell was quite tall (well over six feet), large of frame, and heavy. He was not graceful. He always walked fast; I never saw him dawdle. Even when striding fast, he thought hard or talked much. He wore his hair in a short, stiff Prussian manner, and his erudition in a bristly, battle-ready posture.

He detested small talk and loathed clichés. He sang out "Greetings!" instead of "Hello." I never heard him tell a joke, but no one was a happier audience for the risible. His laughter was uproarious. He adored humor, and doted on anecdotes, but I never heard him tell a story. He venerated the analytic, disparaged the discursive, and forever exalted the scientific. I sometimes thought he yearned to solve all problems—emotional, political, sociological—with equations.

When I first shook hands with him, I found his palms soft and slightly damp. These were not the hands of a man who ever wielded a hammer or caught a baseball.

No one I ever knew was such a tireless taker of notes. His bookshelves were lined with odd volumes and erudite journals, in the margins of which he had scribbled his own hieroglyphs, cryptic equations, approving exclamation points, or disgusted dissents ("Bah!" . . . "Nonsense!" . . . "Data?" . . . "Cf. Cannon . . . in Wallas . . .").

The university community contained a considerable number of smokers (students and teachers), but Harold never so much as touched a cigarette, cigar, or pipe. Alcohol was another matter: He imbibed whiskey exceptionally well. In over fifty years, I never saw him drunk, or heard him bleary. And that included prolonged stays at my house in California or Connecticut or Washington, where he felt much at home with my wife and children and fiery waters.

Once after a long, elaborate dinner in New York, I miserably confessed that I wanted to go back to my hotel. "Too much brandy . . . ," I muttered. With the utmost gentleness, Harold guided me, saying quite quietly, "One must, from time to time, defer to the demands of the soma." I do not think he could bring himself to utter so trite a word as "drunk."

He knew people everywhere in the world, it seemed. He numbered his friends in the dozens, and his admirers in the hundreds. He also had many critics, detractors, and adversaries: Harold's propensity to sarcastic deflation, icy disparagement, and thinly concealed contempt cost him dearly.

He was, essentially and quite oddly, shy. No one of my acquaintance has ever been so parsimonious about the revelation of personal data. When asked a personal question, he would hem and haw and evade; sometimes his face would flush with embarrassment in as many hues of red as could be found in American radical movements from 1932 to 1941.

Of all the people I have known, Lasswell was the one most free of prejudice—*any* kind of prejudice: against creeds, colors, races, foods, customs, religions, mores, habits, hang-ups. He seemed only to despise stupidity. And he hated only those who hated, those who would use violence or terror to gratify their meannesses of soul. He was also, of all I knew, the one most totally and unswervingly dedicated to democracy. For years, during the formative *Stürm und Drang* of the American Civil Liberties Union, Harold was a bulwark of principled, constant, and unabashed support. One of his lesser-known works, *Democracy Through Public Opinion,* is shot through with democratic fervor. His radio dialogues with T. V. Smith, of the university's department of philosophy, were models of pedagogy and insight. He talked as if he had been on intimate terms with Plato, Montesquieu, Jefferson, Holmes.

· III ·

"H.D.L.," as he signed himself, was born in 1902 in Donnellson, Illinois (population about 300). He was raised in Decatur and other small towns in Illinois and Indiana. His father was a Presbyterian clergyman, his mother a schoolteacher. "Prominent people," he once told me, "seemed to drift to our dinner table. As a boy I listened to my father discuss politics with the likes of William Jennings Bryan or candidates for the state senate."

He had excellent teachers in secondary school. He was an insatiable student. He spent his summers in Indiana, visiting an uncle who was a physician. This uncle, baffled by his inability to relieve a patient of a paralysis of the arm that had no physical cause, had heard of the work of a physician in Vienna who was curing cases of "hysterical paralysis." The Indiana physician wrote to Europe and ordered some books by Sigmund Freud. Young Harold, then fourteen, read them. "They seemed sensible to me," he once said. "Indeed, it was not until I was a junior at the University of Chicago that I discovered that Freud was controversial."

He came to the University of Chicago on a scholarship at the age of sixteen. The department of political science at that time was under the chairmanship of Charles E. Merriam, who had been trained at the University of Berlin and Columbia University. His education was of high quality but strictly conventional, yet Merriam was immensely curious and intellectually adventurous. He was fascinated by Harold Lasswell. After his doctoral dissertation and his appointment to a teaching post in the department, Lasswell went to Europe—with Merriam's sponsorship—on a fellowship in 1927–28.

In Vienna, Lasswell met many of the world's leading psychoanalysts. He was himself briefly psychoanalyzed by Theodor Reik, a protégé of Freud. In Berlin, Lasswell sat in on a seminar (in German, in which he was thoroughly at home) on quantum theory, with several of the great nuclear physicists of the time. (He was familiar with the work of Einstein, Planck, Schrödinger, and Heisenberg.)

Back in Chicago, Harold persuaded Merriam to recommend him for another fellowship—to serve as an intern in the psychiatric ward of the Massachusetts General Hospital in Boston. Lasswell not only became a working intern; he plunged into intensive studies of physiology, hematology, cognition, neurology. He became a close friend of the brilliant Harry Stack Sullivan, and a faithful devotee of Dr. Sullivan's provocative "inter-personal" theory of human relations. Lasswell also became a friendly exponent of the work of Dr. Lionel Blitzsten with schizophrenics, and the broadened psychoanalytic theories of Franz Alexander, whom he persuaded to give a series of lectures in the Social Science Research Building.

At some point, Lasswell passed enough examinations at Chicago's Psychoanalytic Institute to become a certified "lay analyst," i.e., a practitioner of psychoanalysis without formal medical qualifications. Soon he had three or four "analysands" trekking to his office in the Social Science Building. An assistant hidden from the patients operated one of the primitive sound-recording devices of the time.

One of the most striking and original of Harold's early papers reported his correlations of verbal free-association and—skin-tension. He used a sensitized plate to measure the heat of the skin as it varied according to the "verbalizations"—the voiced emotions or charged silences—of volunteers. It was a contribution to psychosomatic research, for it vividly confirmed the close relationship between feelings and bodily response.

Lasswell longed to make psychoanalysis a scientifically respectable discipline, a rigorous method and verifiable theory for observing psychological phenomena and for classifying observations and data such as dreams, delusions, paranoid projections, verbal patterns, mundane "mistakes" in anything from nomenclature to anatomy. The road from these endeavors to the study of politics both mystified and flabbergasted many a teacher of political philosophy, political science, party systems, public administration, constitutional law—and the rest of the then-respectable divisions of the academic study of political science.

· IV ·

Harold Lasswell's absorption in psychoanalysis took place at a time when the subject was little known or respected in American universities; it was ridiculed even in departments of psychiatry in sophisticated medical schools.

In the larger field of the social sciences, Lasswell became a unique and emphatically controversial pioneer, not only by undergoing psychoanalysis himself, and by the intensive study of its literature—then mostly in German—but by his bold efforts to apply psychoanalytic and new sociological theories to the interpretation of political phenomena.

In late 1928 and in 1929, Lasswell consulted with the psychiatric directors of important mental institutions in the United States in an effort to obtain data about patients who had been active in politics or government. In the search for data about political activity, the sort which could be objectively studied within the categories of psychoanalysis, he also conducted "depth interviews," interviews using the psychoanalytic technique of "free association" on a number of persons who had been politicians or elected officials.

The first important result of these explorations was *Psychopathology and Politics,* published in 1930. It was a landmark work which antedated works by Margaret Mead, Ruth Benedict, John Dollard, and other social scientists who later came to be known as the founders of the study of "character structure," and of the relationship between personality, culture, and politics, i.e., the distribution of status, power, wealth, or security. Lasswell's depiction of the varying personality structures of the political theorist, bureaucrat, organizer, and demagogue opened entirely new vistas to students of politics.

Lasswell was one of the first Americans to become well acquainted with the school of sociological political science which had been developing in Europe under Max Weber, Vilfredo Pareto, Karl Mannheim, Gaetano Mosca, and Roberto Michels—men who studied governments and politics not so much by the investigation of laws, constitutions, formal tables of organization, and public administration, but through the observation of what really happens in the conflicts and compromises of power exercised in political arenas.

In the first half of the 1930s, Lasswell published two books which remain, I think, among the most striking produced by any academic in the second quarter of the present century: *World Politics and Personal Insecurity,* and *Politics: Who Gets What, When, How.*

The latter was brilliant, bold, sardonic—but schematic. Yet its arresting title and realism have found their way into the common idiom of political thought.

World Politics and Personal Insecurity, with its galvanizing title, is a book of great originality whose entire richness and anti-Marxist repercussions have not been appreciated by subsequent writers, partly because of the startling connections Lasswell draws between phenomena and events which are not ordinarily seen to be connected, and partly because of Lasswell's unfamiliar and often sardonic terminology.

The rich harvest of Lasswell's studies were greatly fertilized by his colleagues at Chicago: Robert Park, Edward Sapir, T. V. Smith, Frank Knight, Robert Redfield, several psychologists and physiologists, and Charles Merriam—who even if he could not follow Lasswell in his imaginative flights into the greatly expanding universe or the profoundly engrossing unconscious, was proud of, and usually indulgent toward, H.D.L.

Lasswell wrote an essay, early in 1935, on why Hitler's hysterical and confused messages appealed to the middle class of Germany: that analysis still seems to me the most acute revelation of the lure of Nazism in the literature. Harold also produced analytic gems for the new *Encyclopedia of the Social Sciences:* on "Bribery," "Chauvinism," "Feuds," "Morale."

His major books—*Psychopathology and Politics, Politics: Who Gets What, When, How, World Politics and Personal Insecurity*—are immensely impressive in the sweep of his knowledge and the audacity of his interpretations.

He published many trenchant essays on public opinion, international relations, and the dynamics of revolutions. He had a luminous gift for memorable phrases: "the garrison state," "the revolution of rising expectations," "the world revolution of our time." He referred to politics as "the displacement of private affect onto public objects." To become a revolutionist involves a profound "rupture of conscience." All societies become organized in "the pyramid of income, safety, and deference."

· V ·

It took me years to discover why Lasswell resorted to his involuted and outlandish lingo: he was entirely at home with it. It was, indeed, his natural patois. When Lasswell thought, wrote, or spoke, he became euphoric. He drew upon an astounding vocabulary with phenomenal speed, exactitude and—intoxication. Only after a long time did it dawn on me that whereas most men use language clumsily, in an effort to express banal ideas, Harold used words brilliantly to conceal his feelings and to elaborate his most complex ideas. I think he had a passion to be comprehended but intricate defenses against being understood. He resisted intimacy. Harold was by all odds the most interesting man he ever knew.

I never heard him say, "I don't know." I often heard him say, "We know so little about this." That meant that man's accumulated knowledge had not yet reached the point where an answer was possible. If it had, Harold would, clearly, have known it.

His intense interest in everything drove him to seek some all-inclusive scheme for encompassing anything. But just as some men have no eye for color, Harold had an imperfect gauge for proportion. He would devote as many words in conversation to chiropody, should it happen to get on the roller coaster of his speculations, as to imperialism. His work has remarkable range, pyrotechnic passages, profundity, brilliance, antiseptic strictures, intoxicating suggestiveness, and insight—but it is haphazard in its proportion and uneven in its focus. His sentences or paragraphs stand up better than his books.

· VI ·

With all his achievements as a teacher and scholar at the University of Chicago, Lasswell's career there came to a dismaying end in 1938, when President Robert Maynard Hutchins "let it be known" that neither Lasswell nor Harold Gosnell, another protégé of Charles Merriam, could hope for promotion to the rank of full professorship. It was a strange judgment on the part of Hutchins, whose acute appreciation of intellectual quality was in this case misguided.

It was a disastrous blow to Lasswell. One of the few times I ever heard him speak bitterly was his remark that Merriam had not "stood up" for him, and that "the Chief," deep down, feared to have men more brilliant than he in the department he royally ran.

For a long time Lasswell was without a solid academic base. He faced humbling and uncertain prospects—at the age of thirty-six. His failure to receive a flood of invitations from other universities depressed and confused him. He was paying the price for having been conspicuously undiplomatic within the academic hierarchy—which he had never ceased to puzzle, mystify, or offend. Some had always dismissed him as an eccentric, an intellectual snob, a philosopher *manqué,* or as a half-baked pseudo-psychiatrist who acted as a condescending political scientist. Personal vendettas did not help him. (He once reviewed a book for the *American Political Science Review* in one word: "Rhetoric." He asked me, before submitting it, what I thought of it. I said, "It's too long." I meant, "Better not publish it at all." But he did.)

In New York, Lasswell wrote a series of programs for radio, dramatizing traumatic moments in the lives of Caesar, Muhammad, Napoleon, and others to explain their conduct and their careers. The series was a novel application of psychoanalytical knowledge and a striking example of Harold's capacity to be flawlessly lucid.

After six years of uncertainty, he became professor at the Law School of Yale University (largely through the efforts of Myres MacDougal).

· VII ·

To me, Lasswell was the most imaginative, fertile, and intrepid social scientist of his generation. This may sound strange to those who did not know him. He irritated many by his obsessive propensity for monologues, his helpless parade of awesome erudition, his sardonic dismissal of the mediocre, his impatience with the conventional, his ceaseless, tireless verbal pyrotechnics.

How do I rate him as a teacher? For 90 percent of his students, Harold was not so much a teacher as a torrent. They could no more understand him than they could understand the *Principia Mathematica.* And Harold, easily bored by adolescents in a classroom, often responded with conceptual reveries too intimidating to convey meaning to any but equally imaginative explorers of the new and the problematic.

For another 5 percent of his students, Lasswell was an unnerving comet who had roared in from some alien heaven of the intellect. He despised the narcotic drone and tranquilizing platitudes of ordinary pedagogy. He sought in students brains, discipline, endless curiosity, and the audacity to examine even the most hallowed of subjects with unyielding zest, detachment—and skepticism.

And to the remaining 5 percent, Harold was an eye-opener, a liberator of the mind, a widener of horizons unlike anyone they would ever run into again.

All of us who were enriched by his influence—Nathan Leites, Philleo Nash, Bruce L. Smith, Gabriel Almond, V. O. Key, Renzo Sereno, Herbert Goldhamer, and many others—were electrified by his insights and his confident command of an extraordinary range of subjects. His analyses of the means by which rulers and agitators seduce audiences and themselves, or manipulate the beliefs of their subjects; his work to develop refined techniques for the study of propaganda; his striking efforts to understand the structure and dynamics of public opinion; his ideas about the political consequences of "the foci of attention"; his single-handed invention of "content analysis"; his versatile adaptations of clinical psychology to political and social institutions—all these were serious contributions to political science.

There was nothing which Harold did not find fascinating. He collaborated with an anthropologist in the study of an Andean village; he studied the symbolism of sun dances in an American Indian reservation; he studied aggressive behavior among the recipients of unemployment relief payments in Chicago; he wrote a large book on the propaganda devices of the Communist International; he collaborated with a philosopher (Abraham Kaplan) on a technical semantic study of political terminology.

Lasswell was easily beguiled by an idea. He was often excited by what interested no one else. His passion to be dispassionate drove him to adopt the stance of a surgeon and the style of a cynic: hence, social conversation struck him as "the production of propitiating noises"; a speech by a ward-heeler at a wake became an example of banal "symbol manipulation." Much of this was meant to illuminate via the shock of irony, and was sometimes both elegant and witty, but sometimes it used a sledgehammer to swat fleas.

Lasswell was often exhausting, but always inexhaustible. This I attribute to his phenomenal capacity for work, and his utterly endless reservoir of enthusiasm. He had a ravenous appetite for every conceivable aspect of living—and thinking.

I once asked Sir Isaiah Berlin whether he had ever met Lasswell. (I was sure he knew Lasswell's work.) Berlin nodded and said, "Queer duck." That is all he said.

Harold might very well have been a queer duck. But I learned, or was encouraged and jolted and inspired to learn, more from him than from anyone I ever met. One cannot easily measure, or hope to repay, such indebtedness.

24

EDWARD LEVI

R O B E R T   H.   B O R K

FOR GENERATIONS of its graduates, to think of the University of Chicago is inevitably to think of Edward Levi. That is, of course, especially true of the alumni of the Law School but by no means of them alone. Edward Levi is largely a product of the University but it is equally true that much of today's University is the product of Levi. He received his elementary and secondary education at the Laboratory School, his undergraduate training in the College, his legal training in the Law School, and then, after service in the Department of Justice, became, successively, professor of law, dean of the Law School, provost of the University, and, finally, its president. Rarely have a man and an institution been so identified. It must be even more rare that the identification proves so beneficial to both.

Though it would be difficult to prove, it has always seemed to me that those who not only attended but were shaped by the University of Chicago have a special quality, not merely of intellect but of respect for ideas and their rigorous examination, an absence of sentimentality coupled with profound regard for the virtue of intellectual honesty. Having said that, I must admit that notable exceptions spring to mind, but Edward Levi is not one of them. Though the Levi career extended well beyond the University, he is so rooted there, so integral a part of it as it is of him, that he seemed to take Chicago's strengths with him wherever he went.

So wide-ranging has been Levi's career that the tributes carried in the *University of Chicago Law Review* in 1985 had to be divided into separate pieces on the man as professor, dean, and attorney general of the United States. (It is difficult to know what to make of the omission of his service as provost and then president of the University. Perhaps the editors thought that if it wasn't law, it didn't count.)

· I ·

Assessments focusing on the man's extraordinary accomplishments necessarily miss much of his distinctive personal style. Let it be said at the
outset that Edward Levi is an exceedingly complex man. (One of his few
entirely predictable reactions is irritation at tributes paid to him, such as
this one.) His mind has, at a minimum, a double aspect. This was apparent
in his teaching, it remains so in his writings, and it is today apparent in
every conversation with the man. By a "double (or multiple) aspect" I
mean that he is keenly aware of the complexities of ideas and of the world,
suspicious of overarching systems, and hence very hard to pin down to
many certainties. That does not mean he cannot act—or he would never
have been the successful administrator he repeatedly proved to be—or
that he was not certain about a few fundamental values, including those of
the law. But it does mean, in his writing as in his speech, his full meaning is
sometimes elusive and his pronouncements are occasionally delphic. On
days when he is at the top of his form, all of his pronouncements are delphic. These qualities of mind make for richness of thought, teaching, and
writing, and certainly contributes to his irony and wit. That wit is not always gentle but it is always germane and not, I think, employed for its own
sake, though Edward himself enjoys it.

Those who have known Edward Levi at various times and in various contexts frequently give different accounts of the man. I think that is the case
because to excel in different fields—fields as diverse as teaching in a university and running the Department of Justice—is to adopt the styles appropriate to each. The trial lawyer, the appellate advocate, and the negotiator are
likely to display very different demeanors. So, too, the teacher, whose object
it is to provoke thought and argument, and the administrator, whose goal is
to lead others to desired objectives without provoking opposition, adopt
very different personae. Hence it was, I think, that Edward Levi left very
different impressions on people in his various roles. I observed him in both
his teaching and his administrative capacities. He was my first law professor
and my last attorney general. The contrast in styles was marked; the achievement in each was the same: top of the line.

· II ·

Edward Levi was, quite simply, the greatest classroom teacher I have ever
seen. There is no point in pretending to a balance and moderation of view
on the subject. It would be artificial. As a student at Chicago and a professor

EDWARD LEVI

at Yale, I saw a great deal of teaching, and it is useless to argue with me on this point. That opinion of his performance was, I believe, universally held by his students. Our first experience of him came on the opening day of the first year of law school in his course on the "Elements of the Law." We were quickly and incisively informed of our current gross intellectual inadequacies and of the dizzying heights we would reach in the next three years at the school. We believed half of that. Those of us who had come from the college of the University of Chicago, whose curriculum was then much influenced by Robert Hutchins, anticipated some relief from the steady diet of Aristotle, Plato, and others now disparagingly known as "dead, white, European males." We had not that objection to them, but there is in such matters, for most people, a point of sufficiency. But there we were, in "Elements," reading Plato and Aquinas once more. Not only that, but in the course materials Levi had put together, seeing Aquinas being played off against transcribed debates of the Illinois legislature, decisions by various state and federal courts, and the wisdom of newspaper columnists such as Westbrook Pegler.

"Elements" was an imperialistic course. It canvassed the major ideas of the law and in the process anticipated the most interesting material in the courses we would take later in our three years. But what made the course a success was not so much its undoubtedly fascinating material as the way Levi juggled, dissected, juxtaposed, reassembled, and displayed the most unexpected connections between the ideas of the law. Ideas seemed to ricochet around the room, leaving a number of wounded in their paths. This was done in rapid-fire questioning of students, a questioning that could be painful but invariably uncovered a point most of us had never considered. The point was then turned upside down and refuted in more rapid-fire questioning. Most of us came to wonder what it was we were supposed to believe.

"Elements" was a mystery course. There were 100 students in that course and one professor, and it was unclear whether the mystery enshrouded 100 persons or 101. There was no way to find out. When pressed as to "the truth," Levi deployed one of his most effective weapons, silence and a Mona Lisa smile. (He was also said to resemble Groucho Marx. He did not, really, and the comparison would have been a calumny but for one of Levi's other devices: his way of waggling, simultaneously, an enormous cigar and his eyebrows to deflate overly passionate bursts of student oratory.) The mystery was actually one of the points of the course, and entirely natural to a man who saw complexity where others sought simplicity.

The great questions, including the great questions of the law, do not lend themselves to certain answers. We were led into a discourse that, if we wished, we could pursue to the end of our lives.

I have mentioned that there was a certain amount of pain associated with the class. Levi did not tolerate slow responses, silly answers, or opinions held on sentimental rather than intellectual grounds. Remarks such as "Put pennies on that man's eyes" were not infrequent. He had an extensive repertoire of such encouragements to clear thinking. I do not wish to convey a sense of bluntness, much less brutality, but there was certainly, as there should be, a price to be paid for sloppy thought. Most of the wit was situational, arose out of the particular turn of the argument, and cannot easily be recaptured. Levi had the facility, through questioning, to lead a student to affirm what a moment ago he had fervently denied. Such episodes were so deft that the class often broke into applause and the student himself usually appreciated the lesson. Some of us enjoyed the rigors of the classroom hour, some did not. I did. But that rigor served a valuable purpose, the way the shock of boot camp serves to snap new recruits out of indolent civilian habits. We were to learn to think logically, respond quickly, and turn ideas around. A student would advance an argument, another would be asked to rebut it but would say he could not because he agreed. "For ten thousand dollars, refute the argument." That suggestion had a remarkably stimulating effect on the thinking of lawyers-to-be.

Levi's mind is quicksilver and he greatly admires intellectual speed. I once had the temerity to suggest that a man he admired was a bit of a charlatan. He replied, "Perhaps, but he's so fast." It was the admiration of one intellectual gunslinger for another. Nor is that derogatory. Gunslingers, as we know from the movies, can be virtuous and valuable men.

Having mentioned the mystery and the occasional wounded ego that attended the "Elements" course, I should say that it was far and away the most popular course I have ever known. It is the custom for students to applaud at the conclusion of a course, and law teachers develop very sensitive ears to the decibel level. Sometimes the applause is perfunctory, sometimes enthusiastic, very occasionally absent altogether. I was three years a law student and fifteen years a professor and I have never seen anything like the end of Levi's class in "Elements of the Law." In the Law School building of those days, the professor was in the well of an amphitheater and had to walk up through the middle of the class to leave the room. As Levi closed his book and started up, the entire class rose to its feet in a thunderous standing ovation. They applauded wildly, stamped their feet, threw books and papers in the air. Though Levi had not courted popularity, he had produced a triumph.

Five years after graduation a reunion of that class met in the law school's auditorium. Levi, seated in a chair on the stage, spoke extemporaneously, praising the class in one sentence and taking it all back in the next. The class was delighted. Men were nudging their wives—in those days the class was almost entirely male—whispering, "See what I told you."

· III ·

Levi wrote in the fields he taught. *An Introduction to Legal Reasoning,* first published as an article and then as a slim book, was read by scholars and students inside and outside the law. We pored over it as seminarians do Holy Writ. The book explicates the nature of legal reasoning, the role of analogy, the syllogistic quality of legal argument and the logical fallacy that necessarily inheres in it (as I recall, it is the fallacy of the undistributed middle term), and the differences between judicial reasoning relating to common law, statutory law, and constitutional law. Levi destroyed claims of the scientific quality of the theory of precedent in an article entitled "Natural Law, Precedent, and Thurman Arnold."

Levi's other primary field is antitrust. He wrote the definitive intellectual demolition of the Robinson-Patman Act, which purports to control price discrimination in the service of competition. With Aaron Director, in another article, he explored the paradoxes and unsatisfactory quality of antitrust doctrine generally. Later, when I came to write in the field, Levi thought my arguments and conclusions too certain, and I must concede at least an outside chance that he is right, though I have never been sure whether he actively disagrees on fundamental points or is merely uneasy, as he is uneasy with all attempts to construct a complete system.

The relationship with Aaron Director is worth at least an article in itself, for it resulted in what has come to be called the "law and economics movement." There have been a great many "law and . . ." ventures but none remotely approaches the success of the economic analysis of legal doctrine and legal institutions. The Chicago Law School was the first to put an economist on its faculty; Director's predecessor in that capacity was Henry Simon. Levi brought Director into the antitrust course to provide an analysis of the case law. Though the basic antitrust statute, the Sherman Act, was then almost sixty years old, this was, incredibly, the first time a first-class price theorist had looked systematically at what judges had developed and fondly imagined to be economic reasoning. Antitrust, dealing with competition and monopoly, was the natural place for economics to find its initial lodgement in the law. But the success achieved there stimulated the application of economic analysis to other branches of the law, sometimes with more, sometimes with less, success, depending upon the amenability of the area to this form of reasoning.

Levi occasionally seemed a bit ambivalent about the enterprise, perhaps because of his ambivalence about doctrines that seemed to him not sufficiently to allow for ambiguity. Nonetheless, he encouraged the intellectual effort, hired people to engage in it, and supported the establishment of the influential *Journal of Law and Economics*. His support was strong and critical to the success of the endeavor. What came to be known as the "Chicago school," was in fact merely the application of rigorous economics to the law. That it started at Chicago rather than elsewhere is to be attributed to the combination of Levi and Aaron Director.

· IV ·

Despite this and other examples of intellectual vitality on its staff, in the late 1940s the Law School of the University of Chicago was in decline. The faculty had areas of great strength but also, it must be said, pockets of considerable weakness. The decline in the school's ability to attract first-rate students was for a time masked by the return of the veterans of the Second World War. Over 100 of us entered in 1948, about the capacity of the school at the time, and, as student bodies go, it was a mature, intellectually vigorous group. I left for the service once more in 1950 and, upon returning in 1952, found a startlingly different class, smaller, less mature, and intellectually more passive. The veterans' pool now being exhausted, the school was learning its real drawing power. But Edward Levi had become dean in 1950 and a thoroughgoing renovation was already under way—of the physical plant, the teaching staff, the student body, and, most important, of the morale of the entire institution. There was, in candor, much room for improvement in all four.

The old Law School had its charms; a building of somewhat grim medieval aspect and a dim, uncomfortable, and inconvenient interior, it fitted my idea at the time of a proper temple of the law. It was seriously inadequate in classroom space, offices, and library facilities. Levi embarked on a fundraising campaign that was enormous for a school of that size, and ultimately built the new Law School on the south side of the Midway. The main building is a striking glass structure designed by Eero Saarinen. It was one of Levi's more remarkable accomplishments that he managed to wring four separate dedication ceremonies, complete with major national figures as speakers, out of a single building.

The teaching body of the Law School already had a solid, even spectacular, core. Aside from Levi and Director, there were men such as Walter Blum, Harry Kalven, and Bernard Meltzer. These were close friends of Levi's and supported the dean, as not all teaching bodies do, in his efforts. Soon such well-known scholars as Karl Llewellyn, Kenneth Culp Davis, and Roscoe Steffen were lured from other schools and gave Chicago added attractiveness. Younger teachers were recruited, and the teaching staff that emerged was among the most lustrous and intellectually productive in the nation.

All of this, of course, began to attract more and better applicants for places in the entering classes. But Levi, not disposed to wait upon gradual progress, began a program of national scholarships that brought in a very high-quality student body in a relatively short time. I had joined a prominent Chicago law firm which had not particularly sought Chicago graduates in the past but now began eagerly to recruit them.

The moral and intellectual excitement of the school was enhanced by a series of programs that brought speakers prominent in the law to the campus. At one such occasion, Levi was described by Thurman Arnold, his old boss at the Antitrust Division of the Department of Justice, as the "tutelary divinity of this great theological seminary." By that time it seemed to us an accurate assessment.

· V ·

Levi's performance as dean led to his becoming the University's first provost in 1962, under President George Beadle. By this time, my direct observation of Levi's work had ended, but I think I know how he must have operated in the higher reaches of university administration by what I saw of him later as attorney general of the United States during Gerald Ford's presidency.

In 1968, President Beadle left and the trustees of the University made Edward Levi president. It was a fitting culmination to an academic career that had, from first to last, been rooted in the University of Chicago. Levi's particular strength was that he was able to deal effectively, and on their own terms, with groups as diverse as the teachers, the alumni, leaders of bench, bar, and business, and with the city administration. He developed a particular admiration for Mayor Richard J. Daley, who worked effectively with all of the city's diverse constituencies and was particularly helpful to the University of Chicago during a lengthy period of neighborhood transition and rebuilding. Daley was once asked why he was so cooperative with the University, many of whose teachers could not appreciate his virtues, and he said, "Because it is the only great university with Chicago in its name."

Those were troubled times at the University. Not only did the deterioration of the surrounding neighborhood threaten its ability to attract the best teachers and students but in the late 1960s student turmoil broke out as it did at almost all universities. Chicago, under Levi, handled it far better than most. When the main administration building was seized and occupied, the University waited the radicals out and then, unlike other universities that remained supine, instituted disciplinary hearings that resulted in a number of expulsions and suspensions. It was a salutary reaffirmation of the purposes of a university and the limits of acceptable behavior within it. Levi was determined to perserve the intellectual culture that had come into his keeping. If Edward Levi is in large measure a product of the University of Chicago, it is equally true that much of today's University, much more than new buildings and faculty, is attributable to Edward Levi.

· VI ·

Events elsewhere were to take Levi away from Hyde Park. By 1973, the presidency of Richard Nixon was unraveling, a process that I observed at first hand from the position of solicitor general of the United States, and, for a brief period, as acting attorney general. In the summer of 1974, President Nixon resigned and Vice President Gerald Ford, who succeeded to the presidency, proceeded to restaff the executive branch. The incumbent attorney general, William Bart Saxbe, was reassigned as ambassador to India and President Ford asked Edward Levi to become the new attorney general. I was extremely pleased but a trifle apprehensive on Edward's behalf. Those were turbulent times in Washington and it was not entirely clear that the town's blood lust had dissipated. In just over a year, the Department of Justice had known three attorneys general, not counting my time as acting, and three deputies attorney general. The turnover of assistant attorneys general had also been high. The department was badly in need of stability.

Edward came to the Department of Justice at a time, moreover, when some of its major branches, as well as other institutions in the executive branch with whose performance the department should have been concerned, had been allowed to edge out of control, to develop attitudes and habits worrisome in a country devoted to the rule of law. I do not mean to suggest wholesale lawlessness, a charge made by some congressional and journalistic demagogues. Nor was it true that what was worrisome had developed only during the Nixon years. The problems went back much further than that. Yet these were fundamentally sound institutions whose vigor as well as integrity were essential to the American society.

Reforming entrenched practices in government is not easily done. No headway might have been made with executive branch agencies outside the department, or indeed with some organizations in, if not of, the department, if Levi had not had the president's confidence and complete backing. It is incorrect to suppose that an attorney general has merely to give orders to correct matters in the Department of Justice. Like a major university, the department is a sprawling collection of fiefdoms and baronies: the various divisions, each headed by an assistant attorney general (Criminal, Civil, Civil Rights, Tax, Lands and Natural Resources, and so on), as well as the Federal Bureau of Investigation, the Bureau of Immigration and Naturalization, the Bureau of Prisons, and much more. It is reasonable to suppose that the experience of heading a major university stood Levi in good stead in Washington. Aside from the normal—and high—degree of organizational inertia, the department's baronies have a capacity for deliberate, if often oblique, resistance. Those who disagree with an attorney general's policies possess all the resources of obfuscation, ambiguity, recalcitrance, pretended misunderstanding, professed inability to pinpoint responsibility, and all of the other devices familiar to bureaucrats the world over. Moreover, each of the fiefdoms with its own agenda is likely to have allies on the outside, in the press, in Congress, in the manifold "public interest" organizations, and even elsewhere in the administration. If their agendas are threatened by an attorney general, they will leak word of the fact, or their versions of the fact, and hostile stories will appear, congressmen and their staffs will call and write.

Levi and I once had what was supposed to be a highly confidential conference with the head of a division who disagreed with a course of action we were contemplating. Despite his promise of confidentiality, that assistant attorney general was seen in the halls as soon as the meeting ended giving his version of the meeting to several members of the press. The next day's stories, not surprisingly, portrayed him as the sole defender of truth and justice at the meeting.

The national media were uniformly respectful of Levi's integrity and intelligence but sometimes disagreed sharply with his policies. One morning I found him in his office grumbling about an uncomplimentary, and uninformed, story in the *Washington Post*. I said, "Don't worry about it, Ed. They've said much worse things about me." He said, "Yes, but it didn't feel the same when they said it about you." (One of Edward Levi's few entirely predictable reactions is irritation at tributes paid him, but he demonstrates balance by displaying equal irritation over unfriendly pieces.)

An attorney general's policies are thus frequently compromised, deflected, or even reversed in the process of their transmittal and application. All of this means that an attorney general is held responsible for much more than he actually controls. It also means that reforming institutions which do not believe they need reform requires patience, subtlety, and light but unrelenting pressure.

Though I had known Edward Levi as a teacher and scholar, I had never witnessed firsthand his style of management. That was a revelation. He practiced administration by discussion, often by seminar. In that way he undertook the enormously arduous, politically difficult, and intellectually demanding task of reform. He did this without the fanfare, recriminations, and moral posturing that would have made him enormously popular with the press and that segment of the public which thinks real reform inseparable from confrontation, firings, and the public utterance of pieties.

Though Levi made it plain that reform was coming, the very process of discussion, and the demonstration that he was alert to real problems, gained the confidence of the various organizations. With them he engaged in a process of rethinking their missions, identifying their difficulties, and redefining the appropriate limits to their discretion. The FBI under J. Edgar Hoover, for example, had often failed to distinguish between a subversive organization's illegal underground activities and its legitimate role in open political processes. There were instances in which the legitimate role was subjected to surveillance or even disrupted by covert actions. Levi ended that. (Ironically, one organization sued him personally because a surveillance was continued for a brief time before he reached the matter, studied it, and ordered the surveillance ended.) In particularly delicate areas, written procedures were worked out that closely defined what might or might not be done. Where the problems did not allow for detailed definition, the regulations located responsibility, required periodic reviews, and limited the uses that could be made of information.

Edward Levi thus introduced reforms and reorganizations that brought several institutions of government into conformity with legal principles and did it without destroying their morale or effectiveness. It was a job that the country badly needed, though it was done so quietly that the country remained almost entirely unaware that it was accomplished and what was owed in gratitude to the man who did it.

The attorney general's share of the regular work of the department, at least where major or sensitive decisions were concerned, was carried on in much the same fashion. I saw Levi making decisions about prosecutions, about desegregation remedies, about the drafting of legislation, and about the interaction of the demands of the Constitution with the imperatives of national security. These decisions were not made by the attorney general alone nor even just with the advice of people directly responsible in the area involved. He brought into the discussion people within the department whose judgment he valued, and even occasionally brought in as discussants persons from outside the department whose discretion and wisdom he trusted and admired. This was not a device for avoiding responsibility, for Levi often went against the advice he was given. It was, rather, a way of ensuring that every aspect of a problem had been uncovered and weighed. These small conferences were like good seminars and the decisions made reflected sensitivity to individuals as well as to competing institutional claims and the basic values of law. Though there was humor even in the gravest discussions, Levi on these occasions displayed no ambiguity and made no delphic pronouncements but explored problems with acute awareness of all their ramifications.

To take a single example, one of the most difficult decisions for any government lawyer is the decision in a close case not to prosecute. For some reason, people generally regard the decision to prosecute as somehow heroic, even though the prosecutor risks little himself. Prosecutors further down in the department wanted to ask a grand jury for an indictment, which they certainly could have gotten, but Levi was troubled. The man in question, a high-ranking government official, had acted in a national security matter in a way that seemed appropriate to most people at the time. But standards of conduct and public morality had undergone a sudden shift. The question was whether to apply the new expectations retroactively. It was not, strictly speaking, a legal question but an issue of justice to the individual. Levi presided over several extended small-group discussions, and in the end the consensus, which was not quite unanimous, was that, though we could get an indictment and had a good chance of obtaining a conviction, the department should not go forward. A decision the other way would have gained favorable publicity for the department and the attorney general, but the decision taken was the correct one, because it was just.

The quality of decision-making determines the integrity and vitality of an institution. In the case of the Department of Justice that quality also determines the degree to which justice is done. The quality of decision-making in Levi's tenure as attorney general was superb. I regret only that, of necessity, it could not be made visible to the public.

Edward and Kate, who greatly assisted his career in all of its phases, are back in Hyde Park, vital members of the university community once more. I like to think of them there—the University would not be itself without them—and look forward to our next meeting, though, given that I have just written a tribute, I do so with some apprehension.

25

RICHARD MCKEON

1 9 0 0 – 1 9 8 5

E L D E R   O L S O N

THORNTON WILDER and Ronald S. Crane both urged me to study with Richard McKeon. He was a professor of philosophy newly brought to Chicago from the department of philosophy of Columbia University by Robert Maynard Hutchins. I must confess that I was not greatly enthusiastic about taking a course in philosophy. Philosophy, when it meant other than one's personal code of life, did not mean much to me. I had read Plato's *Republic* and several of his Dialogues, finding them merely charming, if odd, conversations; Aristotle's *Poetics,* which I thought nonsense from start to finish; chunks of Nietzsche and Schopenhauer, both of whom I despised; and a few other things, like Will Durant's *The Story of Philosophy.*

· I ·

Nevertheless, not one to disregard counselors proven good, I duly enrolled in a course called, if I remember correctly, "The Intellectual History of Western Europe." Promptly at 3:30 a strong-looking man of above average height entered the room in Classics, ascended the dais, and took his place at the lectern. He had brown hair that might have been curly had it not been cropped almost to a crew cut, a furrowed brow with bushy eyebrows, horn-rimmed glasses, and above a firm mouth and jaw, a mustache (destined to disappear in a week or two). His lips were curled slightly in what could have been the beginning or the ending of a smile. He glowered briefly at us, adjusted his notes and his glasses, and began to speak in a pleasant, somewhat husky baritone voice.

The course—a lecture course—was a year-long one, ranging from antiquity to modern times. It was organized around the perennial problem of knowledge. We had barely finished the first week when I made a startling

300

RICHARD McKEON

discovery: *I did not really know how to read!* I had been reading Plato simply for pleasure, with only a faint notion of the underlying argument. I had been like a water-skier, concerned only with the surface he was skimming over; now I was looking through a glass-bottomed boat at the undreamt-of submarine events going on below. Ascending dialectic? Descending dialectic? Combination? Division? I was suddenly in a very strange world.

I think the mark of a truly great professor or teacher lies not only in what is taught or how it is taught but also in what happens in the mind of a receptive student. This is of course a subjective matter, and has to be described as such. It is certainly a process of ever-widening vistas, one in which, to use Pope's words, "Hills peep o'er hills, and Alps on Alps arise." More importantly, it is as if the student were being given an instrument, like a telescope or a microscope, to improve perception—even, to state it more strongly, new organs of perception.

That is what it was like to study under Richard McKeon. He went from philosopher to philosopher, showing the form the problem took for each, shifts in the meanings of terms, the philosophic method entailed, the workings of the arguments. Contrasting the methods and, so to speak, their points of suspension, he seemed almost to be making a series of dialectical "cat's cradles." From the first he had invited us to interrupt his lectures at any time for questions, further discussion, even challenges, but if a student took this as an invitation to begin a lecture of his own, McKeon cut him short and settled the issue in seconds. It was amusing to see someone forced in a moment or two to admit that a proposition which he had just called "trivial" or "preposterous" was in fact a profound philosophic truth, and McKeon himself seemed always amused, ending the matter with a benign but faintly ironic smile.

Challenges were most frequent during the second quarter, which dealt with the medieval period. In one instance a student began, "But *all* medieval philosophers held that—" etc., etc., and McKeon stopped him by simply saying, "Name *one.*" During this quarter we were using as texts McKeon's own *Selections from the Medieval Philosophers,* as well as some publications of the Society for the Propagation of Christian Knowledge, but in my usual way I went beyond these, reading widely in Augustine, Jerome, Aquinas, and the *Patrologia Latina.*

By the end of the course I was convinced of the futility of discussing the meaning of a term, or the truth or falsity of a proposition, apart from its methodological context. I have mentioned McKeon's careful attention to changes in the meanings of terms; his essay, "Literary Criticism and the

Concept of Imitation in Antiquity," reprinted in *Critics and Criticism,* is a remarkable example of this. I was convinced of two other things: that I had better study logic to beat the band, and that I absolutely needed more work with McKeon.

Accordingly, I enrolled in his course in the *Nicomachean Ethics* of Aristotle. I had spent the interval studying logic and reading everything on ethics I could lay my hands on, including Aristotle, and I thought (with an ironic little smile of my own) that I was now loaded for bear. I could not have been more wrong. If I had been greatly impressed before, I was now utterly stunned. I do not think I am easily cowed, but it was six weeks before I dared open my mouth. There is always a certain rivalry, I think, between an eager student and his respected professor; I was shorn of all hope of it.

It is impossible to describe that course; let this suffice. After preliminary sessions devoted to various accounts of Aristotle's life and the editorial fortunes of his works, a review of the whole corpus and the philosophic system involved in it, McKeon began an elaborately detailed analysis of the argument of the *Ethics,* working from the Greek text and taking that apart almost word by word. I had never seen anything like it for minuteness, precision, and erudition.

· II ·

I was to take many more courses with him, in Plato, Aristotle, and others. However, I went to his office only twice in all that time: once when I had a problem in the *Ethics,* and once to ask him about classical and medieval treatises on prosody (my doctoral dissertation, of which he was one of the readers and advisers, was on a theory of prosody). In consequence, I did not know him as a person rather than as a professor until the night of my final oral, when he invited all of the participants to his apartment following the examination.

His wife Muriel met us at the door. I have never known a more wonderful person than Muriel McKeon. She seemed truly to radiate love and understanding. When she learned that Ann (my then wife) and I had had a baby girl the previous year, she took me in to see their son Peter, who was about the same age. (Peter was dutifully fast asleep.)

It is hard to say when some friendships begin; at any rate, the McKeon family and the Olsons became fast friends, entertaining one another frequently with dinners and parties. Muriel often brought Peter to play with our Annie, and sometimes on Sundays both families walked together.

I soon learned that McKeon's gruff manner was only mock-gruff, one of many put-ons dictated by his quirky sense of humor. It concealed a warm, gentle person whose playfulness vanished if he thought something was troubling you, to be replaced by instant concern. Friendships were clearly of great importance to him, though he would never allow them to influence professional decisions.

He and I somehow formed a habit of taking long late nocturnal walks together, making great loops around Jackson Park, at least once a week. On these we usually discussed philosophy or argued amicably, or both. He delighted in this intellectual fencing, as I did. My original awe of him had long since given way to an even more solidly founded esteem, and we debated as equals. I remember especially a spirited defense of Nietzsche, and another of Schopenhauer, against my own furious attacks. Curiously, we never talked much about Aristotle, except that I tried frequently, and vainly, to persuade him to publish his magnificent analyses of Aristotle's arguments.

I think I know, now, why he would not. He wanted no one to come away from his lectures or writings with a fixed mind—a mind, that is, moving in channels which he had pre-cut. He detested parroting; if a student played parrot, he would instantly challenge him, questioning the very statement he himself had made only moments before. There was an extraordinary trio of lectures on William of Ockham. In the first of these he portrayed Ockham as a simon-pure, thoroughgoing Aristotelian. In the second, he showed him to be anything but that. In the third he pointed out both the Aristotelian and the non-Aristotelian elements in Ockham. Dumbfounded like the rest of use, one student demanded, "*What* are we supposed to think?" Smiling, McKeon said, "You are supposed to *think*." I am told that he once dealt with Aquinas in the same fashion.

The minute analyses of arguments always stopped abruptly; we were to continue them; he was merely illustrating what could be done. For example, only the first book of the *Ethics* was given full treatment; the latter books were touched on only in crucial places. The final examination consisted of one question: "Give a general outline of the entire work." He preferred hints to flat-out statements; he wanted to activate intellect and imagination rather than memory, though he thought the last faculty has been much under-cultivated in modern education.

Again and again he illustrated how a proposition false in one dialectical context may be true in another, and vice versa. Thus, in teaching Plato's *Republic,* he pointed out that the definitions of justice refuted by Socrates in Book I—where the context is one of the relation of individual to individual—become true in the later books, where the context involves the relation of the individual to the Ideal State. For example, Thrasymachus' definition of justice as "the interest of the stronger," false in Book I, later becomes true, for the State is stronger, and the Ideal State is just. Thrasymachus himself, McKeon pointed out, abandons his early ferocity and becomes mild, illustrating the influence of philosophy upon character. McKeon made us aware, too, of the possibility of diverse valid logics and dialectics and of variations in warrants of inference.

He drew heavily on the methodological differences between Plato and Aristotle; the method of the former he called "holoscopic," that of the latter, "meroscopic." He told me that this was the most important distinction he ever made; he was to develop it later to astonishing complexity. He would lay out the intricate apparent agreements and disagreements of different philosophies, sometimes in bewildering diagrams that resembled the cat's cradles of which I have spoken. I told him once that in his constant balancings of one philosophy against another, he was a "maker of philosophic mobiles." He nodded, pleased, and laughed.

· III ·

Friends though we were, the differences in our temperaments—not to mention minds—were so great that it was impossible for either to understand the other completely. I remarked once that we were two men walking in the same direction on opposite sides of a thick glass wall, able to communicate only by hand-signs which were bound to be misinterpreted, and he agreed. It was perhaps that very sharpness of difference that led him to ask me to teach a tandem course with him, with texts ranging from Thucydides and Lucretius to Edward Albee and Wallace Stevens. He taught Thucydides as if the history were fiction, I taught it as history; he taught the *De Rerum Natura* as poetry, I taught it as philosophical argument. And so on, throughout: difference, difference.

This much we had in common as teachers: we both were aware that we were not merely teaching students as students, but present students as people of the future. We did not teach *answers,* though we had them and gave them; we taught problems and methods of solving problems, for answers come and go, but problems and methods of solving them remain. Students were not to think as we thought, but to *think*.

After my retirement from the University of Chicago, we naturally saw less of each other, for my wife and I moved at once to New Mexico, but I was able to return now and then for a lunch, a dinner, or a visit. I remember one walk with him to his office, during which we both laughed about the myth of "the Chicago School of Neo-Aristotelian criticism." McKeon had certainly supplied some of us with philosophical bases for what we wrote but had hardly ventured into literary criticism himself. I doubt that he had much interest in criticism, ours or any other; I was astonished to find him saying, in his final published article, that the "Chicago critics" had eschewed theory and restricted themselves to practical criticism. What the devil did he think I had been doing for decades? I had given him, along with everything else I had published, no less than three volumes of theory. I suppose he never read them.

· IV ·

The last time I saw him alive, we ran into each other almost on his doorstep (I was coming to visit him), and I nearly did not recognize him; he had grown a beard, and looked like one of his own medieval philosophers. He had had a heart attack while in Europe and had obviously been ill since, but he was as alert and cordial as ever. When I left his house, his last words to me (delivered with a wry grin) were, "No more of those long walks around Jackson Park for us!"

I want to say something about him that I am perhaps not entitled to say, for I cannot claim to be a philosopher. Nevertheless, I am not unread in modern philosophy, and in any case, have a right to my opinion. I would say without hesitation or qualification that Richard McKeon was one of the greatest of modern philosophers. He produced no philosophy, as such, of his own, no system of doctrines; what he did produce was something that I have likened elsewhere to a Copernican revolution; not a philosophy, but a *meta-philosophy* which, in its systematic display of the oppositions and correlations of diverse philosophies, adumbrated a matrix from which all valid philosophies were generated, as well as a general dialectic explaining how the diverse dialectics operated. He produced, thus *a* key—hinting at *the* key—to all philosophy. If I am correct in this, he had made one of the greatest discoveries in the history of philosophy.

It is impossible for me to assess my debt to him, or to disentangle in my work what was his from what is mine. As I once wrote, "If I have ever said anything of value about the *Poetics,* I should gladly see it attributed to him, rather than cheat him of one particle of his due." This in spite of the fact that I never studied the *Poetics* with him.

To study under him was the rarest of privileges. To have had his friendship was an honor I must still endeavor to deserve.

26

FRANKLIN CHAMBERS MCLEAN

1 8 8 8 – 1 9 6 8

RICHARD L. LANDAU AND PAUL HODGES

ORGANIZER, administrator, scientist, and humanitarian in advance of his time—these were some of the activities that have earned Franklin McLean his place as a leader of medical education in the United States in the twentieth century. By the time he reached the age of forty-three he had started two medical schools. Not the sort of fly-by-night schools that Abraham Flexner had been attempting to have closed, but innovative and enduring institutions which made their mark. Although Franklin McLean would in all likelihood have preferred to be remembered as a distinguished investigator and scholar, it is his relatively short career as an administrative leader which will be appreciated here. With the exception of Flexner, it would be difficult to name an American of this century who could equal McLean's impact on our system of medical education. His influence can, of course, be ascribed to the much-copied clinical arrangements which he created on the campus of the University of Chicago.

· I ·

Although at least three-fourths of his life was spent as a resident of Illinois, Franklin McLean earned a remarkable international reputation. He was born in Maroa, Illinois, and spent the first sixteen years of his life there. He was educated in a one-room school and arrived at the University of Chicago in 1905 without a high school diploma. The University was then just thirteen years old. He received his bachelor's degree in three years and an M.D. and Ph.D. in 1910. His clinical work was done at Rush Medical College; his research was done under A. J. Carlson in the department of physiology. His father, who had also received his medical degree from Rush Medical College, had instilled in Franklin the ambition to become

307

both a physician and a professor of medicine at the University of Chicago. Young McLean served his internship at Cook County Hospital. When that was finished, he left to become a professor of pharmacology at the medical school of the University of Oregon, which was one of those severely criticized by Flexner.

After one year at Oregon, he spent another working in the laboratory of Otto Loewi at the University of Graz. On returning to the United States in 1914, he visited the Rockefeller Institute where he immediately impressed Rufus Cole, the director, Alfred Cohn, and Donald Van Slyke, who had just read McLean's paper on the measurement of blood glucose. He started to work at once in Cohn's laboratory on methods of evaluating renal function, and spent many hours with the Rockefeller group, which included Flexner, discussing their ideas on the future of medical education. Obviously Franklin did more than listen. His brightness and the freshness of his thought so impressed them that he was selected, at the age of twenty-eight, to plan and manage the Peking Union Medical College which the Rockefeller Foundation had decided to start in its effort to improve the quality of medicine practiced in China.

· II ·

Architecturally, the Peking Union Medical College was designed in a manner that would maximize the convenience for a staff which would be expected to teach, practice Western-style medicine, and carry out fundamental medical research—much of it on the diseases indigenous to China. While awaiting the completion of the building, he went to France to serve in the American Expeditionary Force in the First World War. At the end of the war, he returned to the United States to find the staff for the medical college in Peking. This done, he proceeded to China to open and direct the new medical school. Almost from the opening day, he found as much time as possible free of administration to continue his research on renal function and electrolyte metabolism. In 1920, he gave up the directorship of the Peking Union Medical College to become the chairman of its department of medicine. Thus, he was able to spend even more time in the laboratory.

A few months before the scheduled termination of his China duty, he met a strikingly attractive young obstetrician, Helen Vincent, who had been sent to join the staff of the medical college. They were soon married and returned to the United States in 1923. She changed her specialty to psychiatry and eventually became the doyenne of psychoanalysts in Chicago.

FRANKLIN CHAMBERS McLEAN

On his return to New York, Franklin McLean learned that he had been selected by the Rockefeller group to start the detailed planning, staffing, and ultimately the initial directorship of the new medical school to be established at the University of Chicago. William Rainey Harper had affiliated the University of Chicago with the already existing Rush Medical College in 1896 in order to provide for the clinical training of those students who took their two years of basic science at the University of Chicago. It had, however, long been the aim of the University to establish a full-time clinical teaching staff and an institution to house it on the main campus. There had been delays because of insufficient financial resources and the First World War. However, by 1922, with the active assistance of Dr. Frank Billings, who was the outstanding internist in Chicago, and with the financial support and encouragement of the Rockefeller Institute and Foundation, the University was ready to proceed. With the promise of a substantial gift by a wealthy relative of Dr. Billings, the planning of Albert Merritt Billings Hospital and the University of Chicago Clinics could be started.

· III ·

Franklin McLean was appointed to be professor of medicine in 1924, in order that he might have a major influence in the development of the new institution. He was influential in changing the proposed site of the new hospital from the south to the north side of the Midway Plaisance so the offices and laboratories of the clinical departments could be close to the laboratories of the departments of the basic sciences, on the University campus. The plan for the new hospital and clinics was modeled to some extent on the plan which had been followed at the Peking Union Medical College. The essential feature was the location of offices of the teaching staff and their laboratories in close proximity to the hospital and clinics where they were to see and care for their patients.

The University of Chicago, the Rockefeller Foundation and Institute, and Franklin McLean were emphatic in their agreed aim of having a unique full-time clinical teaching staff devoted to clinical research and medical scholarship. There was to be no medical school as such. The two original clinical departments of medicine and surgery were formed as new science departments within what became in a few years the division of the biological sciences. Patient care was added to the usual research and teaching functions of the scientific departments. There were in addition two exceptional aspects of the relationship of the academic medical staff to the University. Their contracts called for four quarters of service each year instead of the usual three and prohibited the acceptance of fees for service outside the institution. (In the early 1940s, Robert Hutchins, then president of the University, attempted to extend this system by the introduction of the four-quarter, full-time contract to the rest of the University. He was unsuccessful.)

Dallas Phemister was appointed to the chairmanship of the department of surgery. He responded with enthusiasm to the novel organization and aims of the new institution; he set about appointing physiologists and anatomists to his clinical staff to assure that the new department would be genuinely oriented towards research. His outstanding success as chairman of the department of surgery was essential to the survival of the new organization. Without the accomplishments of Dallas Phemister, Franklin McLean's directorship of the new clinical side and his chairmanship of the new department of medicine would have come to naught.

Once the new medical building and its clinical teaching and research staffs were in operation, it was assumed that one way or another the hospital and clinics would survive. As a matter of fact, during the difficulties of the first few years, which included the beginning of the great depression, the hostile Rush Medical College offered to take over the University of Chicago hospital and transfer to it all of their activities from Presbyterian Hospital.

The real measure of McLean's accomplishment is thus not that the institution survived but that almost sixty-five years after the doors of Billings Hospital opened in 1927 his aims are still the aims of the department of medicine; the traditions he set in motion still persist almost unchanged. Moreover, while holding to its course, his institution has grown and adapted itself to the changes in medical practice which have resulted from spectacular scientific advances and altered patterns of financial support of medical care. (A Commonwealth Fund study completed in 1990 showed that the satisfaction of patients at the University of Chicago exceeded that of all the other academic medical centers dealt with in the survey.) A larger fraction of University of Chicago graduates in medicine have full-time academic appointments in the teaching of biomedical subjects than those who graduate from any other American medical school. The institution has been widely emulated, and the department of medicine has provided leadership in the country as a whole, although not so many of its present teachers are aware of this.

Franklin McLean drew most of his new staff from the Peking Union Medical College, the Rockefeller Institute, and Chicago. He sought and received guidance from his Rockefeller mentors, Cole and Cohn. But the decisions were his. When one of his advisers hinted that he was being too provincial in his appointments, he responded that the medical schools of the eastern seaboard had already appointed, and were holding on to, the scientists of that part of the country.

With some emphasis on infectious disease research, which was appropriate at the time, all the important subspecialties of medicine, including radiology, neurology, and psychiatry were provided for in the original department of medicine faculty. McLean did not really practice medicine himself. This was a striking departure for the head of a department of medicine of that era, who was expected to be first of all an outstanding and fully rounded clinician and teacher. Exceptional competence in research was not among the usual qualifications for chairmen or heads of departments of medicine in 1927. As a matter of fact, many heads of departments did not even hold full-time, salaried academic appointments at that time.

From the time the doors of the institution first opened, McLean devoted as much time as he could to his research. After three years he resigned as chairman of the department of medicine, while remaining director of the clinics. The next chairman was Russell Wilder, a distinguished endocrinologist from the Mayo Clinic. He returned to Mayo after just two years, and after a short hiatus with O. H. Robertson as acting chairman, George Dick, a very prominent Chicago internist and research worker in streptococcus was appointed to take the post. Dick refused to accept the appointment if McLean were allowed to have an office and laboratory within the hospital and clinics building. Franklin McLean acceded to this egregious demand by accepting an appointment as professor of pathological physiology in the department of physiology. He moved his laboratory to Abbott Hall where he remained an active investigator and scholar until his death at the age of eighty.

· IV ·

How could McLean, in such a short time, have had an immense impact on the future of his department and American medicine? His appointments policy was perhaps the most important factor. He made few errors in the choice of the relatively young persons whom he persuaded to join him. Despite their different interests and emphases all were dedicated to the idea of the kind of department he wished to have; they were more than willing to make the financial sacrifices imposed by their appointments as full-time academics without any income from professional practice. All wanted to pursue a research career, and in this regard Franklin McLean certainly made himself a model to emulate. It was also critically important that he did not establish a hierarchical mode of chairmanship. Somehow he made clear to his colleagues that they could follow their own scientific bent. There was no competition between subspecialties; a person in one subspecialty was not regarded as being in competition with colleagues in other areas of specialization. McLean managed to avoid the strains which are common in universities. Success in his department was like success in golf; one tried to beat the course—not his colleague.

McLean was many years ahead of his time in appreciating the importance of academic clinicians having close working relations with basic scientists. Although some basic scientists have long maintained that what the clinician wanted was a scientific "handmaiden," this was far from Franklin's intent. What he envisaged was an institution with independent nonclinical scientists whose research interests were served by close association with internists, and who would collaborate with clinicians when the circumstances warranted. McLean persuaded Albert Lasker to finance such a venture with a grant of one million dollars. Thus, the Lasker Foundation was established, well supplied with funds for technical assistance and several scientists. A. Baird Hastings, an outstanding young biochemist who later became the pillar of Harvard's biochemistry department, headed the Lasker Foundation while serving as professor of biochemistry in the department of medicine. He subsequently appointed two additional biochemists. They felt at home in McLean's department of medicine, carrying out independent studies, participating fully in seminars, and collaborating from time to time with one or another of the clinicians. Today most of the ten sections of the department of over 100 members find the availability of such basic science members, and the resulting opportunities for collaboration, essential for their own success.

When the medical center started, it was clear that there would be no patients unless they were cared for by the academic staff. There were no "courtesy staff members" to admit their private patients; this is a frequent pattern elsewhere. There were virtually no referrals of patients. Physicians in Chicago were anything but friendly because patients at the medical center were charged. The institution was accused by the Chicago Medical Society of practicing "socialized medicine." To compete successfully, the staff had to include excellent practitioners—not just aloof consultants. The original plans had intended that all patients should be "free," but such generosity could not be afforded, and McLean and Phemister persuaded the board of trustees of the University to allow professional fees. This change in plans was severely criticized by Abraham Flexner, who believed that only patients who did not pay a fee could be utilized in this manner. But it did not turn out to be a handicap; the conduct of the academic medical men and women demonstrated that, when handled tactfully, paying patients could contribute to the instruction of students, residents, and interns, and were more reliable research subjects than the often uneducated poor. The status of paying patients is no longer a basis for discrimination of this sort in any of America's medical schools.

The organization of the subspecialties of the department of medicine developed very rapidly. It was efficient. If one were expected to practice, teach, and investigate, it became natural for the members of the academic staff to try to restrict their practice to the general area in which they carried out research. To appreciate the problems in gastroenterology one had to see a good number of such patients, said Walter Palmer, who was the first to establish a specialty in a clinic. It soon became obvious that this specialization was advantageous to teaching, scholarship, and investigation. Russell Wilder said, just about three years after the institution opened, "For the purposes of carrying out its clinical and teaching duties and research, the department of medicine is loosely divided into sections. It is our opinion that the advantages of the specialization which this sub-division involves outweigh the disadvantages; the patient benefits from it medically, receiving more expert medical attention than he would in the field of medicine concerned. The student benefits by receiving the latest instruction in each separate field; and the study of disease and the advancement of knowledge should be promoted more efficiently." With some variation, this division of responsibility among subspecialties is now the prevailing pattern throughout academic departments of medicine in the United States.

· V ·

McLean's forced transfer to the department of physiology was beneficial to his research. At the time he was collaborating with Baird Hastings and Emmet Bay on the influence of electrolytes on the cat's heart. McLean's removal forced the abandonment of this study, because there was no constant-temperature warm room in Abbott Hall. The heart of the cold-blooded frog became the subject of investigation. This enforced shift led to the bioassay procedure for precisely determining the amount of ionized calcium in a biological fluid and the renowned nomogram widely utilized for many years for estimating the ionized calcium level in plasma. McLean collaborated with William Bloom of the department of anatomy in pioneering studies on the dynamics of bone metabolism and the influence of the female hormone on bone growth and development. He devoted his remaining years to becoming one of the world's experts on bone metabolism. Through Dr. Marshall Urist, his "surrogate son," he became a consultant and adviser to orthopedic surgeons the world over. During the Second World War, his administrative skill was called upon again. He headed the Toxicity Laboratory at the University of Chicago which carried out much classified work on noxious chemicals and their biological effects. Some of these studies led to the first use of nitrogen mustard for the successful treatment of lymphomas.

· VI ·

Franklin McLean was a very unusual person. He obviously relished the opportunities presented by academic administration. One might guess that the primary stimulus for accepting these opportunities was to realize an ideal. As an administrator, he took his duties very seriously but he did not impose himself. He was not authoritarian in his relationships with his academic colleagues. His colleagues in his department were allowed to carve out their own niche in both research and clinical practice. He certainly had an administrative vision, but he was sufficiently pragmatic to compromise or pull back somewhat when circumstances demanded it. It was not always possible to recruit the ideal person for a particular post. When the success of the organization urgently required that a particular position be filled, and the most desirable person could not be appointed, he compromised to appoint the best person available.

· VII ·

In his social views, Franklin McLean was more flexible than Dallas Phemister. He could adapt to and accept circumstances which Dr. Phemister found intolerable. He became a close friend of the philanthropist Julius Rosenwald and became one of his closest advisers on how his foundation could most effectively advance the educational opportunities of Negroes. At that time, he understood that Billings Hospital could not open its doors widely to the black community. Occasional blacks were admitted to the medical school. From the start until many years after he left the directorship, McLean accepted the responsibility of carefully screening black applicants with the help of trusted friends in the black community. Every black student who entered with his help had to succeed, and all of them did. McLean's feeling of obligation to blacks was partially satisfied by arrangements which he negotiated for members of the department of medicine to give some of their time to consult and teach the black staff members of the nearby Provident Hospital. When black medical educators came to Chicago for conferences, Franklin and Helen McLean usually invited them to stay at their home to avoid the embarrassment of discriminatory practices in the leading hotels and restaurants.

In his later years McLean was always available for scientific discussions with his colleagues. He was particularly hospitable to young colleagues and was always delighted when one of them brought him a problem or sought his opinion. During his last illness one of us (R.L.L.) invited him to join the regular Saturday morning endocrinology conference attended by students, house staff, and members of the faculty. It was suggested that we would all like to hear about the formative years of the institution. He came with his wife after being discharged from the hospital. Typically he could not be coaxed to talk about the early days. Rather, he took extreme delight in relating how he "crawled through neurology texts" to be the first to make the diagnosis of his ideopathic cerebellar degeneration which was seriously handicapping him.

Many would assume that his removal from high administrative responsibilities after such brief tenure would lead to considerable bitterness. If Franklin McLean harbored such feelings, he effectively concealed them from all of his friends. His silence about difficulties in organization and appointments—there must have been many—was in all likelihood a manifestation of his special wisdom. It should be recalled that he also gave up administration in China with no comments or regrets.

The man from Maroa who went to church every week during the first sixteen years of his life may not have retained the religious beliefs which were preached at his church. But he did have deeply felt convictions on which he acted. One of these was his belief that clinical medicine is a scientific discipline most effectively advanced and taught in a university. For this the University of Chicago is grateful. The Argonne wing of the medical center, originally built by the Atomic Energy Commission for nuclear research has been renamed the Franklin McLean Memorial Institute in his honor.

27

MARIA GOEPPERT MAYER

1 9 0 6 – 1 9 7 2

R O B E R T   G.   S A C H S

WHEN IN 1963 she received the Nobel Prize in physics, Maria Goeppert Mayer was the second woman in history to win that prize—the first was Marie Curie, who had received it sixty years earlier—and she was the third woman in history to receive the Nobel Prize for scientific work.

The Nobel Prize was awarded in recognition of her major contribution to the understanding of the structure of the atomic nucleus, the spin-orbit-coupling shell model of nuclei. Her discovery was made at the Institute for Nuclear Studies at the University of Chicago, which she joined in early 1946. The institute was one of three interdisciplinary institutes which were established after the war and which placed the University in the forefront of new developments in the sciences. (The other two were the Institute for the Study of Metals, now the James Franck Institute, and the Institute for the Study of Radiobiology, which is no longer in existence. The Institute for Nuclear Studies is now the Enrico Fermi Institute.) The environment of the institutes was set by the interests of the remarkable group of physicists and chemists who were assembled in them. In the Institute for Nuclear Studies those interests encompassed a broad spectrum of key questions in physical science. The spectrum was especially well suited to Maria Goeppert Mayer's talents, the same talents that led her to make the discovery for which she received the Nobel Prize.

· I ·

Maria Goeppert was born on 28 June 1906 in Kattowitz (now Katowice), Upper Silesia (then in Germany), the only child of Friedrich Goeppert and

This is an expanded version of an article that appeared in the *Biographical Memoirs* series (vol. 50), of the National Academy of Sciences and is used with the permission of the Academy.

his wife, Maria, née Wolff. In 1910 the family moved to Göttingen, where Friedrich Goeppert became professor of pediatrics. Maria spent most of her life there until her marriage.

On 19 January 1930 she married Joseph E. Mayer, a chemist who also was eventually a distinguished member of the faculty of the University of Chicago. They had two children: Maria Ann, now Maria Mayer Wentzel, and Peter Conrad. Maria Goeppert Mayer became a citizen of the United States in 1933. She died on 20 February 1972.

Both her father's academic status and his location in Göttingen had a profound influence on her life and career. She was especially proud of being the seventh consecutive generation of university professors on her father's side. Her father's personal influence on her was great. She is quoted as having said that her father was more interesting than her mother: "He was after all a scientist." She was said to have been told by her father that she should not grow up to be a woman, meaning a housewife, and therefore decided, "I wasn't going to be *just* a woman" (Joan Dash, *A Life of One's Own* [New York: Harper and Row, 1973], p. 231).

· II ·

The move to Göttingen came to dominate the whole structure of her education. The Georgia Augusta University, better known simply as "Göttingen," was at the height of its prestige, especially in the fields of mathematics and physics, during the period when she was growing up. David Hilbert was an immediate neighbor and friend of the family. Max Born came to Göttingen in 1921 and James Franck followed soon after; both were close friends of the Goeppert family. Richard Courant, Hermann Weyl, Gustav Herglotz, and Edmund Landau were professors of mathematics.

The presence of these giants of mathematics and physics naturally attracted the most promising young scholars to the institution. Through the years, Maria Goeppert came to meet and know Arthur Holly Compton, Max Delbrück, Paul A. M. Dirac, Enrico Fermi, Werner Heisenberg, John von Neumann, J. Robert Oppenheimer, Wolfgang Pauli, Linus Pauling, Leo Szilard, Edward Teller, and Victor Weisskopf. It was the opportunity to work with James Franck that led to Joseph Mayer's coming to Göttingen and gave him the chance to meet and marry Maria.

Maria Goeppert was attracted to mathematics very early and planned to prepare for the university, but there was no public institution in Göttingen serving to prepare girls for this purpose. Therefore, in 1921 she left the public elementary school to enter the Frauenstudium, a small private

MARIA GOEPPERT MAYER

school run by suffragettes to prepare those few girls who wanted to seek admission to the university for the required examination. The school closed its doors before the full three-year program was completed, but she decided to take the university entrance examination promptly in spite of her truncated formal preparation. She passed the examination and was admitted to the university in the spring of 1924 as a student of mathematics. Except for one term at Cambridge University in England, her entire career as a university student was spent at Göttingen.

In 1924 she was invited by Max Born to join his physics seminar, with the result that her interests started to shift from mathematics to physics. It was just at this time that the great developments in quantum mechanics were taking place, with Göttingen as one of the principal centers. In fact, Göttingen might have been described as a "cauldron of quantum mechanics" at that time, and in that environment Maria Goeppert was molded as a physicist.

As a student of Max Born, a theoretical physicist with a strong foundation in mathematics, she was well trained in the mathematical concepts required to understand quantum mechanics. This and her mathematics education gave her early research a strong mathematical flavor. Yet the influence of James Franck's nonmathematical approach to physics certainly became apparent later. In fact, a reading of her thesis reveals that Franck already had an influence at that stage of her work.

She completed her thesis and received her doctorate in 1930. The thesis was devoted to the theoretical treatment of double-photon processes. It was described many years later by Eugene Wigner as a "masterpiece of clarity and concreteness." Although at the time it was written the possibility of comparing its theoretical results with those of an experiment seemed remote, if not impossible, double-photon phenomena became a matter of considerable experimental interest many years later, both in nuclear physics and in astrophysics. Now, as the result of the development of lasers and nonlinear optics, these phenomena are of even greater experimental interest.

· III ·

After receiving her degree, she married and moved to Baltimore, where her husband, Joseph Mayer, took up an appointment in the department of chemistry of Johns Hopkins University. Opportunities for her to obtain a normal professional appointment at that time, which was at the height of the depression, were extremely limited. Nepotism rules were particularly stringent then and prevented her from being considered for a regular appointment at Johns Hopkins; nevertheless, members of the department of physics were able to arrange for a very modest assistantship, which gave her access to the University facilities, provided her with a place to work in the physics building, and encouraged her to participate in the scientific activities of the University. In the later years of this appointment, she also had the opportunity to present some lecture courses for graduate students.

At the time, the attitude in the department of physics toward theoretical physics gave it little weight as compared to experimental research; however, the department included one outstanding theorist, Karl Herzfeld, who carried the burden of teaching all of the theoretical graduate courses. Herzfeld was an expert in classical theory, especially kinetic theory and thermodynamics, and he had a particular interest in what has come to be known as chemical physics. This was also Joseph Mayer's field of interest; under his and Herzfeld's guidance and influence, Maria Mayer became actively involved in this field, thereby deepening and broadening her knowledge of physics.

However, she did not limit herself to this one field but took advantage of the various talents existing in the Johns Hopkins department, even going so far as to spend a brief period working with R. W. Wood, the dean of the Johns Hopkins experimentalists. Another member of the department with whom she had a substantial common interest was Gerhard Dieke. The mathematics department, which was quite active at that time, included Francis Murnaghan and Aurel Wintner, with whom she developed particularly close connections. However, the two members of the Johns Hopkins faculty who had the greatest influence on her were her husband and Herzfeld. Not only did she write a number of papers with Herzfeld in her early years there, but they also became close, lifelong friends.

The rapid development of quantum mechanics was having a profound effect in the field of chemical physics, in which she had become involved, and the resulting richness and breadth of theoretical chemical physics was so great as to appear to have no bounds. She was in a particularly good position to take advantage of this situation, since no one at Johns Hopkins had a background in quantum mechanics comparable to hers. In particular, she became involved in pioneering work on the structure of organic compounds with a student of Herzfeld's, Alfred Sklar, and in that work she applied her special mathematical background, using the methods of group theory and matrix mechanics.

During the early years in Baltimore, she spent the summers of 1931,

1932, and 1933 back in Göttingen, where she worked with her former teacher, Max Born. In the first of those summers, she completed with him their article in the *Handbuch der Physik,* "Dynamische Gittertheorie der Kristalle." In 1935 she published her important paper on double beta-decay, representing a direct application of techniques she had used for her thesis, but in an entirely different context.

Later, James Franck joined the faculty at Johns Hopkins and renewed his close personal relationship with the Mayers. The Francks had left Germany because of their objections to Nazi rule. Maria, who was very close to them, undertook the task of finding a place for them to live. She found a lovely house for them near her own home in Roland Park, a section of Baltimore that was known at the time for its severe real estate covenants against Jews. She told me long afterward about how pleased she was to have found such a nice place for them and in such close proximity as to remind her of the Göttingen days. I asked her how she had managed it in spite of the restrictive covenant. Her response was that she simply didn't tell the real estate agent that the Francks were Jewish, and, of course James Franck was not familiar with the euphemism for "Jew" (probably "Eastern European") that appeared in the contract he had to sign. She thought that it was a great joke on the snobs of Roland Park. From what I know of Franck, I imagine that he would not have been content with the arrangement if he had known about it.

Edward Teller also came to the United States in reaction against the policies of the Nazis, and he became a member of the faculty of George Washington University, in nearby Washington, D.C. Since he had already made many important original contributions to molecular physics and he had a very close working relationship with Franck, Maria was naturally drawn to discuss her work with him. She found him to be an unusually stimulating physicist and looked to him for guidance in the developing frontiers of theoretical physics.

When Herzfeld left Hopkins in 1936, the physics department no longer had a theoretical physicist on its faculty. Maria took over the teaching of some of the theoretical courses. Since, at that time, she and Joseph Mayer were writing the book *Statistical Mechanics,* published in 1940, she taught that subject in the physics department (while Joe taught it in chemistry).

It was at about this time that I, as a graduate student, was looking for a faculty member to serve as my thesis adviser. I wanted to be a theoretical physicist but was in a quandary because there was no one on the faculty to provide guidance. I discussed the problem with sympathetic members of the faculty, including Franck, who advised me to become an experiment-alist because, he said, "There are already so many Jewish theoretical phys-icists that you would have a very difficult time finding a job." However when I raised the question of the possibility of working with Maria he agreed that she was fully qualified for the role. I also talked to Herzfeld when he returned for a visit and he, too, agreed about her qualifications but warned me that her position was such that she might not have the kind of influence that would help me to find a job.

When I finally asked her if she would take me on as a student she re-sponded very positively but said that it would require a special dispensa-tion from the department of physics to make it official. The department formally agreed to the arrangement and I became her first bona fide gradu-ate student. The first thing she said to me in our opening discussion of research problems was: "Any young man starting out in theoretical physics at this time *must* work in nuclear physics, where all the exciting new things are happening." But she said that since she herself hadn't worked in the field she had no problem to suggest. "Therefore," she said, "we'll go over to Washington to see Edward Teller. He'll tell us what you should do." He did, and our resulting joint work was her first publication in the field of nu-clear physics. My thesis problem was also selected with Teller's help, and she gave her guidance throughout that work, suggesting application to this problem in nuclear physics of techniques of quantum mechanics in which she was so proficient. These two forays into the field were her only activi-ties in the physics of nuclear structure until after the Second World War.

When she had the opportunity to teach graduate courses, her lectures were well organized, very technical, and highly condensed. She spent little time on background matters or physical interpretation. She was not a good lecturer. She spoke in abrupt, clipped sentences in a very soft, almost inau-dible voice. She distracted the students by smoking one cigarette after an-other. In fact she and Joe were such heavy smokers that they bought cigarettes by the carton, and they both had the reputation for distracting the students by confusing the cigarette with the chalk. It sometimes did happen that one of them would, in the course of a lecture, try to smoke the chalk and write with the cigarette. These habits carried over to their period in Chicago.

Her approach to quantum mechanics, having been greatly influenced by Born, gave preference to matrix mechanics over Schrödinger's wave mechanics. She was very quick with matrix manipulations and in the use of symmetry arguments to obtain answers to a specific problem; this ability stood her in good stead in her later work on nuclear shell structure, which led to her Nobel Prize. She appeared to think of physical theories, in general, as tools for solving physics problems and was not much concerned with the philosophical aspects or the structure of the theory.

Her facility with the methods of theoretical physics was overwhelming to most of the graduate students, in whom she inspired a considerable amount of awe. At the same time, the students took a rather romantic view of this young scientific couple, known as "Joe and Maria," and felt that it was a great loss when they left Johns Hopkins to go to Columbia University in 1939.

Although, as a student, I was not privy to academic politics at Johns Hopkins I heard later that, after she had been at Hopkins long enough to demonstrate her qualifications as a theoretical physicist, an attempt was made to persuade the Hopkins administration to appoint her to the faculty of physics. The word was that the proposal was rejected at the highest levels of the administration. The refusal by the same administration to promote Joe to tenure—he was an associate professor without permanent tenure—in spite of his widely recognized research and teaching accomplishments led to their move to Columbia.

· IV ·

At Columbia University, where Joseph Mayer had been appointed to an associate professorship in chemistry, Maria Mayer's position at first was even more tenuous than at Johns Hopkins. George Pegram, the chairman of the department of physics, arranged for her to have an office, but she had no appointment. Jacob Bigeleisen, who worked with her at Columbia and later at the University of Chicago, says: "When Maria Mayer was rejected for any type of appointment in the physics department, Harold Urey, who was chairman of the chemistry department at Columbia, arranged for her appointment as lecturer in the department of chemistry. This was more than a pro forma appointment. She had an office in Chandler Laboratory and she participated in both undergraduate and graduate teaching in addition to carrying out her own research. . . . At the graduate level she shared the lectures in [Joe's] course on statistical mechanics. Their successful book [on that topic] had just been published by Wiley."

In regard to her reception at Columbia, he goes on to say that she "properly resented the fact that she was turned down for any type of an appointment by George B. Pegram, chairman of the physics department at Columbia in 1939, when Joseph E. Mayer was appointed associate professor of chemistry. She never forgot this insult and the discrimination she suffered."

The move to Columbia was the beginning of a close relationship between the Mayers and Harold Urey and his family, a relationship which was to continue throughout her life, as they always seemed to turn up in the same places. In later years (in particular at the University of Chicago) Urey was apparently a mentor to Joe, with a tie strengthened by the fact that Urey had also been a member of the department of chemistry at Johns Hopkins. He left there the year before the Mayers arrived, and the rumors were that there was some similarity between the circumstances of his departure and Joe's.

It was at Columbia that Maria first came under the influence of Enrico Fermi, although she had already met him in her first summer in the United States (1930) at the University of Michigan Summer Session in Physics. Since both of them were at the University of Chicago after the war, Fermi's influence played a continuing role in her research for the remainder of his life.

Maria's scientific career was also greatly influenced by Edward Teller's move to Columbia in 1941 because it gave her the opportunity to renew a working relationship in physics with him which again carried over to Chicago when both of them moved to the Institute for Nuclear Studies. Already when I was her student she had indicated that she considered him to be one of the world's most stimulating theoretical physicists. That is why she took me to Teller to seek help in identifying interesting problems of nuclear physics.

At Columbia she quickly put to work her talent for problem solving when Fermi suggested that she attempt to predict the valence-shell structure of the yet-to-be-discovered transuranium elements. By making use of the very simple Fermi-Thomas model of the electronic structure of the atom, she came to the conclusion that these elements would form a new chemical rare-earth series. In spite of the oversimplifications of the particular model, this subsequently turned out to be a remarkably accurate prediction of their qualitative chemical behavior.

In December 1941, she was offered her first real position, a half-time appointment to teach science at Sarah Lawrence College; she organized and presented a unified science course, which she developed as she went along during that first presentation. Then in February 1942 she was recruited by Harold Urey to work part-time in a research group devoted to separating U-235 from natural uranium as part of the work toward the atomic bomb. This ultimately became known as Columbia University's Substitute Alloy Materials (SAM) project. This second half-time job gave her an opportunity to use her knowledge of chemical physics. Her work included research on the thermodynamic properties of uranium hexa-fluoride and on the theory of separating isotopes by photochemical reactions, a process which, however, did not develop into a practical possibility at that time. (Much later, the invention of the laser reopened the possibility.) She divided her time between Sarah Lawrence and the SAM laboratories until the summer of 1944, when she dropped her teaching appointment to work full time at SAM.

Her early work at SAM included a collaboration with Teller on problems in chemical physics. It was also on this research program that Jacob Bigeleisen was led to work with her after he joined the SAM laboratories in June 1943. He says, "In the work on the feasibility of a photochemical process, Maria Mayer did all of the analyses of the spectra while the program was carried out at Columbia and exerted a major guiding influence on the direction of the program, which had a total of 15 scientific personnel over the life of the program—the calendar year 1943."

He goes on to comment on how quickly her mind acted:

Maria Mayer returned [after recuperation from a gall bladder operation] to work on a Monday in December 1943. She came to see me and asked me how far along I was with the final report [on photo-chemical isotope separation]. I told her I was not working on it. She asked me what I was doing. I showed her the progress I had made on an alternate . . . method of calculating isotopic partition function ratios, which could then be used to calculate chemical exchange enrichment factors. After listening to my approach . . . she said it was interesting and would I mind if she joined me in this project. I was new to this field and was delighted that she found my work sufficiently interesting to work on it with me. Her next sentence was a suggestion which completed the formulation of the concept of an isotopic reduced partition function ratio that revolutionized the field of isotopic chemistry. Ultimately it has opened up the new field of isotopic geology and led to major applications in biology and chemistry and practical applications in isotopic separation processes.

Although Edward Teller moved to the University of Chicago nuclear chain reaction project—the Metallurgical Laboratory—in 1942 and thence to Los Alamos, he maintained his contact with Columbia and visited the SAM Laboratories from time to time. Maria told Bigeleisen about one such visit of which Bigeleisen had been unaware. He says that she told him "that she had prepared a summary document on the statistical mechanics problem [that they had been working on together]. Kilpatrick [supervisor of the project on which they were working] asked Teller to review the document. . . . Teller understood the problem and praised the work. After Teller's visit, Kilpatrick called [her] in and she subsequently told me about that interview. Kilpatrick said that our work was correct, Teller approved it. Maria Mayer then added 'Imagine! They trust Teller but not me!'" It clearly bothered her that even at that stage of her career she did not have the recognition that she so richly deserved as an authority in her field.

Teller demonstrated that he recognized her as an authority, by arranging, at about this same time, for her to supervise a program at Columbia referred to as the Opacity Project, which concerned the properties of matter and radiation at extremely high temperatures and had a bearing on the development of the thermonuclear weapon. In this connection, in the spring of 1945, she was invited to spend some months at Los Alamos, to work more closely with Teller's group there. (At the same time her husband was on a trip to the battle of Okinawa, on a mission for the Ordnance Department.)

In order to make this visit Maria had to pass a severe security screening procedure. Bigeleisen says that at SAM they "had access only to that information which pertained to their immediate assignment. If you did not infer from the open scientific literature that this project was somehow related to the production of an atomic bomb, you did not find this out by working at the SAM Laboratory. You were given no information that there were projects at Berkeley, Chicago, Hanford, Iowa State College, Los Alamos and Oak Ridge which were all part of this effort."

· V ·

In February of 1946, the Mayers moved to Chicago, where Joe had been appointed professor in both the department of chemistry and the newly formed Institute for Nuclear Studies of the University of Chicago. At the time, the University's rule against nepotism did not permit the appointment of both husband and wife in academic posts, but Maria became a voluntary associate professor of physics in the institute, a position which gave her the opportunity to participate fully in activities at the University.

They moved into one of the wonderful old mansions in the Kenwood neighborhood, near the University and took up their prewar mode of life. That included renewing her principal avocation, which was gardening. She was an enthusiastic gardener and very proud of her garden in Chicago. She often insisted that out-of-town visitors to her house take the time to admire it, whether or not they were interested in gardening.

Maria told me that she enjoyed the house and living conditions almost as much as she had enjoyed those in Baltimore, where she also had a lovely garden. The house became a center of hospitality for their colleagues, especially on New Year's Eve when they had an annual party of memorable proportions. There always was dancing because Maria enjoyed it, a throwback to their life in Göttingen. The party was also enlivened by their insistence on maintaining the German tradition of live candles on the Christmas tree—a real challenge to the fire department (and to their guests)!

The institute had pulled together a stellar assembly of physicists and chemists, including Fermi, Urey, and Libby, as well as Teller and the Mayers. Gregor Wentzel joined the department of physics and the institute later, and the families quickly became very close, one outcome being the joining of the families by marriage of Maria Ann to the Wentzel's son.

Subrahmanyan Chandrasekhar, who had been in the department of astronomy for many years, also joined the institute. A stream of young and very bright physical scientists poured into the institute and the atmosphere was stimulating to the extreme. To add to this exciting atmosphere, which in some ways must have been reminiscent of Göttingen in the early days, Maria's former teacher in Göttingen and friend at Johns Hopkins, James Franck, was already a member of the department of chemistry at the University.

The activities of the institute reflected the interests of the leading lights, interests that were very broad indeed, ranging from nuclear physics and chemistry to astrophysics, and from cosmology to geophysics. The interdisciplinary character of the institute was well suited to the breadth of Maria's own activities in the past, so that her Chicago years were the culmination of her variety of scientific experience.

My impression is that, in spite of the absence of a salary, Maria felt that she was recognized by the faculty of the institute as a fully qualified participant in its affairs. I know that she participated in the notorious candidacy examinations in physics that determined whether a student could go on to a doctorate. The early examinations were extremely difficult because the standard was set by the immediate postwar groups of students. These groups included four persons who subsequently received the Nobel Prize in physics and thirteen who have been elected to the National Academy of Sciences. At the time I remarked to Maria that these examinations were likely to drive some very good potential physics students away from the University. Her response was: "We are interested only in the future Heisenbergs!"

She also taught physics courses at the University occasionally although her reputation as a teacher was much the same as it had been at Johns Hopkins. This is confirmed by Bigeleisen's comments on her teaching which indicate just one difference from the earlier days; she, and presumably Joe, had switched to denicotinized Carl Henry cigarettes! Bigeleisen surmises that "her main problem [with lecturing] was that her delivery could not keep pace with her mind."

According to Bigeleisen, Maria had enough influence to arrange for him to be appointed a fellow of the institute. And he says that because she felt that there was something lacking in the formal graduate physics course program at the University, "She proposed that the Institute for Nuclear Studies recruit Professor Gregor Wentzel from the ETH in Zurich [to take on] the principal responsibilities for advanced courses in Quantum Mechanics. With Fermi's support this suggestion was accepted by the Institute members and Wentzel joined the Institute and the Physics Department in the fall of 1948." Her judgment was certainly vindicated by Wentzel's wonderful contributions to both research and teaching at the University.

When Maria moved to the University of Chicago, the Opacity Project moved with her, giving her the opportunity to continue directing this group. It was accommodated in the postwar residuum of the Metallurgical Laboratory of the University where, in its heyday during the war, the initial work on the nuclear chain reaction had been carried out. She was appointed as a consultant to the Metallurgical Laboratory so that she could continue her participation in this project, and several students from Columbia worked on the project under her guidance. Among these students was Rudolph Sternheimer, who later earned his Ph.D. at the University of Chicago under Teller's guidance.

In keeping with Maria's interest in chemical physics, she at first turned her attention to completing and publishing, with Bigeleisen, the work on isotopic exchange reactions that they had started at SAM. The declassification of some of their work allowed them to publish it and to discuss it freely. Urey, who also had joined the institute, was particularly interested in their work on isotopic effects on the thermodynamics of gases, and he along with one of his students had carried out systematic calculations on such effects for isotopic molecules of the light elements. He presented this work in his lecture on "The Thermodynamic Properties of Isotopic Substances," a lecture he gave on several occasions during his postwar travels in England, Switzerland, and Israel.

The first time he gave the lecture was at the first postwar colloquium of the department of chemistry at Chicago. On very short notice, just the morning before the lecture, Urey asked Maria to carry out, for him to use in his presentation, a calculation relating to the separation of the chlorine isotopes. Maria and Bigeleisen set up the problem using the new method they had developed at the SAM Laboratories, the method "that revolutionized the field of isotopic chemistry," and delivered the result to Urey by 2:00 P.M. Bigeleisen says of the lecture that when he "came to the theory of the difference in thermodynamic properties of isotopic substances, Urey said that an exposition of the theory was beyond the scope of the lecture and interested parties should attend Professor Joseph Mayer's course on statistical mechanics. Maria Mayer turned to me (I was sitting between Joe and Maria) and asked in a loud stage whisper 'What's wrong with *my* course?' She was giving a course on statistical mechanics in the department of physics and was codiscoverer of the theory Urey was using!"

This was not to be interpreted as a protest against Urey for discrimination since Urey was one of her strong supporters and it is well known that he was one of the early fighters against any form of discrimination. It is more likely that it was Maria's advertisement for the physics course versus the course in the chemistry department. As a member of the department of chemistry Urey would have been aware of the latter but probably not of the former. And Maria had good reason to be proud of her leadership role in the application of physics to chemistry, a role which was emphasized by Urey in his subsequent lectures.

The Metallurgical Laboratory went out of existence to make way for the Argonne National Laboratory on 1 July 1946, under the aegis of the newly formed Atomic Energy Commission. I was a charter member of the scientific staff of the new laboratory with the responsibility of building a theoretical physics division. At the time it was very difficult to recruit first-rate theoretical physicists because all of the major universities were competing for them in order to rebuild themselves for the postwar period. But Maria's situation offered me a golden opportunity. I went to her and asked: "Maria wouldn't you like to be earning some money for your work?" Her response: "That would be nice." I said: "Why don't we arrange a half-time appointment for you at Argonne as a Senior Physicist?" MGM: "But I don't know anything about nuclear physics [which at the time was the principal thrust of the basic research in physics at Argonne]." RGS: "Maria, you'll learn." She accepted a regular appointment as Senior Physicist (half-time) in the theoretical physics division of the newly formed laboratory and I, her former student, became her "boss." She also gladly accepted the opportunity to learn what she could about nuclear physics.

She continued to hold this part-time appointment throughout her years in Chicago, while maintaining her unpaid appointment at the University. The Argonne appointment was the source of her financial support during this very productive period of her life, a period in which she made her major contribution to the field of nuclear physics, the nuclear shell model, which gained her the Nobel Prize.

Since the mission of Argonne National Laboratory at the time was, in addition to research in basic science, the development of peaceful uses of nuclear power, she also became involved in applied work there. She was the first person to undertake the solution by electronic computer of the criticality problem for a liquid-metal breeder reactor. She programmed this calculation (using the Monte Carlo method) for ENIAC, the first electronic computer, which was located at the Ballistic Research Laboratory, Aberdeen Proving Ground (where Joe had worked during the war and was therefore in a good position to provide the contact). A summary of this work was published in 1951.

While carrying on her work at Argonne, she continued her work as a volunteer at the University of Chicago by lecturing to classes, serving on committees, directing dissertations, and participating in the activities at the Institute for Nuclear Studies.

Among the many topics being discussed at the institute was the question of the origin of the chemical elements. Teller was particularly interested in this subject and induced Maria Mayer to work with him on a cosmological model of the origin of the elements. In pursuit of data required to test any such model, she became engaged in analyzing the abundance of the elements and noticed that there were certain regularities associating the highly abundant elements with specific numbers of neutrons or protons in their nuclei. She soon learned that Walter M. Elsasser had made similar observations in 1933, but she had much more information available to her and found not only that the evidence was stronger but also that there were additional examples of the effect. These specific numbers ultimately came to be referred to as "magic numbers," a term apparently invented by Wigner.

When she looked into information other than abundance of the elements, such as their binding energies, spins, and magnetic moments, she found more and more evidence that these magic numbers were in some way very special and came to the conclusion that they were of great significance for the understanding of nuclear structure. They suggested the notion of stable "shells" in nuclei similar to the stable elecron shells associated with atomic structure, but the prevailing wisdom of the time was that a shell structure in nuclei was most unlikely because of the short range of nuclear forces as compared to the long-range Coulomb forces holding electrons in atoms. There was the further difficulty that the magic numbers did not fit simpleminded ideas associated with the quantum mechanics of shell structure.

There were attempts by various theoretical physicists to describe the shell structure by an independent particle model in analogy with electron shells in atoms, using the orbital angular momentum as the essential quantum number. The order of the levels simply did not come out right. Eugene Feenberg tried to make this right by introducing for the average potential acting on a nuclear particle a "wine bottle potential" having a bump in the middle like the bottom of a wine bottle. He suggested that the bump would change the order of the levels in just the right direction. I happened to see Maria a short time after this paper came out and she said, "Feenberg apparently has forgotten that the Sturm-Liouville theorem shows that such a change in the shape of the potential can never change the order of the levels." As students, all of us had learned about this theorem which relates to a class of problems arising in quantum mechanics, but I was surely not familiar with the result she was stating so I was not too surprised that Feenberg wasn't aware of it either. However it took only a small effort to confirm her result. (Later I gave the proof, which is simple but does not appear in any textbook on quantum mechanics with which I am familiar, in an appendix to my book *Nuclear Theory*.)

Because of this theorem she was sure that the answer must lie in a different direction. Until she knew in what direction she should search, she persisted in checking further evidence for shell structure, such as nuclear beta-decay properties and quadrupole moments, and in trying to find an explanation in terms of the quantum mechanics of the nuclear particles. In this she was greatly encouraged by Fermi and had many discussions with him. She was also strongly supported by her husband, who acted as a continual sounding board for her thoughts on the subject and provided the kind of guidance that could be expected from a chemist who, in many ways, was better equipped to deal with phenomena of this kind than a physicist. The systematics of regularities in behavior with which she was faced has great similarity to the systematics in chemical behavior that had led to the classical development of valence theory in chemistry, and whose fundamental explanation had been found in the Pauli exclusion principle.

It was Fermi who asked her the key question, "Is there any indication of spin-orbit coupling?" whereupon she immediately realized that that was the answer she was looking for, and thus was born the spin-orbit-coupling shell model of nuclei.

Her ability to recognize immediately that spin-orbit coupling could be the source of the numerology was a direct consequence of her mathematical understanding of quantum mechanics and especially of her great facility with the numerics of the representations of the rotation group. The ability to identify instantly the key numerical relationships was most impressive, and even Fermi was surprised at how quickly she realized that his question was the key to the problem.

Joseph Mayer gives the following description of this episode: "Fermi and Maria were talking in her office when Enrico was called out of the office to answer the telephone on a long-distance call. At the door he turned and asked his question about spin-orbit coupling. He returned less than ten minutes later and Maria started to 'snow' him with the detailed explanation. You may remember that Maria, when excited, had a rapid-fire oral delivery, whereas Enrico always wanted a slow, detailed, and methodical explanation. Enrico smiled and left: 'Tomorrow, when you are less excited, you can explain it to me'" (Dash, *A Life of One's Own,* n. 3).

Because he had raised the question about spin-orbit coupling, Maria felt that Fermi should be a co-author of the publication of the idea but Fermi disagreed. He said, "No. Because, you see, I am a famous man. If I put my name on it, it will always be attributed to me—and it is really not my work, it is yours."

While she was preparing the spin-orbit coupling model for publication she learned of a paper by other physicists presenting a different attempt at an explanation and, as a courtesy, she asked the editor of the *Physical Review* to hold her brief letter to the editor in order that it appear in the same issue as that paper. As a result of this delay, her work appeared one issue following publication of an almost identical interpretation of the magic numbers by Otto Haxel, J. Hans, D. Jensen, and Hans E. Suess. Jensen, working completely independently in Heidelberg, had almost simultaneously realized the importance of spin-orbit coupling for explaining the shell structure, and the result had been this joint paper.

Although she and Jensen came to the same phenomenological description of the shell model, it was Maria who made the significant theoretical
observation that the particular "j-j coupling" scheme that was successful
could be accounted for by a very short range (actually zero range) force
between pairs of nuclear particles. This result is particularly amusing because it was the short range of the forces that was originally believed to
exclude a shell structure for nuclei.

One of Maria's first students at Chicago, Steven Moszkowski, says that
her simple model that led to this pairing effect is one of her major contributions to the theory of nuclear structure. His statement is: "I think it is fair
to say that Maria Mayer made three seminal contributions to the nuclear
shell model: 1. The discovery of the magic numbers in their modern form.
2. How spin-orbit coupling helps to account for the magic numbers. 3. A
simple model for the pairing effect, which makes the single [independent]
particle model possible."

The third item refers to the j-j pairing model, and Moszkowski goes on
to reminisce about that:

> One day I was in her office, together with Dieter Kurath [another one
> of her early students at Chicago], and she was telling us about some
> remarkable results that she had found concerning pairing. The results
> she found exciting involved three particles in this [the f 7/2] shell. The
> state which gives the lowest energy has a total J of J=7/2, but what was
> interesting was the expression for the energy. As I remember it, it was
> a rather complicated fraction. The numerator was 4004 and the de-
> nominator 1001, so the result is 4, which happens to be the same as for
> the two-particle case. In other words a rather tedious calculation gave
> a very simple result! I found all this very intriguing, and though my
> own work with Maria Mayer was along different lines, I decided to
> come back to it one day. Shortly afterwards, Igor Talmi was able to
> reproduce this and many other results using very elegant group theo-
> retical methods developed originally for atomic physics by his teacher,
> Racah. They had discovered that pairing is related to a particular sym-
> metry, called symplectic symmetry.

In spite of her early interest in mathematics and especially group theory, there is no evidence that Maria ever knew about or used the symplec-
tic symmetry group, which was introduced into mathematics and physics
(and named) by her good friend Aurel Wintner at Johns Hopkins while she
was there!

Dieter Kurath tells another, related, story about the j-j coupling:

there was a question of what would be the ground state J of a configuration of 3 nucleons in a j-level. G. Racah had published a note evaluating the expectation value of the Majorana (space exchange) operator and found that the lowest state had $J=j-1$, contradicting Maria's rule that $J=j$. We had done some calculations with the Majorana operator multiplied by $V(r)$ and had varied the range. This showed that Racah tacitly assumed infinite range for the force and that the levels crossed as a function of range. The thing that I remember about this incident is that when we realized the result, she said 'Let's publish this quickly before Racah finds out that he has made a mistake!' This shows clearly that though she was shy she was very competitive.

Kurath joined the physics division at Argonne and was one of the people who helped form the shell-model theory group there. This group worked with Maria until she left Chicago. Members of the group became known in their own right as experts on theoretical problems of nuclear structure.

Maria attracted several graduate students and postdoctoral research associates to work with her on the shell model while she remained, part-time, at the University. Several joined the Argonne group after they graduated or completed their postdoctoral appointments. Her relationships with them were evidently rather informal. Moszkowski tells of an experience at a 1951 conference on nuclear structure at the University that illustrates her attitude. He arrived at the conference too late to find a seat. Maria and Hans Jensen were sitting together and they bailed him out by inviting him to sit on the armrest between their seats. He says "Here was Moszkowski sitting just in front of (and slightly above) Mayer and Jensen!" This is in keeping with her attitude when I was her student, but then there was less of an age difference (and she was not so well known) so that it was not so surprising to me.

Maria Mayer and Jensen were not acquainted with one another at the time of their discovery, and they did not meet until her visit to Germany in 1950. In 1951, on a second visit, she and Jensen had the opportunity to collaborate on further interpretation of the spin-orbit-coupling shell model, and this was the beginning of a close friendship as well as a very productive scientific effort. It culminated in their book, *Elementary Theory of Nuclear Shell Structure* (1955). They shared the Nobel Prize in 1963 for their contributions to this subject.

The writing of their book went very slowly for reasons that must have had more to do with Jensen's style than with Maria's. I know that she expressed some degree of frustration about it to me when I asked her when to expect publication. I was interested because in 1951 I undertook the writing of my book *Nuclear Theory* and wanted to incorporate in it some discussion of the shell model.

In particular Maria had presented results on the quadrupole moments of nuclei but had never revealed her derivation of the formula for the moments. Since I wanted to include the derivation in my book, I undertook the treatment of the problem along with Wendell G. Holladay, a student of mine at the University of Wisconsin at the time. We came up with a rather neat derivation that agreed with her results, and I assumed our derivations were the same. But since she seemed to be in no hurry about publishing it, we wrote a little paper about it, sent her a copy, and I raised the question with her whether we should publish it. (I wanted Holladay to get some credit for his work.) However she asked me not to do that because it was going to be presented in her book with Jensen which was on the verge of being published, so I acceded to her wish but went ahead and included it in the manuscript to my book as an appendix. She evidently was too optimistic about getting Jensen to finish his part because it was about three years later (and two years after mine) that their book was published. I was then very surprised to find that our derivation was quite different than theirs!

Following her discovery of the shell model and the j-j coupling scheme, Maria, her students, and her associates devoted most of their attention to problems of nuclear structure and behavior. She did produce a paper with Teller on the origin of the elements, the work that had started her on the road to her important discovery. Also, shortly after the discovery of parity violation she made an excursion into fundamental particle physics with Valentine Telegdi on alternatives to the two-component neutrino theory. Otherwise her style changed from the eclectic style reflecting broad interest in many kinds of physics to a single-minded concern with the consequences of the shell model.

After Fermi's death in 1954, other members of the Institute for Nuclear Studies who had provided so much stimulation for her left Chicago. Teller had gone earlier, in 1952, Libby left in 1954, and Urey in 1958. In 1960 she accepted a regular appointment as professor of physics at the University of California at San Diego when both she and her husband had the opportunity to go there.

Her appointment as a full professor in her own right at a major university was very gratifying to her, and she looked forward to the stimulation of

this newest interdisciplinary group of scientists that was being drawn together there. However, shortly after arriving in San Diego, she had a
stroke, and her years there were marked by continuing ill-health. Nevertheless, she continued to teach and to participate actively in the development and exposition of the shell model. Her last publication, a review of
the shell model written in collaboration with Jensen, appeared in 1966;
and she continued to give as much attention to physics as she could until
her death in early 1972.

28

CHARLES EDWARD MERRIAM

1 8 7 4 – 1 9 5 3

G A B R I E L   A.   A L M O N D

CHARLES EDWARD MERRIAM was the founder and leader of the "Chicago school" of political science. He was an active member of the University of Chicago for almost half a century. He began his career as a "docent," then the lowest academic rank at the University of Chicago, in the year 1900–1901, and retired from active service as the Morton Dennison Hull distinguished service professor of political science in 1940. He continued to occupy his office in retirement, offer seminars, and meet students for the better part of the 1940s.

· I ·

He was born in the small town of Hopkinton, Iowa, the second son of a storekeeper of New England Scottish Presbyterian background. He was educated in the local Lenox Academy and the University of Iowa. Beginning with an interest in a career of law and politics, he shifted to the discipline of "government" then just in process of separating from history in American universities. He took his doctorate at Columbia, with a year in Germany at the University of Berlin, where he studied the *Staatswissenschaften*. At Columbia he studied public law and political theory. He was a young graduate student at the time of the Seth Low reform campaign against Tammany Hall in 1897. Seth Low was then president of Columbia University, and a large part of the student body entered the campaign, including Merriam, who gave campaign speeches from the back of a wagon. He brought to his University of Chicago career this mixture of influences and experiences—a boyhood in post–Civil War, small town, Middle West America; an exposure to Scottish Covenanter Presbyterianism, particularly through his mother; an encounter with Tammany Hall and the urban reform movement; and Germanic scholarship.

CHARLES EDWARD MERRIAM, 1911

He inspired and edified many generations of undergraduates by his example of combining teaching and doing, and he sent several dozens of Ph.D.'s to teach in other major universities. The department of political science which he shaped in the 1920s and 1930s, largely from his own ideas and experiences, and which he staffed with his own graduate students, significantly shaped the model of modern political science in the United States, spreading to Europe more recently, and in the last years to China and the Soviet Union.

As the leading figure in the founding of the Social Science Research Council, and as the chairman of its board of directors in its early years, he made an important contribution to the modernization of the social sciences. It was this organization which spread the culture of rigorous empirical research to the various social science disciplines, and to the centers of higher education both here and abroad.

As a young man teaching municipal government at the University, and serving as alderman of the Fifth Ward, he fought for civic reform and for the professionalization of municipal government. He left a lasting legacy in the establishment of professional associations of local government officials, located in the "1313" building on the campus of the University of Chicago. As his reputation grew he played a similar role at the national level, serving on such bodies as President Hoover's Commission on Recent Social Trends, President Roosevelt's Committee on Administrative Management, and the National Resources Planning Board, agencies which were concerned with bringing modern scientific knowledge to bear on social policy and with the development of honest and effective management practices. The unifying theme of his professional career was the development of the sciences of politics and society in the service of democracy and the public welfare.

He was a politician and statesman in both academic and public life in the very best senses of those terms. Though he spent much time first in the city hall of Chicago, and later at meetings of the Social Science Research Council, foundations, and various commissions in New York, Washington, and elsewhere on the East Coast, he was always available to students, and maintained an intimate and active university and departmental life. By the time I came to know Charles Merriam, first in 1930 as an undergraduate member of one of his seminars in political theory, he had already passed the scholarly "point of no return," though he cherished the belief throughout his career that he would return to creative scholarship in his later years. He suffered the fate of many multiply talented persons. His students could realize his dreams and designs of creative scholarship. But once he and others became aware of his gifts in dealing with the rich and the powerful, and his imagination and energy as a builder of institutions, he was drawn away from scholarship; he was attracted by essentially political roles as an evangelist of political and social science, as a builder of coalitions in the University, in the national life of the social sciences, and in local and in national politics in behalf of liberal reforms.

He was active in the Bull Moose wing of the Republican party, in the short-lived interlude of the Progressive party, and he became one of the intellectual stalwarts of the New Deal. For a brief period during his mayoral campaign in 1911, there was thought of him in presidential terms, as the "Woodrow Wilson of the West." The frequency and length of his long-distance telephone calls waxed and waned as election days neared and receded. During prohibition years he kept two bottles of Johnny Walker Black Label in a filing cabinet to toast an influential visitor, or a successful colleague.

· II ·

The idea of the scholar in politics ran into conflict with trends toward graduate training and professionalization in American universities early in the century. Merriam's department chairman and then president of the University, Henry Pratt Judson, actively opposed Merriam's ventures into politics. Merriam had been appointed on the basis of his early work on the history of political theory as it was represented in his doctoral dissertation on theories of sovereignty, and in his early book on the history of American political theory. There was the promise of productivity and originality in these early studies.

The first book in the empirical "behavioral" type of political science which he began to foster in the 1920s, was a study of "non-voting" in Chicago, based on a large-scale survey which included some 6,000 respondents. It was a departmental venture employing graduate students as interviewers. It was conducted and written jointly by Merriam and Harold Gosnell; the first chapter, which dealt with survey and sampling methods, and questionnaire construction, was written by Merriam. Harold Lasswell's studies of communication and propaganda and political psychology were foreshadowed by Merriam's wartime service in directing the United States information program in Italy, and by his fascination with the phenomenon of leadership.

The Merriam that I encountered from 1933 to 1938 as a graduate student in the department was surrounded by his former students—then assistant and associate professors. These included Harold Lasswell, Harold Gosnell, Frederick Schuman, and Carroll Wooddy. Closer to being peers were Leonard White and Quincy Wright, the first a specialist in public administration, and the second a specialist in international relations. But Merriam had no real peers in the department. His friends and colleagues referred to him affectionately, but respectfully, as "the chief."

The department was patriarchal in structure. Merriam served on many dissertation committees, but the detailed supervision was done by Lasswell, Gosnell, L. D. White, and others. Merriam would approve the topic and have some general idea of the drift of the project. There was a rite after the oral examination on the dissertation when Merriam would invite the neophyte to have a drink at the bar of the Shoreland Hotel. I recall a long walk with the "chief" in the hot sun of the late spring, up 59th Street to Lake Shore Drive, and along the Drive to the then stylish Shoreland Hotel with its beautiful view of the lakefront. It had the only air-conditioned bar in Hyde Park. I still have a letter which he sent me in 1939, a few months after I received my degree, addressed for the first time to "My Dear Doctor Gay."

· III ·

He prided himself on being a good judge of people. His patronage was extensive. He touched the lives of many, if not most, of the scholars who became prominent in the social sciences in the 1920s to the 1950s. Within our own department, he was curious about everybody and treasured little bits of information which he could use to tease us. When I first presented him with the plans for my doctoral dissertation on the elites of New York City, he smiled and said, "The desert is full of bones." He went to many weddings, including mine. It pleased him to be instrumental in helping the children of immigrants to enter careers in American society and shared in the joy of their parents. He was sensitive to the pain of immigrant parents as their children became assimilated in an alien culture. He urged us to be our brothers' keepers. If we were successful, we were reminded that "so-and-so" had a writer's block or other troubles, and needed help. As I left the university in 1939 he gave me such an assignment, and reminded me of it intermittently over the years.

He was a man who combined courage and prudence. He turned the notion of political prudence into a political science concept. It came out of the historical experience of the populist and progressive movements in which he had participated, movements that had minimized the importance of political institutions such as parties, and such governmental arrangements as the separation of powers. The notion of political prudence to

Merriam was very much like Max Weber's "ethics of responsibility," the idea that politicians had to assume responsibility for the consequences of the causes and goals which they advocated, whether these consequences were intended or not. The social sciences, and political science in particular, had the job of anticipating the consequences of different political structures, political decisions, and public policies.

As to his courage, it was Merriam who went to the home of W. I. Thomas, his colleague from the department of sociology and author of the *Polish Peasant in Europe and America,* when he was in disgrace because of a sexual scandal, and took him by the arm to the Quadrangle Club to reunite him with his friends. And it was Merriam who defended his young colleague Frederick Schuman and others accused of subversion in the mid-1930s. It was he along with others who prevailed on the drugstore millionaire, Charles R. Walgreen, who had been hounding the university for harboring radicals, to support a lectureship on American institutions.

He was a tall man with a shambling walk. He spoke with something of a nasal twang, a bit from the side of his mouth. He enjoyed recalling childhood experiences with another colleague, Louis Brownlow, who also had a midwestern, small-town background, even imitating the accents and repeating the homilies to which they had been exposed. He used to walk up the stairs, scorning the elevator, to his third-floor office. There, with his personal library, he had an old typewriter on which he typed his manuscripts. He did a lot of writing during the summer months, and used to come to work in the cool of the early morning. V. O. Key, Jr., who occupied the office next to him was an even earlier riser, and had done a day's work before nine or ten o'clock. There was an office for the departmental secretary, another office for a research associate, occupied at different times by such senior graduate students as V. O. Key, Jr., Herman Pritchett, and Albert Lepawsky. There was in addition a large office occupied by three or four younger research assistants, who, while working on their dissertations, might be employed part-time in research for the Study of Recent Social Trends, the Committee on Administrative Management, or the National Resource Planning Board. He would come out of his office at odd moments, to banter with his students, pass on a political confidence, or tell a story. He had periods of self-doubt and melancholy, when he especially needed affection and response.

He ran an evening advanced seminar where we read our chapters as we worked on our dissertations, and where Merriam would occasionally read or discuss projects on which he was engaged. In whimsical and melancholy moments, he presented his thoughts and moods as though written

by his dog, Carlo. Carlo was the name of a pet dog of Merriam's early boyhood who had to be left in Hopkinton, when the family tried living in California for a few years in the 1880s. The legend was that the dog languished
and died of loneliness. Carlo seemed to have become a vehicle for Merriam's fantasies and regrets.

· IV ·

The local stage on which Merriam performed was the Social Science
Research Building facing the Midway on 59th Street near the corner of University Avenue. It was built around the same time that the social sciences
were acquiring a national coherence through the formation of the Social
Science Research Council. He had been largely responsible for soliciting
the gift from the Laura Spelman Rockefeller Memorial for the construction
of this first building on any American university campus devoted solely to
the social sciences.

His somewhat younger colleague in sociology, William Fielding Ogburn, was chairman of a committee to decide upon the appropriate symbolism—iconography, mottoes, and quotations—for the adornment of the
building. Recommendations were solicited from all the social science departments. There was a battle over this, reflecting differences in the ideas
of social science among the departments and scholars in the social sciences. The most popular motto for the prominent place on the side of the
building facing the Midway was Aristotle's *Anthropos Zoon Politikon* (man
is a political animal), but Ogburn, a strongly statistical brand of sociologist,
preferred to adapt a statement of Lord Kelvin in the form: "When you cannot measure, your knowledge is meagre and unsatisfactory." Such a strong
identification with quantification was foreign to Merriam's view of the social sciences. He was abroad at the time these decisions were being made,
and the chairman of the committee on symbolism won the day. Merriam's
wrath on his return when he found an adaptation of the maxim from Kelvin carved in stone was unavailing, as anyone passing the front of the
building can witness.

The five-story building, Gothic in style and appurtenances, housed the
departments of anthropology, economics, political science, sociology, and
parts of social service administration, education, philosophy, and psychology most closely associated with the social sciences. There was a lecture
hall on the first floor (where recorded classical music was played during
the noon hour), rooms for seminars and classes, and a statistical laboratory
presided over by Ogburn on the fifth floor.

It was an intimate setting. In the course of a graduate career spanning four or five years one would encounter all the inhabitants of the building at one time or another in the halls, on the stairs, in the elevator, or in a large seminar room on the second floor where tea and cookies were served every afternoon at four o'clock. Graduate students in political science shared offices and mingled with sociology, anthropology, and economics students. The building suited and fostered the interdisciplinary culture which Merriam cherished.

· V ·

The productivity of the department accelerated from the early years of Merriam's chairmanship to the final ones. The first half of the 1920s was the period of the pioneers identified with the quantitative voting studies of Harold Gosnell, the psychoanalytic and sociological studies of Harold Lasswell, Frederick Schuman's innovative work in international relations, and studies of attitudes toward public employment of L. D. White. The more visible leaders of the second generation were V. O. Key, Jr., at work in the early 1930s on the techniques of "graft" in American politics; Herman Pritchett, who made an early field study of the organization and politics of the Tennessee Valley Authority; and Albert Lepawsky, who led a cohort of graduate students in studies of the politics of the metropolitan region of Chicago, Lepawsky specializing in the judicial system of the region.

Among the Ph.D.'s of the later 1930s were Victor Jones and John Vieg, who were at work on the government of the metropolitan region of Chicago and the mode of government of its educational system; William T. R. Fox, who was associated with Quincy Wright in his studies of war; David Truman and Avery Leiserson, later important contributors to the theory of political parties and pressure groups, whose dissertations were supervised by L. D. White. Leo Rosten did his celebrated study of the Washington press corps under Merriam's and Lasswell's supervision in these years. The later Nobel laureate, Herbert Simon, came in at the end of this cohort, and was already pioneering in the measurement of administrative performance in the late 1930s. My own work in the early and middle 1930s dealt with the politics of the unemployed during the depression, which I did in association with Harold Lasswell, and with the social and political characteristics of the business elites in New York City, which I did under the supervision of Gosnell and Lasswell.

The "myth" of the Chicago school has somewhat exaggerated its innovativeness. Some of the dissertations that were done during these decades were rather conventional descriptive studies of governmental institutions, political processes, and political ideas. But for just about every one of the graduate students of that time, the boundaries of the discipline of political science had been broadened and deepened. We were aware that we were members of an innovative department, and most had feelings of pride in breaking new ground and developing unconventional insights into the explanation of political behavior. Early anxieties that the bearers of the label of the University of Chicago would not fare well in the job market for political scientists because of this reputation for innovation were quickly allayed after the war years, when a University of Chicago degree acquired a special cachet.

During its best years it was a harmonious department, and this could be attributed to Merriam's personality and his style of management. The department encouraged risk, rewarded merit, eschewed stuffiness, and mocked a bit at conventionality. Envy and malice, not unusual in academic settings, were mitigated by Merriam's combination of generosity and optimism.

Merriam's department of political science did not survive his retirement. Even before that event, Lasswell, Gosnell, and Schuman had left for other universities or government service. The department which emerged in the 1940s and 1950s was sharply divided between a humanistic wing led by the refugee political philosopher Leo Strauss and a group consisting of survivors of Merriam's department. It is ironic that just as Merriam's type of political science was waning at the University of Chicago, it was becoming dominant nationally. What was missed at the University of Chicago—even as the first atomic pile was being tested in Stagg Field—was that the decades after the Second World War were to become the era of "big science," and that the social sciences and political science would not escape the powerful draft of the great discoveries and developments in physics and biology. What Merriam had pioneered in the 1920s and 1930s—the idea of research as having an equal, or greater, claim on the university with teaching, well-supported team research and research programs, reductionist strategies in research designs, and quantification—rapidly became the dominant model to emulate at leading universities. Though Merriam never referred to his type of political science as "behavioral political science," and probably would have been uncomfortable with the term, it was under this name that the influence of the Chicago school was diffused after the Second World War to other major universities.

· VI ·

The Chicago school is generally acknowledged to have been the founding influence in the history of modern political science, and Charles E.
Merriam is generally recognized as the founder and shaper of the Chicago
school. Hence there may be a point in expatiating a bit on the kind of "science" Merriam thought he was fostering in the early 1920s when he began
to prophesy and exhort. I draw on Merriam's book *New Aspects of Politics,*
published in 1925, and on the second and third editions, published in 1931
and 1970, which contained other writings from this early period and later.

He spoke and wrote in the rhetoric and logic of prophecy. But though
he was a prophet, he was not of the desert breed, not an ascetic. As a major
entrepreneur in the financial patronage of social science, and one of the
inventors of the weekend conference, he appreciated worldly enjoyments.
Like the prophets, he attacked his complacent colleagues for cultivating
the forms rather than the spirit of their calling. He exhorted them to live
up to their obligations, spelled out the rewards of virtue, and specified the
professional way of life leading to these rewards.

The false prophets were scholars like Harold Laski and Charles Beard
who ridiculed Merriam's emphasis on political psychology, organized research, and quantification. In his manifesto of the early 1920s he wrote, "I
am not unmindful of the significance of the study of the history of human
experience; nor, trained in public law, am I unmindful of the value of the
juristic approach to the problems of political theory and practice. . . . In
suggesting that politics sit around the table with psychology and statistics
and biology and geography, I am not suggesting that we ask our older
friends to go. Only this: politics must follow its problem wherever the
problem leads."

Merriam was a believer in the Enlightenment and in progress. Scientific
knowledge was to be the instrument of professional progress. Political science was to move beyond its historical, legal, and philosophical methods,
cultivated by individual scholars in their libraries, and become a more
powerful explanatory discipline, drawing on the other sciences—social,
natural, mathematical. These emerging sciences of politics and society
would lead to a new "political prudence" which would make possible "the
conscious control of human evolution toward which intelligence steadily
moves in every domain of human life."

He saw these transformations of political science as continuous with the
tradition of the discipline. He offered the solace of a new political theory

to the political theorists and the more conservative political scientists of his generation. He wrote in 1931, "It may reasonably be expected that a new synthetic philosophy will emerge, fusing the material now found scattered throughout the natural sciences, the social sciences, the humanities, into a new interpretation with perhaps a new logic. But 'science' will be inside, not outside, this new philosophy when it appears. . . . [H]ere the adventurous political theorist may find full sweep for his analytic and synthetic faculties weaving together the new data developed by modern research."

Merriam's view of the contributions which the other sciences would make to political science recognized the dangers of reductionism. The logic of his prophecy began with the argument that political theorists had always been concerned with the effects of psychological, sociological, economic, biological, and geographic variables on the characteristics of states, statesmen, and citizens. Given these concerns in the traditions of political science, it was really not much to suggest that, as our knowledge increased, political science would replace the primitive and intuitive bodies of knowledge contained in traditional psychology, sociology, anthropology, biology, and the like with more reliable insights resulting from more recent scientific achievements. He specified the various aspects of political science which might be illuminated and made more rigorous and exact by the introduction of this knowledge. At the end of each such analysis he confronted the danger that political scientists going deeply into the various social sciences might become lost, tending to reduce political phenomena to the terms of the contributing sciences. He answered this fear by arguing, "better be lost for a while in order to return to the discipline and enrich it."

Merriam was especially positive about the possible contributions of psychology to the new political science. But he did not view psychology as the primary science and politics as the secondary one. "What we are really striving to achieve," he wrote in 1924 "is neither psychology nor psychiatry as such, nor biology as such, nor economics as such, but the development of scientific method in the observation, measurement, and comparison of political relations." Psychology held out special promise for Merriam. He urged, "[M]ay we not intensify our study of the political man, the political personality, of his genesis, environment, reactions, modes of adaptation, and training, and the groups of which he is a part, and of the complicated political process, to a point where the preconceptions of politics will be given a far more definite fact basis, and practical prudence a far surer touch in its dealings with the problem of the state?"

In counseling colleagues and graduate students to take risks in their research he openly acknowledged the possibility of having to take a few casualties. "It may be said that the lines of inquiry suggested are not appropriate for political scientists, because they carry us out of our accustomed territory, and we may be lost in the desert. . . . [A] certain number of explorers must always be lost, especially if they advance too far or too fast."

In his treatment of quantification, Merriam makes the point that modern statistics had its origins in the study of affairs of state, so that the complaints of some of his contemporaries, at his urging that political science move in quantitative directions, were really quite inappropriate. He spoke of the census as a revolutionary invention making possible a surer grasp of social structure, social change, and of the performance of government. Acquiring skills in quantification forced social scientists and political scientists to relate their ideas to the real phenomena to which they were supposed to refer. He understood the importance of redefining concepts more precisely to make them more usable in research. He saw in the development of correlational analysis the possibility of generating testable theories of the relationship between various social properties such as sex and economic status and political opinion and voting behavior. He took great pride in what must be the first modern behavioral studies in political science—the "nonvoting" studies by Harold Gosnell, the "prestige value of public employment" studies by Leonard D. White, and Lasswell's trail-breaking clinical case studies in *Psychopathology and Politics*. He particularly relished the experimental aspects of Gosnell's study, and the depth psychological ventures of Lasswell.

In his argument for the self-evident character of the importance of quantification in the study of politics he pointed to such measurable phenomena as the vote, the legislative roll call, judicial decisions, various aspects of the administrative process, the military services, the educational system as "teeming with definite facts susceptible of relationship to other sets of social facts. In the case of public institutions, experiment may be carried out and situations varied for the purpose of determining the effect of the various factors in behavior. No richer material is found than in the domain of political operations. Furthermore when the minute study of political operations and traits is begun, the number of feasible statistical relationships is of course very largely increased."

Merriam confronted those colleagues concerned that political science might be lost in number-crunching with the answer "Possibly so. It may well be that politics must lose its way before it finds itself again in the modern world of science." If Merriam were alive today and a regular reader of the *American Political Science Review*, I am not quite sure what conclusions he might reach about the present state of the quantitative study of politics. Would he say, "It is wholly improbable that politics will be absorbed in statistics," or would he say, "It may be disastrous if political investigators rush into the collection and quantitative measurement of facts without preliminary consideration and statement of what we call 'the problem', and without certain hypotheses . . . which the proposed examination of facts might be expected to prove or disprove." These two statements—one confident and one apprehensive—appear in adjoining pages of the same chapter on "Politics and Numbers" in *New Aspects of Politics*.

Rereading these documents of the early history of the scientific movement in the study of politics, one cannot escape an impression of an age of innocence. The writing had a simple and confident quality about it. The growth of scientific knowledge held out the prospect of increasing humanity's capacity for understanding, explaining, and improving the political process. When the first edition of *New Aspects* appeared in 1925, the Bolshevik Revolution had not as yet taken on its sinister Stalinist form, and Italian fascism was still being admired for its enforcement of railroad schedules. The depression was a few years off, and national socialism was not as yet taken seriously. When the second edition of *New Aspects* was published in 1931, a sense of menace appears in some of the more recent writings included in the book, but the basic optimism persists.

In the 1990s, a century after the founding of the University of Chicago, and half a century after his retirement, we recognize that there was a naive quality in Merriam's prophecy; just as there was naiveté in the appreciation of science and technology as it developed in Merriam's time. It was a version of science and progress that came before the nuclear threat, before the menace of overpopulation, before pollution and toxic waste, and before ozone depletion. The descendants of Merriam in universities both here and abroad pursue his combination of scientific research and responsible public policy analysis, but without his unequivocal confidence that it would result in "the conscious control of human evolution toward which intelligence steadily moves in every domain of human life."

This essentially was the vision of Charles E. Merriam, whose activities in the first half of the present century left a deep imprint on the University of Chicago and on the profession of political science as it developed nationally and internationally in the subsequent decades.

29

ARNALDO MOMIGLIANO

1 9 0 8 – 1 9 8 7

J A M E S   W H I T M A N

ARNALDO MOMIGLIANO, one of the leading historians of the twentieth century, came to the University of Chicago in 1975 as Alexander White Visiting Professor, after his retirement as professor of ancient history at University College, London. He returned every year thereafter until his death in 1987. Chicago was the last of several universities in which Momigliano spent the life of exile from his native Piedmont.

· I ·

Born in 1908 into a very old and very scholarly Jewish family in Caraglio (Cuneo), Piedmont, Momigliano enjoyed a stellar early success in Italy, culminating in his appointment as professor of Roman history in Turin in 1936. He was the author, at the age of twenty-eight, of more than one hundred and fifty learned publications. Early success, however, was followed by more than a decade of harsh difficulties. As the Italian fascist regime, in imitation of German national socialism, enacted anti-Jewish laws in 1938, Momigliano was dismissed from his professorship. He made his way, with his wife and daughter, to Oxford, where he benefited from the help of Hugh Last and Isobel Henderson. Thus he escaped the fate awaiting so many Jews on the Continent, among them his parents, who died in a Nazi extermination camp in 1943. But he left behind a life of established academic success for one of harsh poverty and utter uncertainty regarding his professional prospects.

He did not reestablish himself in a leading academic position until 1951. In 1946, he returned briefly to Italy, where he was offered an appointment in Turin. Benedetto Croce also offered him, at the same time, the directorship of the new institute for historical studies which Croce himself had founded in Naples. Momigliano did not, however, feel able to return permanently to Italy. Although he retained his Italian citizenship, he returned to voluntary exile in England, as first lecturer, then reader, in the University of Bristol. In 1951 he was elected to succeed A. H. M. Jones as professor of ancient history at University College, London—a position in which, at the age of forty-three, he could follow the settled life of research and teaching that he might by rights have expected to begin fifteen years earlier in Turin.

During the subsequent twenty-four years in London, Momigliano made himself not only honored, but beloved. He attracted gifted pupils to his seminars, conducted not only at University College but also at the nearby Warburg Institute. These seminars, widely described in the memorial essays published after his death, were centers of the intellectual lives of innumerable scholars at all levels. He continued to produce scholarly work at the prodigious rate he had maintained since the age of eighteen. Indeed, he flourished in his London exile, presenting the world with the model of a great scholar. He ranged over an astonishingly wide scholarly territory. He showed himself the master of archaic Roman history, of the religious and intellectual history of late antiquity, of the history of historiography, and more. If pressed, perhaps one could say that certain subjects lay at the heart of his interest: the importance of religious beliefs in the making of human activity, and the consequent necessity of integrating the history of religions with the general history of humanity; the history of liberty in antiquity, about which a book projected since his early years in fascist Italy was never written; above all, the interrelations of Jews, Greeks, and Romans in the ancient world. But, in the last analysis, he had no single subject. He read all and weighed all.

In 1975, he was again obliged to give up his professorship—this time, because of mandatory retirement. He was, for a time, an associate at All Souls College, Oxford, and he kept his book-crammed flat in London. But he made his principal new academic seats away from England, at the Scuola Normale Superiore di Pisa for one term each year and, for two quarters of each year, at the University of Chicago. Thus he came to the University of Chicago in a kind of new voluntary exile, after the loss of his second professorship.

· II ·

He came in full vigor, writing at his accustomed great pace until his death in 1987, leading weekly seminars and giving a lecture series every

Arnaldo Momigliano

spring. He seemed entirely at home, not only honored, but, as he had been in London, beloved. He attracted a circle of admirers drawn from graduate students and faculty on all levels. Indeed, he was approachable by all in Chicago who wished to meet a great scholar. His learning was awe-inspiring, and he was of course a bit of an intimidating figure. But he was never a forbidding figure; quite the contrary, he was plainly delighted to meet and converse with the hungry scholarly souls who find their way to the University of Chicago.

When I joined his circle in his later years at Chicago, he was an old man, but an astonishingly vigorous one. He walked rapidly between the few places he frequented on campus, generally immersed either in conversation or in thought. He would occasionally pull up short when struck by some comment; otherwise he barreled along at a more rapid pace than many of us could match. His haunts were the bookstores, of course, and a couple of local eating places. In the Agora, a restaurant on Fifty-Seventh Street, now defunct, he always had cheesecake. In the coffee shop in the Reynolds Club he experimented, roving widely over the baked goods.

It was in these eating places that he got to know students and admirers. He tried, against American resistance, to insist that everybody at the table eat something sweet. The common eating of sweets created a startlingly friendly, and often merry, atmosphere at Momigliano's table. If Momigliano had no equal in his scholarship, in his sweet tooth he was one among many. Accordingly we could all sit together comfortably with him, taking in the learning he offered in thickly accented English, a charming, somewhat ill-shaven, in dress somewhat disheveled, septuagenarian genius of scholarship, with an enthusiasm for stale pastry and young minds.

He had offices both in the department of classics and in Regenstein Library; but he rarely worked in either of them. He was a man of the library, not of the office, and he often expressed the view that scholars should be chained to their places until they had finished their work. Most nights, until midnight or so, he could be found at the same table by the reference section on the fifth floor of Regenstein, a few books and a pad of paper before him. Firm in the belief that books should sit on the shelf, available to readers who needed them, he rarely checked them out. At the end of the evening, it was his general practice to return books—particularly primary texts—to their place in the stacks; it was only with great effort that some of his students convinced him that it was acceptable practice to leave books sitting at one's place overnight.

If his research continued into the night, so too did his teaching. He generally took a break at 10 P.M. or so, to chat with students. Typically, he would suggest coffee—"the cup of wisdom," as he called it—and, of course, pastry. Sitting in the noisy basement snack room of Regenstein, he would examine advanced students whose topics interested him on their readings. The discussion would frequently raise some question answerable only by consulting the *Enciclopedia Italiana* or the *National Union Catalogue,* and after coffee he would move upstairs to the reference section to hunt down facts, names, dates of publication. After that followed another hour or so of work. At midnight he might invite a student to walk him home over the hundred yards or so to the Quadrangle Club—time during which his teaching continued unabated.

Living this daily routine, he seemed entirely at home at the University, and he frequently expressed his preference for Chicago over other American universities.

· III ·

The students and faculty of Chicago, for their part, made it clear how much they welcomed him. His lectures attracted remarkably large audiences. Teachers from many departments attended them regularly. Students at the University of Chicago loved learning and wanted to witness a great scholar, even one whose lectures soared beyond any knowledge of the ancient or modern world they might have brought to the large hall they filled.

Like his lectures, his seminars attracted teachers and students from all conceivable departments of the University. The participants included theologians, religious historians, classicists, literary critics, even sociologists. Indeed, as he occasionally declared, what made Chicago such a pleasant place for him was, as much as anything else, the regular interchange between members of different departments. Perhaps most important to him, in his wide-ranging academic acquaintanceship at the University, were the historians of religion, whose accessibility and integration into the larger scholarly community made it possible for him to break down the distinction between ecclesiastical and political history which he had denounced since the publication of his famous essay "La Formazione della moderna storiografia sull'impero Romano" (1936).

The seminars he led for this broad assortment of Chicago scholars were rather different from those he led at Pisa. At Pisa, Momigliano led seminars on the great German scholars of the end of the last century: Usener, Wilamowitz and others. The Pisa seminars were clearly given for a commu-

nity of advanced specialists in ancient history, and in particular to a community of specialists in ancient religions. At Chicago, by contrast, his
seminars were usually on more general themes in ancient history and in
the history of scholarship, addressed to a less specialized community: Philology and Hermeneutics in the Nineteenth-Century; Antiquarianship and
the Antiquarian. These seminars typically included only one paper read by
Momigliano himself; on other weeks a paper was read by some other
member of the seminar. But that hardly meant that the seminar was not
still Momigliano's show. For every week when Momigliano himself did not
present a paper, the great moment was when he commented on the paper
read. It was an extraordinary impromptu weekly disquisition that Momigliano offered, in part a comment on the paper before the seminar, but in
large part a fresh approach to the topic by Momigliano himself, learnedly
marshaling what was known on the subject, but always (as was Momigliano's constant practice) emphasizing what was not known.

And of course his own papers and lectures always inspired awe. To the
end, this remained particularly true of his papers on the ancient world, in
which his vast learning and startling ability to see connections between
various isolated fragments of evidence was most notably on display. It was
impossible not to marvel at the quantity and variety of the evidence that
Momigliano "controlled," to adopt his favorite word. His erudition had
none of the ponderousness one associates with the erudite; far from pon-
derous, he was magically deft, moving from fact to fact without any evident
effort.

· IV ·

To say that Momigliano was at home at the University of Chicago is, of
course, not to deny that he sometimes rather dwarfed the place. He was a
scholar of a grander type than any university could ordinarily hope to have
on hand.

Nevertheless, most of the time he acted as though the University (and
indeed the world at large) were made up of scholars as profound as himself. Unmatched as he was, he nevertheless chose to behave as though he
moved among equals. All who encountered him in Chicago—as elsewhere—remember his odd habit of presuming that his interlocutor, whoever that might be, possessed great learning. "As you know . . ." was the
phrase one heard from him more often than any other; it was invariably
followed by some fact or some text or some scholarly interpretation that
one did not know at all. In part, perhaps, this practice satisfied some desire
of his own, to pretend that he was living in more learned company than

was in fact the case—that he was still in the wartime Oxford of Fraenkel, Pfeiffer, and the rest of the spectacular collection of refugees among whom he had found himself after 1938.

But one suspects that his "as you know" was at bottom an effort to uphold scholarly standards, by presuming the level of learning he thought it appropriate to expect. It was, of course, too much to expect. No one was up to Momigliano's standard—not in London, not in Chicago. So it was that, while Momigliano always maintained the courteous fiction that everyone present with him was deeply learned, he could occasionally surrender to a fierce irritation at the ignorance of absent others. Nothing distressed him quite so much as the spectacle of the pompous scholar who was out of his depth. Momigliano's students quickly learned that to please him, they had first of all to have a decent sense of the limits of their own knowledge; they quickly learned to honor the maxim of Gottfried Hermann, which Momigliano made his own: "Est quaedam etiam nesciendi ars et scientia."

It was when he expressed his distress at the sad state of the "ars nesciendi" that his Chicago circle came to know Momigliano the philosopher (or perhaps, better, methodologist) of history. The dissatisfactions that he vented from time to time in Chicago belonged to a lifetime of effort at keeping historians methodologically honest. Momigliano was always something of a reluctant philosopher of history, concerned much more to defend sound practices than to propagate some view of his own. He was drawn into methodological battle as a young man in fascist Italy—notably, for example, in his response to Mario Attilio Levi's *Roma negli studi storici italiani* of 1934. Levi, later second on the list for the Turin chair that became Momigliano's, had written of the necessity for conforming the interpretation of the Roman past to the needs of a fascist present. The young Momigliano replied, "It would be well for professional historians to leave off these generic affirmations, of which we have heard quite enough, and get on with their job, which it is superfluous to define" (quoted in L. Canfora, *Ideologie del Classicisimo* [1980], p. 97; Canfora's book, it should however be added, was not one that Momigliano approved of). It would be hard to match the rhetorical force of this contemptuous refusal to argue method with thugs.

But in later years it evidently became clear to Momigliano that, for better or for worse, the job of the historian did indeed need, for the health of the profession, to be specified. His immense body of reviews, his magnificent work as historian of historiography and of classical studies, his few but remarkable essays on philosophy of history, constituted the leading corpus of methodological definition produced over the past several decades. Yet always one had the sense that methodology was a chore for him, a necessary but secondary labor. Momigliano was a scholar, a weigher of evidence, who felt obliged to define "the task of the professional historian" only when he saw professional historians unmindful of their task, or incapable of performing it properly.

By the time he came to Chicago, a changing tone in his methodological writings made it clear that he was finding far too many over-ambitious scholars. In his last years in London, his prime concern, as expressed for example in his well-known essay "Le regole del gioco nello studio della storia antica" (1974), had been to insist that historians must have proper command of the primary evidence. By the time I came to him in 1982, by contrast, Momigliano's view had darkened a bit. It was in 1982 that, moving beyond both the sovereign disdain he had shown in dismissing the work of fascist historians, and the calm insistence on mastery of the evidence he had expressed a decade earlier, he published his *New Paths of Classicism in the Nineteenth Century,* with its impatient opening line: "In our time there is a great danger that those who talk most readily about historians and scholars may not know too much about history and scholarship."

The impatience he expressed in print was the impatience he expressed in conversation—in particular, in his often expressed worry that command of scholarly fundamentals, most notably knowledge of the Latin language, was perilously weak. His distress with the overblown ambitions of ill-prepared scholars was the first thing I encountered. I came to him at the beginning of the spring quarter, 1982. He had just arrived at Chicago for the quarter. He sat with me in the small waiting room of the Quadrangle Club; listened scowling to my plans for work in the history of classical scholarship; and forcefully discouraged me from working on such a subject without far better training in classical scholarship than I possessed. He left me with little doubt that he would not care to work with a weakly trained young American with grandiose ambitions for writing scholarly history. I heard more such harsh judgments later, during a long effort to win his confidence.

Nevertheless it should be said that he spoke harshly only of those who were not up to their task as scholars; of their failures as human beings he was forgiving. And it should be said again and again that he loved the University.

· V ·

During his last few years at Chicago, he was acutely aware of the deterioration in his health. Nevertheless he continued to work at a remarkable pace; surely there have been few scholars so afflicted by the sense of impending death who have continued to work so unremittingly. He suffered a severe heart attack in the spring of 1987. Action by colleagues and care at the University of Chicago hospital saved his life, but only for a few months more. He returned to London in mid-summer, but never regained his strength, dying on September 1 of that year, a few days short of his seventy-ninth birthday.

He left little of the sort of marks on the University that could be detected by an administrator. He directed few doctoral students; America simply did not offer him students with an adequate preparation. Nor did he teach, precisely speaking, in the classroom. But it would be untrue to say that he left no mark at all, quite the contrary. He was available to all serious students wise enough to come to him for guidance and learned direction. They looked upon him as an omniscient and kindly sage. He left, moreover, any number of persons who could feel that, having encountered Momigliano, they had been made aware of the great tradition of scholarship. The deepest mark he left was the sense of an empty place which followed his death, and which still persists among all who knew him.

30

ROBERT SANDERSON MULLIKEN

1 8 9 6 – 1 9 8 6

R. STEPHEN BERRY

ROBERT S. MULLIKEN was a quiet, soft-spoken man, yet so single-minded and determined in his devotion to understanding molecules that he came to be called "Mr. Molecule." If a single person's ideas and teachings dominated the development of our understanding of molecular structure and spectra, that person surely has been Robert Mulliken. From the beginning of his career as an independent scientist in the mid-1920s until he published his last scientific papers in the early 1980s, he guided an entire field, through his penetrating solutions of outstanding puzzles, his identification and analysis of the new major problems ripe for study, and his creation of a school, the Laboratory of Molecular Structure and Spectroscopy, or LMSS, at the University of Chicago, in its time the most important center in the world for the study of molecules.

· I ·

Mulliken epitomized the eclectic in his scientific style. He considered himself neither a theorist nor an experimentalist—although he carried out both experimental and theoretical research—but an interpreter of observations. With this attitude, he was free to call on any techniques, ideas, or approaches, whatever best suited the problem at hand. Until the experimental work of his group closed down with his official retirement, his laboratory always had experimentalists studying electronic spectra of molecules. The basement of Eckhart Laboratory was the spectroscopy laboratory, with several instruments, including a very awkward, homemade spectrograph for work in the far or "vacuum" ultraviolet and two other very large instruments, "Paschen circles" with 21- and 30-foot radii for the focal curve, literally using rather large rooms as the inside of their cam-

ROBERT SANDERSON MULLIKEN, 1984

eras. These were used for fairly high-resolution spectroscopy until the advent of laser techniques, which came into use just when the LMSS was discontinuing experimental work.

Although the LMSS and Robert Mulliken himself did not participate at the leading edge of the experimental methods that now dominate the field, the opposite was the case regarding the role of computations in molecular science. In 1950, Mulliken committed his group to the development of computational methods for finding molecular properties. He foresaw the role that computers could fill in transforming quantum mechanics from a formal analytic tool and a guide for simplifying models into a quantitative tool with powerful predictive capabilities. In an article written in 1958 with his protégé and subsequent colleague, Clemens Roothaan, he said, "Looking toward the future, it seems certain that colossal rewards lie ahead from large-scale quantum-mechanical calculations of the structure of matter. . . . And gradually, reliable computations even of quantities now inaccessible or poorly accessible to experimental observation will come more and more into the picture. . . . We think it is no exaggeration to say that the workers in this field are standing on the threshold of a new era."

Between 1950 and 1958, there was a qualitative change in the way computations were done. In 1950, almost the only devices available to aid computations were electrically driven mechanical calculators; some laboratories still used hand-cranked calculators. By 1958, machines such as the IBM 650 and the larger, faster Remington-Rand 1103 and Univac Scientific were available to research workers in LMSS and some places elsewhere. This meant, in Mulliken's words in 1958, "the entire set of calculations which took [Charles] Scherr (with the help of two assistants) about a year, can now be repeated in 35 min," and we know that was only the beginning.

Mulliken was not alone by any means in his belief that computational molecular science was a large part of the future of the field. His close friend from their postdoctoral days in Cambridge, Massachusetts, John C. Slater, was one of these; he founded a group at the Massachusetts Institute of Technology in friendly rivalry with the LMSS. Others with large, active groups included Masao Kotani in Tokyo and Per Olov Löwdin in Uppsala. S. F. Boys worked at Cambridge University, with only occasional students or postdoctoral associates, but made seminal contributions well recognized later. But it was the LMSS to which the pilgrimages were made. A striking majority of the important contributors to molecular theory and molecular computation spent some period as student, postdoctoral associate, or visiting faculty member in Robert Mulliken's group at the University of Chicago. One of Robert's favorite stories of this phenomenon concerns Professor Saburo Nagakura, later the director of the Institute for Molecular Science at Okazaki, Japan, president of Graduate University for Advanced Studies, Yokohama, Japan, and recipient of the Order of Culture, the highest award given in Japan for scientific or cultural contributions. Robert had written to Nagakura, already a professor, asking whether the latter had anyone he could recommend to come to Chicago as a postdoctoral associate to do experimental work. Nagakura replied by asking whether it would be all right if he himself came in that capacity. So, in 1965–66, he did!

In that period when Mulliken became completely persuaded of the power of computation from first principles, his allies notwithstanding, there were other strong opinions in opposition. Those who believed in elementary models and simply calculable, semi-empirical descriptions expressed deep reservations about the role of "big" calculations. They questioned both the feasibility of accurate computations for all but the simplest molecules and the extent of new physical insight that could be gained from a knowledge of elaborate wave functions and some predicted values of observables. One confrontation of the two factions occurred at a conference in Boulder, Colorado, in 1960. The proceedings of this conference were published in October 1960 in *Reviews of Modern Physics*. The division of viewpoints now seems shortsighted, because it seems so clear today that both approaches have important uses. But at that meeting, Charles Coulson, professor of theoretical chemistry at Oxford, in his summary talk, divided theoretical chemistry into two populations, Type 1, which believed the future lay with computations, and Type 2, which chose simple and semi-empirical models. Coulson, having made important contributions to both aspects, tried to be as tolerant as possible toward both, but his sympathies seemed to us young Americans to be with Type 2, the favorite of almost all the British scientists except Boys and a few young iconoclasts. Mulliken, despite his belief in large-scale computation, straddled the field, continuing to carry out simple, interpretive studies; there were often people working in the LMSS on semi-empirical models.

Chicago and the LMSS became, ultimately, the most important center for molecular computations. The facilities were remarkably good; when I asked Enrico Clementi in the mid-1960s about the quality of the computing facilities at IBM (where he then was) and at Chicago, Enrico said without hesitation that Chicago's were the best in the world; "after all," he said, "you are customers!" Clemens Roothaan was in charge of the Computation

Center. Always a zealous believer that users should understand how their machines operate, he was a strong, encouraging influence on aspiring scientists for whom such knowledge would enable them to use computers at the limits of their capabilities; but he seemed something of an ogre to users who wanted computers to be black boxes operating with reliable, "canned" programs. The students in the LMSS typically became very skilled programmers, in addition to well-educated molecular scientists.

Mulliken himself left the programming and the machine operations to others until 1970, when he spent a summer working at the IBM laboratory in San Jose, California. This laboratory had collected several alumni of the LMSS—Douglas McLean, Clementi, Yoshimine and Bowen Liu—a group known as the "Chicago Mafia." Robert learned to write and execute programs that summer, at age seventy-four. He had, of course, done roughly the same kinds of computations by hand years before. But the power of the computer enabled him and everyone else to realize some of the accuracy that he and Roothaan had anticipated. Sometimes the results were counterintuitive, at least counter to the intuitions we had all built up during the precomputer years. At lunch at the Quadrangle Club early that autumn of 1970, shortly after his return, Robert turned to me and said, with the naive wonderment so characteristic of his discussion, "You know, I don't think I understand molecular orbitals very well." This, from one of the two people who did most to develop the concept of molecular orbitals and integrate them into all the thinking about molecular structure since the late 1920s.

The roll of scientists who worked in his group illustrates what an institution Robert Mulliken created. When the LMSS was established, Robert was "big boss," Clemens Roothaan was "little boss," and Bernard Ransil was "straw boss." Others who were in the group at one time or another included W. C. Price, Christopher Longuet-Higgins, Jacob Bigeleisen, Leslie Orgel, Harrison Shull, Michael Kasha, Klaus Ruedenberg, Yoshio Tanaka, Harden McConnell, Norbert Muller, Robert G. Parr, Gerhard Herzberg, Alf Lofthus, Philip G. Wilkinson (who was primarily responsible for the vacuum ultraviolet spectroscopy), John Platt, W. Kolos, Hiroshi Tsubomura, T. Namioka, F. A. Matsen, Martin Gouterman, John Murrell, P. K. Carroll, A. C. Wahl, Paul Bagus, Willis B. Person, Anthony Merer, Joel Tellinghuisen, Marshall Ginter, Paul Cade, and Juergen Hinze, as well as Scherr, Nagakura, Clementi, McLean, and Yoshimine. Robert enjoyed learning from all his faculty colleagues, whether they were, roughly, contemporaries, like Weldon Brown and G. W. (Bill) Wheland, or the most junior members. He lunched almost every day at the Quadrangle Club, usually with either the physicists or the chemists. A carpet of his hangs there now on the wall of the dining room above the "chemists' table."

· II ·

Robert's background led him naturally into academic science. He was born in Newburyport, Massachusetts, in a house built by his great-grand-father about 1798. His father, Samuel Parsons Mulliken, was a professor of chemistry at Massachusetts Institute of Technology, which made him a daily commuter between Newburyport and Boston. Samuel Mulliken and his childhood friend and later colleague, Arthur A. Noyes, were strong influences, stirring Robert's interests in science. As a high school student, Robert decided against philosophy as a career and decided for science. He attended MIT as an undergraduate, receiving the degree of bachelor of science in chemistry in 1917. He then did a wartime service studying poison gases in a laboratory at American University under the direction of a Lieutenant James Bryant Conant, then of the Chemical Warfare Service. Mulliken entered the Chemical Warfare Service himself, rising to private first class, but left when he contracted influenza in 1918. When he recovered, he worked for the New Jersey Zinc Company until he entered graduate school at the University of Chicago in autumn of 1919.

As a graduate student in chemistry at Chicago, Robert worked under the direction of W. D. Harkins, first on surface tension and then on isotope separation, particularly of mercury isotopes. The method used in his thesis was "irreversible evaporation" and distillation. Robert found that a dirty surface on the mercury aided the separation considerably; this concept, later called a boundary layer or diffusion membrane, played an integral role in the Manhattan Project. Robert conceived and tried centrifugation but, as he said fifty-five years later, the centrifuge was simply too crude. He also considered photochemical separation but never published anything on the subject.

At Chicago, Robert became interested in the interpretation of valence and chemical bonding through the papers of Irving Langmuir and G. N. Lewis. He encountered the old quantum theory through two enthusiastic courses of lectures by Robert A. Millikan, but was uneasy about the theory; "a disorganized chaos" was the description Mulliken used for it in reminiscences written in 1965. Nevertheless Robert succeeded in applying it in 1924–25 to the interpretation of a particular molecular spectrum, assigned initially by Wilfred Jevons to the boron nitride molecule BN. Mulliken showed that the spectrum was that of boron oxide, despite the preparation involving no apparent oxygen-containing substances. Jevons was pressed by a zealous department head to publish a note insisting on the initial assignment. Then, at the urging of R. T. Birge, Mulliken wrote directly to Jevons, visited him in England in 1925 and the two men settled the matter amicably and remained friends thereafter. It was in the analysis of the boron oxide spectrum that Mulliken pointed out that the best representation of the data required that the molecule's state of lowest energy kept a half-quantum of vibrational energy, rather than none at all. This was shown about two years later to be a necessary consequence of quantum mechanics and the uncertainty principle.

Robert held a National Research Council fellowship at that time and was working at Harvard after he completed his doctorate in 1922. He had wanted to study beta-ray spectroscopy with Ernest Rutherford at Manchester, but the fellowship board felt that his physics background was not strong enough and urged him to select a more chemical topic. Consequently he carried out many experiments in molecular spectroscopy largely under the guidance of E. C. Kemble and F. A. Saunders. At that time, a coterie of enthusiastic young American scientists came together in Cambridge, a group including Mulliken, Samuel Allison, F. A. Jenkins, J. R. Oppenheimer, John Van Vleck, Gregory Breit, Harold Urey, and John Slater. They were not all in Cambridge at the same time but, for the most part, knew one another, and there were several close friendships among them.

Like most of that group, Mulliken made his early pilgrimage to Europe in the summer of 1925. This was just at the threshold of quantum mechanics. Robert, like several of his contemporaries, had been trying to give an organization to the states and spectra of diatomic molecules. This subject was, from his later reminiscences, a lively part of many of the discussions he had with colleagues and distinguished senior scientists in London, Oxford, Cambridge, Copenhagen, and, perhaps most important, Göttingen. There he met Max Born, James Franck, Otto Oldenberg, Hertha Sponer, V. Kondratiev, V. I. Semenov, A. Terenin, and especially Born's assistant, Fredrich Hund. The relationship between Mulliken and Hund became one of the most fruitful in the twentieth century, in the history of the interpretation of the structure of matter and the nature of chemical bonds.

Even in 1925, a year before the first papers were published on quantum mechanics, Mulliken and Hund began to conceive an analogue for molecules of the *Aufbauprinzip* introduced by Niels Bohr to explain the structures of atoms and the periodic table. Their notion was that electrons in molecules would have quantized orbits like those introduced by Bohr and developed by Sommerfeld. These orbits would define successive shells, like their atomic counterparts. However the orbits in molecules would extend throughout the molecule, encircling two or more nuclei. After their meeting, Mulliken and Hund corresponded and both published on the subject in 1926 and 1927. But as soon as they knew of the matrix mechanics of Heisenberg and the wave mechanics of Schrödinger, both realized that would be the correct direction for them. Mulliken probably learned first about Heisenberg's work from a lecture in 1926 by Max Born. He felt quite inadequately trained, especially in mathematics, for this new kind of physics—although it seems now like something he could have learned in a week or two. Schrödinger's formulation, which was based on the second-order differential equations that everybody learned, "was somewhat of a relief that it wasn't so bad."

Mulliken returned to Göttingen in 1927, after the hydrogen atom had been worked out by Pauli with matrix mechanics and by Schrödinger with wave mechanics. That summer was the time Hund and Mulliken developed their basic interpretation of the spectra of diatomic molecules and their generalization of atomic orbitals, the standing-wave, stationary states of electrons in atoms, to "molecular orbitals," the molecular counterparts. Robert's strengths were a deep knowledge of molecular spectra and a capacity to invent phenomenological and empirical interpretations; Hund brought quantitative and mathematical insights, a greater mastery of the new theories and a specific vector model for quantum systems. They shared a view of stationary states of electrons in molecules and of the analogy between atoms and molecules. By 1928, they had both written their first papers, which went beyond the old quantum theory, and molecular orbitals were born. Remarkably, especially in light of their long friendship and profound mutual respect, the two men never published a joint paper.

Also during the summer of 1927, in Zurich, Mulliken met Schrödinger, whose chair, Mulliken recalled later, collapsed during their conversation. Schrödinger introduced him to W. Heitler and F. London, who were just developing their electron-pair theory of the chemical bond. This approach, close to Langmuir's and Lewis's, was to become a rival to the molecular orbital approach until John Slater, some years later, showed that both were approximations and suitable starting points from which a common, accurate theoretical picture could be achieved. Upon seeing it for the first time, Robert was not enthusiastic. However he was deeply engaged in developing his own ideas and did not care to stop to learn, evaluate, and incorporate such different ideas from others. Linus Pauling and John Slater, however, quickly absorbed the ideas, and the Heitler-London-Slater-Pauling valence bond theory became another item in the theorist's bag of tools. There were difficulties inherent in valence bond theory that did not appear in the Hund-Mulliken molecular orbital theory, which Mulliken recognized. Mulliken objected particularly to how "Pauling made a special point in making everything sound as simple as possible and in that way making it [valence bond theory] very popular with chemists but delaying their understanding of the true [complexity of molecular structure]." Mulliken's respect for Hund and Slater endured throughout his life; he felt that his Nobel Prize should, most properly, have been shared with them.

Between the two trips to Europe, Mulliken became an assistant professor in the department of physics at New York University. In 1928, he refused the chairmanship of that department, thinking himself quite unfit for the job. He also refused a professorship in the department of physics at Johns Hopkins offered by R. W. Wood. Instead, he accepted an associate professorship in the department of physics at the University of Chicago, under Arthur H. Compton. He acknowledged later that his decision was heavily influenced by the warm feelings he held toward Chicago from his days as a graduate student. The University of Chicago remained his academic home, and Hyde Park his domicile, until about two years before he died.

In the summer of 1929, Robert met Mary Helen von Noé, the beautiful daughter of a well-known professor of paleobotany at the University of Chicago, the man who designed the underground coal mine at the Museum of Science and Industry. She, an aspiring water-colorist, and he, the brilliant, rising young physicist, were married on Christmas Eve of the same year.

Robert held a Guggenheim Fellowship at that time and decided to split it into two six-month segments. The first, in spring of 1930, must have been the time of the honeymoon, during which, Mary Helen claimed, molecular orbital theory was born. Our chronology would probably put it almost three years earlier, in 1927. Among the many places on the itinerary, the 1930 trip took the couple to Leipzig, where Hund, Heisenberg, Peter Debye, and Hückel were, and Edward Teller, too, then Heisenberg's assistant. Mulliken talked with them all, especially Hund and Teller, continuing the productive dialogue with Hund and engaging Teller, later a colleague at Chicago, in molecular problems, to which Teller later made a wide variety of very important contributions. Mulliken himself was deeply immersed in interpreting molecular spectra, writing a series of articles on the halogen molecules and another series for *Reviews of Modern Physics* which gave molecular electronic spectroscopy the coherence he had been seeking since the early 1920s. Mulliken later noted that he did not bother to go to a "screaming, roaring speech" by Adolf Hitler.

The Mullikens used the second half of the Guggenheim Fellowship during the autumn and winter of 1932–33. Heisenberg, Hund, and Teller were still in Leipzig. This time, the atmosphere was distinctly more ominous; Hund was predicting the inevitability of Hitler's accession to power. There was a similar premonition in Göttingen and Berlin. A visit to Darmstadt with Gerhard Herzberg ended the German segment of the trip and cemented the long-standing close relationship between the two men. (Herzberg later came to the University of Chicago before going to the National Research Council of Canada.) The Mullikens left Germany and were in Austria on 5 March, the day of Hitler's electoral victory; the next day, they crossed Germany to go to Amsterdam. Mulliken does not mention visiting Hund again until 1953 in Frankfurt; Hund had remained in Leipzig and then moved to Jena, both in East Germany, but was able to move to Frankfurt to accept a professorship there in about 1950.

Robert's profound influence on molecular science evolved partly through the several monumental series of articles he published, beginning in 1926 and continuing until his death. The first, a series of eight papers on "Electronic States and Band-Spectrum Structure in Diatomic Molecules," was designed to organize the subject; the series in *Reviews of Modern Physics,* "Interpretation of Band Spectra," carries that analysis further, making it more encompassing and more penetrating. That series remains a standard text on the subject. Between the two he wrote a three-paper series, "The Assignment of Quantum Numbers for Electrons in Molecules," which shows the influence of Hund. Mulliken went beyond diatomic molecules with the long series—fourteen papers—entitled "Electronic Structures of Polyatomic Molecules and Valence," which appeared between 1932 and 1935. A series of ten papers on intensities of electronic spectra appeared in 1939–40. After the Second World War, he wrote three more series. One dealt with the distribution of electronic charge in molecules and its relation to chemical bonding.

The next series, which overlapped the charge distribution series in time, took Mulliken into an area altogether new for him, the spectra of molecules in solution. A puzzling spectrum of iodine dissolved in benzene was reported in 1949 by Joel Hildebrand and H. A. Benesi; Mulliken was tantalized by the observation and told Hildebrand, "I bet I can explain that spectrum." After one false start, he did explain it, in terms of what is now called a "charge transfer band," an intense spectral band system due to the production by light of two ions bound together from two neutral molecules. The insight that explained the iodine-benzene spectrum led to the series "Molecular Complexes and Their Spectra" and to a book, written with Willis Person. This series has had ramifications for many aspects of photochemistry and photobiology. The last series he wrote became remarkably influential, changing much of the interpretation of molecular spectra in the ultraviolet; this set of seven papers dealt with molecular Rydberg spectra, spectra in which one electron is excited to an orbit (strictly, orbital or standing wave state) large enough to be well outside the core formed by the nuclei and the other electrons.

Certain topics aroused Robert's interest early and intrigued him throughout his career. One pervasive theme was the spectrum and structure of ethylene and species related to it. He pointed out in 1935 that the lowest excited state of ethylene had to be a "triplet," a state in which the molecule is magnetic. The idea was not readily accepted, but eventually it became a basic concept for the interpretation of not only the behavior of ethylene but of most small and medium-sized molecules. Mulliken was always adept at seeing connections between seemingly unrelated observations and systems. He recognized the close relationship of the molecules of ethylene, formaldehyde, and oxgen, and the differences and similarities their spectra should—and do—show. He did miss one finding when he was interpreting the spectrum of oxygen in 1932. He left unassigned some weak lines which W. F. Giauque and H. S. Johnston soon showed were due to the isotopes of oxygen with mass numbers 17 and 18 instead of 16. This led to the award of a Nobel Prize to Giauque. Thereafter, Mulliken was very careful to pay as much attention to weak bands as to strong ones!

· III ·

He was rarely quick to react to sound new ideas, but he listened to them and absorbed them. The people working in his group learned soon after they arrived that Robert's characteristic "Mmmmm . . ." followed by a long draw on his cigarette, usually with a slight nod, meant that the ideas were going in, to be processed and discussed when Robert had something substantive to contribute to them. It might be days or months, but he usually had something important to add.

I recall a lunch-table discussion with Robert in about 1975 concerning ethylene. He and I had been talking, off and on, about the topic and he was rereading old papers of his own. On this occasion, he described how he thought he had discovered a mistake in an early, central paper. However, he said, he studied it very carefully and decided that he had correctly meant precisely what he had said. It was as if the author were a different person, whose subtlety he was able to admire. His care for precision frequently generated a formidable array of footnotes in his papers. The footnotes sometimes contained the essential steps in his line of reasoning. In lecturing, he maintained the same concern for precision; consequently he would digress from his main line into clarifications and clarifications of the clarifications, so that those in his audiences who were not aware of his style sometimes lost track of the point—to say the least. But his papers were, and remain, remarkable for their capacity to convey detailed information with percision and clarity. My own research director, William Moffitt, said to me that he learned more, as a student, reading Robert Mulliken's papers than from any other source. Moffitt had been a student of Charles Coulson, in turn a student of John Lennard-Jones, both of them masters of clear scientific writing, so Moffitt's comment carried great weight with those of us studying with him.

During the Second World War Robert was in charge of the Information Division of the Metallurgical Laboratory, the portion of the Manhattan Project at the University of Chicago. Superficially he seemed to stay shyly aloof from human affairs; by his own admission, he "dehumanized" himself as a young man. In reality, he later tried consciously, and with success, to "rehumanize" himself. In 1944, he and Eugene Rabinowich produced a key chapter of the "Report on Nucleonics" from the Metallurgical Laboratory, an assessment of what the world would be like with nuclear weapons. This chapter became the forerunner of the famous Franck Report. During the late 1960s and 1970s, he became very concerned about population growth and its implications for the world's resources. This stimulated him to write and speak publicly about "NPG" or negative population growth, which he believed would be necessary.

· IV ·

Robert always enjoyed finance and investment. One could be sure of a lively lunch conversation with him by bringing up some question about stocks and bonds, as sure as if one raised a question about molecular spectra. He applied the same combination of analytical and intuitive insight to securities that he did to molecules. He was conservative politically and in his investments. He was not conservative at the wheel of a car; he managed to surprise and sometimes shock postdoctoral fellows who traveled with him to meetings in Columbus—the famous and still-continuing meetings on molecular spectroscopy— and elsewhere. His wry sense of humor sometimes showed when he was driving; on one occasion, with two distinguished scientists, L. Oosterhoff and J. C. Slater, as his passengers, he stopped at a stop sign on a road in the middle of empty farmland . . . and waited and waited. When John Slater finally said "Robert, I think you'll have to go on across," Robert replied "That's the trouble with these road signs. They say 'Stop' and then they don't say what to do after that."

One story that became well known partly through Robert's own retelling is the story of his stolen car. Late in the autumn of 1982, he drove from his apartment to the house of the University president, where he parked his car in the small lot. At the end of the evening, it had begun to snow so he accepted a ride home. The next day, he came down and did not find his car in its usual place, so he reported it stolen. After a few weeks, the insurance company paid him in full for loss of a stolen car. Several months later, when the snows had melted, Robert received a telephone call from the University police, asking him to please move his car. "My car?" asked Robert, puzzled. "Yes, it is in the lot next to the president's house."

We who were close to Mulliken and his group discovered that one way to learn how his thinking worked was to use the remarkable collection he assembled under the name of "the reprint collection." But it was far more than a categorized collection of reprints and preprints available to everyone. The papers there were filled with Mulliken's handwritten comments, and there were many drafts, unpublished reports, and especially letters exchanged between Mulliken and the innumerable authors represented there. We all knew that soon after publishing anything connected with molecular spectra or structure, we would receive a postcard requesting a reprint, with the rubber-stamped signature of Robert S. Mulliken, sent at Robert's direction by his secretary, Helen Barileau. And that soon thereafter, the reprint would be added to the collection.

· V ·

Robert continued to travel until almost the last year of his life. He spent several years, beginning in 1965, dividing his time between Chicago and Tallahassee, where he spent winter quarters at Florida State University, at the instigation of Michael Kasha. Early in the morning after his first arrival in Tallahassee, after a hot, arduous drive from Chicago with Mary Helen, Robert learned of his Nobel award. During the inevitable interviews immediately following, he was asked if he was excited. "Mmmmm . . . no, not particularly, I don't see anything to be excited about. After all, I don't even know if it's true; all I've heard is just from a newspaper reporter."

He held many other visiting appointments such as Baker Lecturer at Cornell in 1960 and Silliman Lecturer at Yale in 1965. He received virtually every major award of the American Chemical Society and its sections, including the J. Willard Gibbs Medal, the Gilbert N. Lewis Medal, the Theodore W. Richards Medal, the Peter Debye Award, the John G. Kirkwood Award and the Priestley Medal. The last of these, the highest award of the American Chemical Society, was one of his most prized honors. And of course Robert's Nobel award, which was given in 1965, was something he dearly prized.

Robert's readiness for new ideas and observations, coupled with his natural caution and physical intuition, made him a unique personality in science. He loved new challenges and puzzles but sensed which were worth pursuing and which were artifacts. I watched at one conference when an enthusiastic young experimentalist explained his latest results to Robert, who listened attentively, obviously thinking as he listened. When the exposition was over, Robert replied, nodding his head, "Hmmmm; very interesting . . . [long pause] . . . if it's right." He was ready for the unexpected, but he was in tune with nature, and knew inside himself what was real and deserving of his acute thought. He set a style and a standard that are as much his legacy as the body of scientific understanding he created.

31

A. LEO OPPENHEIM

1 9 0 4 – 1 9 7 4

E R I C A   R E I N E R

NAVIGARE NECESSE EST, VIVERE NON. This was Leo Oppenheim's favorite quotation, and a motto for his work and his life.

· I ·

The University of Chicago owes its greatest debt to Oppenheim for the Chicago *Assyrian Dictionary*, the task he was engaged in for the twenty-seven years he spent at the University, from his appointment in 1947 to his death, at the age of seventy, in 1974. But the realization of this long-standing project must not obscure or overshadow the multiple ways in which Oppenheim contributed to the intellectual life of the University. He did this not by holding administrative jobs or by participating in committees but by being an avid participant in discussions, raising questions and keeping close ties with resident and visiting scholars, such as Arnaldo Momigliano and Michael Polanyi; and by attending, and urging his junior colleagues to attend, the gatherings we knew as the Near East Club, held at the Oriental Institute over beer and pretzels, and of the Philological Society of the division of the humanities, with somewhat heartier post-colloquial fare. He was no less interested in maintaining relations with the other divisions, especially with the anthropologists. Indeed, he claimed to be a "cultural anthropologist" who happened to study a dead civilization.

This image surfaces in the subtitle of his *Ancient Mesopotamia: Portrait of a Dead Civilization* (1964; second revised edition, 1977). In a memorial tribute to Oppenheim, Robert McC. Adams wrote that "I have always been struck by the firmness of his insistence, in the subtitle of *Ancient Mesopotamia* and elsewhere, that his subject was a 'dead' civilization. Surely, one wanted to respond, all human societies and achievements have had

A. LEO OPPENHEIM

issue in which they remain in a sense living—and Mesopotamian civilization far more than most. Only gradually did I come to understand that, for him, the death of his subject matter was somehow a precondition for its productive study, which then had to involve its painstaking, conscious recreation as a formed thing of the mind. The separation of the scholar from the object of his study, across an immense gulf of time, circumstance, and cognitive differences that was not to be bridged, was a part of the lonely and yet also necessarily collaborative and interdependent grandeur of scholarship itself."

Oppenheim called himself a cultural anthropologist in part so as to dissociate himself with the often sterile pursuits of the "pure" philologists and in part to claim citizenship in a discipline he admired without overlooking its flaws. From anthropologists he took not their jargon—even though he could use it as well as anyone—but their preoccupation with the culture as a whole. The ideas he gained from his readings in history or anthropology owed nothing to the ideas expressed in the books he had read; rather they started a train of thought that led in some unpredictable directions.

It is also with anthropologists that Oppenheim shared the ways of abstract thinking, without indulging in piling words upon words like those whom he, albeit only orally, jocularly accused of denuding the forests with their need for paper. And whenever he had completed a work that demanded rigorous abstract thought and categories, he announced that he would make a text edition, thus returning, like Antaeus to the earth, to the essential groundwork, the philological analysis of texts. In this field his main publications were the *Assyrian Dreambook* (1956), the instructions for producing colored glasses (in the "glass book" published in 1971 under the sponsorship of Corning Glass), and a large number of articles giving the *editio princeps* of many texts, legal, administrative, and scientific. Unfinished, alas, remained the reedition of the reports written to Assyrian kings of the eighth and seventh centuries on astronomical observations, on which he spent many weeks, collating the originals, in the British Museum.

· II ·

My colleague J. M. Renger and I surprised him with a *Festfiche* on his seventieth birthday. He disliked *Festschriften* but was intrigued by any new technological advance, so we hit upon the idea of collecting his most significant papers on microfiche. We divided his scholarly contributions into the broad categories of cultural history, social history, science and technology, religion, and linguistics. A surprising number of his early papers had to be included, not out of antiquarian interest but simply because they were still the only—and best—word on the subject. An equally surprising number of papers were pathbreakers. Oppenheim's inclination was to open up new perspectives and new fields and methods of research, leaving to others the job of gleaning; he did not wish to pontificate and thereby close doors to the young and their new ideas.

Oppenheim's renown extended beyond the confines of the field of Assyriology, or even ancient history, as shown by his participation in the various International Congresses of Economic History and especially, in 1954–55, in the seminar on economic aspects of institutional growth led by Karl Polanyi at Columbia University. He created, by introducing new terminology, a framework which has continued to serve new generations of scholars: the "great organizations," to refer to the role of the palace and the temple; the "stream of tradition," to designate the basic texts of Mesopotamian culture transmitted by generations of scribes, as opposed to the ephemeral records of everyday life preserved in tens of thousands of letters, court records, contracts, and administrative texts. The everyday records intrigued him inasmuch as they shed light, on the one hand, on the ancient material culture and technology, an area he felt sympathetic with, as he too was clever with his hands; and on the other hand, on many an underlying personal and political rivalry that does not surface in royal inscriptions and other similar public documents. Having written *Portrait of a Dead Civilization,* he wrote portraits of individuals in *Letters from Mesopotamia;* the nature of these letters as portraits is given away by the illustrations he asked his art historian colleague Maurits van Loon to provide from various periods of Mesopotamian history. The idea of presenting Mesopotamian society under the unusual aspect of the direct testimony of letters written by private persons as well as by officials and kings was typical of a mind always bent on innovation, *Letters from Mesopotamia* serving as a counterpoint to the abstract presentation of *Ancient Mesopotamia.* All of Oppenheim's works were in some sense programmatic. In *Letters* he grappled with the problem of translation from one language, a dead and structurally divergent language, into English; in *Ancient Mesopotamia* with the wider issue of translating the parameters of one civilization, again one that has been dead for millennia, into those of another, contemporary one.

· III ·

In later years, he was intrigued by Mesopotamian scholars and scientists and probed their intellectual attitude to their disciplines. This topic, first broached at the conference organized in Venice in 1973 by *Daedalus,* and published in that journal as "The Position of the Intellectual in Mesopotamian Society" in 1975, was the subject of his lectures at the Collège de France in the spring of 1971; these have remained unpublished. From this perspective, entire areas of Mesopotamian thought, such as divination, that had been considered as pertaining to religion at best, have been placed among the scientific disciplines, and thus have become respectable subjects of research by younger scholars.

Oppenheim liked to work under pressure but the pressure was self-imposed. It is true to say—as he often did—that he was driven by his daimon. He could place on his desk half a dozen trays with thousands of dictionary file-cards illustrating the uses of a word and put order in the chaos in less than a day. He had a comprehensive view of the word, of a text, and of the entire civilization he was passionately studying, as his *Ancient Mesopotamia* eventually demonstrated. The prescriptions for the means of producing colored glasses told him about the attitudes of craftsmen and scholars just as the predictions from dreams laboriously collected into handbooks and the rituals prescribed for averting their ill portents told him about the fears and aspirations of the common man. He has been described as a complex mind; indeed his mind was working in several layers, and so what he saw acquired a depth that was transparent to him alone. He was struck by the atypical, and had to find out what was behind it. He could not read a text the same way twice, or even write it down twice the same way, and so, inevitably, he was often accused of inconsistency.

What Oppenheim had said about Mesopotamian civilization never satisfied him. He came at it again and again from different angles, whether it was in connection with the Dreambook, or in his long quest on the position of the intellectual in Mesopotamia, that he approached in his various papers and lectures but that he did not live to incorporate into the synthesis he had planned in connection with editing the "Reports of the Astrologers" to the Assyrian kings. We can have an idea of what we missed through the sketch he gave in *Centaurus,* in the volume dedicated to Otto Neugebauer, the scholar whom he admired most.

He also admired "il miglior fabbro," Benno Landsberger, but he never begrudged appreciation for his peers and juniors alike. He encouraged, indeed pushed, students and young colleagues. In fact, he used to say, "I do not teach students: I teach future colleagues." And teach he did, many times giving courses not listed in the *Announcements* of the University, and during the summer for eager visitors.

· IV ·

Summers were a special time for him and his wife, Lilly, especially when they went to their farm in Michigan, usually on weekends but for longer periods during the summer. There he cut grass with a tractor-mower, planted thousands of pine trees, and in between typed page after page of the current book. In such a way did he hope to spend his "retirement" years in Berkeley, and for one brief year did so: from his study, at his enormous desk, he overlooked the bay; then he would get up and walk in the streets on the hill, observing with special pleasure the progress of a construction site, and thinking about the next page, the next chapter, the next task.

He enjoyed watching builders and would have no doubt made an excellent architect, as he had a special knack for a layout, a blueprint, a talent that made any manuscript of his—including the heavily marked-up drafts of dictionary articles—pleasant to look at; the arrows and lines of his insertions always went to the place aimed at directly, not contortedly like mine and others.' He took pleasure in working with his hands and was intrigued by solutions to technological problems, modern as well as ancient, as the titles and subject matters of a number of his articles and books testify. He had begun a book on the material culture of the Neo-Babylonian empire, wherein an astounding number of data are collected and explained, but he abandoned the project, not so much because of the more important commitment to the *Assyrian Dictionary* but, I suspect, because for him the solutions were of interest principally as they reflected attitudes of Mesopotamian man, in relation to his environment and to his social and religious organization. Eventually, it was in a variety of articles that he dealt with the adoption of influences and techniques by Mesopotamian man, especially from what he was wont to call the "barbaric West"; the importance of this area has been splendidly demonstrated by the discoveries, after his death, of the cultures of Ebla and Emar in Syria.

Oppenheim's attitude toward the latest technological devices belied the image of the stolid philologist. Before it had been considered by most other projects, he investigated the possibility of using electronic means of inputting for the dictionary, and I recall our meetings both with the director of the University of Michigan's *Middle English Dictionary,* which at that time also used handwritten file-cards, and with the computer experts at the University of Chicago. When told that to change over to computers, which at that time, in the mid-fifties, were clumsy beasts, would mean suspending work for three years at least, he decided he would not sacrifice that time, and indeed publication of the Chicago *Assyrian Dictionary* continued with a regularity that amazed, and often dismayed, more cautious colleagues.

· V ·

The difficulties in writing about a teacher and close friend have been well expressed by E. M. Uhlenbeck, writing on Roman Jakobson: "a large part of the more recent period falls within one's own period of scholarly life, so that one has become familiar with many of the relevant writings. However, even for that period, one is confronted, to one's surprise, with uncertainties and doubts about seemingly simple matters. To gauge the influence of one scholar upon another turns out to be a subtle task which only rarely can be fulfilled to one's own satisfaction. And at every step one becomes painfully aware that a linguist is not automatically also a historian or a psychologist." It is equally difficult for me, from my perspective, to speak of Oppenheim's role in bringing the Chicago Assyrian Dictionary Project from project to reality. The project had been initiated in the 1920s with the grandiose aim of producing a thesaurus, comparable to the Latin thesaurus then in progress and especially to the contemporary Berlin Egyptian Dictionary. It was conceived as a collaborative project, with scholars from the United States and abroad providing manuscripts, while the collection of the material on file cards was centered in Chicago. After several reorganizations, both before the Second World War (which caused a halt in the progress) and after, it became evident that to hold off until all the material had been incorporated in the files and all the articles had been written was an unrealistic goal. Many eminent scholars had worked on the project over its first thirty-odd years and had prepared the files and much of the methodology that would produce the Chicago *Assyrian Dictionary.* Yet none of them believed that the project was ready to go to press, and thus a number of auxiliary projects were planned and even published, except the *Dictionary* itself. It took Oppenheim's courage, persistence, and willingness to break with the past and even with colleagues close to him to persuade some of his colleagues and the then director of the Oriental Institute, Carl Kraeling, that the time had come to publish, even if the staff had to learn as it went along. The clash this plan caused among the editors of the Chicago *Assyrian Dictionary* has been described, albeit in muted form, elsewhere. It suffices to say that Oppenheim's point was won, supported by the senior, and then greatest, scholar in the field, Benno Landsberger, and especially by Carl Kraeling, the director of the Oriental Institute. At that time I was a junior, but brash, research assistant, and I believed in Oppenheim. I would like to think that my support encouraged him in his fight. And so it came about that Oppenheim was appointed editor-in-charge and director of the Assyrian Dictionary Project in 1955, and the first volume, letter H, which had been in the works as a trial project, was effectively published in 1956, to be followed speedily by the fortunately small letter G bearing the same imprint of 1956.

Oppenheim was the first to admit that the product would be uneven and flawed, but he was sensitive to the ridicule that would have befallen the project if publication would not have ensued. But he was not a director who was only a taskmaster. He led by example: coming early, staying late, working on Saturdays—and only rarely did he use Saturdays to finish one of his own manuscripts; he used to say, echoing Michael Polanyi, that one can teach only by example. At the same time, he encouraged the younger members and the postdoctoral fellows who were invited to work on the *Assyrian Dictionary,* to start their own projects—by working evenings and weekends, of course—so that they could take away from Chicago a personal accomplishment. Many an Assyriological book had its beginnings under these conditions, or was brought to completion with Oppenheim's critical reading of the manuscript. To those who had no project of their own, he often suggested projects that needed to be done. And it was not only their intellectual well-being that he cared for: friends, students, and colleagues found a hospitable table at the Oppenheim's home, at small gatherings and such events as the Krampus-parties on the day of St. Nicholas. He was gregarious, but he dreaded "Waste Land" parties.

· VI ·

He himself considered that his lasting contribution would be the *Assyrian Dictionary. Scripta volant,* as he used to say. He believed that his various studies on Mesopotamian culture represented essentially one man's viewpoint.

This is hardly true. One cannot and should not work in the field without again and again going back to what Oppenheim wrote, on whatever subject he touched. And he touched on a great variety of subjects, all of which he showed in a new light. Often a single text led him to draw a large panorama of the historical and cultural life in Ancient Mesopotamia—to draw and redraw, even after the supposedly complete picture he gave in his book by that name. As we said in the foreword to the "Festfiche": "Current approaches to Assyriology have been decisively shaped by the work of Oppenheim. . . . Texts for him are only means to understand cultural history, and he has thus greatly helped to establish Assyriology as a discipline of the cultural sciences. Contemporary cultural and anthropological approaches to the classical work have influenced his thinking in many other ways too, as have the contributions of anthropologists of a variety of schools from Claude Lévi-Strauss to the Chicago school of anthropology."

Leo Oppenheim had few of the honors that today come more easily to ancient historians and even Assyriologists, such as election to membership in prestigious learned societies or honorary degrees. Of course he was elected president of the American Oriental Society, he was invited to lecture at many universities and to teach as visiting professor at the University of California at Berkeley. He was asked to participate in seminars such as the one organized by *Daedalus* in Venice, and to collaborate with scientists and art historians under the auspices of Corning Glass. Our University, though somewhat tardy in its appreciation, did appoint Oppenheim, in 1969, to the newly created John A. Wilson professorship, and in 1964 Oppenheim was among the first recipients of the Laing Prize, awarded annually by the University of Chicago Press, for his *Ancient Mesopotamia*. Among his honors he especially treasured the invitation to give a series of lectures at the Collège de France in 1971, even though the pleasure of living in Paris was commingled with the bittersweet memories of his first stay in France, after leaving his native Vienna to escape the Nazi persecution, during the Vichy years.

32

ROBERT E. PARK

1 8 6 4 – 1 9 4 4

E D W A R D   S H I L S

ROBERT PARK was known to me well before I came to Chicago. I came to Chicago largely because of his association with it.

In the autumn of 1933, after about a year as a social worker in the Black Belt of Chicago, I became a research assistant to Louis Wirth at the University of Chicago, on the basis of my ability to read German more or less easily. I studied the "Green Bible," the *Introduction to the Science of Sociology* by Park himself and his sweet, shy collaborator, Ernest Burgess. Park was still traveling in the Orient at that time. In the autumn quarter of 1934 or in the winter quarter of 1935, he gave his last course on "Collective Behavior"; it was given in Rosenwald in a room cluttered with maps. I was a regular attendant.

· I ·

Park was all that I thought a great American professor should be. Unlike what I thought German professors were, he did not speak as if he knew all there was to be known. It was clear at once that he was a "seeker," excited by the search. He was unlike German professors in another respect: he was clean shaven. He was almost entirely bald; he had a thick fringe of white hair around his baldness. He was about 5′ 10″ in height but looked shorter because he leaned forward like a curious animal—a bear, perhaps. He was broad-shouldered, deep-chested. He had a deep growling voice when he spoke loudly. In conversation his voice was as low as a whisper. At least in the years I knew him, it had a wheezy tone. His speech was always slow but animated by the vision which it sought to carry.

An earlier version of this essay appeared in *The American Scholar* (Winter 1991), pp. 120–27, and is used with permission.

In teaching, Park growled as he paced up and back across the front of the room. He always looked into the distance when he spoke; he spoke slowly as if he were reading out his thoughts from a distant script which he could not easily decipher. Sometimes he spoke as if from the midst of things he was talking about. He did not lecture to us; we were just present while he pondered aloud on what he had seen or was seeing while he spoke. This course must have been partly a seminar, because I remember that I delivered a paper there on the socialist and communist movements—the course gave much attention to social movements since they were forms of collective consciousness, the growth and transformations of which were of major interest to Park throughout his life. My presentation was a success and Park singled me out for special attention. That was his way. If a student's subject interested him, he did not limit his interest to the classroom.

That was how I came to have the privilege of walking home with him after class. He lived on the east side of Dorchester Avenue between 56th and 57th Streets in a tall, then relatively new building—it is still there. He spoke to me all the way home and sometimes he stood for a few minutes in front of the building before going in, continuing to tell of his observations and reflections.

Park spoke from time to time of consensus, of social unity such as exists in a mob with a common mood, or *Stimmung*. He thought that the mob or crowd, released from the control of institutions, manifested certain features of the "emotional unity" which was a fundamental, elementary form of the life of society under more ordinary circumstances. In his idea of moral order, inchoately expounded by him and inchoately apprehended by me, he went more deeply than any other sociologist of his time or since into the fundamental substratum of the bonds which form individuals into societies.

Park combined this brooding reflectiveness about the basis of society with a passionate sensitivity to the humble facts of ordinary life. Harold Lasswell once wrote of "his respect for creative interplay between hours of high abstraction and days of patient contact with humble detail." He loved to walk the streets to watch ordinary human beings, to strike up conversations with them, to ask them questions, and to ponder on their lives. When a student did a dissertation under him, he lived in that student's subject, imposed himself on the student, went to the district or the institution where the student was doing his fieldwork, adding his own observation to the student's. He cross-examined his students and thought aloud with

ROBERT E. PARK

them about the things he and they had observed. If a graduate student worked on an interesting subject—usually a subject suggested by him— he interested himself unrestrainedly in the student's work. He was able to do this for several students at the same time. That is how it happened that the monographs in the University of Chicago Sociological Series were published from the dissertations which he supervised by authors who never afterward wrote anything of any interest whatsoever. He had no reservations about telling a student, "I am interested in you." He once said that to me. I wish that I had taken greater advantage of that interest.

If students faltered, Park kept after them with prodding, inquisitive kindness and sometimes with brutality. One graduate student in the department, a Negro, had formerly been a policeman in a large city of the Northwest. His name was Horace Cayton. He had aroused the interest of one of Park's former students, Jesse Steiner, who was then teaching at the University of Washington where he was head of the department of sociology. He took an interest in Cayton and sent him to work under Park for an advanced degree. He was a thick-chested, large man, of the shape which used to be characteristic of American policemen; he was also a jovial, charming person, and quite clever, and Park wanted to make something of him. Park farmed him out to Harold Gosnell, then in the department of political science, who was writing a book on Negro politicians—later the book turned out to be a minor classic. The former policeman did much of the fieldwork but he was not always a faithful worker; there were periods when he was indolent, too convivial, or pursued women. One day, having heard from Gosnell that Cayton was neglecting his duties, Park went to his room and took him to task for his waste of his talents. Park launched into him—Cayton was then a man of about thirty-five. He started with reprimands, then began to shout at him; finally Cayton burst into tears. There the interview ended and the crushed object of Park's censure was left alone in his room, much the worse for the encounter. About an hour later, Park appeared at the man's door, to cheer him up and to apologize for having spoken to him so roughly. He explained himself by saying that Cayton would benefit from the hiding he had received. "Conflict brings out what's in a man" was his final consolation to the sorry fellow. But Park never lost interest in him. Park never lost interest in any of his students. He was as interested in them as he was interested in their subjects.

Park was not a lucid expositor of his own ideas; he proceeded by giving hints about glimpses, but his growling ruminations about what he glimpsed were so vivid and so emphatic, so many-sided, that I understood things from him which he never said. On our frequent walks home after his class—about three-quarters of a mile from the University—I had many opportunities to hear him recalling and reflecting on what he had seen. Having been in the Orient for much of 1932 and 1933, he would tell me about what he had seen there and what it signified. Rickshaw pullers, street vendors, small shopkeepers, priests and temple custodians, gamblers— everybody and everything interested him. He wanted to set going a series of investigations into the life of society in Peking (now Beijing) such as he had instigated in Chicago. The whole world was interesting to him; he created his sociological thought to describe and explain what he had seen. There were not many American newspaper reporters and city editors in the Middle West who went to Berlin and Heidelberg to write dissertations to enable them to make theoretical sense of what they had seen as newspaper men. Park was a seeker all his life.

In 1933 and 1934, after his return from China, he wandered about the streets of Chicago in districts through which he had tramped in the past, observing and reflecting unceasingly. He was then about seventy years of age, a powerful presence, a sort of sociological Tom Lingard. He spoke to me with horror of what he had just seen on the West Side after his return. In what was then the idiom of American sociology, he spoke to me with horrified astonishment of some of the younger inhabitants of one of those areas: "They have no norms; they have no norms at all." He did not intend to be prophetic but he was. I said very little in response to the interesting things he told me.

Although he retired after this last course, Park continued to come to the department of sociology on most days, until about 1935, and I saw a lot of him because he came frequently into Louis Wirth's room while we were revising the translation of Karl Mannheim's *Ideologie und Utopie,* which Wirth had asked me to do. Park would come into Wirth's room several times each day when he was at the university, usually very excited about some new aspect of an old idea which had occurred to him or some "interesting" new fact he had discovered while reading or writing. He would stay for about five or ten minutes excitedly recounting his newest insight. When the excitement passed, he went back to his room. Sometimes this happened several times within an hour. He never sat down, but paced back and forth in the small room, in a lumbering ursine movement, gesticulating with both hands outstretched in front of his chest, moving up and down, as if he were measuring something. (Louis Wirth acquired this particular gesture.) I cannot recall the things he said, but I received from those frequent interruptions a sense of Park's unquenchable wonderment and curiosity. I also came to understand why Park's writings are so incoherent. Wherever an idea came to him in the course of writing it, he transferred it to conversation, talking until he used up his stimulation. He would then go back to his manuscript and would begin again where the conversation had left off. I am not certain of this, but after seeing him in action so often in this way and reading his penetrating but discontinuous essays, this explanation seems plausible to me.

He continued to read the most miscellaneous books which seemed to bear on his interest in "the unity of the crowd," the power of the normative element in human action, the mechanisms which maintain conformity, the incessant disruptions of order in every sphere of social life. The movement to and fro of ethnic groups between assimilation and conflict was one of the subjects with which his theoretical ideas were in constant interaction.

· II ·

Robert Park was born in Harveyville, Pennsylvania, on 16 February 1864 by the accident that his father was then serving in the Union army. After the war, the family settled in Minnesota where the senior Park became a prosperous grocer. His father wished him to enter and to take over his business but Park wished to go to a university. In 1883, he went to the University of Michigan, then the most outstanding state university in the country, bearing the influence of the German university ideal—in part directly received by numerous teachers who had studied in Germany and in part indirectly by teachers who had taught or studied at Johns Hopkins University. At Michigan, Park was interested in philosophy and German literature, particularly Goethe. He studied philosophy under John Dewey and absorbed a great deal from Dewey—evolutionary naturalism and German idealism. From Dewey he came to see human beings as biological organisms set in the order of nature, competing with each other within their own species, and as a species against other species; he also learned from Dewey to see human beings not only as biological organisms but as members of a society, held together not only by rational calculation and contract but by common culture and common moral ideas, by a cognitive and moral consensus. These fundamental conceptions of the life of man on earth as a biological organism in an ecological order and as a human being capable of intelligent discourse, rationality, and morality and participating in a collective self-consciousness, remained in Park's mind for the rest of his life and pervaded his outlook as a sociologist.

On graduation from the University of Michigan, Park became a newspaper reporter. School teaching, which he tried for a short time in his home town, Red Wing, Minnesota, was not stimulating. The legal and clerical professions seemed to him to be, in prospect, too constraining intellectually. He chose to become a reporter, first in Minneapolis, later in Detroit and Denver, and then in New York. He returned to the Middle West, becoming a reporter and editor, and then he came to Chicago where he continued his work as a reporter and served also as a drama critic.

The variety and poignancy of the life of great cities fascinated him. He had a curiosity to come into contact with the facts of human life. What appeared chaotic also seemed to exist as a pattern. He seems to have taken pleasure in feeling himself to be a sentient participant in an immense and complex organism.

He had a rich and diverse sympathy with all sorts and conditions of human beings, an aesthetic or moral pleasure in the facts of their daily existence. A pleasure in contemplating the drama and conflicts of large events existed in him together with detachment. Everything that happened interested him; he did not respond censoriously to the things he saw. They were all part of the large process to which Dewey referred and the intellectual unraveling of which was Park's objective then and for the rest of his life.

· III ·

His years as a journalist did not diminish his fascination with the intricate multifariousness of life but they left him dissatisfied. Journalism showed him the "many" and the "flux" of things but it did not enable him to see the "one" in the many or to detect the constant pattern that lies under the flux. He decided to give up journalism and to study philosophy, which had been one of his main interests—with Dewey as his guide— when he was a student at the University of Michigan. He went first to Harvard; while there, he decided that he must go to Germany, as so many Americans of the last century had done in order to qualify themselves as properly trained for academic life. Park was different from the others who went in that he was rather older than the average American student in Germany and he had no definite goal of an academic career before him. It is possible that Hugo Munsterberg, who was then teaching at Harvard, helped him to make the decision to go to Germany but that was not really necessary since it was the normal thing for a man with aspirations to master a branch of academic knowledge.

He went first to Berlin in 1899; there he came into contact with the brilliant *Privatdozent* Georg Simmel, who was lecturing in sociology. It is uncertain what led him to Simmel. It is possible that he knew about Simmel from the *American Journal of Sociology,* where Albion Small, as editor, had formed an advisory editorial board of eminent sociologists of the time and of which he made Simmel a member. It is possible that having tried Friedrich Paulsen who was the professor of philosophy—and a very close friend of Tönnies—and found him not especially interesting, he tried Simmel as an alternative. Simmel was a very popular teacher and Park might have learned his name and merits from other students. Whatever the mode of his coming upon Simmel, when he did so there was an almost immediate recognition of an affinity of interest and understanding. I do not know whether he ever had a conversation with Simmel; he never mentioned to me anything as direct as that in his references to Simmel. It might be that with all his toughness as a reporter he was shy about speaking with Simmel in his poor German. The simplicity of the notes which he took in Simmel's lectures might indicate that his comprehension of spoken German was not very good. Nevertheless, in Simmel's sociological ideas he found some of the general propositions he had been seeking. He was drawn on by Simmel's accounts of social differentiation and the division of labor, of the spatial distribution of social activities and institutions and the coordination of those spatially dispersed phenomena, by the prominence Simmel gave to conflict and by his view of the individualizing and differentiating character of urban life, of isolation and coordination. These were some of the things that Park had been trying to grasp in his years as a journalist. Simmel gave a focus to his curiosity but could not satisfy it. Park never reached such a point of satisfaction at any time in his life. He was never content with what he already knew; he always wanted to know more and grasp its essence.

By accident, he encountered a small book by a Russian, resident in Heidelberg and a friend of Max Weber. The book was *Gesellschaft und Einzelwesen;* the author was Bogdan (Theodor) Kistiakowski. It was just the thing Park wanted. It dealt with the individual and society, a coupling of terms which has lost its meaning through their latter-day superficial moral-philanthropic juxtaposition. For Park, who was always concerned with the absorption of the individual into the collective self-consciousness— the "moral order" in his later usage—the book helped to precipitate his interest which had been accumulating over a decade of experiences as a reporter and during his philosophical studies at Harvard. Wilhelm Windelband, then professor of philosophy at Strassburg, was one of the persons to whom Kistiakowski's book was dedicated. (The other was Simmel.) Park went to Strassburg and began to write a doctoral dissertation under Windelband on a topic basically similar to that of Kistiakowski. When Windelband was called to Heidelberg, Park went with him. There is no evidence of any personal connection between pupil and supervisor. Windelband was a great figure in Germany in those years by virtue of his still valuable history of philosophy and his views on the similarities and differences between history and science. Park seems to have had little or no personal contact with him, although Windelband was a kind man and well-disposed towards students. Park attended lectures on the European peasantry by G. F. Knapp. This was useful to him because it gave him knowledge of a mode of life very different from the life of the big cities which he knew as a journalist. It was also a good basis for his sympathetic understanding of the Negro peasants in the United States.

The dissertation was entitled *Masse und Publikum*. (It was published in 1904 and reprinted, on my suggestion, in an English translation nearly three-quarters of a century later.)

When Park returned to the United States in 1903, he became an assistant to Royce and Munsterberg. In 1904, he met Albion Small, to whom he had sent an inscribed copy of his dissertation, now in my possession. Small offered him a very minor post at Chicago in the department of sociology; it was only for a summer term. Park rejected it, perhaps because it did not offer the prospect of a career, or perhaps he had found academic life boring—he had found Harvard that way—and too remote from the daily life of society.

Whatever his grounds for the rejection of Small's invitation, he was at loose ends. Through an accidental encounter with a missionary, he learned of the formation of the Congo Reform Association. He was offered the secretaryship of the association and accepted it. He was very active in the production and publication of articles about the Congo, but he did not like to be so closely associated with missionaries, Roman Catholic and Protestant. Nevertheless, the year of experience in the Congo Association was an enrichment of his stock of knowledge. Henceforth, the expansion of European civilization into traditional and primordial societies became one of the major themes of his thought. He had to think about empires, about the transformation of primordial societies and the significance of ethnicity. His new knowledge fitted into his earlier interests and extended them. His experience in dealing with the Congo had another effect on his career. It brought him into contact with Booker Washington and this opened his horizon to enable him to incorporate the American Negro into his earlier interests.

He was amanuensis, counselor, and press agent for Washington for about seven years. He lived in the South and came to see a new side of American society and of world society of which he had been only dimly aware hitherto. He traveled to Europe with Washington and he wrote *The Man Down Under,* a book on the European lower classes of which Washington was nominally the author and Park the real author. He helped Washington with other books and in the course of his work with Washington became intimate with the life of the blacks of the South. It enriched his sociological understanding. That was possible only because he was entirely free from prejudice about race and color. W. I. Thomas said that Park was as free from prejudice as any white man could be. While he worked for Washington nine months of the year, he left his family in New England, spending only the summer and holidays with them. Under the urging of his wife and children, he decided that his mode of life had to change. It was difficult for him to separate himself from Tuskegee Institute and from Booker Washington. Park's sympathies were inexhaustible and they went out in full measure to Negroes, and to everyone for that matter. Although he did depart from Tuskegee—a step from which Washington tried hard to dissuade him—he never lost his interest and pleasure in being among Negroes. (He spent the last nine years of life living in Nashville, Tennessee, at Fisk University where his pupil and friend Charles Johnson was president.)

The line of succession of the phases of Park's life was, despite the vagaries of his professional career, as straight as the line of growth of his intellectual interests and accomplishments. It was a line of continuous expansion of experience and knowledge in very diverse situations, all in the service of his striving for a coherent, internally consistent, and constantly deepening understanding. His role in the Congo Reform Association brought him into touch with Booker Washington and Tuskegee Institute. These in turn brought him into touch with W. I. Thomas, who was then professor of sociology at the University of Chicago. He had read Thomas's writings on "folk psychology" and on German-Polish border relations, which were especially interesting to Park because they touched on the peasantry and agricultural labor. Park invited Thomas to a conference he was organizing for Washington; Thomas accepted the invitation. Thomas, a man of very outstanding intellectual powers, was free from prejudice about many things. (This ultimately led to his undoing.) He saw in Park another man with universal sociological curiosity, a man remarkably free from the prevailing ethnic prejudices as well as one who had uncommon gifts—not yet really openly visible—as a sociologist. He prevailed on Park to come to the University of Chicago.

This was the end of Park's life as a wanderer. It did not mean the end of his life as a intellectual wanderer. His career as a university teacher—and his family—might have tied him down to one place but neither could tie down his curiosity and imagination.

· IV ·

Park began his academic career when he was nearly fifty years of age. He was kept on a narrow leash by the president of the University of Chicago, Harry Pratt Judson, Harper's successor and very different from Harper in his parsimoniousness and self-righteousness. Judson was a political scientist who had tried to put order into the financial affairs of the University of Chicago after the disorder in which they had been left by Harper when he died in 1906. Judson was an ungenerous person who probably did not think well of Thomas for his unconventional declarations about sexual relations—it was Judson who dismissed Thomas from the University in 1919 immediately after the disclosure in the press of his act of adultery.

Park was not exactly welcomed by Judson. He was paid an annual salary of $500 for teaching a single course. This did not dampen Park's enthusiasm for teaching. He taught more than he was paid for. After several years, the president sent a statement to the department of sociology permitting him "to give a course in the winter quarter without salary." It was only in 1919 that the president agreed to raise Park's salary to $1,000 per annum and granted him the title of "professorial lecturer."

Park remained in that status until 1923, when he was elevated to a full professorship, following Judson's retirement. Park did not allow himself to be discouraged by the lack of sympathy in the University administration. He did not care about the money since he had inherited a large sum from his father.

He plunged into academic life with the same unquenchable curiosity as he had manifested in each of his earlier occupations. He made himself familiar with the city of Chicago, walking its streets, stopping to look at whatever interested him, speaking to whomever he pleased. He was once more a reporter, but this time he had no deadlines, and he did not have to confine himself to "digging-out" facts. He could exercise his freedom of imagination. His imagination had a great deal to work on. There were the years of reporting about the life of several large cities. There were the years of preoccupation with Negroes after a year of informing himself about European expansion into Africa. There was also his old interest in the one and the many, the individual and his collectivities, his rational decisions and rational actions and their intricate relations with primordially dominated decisions and primordial collectivities. He began to expand his imagination into theories in which he had always been interested.

Becoming a sociologist in a department of sociologists brought all these things together. His self-imposed responsibilities as a teacher—he always taught subjects which interested him—added a factor hitherto absent, namely, students who already had committed themselves to being interested in society or who were willing to allow themselves to be made interested by their teacher's own passionate interests.

The department of sociology at the University had graduate students from the very beginning. Some of them had once begun training for the clergy, others came from families of clergymen. Many of them were already teaching at small colleges. Sociology was becoming established at state universities and liberal arts colleges and there were opportunities for employment in those institutions. In Chicago at that time there were municipal and state institutions in which sociologists-in-training could find part-time employment which enabled them to support themselves financially while pursuing their graduate studies.

Chicago was the ideal place for the kind of sociological point of view developed by Thomas and Park. The doctoral dissertations reported on the research inspired by their ideas and carried out under the inquisitive, overpowering, and intensive supervision which Park gave to his students and under the gentler, less imposing, but no less insistent supervision of Ernest Burgess. This combination of diligent students and brilliant and unremitting supervision produced many impressive, instructive, and illuminating monographs. These monographs, some of them published in the University of Chicago Sociological Series by the University of Chicago Press were the realization in concrete, fragmentary form of the profound understanding of society which Robert Park offered.

Unfortunately, Park's universal curiosity and his never relaxing wonderment did not find adequate expression in his own writings. He was full of projects which he never succeeded in advancing. He wrote many valuable introductions to the books of his protégés and he wrote about a dozen essays full of profound insights. But he could not quite put his vision into lasting words. His students who were formed by him and who were inspired by his vision as long as he "sat" on them, were unable to carry on his work, elaborate his ideas, systematize them, and go on applying and extending them. For some reason, sociology attracted very few graduate students who could go on producing on their own. The authors of the classic monographs wrote very little after they left Chicago. Perhaps the times were too disheartening, perhaps sociology did not attract first-class graduate students, perhaps Park was too powerful, too unrelenting a supervisor. In any case, the "Chicago school" faded out after his departure.

· V ·

Robert Park was a "seeker." He was no ordinary professor; he found it difficult to sit still. Too much in the world interested him. His most frequent remark about things which he read and observed was that they were "very interesting," with accent on the first "t." He had a sense that what interested him belonged in a larger scheme of interpretation, but the interestingness of concrete events could not always or even frequently be bound down and articulated. I had the impression that he cared more for the search for answers than for the answer itself. It was the journey, not the destination, that mattered. Perhaps that is the right attitude for a great scholar. The destination is always receding anyway. That was true of Park's theories. That is why Park's vision of society—a very profound and true one—could not be passed on easily to succeeding generations of scholars. He never succeeded in putting together his views about human ecology and his views about collective consciousness. That was a great loss.

Park read omnivorously, even up to his very last years. But he was too restless to put his profound and stirring visions and insights into orderly form; he always wanted to learn something more.

His work would have had a longer life if he had been able to draw on Max Weber's writings in *Wirtschaft und Gesellschaft* and the *Gesammelte Aufsätze zur Religionssoziologie* and if he had studied and pondered Durkheim's and Mauss's writings. Robert Park worked within the same traditions and his ideas are harmonious with theirs and would have enriched them. He was on the right track but he was a seeker who never arrived at what he was seeking. The task remains to be done. It is worth doing.

His writings, despite the fundamental coherence of his outlook, failed to give a sufficiently clear formulation to that coherence. Yet the coherence was there. One could not fail to apprehend it when one heard him speak in a seminar or at a lecture. That was why hearing him deliver a lecture or make a comment in a seminar or in a conversation in the course of a walk was such an exhilarating intellectual experience. But to put it into systematic and precise form was another matter. Still, taken all in all, I never met anyone else who impressed me as lastingly as he did. He was a marvelous man.

33

DALLAS B. PHEMISTER

1 8 8 2 – 1 9 5 1

CHARLES HUGGINS

DALLAS BURTON PHEMISTER was a son of Illinois. He loved the prairies, the huge cornfields, the great rivers and lakes of our fertile lands. He adored the University of Chicago. It was the destiny of Dallas Phemister to launch the brand new Billings Hospital with its splendid surgical laboratories. The new facility opened its doors on 1 October 1927. He had selected the entire faculty of surgery. He had gambled on youth in the new department of surgery.

The ideas of Dallas Phemister had a great impact on the development and course of surgery in America. No longer were the cash box and clinical service dominant in the first-rate facility; investigation was introduced and fostered. In this essay I shall try to convey the essence of Dallas Phemister as surgeon, scientist, teacher, and human being.

· I ·

Dallas Phemister was born on 15 July 1882 on a farm in southern Illinois near the coal mines of "bloody Herrin County," so called because of labor unrest and violent crimes. He attended a country school near Carbondale and after graduation from high school continued his education at the Normal School of Indiana. While there he decided to become a physician and entered Rush Medical College, a branch of the University of Chicago. In this way began a love affair between student and university which was to last lifelong. After graduation with the M.D. from Rush in 1904—Dallas Phemister was then twenty-two years of age—he served an internship for one year at the Cook County Hospital in Chicago. Then he entered the private practice of medicine in LaGrange, Illinois, continuing at the same time his interest in teaching and research as a voluntary member of the surgical faculty of the Presbyterian Hospital of Chicago.

The most disagreeable and unpleasant task for the junior surgeons was the care of children with osteomyelitis (infection of bone due to staphylo-coccus). It was a tearful and necessary daily task which persisted for years; it involved the change of dressings of the infected bones of the sick chil-dren. This project assigned to Dr. Phemister was fruitful and necessary but it was an unparalleled opportunity to observe the growth and death of bone.

In this period of American medicine, advanced training in the medical sciences was available only in Europe. After five years of private practice, Dallas Phemister went abroad, where he studied in London, Vienna, Berlin, and Paris. He was greatly impressed with the history and culture of the foreign capitals but his greatest interest arose in learning the new tech-niques for the study of bone.

The *Wanderjahr* of Dallas Phemister was financed by his own meager savings from private practice. He worked with great industry and intelli-gence in the laboratories of the medical sciences. He found that his experi-ences in Europe were of priceless importance in studying history and foreign languages as well as the medical sciences. Soon he became fluent in conversation in French and German, which he practiced, especially with German-born natives, upon every opportunity, lifelong. Some years later, one of his young assistants said: "If I needed an operation I should cer-tainly ask Dr. Phemister to perform it, but prior to the operation I would take a short course in German."

In 1911 Dallas Phemister returned to Chicago to resume his teaching positions at Rush. Soon he established a professional association with the famous surgeon Arthur Dean Bevan, chairman of surgery at Rush.

During the First World War, Dr. Phemister served in the Presbyterian Hospital unit with the military rank of major. He was head of an operating team which served behind the lines at the battles of Chateau Thierry and the Argonne. At the end of the war, he returned to Rush Medical College where he soon became professor of surgery. Although he carried on a large private practice, he devoted much time to teaching and research with his students. Many of his contributions to our knowledge of bone and joint diseases owe their inception to this phase of his life.

In 1927, Dallas Phemister became the first professor of surgery in the new Billings Hospital at the University at Chicago, a position he held until 1947 when he became professor emeritus. His scientific studies covered a wide field of interests. Among the orthopedic subjects he studied in great detail were: osteitis deformans, bone cysts, eosinophilic granuloma of bone, growth in epiphyses in man, bone necrosis and repair, creeping sub-stitution, operative arrest of longitudinal growth of bone, bone and peri-osteum transplantation, ectopic osteogenesis, primary point of infection in

Dallas B. Phemister

tuberculosis of the hip joint, surgical shock, giant cell tumors of bone, chondrosarcoma, and osteosarcoma. In addition to his studies on bone, his greatest contribution was in the study of the alimentary tract. With his pupil, William E. Adams, he performed the first resection of cancer of the esophagus with anastomosis. Also, he made important contributions to the study of gall stones.

· II ·

Dallas Phemister was tall, handsome, and dignified in appearance. He was mild in manner but strong. The first day in the new Billings Hospital he issued an order: "There will be no storming in the operating rooms," and there was none. The work of the department of surgery was underway at 8:00 A.M., six days a week, and continued for long and happy hours all day and the early part of the night. There were three formal sessions, each of one hour each week, viz: Tuesday, surgical pathology; Thursday, discussion of original work in the department; Saturday, post-operative demonstration of recently operated cases with discussion of clinical results.

Dallas Phemister was a modest man; his friends and acquaintances were found in all walks of life. He was respected for his honesty, industry, and altruism. Dr. Phemister had a deep and continuing interest in all of his young surgical disciples. The important facet in development of surgery was the *Arbeitskreis*. Dallas rejoiced when any of his young surgeon-pupils had success of either major or minor significance. Dallas was father confessor to all of us.

The department of surgery under Phemister was notable as the first in America in which each member served on a whole-time salaried basis. Each surgeon worked on problems, directly or indirectly, related to surgery. The motto of the surgical department was: "No man shall be permitted to teach unless he is engaged in research."

It was a delight to be a member of the Phemister department: zest and enthusiasm abounded. Often at 8:00 A.M. Dr. Phemister would knock on the door of members of our surgical staff to ask, "What have you discovered today?" Every Wednesday at 12:30 P.M. there was the staff luncheon, usually for ten or twelve of our senior surgical staff. There was good talk about the surgical craft, and many of the world's most highly respected surgeons participated in lively discussion while guests of the department and of Dr. Phemister.

It has been said that Dallas Phemister was the last of the general surgeons. Certainly he was one of the earliest academic surgeons.

34

A. R. RADCLIFFE-BROWN

1 8 8 1 – 1 9 5 5

F R E D   E G G A N

A. R. RADCLIFFE-BROWN came to the University of Chicago in the autumn of 1931 as a visiting professor of anthropology to replace Edward Sapir, who was going to Yale as a Sterling professor to start a new department of anthropology and linguistics. Sapir had come to the University in 1925 from Ottawa, where he had been in charge of Canadian studies in anthropology for some fifteen years, to join Fay-Cooper Cole in setting up a graduate program in anthropology, and to separate anthropology from sociology, with which it had been linked since the founding of the University in 1892.

I had come to the University in 1923 from Deerfield-Shields Township High School on the North Shore, where I had become interested in physics and chemistry. In the 1920s, the University of Chicago had a normal undergraduate program with champion football and basketball teams and a varied social life—all for a tuition fee of $60 per quarter! But the graduate program was outstanding. The first comprehensive poll of scholarly opinion in 1925 showed Chicago in first place in the country so far as graduate departments were concerned, with the department of sociology leading an outstanding group of social science departments.

The social sciences were beginning to expand in the mid-1920s and Cole and Sapir soon attracted an excellent group of graduate students, and Sapir became a leader in the growing program of interdisciplinary research in the University, in the newly organized Social Science Research Council and the committees of the National Research Council. (Regna Darnell has a half-dozen chapters in her recent biography of Edward Sapir covering his years at Chicago and elsewhere, and the important role he played in social science research and training.) Our Social Science Research Building, dedicated in 1931 and the first in the United States, was given in recognition of these activities.

In the meantime Robert Maynard Hutchins came in 1929 as president of the University, replacing Max Mason, who went on to head the Rockefeller Foundation, and Hutchins began his efforts to reshape the University. The divisional structure was put in place, and the College was established and given independent status with regard to faculty and budget. The department of anthropology was established in October 1929, with Cole, Sapir, and Redfield as the main teachers and a promise of one million dollars from a wealthy Chicagoan; the gift evaporated with the stock market crash a few weeks later.

Hutchins had a low opinion of the social sciences, but Beardsley Ruml, the first dean of the division, provided funds and instituted faculty seminars on various topics of interest, and the social sciences maintained their momentum in the face of the depression which dominated the 1930s. When Ruml retired from the deanship, Hutchins appointed Robert Redfield, then an associate professor of anthropology, to succeed him as dean of the social sciences, a position which he held until after the Second World War.

I had graduated in 1927 with a major in psychology and a minor in anthropology and continued for another year when I received an M.A. in psychology. But I had determined to take my doctorate in anthropology, so I taught for two years and saved enough money to provide for further graduate work. I returned to the University in the summer of 1930, with the intention of specializing in archaeology and ethnology. When Sapir was offered a Sterling professorship at Yale a year later to develop a new department of anthropology and linguistics with ample funds for graduate students and staff, we were all sorry to see him leave.

· I ·

Radcliffe-Brown, who came in 1931 as a visiting professor, remained at Chicago until 1937, when he was called to Oxford to develop work in social anthropology; his professorship, which was newly created, was attached to All Souls College. We students knew little about him, other than that he was the author of *The Andaman Islanders* (1922) and had just come from five years at the University of Sydney where he had been the first professor of social anthropology, in charge of research on the Australian aborigines. Initially he was very British—with a cape and a monocle—and it took us some time to discover that he was a founder of social anthropology, along with Bronislaw Malinowski, whose monographs on the Trobriand Islanders were establishing functionalism as a basic theoretical position in anthropology.

A. R. RADCLIFFE-BROWN

During his first year Radcliffe-Brown was both flamboyant and distant. He was contemptuous of our steam-heated buildings and had the radiator removed from his office, and then sat with his overcoat on while talking with students during the Chicago winter. The following year he had the radiator reinstalled. I took his classes with some reluctance, since I had taken most of the courses I needed, but his courses on Africa and Australia aroused my interest. Radcliffe-Brown was an excellent lecturer and had developed an anthropological point of view which was novel, in that it centered on the social system and was concerned with social structure and social integration as the bases for understanding culture and its development.

· II ·

Radcliffe-Brown had been born in 1881 in Birmingham, England; when he was five his father had died, and he had been raised by his maternal grandmother whose name he ultimately added to his natal name of Brown. As a boy he had suffered and recovered from tuberculosis, and then had gone to King Edward's school in Birmingham, and on to Trinity College, Cambridge, where he won an exhibition and took a first in the Moral Sciences Tripos, then including philosophy, psychology, and political science. He worked in psychology under W. H. R. Rivers, who had been a member of the Torres Straits expedition, organized by A. C. Haddon, a zoologist, in 1898–99, which turned Rivers and Haddon towards the new science of anthropology. Other influences on Radcliffe-Brown came from Frazer, Russell, and Whitehead, among others.

Radcliffe-Brown became Rivers' first student in anthropology in 1904 and was sent to the Andaman Islands in 1906–8, where he wrote his fellowship thesis on the Andaman Islanders; and later to Australia when he began his studies of the Australian aborigines. He was in Australia for a meeting when the First World War broke out and was sent to Tonga as minister of education; from there he went to South Africa where he was a museum curator. In 1921 he was appointed to the Foundation Chair in the University of Cape Town to develop social anthropology and establish a training program in African languages and cultures.

In 1926 Radcliffe-Brown left South Africa to occupy a similar position in Sydney. His early field research in Western Australia had led him to concentrate his research program on the complex systems of kinship and marriage and on totemism and other aspects of aboriginal religion. With adequate support from the Australian government and the Rockefeller Foundation, he was able to send graduate students into the field, including some from America; to write a major study of the "Social Organization of Australian Tribes"; and to found the journal *Oceania*. But with the onset of the worldwide depression in 1929–30, research funds from the Rockefeller Foundation decreased, and Radcliffe-Brown accepted the invitation to come to Chicago, stopping briefly in London to give a presidential address to section H of the British Association for the Advancement of Science's centenary meeting on "The Present Position of Anthropological Studies."

The brand of social anthropology that Radcliffe-Brown practiced and taught came to be called "structural-functional" and was based originally on the work of Emile Durkheim and his followers in the *Année Sociologique,* which he discovered after his Andaman research and applied to the interpretation of their ceremonials and their myths and legends. During his stay at Cape Town, he had emphasized the practical problems that faced the South African government in its treatment of the native tribes— problems that are only now being addressed in a serious manner. In Australia, he provided basic study of Australian social organization which still guides much of Australian research.

· III ·

In Chicago, with his visiting professorship being made a permanent one, Radcliffe-Brown became Americanized in many respects. He had been known as "Rex" to his friends and associates in Australia, but in Chicago he became R.-B. Our Chicago program in anthropology followed that of Franz Boas, with four fields or subdivisions: physical or biological anthropology, ethnology, archaeology, and linguistics. To these we added social anthropology, primarily concerned with social systems and social structure, and emphasizing comparison and a search for scientific generalizations.

I became his first research assistant in 1931–32. He had read Lewis H. Morgan's *Systems of Consanguinity and Affinity of the Human Family,* published by the Smithsonian Institution in 1871, and he asked me to begin the collection of data on kinship and social organization of the North American Indians. I covered the literature on the Southeast, Plains, and Southwestern tribes, and was followed by Sol Tax and Philleo Nash in succeeding years. In 1932 I secured a Laboratory of Anthropology Field Training Fellowship, along with graduate students from Columbia, Yale, and Harvard, for work on the Hopi Indian reservation in Arizona, where I concentrated my attention on the kinship system and ultimately wrote a doctoral dissertation on the "Social Organization of the Western Pueblos"

(1933). With the thesis I became a social anthropologist, and with comparable studies by other graduate students our department became known for its emphasis on social organization and related fields.

Since few teaching positions were available in the 1930s, R.-B. had arranged for me to go to northwestern Australia on a postdoctoral fellowship from the Australian National Research Council, and Raymond Firth came through on his way to London and provided me with some details. But the prospect was canceled when President Roosevelt devalued the dollar by going off the gold standard in March 1934, reducing the value of grants from American foundations by about half. However, Cole came to my rescue by securing funds from the University and friends to send me to the Philippines for a year to study what had happened to the Tinguian, a group that Cole and his wife, Mabel, had lived with in 1907 and 1908. I left in late May of 1934 and returned in October 1935, beginning a relationship that I continued during the Second World War and developed into a research program after the war.

Radcliffe-Brown left for a four-month's visit to China in late 1935 at the invitation of Professor Wu Wenzao, an old friend, who invited him to lecture at Yenching University and other places in China. Here he had a major influence on a number of younger scholars and his lectures were translated and published in a special volume of the Chinese Sociological Circle.

· IV ·

R.-B. served tea in his apartment almost every afternoon, to which he invited visitors and faculty members. He had brought a set of Chinese furniture from Australia, and he always served Chinese tea, usually *lung ching cha,* and the rituals were the same each time. Here R.-B. was at his best and the conversation was varied but always interesting. Frequently we would end up at a Chinese restaurant where we ultimately learned to eat with chopsticks and sometimes even won a round of "scissors and stones."

Often there were visitors from Great Britain, France, or Australia. When Malinowski came to Chicago, he and R.-B. were usually on their best behavior. As co-founders of social anthropology, they were united against their American contemporaries who were more historically and psychologically oriented, but between themselves there were differences of emphasis and theory. R.-B. recognized that Malinowski was a better field worker than he was and he had sent his best students to Malinowski in earlier years, but he considered himself a better theorist. On one occasion I experienced Malinowski's use of research assistants. He asked me to provide him with a list of some of the major events in American anthropology during the past year. Flattered, I responded with several pages of notes, whereupon he called in the departmental secretary and dictated an article for the yearbook of the *Encyclopaedia Britannica*. As a young man, R.-B. had proclaimed himself an "anarchist" as a result of a friendship with Prince Peter Kropotkin, and he entertained the idea that Shakespeare's poems and plays had been written by somebody else. In South Africa and Australia he represented himself as an authority on almost everything, but in Chicago he restricted himself largely to anthropology.

In 1935 William Lloyd Warner, who was a student of Robert Lowie and had been recruited by R.-B. for a study of the Murngin of northern Australia in 1927, came to Chicago from Harvard to join the departments of sociology and anthropology, and that same year the department found a place for me as an instructor on my return from the Philippines. Here I could point out to R.-B. that he was using "culture" in a different way than were most American anthropologists. He didn't change the title of his favorite introductory course—"The Comparative Science of Culture"—but he would often say: "let's put 'culture' on the shelf," affirming his view of social anthropology as the comparative study of primitive society.

When William F. Ogburn came to the department of sociology from Columbia, he renewed an earlier acquaintance with R.-B. and they sometimes went to the lectures at the Adlerian institute in the Chicago Loop. Malinowski had a strong interest in psychoanalysis and Freudian theory but R.-B. seldom mentioned Freud, preferring apparently the ideas of Alfred Adler. Even Roheim, who had carried out field research on Australian totemism, was never seriously discussed in class or elsewhere.

Radcliffe-Brown had a long-time interest in applied anthropology, and had made it an important part of his lecturing and writing in both South Africa and Australia. In Chicago, John Collier's program of Indian reform, which he put into effect as Commissioner of Indian Affairs in the 1930s, attracted R.-B.'s attention when Collier recruited anthropologists as advisers and participants. I had visited one of Collier's conferences with the Navajo on the Indian Reorganizations Act in 1934 and talked briefly with Collier. Later that year, when I was in the Philippines, I received several letters from R.-B. indicating his own interest in the possibilities in the Indian Service, for which he wrote an article on "Anthropology and Indian Administration" for *American Indian Life* (1935). John Provinse, a fellow student who had studied Plains Indian law under R.-B.'s guidance, did enter the Indian Service and ultimately became assistant commissioner of Indian affairs; and Philleo

Nash was appointed commissioner of Indian affairs during the administration of President Kennedy. Sol Tax's "action anthropology" was apparently developed independently of Collier's earlier program.

As Radcliffe-Brown's interests in North American social organization increased, he attracted graduate students who began to do fieldwork and write theses under his direction. Sol Tax made a study of the Fox Indians, which he prefaced with a history of the study of social organization entitled "From Lafitau to Radcliffe-Brown." Gilbert McAllister wrote on Kiowa-Apache social organization, Morris Opler on Chiricahua and Mescalero kinship and social organization, and William Gilbert on Eastern Cherokee social organization. After my thesis on the Hopi and the Western Pueblos, I made a briefer study of the Choctaw and their neighbors in the southeastern states, and the Cheyenne and Arapaho kinship systems in Oklahoma. These formed the basis for seminar discussions and were partly published in *Social Anthropology of North American Tribes* (1937), presented to R.-B. when he left for Oxford, and reprinted with additions in 1955. Here R.-B.'s contributions to social anthropology have their clearest expression.

In addition, there were debates between Radcliffe-Brown and Ralph Linton over the relative value of historical and scientific studies of American Indians, arranged by Sol Tax, who had been a student of Linton's at Wisconsin before coming to Chicago for graduate work; and controversies in the *American Anthropologist* between R.-B. and Alfred Kroeber with regard to the significant kinship terminologies in California and elsewhere, and with Alexander Lesser over the meaning of functionalism.

During the 1930s, also, Radcliffe-Brown prepared a new edition of *The Andaman Islanders* (1933), and wrote some of his best papers, such as "The Sociological Theory of Totemism" (1930), "Primitive Law" and "Social Sanctions" for the new *Encyclopedia of the Social Sciences,* and "Patrilineal and Matrilineal Succession" in the *Iowa Law Review* (1935).

In 1936, the social science division of the University of Chicago sponsored a series of lectures on the nature of the social sciences, beginning with the department of anthropology. Radcliffe-Brown chose to lecture on "The Development of Social Anthropology" and W. L. Warner described "Contemporary Social Anthropology" including his own work on "Yankee City" and that of his students on "Deep South" and Chicago. Here R.-B. traced the early sources for social anthropology to the philosophers of the seventeenth and eighteenth centuries, particularly to Montesquieu and the Scottish philosophers he influenced. As the first student of W. H. R. Rivers in anthropology at Cambridge and under the later influence of Durkheim and his followers, he shifted from a concern for the origins of social institutions to an interest in their nature, which he sought to discover through a comparison of variant forms in different groups. "So long as the students of jurisprudence, economics, political science and sociology concentrate their attention on one type of society and on some particular aspects of these societies, it is left to the social anthropologist to study society in general and as a whole, and it is therefore left to him to discover the fundamental concepts in terms of which these social phenomena of all kinds can be scientifically described and explained."

This conclusion attracted some graduate students and colleagues and repelled others. Morris Opler, who had come to study under Sapir, found himself writing a comparative study of Chiricahua and Mescalero Apaches for his dissertation under R.-B.'s supervision, but he never accepted the latter's conception of social anthropology, carrying out his post-doctoral research on Southern Athapaskans with the assistance of Harry Hoijer, who had taken Sapir's place in the department of anthropology. But most students were attracted to R.-B. and he increasingly attended student parties and gatherings where he sometimes danced around a small fire in a metal wastebasket, yipping an Andamanese song.

During the lecture series on the social sciences, Radcliffe-Brown listened to Mortimer Adler's thesis that there was only one possible social science and its name was psychology, and asked for an opportunity to reply. Adler had laid great stress on Aristotelian propositions, so R.-B. went back to Heraclitus. His seminar on the nature of a natural science of society was a brilliant performance, delivered with no notes beyond a mimeographed set of propositions, and was recorded by Warner's secretary, who transcribed it in some 150 pages of text. For those of us who were here in the spring of 1937 it was a memorable occasion. R.-B. had just accepted the newly created chair in social anthropology at Oxford University, so this was a farewell performance. Of particular significance was R.-B.'s discussion of the social system and its characteristics and his challenging conclusion that no science of culture is possible since culture can only be studied as a characteristic of a social system.

We urged that he let us publish the text as he presented it, but except for a mimeographed edition of limited circulation, he asked us to wait until he could revise it. But the onset of the Second World War in Europe and his later ill-health interfered, and he only revised the first section before his retirement just after the war and his death in 1955. Soon after his death we arranged for its publication as *A Natural Science of Society* (1957), which provided his vision of what social anthropology should become.

In Chicago we had put together a collection of our contributions under the title *Social Anthropology of North American Tribes, Essays in Social Organization, Law, and Religion Presented to Professor A. R. Radcliffe-Brown upon the Occasion of His Accepting the Chair of Social Anthropology at Oxford University* and published by the University of Chicago Press (1937). Robert Redfield, in his introduction, noted that "this book marks the conclusion of an important episode in the recent history of anthropology—the immediate presence and participation of A. R. Radcliffe-Brown." He went on to state that "Professor Radcliffe-Brown brought to this country a method for the study of society, well defined and different enough from what prevailed here to require American anthropologists to reconsider the whole matter of method, to scrutinize their objectives, and to attend to new problems and new ways of looking at problems. He stirred us up and accelerated intellectual invention and variation among us."

· V ·

The onset of the Second World War came soon after Radcliffe-Brown's arrival at Oxford, but Evans-Pritchard, Meyer Fortes, and Max Gluckman joined him in developing a graduate Institute of Social Anthropology, before going off to wartime service, and later to chairs at Cambridge and Manchester. R.-B. was sent by the British Council to Brazil to establish social anthropology in the Escola Livre de Sociologia e Politica de São Paulo, where he remained two years, returning in 1944 to Oxford where he taught until his forced retirement through postwar regulations. This was a bitter blow since, as a fellow of All Souls, he had expected to stay on for a longer period. Professor Evans-Pritchard took his place and R.-B. went off again—to King Farouk I University in Cairo, and later to his brother in Grahamstown, South Africa.

In the meantime Radcliffe-Brown's influence was felt in *African Political Systems,* edited by Meyer Fortes and E. E. Evans-Pritchard (1940), and *African Systems of Kinship and Marriage,* edited by A. R. Radcliffe-Brown and Daryll Forde (1950), and by the founding of the Association of Social Anthropologists of the Commonwealth in 1946, with Radcliffe-Brown as its first president. A volume of studies presented to A. R. Radcliffe-Brown and edited by Meyer Fortes was published at the Clarendon Press in 1949 and entitled *Social Structure,* with contributors from both the United States and Great Britain.

In America, after the war, social anthropology became popular; it came to rival cultural anthropology in the numbers of its adherents. But a consensus was reached in the 1950s to call the two "socio-cultural anthropology," rather than dividing them, as in Great Britain and the Commonwealth. In Chicago we maintained the distinction in our program, and for two decades after the war the department of anthropology ranked first in American scholarly opinion. In the 1970s we began a series of informal seminars which have resulted in a new appreciation of Radcliffe-Brown; some of the seminars were presented by visitors from other countries who had been associated with R.-B. as students or colleagues and others by members of our Chicago department such as Milton Singer and George W. Stocking, Jr. British scholars such as Adam Kuper have published *Anthropologists and Anthropology, The British School 1922–1972* (1973), and *The Social Anthropology of Radcliffe-Brown* (1977); and Ian Langham, a historian of science in Australia, has written *The Building of British Social Anthropology, W. H. R. Rivers and His Cambridge Disciples in the Development of Kinship Studies, 1898–1931* (1981), in which Radcliffe-Brown has a prominent place. More recently, in *Functionalism Historicized,* Stocking has edited a series of essays, including his own on British social anthropology (*History of Anthropology,* volume 2, 1984), which deal with Durkheim and Radcliffe-Brown and with Radcliffe-Brown and British social anthropology in both a critical and appreciative manner. And Milton Singer has a seminal essay on "A Neglected Source of Structuralism: Radcliffe-Brown, Russell, and Whitehead" (in *Semiotica* 48 [1984], pp. 11–96), which developed from our series of seminars on R.-B.

I never got to England while Radcliffe-Brown was still alive, but Evans-Pritchard invited me to All Souls College as a visiting fellow in 1970, his last year as professor in the Institute which R.-B. founded. Evans-Pritchard had followed R.-B.'s program for a few years after the war but had then returned to his earlier historical interests and given up R.-B.'s interest in a natural science of society. But in the common room at All Souls and in the King's Crown pub I could see the setting and hear of the events and discussions that had molded R.-B. at Trinity College. Oxford is still distrustful of anthropology, thinking it a subject not suitable for undergraduates in the colleges but acceptable for graduate students. In a different environment at Chicago, R.-B. was able to create a program with a more universal appeal.

We had invited R.-B. as a speaker and honored guest for the twenty-fifth anniversary of the Social Science Research Building and had planned to present him with an honorary degree on that occasion. He consulted with his doctors, who decided he should not make such a long trip, but he wrote about how much it would have meant to him to be in Chicago again with his old friends and students. But it was not to be. He had passed three-score and ten and was content—but the tuberculosis that he had fought as a boy had weakened his lungs. He sent us his best wishes for the occasion. He died not long after, but his influence continues in his books and teachings, and in the growing significance of what anthropology might become, if his vision becomes a reality.

35

ROBERT REDFIELD

1 8 9 7 – 1 9 5 8

MILTON SINGER

 SOON AFTER he was appointed president of the University of Chicago in 1929, Robert Hutchins submitted a one-page memorandum, which was accepted by the faculty senate and approved by the board of trustees, for the administrative reorganization of the University. The proposed reorganization essentially consisted of grouping the various academic departments, the undergraduate College, and the professional schools into separate divisions. Each division and school was to have its own dean responsible directly to the president. Mr. Hutchins's proposal set the framework for the administration of the University ever since. One obvious objective of the reorganization was to unify and centralize the University's administration. Another, more implicit, objective was to rein in the independent powers of the academic departments over appointments, curricula, and degree requirements.

Many of the successes—and failures—of Hutchins's administration from 1929 to 1950 depended on the quality of the deans he appointed to administer each of the divisions and schools. A dean's administrative efficiency, educational credentials, and personal style became decisive for the mediation of Hutchins's leadership to the faculty, students and staff, and professional and general public. In the case of the division of the social sciences, Hutchins was particularly fortunate to appoint as dean Robert Redfield, a young professor in the department of anthropology at the time, after several other temporary expedients did not work out.

· I ·

When appointed as dean in 1934, Redfield was just six years past the receipt of his doctorate and was doing research in Yucatan, but he was already a "veteran" of the University of Chicago, having graduated from its

413

Laboratory School, the College, the Law School, and its combined departments of sociology and anthropology. He was also an "insider" so far as family and residence were concerned. Born in Chicago in 1897 of a lawyer father whose "old American" great-grandfather settled in Illinois in 1833, and whose mother was the daughter of the Danish consul in Chicago, he represented the kind of family which acquired a strong identification with the University. The fact that he married a fellow student, Margaret Park, who was the daughter of Robert E. Park, professor in the sociology department, did not weaken that identification.

It would be too facile to say that Redfield was qualified to become dean of the division of the social sciences by family and residence, education and professional training. His personal qualities and personal style had a great deal to do with his longevity in the dean's office from 1934 to 1946. Among those who have had some personal contact with him as colleagues, students, staff, personal friends, and relatives, there is unusual consensus that Redfield was somewhat formal and precise in speech and writing, very punctual about appointments, quick to comprehend another's words, fast in his physical movements, a good listener in the classroom and out, courageous in speaking out against racial and religious discrimination and for political and academic freedom, an idealist and optimist about the future of the human race.

The interpretation of Redfield's formal speech mannerisms as expressions of arrogance or condescension was usually quickly dispelled by experience of his willingness to listen to the opinions and to read carefully the writings of other persons. He had an unfailing habit of acknowledging student papers and other communications. The comments on his rickety typewriter usually concluded with a question, and gave one a sense of listening to his fast-paced oral comments.

A former student's sketch, about 1951, of Redfield's listening to a longwinded seminar report conveys how intently he would listen, even to reports he did not agree with. At the end of one such report, after his questioning elicited a sparkling discussion, I asked him how he managed to snatch victory from a near defeat. He answered that he usually kept at the back of his head two questions for such reports: "Is it true?" and "What of it?"

The speed of Redfield's reactions, physical and intellectual, became legendary around the Social Science Research Building. Professor Everett Hughes, a classmate, colleague, and friend of Redfield told the following story at the symposium in Worcester in 1974:

ROBERT REDFIELD, 1951

> One summer . . . when we were up in Michigan, Park came over and
> tapped on our window. He said, "I have got something to think through,
> and Redfield is too damn fast. I keep trying to think things over."

Was Redfield's style also too fast for the people he studied in the field?
Asael Hansen, the sociologist and former student of Ralph Linton at Wisconsin, who with his wife did the fieldwork in Merida for the Yucatan
study, reported that he was discouraged when Redfield once showed him
in the field a two-page summary of the project which would have taken
Hansen two or three days to prepare; Redfield whipped it up in a half hour.
Hansen, however, was at pains to qualify the portrait of Redfield as a
"speed demon" in the field. Hansen recalled at the same symposium that a
former Chicago Ph.D. described Redfield's brisk manner with students in
his office and then wondered how he could do fieldwork with the slower-
paced Yucatan peasants. Hansen's amended reply to the question gives a
valuable insight into Redfield's style of doing fieldwork as well as his
personality:

> Redfield knew perfectly well when he was at the University of Chicago
> and when he was in back-country Yucatán. He was fully aware of the
> vast culture differences between the two. I alluded to his great pa-
> tience as he was being "processed" for entering Mexico. In Dzitas I
> was present during one of his interviews. The interviewee was greeted,
> invited to sit down, and asked about his health. The questioning was
> clear but not direct and never abrupt. Initial phrases were sprinkled
> with "it is said" or "I have been told" or "Don Fulano seems to hold,"
> and so on—followed by "What do you think?" or "How does it look to
> you?" The man appeared comfortable and to be enjoying the talk. I
> could see information piling up, all freely given. At no point did I note
> evidence of the awful sign, "What does this man from the United
> States want me to say?"

Some future biographer will undoubtedly note the contrast, if not the
conflict, in Redfield's personality between his compulsive punctuality, precision, and formality of speech, and his interest in the thoughtful and
reflective informants, even in peasant communities, or the emphasis he
placed on such concepts as a people's "world view" and on the role of
ideas in anthropological theory. Redfield was willing to accept responsibility as a leader for a wide range of activities and, at the same time, he felt
acutely the limitations of time and energy. All of these official responsibilities combined with the organization and content of an ambitious research

program in Yucatan, and, somewhat later, travel to China and India, the Ford project, and invitations to deliver several series of public lectures in Frankfurt, Cornell, London, Paris, Uppsala, Cambridge, Swarthmore, Santa Barbara—all of which he accepted—would have created some problems for any reasonably conscientious person.

A description of Robert Redfield as a person which I have found illuminating and consistent with my own more episodic impressions was given by Robert Hutchins at the memorial service for Redfield in 1958: "The implied rules of the educational conversation are both intellectual and moral. They say 'Use reason,' and they say, 'Be fair and generous.' These words are a description of their author. Because he was reasonable, fair, and generous, he helped us all to be better than we could otherwise have been."

· II ·

Redfield's professional reputation among anthropologists and social scientists was largely based on his pioneering studies in a Mexican village, Tepoztlán and in Chan Kom, a Maya peasant village, as part of a folk to urban continuum in Yucatan. In the fieldwork for these studies he was accompanied by his wife and at least one of the children on each trip. In addition he was assisted by Alfonso Villa Rojas, a local schoolteacher, who collaborated in the fieldwork in Chan Kom and also did a study of the tribal village of Tusik; and by Asael Hansen and his wife, who did the fieldwork in the capital city of Merida. Most of the Yucatan fieldwork was done between 1931 and 1934 before Redfield was appointed dean of the division of social sciences. Monographs on Tusik and Chan Kom and several journal articles appeared before Redfield published the comprehensive summary volume, *The Folk Culture of Yucatán* in 1941.

The anthropologist Oscar Lewis, in his restudy of Tepoztlán published in 1951, twenty-one years after Redfield's published study, said that Redfield idealized the community by concentrating on the Barrio fiesta cycles, rituals, weddings, and folk ballads. He omitted, said Lewis, the poverty, conflicts between individuals and the misery of the villagers. Redfield himself praised Lewis's monograph on the dust jacket and added that, given his own earlier study, the addition of Lewis's work provided "a stereoscopic vision" of Tepoztlán. The dramatic disagreement between the two anthropologists stimulated a controversy among social scientists and popularized restudies. Redfield himself did a restudy in 1948 of Chan Kom and was also stirred by Lewis's criticism to restate his theory of the folk-urban continuum and the reasons for the disagreement. His restatement in *The Little Community: Viewpoints for the Study of a Human Whole* (1955), particularly in the chapter "A Combination of Opposites," also suggested some general lessons for social scientists to learn from this disagreement.

Redfield agreed with Lewis about the kind of differences that existed between the two books. He also agreed that these differences were not completely attributable to the lapse of time or the greater number of informants and experts which Lewis had used. The essential difference, Redfield suggested, was accounted for by the different "hidden questions" which each anthropologist brought to his study.

> There are hidden questions behind the two books that have been written about Tepoztlán. The hidden question behind my book is, "What do these people enjoy?" The hidden question behind Dr. Lewis's book is, "What do these people suffer from?"

Given his own book, Redfield found Lewis's book very valuable:

> Not only because it makes good use of the resources and procedures and research developed since 1926, but also for the reason that Lewis is especially interested in the problems of economic need and of personal disharmony and unhappiness, topics which I did not investigate.

As for Lewis's application of Redfield's folk-urban continuum theory to Tepoztlán, Redfield regarded that as an anachronistic exercise:

> When I went to Tepoztlán I did not have "the concept of the folk-culture and folk-urban continuum," as Lewis suggests. I began to develop the concept as I wrote the book about Tepoztlán, but the concept was not really apparent to me until several years later.

Ironically, despite Lewis's criticism of Redfield's folk-urban theory, Lewis's conclusions from his restudy generally supported the conclusions of Redfield's studies in Yucatan, as the following quotation from Lewis's monograph indicates:

> On the whole, many of our findings for Tepoztlán might be interpreted as confirming Redfield's more general findings for Yucatán, particularly in regard to the trend toward secularization and individualization, perhaps less so in regard to disorganization.

Lewis's critique of Redfield's theory of the folk-urban continuum may have been anachronistic as applied to the Tepoztlán book. The critique was more relevant to Redfield's studies of Yucatan in the 1930s and their summarizing volume, *The Folk Culture of Yucatán,* which explicitly formulated and applied the folk-urban theory to four Yucatan communities—a tribal village (Tusik), a peasant village (Chan Kom), a small railroad town (Dzitas), and the capital city of Merida.

Redfield was quite aware of the role of the personal style and the personality of the ethnographer in the writing of ethnography. He discussed this question in his lectures on the *Little Community* in 1955, in the context of the controversy with Lewis and in that of the personality-and-culture theory. He was also interested in exploring the possibility, suggested by Kroeber, of using literary portraiture as a method of writing ethnography. Yet in one of the very last lectures he wrote, "Art and Icon" (1958), he made it clear that aesthetic criteria for describing a work of art, such as a Dogon carving, were different from an ethnographer's description of the same object.

· III ·

In 1953 when Senator McCarthy's investigation intimidated many academics from speaking out, Redfield published a popular article in the *Saturday Review* called "Does America Need a Hearing Aid?" The article stated the case for an affirmative answer in terms of the urgent need for national security, mutual understanding, and conversation between the superpowers—and between the nations of the world.

> Mutual security depends on mutual understanding, and for understanding you have to have a conversation. . . . At home and abroad to talk and then to listen, to listen with the help of reason and then reasonably to talk, is to strengthen us just where we can be so much stronger than the Soviets. It is to build the community of free minds, "the civilization of the dialogue."

By "a conversation of cultures," and a "civilization of the dialogue," Redfield did not mean just an oral, face-to-face conversation. He included all modalities of communication—writing, reading, photography and film, the performing and plastic arts, and all the cultural media that can be made available to facilitate communication across cultures and disciplines.

Redfield concluded in the article in the *Saturday Review* that Americans need to listen to changing national moods, persisting national characteristics, and underlying human nature of the different societies that meet in the "Big Room" of the world. In fact, by 1953 he had already spent two years organizing an interdisciplinary and multinational scholarly program to develop the cultural hearing aids and radars that Americans and others needed.

In 1951, the Ford Foundation made a substantial grant to the University of Chicago for evaluating and developing methods to characterize and explore living civilizations, with a view to improving international understanding and international security. The scope of the project was interdisciplinary and international but was based at the University of Chicago under Redfield's direction. I was invited by Redfield to serve as associate director. From 1951 to 1953 contacts were made with relevant research programs in the United States and Europe. With the assistance of Gustave von Grünebaum, an historian of Islamic civilization, John Fairbank and Arthur Wright on Chinese civilization, Eliseo Vivas, a philosopher of aesthetics and ethics, and Harry Hoijer, a linguist, these preliminary explorations generated several conferences and publications. Much useful information was digested and discussed in a continuing seminar at the University of Chicago on the comparison of cultures. This seminar also became a forum for the presentation and critical evaluation of concepts and methods for characterizing and comparing civilizations by members of the staff of the project and invited visitors. Some of the concepts which received particular attention and intensive discussion in the seminar were "worldview," "total cultural pattern," "ethos" and "value system," "group personality," and "the self."

By 1953, we decided to concentrate many of the project's resources on the study of Indian civilization because of the interest and availability of anthropologists who had recently done Indian village studies, and of social scientists and humanists who were willing to collaborate in multidisciplinary studies of a civilization. In a Chicago seminar on Indian village studies in 1954, which took its point of departure from a typescript of Redfield's lectures on "The Little Community," the participating anthropologists concluded that while village studies can be used as points of entry for a study of Indian civilization, they were not the only available points of entry for a study of that civilization. A companion two-day conference canvassed the needs and opportunities for Indian studies. In a joint paper on "The Cultural Role of Cities" which Redfield and I presented in 1954 at a conference on urbanism organized by Bert Hoselitz, we sketched somewhat speculatively a conceptual framework for studying the formation and transformation of cities within the time-perspectives of particular civilizations, including that of India. In this paper, Redfield formulated his conception of a civilization as a historic structure of interacting little and great traditions, little and great communities. Although neither I nor Redfield had yet visited India when we wrote the paper, the hypotheses suggested in it, when combined with M. N. Srinivas's concepts of "sanskritization" and "sanskritic Hinduism" from his monograph on the Coorgs (1952) provided a fruitful approach to my studies in Madras.

Redfield introduced the concept of "a social organization of tradition" to link with "the structure of tradition" in a formulation that extended and paralleled Radcliffe-Brown's and Firth's conception of "social organization" as the assembling of elements of a "social structure" in particular instances of social action. For Redfield the "structure of tradition" included the learned and systematized knowledge and cosmology of a culture ("the great tradition") as well as the folk beliefs and worldviews of the folk ("the little tradition"). The interaction of the two levels of tradition could be observed and studied in the teaching and practices of ritual specialists in ceremonies and rites as well as in discourses and other kinds of "cultural performances" and texts in context.

Changes in both "great traditions" and "little traditions" could be studied, Redfield believed, through archaeological, historical, and social anthropological data. He said that at the time he did his Mexican studies, the indigenous "great traditions" had already been decapitated. In oriental civilizations, Redfield believed that it was still possible to study their great traditions in villages, "from the bottom up." His own plans to do such village studies in China in 1949 and in India in 1955 were frustrated. But his vision of a social anthropology of civilizations has animated the research of Mandelbaum, Marriott, Cohn, and others in India, Spiro in Burma, Tambiah in Thailand, Geertz in Indonesia, and that of many other anthropologists, historians, and archaeologists of civilizations. By 1951, Redfield was already moving away from a synchronic, functionalist comparison along the folk-urban continuum and towards direct historical studies of a folk-civilization continuum in China, the Middle East, and India.

This proposal for a study of civilizations as historic structures of little and great cultural traditions appeared to Redfield as a feasible way to approach the larger civilizational systems "from the bottom up," through "studies of the small communities of peasant or natural peoples." Citing scattered anthropological community studies in different parts of the world, Redfield envisaged far-reaching changes in the methods and scope of social anthropology.

In China, India, or Mexico each village chosen for intensive study represents not only an instance of social structure or social organization within itself but also a persisting and characteristic level or dimension of the whole historic civilization.

· IV ·

The achievements and impact of Redfield's Ford Foundation project were mostly educational. They were most immediately evident at the University of Chicago, and quickly spread to other universities and colleges. The "crash" language and area programs of the Second World War were replaced by programs concentrating on specific civilizations with the help of the several disciplines in the languages, literatures, history, social sciences, and natural sciences relevant to the study of each civilization. The College at the University of Chicago instituted full-year introductions to Chinese, Indian, and Islamic civilizations in 1956. Redfield opened the Indian civilization course with a lecture on how to think about a civilization. In short order these courses and their staffs became the nucleus for programs leading to elementary and advanced programs supervised by interdisciplinary committees. Financial support from the Carnegie, Rockefeller, and Ford Foundations, together with government funds from the Office of Education, kept pace with the expansion and made it possible.

Redfield's model for the study of civilizations became popular and was applied in Far Eastern, Near Eastern, African, Greek, and European studies, among others. By the early 1960s, Redfield's proposal made in 1944 for the long, intensive study of civilizations with the help of specialized disciplines had become an educational reality. Not surprisingly, Redfield's thinking and writing about these developments also changed his conception of anthropology. The folk-urban continuum was transformed into a folk-civilization continuum. The "primitive isolates" of classical anthropology in simultaneous side-by-side comparison were now to be replaced as objects of study by histories of the formation and transformation of peasant villages and cities. Archaeological, prehistoric, and historic perspectives were now considered relevant for "a social anthropology of civilizations." Most striking, perhaps, was that his earlier view of societies as "natural systems," while not completely abandoned, would be succeeded by a view of societies as cultural and symbol systems. Equally striking was his acknowledgment of the influence of the anthropologist's personality and values on both the field observations and their interpretations.

The first educational fruits of Redfield's program for intercultural studies began to appear around 1955, when a Chancellor's Committee on the College Curriculum recommended to the College Council that three year-long introductions to, respectively, Chinese, Indian, and Islamic civilizations be added in 1956–57 to complement the course in Western civilization. At least three members of the Chancellor's committee, William McNeill, Frank Chase, and I, strongly supported the recommendation and persuaded the other members of the committee. McNeill, an historian, himself took the lead in elaborating the course on the history of Western civilization in the College. Freshly returned from my first trip to India where I had gone to enlist Indian scholars and to undertake some field research in Redfield's project, I was eager to make the study of non-Western civilizations a part of a liberal education. Frank Chase, who was chairman of the department of education, approved the educational guidelines of the proposal and supported it. Dean Chauncy Harris and Robert Street gave their support.

Although occasional courses in Chinese, Sanskrit, and Islamic studies had been given earlier, by Creel, Bobrinskoy, and von Grünebaum, respectively, these three introductions were the College's first organized interdisciplinary introductions to non-Western civilizations designed as integral ingredients of a general liberal education for undergraduates. With the help of a three-year grant from the Carnegie Corporation, these courses soon became the hub around which much new thinking, materials, teaching, and research were developed. They also became a kind of model for the study of many other civilizations. In the Committee on Southern Asian Studies, senior members of departments in the social sciences and humanities who had had opportunities for travel and research in South and Southeast Asia (e.g., Eggan, Hauser, Hoselitz, Lach, McKeon, Shils, White) were joined by outstanding younger scholars such as van Buitenen, Dimock, and Ramanujan; Weiner and Hay; Cohn and Marriott, not only to teach in the introductory courses but also to design and teach more advanced courses. Substantial grants from the Ford Foundation and the U.S. Department of Education in the late 1950s made possible the creation of a center for Southern Asian studies, and a department of south Asian languages and civilizations in 1966.

These developments began to fulfill in some measure Robert Redfield's vision, articulated as early as 1944, of how the wartime language and area-studies programs could be converted into "an intensive study of the important world civilizations with the aid of the specialized disciplines." The practical realization of Redfield's vision depended in part on two institutional circumstances: the existence of the College within the University, and the administrative freedom to organize interdepartmental committees and programs.

By 1956, when course in the Introduction to Indian Civilization was inaugurated, Redfield was too ill to participate. He did, however, give the enterprise his blessing with an introductory lecture, "Thinking about a Civilization," which was included in the volume of readings. This lecture prefigured the three lectures on civilization he delivered two years later, in 1958, at the Center for Advanced Study in the Behavioral Sciences. These lectures represented his last thoughts about a social anthropology of civilizations, although not quite the full reach of the little book on civilization he projected in the table of contents he sent me shortly before he died.

The results of these exploratory activities were reported and discussed in a continuing seminar on "The Comparison of Cultures" which met biweekly at the University of Chicago. Students as well as teachers participated in these seminars, and visitors from abroad and the United States were often invited to speak there. During the first year of the seminar in 1951, three French students who had come to study with Redfield were active contributors. One of these, Claude Tardits, translated and commented on some of Marcel Griaule's Dogon studies. Another, Michel Mendelsohn, prepared a comprehensive bibliography of worldview studies and then went on to do a field study in Guatemala. Eric de Dampier acquainted us with scholars in France.

Independent field research in Meso America was also undertaken by Charles Leslie in Mitla, Mexico, and by Calixta Guiteras Holmes, a former student of Sol Tax, on the worldview of a Tzotzil Indian. Redfield's supervision of these studies was interested and constructive. A letter he wrote for Mendelsohn suggesting how to collect field information about worldviews, which was later sent to Calixta Guiteras Holmes with additional comments, is characteristic.

By 1953 the results of exploratory conferences and original research were beginning to appear. Through an agreement with the University of Chicago Press and the American Anthropological Association negotiated by Sol Tax, who was at the time editor of *The American Anthropologist,* a monograph series called "Comparative Studies of Cultures and Civilizations" and jointly edited by Redfield and myself was launched. About ten volumes appeared in the series during the life of the project, from 1951 to 1961. Redfield's lectures at Uppsala were published in the series in 1955 as *The Little Community.* The publication arrangements gave assurance that results of the project would become known to a professional audience of anthropologists and social scientists, as well as to a wider public.

· V ·

Early in 1953 when we discussed the preliminary publications, Redfield expressed some regret that they tended to focus on high culture and "the great tradition" of a civilization and to slight the "little traditions" of the folk. At that point I suggested that a concentration on Indian civilization for about five years would probably yield the kind of insight into the relations of the great and little traditions Redfield was after. The availability of indologists, and anthropologists who were doing village studies made the suggestion a feasible one. After Redfield accepted it, it was decided that I and my wife should prepare for a trip to India in 1954–55 by attending classes at the South Asia Regional Studies program at the University of Pennsylvania during the autumn of 1953, and classes in South Asian anthropology offered by Professor David Mandelbaum at Berkeley during the winter of 1954. On our return to Chicago for the spring quarter of 1954, we would devote the "Comparison of Cultures" seminar to "Village India" with about six anthropologists who had recently done village studies. A two-day conference on some needs in Indian research to follow the seminar on "Village India" was also planned.

By September of 1954 we felt almost ready to start on our first trip to India by way of Cambridge University, where the International Congress of Orientalists was scheduled to meet. At the two-day Chicago conference, the Indian linguist and educator, Professor S. M. Katre, who was present, invited Professor W. Norman Brown and myself to continue our discussion about interdisciplinary Indian studies at the Deccan College Research Institute soon after we were to arrive in India in 1954. The Redfields also planned to travel to India the following year and would undertake to enter Indian civilization from the ground up in an Orissan village.

These 1953 plans now sound a bit speculative and unrealistic. But as it turned out, the world was then peaceful and predictable enough to permit most of our plans to be realized. The only significant event that was not realized was the Redfields' village study. Redfield addressed a conference in Madras organized in 1955 by Professor A. Aiyappan, the superintendent of the Madras Government Museum and a former student of Malinowski in London. In Calcutta, Redfield became ill while purchasing camping equipment while guided by Professor Nirmal Kumar Bose and Dr. Surajit Sinha. A doctor in Calcutta who examined Redfield told him he had too many white blood cells and urged his wife to take him directly home. In Chicago, the physicians in Billings Hospital diagnosed his illness as lymphatic leukemia.

· VI ·

Over the three years from 1955 to 1958, although in and out of the hospital for diagnosis and treatments, and aware that he was suffering from an incurable disease, Redfield continued to conduct seminars, deliver public lectures, read papers, meet students and visitors, keep up an active correspondence, write articles, and read proofs. In February of 1958, Redfield and his wife went to the Center for the Advanced Study of Behavioral Sciences in Palo Alto to give three lectures on civilization to a seminar on the comparative study of civilizations. David Mandelbaum and I, who were both fellows at the center that year, had organized the seminar and invited Redfield, Kroeber, von Grünebaum, Wright, and Nirmal Kumar Bose to participate. In addition, Ethel Albert, Kenneth Burke, Bjore Hansen from Sweden, Talcott Parsons, and Charles Wagley participated actively in the seminar as regular fellows of the center. This seminar produced some lively discussion and papers, all of which were published by their authors.

Soon after his return from California, Redfield was back in the hospital. In a letter written about a month before he died, he wrote of his pleasure at receiving a copy of Kroeber's comments at the center, which I had s him. He also expressed his intention to write:

. . . a small book on civilizations, perhaps ten essay-like chapters, something like—but in the end probably not much like—the following:

I. A Civilization as an Object (a formed thing of the mind)
II. Cultures and Civilizations: Class and Subclass
III. Criteria (class and continue)
IV. Structures in History (Societal or Cultural)
V. Community, Region, Class, Estate
VI. The Cultivation of Tradition and Self-image: Knowledge
VII. The Cultivation of Aesthetic Discrimination
VIII. The Cultivation of Moral Judgment
IX. The Creativity of the Civilized
X. The Civilization of the Untraditional

Redfield's death of leukemia on 16 October 1958, robbed him of the opportunity to write that small book on civilizations. Perhaps it will console readers to learn that he left in his writings a paper trail of clues to some of the things he might have said in each of the chapters he projected for that book. A few suggestions will illustrate the rich possibilities. The subjects of the first three chapters he discussed in the three lectures on civilization at the center at Palo Alto in 1958. The chapter on "The Cultivation of Tradition and Self-image: Knowledge" must refer to his persistent interest in describing the worldview of a civilization conceived of both as a self-image and a distinctive organization of knowledge. His writings return to this theme many times and reflect some influence of the French conception of culture as *connaissance*. The chapter in *Peasant Society and Culture* on "The Social Organization of Tradition" embodies some of his later formulations in the context of a discussion of how "the great tradition" was cultivated and transmitted in Indian civilization.

"The Cultivation of Aesthetic Discrimination" does not loom very prominently in Redfield's works. Despite his occasional agreement with Kroeber that literary portraiture should be explored as a technique for ethnographic description. Redfield did not regard aesthetic appreciation as a substitute for ethnographic description. He discussed the difference between the two genres in some detail in one of his last papers, "Art and Icon," which applies Peirce's conception of an iconic sign to a Dogon carving of twins as an object of primitive art and as an ethnographic object.

"The Cultivation of Moral Judgment" was a subject that Redfield took very seriously. It turns up in his discussions of the distinction between "the technical order" and "the moral order" in *The Primitive World and Its Transformations*. More specifically it received attention in his lectures in Frankfurt on the role of morality and value judgments in the social sciences and in the sketches of Chan Kom's peasant ethos and peasant conceptions of the good life.

Redfield was interested in the problems of describing the morality and value of different cultures, and invited at least two professional philosophers who shared that interest to the seminar on the comparison of culture; they were Richard Brandt, who spoke on Hopi ethics, and F. G. Friedman, who spoke on the South Italian peasant worldview. In the end he attached the greatest importance to the question of the role of moral and value judgments made by social scientists. His own disposition to make such judgments was well known through his many public lectures and writings about racial and religious discrimination and quotas in education, and on a wide range of public policy issues. Between 1943 and 1953 he appeared at least once a year on "The University of Chicago Roundtable," where he conversed with Prime Minister Nehru, Bertrand Russell, James Conant, and other public figures. These appearances Redfield generally regarded as fulfilling the duties of a good citizen and human being, as separate from his role as a social scientist or anthropologist. By the end of the Second World War, however, he was no longer sure that such a separation was possible or desirable, as his lectures at Frankfurt in 1949 testified. He confesses unequivocally his inability to make the separation and declares his commitment to scientific humanism and to a humanistic science in his lectures at Cornell on *The Primitive World and Its Transformations*. After agreeing with Kroeber that on the whole mankind has come to act more decently and humanly, and praising a Huron Indian for acting against his people's custom, Redfield confesses that he can no longer separate his scientific judgments from his human judgments; then follows a remarkable reconciliation of cultural relativism with scientific objectivity:

> All the rules of objectivity I should maintain: the marshaling of evidence that may be confirmed by others, the persistent doubting and testing of all important descriptive formulations that I make, the humility before the facts, and the willingness to confess oneself wrong and begin over. I hope I may always strive to obey these rules. But I think now that what I see men do, and understand as something that human beings do, is seen often with a valuing of it. I like or dislike as I go. This is how I reach understanding of it. The double standard of ethical judgment toward primitive peoples is a part of my version of cultural relativity. It is because I am a product of civilization that I value as I do. It is because I am a product of civilization that I have both a range of experience within which to do my understanding-valuing and the scientific disciplines that help me to describe what I value so that others will accept it, or, recognizing it as not near enough the truth, to correct it. And if, in this too I am wrong, those others will correct me here also.

Although upset by the predicted global destruction of agriculture by nuclear bombs, he did not join in the chorus of strident, apocalyptic voices that have become so numerous and insistent since. Instead, his considered opinion became thoughtful, constructive, and ultimately hopeful for the future. This attitude was expressed in the paper "Talk with a Stranger" published in 1958. This paper used the literary device of imagining a conversation with a mysterious stranger from another world. It is always risky to identify the "I" in such documents with their author; yet there is an internal consistency between Redfield's literary persona and his appeal to some words of Camus about the capacity of the human spirit to learn from experience, to mature, and to survive.

· VII ·

In his history of the department of anthropology at the University of Chicago, George Stocking has written that "although the onset of Redfield's fatal illness forestalled his own participation in the Indian research, and the proposed manual for a comparative social anthropology never appeared, the Ford project left enduring fruit." While a "manual" on how to compare civilizations was never published, I have suggested that practically every topic included in the proposed outlines for such a book was extensively discussed in the published papers, books, and book chapters that were generated by the project. The "enduring fruit" in the form of new courses in non-Western civilizations, and "a strong South Asian Studies Center . . . at Chicago" also had a far wider significance than reorganization of curricula and research at the University of Chicago. Not only did Redfield's model for the comparative study of civilizations as historic structures of great and little traditions stimulate new research and teaching on many non-Western civilizations at Chicago and elsewhere; it also reinvigorated the studies of American and European civilizations. Redfield's approach moved anthropology and other social sciences towards more humanistic models which added history and archaeology, cultural symbolism, ethical and aesthetic valuations to the prevailing causal and functional models.

We come, almost full circle, to consider anew the evolution of whole cultures and societies: the regularities in their transformation which are of such magnitude as to regard the later focus as "emergent," as representing a new level of existence. Once more our interest is both historical and generalizing.

36

MAX RHEINSTEIN

G E R H A R D   C A S P E R

CHAPTER 7 OF Max Weber's *Wirtschaft und Gesellschaft* is entitled "Sociology of Law." Its data are taken from almost anywhere and any age. Its range is formidable, its German impenetrable at times even for the German reader. My first attempt to work through it was made in a deck chair on a boat as I traveled from my native Hamburg to New York. I struggled for eight days but, on arrival in New York, had to admit defeat. A few weeks later, however, while a student at Yale, I discovered the key to Finnegans Wake—an annotated American edition of Weber's writings on the sociology of law. In its preface the editor stated his hope to have produced an English text "which is not only accurate but also more readable than the German original." This was obviously the book I needed. It was also my first encounter with Max Rheinstein.

· I ·

In the preface, Rheinstein identified himself as having had "the privilege of attending classes of Max Weber's at the University of Munich." When he undertook to edit *Max Weber on Law in Economy and Society,* Max Rheinstein was in his fifties, a scholar of world renown. The commitment to scholarship, and the generosity and loyalty expressed in his shouldering the burden of editing, introducing, annotating, and, jointly with his colleague Edward Shils, translating Weber, were typical of Max Rheinstein. So was the splendor of the accomplishment.

In order to make the text fully intelligible and useful, Rheinstein wrote, it had to be commented upon. "As the readers will observe, the range

This essay first appeared in the *University of Chicago Law Review* 45, no. 3 (Spring 1978), and is used with permission.

Max Rheinstein

of Weber's knowledge was phenomenal. . . . Weber draws upon Hindu, Chinese, Islamic or primitive Polynesian law just as well as on the legal systems of Rome, England, medieval Europe, or modern Germany, America, or France. In many, if not in most cases, he hints at the phenomena referred to rather than explain them." It was Max Rheinstein who did the explaining for us. Who else could have? The range of his knowledge was equally phenomenal. And it was available to his colleagues and students, without the slightest diminution, until his death at age seventy-eight.

In the preface to *Max Weber on Law in Economy and Society*, Rheinstein also queried how the reader can know whether Weber is correct in all those statements which he uses as the basis of his generalizations and conclusions. "They had to be checked and their sources had to be found. . . . Not even Max Weber could be expected to be infallible, but the number of serious mistakes turned out to be unbelievably small." Rheinstein checked Weber. But even Max Rheinstein cannot be expected to be infallible. Who will check his sources? Only he himself could.

The Max Rheinstein bibliography includes some 350 titles covering his major substantive fields—family law, decedents' estates, and the conflicts of laws, as well as comparative law and legal theory. The bibliography attests not only to the universality of his knowledge and learning about substantive law, but also to his empiricist attitude towards legal scholarship. The latter is perhaps best expressed in his last book, *Marriage Stability, Divorce and the Law* (1972). The work is concerned with how divorce law works, or rather does not work, in industrial societies of the twentieth century. The data are drawn from various countries and include almost everything of empirical importance, from legislation and statistics to complex cultural data not amenable to quantitative analysis.

· II ·

Rheinstein was born in Bad Kreuznach in 1899. He grew up in Munich and graduated from the Wittelsbacher Gymnasium in 1918. He then studied law at the University of Munich where he was awarded his doctorate summa cum laude in 1924. His published dissertation was on the subject of third-party interference with contractual relationships in English law. In 1926 Rheinstein moved to Berlin to join the research staff of the Institute for Foreign and Private International Law that Ernst Rabel had newly founded within the Kaiser Wilhelm Gesellschaft (after the Second World War renamed the Max Planck Society). He began to teach at the University of Berlin in 1931 and published a major work on the structure of contractual obligations in Anglo-American Law in 1932. (A reviewer at the time said, "If only an American lawyer could tell us as much about the German system of contract law.") In the fateful year 1933 he went to the United States to take up a Rockefeller fellowship at Columbia and Harvard. Rheinstein did not return to Germany until 1945 (as an American citizen and a member of the legal division of the United States Military Government).

His affiliation with the University of Chicago—where he remained even beyond his formal retirement in 1968—began on January 1, 1935, with the status of visiting assistant professor of law. It had initially been made possible by the joint financial support of the Rockefeller Foundation and the Emergency Committee in Aid of Displaced German Scholars. The attribute "visiting" was dropped in 1936. Dean Harry Bigelow's letter of invitation makes it clear that Rheinstein was brought to Chicago in order to teach comparative law. While the subject matter was a rarity in American law schools at the time, it had a well-established place in Chicago. As Rheinstein wrote in a 1974 letter to friends of the Law School: "Instructional and investigative work in foreign and comparative law has been carried on at the University ever since the beginning of the Law School in 1902. Ernst Freund was a charter member of the faculty. He was trained in both American and German law, and he was well at home in Roman law and in the French system. [He] was the constant bridge between the legal scholars of the United States and of Europe." Ernst Freund had died in 1932. Rheinstein succeeded him as "the constant bridge." The worldwide recognition that over the decades came to him as Max Pam professor of comparative law found expression in honorary doctorates, memberships in international scholarly associations, foreign decorations, countless invitations to lecture, and the like. On his seventieth birthday, Ernst von Caemmerer, Soia Mentschikoff, and Konrad Zweigert published a two-volume *Festschrift* that contains fifty-five contributions ranging from legal theory, comparative law, and conflicts of law to contracts law and family law.

· III ·

At Chicago Rheinstein easily worked within the framework of a university whose law school is closely linked to its other parts. Rheinstein's report in 1943 to the Max Pam Trustees makes the point charmingly as he refers to a course about the sociology of law: "[T]he course has been open to students not only of the Law School but also of other departments of the University. The presence of students of sociology, political science, history, education, social service, and divinity has been a stimulating influence;

particularly valuable contributions were made by members of the staff of the Oriental Institute who participated in the course in pursuance of their research work in cuneiform laws."

In the world of the American law school which precariously pursues both "is" and "ought," Rheinstein was committed to being, in Max Weber's words, a teacher, not a leader. At what happened to universities the world over in the wake of the sixties, he looked with bemusement. Teaching did not, for him, include politics. And a splendid teacher he was, as can be measured by the admiration, friendship, and warmth which the generations of his former students express. Rheinstein was not only an important mediator for the many foreign students at the University of Chicago Law School, but he also transformed the teaching of foreign law to American students into a disciplined enterprise of high quality and seriousness. This was accomplished in the specialized courses of the Foreign Law Program as well as by the comparative perspective he provided in such "regular" courses as family law. As one of his former students told it: Chicago was the best of times because of "Max inviting us to share his pleasure and knowledge of the law. He spoke about the family law customs of a remote canton of Switzerland as if it were a pristine laboratory in which to view a rare species of creature."

One of the qualities which endeared Max Rheinstein to students and colleagues was his intellectual curiosity. Conversations with him were never one-way. His eagerness to learn from the student usually surpassed the student's eagerness to learn. His attitude was one of live-and-let-live. He was friendly to the extent of being most reluctant to say anything critical of personal acquaintances. As Andreas Heldrich, of the University of Munich, once put it, "When he did express some cautious skepticism concerning a colleague, we knew that that unfortunate fellow had no redeeming feature whatsoever."

· IV ·

Rheinstein's scholarly curiosity and appetite for life, shared, supported, and gently watched over by Lilly Rheinstein, whom he had married in 1929, brought him to travel all over the world. Once asked by his law-school colleague Kenneth Dam what he would have done had he not become a professor, he said: "Oh, I would have been a travel agent." Max Rheinstein filled the somewhat empty and sterile notion of a world citizen with color and richness. He could do so easily, because he had the one quality which I suspect is indispensable for bridging cultures: he was a patriot, or to use a German expression, "ein Lokalpatriot." The two places where Rheinstein had his moorings were Munich, his hometown, and Chicago, the city which had become his refuge from the Nazis. Most of his adult years were spent at the University of Chicago until he moved, shortly before his death, to a retirement home in Palo Alto. Max Rheinstein died on July 9, 1977, four days after his seventy-eighth birthday, in Badgastein, Austria, where at the end of June, the Rheinsteins had gone, as often before, from Munich.

To Munich the Rheinsteins returned every summer—to the "Royal Bavarian Capital" where he grew up during the last decades of 750 years of Wittelsbach rule. Looking back in a vignette entitled *Royal Bavarian,* Rheinstein wrote about his years spent in "Royal Bavarian" schools: "Judging from what life required in later years of change, uncertainty, demands and troubles, that schooling cannot have been bad. . . . [We] learned to think, logically, autonomously and critically. We became conscious of the Great Tradition, acquired a sense of history and with that, perhaps, a degree of conservatism, but conservatism of the liberal, Royal Bavarian kind. . . ." In part, Max Rheinstein's humanism, zest for life, and his openness to the world reflected the vitality of his hometown at the beginning of the century.

Weber's "Wissenschaft als Beruf" concludes with two famous sentences: "We shall set to work and meet the 'demands of the day,' as men as well as professionally. This, however, is plain and simple, if each finds and obeys the daimon who holds the fibers of *his* life." Max Rheinstein met the demands and found his daimon.

37

LEONARD JIMMIE SAVAGE

1 9 1 7 – 1 9 7 1

W. A L L E N   W A L L I S

 IN MY FILES are two appraisals of Jimmie Savage, one written in 1950, the other in 1960.

The first, to the Guggenheim Foundation, said,

Dr. Savage is brilliant and scholarly, has broad and varied interests, and knows a number of fields rather deeply. He is in addition a remarkable personality, vitally stimulated and interested by, and stimulating and interesting to, others. His basic training is in pure mathematics, but fundamentally he is equally interested in empirical science, whether physical, biological, or social. Statistics, in which he began to work about 1944, has provided a suitable meeting ground for his formal-abstract and his empirical-inductive interests. At least two of the several contributions he has already made to Statistics are of major importance, and have stimulated a flow of papers by others. In addition, he has published significant papers in economics, biology, and medicine. It is quite possible, though obviously too early to predict, that he will become one of the great figures of his generation in the field of Statistics.

Ten years later, responding to a query from Michigan State University, two sentences sufficed:

Leonard J. Savage . . . is one of the few truly great minds in American scholarship today. It is doubtful that there is another person who has such extraordinarily deep understanding of such an extraordinarily diverse range of subjects.

This essay first appeared in *The Writings of Leonard Jimmy Savage, A Memorial Selection* (Washington, D.C.: American Statistical Association and the Institute of Mathematical Statistics, 1981).

Leonard Jimmie Savage

These views were by no means unique with me. Almost everyone who knew Savage well would have regarded them as simple factual statements, requiring only a modicum of perspicacity.

John von Neumann, for example, wrote in 1949,

> I consider him a very gifted mathematician who would rate quite high in the mathematical fraternity on the basis of his ability within Mathematics proper if he had chosen to concentrate on this. He has, however, taken a great interest in a number of applications of Mathematics, and quite specifically, in . . . its application to Economics, some social phenomena, and Biology. The work he did in these fields, especially in Chicago, struck me as very excellent. His further ideas, I am convinced, are very promising, and his scientific personality cannot simply be assessed on the basis of his publications to date alone.

Similarly, Milton Friedman wrote in 1964, after he had been associated with Savage for twenty years,

> Jimmie is one of the few really creative people I have met in the course of my intellectual life. He has an original, independent mind capable of throwing new light on whatever problems he looks at. He also has a wide ranging curiosity. In whatever fields he turns his mind to, he gets new insights, ideas, and approaches. . . . Here is one of those extraordinary people of whom there are only a handful in any university at any time.

At a party of statisticians in Albert Bowker's garden at Stanford one summer afternoon in 1950, the conversation moved from topics in the history of statistics to speculation about what, if anything, going on currently would prove of interest to statisticians in the future. After listening thoughtfully, David Blackwell said, "Of all the things going on in statistics today, the only work sure to be significant fifty years from now is Savage's." Abraham Girshick gave a hearty assent, as did several others, although one eminent mathematical statistician turned away, incredulous.

· I ·

Jimmie Savage's two most striking characteristics were a powerful intellect and a powerful personality. A third conspicuous trait was eyesight so poor that it met some legal definitions of blindness. All three of these traits were recognized in the first three or four years of his life.

He was born in Detroit on November 20, 1917, his parents' first child. Because his mother was seriously ill, there was a delay in naming him.

Eventually the name Leonard was chosen, an adaptation of his paternal grandfather's Hebrew name. During the delay in assigning a name, a nurse resorted to calling him Jimmie, writing it with the final *ie* on hospital records; thereafter everyone followed her example. Years later, Jimmie insisted that his father get a court order making the name legally Leonard Jimmie Savage. (A court order was needed in any event to legalize the name Savage, since the family name was Ogashevitz when Jimmie was born and the subsequent change by his father did not apply automatically to the children.)

His father, Louis, was the most significant figure in Savage's life. His respect and love for his father had extraordinary depth and duration. Except for Louis's unwavering devotion and support, continuing throughout Jimmie's life, sometimes under circumstances that would have broken the spirit of Job, Jimmie would not have had as productive a life nor as happy a one. His greatest work, *The Foundations of Statistics* (published in 1954 with a revised edition in 1972), is dedicated to his father.

Louis Savage had almost no schooling. He was born in Detroit in 1893 to parents who had come from an area that then was in Russia but now is in Poland. They were extremely religious Orthodox Jews, and Louis's father was highly educated religiously. When Louis was seven, his father died. His mother, in order to keep her five children together, started a small store in which Louis worked. He attended school occasionally until he was ten, but then quit in disgust because he was so much better than the teacher at the only subject he considered useful, arithmetic.

Jimmie's mother, Mae Rugawitz Savage, had graduated from high school and was a nurse. She recognized Jimmie's affinity for books early, and kept him supplied. His congenitally poor eyesight (a combination of nystagmus and extreme myopia, shared—though in milder degree—by his younger brother, Richard, and by two maternal uncles) kept him from most of the normal activities of children. When he was two, however, he could recognize every make of automobile, having learned them from pictures. When he was three-and-a-half he could read well, which is what he did for much of the rest of his life. When he was five his mother bought him a children's encyclopedia, the *Book of Knowledge,* and he devoured it.

When Jimmie was five, just before he started school, a pediatrician, who thought his intelligence was so high that special schooling would be appropriate, arranged for a mental test. At one point the tester asked Jimmie about his father's occupation. Because a neighbor's child frequently discussed family affairs in an indiscreet way, Louis and Mae had taught Jimmie that family affairs are private; thus his reply to the question about what his father did was, "That is one subject that we will not discuss here." Louis felt it necessary, when Mae told him of this, to establish that he was not a bootlegger, it being the era of prohibition.

Louis Savage actually was in the real estate business, and he remained active in it until his death in June 1972. His chief activity was developing new housing tracts. During the Great Depression of the 1930s he built and sold shell houses—sometimes as many as fifty per week—that a person could buy for a thousand dollars and finish while living there, thus employing himself gainfully when industrial jobs were not available. Jimmie once remarked that he had complete faith in his father's ability to earn an extra ten thousand dollars any time a member of the family seriously needed it.

Jimmie had a deep interest in the business: its social significance, the risks and opportunities, the kinds and amounts of information available, the personal relations, the techniques of negotiation, and the subtle and complex ethical issues. This intellectual interest in his father's business contributed beyond question to the sophistication and power of Savage's professional analyses of decision making. It also accounts, in part, for the fact that he never fell into the puerile rejection of business, capitalism, flag, and father that afflicts so many intellectuals, even though their abilities, opportunities, tastes, and values, like Jimmie's, are derived from those sources.

As a child, Jimmie was isolated not only by his eyesight but by his parents' fears of kidnapping, which was not uncommon in Detroit during the prohibition era. They built a wall around their yard, and had a governess for Jimmie. He got along with his two sisters so badly that one year he was sent away to boarding school—one of the unhappiest years of his life. His closest friend was his dog, who walked him to school every day and then returned at the correct time to walk him home. The dog was poisoned when Jimmie was ten or eleven years old, and Jimmie was distraught for weeks. Later he had a bulldog named "Bootsie" who was wonderful with children, but bit postmen and all delivery-men, and so had to be given away—another tragedy for Jimmie.

· II ·

When Jimmie finished Central High School in Detroit, the school refused to recommend him for college. His homeroom teacher said he would be unable to do college work because he never paid attention in class—an impression probably generated by the fact that he did not usually stare in the direction of things he could not see. (This teacher was later a student in one of Jimmie's classes; presumably she paid close attention at all times.) Through personal friendships, Louis was able to get Jimmie admitted on probation to Wayne University as an engineering student. In his year there he established a good enough record to be admitted on probation to the University of Michigan. There he caused a fire in a chemistry laboratory and was expelled. Louis Savage broke down in tears when he went to get Jimmie, for he had always been determined that, in his words, "even if I had to steal, my son would have an education." Jimmie too was in tears.

The mathematician G. Y. Rainich happened on this tearful scene, and through his intervention Jimmie was allowed to take a course in analytic geometry. His grade was only C, but later he got B's in calculus and differential equations. Then, beginning with two courses under R. L. Wilder, one in the foundations of mathematics and the other in point sets, he obtained A's in all the rest of his mathematics courses, undergraduate and graduate. He always felt that Wilder's course on foundations had opened a wonderful new world, and he spent much of the rest of his life reveling in that world, marveling at it, and enriching it.

Savage received the Bachelor of Science degree in 1938 and the Doctor of Philosophy in 1941, both in mathematics at the University of Michigan. He was elected to Sigma Xi, and awarded a Horace Rackham Fellowship for postdoctoral study.

In 1950 he summarized his professional career of the 1940s as follows:

> My dissertation for the Ph.D. degree at the University of Michigan was on applications of vectorial methods to metric geometry (in the sense of the Menger school), especially with a view to the merging of metric geometry in that sense with differential geometry. Professor S. B. Myers at the University of Michigan sponsored my dissertation, but I was also particularly close to R. L. Wilder there.
>
> Immediately after receiving the degree, I spent an academic year at the Institute for Advanced Study in Princeton where I continued to study pure mathematics generally and particularly in the direction of my dissertation. I had the good fortune there of solving a problem in the calculus of variations which was recognized to be of some difficulty. John von Neumann and Marston Morse are the professors there with whom I had most contact.
>
> While teaching at Cornell the succeeding year (1942–43), I studied some but did no fruitful research.

The summer of 1943 was spent at Brown University in relatively elementary study of hydrodynamics and electricity and magnetism.

From the fall of 1943 to the fall of 1945 I worked under the Applied Mathematics Panel on varied and often interesting problems. It was in the course of this experience that I first learned something about mathematical statistics.

During the academic year 1945–46 I worked at New York University on relatively academic applied mathematical problems, especially problems of compressible flow. My work there was closely guided by K. O. Friedrichs.

While at New York University I applied for and was granted a Special Rockefeller Fellowship to study applications of mathematics to biology. The fellowship was spent from June 1946 to June 1947 at the Woods Hole Marine Biological Laoratory and at the University of Chicago, largely in reading and in consulting with biologists about numerous small problems.

Since June of 1947 I have been employed at the University of Chicago in two slightly different capacities, except for summer visits to the Rand Corporation in Santa Monica, California, and the Biology Division of the Oak Ridge National Laboratory, where I did research much like that which I do at the University.

My research here has been largely in applications (mainly statistical) of mathematics to biology, but for the past three years I have been teaching mathematical statistics, and some of my research has been in that field. The work in biology, while constructive, has tended to be intellectually rather elementary, so that, though I expect to continue actively in biology, most of my research for the next several years is likely to be in the more academic aspects of statistics and the closely related field of probability.

> In 1963, he was awarded the honorary degree of Doctor of Science at the University of Rochester. Also receiving honorary doctorates were George W. Beadle, Arthur F. Burns, Dwight D. Eisenhower, Harold Hotelling, Frank H. Knight, and Warren Weaver, all of whom were older than Savage and already famous. Each, except Eisenhower, was asked to give a brief, informal scientific autobiography. Savage is worth quoting in full from the transcript, which includes some impromptu remarks.

I accepted my role here reluctantly because I envisaged that no matter how small the group might be, it was going to be uncomfortable for me, and I took the assignment seriously. I am a man of very many words. If I were to speak extemporaneously, I could probably hold myself spellbound for an hour, and that wouldn't be loyal to the cause; so I am going to read a moment. I might explain that I didn't prepare any general conclusions about education, and the role of chance and system in it. . . .

Rather than pretend to tell in 10 minutes how I came to be a statistician, I am tempted to discuss how little anyone knows of his own genesis and why even that little cannot be easily expressed. Mention of people, institutions, and publications of great influence would alone take a long time. But I shall try to do as I promised.

Original biological endowment must be half the story. What I can say about mine is that I've been pretty healthy, that my eyes are too weak for much mischief, but strong enough for interminable reading at a moderate pace. My grandparents, who were hopeful immigrants from a cruel country, in the élan of the great American melting pot ethic, came down to me in many ways through my father and mother, giving me some disposition to reach for the stars.

Much of my middle childhood was vicariously spent in 19th century England with a starry-eyed, unalphabetized children's encyclopedia. The influence of these romantic volumes on my outlook and personality is inestimable.

The daily disciplines of social life at school were somehow hard for me. On graduation from high school, most of the teachers and some other experts who had measured my I.Q. and found it substantially below normal, were agreed that I was not college material. My parents and I, though we knew little about the issues, were strongly of the opposite opinion, and after an awkward year or two, I was finally established in good standing at the University of Michigan.

It was to study science that I wanted to go to college, and this desire was not quite without foundation for I had had some genuine tastes of science and had a smattering of qualitative scientific knowledge. But my ignorance of actual scientific life was such that the only scientific careers known to me were in medicine, engineering, and commercial geology. I didn't grow up in a small town, I grew up in Detroit; but that's how it was: I wanted very much to know about science and didn't know that there were scientific professions.

So I enrolled in chemical engineering. And the one semester of orientation in that subject is one of the many educational accidents for which I count myself lucky. I was soon aiming toward a doctorate in academic chemistry. My chemistry teachers, though, saw that my clumsiness was about to bring the laboratory roof down and they insisted on an honorable but firm and prompt discharge from the department.

Thus, in my junior year, I found myself systematically canvassing the university for a new major. That was very interesting. I went from department to department and asked them what you need to do to be in that line of business. The biologist said you simply had to draw, and I said I couldn't, and he said we don't want you.

Finally, I got to physics, which I didn't know anything about. The chairman of physics, who was as hard of hearing as I was of seeing, welcomed me warmly and told me to borrow data from other students if I had any difficulty in the laboratory. He was very serious and grave about that and he said that any student worth his salt around here can steal enough data to get through our laboratory test.

Physical theory astonished, puzzled, and entranced me—the more so because of my preconception that I must already know something about it. After all, I had already had high school physics, but not having had any quantitative experience, I just had no idea what physics really was. I mention a particular introductory book on physics by Richtmeyer. It just happens to be a book that I spent many hours with. It could well have been another, no doubt. This book was inscrutable to me in its mathematical details, but it abruptly opened my eyes to the fantastic achievements and aspirations of theoretical physics, with which the University of Michigan at that time was simply bubbling over.

In those days, mathematics was for me a half-understood welter of formulas that had to be endured for physics' sake. Things began to change with a famous course at the University of Michigan under R. L. Wilder, on the foundations of mathematics. Even so, the formal switch to mathematics that I made in my senior year was a tactful detour to theoretical physics. That is, it was intended to get me out of the examination in the laboratory course on heat. But it was perhaps a bad thing to do. The hook was set, and by the next year becoming a mathematician seemed to me the most desirable and the most unattainable thing in the world.

The stumbling block to becoming a mathematician appears in retrospect to have been a modest, but certainly important, topic in mathematics, commonly called linear algebra. Nothing then written about it got through to me, and little does today. I have re-read the books that puzzled me then, and I don't see how anyone can read them. But, there was a course by a man who I think is a great teacher, G. Y. Rainich, which made linear algebra perfectly plain and simple. A new world opened; half of mathematics opened with just one course. My self-confidence at that time was almost overexpanded by an intangible pat on the back by the mathematics department, and so I was a serious mathematics student.

Finding a thesis was an ordeal for me. I had always been a pure spectator in science. Though I aspired to participate, I had no real conviction that I could.

The post-doctorate year at Princeton was good for me in some ways, not the least of which was some contact with the great communicative mind of John von Neumann. I might have stayed on as von Neumann's academic assistant, but by the spring of 1942 it was intolerable not to be doing something about the war. This led to a year of teaching calculus and spherical trigonometry to pretty unwilling students and then, thanks to an introduction to Warren Weaver, I found myself in more direct war work. This showed me that I was not only interested in the work of non-mathematicians, but that I could be useful to them. It would have been impossible at that time not to have learned something about statistics, for I was stationed at the Statistical Research Group at Columbia, which was directed by Harold Hotelling and Allen Wallis, and was one of the greatest hotbeds statistics has ever had.

After the war, I tried to set myself up as a mathematical consultant to university biologists as a way of being in touch with both empirical science and mathematics. I had no training at all in biology. I had had a friend at the University of Michigan who was a human geneticist and talked to me about that beautiful subject. At Princeton, I found a cheap copy of *The Origin of Species* and that was about all I was equipped with for going into biology, but I thought I could do it anyway because there weren't so many mathematicians who wanted to do something like that.

Nine clients out of 10 wanted help in statistics and I soon found myself officially a statistician and in a statistics department, and my current specialty is the philosophical foundations of statistics. That fits me very well and it offers wide prospects, but it may not be my last specialty.

· III ·

Warren Weaver had a profound influence on Savage's intellectual development at the critical turning point in his career, 1943–46. Weaver, a vice president of the Rockefeller Foundation, during the Second World War was head of the Applied Mathematics Panel of the National Defense Research Committee. (The NDRC was the physical science and engineering division of the U.S. Office of Scientific Research and Development.) In 1943 Weaver put Savage into a group at Brown University working in classical mechanics under R. G. D. Richardson. In 1944 Weaver arranged for Savage's transfer to the Statistical Research Group at Columbia. Weaver was responsible for Savage's spending the first year after the war under Richard Courant at the Institute of Applied Mathematics (now the Courant Institute) at New York University. And Weaver provided the Rockefeller Fellowship that took Savage to the Institute of Radiobiology and Biophysics at the University of Chicago in the fall of 1947, a year after Milton Friedman and Allen Wallis, his colleagues at the Statistical Research Group, had joined the Chicago faculty.

Savage described the Statistical Research Group as "one of the greatest hotbeds statistics has ever had." How could it have been otherwise with a group which included Albert Bowker, Churchill Eisenhart, Milton Friedman, Abraham Girshick, Harold Hotelling, Frederick Mosteller, Jimmie Savage, Herbert Solomon, George Stigler, Abraham Wald, Allen Wallis, and Jacob Wolfowitz? I list this dozen because each has been president of the Institute of Mathematical Statistics, the American Statistical Association, or the American Economic Association. Friedman and Stigler have received Nobel Prizes and Mosteller has been president of the American Association for the Advancement of Science. There were others who elevated and enlivened the intellectual atmosphere and the group was in close touch with other groups under Weaver that included Richard Courant, Kurt Friederichs, Saunders MacLane, Jerzy Neyman, Mina Rees, James Stoker, John Tukey, Samuel Wilks, and John D. Williams.

The Statistical Research Group published three books. Savage made important contributions to two of them. He, Frederick Mosteller, and Milton Friedman, with Friedman in charge, did most of the actual writing of a monograph on *Sampling Inspection.* Copies of this 395-page book were distributed ninety days after the project started; since innumerable computations and policy decisions were required, not to mention typing and proofreading, this left very little time for the actual writing. From Friedman, Savage learned a great deal under high pressure about the use of the English language. While later he was grateful to Friedman, at the time he could not contain his exasperation and probably hoped never to see or hear of Friedman again. Savage ridiculed as overpunctilious pedantry Friedman's insistence on changing such phrases as "in most applications" to "in many applications." Friedman maintained—correctly, of course— that "most" means more than half, and to know whether something is more than half would require statistical data that did not exist.

The ultimate effect of this experience with Friedman was that Savage worked hard at developing his literary style. He became as meticulous in his choice of words as in his choice of mathematical notation, as elegant in his fashioning of sentences as in his fashioning of equations, as orderly and rigorous in his structuring of paragraphs as in his structuring of theorems. His style, whether in a note scribbled on the margin of a manuscript, in a letter, or in a technical treatise, came to have an eighteenth-century quality that was a pleasure in itself. For the rest of his life he remained a close friend, strong admirer, and occasional collaborator and coauthor with Friedman.

· IV ·

Typical of Savage in style and substance is a letter he wrote in 1958 to Dennis V. Lindley, whom he admired professionally and liked personally. Lindley had sent Savage a draft of his review, later published in *Applied Statistics* (1958, pp. 186–98), of Lancelot Hogben's then-new book on *Statistical Theory*. Savage responded with seven single-spaced pages containing twenty-four numbered points, some stylistic, some technical, some philosophical. (This was typical of the way he would throw himself whole-heartedly into a friend's work when asked. In 1955 he did an even more thorough job on the manuscript of an entire book that I wrote with Harry Roberts.) The letter to Lindley opens with a page that illustrates Savage's style and his personality:

> I have been reading your review of Hogben's book with great interest and will be glad to let you have my reactions for whatever benefit they may be to you, without of course expecting you to see everything through my eyes.
>
> The reaction that weighs most heavily in my own mind is an objection against a fault that may not be in your manuscript but only in my own head, and that may not even be a fault even if it really is present in the manuscript. You seem to betray a positive dislike for Hogben, a willingness if not a positive desire to infuriate him; you seem to be sarcastic and jocular at his expense. Perhaps this is not true at all. I myself have a firm antipathy to Hogben, which I think has some rational basis, but which I am certain, from its emotional strength, must also have some basis in irrationality. Thus, it may be that I only seem to see in your writing what I would have the greatest difficulty keeping out of my own.
>
> On the other hand, the tradition of book reviewing, especially in certain fields, condones frankness and even sarcasm. I don't myself see how sarcasm really can properly be condoned, but the case for frankness is of course plain. It is supposed to be the reviewer's duty to

tell the public the truth, without regard to the feelings of the author. This argument is valid, but it seems to me to put the reviewer under a heavy responsibility to distinguish between duty on one side and cruelty and carelessness on the other, such as is borne by those who fight the enemy, spank the naughty child, and eviscerate the ill. It is my opinion that, at least in reviewing scholarly books, the reviewer should lean over backwards to spare the feelings of the author without, of course, deceiving or even misleading the public.

In the Soviet Union, this attitude is held to be sissified; people are supposed to give and take frank, bald criticism. I don't think this has worked out so very well for the Russians, and even if it had, a practice good for the Spartans need not be good for the Athenians. You know yourself how much harm a few xenophobic American reviews did to relations between American and British statisticians. I believe it would be quite missing the point to suppose this harm flowed not from the hostility of the reviews, but only from the objective errors in them.

Another paragraph in that letter throws light on Savage's basic attitude toward statistics:

Perhaps "crisis" is not the very best word that Hogben could have used, but it does not seem to me as ill-chosen as it does to you. "Revolution" might be a better term, for I think, not that we've come to insoluble difficulties, but that we are beginning to see how to solve our difficulties. You say that statistics has until recently been too young to analyze its own foundations. I would say that it had until recently been sleeping under the hypnosis of plausible catchwords presented by its great men without rational support. Perhaps, in a science, that's the same thing as being young. When last I saw you I might have subscribed to your suggestion that there is enduring value in the t-test, the analysis of variance, and other gadgets of everyday statistical life. Even now, I concede that at least some aspects of some of these things will be with us for a long time, but I now think that a good deal of practical everyday statistics is in for revision. My own statistical practice seems to have been affected by Bayesian ideas, and I think that it will become even more so with familiarity and as the necessary technical ideas are worked out by various people.

A final quotation from the 1958 letter to Lindley:

I am reminded when I see expressions like post- and pre-Savage that you are turning too much limelight on me. A reader familiar with Ramsey, Jeffreys, de Finetti, and Good has not really so much to learn from Savage. I think, as you seem to, that my main contribution has been to emphasize that the theory of subjective probability finds its place in a natural theory of rational behavior.

· V ·

Savage spent fourteen years, from 1946 to 1960, at the University of Chicago, first in the Institute of Radiobiology and Biophysics, then in the department of mathematics, and finally, beginning in 1949, in the department of statistics, of which he was chairman from 1957 to 1960. Professionally, those were the happiest and most fruitful years of his life. But in an effort to preserve his marriage, he moved to the University of Michigan in 1960. He had married Jane Kretschmer in 1938, and they had two sons, Sam Linton, born in 1944, and Frank Albert, born in 1954. Sam developed interests somewhat akin to his father's, to Savage's pleasure.

The move to Michigan failed in its purpose; the Savages separated in 1963 and were divorced in 1964. Because Jane decided to remain in Ann Arbor, Jimmie moved to Yale, after spending the academic year 1963–64 at the Center for Advanced Study in the Behavioral Sciences. At the Center he met Jean Strickland Pearce, whom he married in 1964.

It is a reflection on our principal university departments of statistics that, although Savage was clearly one of the most original and profound statistical thinkers of his generation, he never received an invitation to join one of those departments. At Chicago and Yale he participated in the creation of new departments of statistics; at Michigan he was in the mathematics department. In 1960 and again in 1964 all the leading department heads knew that he needed a job, yet none made him an offer. Savage was never bitter about such things; for example, he once shared an office with a mild anti-Semite and did not reveal that he was Jewish until the end of the year, because he wanted to understand how such a person feels and thinks. Yet it hurt him deeply that the Chicago statistics department, which he had helped to create in 1949 and preserve from annihilation in 1959, refused to have him back in 1964, even though other departments at Chicago did extend enthusiastic invitations.

The department had been sorely tried by Savage during his last year at Chicago, when he was in a state of intense psychological turmoil resulting from the compounding of several distressing factors. One was that he had decided to leave what he recognized to be an ideal environment for him. Another was the marital situation that had led to the decision to leave. A third factor was a decision by the university administration to abolish the statistics department. The department did not know of this decision, and

Savage helped greatly in getting it reversed, but only at a high cost in time, energy, and emotion. Still another factor was the intellectual and moral distress caused by what Savage misinterpreted as indifference by his colleagues to his radical new ideas, ideas which they did not refute but which if accepted would render obsolete much of the corpus of applied statistics that was their stock-in-trade.

A fifth factor was intense internal conflict arising from the impossibility of practicing what he preached—that is, an impossiblity arising from the lack of adequate statistical technology to fit the new theoretical foundations he had laid. This was the same conflict that explained some of the apparent indifference of his colleagues to the new foundations. Despite all this, the department did its utmost to persuade him to stay; and he himself, as he was about to leave Chicago in 1960, wrote to Raj Bahadur, "For a person who wants to do original, realistic, and critical work in statistics there is no atmosphere anywhere in the world today to compare with this Department. I say so in a moment of unusually complete information." One may conjecture that Savage's behavior in 1959–60 perhaps paralleled the childhood behavior which had led his family to send him away from home to boarding school. But the family welcomed him back.

As it turned out, Yale proved much to his liking, especially the close association with Frank Anscombe, whom he had held in high personal and professional regard from the time they first met and to whom, in fact, Savage had enthusiastically offered a professorship at Chicago. The agreeable professional circumstances during the seven Yale years, and above all his great happiness with Jean, combined to make the last period of Savage's life personally the happiest.

Savage received few formal honors and awards, but of course he died at the age of fifty-four, when such things normally are just beginning. The Institute of Mathematical Statistics did confer three honors on him: the presidency for 1957–58, the Fisher lectureship for 1970, and the Wald lectureship for 1972 (which he did not live to deliver), and the University of Rochester awarded him an honorary doctorate in 1963. Since his death, three additional honors have been established in his name, a professorship at Carnegie Mellon University, an assistant professorship at the University of Chicago, and an annual dissertation prize by the National Science Foundation-National Bureau of Economic Research Seminar on Bayesian Inference in Econometrics and Statistics. Almost half of the articles (eighteen of forty) on "Utility" and "Probability" in *The New Palgrave* refer to Savage's work.

· VI ·

This essay is in some respects too lengthy, in some respects too brief. I would have liked to add something about Savage's administrative talents and persuasiveness; about his personality; about his pleasure and pride in the statistical work of his younger brother, Richard; about the breadth and depth of his knowledge in art, archaeology, anthropology, economics, history, literature, and music, as well as in all of the sciences (he was offered faculty appointments in departments of biology, economics, management, mathematics, and physics); about his accommodation to his poor vision (when walking alone he would wait to cross a street for five or ten minutes, if necessary, without apparent impatience and he did not hesitate at a public lecture to go onto the platform and peer at the blackboard through a high-powered monocular); and about his hobbies and recreations (photography, travel, swimming, reading aloud, pemmican, and ambergris). But it would be beyond my capacity to portray his charm, his wit, his zeal, his curiosity, his intelligence, his eloquence, his enthusiasm, his generosity, his intensity, his subtlety, his complexity, his simplicity, his loyalty, or his colorfulness. He had great joy in life; and he brought great joy to many lives. He was a deep friend, a true one, and a strong one. He was an authentic genius and a towering personality.

I conclude with the opening and closing passages of a short story by Nathaniel Hawthorne, "David Swan." Jimmie sent these to me in 1963 when he was writing the autobiographical essay quoted earlier. If they were appropriate then, they are peculiarly appropriate now.

> We can be but partially acquainted even with the events which actually influence our course through life, and our final destiny. There are innumerable other events, if such they may be called, which come close upon us, yet pass away without actual results, or even betraying their near approach, by the reflection of any light or shadow across our minds. Could we know all the vicissitudes of our fortunes, life would be too full of hope and fear, exultation or disappointment, to afford us a single hour of true serenity.
>
> Sleeping or waking, we hear not the airy footsteps of the things that almost happen. Does it not argue a superintending Providence, that, while viewless and unexpected events thrust themselves continually athwart our path, there should still be regularity enough in mortal life to render foresight even partially available?

38

JOSEPH JACKSON SCHWAB

1 9 0 9 – 1 9 8 8

L E E   S.   S H U L M A N

JOE SCHWAB TAUGHT. Whatever else he accomplished as educational theorist, philosopher of science and education, and curriculum developer, when graduates of the College of the University of Chicago think about the greatness of the teaching they received at the University, they think of Schwab.

Joseph Schwab died on April 13, 1988, in Lancaster, Pennsylvania. He left behind a legacy of teaching and scholarship that will influence many fields of education. The University of Chicago Press published his volume of collected papers, edited by Ian Westbury and Neil Wilkof, entitled *Science, Curriculum, and Liberal Education*. These three topics certainly cover the domains in which he made his most significant contributions. Yet properly to appreciate both the sources of his wisdom and the fields of his substantial influence, I would have to entitle this reminiscence "Joseph Schwab: Science, Curriculum, Liberal Education . . . and the University of Chicago." In a real sense, the University of Chicago remained a not-so-silent partner in all of his achievements and a continuing beneficiary of his many accomplishments.

Joe Schwab played a central role in my personal and professional life for about thirty years. During that period, as teacher, mentor, colleague, critic, gadfly, and friend, he influenced my ways of thinking and seeing, of teaching and of learning, in a manner I am still discovering. As I continue to meet his former students from Chicago, I find that I am not alone. This extraordinary scholar and pedagogue shaped those he taught in a profound and unforgettable manner.

He was a Southerner who moved North; a biologist turned educator; a Deweyan in the Aristotelian and Thomistic environment which existed in parts of the University of Chicago when Robert Hutchins was president; an eclectic in a world that valued a unitary theoretical doctrine; and a dedi-

JOSEPH JACKSON SCHWAB

cated teacher in a community that celebrated the pure scholar and scientist. Schwab straddled the chasm between Cobb Hall and Judd Hall, between the Hutchins curriculum he shaped and loved, and the study of curriculum as an object of enquiry in its own right.

Writing about Schwab is a challenge because so much of his impact was personal; it arose in the course of interaction with him. Nevertheless, his writings have left a mark on the teaching of biology, the philosophy of curriculum, and the field of education as a whole. I shall write of Joseph Schwab through a mingling of my personal recollections and my study of his writings, combining reminiscences of his pedagogical and consultative impact with reference to his more formal writings.

· I ·

The following exchange is reported in the proceedings of the Educational Testing Service annual conference on testing in 1950:

> DR. SCHWAB: Dr.—— illustrates very clearly one of the doctrinaire adhesions to which I made passing reference in my talk. One axis of doctrinaire adhesion consisted of a line of which one extreme consisted of persons who felt they deserved the name "no-nonsense" people. The no-nonsense people turn out to be simply people who have honed a problem down until it looks simple. Their "common-sense" view of reality looks good because it is an unexamined notion of what reality is. . . . What is required is conversation. . . .
>
> DR. ——: I call this conversing you are talking about by teachers who don't know much about the facts of life a pooling of ignorance.
>
> DR. SCHWAB: But that is precisely the way in which all research is done, isn't it?
>
> DR. ——: That isn't the way I do it.
>
> DR. SCHWAB: Then I really fear for your results, because it seems to me that the first condition of discovery is recognition of ignorance and [of] the delusion of knowledge; believing that one knows, for instance, what deduction or induction is, or that science is certain, firmly padlocks the door to any reinvestigation of the question of what science is.

That dialogue captures the essence of Joseph Schwab—his directness to the point of insult, his commitment to doubt as the source of wisdom, and his devotion to the "other view" as the key to the growth of understanding.

Schwab's connections with the University of Chicago began early. Born on February 2, 1909, in Columbus, Mississippi, to parents who had originally met in Chicago, he ran away from home immediately after his precocious high-school graduation to attend the College of the University of Chicago at the ripe age of fifteen. He graduated with a bachelor's degree in English literature and physics in 1930 and immediately pursued graduate work in biology. He received his Ph.D. in mathematical genetics in 1939. Even before completing his doctoral work, however, he was identified as an outstanding educator. He received a fellowship in science education from Teachers College, Columbia, in 1937, spending the year studying testing and measurement under Irving Lorge. He returned to Chicago in 1938 as an instructor, while working as the examiner in biology under Ralph Tyler and also completing his dissertation.

Schwab remained on the faculty of the University of Chicago, first in the College alone, later jointly in the College and the department of education, from 1938 until his retirement in 1974. He was professor of education and William Rainey Harper professor of biological sciences in the College. He retired to accept an appointment at the Center for the Study of Democratic Institutions in Santa Barbara, which had been created by one of his Chicago mentors, President Robert Maynard Hutchins. He remained in Santa Barbara until the year before his death.

· II ·

Schwab's most powerful influences were as a teacher, and I write this essay as his student. His pedagogical imprint was pervasive, profound, and lasting. No student could ignore his impact; no student could ever forget his pedagogical power. He eschewed the lecture, though he could be a fine lecturer when he wished. His teaching was superbly Socratic in the classical sense. He posed problems for students, often in the text being read. "What is the author doing?" he would ask. The student would attempt a response. Then Schwab would begin his relentless questioning, pressing the student to reflect on his answer, to apply it to examples, to examine the inconsistencies among his responses. Sitting in Joe Schwab's classes fostered clammy hands, damp foreheads, and an ever-attentive demeanor.

I will always remember a morning in one of his classes, probably the first quarter of Natural Sciences 3 or of "OMP" i.e., Organizations, Principles and Methods, which was the capstone course of the undergraduate curriculum in the mid-1950s. I was sitting near the window in a Judd Hall classroom with a clear view of Rockefeller Chapel. I was nineteen. Schwab asked me to read aloud the opening passage of Book 2 of Aristotle's Physics. "Of things that exist, some exist by nature, some from other causes."

(Naturally, we used Richard McKeon's edition of Aristotle.) "All right, mister, what is the author doing in that sentence?" I provided a careful paraphrase of what Aristotle had said. "I didn't ask what he was saying. What is he doing?" I remember feeling tense. It took what seemed like half an hour—probably no more than ten minutes in reality—for me to understand the difference between what the author said and what he was doing that made what he said appropriate. Now, more than thirty years later, I have not forgotten the distinction, nor the strategy of critical reading that yielded up its meaning.

Schwab not only taught masterfully, he made his procedures in teaching marvelously transparent. He wanted you to understand what he was doing as a pedagogue, not only what he was saying as biologist, philosopher, and educator. He would say, after posing a question that left his students speechless, "Let's see if I can replace that big fat question with a few long skinny ones." And he would then demonstrate his indispensable teaching capacity for breaking down a complex question into a series of steps or components, pursuing each in turn. Yet cleverness was never sufficient in Schwab's teaching; mere brilliance was not enough. An incredible passion for learning enlivened every moment in his presence, whether in class or in a tutorial. You not only learned from Joe Schwab; you came to love and value what you learned with him. His talent as a teacher was not a secret cherished only by his students. He was the first member of the faculty to be cited as a repeated winner of the Quantrell Prize for teaching excellence awarded to outstanding teachers in the College of the University of Chicago.

In 1969, Schwab published the essential ideas behind the pedagogy of the College as he conceived of it. Although, by then, he had been continuously reinventing and practicing this form of teaching for some thirty years, he was motivated to write *College Curriculum and Student Protest* by his shock at the character of student demonstrations at Chicago against the Vietnam War. It was not the political beliefs of the protesters that upset him; he may well have agreed with their political inclinations. He was taken aback by the unwillingness of the student leaders, many of them outstanding students in the College, to permit the free flow of ideas in the critical examination of the foreign policy of the United States. Once the world of Plato's *Republic* was left behind for the hurly-burly of real political struggle, the values of enquiry and dialogue were disdained. Opposing ideas were refuted through angry shouts and severed microphone connections, not solid evidence and reasoned arguments. This caused Schwab to reevaluate the quality of higher education he had been providing and to reiterate the necessary conditions for effective general education.

For Schwab, good teaching rested on the twin foundations of a well-conceived curriculum, with carefully selected and designed materials, combined with forms of pedagogy appropriate to the goals of the curriculum. The reason that the College rejected textbooks as the medium for instruction was that they simplified and predigested the rich complexity of ideas needed to stimulate young minds. Curriculum materials could not be simplistic and schematic if the goal was to draw students into active learning and critical reasoning. The materials had to be sufficiently complex that multiple alternative interpretations could be offered and defended. In this way, with texts that rewarded close reading and a disposition toward interpretation, a proper atmosphere for discussion and debate could be fostered. A primary virtue of "great books" and other original sources was their hermeneutic potentiality; they had demonstrated over the years that they could yield new insights to novel interpretive approaches. Actual cases, especially medical or legal cases, were also highly useful in this regard. They invited enquiry, deliberation, and debate.

Schwab was just as interested in the conduct of class discussions as with the substance of instructional materials. In *College Curriculum and Student Protest,* published by the University of Chicago Press in 1969, he illustrates the approach to teaching he practiced and advocated. His description of a class session that began with the reading of a medical case of a woman who was brought to the physician in a "cretinoid state," can be summarized as follows:

> Schwab opens the discussion with a broad question: What is going on in this paper? What is the author's purpose?
>
> After some hesitations, misconstruals of the question and false starts, one student offers an answer to the question. The teacher probes for clarification, qualification and purpose. The student revises and refines his proposal.
>
> The teacher then calls for an alternative view. A second student now proposes another reading. After necessary clarification of the second proposal, the teacher turns back to the first student and asks her to consider and comment upon the second reading. He then asks Student 2 to reconsider and criticize the first reading.
>
> At that time, other students begin to participate. What began as a debate between two views is steered into conjoint enquiry regarding several alternative readings.
>
> Under the teacher's direction, the number and extent of different readings is reduced and simplified. The discussion then begins to consider its own course, with members reflecting on the path taken by their deliberation.

The class concludes with several alternative proposals remaining on the floor, but these have undergone considerable refinement and analysis.

Schwab comments that in a properly conducted discussion of such an original document or a case, there are two distinct layers of discourse. In the first, the text or case itself is the object of enquiry, as the group moves toward the collection and elaboration of multiple alternative readings. In the second layer, the dialogue becomes reflexive. The students begin to work reflectively on their own dialogue and analyses, treating them as a form of second-order text. They thus alternate between cognition and metacognition, between analyzing the text and analyzing their own processes of analysis and review. In that way, the processes of learning come to mirror the processes of teaching, wherein Schwab regularly would reflect aloud about why he was posing a particular question at a particular moment in the course of the discussion. For Schwab, the processes of teaching and learning were easily as fascinating as the subject matter of the discussions. As he taught, he was simultaneously serving as a powerful teaching model. He not only educated future scholars; he educated future teachers and scholars.

What purposes are achieved in the forms of classroom discussion that Schwab conducted so masterfully? Why would anyone choose to engage in such patently difficult and inefficient approaches to teaching instead of employing the far more economical method of the traditional lecture? Schwab posited four virtues that accompanied teaching organized as discussion.

First, students achieve a mastery of the work that has been analyzed and discussed. After such a thoroughgoing analysis, the document in question—whether the case of a woman in a cretinoid state, an excerpt from Galileo's *Two New Sciences,* or the exposition of a particular historical interpretation—has been apprehended in fact and in principle, with attention to its virtues as well as its flaws.

Second, such discussions provide a student with the opportunity to "enjoy an increment to his command of knowledge in the interest of sense." The student now sees the potential complexities inherent in doctrinaire solutions and becomes more alert to the vulgarity of simple systems such as the seven steps of the scientific method.

Third, the student comes to know what he knows and that he knows. He has learned tactics of analysis and reflection and why they are appropriate, and how to identify new situations that will make use of these same tactics. He thus also comes to understand what he does not know, and the sense of accomplishment that ought to accompany the recognition of the areas of one's ignorance.

Fourth, the student has entered into a community of learning embracing both students and teachers, giving and receiving help with neither undue pride nor undeserved shame, and establishing person-to-person relations which attach affective significance to cognitive operations.

These aspects of a proper liberal education were central for Schwab. The processes of discussion were essential to gain the potential profit of reading worthwhile texts. Lectures, however well delivered, always flirted with the danger of doctrine, of presenting knowledge as definitive and settled truth. The kinds of discussions Schwab valued involved students' emotions as well as their intellects. Students could participate jointly in the creation of understanding as well as in the equally important accomplishment of doubt. The joining of cognition and emotion in learning was significant for Schwab. In his "Eros and Education" he portrays the art of discussion as fostering the blending of thought and feeling in educationally significant ways.

He urgently warned against a "rhetoric of conclusions" dominating educational transactions, preferring instead the honesty of "narratives of enquiry." Schwab valued the realism and humility associated with students coming to understand how knowledge truly grows rather than accepting schematic and false notions about its systematic discovery. They would thus learn, in Schwab's words, that knowledge was "contingent, dubitable and hard to come by."

·   III   ·

Beginning in the late 1950s, Schwab began to work on two quite different curriculum projects. By then Hutchins had left Chicago, and perhaps Schwab's intense involvement in the curriculum of the College had waned. One project, the "Biological Sciences Curriculum Study," flowed directly from his activity as a biologist and science teacher in the College. The other project involved the teaching of the Pentateuch, the first five books of the Hebrew Bible. This project emerged from Schwab's collaboration with a former student, Seymour Fox. Fox, an ordained Conservative rabbi and holder of a Chicago doctorate in education under Schwab, wished to create a Bible curriculum that would combine an emphasis on original sources with a strong Deweyan orientation toward inquiry.

"The Biological Sciences Curriculum Study" was to become the most enduring of the major high-school curriculum reforms stimulated by the shock of Sputnik. Schwab was a creator and inspiration for significant aspects of this curriculum. The brilliantly conceived laboratories in that program were built around "invitations to enquiry," which Schwab designed to reflect his conception of discovery and method in science. His *Teacher's Handbook* for the study remains to this day a masterpiece of writing for biology teachers. But his most pervasive contribution lay in the organization of the program itself, especially in the decision by the program's developers to issue the curriculum in three distinctive versions—dubbed the yellow, the blue, and the green—rather than in only one. This was the only one of the "new curricula" of the 1960s to be published as a set of parallel alternative organizations rather than as a single version.

The reason for the three versions is uniquely Schwabian, and reflects his strong predilection toward respecting the pluralism inherent in all disciplines. The alternate versions of the biological sciences curriculum reflect Schwab's concern that we give proper recognition to the variety of organizations or structures in terms of which disciplines can be created and examined. He insisted that students and teachers understand that disciplines are the outcome of human inventions whose structure varies as a consequence of human decisions concerning starting points, units of analysis, and central questions.

The curriculum writings that inspired the post-Sputnik reforms emphasized the importance of new programs reflecting the "structure" of their subject matters rather than merely comprising loosely organized collections of facts and concepts. The biologists and educators working on the biological sciences curriculum discovered in their deliberations that they were having a terrible time agreeing on one proper structure for biology, 'and thus a single coherent organization for the curriculum. Schwab helped them to see that the root of their difficulty lay in the fact that there were at least three very different ways of knowing biology that coexisted in the community of biologists. The reason most biology texts are such a mishmash is because the authors simply and arbitrarily collapse all of these perspectives together.

What were the three perspectives? One can argue that the natural starting point for biological inquiry and explanation is the individual cell, for it is the building block of all other forms of life or biological structures. To explain any biological phenomenon, therefore, should require that the biologist relate structures and functions to their underlying cellular components. To understand how living systems function is to explain how cells aggregate to form organs, organ systems, and organisms. Thus, biological explanations proceed from below, from the bottom up, from biochemistry, biophysics, and the like. The biological curriculum that flows from that perspective is a molecular or cell biology, which was dubbed the "blue" version of the biological sciences curriculum.

Alternatively, it can be asserted that the organism itself, that entity capable of independent existence and functioning—whether composed of one cell or millions—is the proper unit of analysis. Starting from the organism, one would then seek explanations of how individual organs function to enable the organism's activities, how they are organized into systems and how equilibrium among and within those systems is maintained. Biological explanation would focus on asking how the parts of intact organisms are themselves organized into functioning wholes, and on how different types of organisms compare and contrast with one another as adaptive systems across variations in environment. This organ, organ system, structure-function perspective became the basis of a second biological sciences curriculum, the "yellow" version.

Finally, though by no means exhaustively, one could argue that neither cells nor organisms are adequate as units of enquiry, for each is no more than a part of an even more comprehensive natural whole, which is the community or ecosystem. It is as impossible to understand the workings of any individual organism independent of its ecosystem as it is impossible to define the functions of a cell independent of the organized system of organs to which it contributes. To explain biological functioning, therefore, one must ask about the larger community of which any organism is a part, and reason from the top down, from the largest whole to its constituent parts. The third biological sciences curriculum—the "green" version—took this perspective and stressed the centrality of ecological principles in understanding biology.

These turn out to be extraordinarily important contrasts, and not only for biology. Schwab's message was that in fields where multiple paradigms compete with one another, it is rarely wise to make a forced choice of one over all the others. Consistent with Dewey's warnings regarding the dangers of "either/or" thinking, Schwab argued that each conceptual scheme or structure is probably a way of knowing that yields its own particular types of insights and understandings but is incapable of yielding them all. The way we know is through simplifying, through eliminating, through focusing. Ways of knowing are most importantly ways of *not* knowing.

Full understanding is possible only through permitting alternative views to flourish, compete, and interact.

· IV ·

The Jewish Theological Seminary of New York wished to create an enquiry-based form of religious education that treated biblical texts as both holy and yet warranting historical, critical, comparative, and eclectic analysis. The Melton curriculum presented a remarkable challenge for Schwab: advising on the construction of a curriculum around a text of richness and complexity augmented by centuries of layered commentaries and interpretation and a religious tradition which rested on an unspecified balance between revelation and interpretation, between revealed truth and requisite inference and invention. Schwab's contributions to this curriculum are not widely known outside of Jewish education circles, though Ralph Tyler remarked on this work in his comments during the Schwab memorial held at Bond chapel in May 1989. Nevertheless, the activities surrounding the development of an enquiry-based Bible curriculum may well have comprised the fullest expression of Schwab's conceptions of curriculum.

· V ·

There was a consistent pattern to Joseph Schwab's scholarship as well as his teaching. He distrusted single theoretical solutions to the practical problems of education. This disdain for theoretically unitary positions continued as a theme throughout Schwab's career. In the early 1960s he published an essay called "On the Corruption of Education by Psychology" in which he attacked educators who embraced a particular psychological theory—e.g., group dynamics, operant conditioning, Rogersian psychotherapy—and attempted to erect a complete pedagogical edifice upon it. He argued persuasively that any theoretical position necessarily represents a narrowing of the field, a self-conscious exclusion of important elements of the field from its purview. No practical enterprise such as education could afford to be theoretically univocal because practical work could not tolerate that kind of narrowness or tunnel vision.

Similarly, in his Inglis Lectures at Harvard University, Schwab expounded on the four "commonplaces" of education which he and his colleagues, Ralph Tyler and Harold Dunkel, had been discussing for many years. The commonplaces, a concept he drew from the classical rhetorical tradition of "topics" (hence, commonplaces), were (1) the subject matter; (2) the teacher; (3) the learner; and (4) the milieu. Schwab argued that no comprehensive statement about education could be offered that did not treat, in some fashion, each of the four commonplaces. Education always involved the teaching of something by someone to someone else in some context. To ignore any of the four commonplaces was to risk leaving out a critical aspect of an educational problem.

It was typical of educational rhetoric, argued Schwab, to rest an argument primarily on a single commonplace, thus leaving it fatally flawed. The progressive educators who distorted Dewey were obsessively concerned with the learner, but paid far too little attention to the subject matter or the teacher. The curriculum reformers of the 1960s focused on the subject matter or on the need for our society to compete with the Soviets, but tended to pay little attention to whether their new curricula could be taught or learned by human teachers and their equally human pupils. In the analysis of the commonplaces, Schwab was again concerned with educational arguments that were dangerously incomplete because they placed the narrowness of theoretical perspectives on the broad and multifaceted problems of practice.

Out of this set of ideas emerged the conceptions of curriculum theory and practice that are likely to represent Schwab's most enduring contributions to educational thought. Beginning in 1968, he wrote a series of four papers on "the practical." In those essays he argued that the greatest deficiencies in curriculum deliberations lay in their theoretical character. An eclectic and practical approach was needed to design curriculum.

Schwab was not opposed to training in the theoretical disciplines nor did he disparage their intrinsic value. Any particular discipline can enlighten and improve the capacities of an investigator or curriculum maker. It can also limit the teacher's purview. This becomes particularly problematic in education, since it is a field of study that presents its problems, topics, and issues to its investigators and practitioners in ways that do not readily fold into any one neat disciplinary package.

Schwab argued that the field of curriculum was moribund because relentlessly theoretical solutions were imposed on a fundamentally practical domain. Instead of permitting any single theoretical perspective to dominate the construction of a curriculum, thereby consigning it to an unavoidably narrow and restricted view, he advocated the creation of deliberative forums for curriculum work. In these forums, each of the necessary theoretical and practical points of view would be assured a place at the table and a role in the conversation. Some version of the commonplaces would be useful in defining the minimum variety of viewpoints needed to ensure an adequately comprehensive discussion. Moreover, as he demonstrated in his work on the biological sciences curriculum, even the definition of the subject matter of the curriculum had to be subjected to such an analysis. Whether the subject was the science of biology or the literary analysis of the novel, one had to consider the likelihood that several alternative views of the subject were in competition. His essays on the practical gave a number of examples of how such deliberations might be conducted.

In the late 1970s, Schwab was asked to serve as the final discussant on a distinguished panel of social scientists invited to examine the relationships between the social science disciplines and the theory and practice of education. Nearly all these social scientists stressed the ways in which their investigations in education contributed to the furtherance of their disciplines, as well as the importance that their disciplinary knowledge held for the improvement of education. Schwab would have none of it. He alienated nearly every member of the panel by accusing them of vainly seeking legitimacy under the umbrella of the traditional social science disciplines instead of pursuing educational questions in their own right. He concluded his remarks with the charge that his fellow panelists were simply "whoring after respectability." They were furious, but once again Schwab had made his point. The disciplines were essential to the practice of education, but only if they were ready to relinquish their propriety and become eclectic fodder for the deliberations that were needed.

· VI ·

In 1976, while teaching at Michigan State University, my colleagues and I received a federal grant to establish a national research center for the study of classroom teaching, the Institute for Research on Teaching. The institute brought together scholars from a number of different academic disciplines and curriculum areas to design and conduct research on teaching in elementary and secondary schools. In my role as codirector of the institute, I invited Schwab to come to Michigan State to conduct several weeks of seminars for the members of the research group that would assist them to communicate intelligently across the borders of their respective disciplines. It was one thing to argue for an eclectic, multidisciplinary approach; it would be quite another to accomplish such a collaboration without reinventing the Tower of Babel.

The seminar was quintessential Schwab. About twenty-five scholars and public-school teachers sat around the inner tables. A similar number of graduate students and teachers sat around the outside of the room. On the first afternoon, Schwab distributed the initial reading, the first three chapters of *Genesis*. He said, "Let's read this familiar text together and see if we can figure out what the author had in mind." And so we began.

The seminar met for two hours at the end of the afternoon, three days a week. It was exceedingly rare for anyone to miss a meeting. Using his ubiquitous cigarette as a combination pointer, conducting baton and general pedagogical prosthesis, Schwab led the seminar through a series of readings designed to lay bare their disciplinary or professional premises. We spent three or four sessions after *Genesis* with Faulkner's short story "A Rose for Emily." We read Aristotle's treatment of the elements of biological knowledge, and then studied William Harvey's paper on the circulation of the blood to examine a good example of Aristotelian biology.

Having convinced ourselves of the wisdom of a structure-function biology, rooted in the inherent natures of organisms and their parts, we read a recent article from *Science* on the fascinating topic, "Sex Change in a Coral Reef Fish." The article described a type of fish that lived in communities composed of a single male and many females. Upon the death of the male, the dominant female metamorphosed into a male. We now had to wonder if even categories like gender could be viewed as permanent and unchanging. Was the influence of community membership even more powerful than the "inherent" characteristics of organisms? Thus did Schwab continue his lifelong quest to cure his students, whatever their ages or stations in life, of the malady that some came to call the "hardening of the categories." As with all students who experienced his Socratic pedagogy, no member of that seminar would ever forget the experience.

In 1977, Schwab returned to Michigan State to offer another seminar for the institute faculty, devoted to the study of thinking. He invited me to teach with him and for the first time I was offered an insider's view of the master-teacher in action. What appeared so spontaneous in the classroom was meticulously planned by Schwab. Before each meeting we would meet for a couple of hours and think through the text to be read and its most important questions. We would then rehearse the likely course or courses the conversation might take, the kinds of questions that could provoke the most serious doubts and the counterexamples we could prepare that might prove problematic in response to the generalizations most likely to be offered by our students. He not only thought through the seminar's probable paths like a chessmaster in midgame, he considered explicitly which participants might be counted on to make which contributions.

As we planned together, it was almost as if we were composing an improvisation.

By 1977 he had paid the price for a lifelong smoking habit so inescapably connected to any student's memory of his teaching. To remember Joe Schwab in the classroom was to remember that cigarette in his right hand, gracefully swooping, pointing and underscoring. But his emphysema had by then advanced to a point where he had to forego smoking entirely. An empty pipe replaced the lighted cigarette as pacifier and prop. But it was never quite the same. After the faculty seminar in the fall of 1977, he never again taught a regularly scheduled course.

· VII ·

Two of the most significant influences on Schwab's thinking were Hutchins and Dewey. At first blush, this might seem paradoxical, since in both popular and academic circles these two men were perceived as occupying opposite ends of most continua: Hutchins stood for the importance of great books and eternal ideas, the primacy of a canon the study of which would benefit all learners. Dewey, in contrast, advocated that educators begin with the background, interests, and understanding of the learner, building instruction on a foundation of that interest and understanding. Schwab was never convinced that the differences between the two positions was so very great. Dewey never neglected the importance of systematic consideration of the subject matter; he argued strongly for the progressive organization of the curriculum.

One common concept that both men held dear, and that Schwab placed at the center of his own thinking about education, was that of the democratic community as both a goal of liberal education and a crucible for the creation and testing of understanding. Both Dewey and Hutchins shared a belief in the centrality of democracy for both the pursuit of knowledge and the conduct of a just society. The two commitments were inextricably linked.

I remember spending at least three hours of class time in our graduate seminar on John Dewey reading the rather brief preface to *Experience and Education.*

> All social movements involve conflicts which are reflected intellectually in controversies. . . . the practical conflicts and the controversies that are conducted upon the level of these conflicts only set a problem. It is the business of an intelligent theory of education to ascertain the causes for the conflicts that exist and then, instead of taking one side or the other, to indicate a plan of operations proceeding from a

level deeper and more inclusive than is represented by the practices
and ideas of the contending parties.

Schwab argued that the essence of Dewey's philosophy of inquiry and of
education could be found in that preface and its treatment of "either/or"
thinking. I would argue that the same could be said for Schwab himself.

Dewey argued that human discourse is characterized by controversy
because we are intrinsically incapable of uttering the whole truth and
nothing but the truth. Claimed truth is unavoidably incomplete. Our asser-
tions can never do justice to the full complexity of the world around us any
more than our perceptions and cognitions can grasp the full richness of
any setting. For this reason controversies are both inevitable and desirable.
Individuals or groups will sense the incompleteness of any argument and
oppose it with an alternative that builds on what was left out of the original position, thus advancing the original deliberation and advancing the
analysis.

If the achievement of knowledge is a good thing, then a good society
permits, even fosters the competition between competing views. The
more distant a view from the mainstream, the more likely that it contains a
seed of truth absent from prevailing views. Freedom of speech and the encouragement of open dialogue and debate are therefore not only political
virtues, they are also epistemological virtues. If the survival and flourishing
of a society is dependent, in large measure, on its capacity to seek out what
is warranted and true, then its openness to new and different ideas is
essential.

Schools and classrooms in such a society should be microcosms for the
kind of debate and deliberation needed by the society more generally.
They must be organized to permit, encourage, and model the competition
between ideas. They must discourage dogmatic doctrine. Both the selection of content and the organization of interactions within the classroom
should embody the collaborative and competitive conception of the
search for knowledge.

This Deweyan understanding of the social and democratic character of
education and of society was the theme underlying Schwab's conception of
teaching. It permeated his work. After arriving in Santa Barbara, he wrote a
lovely essay for the *Encyclopaedia Britannica* on "Education and the
State: Learning Community," in which he emphasized the pun of the subtitle.

First, community can be learned. It is not merely a matter of place, of
village or small town, but a body of propensities toward action and

feeling, propensities which can be expressed in many social circumstances.

Second, human learning is a communal enterprise. The knowledge we learned has been garnered by a community of which we are only the most recent members and is conveyed by languages of work and gesture devised, preserved, and passed on to us by that community. . . . Even experience as a form of learning *becomes* experience only as it is shared and given meaning by transactions with fellow human beings.

Those of us who were transformed as we learned in the classrooms, lounges, and halls of the University of Chicago, acquired dispositions toward dialogue, questioning, and deliberation that seem to characterize a "Chicago style" of thinking. Joe Schwab exemplified that style in both method and manner. Through Schwab, we came to experience Chicago as a community of scholars, a community whose members conversed regularly about curriculum and about evaluation, a community of teachers who were scholars and scholars who were teachers. He strove to create that sense in his classes and his curricula. His image of deliberation on the curriculum was such an image of colloquy and enquiry. He taught it to generations of students in the College and in the department of education, and they in turn have passed it on to their own students.

39

GEORGE J. STIGLER

1 9 1 1 –

R O N A L D   C O A S E

"If I had known David Ricardo, I would be better able to understand his written words." So said George Stigler. I had met him on a number of occasions but it was not until I joined the faculty of the University of Chicago in 1964 that I came to know him at all well. As a result, I understand his writings better and I admire them more. What I have not been able to understand is how he does it. But no matter. To quote George Stigler once again: "A superior mind and its products must be the most fascinating of scholarly objects." And I have been fascinated. I wish I had the literary skills to describe George Stigler as a person: his affability, his kindness, his honesty, his jocularity, all of which overlay but do not conceal his inner seriousness. What I feel capable of doing in this essay is to describe George Stigler's work as an economist. But there is much to tell.

· I ·

George Stigler was born in 1911 in Renton, a suburb of Seattle, Washington, but was obviously destined for the University of Chicago. In his autobiography he tells us of the circuitous route that brought him there. He first went to the University of Washington, taking, among others, courses in business administration such as real estate principles. Graduating in 1931, a year which did not afford him much opportunity of putting these principles into practice, he accepted a fellowship at Northwestern University, obtaining, at the end of a year, his M.B.A. After returning to Washington for another year, he made the decision which was to make possible all that he

I am grateful to the Cato Institute for permission to incorporate in the present paper much of what I said earlier in "George J. Stigler: An Appreciation," *Regulation,* November-December, 1982.

would achieve: he went to the University of Chicago to obtain his Ph.D., having been told by his teachers at the University of Washington that Chicago had good economists in Frank Knight and Jacob Viner. They were right. He learned from both of them but it was Knight, under whom he wrote his thesis, who most influenced him. Knight gave him his vision of economics and strongly reinforced what must have been innate in George Stigler, his love of scholarship.

His first academic appointment was at Iowa State University in 1936. In 1938 he went to the University of Minnesota and remained there until 1946. What then happened in 1946 does little credit to the authorities of the University of Chicago. George Stigler was offered a professorship by the economics department but it was subject to approval by the central administration. He met with the president, Ernest Colwell, and was vetoed, the ostensible reason being that he was too empirical. Colwell had been dean of the Divinity School. While it has to be admitted that theology is a subject in which prudence and faith combine to discourage the empirical testing of doctrines, Colwell's decision is nonetheless difficult to understand. It had as a result that Stigler went to Brown University for a year and then joined the strong economics department of Columbia University.

The rejection of Stigler was not all loss for the University of Chicago since it made possible the appointment of Milton Friedman to a professorship in the economics department. It seems that the University administration would not have agreed to this had Stigler's appointment gone through. As it enabled Friedman to come to Chicago, George Stigler has described his failure to be appointed in 1946 as perhaps "my greatest service to Chicago." But Stigler was not to be denied to Chicago, although "God moves in a mysterious way his wonders to perform." Charles Walgreen in 1936 withdrew his niece from the University of Chicago because he had been informed that the University taught free love and communism. I know nothing about the University's teaching on communism but presumably Mr. Walgreen would not have been mollified to learn that the true Chicago view is that there is no such thing as a free love. Eventually, however, Mr. Walgreen was convinced that he had been misinformed and he made handsome amends by endowing a chair in American Institutions. For reasons unknown to me the chair was not filled for many years. Then, in 1956, Allen Wallis, a fellow student of Stigler's at Chicago in the 1930s, a close friend, and an able administrator, was made dean of the Graduate School of Business. In 1958 Wallis offered the Walgreen Chair to Stigler and he was at last welcomed into his spiritual home. Once there he became an

GEORGE J. STIGLER, ABOUT 1960

editor of the *Journal of Political Economy,* established the famous Industrial Organization Workshop, and later, in 1977, founded the Center for the Study of Economy and the State, of which he became the director. In 1982 he was awarded the Nobel Prize in economic science.

· II ·

The Swedish Academy of Sciences stated that it had awarded the Nobel Prize to Stigler for his "seminal studies of industrial structures, functioning of markets, and causes and effects of public regulation." This is just. But this citation, with its long account of Stigler's work, nonetheless conveys an inadequate notion of the character of his contributions to economics. His range of subject matter is wide. He is equally at home in the history of ideas, economic theory, and the study of politics. Even more remarkable is the variety of ways in which he handles a problem; he moves from the marshaling of high theory to aphorism to detailed statistical analysis, a mingling of treatments which resembles, in this respect, the "subtle and colourful" Edgeworth. It is by a magic of his own that Stigler arrives at conclusions which are both unexpected and important. Even those who have reservations about his conclusions will find that a study of his argument has enlarged their understanding of the problem being discussed and that aspects are revealed which were previously hidden. Stigler never deals with a subject which he does not illuminate. And he expresses his views in a style uniquely Stiglerian, penetrating, lively, and spiced with wit. His writings are easy to admire, a joy to read, and impossible to imitate. He is a man *sui generis,* Age shall not wither nor custom stale George Stigler's infinite variety.

In its citation, the Swedish Academy made no mention of Stigler's studies of the history of economic thought, but in them he is, I believe, seen at his best. His first book, *Production and Distribution Theories* (1941), which shows the influence of his great teacher, Frank Knight, is wholly concerned with this subject. Of course, being Stigler, his critical comments, which he rightly suspects some will consider hypercritical, on the handling of the analysis by the great economists whose work he examines, end by being a substantial contribution to economic theory in their own right. This interest in the history of economics and of the men who made it has remained with Stigler, and articles such as "The Development of Utility Theory" or "Perfect Competition Historically Contemplated" (reprinted in his *Essays in the History of Economics,* [1965]) are masterly treatments of their subjects.

Stigler also uses his extensive knowledge of the history of economics to examine more general questions, and in particular to attempt to uncover the forces which have governed the development of economic theory itself. The thesis of his essay "The Influence of Events and Policies on Economic Theory" (also reprinted in the 1965 volume) is striking. He argues that "neither popular economic problems nor heroic events influence much the development of economic theory. . . . The dominant influence on the working range of economic theorists is the set of internal values and pressures of the discipline." Similarly, in his Tanner lectures, given at Harvard in 1980, and reprinted in *The Economist as Preacher and Other Essays* (1982), he argued that

> economists are not addicted to taking frequent and disputatious policy positions. . . . The typical article in a professional journal is unrelated to public policy, and often apparently unrelated to this world. Whether the amount of policy-advising activity is rising or falling I do not know, but it is not what professional economics is about.

The claim that the development of economic theory is not much influenced by current events in the economic world and that the work of the economic theorist is not much concerned with economic policy is not, at first sight, very plausible, but I am convinced that Stigler's conclusions are largely true. While Stigler's knowledge of the history of economics is mainly used, as one would expect, in his historical studies, it never fails to influence his treatment, no matter what subject is being discussed. Unlike most modern economists, his investigation of an economic problem is always enriched by his knowledge of the work of earlier economists.

· III ·

Most academic economists presumably know Stigler, above all, as the author of a very successful textbook dealing with what is now called microeconomics. It first appeared in 1942 with the title *The Theory of Competitive Price*, but in later editions the title was changed to *The Theory of Price* (1946, with revised editions in 1952, 1966, 1987). Though there are many revisions, rearrangements, and substitutions from one edition to another, fundamentally the book has remained unchanged. There must, however, be many who have regretted the disappearance of some of the illustrations to be found in the 1946 edition, such as the extremely amusing account of the difficulties of getting effective collusion on prices among bakers in Illinois. It is not an easy text but it is excellent for anyone seriously interested in training to become an economist. A textbook, however, is not the place to display innovations in economic analysis, and despite the fact that there are some very Stiglerian passages, particularly in the later editions, the Swedish Academy was no doubt right to ignore it when it set out those of Stigler's contributions to economics for which the award was given. The subjects dealt with in *The Theory of Price* are those that one expects to find in a textbook on the theory of price, and even the treatment is, in many respects, quite conventional. Of course, as in all his writing, Stigler's exposition is lively and spiced with wit, but these are not the qualities which lead to a Nobel Prize.

What the Swedish Academy singled out for commendation was Stigler's work in the fields of industrial organization and the economics of regulation. In economics the subject of industrial organization means the study of market processes and the structure of industries. However, for reasons which are not altogether clear to me, it is a field which has come to concentrate on "the monopoly problem" and, more specifically in the United States, on the problems thrown up by the administration of the antitrust laws. The result has not been a happy one for economics. By concentrating on the problem of monopoly in dealing with an economic system which is, broadly speaking, competitive, economists have had their attention misdirected and as a consequence they have left unexplained many of the salient features of our economic system or have been content with very defective explanations. The link with the administration of the antitrust laws has tended to make matters worse by importing into economics the imprecise analysis (if that is the proper word) which abounds in the opinions of the judiciary in antitrust cases.

· IV ·

Most of Stigler's articles on industrial organization (reprinted in *The Organization of Industry* [1968]) are concerned with monopoly and antitrust policy. However, he transcends the weakness of most discussions of these questions by an impressive use of empirical data (as in "The Economic Effects of the Antitrust Laws"), by an analysis more precise and more searching (as in "Price and Nonprice Competition" or "A Theory of Oligopoly"), and by discussing interesting and significant problems (as in "The Division of Labor Is Limited by the Extent of the Market"). Nonetheless, although the analysis proceeds at a much higher level than is usual, it remains true that most of the subjects discussed are those commonly dealt with under the heading of industrial organization. But Stigler is not like the others. Like a mountain raised by a volcanic eruption, standing high and strange in the surrounding landscape, there is to be found in *The Organization of Industry* a paper of a quite different kind. It is his article on "The Economics of Information," rightly regarded as Stigler's major contribution to economic theory, and it is no surprise that it was picked out by the Swedish Academy for special commendation.

Stigler's starting point is that at any one time there exists an array of prices charged by different suppliers for the same good or service. Those wishing to discover the lowest price will engage in what Stigler calls "search." The more suppliers who are canvassed, the lower the price that a buyer can expect to pay. But as there are costs to search and the marginal gains from increased canvassing tend to diminish, there will be an optimum amount of search for each buyer. This conclusion is not invalidated by the fact that the actual dispersion of prices will be affected by the amount of search undertaken by buyers. There are, of course, ways in which search costs can be reduced—by localization, advertising, specialized dealers, firms which collect and sell information, and so on. The analysis throws considerable light on the function of these business arrangements and on the way in which a competitive system operates. Particularly important is that it has led to a greater recognition of the role of advertising as a provider of information. But the effect of the analysis is pervasive. As the Swedish Academy said, "phenomena such as price rigidity, variations in delivery periods, queuing and unutilized resources, which are essential features of market processes, can be afforded a strict explanation within the framework of basic economic assumptions." Economists have started to prove, and can be expected to continue to prove, the implications of Stigler's analysis, and with considerable benefit to economics.

Although Stigler had written on rent controls and minimum wage legislation in the 1940s, it was not until the 1960s that he began writing the articles on the economics of regulation that were reprinted (along with many previously unpublished essays) in *The Citizen and the State* (1975). Three of these articles appeared in 1964. At the end of that year, Stigler gave the presidential address to the American Economic Association on "The Economist and the State." His message was twofold. First, economists, whether they were in favor of limiting government intervention or of expanding it, had not hesitated to express their views on what the role of the state in economic affairs should be, without making any serious attempt at discovering what the effects of government intervention had been and without making a systematic comparative study of the results achieved by private and public enterprise. Second, we now have at our disposal quantitative methods to investigate such questions. "The age of quantification is now full upon us . . . economics is at the threshold of its golden age." Stigler had himself already done extensive quantitative work, his book *Capital and Rates of Return in Manufacturing Industries* having been published in 1963. In the context of his presidential address, what Stigler was calling for was a study, using quantitative methods, of the effects of regulation.

· V ·

One did not have to look far to see what he had in mind. Earlier in 1964 Stigler had published the results of a quantitative investigation into the effects of regulation on electricity rates (written with Claire Friedland). The study could not discover significant effects. Again, in the same year, in the course of reviewing a report on the regulation of the securities markets, Stigler compared the result of investing in new issues in the periods before and after the formation of the Securities and Exchange Commission. No important difference could be detected. In the years which have followed there has been a flood of similar studies investigating the effect of regulation on a wide range of economic activities. Some were directly influenced by Stigler's work. Others were no doubt independently conceived and executed. The results of these studies were uniformly depressing. Either, as in Stigler's studies, no effects of regulation could be detected or, when they could be discovered, the effects, on balance, made matters worse. With regulation, prices were higher, products were less well adapted to consumer demands, and competition was restrained.

About twenty years ago, most economists, under the influence of the writings of Pigou and others, thought of the government as standing ready to put things right whenever the results produced by the working of the market were in some respect defective. This led them to support extensive government regulation. The studies which have been made since then have shown how pernicious the results of regulation have commonly been. It has become difficult to argue with plausibility that the ills of society can be cured by government regulation, and the views of most economists have changed accordingly. Stigler has played a major part in bringing about this change of view.

Stigler has not been content merely to investigate the effects of regulation. He went on to inquire why the regulations are what they are, and this led him to analyze the workings of a political system. His approach was that of an economist, treating political behavior as utility-maximizing, political parties as firms supplying regulation, with what is supplied being what is wanted by those groups (or coalitions) which are able to outbid others in the political market. What each group will bid depends on the gain to be derived from the regulation less the costs of organizing for political action. In practice the highest bidder was very likely to be the industry regulated, and it is not therefore surprising to find that the regulation, as Stigler puts it, "is designed and operated primarily for its benefit." The examination of the interrelationships between political behavior and the economic system has been greatly helped through the creation by George Stigler in 1977 of the Center for the Study of the Economy and the State. It has resulted in the publication of many articles by talented economists who have held fellowships at the Center and has, in consequence, had a considerable impact on the views on regulation held by economists. Acceptance of Stigler's approach (and it, or some variant, has been adopted by many economists) will change the way economists look at regulation since it means, as the Swedish Academy pointed out, that "legislation is no longer an 'exogenous' force which affects the economy from the outside, but an 'endogenous' part of the economic system itself."

Just how much political behavior can be explained in this way seems to me problematical. As I watch people who are engaged in political activities, whether through voting in a parliamentary system or by taking part in political, including revolutionary, movements, supporting with enthusiasm policies which seem likely to greatly harm or even destroy the countries and perhaps themselves, I find it difficult to believe that such behavior is best described as rational utility-maximizing. However, that does not mean that in some areas, and particularly those of most interest to an economist, Stigler's approach may not have great explanatory power. And I think it does. The Swedish Academy spoke with caution about his analysis of the causes of regulation: "it is still too early to assess its ultimate scope." But, in any case, we should not assess the worth of an economist's contributions by deciding whether the profession will ultimately conclude that he is right. All theories will in time be superseded by others and all will, ultimately, come to be regarded as false (or incomplete or irrelevant). What really matters is whether the contribution moves the subject forward, makes us aware of possibilities previously neglected and opens up new and fruitful avenues of research. Stigler's contributions clearly meet this test.

I said at the beginning of this essay on George Stigler that because I knew him I understood his writings better. For those who do not know him there is a way to offset the disadvantage of not knowing him. In 1988 George Stigler's autobiography, *Memoirs of an Unregulated Economist,* was published. In it he tells the story of his intellectual development and sets out his main positions with clarity, with honesty, and with charm. Reading it is the next best thing to a personal acquaintance.

Marshall defined a classical economist as one who "by the form or the matter of his words or deeds . . . has stated or indicated architectonic ideas in thought or sentiment, which are in some degree his own, and which, once created, can never die but are an existing yeast ceaselessly working in the Cosmos." If we use Marshall's definition, George Stigler is a classical economist.

40

MARSHALL STONE

1 9 0 3 – 1 9 8 9

FELIX BROWDER

 AFTER ITS FOUNDATION as a distinguished department by E. H. Moore in the 1890s, the single most decisive event in the history of the department of mathematics at the University of Chicago was the assumption of its chairmanship by Marshall Harvey Stone in 1946. From a professorship at Harvard, Stone arrived in Chicago as the newly appointed Andrew MacLeish distinguished service professor of mathematics as well as chairman of the department. Within a year or two, he had transformed a department of dwindling prestige and vitality into what was once more the strongest mathematics department in the United States—and at that point probably in the world.

This remarkable transformation, which endowed the department with a continuing vitality during the trials of the following decades, is unparalleled, to my knowledge, in modern academic history for its speed and dramatic effect. This was no easy victory on the basis of great infusions of outside money for bringing in men and building research facilities. It was completely a triumph for Stone's sureness of judgment in men and his determination and strength of character in getting done what he knew had to be done.

Stone's account of the transformation that he brought about is unparalleled for its candor and its objectivity (despite the strong flavor of Stone's personality) and for its remarkably open presentation of the process by which academic decisions are reached and leadership exerted.

Within every academic institution, policy leadership follows two patterns. The most common pattern, which is the basis of the ongoing routine of the institution's existence, falls within the rational-bureaucratic mold (to

An earlier version of this essay appeared in the *University of Chicago Alumni Magazine* 69 (Fall 1976) and is used with permission.

use the classical terminology of Max Weber) in terms of rationalized general policies and procedures to be applied uniformly to an array of cases in the context of a balance of special interests and influences. The other pattern, which is less common, is that of charismatic leadership in which the individual judgment and personal qualities of the administrator play a fundamental role in both the choice and nature of the policy decisions which are made and in their acceptance by those who are affected by them. Stone's account gives us a picture of the most highly developed form of charismatic leadership, one which turned out to be enormously successful. What is more interesting about it is the question it raises about the role of charismatic leadership in the search for academic excellence.

To my knowledge, there is no case in which academic excellence in any reasonably high degree has been achieved and maintained without an infusion of charismatic leadership, either public or behind the scenes. Yet to an even greater degree, it has become increasingly incompatible with the growing pressures and struggles of interests intent on dominating the organized life of our universities.

When Marshall Harvey Stone arrived at the University in 1946 to play such a distinctive role, he was a relatively young man (forty-three) and a mathematician of great distinction and great reputation. He had spent most of his academic life at Harvard, getting his Ph.D. degree there in the late 1920s under the dominant personality of the Harvard department, George David Birkhoff, who had himself been a student of E. H. Moore at Chicago. Stone had done fundamental work in a number of widely known directions, in particular on the spectral theory of unbounded self-adjoint operators in Hilbert space and on the applications of the algebraic properties of Boolean algebras in the study of rings of continuous functions. He was an inner member of the country's mathematical establishment, having obtained a full professorship at Harvard as well as such honors as election to the National Academy of Sciences. He was profoundly involved in the growing trend toward putting mathematics research and education on an abstract or axiomatic foundation, and was sharply influenced by the efforts of the Bourbaki school in France in this direction, which achieved a major impact in the years after the end of the Second World War.

Most important of all, Stone was a man of forceful character and unquestioned integrity, with a strong insight into the mathematical quality of others.

Stone's fundamental achievement at Chicago was to bring together a faculty group of unprecedented quality. In the senior faculty he appointed

Marshall Stone, 1952

four very diverse men with widely different personal styles and mathematical tastes. The most important of these was undoubtedly André Weil, the dominant figure of the Bourbaki group, who was, then and now, one of the decisive tastemakers of the mathematical world, as well as a brilliant research mathematician in his own work.

S. S. Chern, who was to be the central figure of differential geometry in the world, was brought from the Princeton Institute for Advanced Study where he has found a haven after his departure from China.

Antoni Zygmund, who became the central figure of the American school of classical Fourier analysis, which he was to build up single-handed, came from the University of Pennsylvania.

Saunders MacLane, who had been Stone's colleague and sympathizer in the abstract program as applied in algebra, came from a professorship at Harvard.

Together with Adrian Albert, who had been Dickson's prize student at Chicago and a longtime member of the Chicago department, these men formed the central group of the new Stone department at the University.

To do full justice to the kind of revolution that Stone brought about in Chicago mathematics, one needs to perform the unedifying task of acknowledging the decay of the department in the late 1930s and early 1940s. The great prestige and intellectual vitality that had been created under the long reign of E. H. Moore as chairman had not been maintained after his retirement from the chairmanship at the end of the 1920s. His successors, G. A. Bliss and E. P. Lane, were not Moore's equals in either mathematical insight or standards. Especially under Bliss's regime, a strong tendency to inbreeding was in evidence, and as the great elder figures of the department died or retired they were not replaced by younger mathematicians of equal caliber. Some of the most promising of those who came into the department soon left. There was one principal exception: Adrian Albert. But despite his distinction as an algebraist in the Dickson tradition, Albert at that time had neither the influence nor the vision to bring about the kind of radical transformation that the department needed and that Stone brought about.

The insight that Stone reveals in his firsthand account of his great achievements and of how they were accomplished provides us once more with a dramatic vindication of the decisive importance of the special qualities of significant individuals as the major agents of the development of academic institutions. In academic terms, Marshall Stone served as a great revolutionary and a great traditionalist. The revolution he made is the only kind which has a permanent significance—a revolution that founds or renovates an intense and vital tradition.

REMINISCENCES OF MATHEMATICS AT CHICAGO

M A R S H A L L   S T O N E

· I ·

In 1946 I moved to the University of Chicago. An important reason for this move was the opportunity to participate in the rehabilitation of a mathematics department that had once had a brilliant role in American mathematics but had suffered a decline, accelerated by the Second World War. During the war, the activity of the department fell to a low level and its ranks were depleted by retirements and resignations. The administration may have welcomed some of these changes, because they removed persons who had opposed some of its policies. Be that as it may, the University resolved at the close of the war to rebuild the department.

The decision may have been influenced by the plans to create new institutes of physics, metallurgy, and biology on foundations laid by the University's role in the Manhattan Project. President Hutchins had seized the opportunity of retaining many of the atomic scientists brought to Chicago by this project, and had succeeded in making a series of brilliant appointments in physics, chemistry, and related fields. Something similar clearly needed to be done when the University started filling the vacancies that had accumulated in mathematics. Professors Dickson, Bliss, and Logsdon had all retired fairly recently, and Professors W. T. Reid and Sanger had resigned to take positions elsewhere. The five vacancies that had resulted offered a splendid challenge to anyone mindful of Chicago's great contribution in the past and desirous of ensuring its continuation in the future.

· II ·

When the University of Chicago was founded under the presidency of William Rainey Harper at the end of the nineteenth century, mathematics was encouraged and vigorously supported. Under the leadership of Eliakim Hastings Moore, Bolze, and Maschke it quickly became a brilliant center of mathematical study and research. Among its early students were such mathematicians as Leonard Dickson, Oswald Veblen, George Birkhoff, and R. L. Moore, destined to future positions of leadership in research and teaching. Some of the students remained in Chicago as members of the faculty. Dickson, Bliss, Lane, Reid, and Magnus Hestenes were among them.

Algebra, functional analysis, calculus of variations and projective differential geometry were fields in which Chicago developed special distinction. With the passage of time, retirements and new appointments had brought a much increased emphasis on the calculus of variations and a certain tendency to inbreeding. When such outstanding mathematicians as E. H. Moore and Wilczynski, a brilliant pioneer in projective differential geometry, retired from the department, replacements of comparable ability were not found. Thus in 1945 the situation was ripe for a revival.

A second, and perhaps even more important, reason for the move to Chicago was my conviction that the time was also ripe for a fundamental revision of graduate and undergraduate mathematical education.

The invitation to Chicago confronted me with a very difficult question: "Could the elaboration of a modernized curriculum be carried out more successfully at Harvard or at Chicago?"

When President Hutchins invited me to visit the University in the summer of 1945, it was with the purpose of interviewing me as a possible candidate for the deanship of the division of physical sciences. After two or three days of conferences with department heads, I was called to Mr. Hutchins's residence, where he announced that he would offer me not the deanship but a distinguished service professorship in the department of mathematics.

The negotiations over this offer occupied nearly a year, during which I sought the answer to the question with which it confronted me. It soon became clear that the situation at Harvard was not ready for the kind of change to which I hoped to dedicate my energies in the decade following the war. However, it was by no means clear that circumstances would be any more propitious at Chicago than they seemed to be at Harvard. In consulting some of my friends and colleagues, I was advised by the more astute among them to come to a clear understanding with the Chicago administration concerning its intentions.

There are those who believe that I went to Chicago to execute plans that the administration there already had in mind. Nothing could be farther from the truth. In fact, my negotiations were directed towards developing

detailed plans for reviving the Chicago department of mathematics and obtaining some kind of commitment from the administration to implement
them. Some of the best advice given me confirmed my own instinct that I
should not join the University of Chicago unless I were made chairman of
the department and thus given some measure of authority over its development. Earlier experiences had taught me that administrative promises of
wholehearted interest in academic improvements were too often untrust-
worthy. I therefore asked the University of Chicago to commit itself to the
development program that was under discussion, at least to the extent of
offering me the chairmanship.

This created a problem for the University, as the department had to be
consulted about the matter and it responded by voting unanimously that
Professor Lane should be retained in the office. As I was unwilling to move
merely on the basis of a promise to appoint me to the chairmanship at
some later time, the administration was brought around to arranging the
appointment, and I to accept it. Mr. Lane, a very fine gentleman in ever
sense of the word, never showed any resentment. Neither of us ever referred to the matter and he served as an active and loyal member of the
department until he retired several years later. I was very grateful to him
for the grace and selflessness he displayed in circumstances that might
have justified a quite different attitude.

Even though the University made no specific detailed commitments to
establish the program I had proposed during these year-long negotiations,
I was ready to accept the chairmanship as an earnest of forthcoming support. I felt confident that with some show of firmness on my part the program could be established. In this optimistic spirit I decided to go to
Chicago, despite the very generous terms on which Harvard wished to retain me.

· III ·

Regardless of what many seem to believe, rebuilding the Chicago department of mathematics was an uphill fight all the way. The University was
not about to implement the plans I had proposed in our negotiations,
without resisting and raising objections at every step. The department's
loyalty to Mr. Lane had the fortunate consequence for me that I felt released from any formal obligation to submit my recommendations to the
department for approval. Although I consulted my colleagues on occasion,
I became an autocrat in making recommendations. I like to think that I am
not by nature an autocrat, and that the later years of my chairmanship pro-

vided evidence of this belief. At the beginning, however, I took a strong line in what I was doing in order to make the department a truly great one.

The first recommendation sent up to the administration was to offer an appointment to Hassler Whitney. The suggestion was promptly rejected by Mr. Hutchins's second-in-command. It took some time to persuade the administration to reverse this action and to make an offer to Professor Whitney. When the offer was made, he declined it and remained at Harvard for a short time before moving to the Institute for Advanced Study.

The next offer I had in mind was one to André Weil. He was a somewhat controversial personality, and I found a good deal of hesitation, if not reluctance, on the part of the administration to accept my recommendation.

In fact, while the recommendation eventually received favorable treatment in principle, the administration made its offer with a substantial reduction in the salary that had been proposed; and I was forced to advise Professor Weil, who was then in Brazil, that the offer was not acceptable. When he declined the offer, I was in a position to take the matter up at the highest level. Though I had to go to an 8 A.M. appointment suffering from a fairly high fever, in order to discuss the appointment with Mr. Hutchins, I was rewarded by his willingness to renew the offer on the terms I had originally proposed. Professor Weil's acceptance of the improved offer was an important event in the history of the University of Chicago and the history of American mathematics.

My conversation with Mr. Hutchins brought me an unexpected bonus. At its conclusion he turned to me and asked, "When shall we invite Mr. MacLane?" I was happy to be able to reply, "Mr. Hutchins, I have been discussing the possibility with Saunders and believe that he would give favorable consideration to a good offer whenever you are ready to make it." That offer was made soon afterwards and was accepted.

There were other appointments, such as that of Professor Zygmund, that also went smoothly, but what would happen in any particular case was always unpredictable.

· IV ·

One explanation doubtless was to be found in the University's hand-to-mouth practice of budgeting. This would appear to have been the reason why one evening I was given indirect assurances from Mr. Hutchins that S. S. Chern would be offered a professorship, only to be informed by Vice-President Harrison the next morning that the offer would not be made.

Such casual, not to say arbitrary, treatment of a crucial recommendation naturally evoked a strong protest. In the presence of the dean of the division of the physical sciences, I told Mr. Harrison that if the appointment were not made, I would not be a candidate for reappointment as chairman when the three-year term expired. Some of my colleagues who were informed of the situation called on the dean a few hours later to associate themselves with the protest. Happily, the protest was successful, the offer was made to Professor Chern, and he accepted it. This was the stormiest incident in a stormy period. Fortunately, the period was a fairly short one, and at the roughest times Mr. Hutchins always backed me unreservedly.

As soon as the department had been brought up to strength by this series of new appointments, we could turn our attention to a thorough study of the curriculum and the requirement for higher degrees in mathematics. The group that was about to undertake the task of redesigning the department's work was magnificently equipped for what it had to do. It included, in alphabetical order, Adrian Albert, R. W. Barnard, Lawrence Graves, Paul Halmos, Magnus Hestenes, Irving Kaplansky, J. L. Kelley, E. P. Lane, Saunders MacLane, Otto Schilling, Irving Segal, M. H. Stone, André Weil, and Antoni Zygmund. Among them were great mathematicians, great teachers, and leading specialists in almost every branch of pure mathematics. Some were new to the University, others were familiar with its history and traditions. We were all resolved to make Chicago the leading center in mathematical research and education it had always aspired to be. We had to bring great patience and open minds to the time-consuming discussions that ranged from general principles to detailed mathematical questions. The presence of a separate and quite independent College mathematics staff did not relieve us of the obligation to establish a new undergraduate curriculum beside the new graduate program.

Two aims on which we came to early agreement were to make course requirements more flexible and to limit examination and other required tasks to those having some educational value.

The streamlined program of studies, the unusual distinction of the mathematics faculty, and a rich offering of courses and seminars have attracted many very promising young mathematicians to the University of Chicago ever since the late 1940s. The successful coordination of these factors was reinforced by the concentration of all departmental activities in Eckhart Hall, with its offices (for faculty and graduate students), classrooms, and library. As most members of the department lived near the University and generally spent their days in Eckhart, close contact between faculty and students was easily established and maintained. (This had been foreseen and planned for by Professor G. A. Bliss, when he counseled the architect engaged to build Eckhart Hall.) It was one of the reasons why the mathematical life at Chicago became so spontaneous and intense. By help-ing create conditions so favorable for such mathematical activity, Professor Bliss earned the eternal gratitude of his University and department. Any-one who reads the roster of Chicago doctorates since the later 1940s can-not but be impressed by the prominence and influence many of them have enjoyed in American—indeed in world—mathematics. It is probably fair to credit the Chicago program with an important role in stimulating and guiding the development of these mathematicians during a crucial phase of their careers. If this is so, the program must be considered as a highly effective one.

As I have described it, the Chicago program made one conspicuous omission: it provided no place for applied mathematics. During my corre-spondence of 1945–46 with the Chicago administration, I had insisted that applied mathematics should be a concern of the department, and I had outlined plans for professors of applied subjects. I had also hoped that it would be possible to bring about closer cooperation than had existed in the past between the departments of mathematics and physics.

Circumstances were unfavorable. The University felt little pressure to increase its offerings in applied mathematics. It had no engineering school, and rather recently had even rejected a bequest that would have endowed one. Several of its scientific departments offered courses in the applications of mathematics to specific fields such as biology, chemistry, and meteorology. The department of physics and the Fermi Institute had already worked out an entirely new program in physics and were in no mood to modify it in the light of subsequent changes that might take place ,in the mathematics department.

However, many students of physics elected advanced mathematics courses of potential interest for them—for example, those dealing with Hilbert space or operator theory, subjects prominently represented among the specialties cultivated in the mathematics department.

On the other hand, there was pressure for the creation of a department of statistics, exerted particularly by the economists of the Cowles Founda-tion. A committee was appointed to make recommendations to the admin-istration for the future of statistics, with Professor Allen Wallis, Professor Tjalling Koopmans, and myself as members. Its report led to the creation of a committee on statistics, Mr. Hutchins being firmly opposed to the pro-liferation of departments.

The committee enjoyed powers of appointment and eventually of rec-ommendation for higher degrees. It was housed in Eckhart and developed informal ties with the department of mathematics.

At a somewhat later time a similar committee was set up to bring the instruction in applied mathematics into focus by coordinating the courses offered in several different departments and eventually recommending higher degrees.

Long before that, however, the department of mathematics had sounded out the dean of the division, a physicist, about the possibility of a joint appointment for Freeman Dyson, a young English physicist then visit-ing the United States on a research grant. We had invited him to Chicago for lectures on some brilliant work in number theory that had marked him as a mathematician of unusual talent. We were impressed by his lectures and realized that he was well qualified to establish a much needed link between the two departments.

However, Dean Zachariasen quickly stifled our initiative with a simple question: "Who is Dyson?" (He was soon to become a permanent member of the Institute for Advanced Study.)

By 1952 I realized that it was time for the department of mathematics to be led by someone whose moves the administration had not learned to predict. It was also time for the department to increase its material support by entering into research contracts with the government.

Fortunately there were several colleagues who were more than quali-fied to take over. The two most conspicuous were Saunders MacLane and Adrian Albert. The choice fell first on Professor MacLane, who served for the next six years.

Under the strong leadership of these two gifted mathematicians and their younger successors, the department experienced many changes but flourished mightily and was able to maintain its acknowledged position at the top of American mathematics.

41

LEO STRAUSS

1899-1973

E D W A R D   C.   B A N F I E L D

 LEO STRAUSS was a great scholar and a great teacher who in his eighteen years from 1949 to 1967 as a professor of political science at the University of Chicago created a school of political philosophy which, nearly twenty years after his death, attracts adherents wherever serious study is done. He brought some of the best minds among the students of his and later days to devote themselves to the thought of the ancients, especially Aristotle and Plato, in the hope of turning political philosophy from the course it has followed since Machiavelli, one that has led, according to Strauss, to "the crisis of our time." His assault on the assumptions of modern thought established a lively new political discipline. This brought him fierce opposition, but not the contempt—he was too learned and too intelligent for that—of those in the tradition that he so vigorously attacked.

· I ·

I believe that I was in the first class that Strauss met at the University of Chicago. Sometimes I wonder what would have happened if I had not been there: could he have given a first lecture?

The classroom was on the third floor of Swift Hall. A few students were on hand to hear the new professor. Strauss was manifestly uneasy. He fiddled with an unlit cigarette; obviously he wanted very much to smoke. (This, I later learned, was not a matter of habit; he suffered from asthma, and medicated cigarettes, ten a day, had been prescribed to make breathing easier). But there was a sign on the wall: *No Smoking*. What to do? He could not bring himself to break the rule; as I was to learn, for him law was something almost sacred. (The epigraph of one of his books includes these words of Macaulay's: "The habit of breaking even an unreasonable law tends to make men altogether lawless. . . .")

Leo Strauss

I ended the impasse by taking the sign down. That action began a lasting friendship and, incidentally, put me in an Aristotelian category—that of the practical man—in which, when I read Aristotle, I was happy to be.

Although I attended many of Strauss's classes I was never properly speaking one of his students. At the time of that first class I was both an instructor in planning (that status was what made me bold enough to take the sign down) and a graduate student in political science; later I became a colleague of Strauss on permanent tenure. I mention this to make it clear that my credentials here are those of an admiring bystander, not a student of political philosophy.

· II ·

A brief biography of Strauss appears in a volume of essays edited by Joseph Cropsey (*Ancients and Moderns: Essays on the Tradition of Political Philosophy in Honor of Leo Strauss* [Basic Books, 1964]), and presented to Strauss in 1964 by former students and associates on his sixty-fifth birthday. I reproduce it here with a few supplementary observations, which are connected with the text of the biography by superscripts as if they were footnotes.

Leo Strauss was born in Kirchhain, Hessen, Germany, on September 20, 1899.[a] He was graduated from gymnasium in 1917 and entered into service in the German army.[b] After the war, he resumed his studies, concentrating on philosophy, mathematics, and natural science, in the universities of Marburg, Frankfurt am Main, Berlin and Hamburg. He took the degree of doctor of philosophy at Hamburg in 1921, his dissertation having the title *Das Erkenntnisproblem in der philosophischen Lehre Fr. H. Jacobis.*[c]

In the years between 1925 and 1932, he held the post of research assistant in the Academy of Jewish Research, Berlin, where he worked in the field of seventeenth-century biblical criticism with special emphasis on the doctrines of Spinoza.[d] He served also as co-editor of the philosophic writings of Moses Mendelssohn while the jubilee edition of Mendelssohn's works was in preparation.[e] In 1932 he left Germany for France as a fellow of the Rockefeller Foundation, an appointment that he held until 1934, by which time he had resettled in England.[f]

In 1938, Professor Strauss removed permanently to the United States and began his career at the Graduate Faculty of Political and Social Science of the New School for Social Research in New York.[g] He remained at the Graduate Faculty until 1949, when he joined the department of political science of the University of Chicago.[h] In 1959 he was designated Robert M.

Hutchins Distinguished Service professor of political science by the university, in which capacity he is now active.[i]

To this information, I add: In 1967 Strauss became professor emeritus but continued to teach at the University of Chicago until 1968. The following year he taught at Claremont Men's College; in 1969 he became the Scott Buchanan Distinguished Scholar-in-Residence at St. John's College, Annapolis, where he served until his death on October 18, 1973.[j]

a. Strauss's father, an orthodox Jew, was a prosperous grain merchant. Once, illustrating the thought that a man's demeanor may be an artifact of a bargaining strategy, Strauss told how as a boy he watched his father deal with the peasants who came to his office to sell their grain. The merchant held a newspaper before his face while a peasant stood first on one foot and then on the other before him. After a rather long wait he suddenly lowered the paper and announced the price in a take-it-or-leave-it tone.

b. Strauss, age sixteen, feigned appendicitis to escape conscription but, unfortunately for him, in the operating room a doctor found that his temperature was normal. He was sent to Belgium as an interpreter. In Chicago Mrs. Strauss kept a small framed sepia photograph of the soldier, looking like a nice boy, on display in their living room.

c. The dissertation, written under the direction of Ernst Cassirer was about an eighteenth-century Romantic philosopher named Jacobi. I have been told that neither Cassirer nor Strauss thought very highly of it.

d. At this time Strauss was an ardent Zionist. Later he decided that the state of Israel, although "a blessing for Jews everywhere," could never solve the Jewish problem because it presented itself as a product of the human mind rather than of the Jewish tradition, i.e., of divine revelation. Being Jewish was a central fact of life for Strauss. He once confided that he could never feel completely comfortable with a non-Jew.

e. From the time of his first work on Spinoza, Strauss wrote in 1962, "the theological-political problem has remained *the* theme of my investigations." The problem—the conflict between the claims of revelation (Jerusalem) and of reason (Athens)—could never be resolved. It was, however, "the secret of the vitality of Western civilization."

f. Strauss left Germany to study in France. Hitler's rise to power prevented his return.

His study of Spinoza led first to Hobbes and then to Maimonides and Farabi. Maimonides convinced Strauss that the great political philosophers had concealed their most important teachings both from fear of persecution and in the belief that certain truths would be harmful to society. The search for esoteric teachings became a hallmark of Strauss's method (when writing his book on Machiavelli, he employed a student assistant who had been an Army cryptographer). The inevitability of conflict between philosophy and society became a constant theme of his thought. It was by way of Spinoza and the others just mentioned that Strauss came to the ancients. Plato and Aristotle, he concluded, had sketched the best political order. It was one that could never be realized but might nevertheless be decisive in the choice between present alternatives.

When he embarked for England Strauss carried with him the German manuscript of his book on Hobbes. It was wrapped in waxed canvas so that, if the ship sank, what he had to say about Hobbes would survive. In England Strauss's eye was caught by a headline in *The Times:* "Public Opinion Favors. . . ." Reading, he found that it was actually the Archbishop of Canterbury who favored whatever it was. "Thank God," he said to himself. "At last I am in a country where public opinion and the opinion of the Archbishop of Canterbury are one and the same."

g. The thirty-nine-year-old Strauss began as a lecturer at the New School. After ten very productive years he became an associate professor.

h. Strauss was recommended to Chancellor Hutchins for appointment by Edward Shils, the chairman of a committee the other members of which were Theodore Schultz and Hans Morgenthau. Strauss had come to Shils's attention in 1936 when he read Strauss's dissertation.

i. That Strauss was "active" is an understatement. He was very busy both as a teacher and as a scholar. In his years at the University he published articles of lasting interest on many topics as well as six important books: *Persecution and the Art of Writing* (1952); *Natural Right and History* (1953); *Thoughts on Machiavelli* (1958); *What Is Political Philosophy?* (1959); *Liberalism Ancient and Modern* (1959); and *The City and Man* (1964). In 1963 he edited (with Joseph Cropsey) a textbook, *History of Political Philosophy,* intended to introduce undergraduates to political philosophy.

· III ·

Strauss presented himself not as a philosopher but as a scholar, an historian of political philosophy. So far as I know he never pronounced in his own name on a philosophical problem. Philosophy, he thought, is for great thinkers, who possess "all the excellences of which a man's mind is capable, to the highest degree"; they are so extremely rare that "it is a piece of good luck if there is a single one alive in one's time." Scholars have a place because the great thinkers disagree: the scholars make a kind of herbarium of the philosophers' doctrines and think them over.

j. Strauss was a productive scholar until the very day of his death. A collection of his *Studies in Platonic Political Philosophy,* edited by Thomas Pangle and published by the University of Chicago Press in 1983, contains a bibliography complete to that time.

· IV ·

Strauss began his career at the University of Chicago with relentless criticism of modernity, the central error of which, he taught, was the belief, which he traced to Machiavelli, that mankind can dispense with the notion of virtue. The distinction between the noble and the base, he contended, is rooted in nature. Its abolition is both undesirable and impossible; men cannot live without it.

In six Walgreen Foundation lectures given in October 1949 (published in 1953 as *Natural Right and History*) Strauss described the fundamental difference between classical and modern ideas of natural right, and he went on to argue that the rejection in our time of both classical and modern natural right rests on a denial of the very principles of rational knowledge. In the light of that rejection, principles, such as those of the Declaration of Independence, come to be interpreted as ideology or myth. This amounts to nihilism, and can lead only to disaster. Aware that there were many social scientists among his listeners, Strauss gave particular attention to the "fact-value" problem. Max Weber, whom he considered the greatest social scientist of the twentieth century, had not, he said, fully understood the problem. Weber's dictum "Follow God or the Devil" Strauss translated as "Strive resolutely for excellence or baseness." A political science that declares discussion of values out of bounds condemns itself to trivialities: it fiddles while Rome burns, he wrote. This is excused by two facts: "it does not know that it fiddles, and it does not know that Rome burns."

Strauss's attachment to the ancients was not at all antiquarian: he had no interest in the daily life of Athens and Jerusalem. The ancients mattered to him only for what the philosophers among them thought and that mattered only as it might help to answer the supreme question: What is the best life for man? "Our present predicament" was the incentive to the study of classical political philosophy; only by going outside the bounds of modern thought would it be possible to reach a "fresh understanding," one untainted by its own confusions. Strauss, it has been said, was more intent on challenging the moderns than on defending the ancients; the classics were for him a means of escaping the corruption of the moderns.

He thought that there is a natural hierarchy of ends—that some things are by nature more praiseworthy than others and that ordinary human understanding—common sense—makes people aware of the difference between the noble and the base. When in my capacity as a student of planning I put to him the problem of budgeting—given limited funds, which should get more, schools or hospitals?—he answered unhesitatingly "schools, because education is more important than health." Later, teasing me for my failure to appreciate the contribution that natural law made to the theory of planning, he remarked that being an honest man I must act on principles. "And natural law," he went on, "is nothing but an attempt to spell out the principles on which honest men act and have acted and will act as long as there are men."

There being unchangeable principles of right and wrong, there must also be a human nature that is essentially unchangeable. Strauss once told with delight of his conversation with a famous anthropologist who had just returned from a South American jungle. The natives, he told Strauss, had been very hospitable: why, a chief had offered to lend him the services of his wife. "Did you accept that amenity?" Strauss asked. "No," the believer in the cultural relativity of moral norms, replied, "I was afraid that he might be jealous."

If human nature is unchanging there cannot be progress in any final sense. It was evident to Strauss that men have not become wiser than they were in the past and that no amount of enlightenment can ever bridge the natural gulf between the wise and the unwise. What is called enlightenment, he wrote, would be better called obfuscation, for genuine knowledge becomes opinion, prejudice, or mere belief when it reaches the unwise.

It follows that no solution of the social problem is possible. The nature of man is such that some people will always have to be coerced and some will always coerce others whether they require it or not. Because desires are both limitless and conflicting, it is impossible that all can be satisfied. These are among the reasons why a perfect regime can exist only in thought. They are also reasons why the qualities of the gentleman and the statesman must be held in high esteem in any society that values freedom and justice.

The liberal ideal, Strauss pointed out, is fundamentally defective. A liberal state must recognize and protect a private sphere, but to do this it must permit and thus in fact foster whatever evils are of a "private" kind, for example racial discrimination. Insofar as it ceases to protect such evils, it destroys the private sphere and so ceases to be liberal.

For Strauss these were philosophic truths, not grounds to find fault with the society in which he lived. He taught the importance of "unhesitating loyalty to a decent constitution" and there was never any doubt that he considered the American Constitution to be a very decent one. Although he had a lively interest in public affairs (he once reproved the *National Review* for a comment he considered unfair to Israel and he once wrote the *New York Times* endorsing the candidacy of Richard Nixon), he never brought partisan issues into his classrooms. For him "the crisis of our time" was essentially a matter for philosophers to think about.

That he lived in an intellectual world that was foreign to most of his colleagues, a world that it was pointless for them to visit as tourists, meant that Strauss had remarkably little contact with other teachers at the University of Chicago. Some distinguished figures, aware that he was a man of superior talents, showed curiosity about him. Strauss was polite, but not forthcoming. His interest was in students, those whose minds were open and receptive.

· V ·

Strauss's success with students was phenomenal. Some of course had enough political philosophy after one class; among the others there may have been some who did not like Strauss, but if so they were very few. Most were charmed and many were enchanted. Here was a man who seemed to know all languages, ancient and modern; who seemed to have read everything worth reading, including—especially—what was between the lines, and to have remembered it all; who seemed to have no ego that required being shown off to a captive audience; who was wholly absorbed in making clear what was often very obscure. . . . How could a student, even one who had little taste or aptitude for political philosophy, fail to stand in awe of such a teacher?

Strauss spoke very softly, his voice hardly more than a murmur. (Was this to keep the students leaning forward in their chairs intent to hear— the effect of a teaching strategy, something like his father's bargaining strategy?) He expected his students to learn to read as he did, searching every line for exactly what was said and also for what was (deliberately?) unsaid, looking for passages in which an author contradicted himself and (because a great thinker would not contradict himself by accident) pondering the meaning of the contradiction. Students were free to question and to comment; if what one said was dull or irrelevant Strauss somehow managed to

convey that fact without injury to the student's self-esteem. "Always assume," he told a prospective teacher, "that there is one silent student in
your class who is by far superior to you in head and in heart." The teacher,
he meant, should have the highest opinion of his duty and responsibility
but not too high an opinion of his own importance.

Gentle as he was, a Strauss class could be perceived as terrifying. "Life-
threatening," according to James Q. Wilson, "because he clearly expected
so much, knew so much, and communicated so indirectly. I never worked
harder in my life than I did when preparing for his seminar a five-page
paper on Kant's 'Essay on Perpetual Peace.' I was trembling when I read it.
When I finished, Strauss asked a question with utmost politeness. I did not
understand a word of it; my mind went blank and my lips were silent.
'Thank you,' he said. I thought I had failed. I got an A."

It is only a seeming contradiction to say that a happy spirit prevailed in
Strauss's classes. Listening to a tape recording made in a seminar on Aristotle's *Rhetoric,* one hears frequent bursts of laughter from the class. Unfortunately the laughter drowns out whatever provoked it, but it is safe to
say that the jokes were not Aristotle's.

Every teacher has some students who, whether he encourages it or not,
become much attached to him and to his teachings. Strauss had many such,
all of them very gifted, and he certainly encouraged their attachment; close
association with "the puppies of his race"—i.e., those who had the potential to be serious thinkers—was an indispensable source of satisfaction to
him. Students who were devoted to what they thought Strauss stood for
were—and are—sometimes derided as adherents of a cult. In fact there
was no possibility of full agreement on what he stood for—unless it was
that dogma and piety have no place in philosophy!—and among his students there was—and is—nothing like unity. Nevertheless those who
wished to follow as closely as they could in his path found that they had a
special handicap to overcome; there are some political science departments which would not—and will not now—consider for an appointment
one who has been corrupted by the teachings of Strauss.

There were no women among the "puppies." A few women wanted to
be, but somehow they did not make it. Strauss did not dislike women; he
could be perfectly charming to them; my wife, for example, found it easy
to have serious conversation with him. But she did not aspire to be a political philosopher. Those who did aspire to that found him difficult.

Although only about twenty to twenty-five books were read in Strauss's
classes, he was not what some may think of as a "Great Books man." Liberal
education is "listening to the conversation among the greatest minds": ten

pages of Herodotus, he wrote, introduce us immeasurably better to the mysterious unity of oneness and variety in human things than many volumes written in the spirit predominant in our age. But herein lies a difficulty, for the greatest minds contradict each other regarding the most important things and who is competent to say which is right? This difficulty, Strauss said, is "so great as to seem to condemn liberal education as an absurdity."

Considering the excruciating care he took in studying the many great works of political philosophy, one wonders how he found time to read anything else. In fact from his early years he read widely in English literature; his book on Hobbes, written in German, makes footnote reference to Thackeray's *Vanity Fair* and *Henry Esmond*. He was very fond, his daughter writes, of the novels of Jane Austen and Disraeli; Macauley and Froude were great favorites as was Churchill's *Marlborough* and Cecil's *Melbourne*. "And, of course, murder mysteries."

· VI ·

Strauss's following continues to grow almost twenty years after his death. If one calls those who sat in his classes "first generation" followers and their students "second generation" followers, one may now speak of a third generation that is beginning to train a fourth. It is interesting that in each generation some Strauss followers have been stimulated by his example to strike out in a new direction and have done original and important studies of American political thought, especially that of the Founders and of Lincoln.

How is the remarkable persistence of Strauss's influence to be explained? In my opinion the answer is this. In his lectures and writings Strauss persistently raised questions of the utmost interest to thoughtful young minds. How ought men to live? He showed that modern thought, by seeing all ideas as mere products of history and custom, renders such questions essentially meaningless. And he demonstrated with his own work that it was worthwhile (even at the cost of learning Latin, Greek, Hebrew, Arabic, and perhaps a few other languages!) to search for ideas that may be true. Perhaps the Strauss following is evidence that men do by nature love the truth.

· VII ·

Socrates, Xenophon recorded, loved to dance alone in a room with seven empty couches. As far as I know Strauss never did anything like that. Occasionally, however, one could glimpse an inner Strauss who was very different from the outer one. He wished, he once said, that he could enter his classroom doing somersaults.

A search committee of the department interviewed for an assistant professorship a man who had just finished a term in a Federal penitentiary for armed robbery. Awaiting demobilization from the Navy, he had discovered that a gang of sailors was stealing narcotics from lifeboats for very profitable resale. In the face of their armed guard he had successfully robbed the robbers. ("A very respectable crime," Strauss remarked.) After lunch at the Faculty Club some of us walked with the candidate. "Who was that sitting opposite me?" he asked. "Leo Strauss." "He had that look in his eye—the look of a man who's planning a break." When we told Strauss of this conversation he was delighted; obviously he liked being seen as someone planning a break.

Strauss was a fan of the brave and virtuous sheriff, Matt Dillon, of the TV serial *Gunsmoke*. No doubt it pleased him to find the principles of natural right dramatically vindicated in the post-Nietzschean world. One suspects, however, that the professor who stood no more than five feet five and—outside of the world of ideas—was the most timid of men, fancied seeing himself in the boots of the strapping sheriff whose six-shooter was close at hand.

"Have lecture, will travel," Strauss used to say, parodying the line of another TV gunslinger.

How much of this side of Strauss was created for the entertainment of his "puppies" and how much was a manifestation of his basic personality or (to use his word) soul? He must have been aware that there were many collectors of Strauss anecdotes; did he sometimes yield to a desire to give them satisfaction?

His utter inability to cope with the practical side of things was notorious. Once a student found him in distress in his office; the desk lamp had gone out; Strauss could not see to work. The student changed the bulb and all was well. "Mr. ——," beamed Strauss (he addressed everyone formally), "You are an electrical genius!" I find it hard to believe that the great man did not know how to change a light bulb, but I doubt that he meant to embroider his myth; most likely he simply liked having people do things for him.

That may explain the business about the light bulb. But how about the library book? It had been charged out to Strauss from the library in Swift Hall; when he got a recall notice he gave the book to a student who offered to return it. A day or two later a librarian called to ask for the book. Strauss was upset. He called the student. What had he done with the book? Returned it to the library. Had he actually handed it to the librarian? Yes. Strauss deliberated. "How do you know that she was not an imposter?" he asked.

Things like that left one wondering whether he was joking. Sense of humor, he once said, is a form of the sense of the ridiculous. "The ridiculous," he went on, "is primarily the strange—the deviation which is innocuous, e.g., to grow a beard on one side of the face. Sense of humor, I think, consists in being open to the ridiculous strangeness of the customary or the normal—of what we ordinarily take very seriously." This suggests to me that Strauss the pixie and Strauss the philosopher saw the same reality and saw it not altogether differently. It may be worth noting in this connection that his jokes were hilarious in their unfunniness; his witticisms, by contrast, were memorable. When a colleague who had been complimented by Chancellor Hutchins asked Strauss if he thought Hutchins really meant what he said, Strauss assured him that he did. "Mr. Hutchins," he said "is much too rude a man to tell a lie."

· VIII ·

I hope enough has been said to convey some sense of the special greatness of Strauss as a teacher, scholar, and human being. Directly and through his writing he enabled many people to see more clearly what it means to be fully human. That such a man flourished for so many years in the United States and at the University of Chicago must be both a source of pride and grounds for hope. To paraphrase a few words of what he said in eulogy of Sir Winston Churchill (whom he thought the greatest man of this century), Strauss's life reminds us to see things as they are—to see them in their greatness as well as their misery, in their brilliance as well as their mediocrity.

42

OTTO STRUVE

1 8 9 7 – 1 9 6 3

S . C H A N D R A S E K H A R

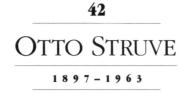THE TWO DOMINANT figures in the development of astronomy and astrophysics at the University of Chicago during the past one hundred years are George Ellery Hale and Otto Struve. Their unique positions in the astronomy of their time and their splendid accomplishments as scientists and as administrators provided for the University a solid foundation on which the future of the department of astronomy could be securely based.

On the occasion of the fiftieth anniversary of the Yerkes Observatory, Struve recounted the "story" of the observatory at a staff meeting on March 25, 1947 (still vivid in the writer's memory). A fuller version of the masterly survey that Struve presented at that meeting was later published in *Popular Astronomy*—a journal that ceased publication not long thereafter. There can be no account of the first fifty years of astronomy and astrophysics at this University that is at once more authentic or more authoritative than Struve's. For this reason, it has seemed appropriate to include Struve's "Story," in a somewhat abridged form, in this volume.

THE STORY OF AN OBSERVATORY

O T T O   S T R U V E

· I ·

During the summer of 1892 a young man of twenty-four was attending a meeting of the American Association for the Advancement of Science at

This account by Otto Struve first appeared in *Popular Astronomy* 55 (1947).

OTTO STRUVE

Rochester, New York. One hot evening a group of delegates were sitting in front of the hotel, trying to keep cool. The young man was in a receptive mood and his ears readily caught a tale that the famous Cambridge telescope builder, Alvan G. Clark, was telling to a group about him. It seems that in 1889, when the Lick Observatory was beginning to create its worldwide reputation, the people of Southern California, then in the uproar of a land boom, felt that their fair territory might advantageously profit by the example of James Lick. So a worthy citizen offered to a local educational institution land then valued at fifty thousand dollars. This was ample warrant, in the judgment of the hour, for ordering a pair of 40-inch glass discs, which in the course of three years had been successfully made by M. Mantois in Paris. But unfortunately the land bubble had meanwhile burst, the gift was worthless, and Mantois was vainly seeking payment of the sixteen thousand dollars at which the discs were valued. Here was a great opportunity, said Clark, for someone to get a large telescope without loss of time. He had tested the glass and found it perfect, and nothing would please him more than to figure a 40-inch objective.

The name of the young man was George Ellery Hale, and this description of the origin of the Yerkes Observatory is quoted, almost verbatim, from an unpublished manuscript which he communicated to the American Astronomical Society. . . .

Mr. Hale had left the Yerkes Observatory long before I arrived in Williams Bay. . . . In 1892 Hale was filled with the exuberance of youth. He had visually observed the solar prominences with a spectroscope at the Kenwood Observatory and he was filled with a simple, but very strong ambition: he must find a way to photograph the prominences without an eclipse. This ambition was gratified when he invented the spectroheliograph. With this new instrument he discovered the large mottled areas in the light of the calcium lines H and K which we call flocculi, and which represent, essentially, those solar prominences which are seen projected upon the disc of the sun. He keenly felt the inadequacy for further study of the flocculi and prominences of his own 12-inch telescope at Kenwood and he determined that he must have a larger telescope.

The opportunity came soon after he had overheard the conversation of Alvan Clark at Rochester. At the suggestion of Mr. Charles Hutchinson of Chicago, the same man who had done so much for Chicago's Art Institute, and for the University of Chicago, Mr. Hale approached Mr. Charles T. Yerkes, who had expressed an interest in the new and struggling educational venture which was the University of Chicago under President Harper.

Mr. Yerkes invited the latter, together with Mr. Hale, to call upon him in his downtown Chicago office, and before the interview was over a telegram had been drafted to Mr. Clark to come to Chicago with a contract for the two lenses.

At first Mr. Yerkes consented only to purchase the objective. There were no funds for the mounting, the dome, or the building. Mr. Harper was reluctant to divert any of the University's limited funds for the observatory, and Mr. Yerkes undoubtedly thought that Mr. Rockefeller's millions should build, equip, and maintain the observatory he had initiated. After several long years of nerve-racking uncertainty this financial problem was solved through the further generosity of Mr. Yerkes. Plans were drawn up in 1894 and construction of the building, as we now know it, was begun in 1895.

In the preceding year Mr. Hale had given careful attention to the choice of a suitable site for the great telescope. The extreme care with which he approached this question is evident in an article in the *Astrophysical Journal* for 1897 in which he summarized the principal questions, the answers by leading American and foreign astronomers, and his own final conclusions. . . . The final choice fell upon a location at Williams Bay, Wisconsin, on the northern shore of Lake Geneva. The opinion of Professor Burnham, who had taken an active part in choosing the site of the Lick Observatory, was taken as final.

In the meantime the Warner and Swasey Company had completed the mounting and exhibited it at the Columbian Exposition at Chicago in 1893. The grinding and polishing of the objective took much longer. It was only in October of 1895 that the two lenses were finished and tested by Mr. Keeler and Mr. Hale. The quality of the star images was found to be excellent. Then there followed a long delay in building the observatory. Finally, on May 19, 1897, the lenses arrived in Williams Bay and two days later, after they had been mounted in the great tube, the first observations were made by Hale, Barnard, and Ellerman. Although the seeing was not very good, many objects were well seen, notably the ring nebula in Lyra, the globular star cluster in Hercules, and the dumbbell nebula. The great light-gathering power of the telescope was well illustrated by the fact that Professor Barnard saw these objects better than he had ever seen them at Mount Hamilton. He also succeeded in finding a new optical companion of Vega which had not been seen elsewhere.

Then in the morning of May 29, only a little more than one week after the beginning of the observations, a cable slipped from its fastening and the entire south side of the rising floor crashed to the ground from a height of forty-five feet. Fortunately, there were no observers on the floor when the accident occurred. Mr. Barnard and Mr. Ellerman, who had been working throughout the preceding night, had gone home at dawn. The telescope must have been severely jarred during the collapse of the floor. It took a long time to reach the objective—at first there were thought to be indications of fine fissures in the glass. Only later was it established that a fine cobweb built in the large tube by a spider had given rise to the peculiar design which looked like fissures. The lens was undamaged. But it took several months for the Warner and Swasey Company to rebuild the floor, and the dedication, at first scheduled for October 1, had to be postponed until October 18.

· II ·

Although Mr. Hale's own work depended primarily upon the completion of the 40-inch refractor, he had from the very beginning intended to add to the equipment a reflecting telescope of 60-inch aperture. A glass disc was purchased by Mr. Hale's father, and optical work on the mirror was soon started in the optical shop of the Yerkes Observatory by G. W. Ritchey. The gift of the mirror by the elder Hale was conditioned upon the University of Chicago being able to raise the necessary funds for the mounting and dome. However, it soon became evident that the University was in no position to undertake additional financial burdens, and Mr. Hale began to look elsewhere for support. His published and unpublished statements, as well as his letters, show a growing concern over financial matters. The observatory had started functioning with an almost ridiculously small staff. . . .

Because of the heavy financial restrictions, Mr. Hale was obliged to guarantee that the operating expenses would not exceed a very small sum during the first year, and this meant that additional money to pay the salaries had to be raised from other sources. In this emergency the Carnegie Institution of Washington came to the rescue. A special grant from the same source brought to the Yerkes Observatory Mr. Frank Schlesinger, whose work on the photographic determination of stellar distances became one of the principal contributions to astronomy of the Yerkes Observatory.

· III ·

If we should now try to evaluate the results obtained at the Yerkes Observatory during the first half of its life we should probably agree that while Hale furnished the stimulus and paved the way, it was the work of others that actually brought in the most important results. In order of significance, as they impress me today, these results are the following:

1. Barnard's photographic work with portrait lenses which culminated in his own and in Ross's magnificent atlases of the Milky Way.

2. Schlesinger's work on stellar parallax and its continuation by Mitchell, Slocum, Fox, Lee, Moffitt and many others.

3. Frost's and Adams's measurements of radial velocities of B-type stars, the discovery of the K-effect, and the recognition of the slow peculiar motions of the helium stars.

4. Burnham's, and later Van Biesbroeck's, systematic visual observations of double stars.

5. A. A. Michelson's experiments with an interferometer (first conducted by him at the Lick Observatory, where the satellites of Jupiter were measured, and then continued at Yerkes, where double stars were measured) and later, his measurement, with Henry G. Gale, of the earth-tides. The pits in which the ends of the long pipes of water were brought in contact with the interferometer, were located north of the observatory and east of the main drive. For many years they stood abandoned and their cave-like interiors fascinated the minds of a younger generation of astronomers. When I arrived in Williams Bay the darkrooms were still full of exposed film showing the regular pattern of the interferometer as the shape of the earth underwent its tidal deformations. The theoretical determination of the rigidity of the earth was carried out by Dr. F. R. Moulton, professor of theoretical astronomy at the University of Chicago, and the whole project may well be regarded as one of the finest examples of cooperative research in America.

6. Nichols's first successful measurement in 1899 of the heat radiation of Arcturus and Vega, with a radiometer mounted in the heliostat room of the Yerkes Observatory.

7. Ritchey's superb photographs of nebulae, clusters, and other objects, with the 24-inch reflector and the 40-inch refractor.

These accomplishments, and many others, at once created for the Yerkes Observatory an enviable reputation. But from the vantage point of fifty years later we cannot escape the conclusion that Hale's own tremendous energy was being dissipated among innumerable projects and that his own scientific brilliance was being expended in administrative functions.

Illness in his family added to the complications, and Hale was forced to spend the winter of 1903–4 in California. Professor Frost was appointed acting director, and the director's residence at Williams Bay was leased by President Harper and his family. Mr. Harper was a great organizer and a great scholar, but it seems incongruous that so soon after the dedication of the observatory the principal residence on the hill and the principal office in the main building should be devoted to the study of linguistics.

It is not clear to me whether Hale expected to return permanently to Williams Bay. The Carnegie Institution had provided him with funds for a temporary expedition to Mount Wilson for solar research, and gradually the expedition began to take on a permanent character. There was a long and somewhat bitter exchange of letters between him and Mr. Harper. But in the end Mr. Hale remained at Mount Wilson and took with him some of the ablest members of the Yerkes staff, notably Adams, Ellerman, Pease, and Ritchey. . . . Mr. Frost was appointed director in 1905, but for many years afterwards Mr. Hale was considered a nonresident professor of astrophysics in the University of Chicago.

The period of Mr. Frost's administration, 1905–32, I can best describe as a period of retrenchment. The loss of the staff was a serious blow, but the gradual transfer of the financial support by the Carnegie Institution from Yerkes to Mount Wilson was even worse. The University, under Presidents Judson and Burton, was dedicated to a program of rigid economy.

· IV ·

In the fall of 1931 Professor Frost underwent a serious operation at Billings Hospital in Chicago, and during his absence I was appointed assistant director. I had only a short time before that been promoted to an associate professorship and was therefore greatly surprised when a letter from Dean Henry G. Gale informed me of this action on the part of the University's Board of Trustees.

By the time I arrived at Williams Bay we were hopelessly out-distanced in astrophysics. Our old spectrograph—the gift of Miss Catherine Bruce in 1901—was equipped with badly annealed prisms of a notoriously opaque and dense Jena flint glass. We had only one moderately satisfactory camera which we exposed óne hour to obtain the spectrum of a 5th magnitude star. With similar dispersion and similar plates we now expose about 15 or 20 seconds at the McDonald Observatory. Our effective limit for spectrographic work was magnitude 5.5, while with the 36-inch Lick refractor equally good radial-velocity measurements could be made to magnitude 8, and Mount Wilson could easily go beyond magnitude 10. In other fields of astronomy we were also surpassed by others.

The 40-inch telescope remained supreme in double-star work and the observatory continued to make important contributions in the wide-angle photography of the Milky Way. In the former, our frequent bad seeing at night was a disadvantage. In the latter, requirements of high transparency made it necessary for the observers to secure a large part of their material at Mount Wilson or Flagstaff. I remember one cloudy night, many years ago, when Mr. Van Biesbroeck and I were waiting in our office for the sky to clear. We were talking about the advantages of large reflecting telescopes for many types of research, and decided to look up convenient places where the climate would be more favorable than at Williams Bay. Reference to the Weather Bureau's reports and to the timetables indicated that a location in the Texas Panhandle, near Amarillo, would be within easy reach of Chicago and would give a vastly larger percentage of clear sky than we normally have in the region around Chicago.

At the request of the University administration I prepared two plans of development. I explained that my own work was concerned with the physical study of the stars by means of their spectra and that progress in this field seemed to depend upon being able to record and explain the many different shapes (or contours) of the spectral lines in celestial sources. For this I needed an instrument of great light-gathering power —a 60-inch reflector might do—equipped with an optically perfect spectrograph, capable of recording on photographic emulsions of great contrast (and therefore of low sensitivity) high-dispersion spectra in different wave lengths.

We were then in the worst stages of the great economic depression of the early thirties, and a few attempts on the part of the University authorities to find a donor in Chicago were unavailing. Then, one day, I happened to remember that some years previously a wealthy banker at Paris, Texas, had left his entire fortune of more than $1 million to the State University at Austin for the purpose of constructing and maintaining a large observatory. Mr. W. J. McDonald, it appeared, had always been interested in natural science, including astronomy.

The University of Texas had no department of astronomy and it was not known whether plans for the observatory were then under consideration. President Hutchins decided to find out. He placed a long-distance call to President H. Y. Benedict at Austin and within a few minutes the two presidents had agreed to appoint me director of both observatories, Yerkes at Williams Bay, and McDonald, which then existed only in our imagination.

The negotiations between the two universities were quickly concluded: Texas would build the telescope and the entire physical plant and would pay annually a fixed amount towards the operating expenses; Chicago would furnish the entire staff and pay the remainder of the operating expenses. I visited Austin on a beautiful, sunny April day, with the bluebonnets in full glory. Dr. Benedict, himself trained as an astronomer many years ago at Virginia, took me on a short drive to show me one or two proposed sites for the observatory in the vicinity of Austin. I remember that for once in my life I regretted that the sky was clear: if it had been cloudy it would have been easier to convince the observatory committee that Austin was no place for a large observatory. Fortunately, Dr. Benedict supported my views, as did several members of the group, among whom I remember with gratitude and affection the vice-president, Dr. J. W. Calhoun, and Professors M. B. Porter and J. M. Kuehne. We finally decided that we would equip a small expedition to locate a suitable site, preferably within the borders of Texas, but if necessary in some other state, or even south of the Rio Grande. In the early summer of 1932 C. T. Elvey and T. G. Mehlin were sent in a specially equipped truck to Texas and points beyond in order to obtain some preliminary observations of seeing. Later, I went to Texas myself and chose our present location on what is now called Mount Locke and what then went under the more poetic name U-Up-And-Down Mountain (from the brand of a neighboring ranch).

The many problems which arose in connection with the construction of the 82-inch telescope are so vividly in my mind that I could fill volumes. Our negotiations with the Warner and Swasey Company lasted for nearly a year, with almost weekly conferences in Williams Bay, Cleveland, or Austin. The outcome remained the same: there was not enough money. Then, after we had finally found a solution for the financial problem (by omitting the office building and placing all darkrooms and offices in the dome) there was a change in the state administration at Austin, and one of the new regents of the University of Texas went to Washington and was told by some "well-wisher" that our design, which was based upon that of the Victoria 72-inch, was completely wrong because supposedly the Victoria telescope had so much flexure that it could not be used at zenith distances greater than 30°.

The mechanical construction of piers, dome, and mounting under the able engineering direction of E. P. Burrell of Warner and Swasey made rapid progress. We had transported the old Yerkes 12-inch refractor to Mount Locke, and Elvey and I used it extensively as a guiding device for a small f/1 Schmidt camera which a Chicago amateur had made for us and which we were using to record the polarization of the light of several reflection nebulae. We also obtained numerous photographs of nebulae with red and violet filters and these gave the first indication that the reflecting particles of nebulae have high albedos with scattering functions of the highly forward-throwing type.

While we were working without dome or shelter, we could see the silvery structure of the dome a short distance above us take shape. The parabolizing of the mirror took six weary years. Mr. C. A. R. Lundin, who as a young man had assisted his father and Alvan Clark in the polishing of the Yerkes 40-inch and whose father had also made the famous Pulkovo 30-inch, was employed by Warner and Swasey. He ranks as one of the most expert opticians in the world, and the fine performance of the mirror, when it was tested by Dr. J. S. Plaskett, gave support to this claim. But the years of waiting were nerve-racking. . . .

Finally, after many disappointing tests, and after enlisting the assistance of Messrs. Van Biesbroeck, Kuiper, and Pearson, we decided that the mirror was ready. It was "chroluminized" by Robley C. Williams at Cleveland, and was installed at the observatory early in March 1939. The first night-tests were conducted by Van Biesbroeck and Kuiper. The first scientific result was an ultraviolet spectrum of the expanding shell of 17 Leporis on March 5. . . . Mr. Kuiper continued observations throughout the remainder of March and April and secured many important results before May 5, the date set for the official dedication. We had several hundred guests and a large scientific colloquium with papers by Milne, Shapley, Hubble, Baade, Trumpler, Bok, Ort, Mrs. Gaposchkin, and many others. The Warner and Swasey Company acted as the host and furnished among other luxuries a rodeo and a complete chuck-wagon dinner for several hundred persons.

· V ·

A few years after my appointment as director, in about 1935, I attended an annual dinner given by the trustees of the University of Chicago for members of the faculty. As I was passing through the receiving line President Hutchins came up to me and asked me to visit him soon at his office. When I did so, a few weeks later, he asked me whether I had given some thought to the question of increasing and improving the staff of the astronomy department and he outlined to me his own policy of building up weak departments through the appointment of only relatively young first-class research workers. Were there such workers available in astronomy? I replied that I could name three or four immediately: Kuiper,

Chandrasekhar, Bengt Strömgren, and one or two others. Mr. Hutchins questioned the wisdom of inviting a mature man of forty, expressing a definite preference for men of about thirty-five, or younger. This was the beginning of a new policy of staff-building which has been at the bottom of most of our organizational changes. I continued going to the president's office and discussing with Mr. Hutchins various questions of personnel. His attitude was always favorable if I could describe a candidate as the best worker in his field. Really good men are so difficult to find that Mr. Hutchins invariably offered to appoint those who merited the designation, irrespective of whether or not their work fitted into the established program of the department: if it did not fit, then the program had to be modified. Questions of salary, equipment, etc., were also secondary in his mind.

. . . Upon my arrival in Williams Bay in 1921 Professor Frost had assigned to me the measurement and reduction of thousands of spectrograms obtained with the Bruce spectrograph for the determination of the radial velocities of the A- and B-type stars. My studies in Russia had been interrupted by four years of military service in World War I, and in consequence I had had only a superficial course in astrophysics (under the late B. P. Gerasimovič). The only kind of spectrum I had an acquaintance with was that of the sun as seen through a small prism spectroscope. My impression of the Fraunhofer absorption lines was of countless narrow and sharply-defined black lines whose shapes or contours had no interest because they were more or less faithful images of the shape of the slit. I was greatly disappointed when I found that more than one-half of the stars I was to measure had a few hazy, broad, and extremely ill-defined features in place of lines, and for some time it was difficult for me to understand how one could measure such features at all. Since then my principal aim has been to explain the great variety of contours of stellar absorption and emission lines, and in a very large measure progress in this field has been an accomplishment of the Yerkes Observatory. Problems of stellar rotation, the Stark effect, turbulence, and collisional broadening, one after the other, held the spotlight. It became apparent that ordinary photographic emulsions did not possess enough contrast to bring out the slight shadings and differences in nuance between different lines, so that the slow Eastman Process emulsion had to be employed despite a factor of almost 20 in the exposure times. This made it impossible at Yerkes to observe with adequate dispersion any but the very brightest stars. A large reflector was urgently needed, and the construction of the 82-inch at McDonald gave me adequate light-gathering power for all those problems in stellar spectroscopy which I had contemplated. I have estimated that with the 82-inch reflector I quite regularly secured in one month of concentrated work a larger amount of observational material, and material of far better quality, than I had secured with the 40- inch in twenty years of work! . . .

The completion of the McDonald Observatory marked the fulfillment of the first task I had set myself in 1932. The other task, equally important and in some respects more difficult, was to reorganize the staff of the department. When I was appointed director the reputation of the institution was upheld by Mr. Van Biesbroeck and Mr. Ross. The addition of Chandrasekhar to the staff gave us our first strong representation in the field of theoretical astrophysics. His influence has expanded enormously during the past ten years, and his recent promotion to a distinguished service professorship in the University of Chicago serves to underline the importance which his work is accorded in our present organization.

The formulation of a plan of research is perhaps the most difficult task of an observatory administrator. In our case this plan was not entirely free; it was constrained by two outside conditions: we were committed to Mr. Hutchins's program of faculty-building, and we were limited in our equipment to instruments of the type of the 82-inch reflector and the 40-inch refractor. . . .

Astronomy is at a threshold. If we continue along the old lines laid out fifty years ago, or even only a short fifteen years ago, we shall rapidly lose our place in science.

After careful consideration of the many questions involved, I decided, a few months ago, to ask the University of Chicago to relieve me of the responsibility of the directorship of the two observatories.

AFTERWORD

S. CHANDRASEKHAR

Struve did not continue very long at the University of Chicago after he relinquished his directorship of the Yerkes and McDonald Observatories in 1947. He resigned in 1950 to become the chairman of the department of astronomy at the University of California at Berkeley. In 1960 he left Berkeley to become the director of the National Radio Observatory at Green Bank (West Virginia), but only for two years. In 1962 he returned to Berkeley as a professor of astronomy while holding visiting professorships at the California Institute of Technology in Pasadena and at the Institute for Advanced Study in Princeton. He died on April 6, 1963.

Soon after his death, I wrote a short notice in the February 1964 issue of the *Astrophysical Journal* recalling his years as the managing editor of the *Journal*. I append that notice below as a renewal of the warm regard I have always had for him.

"Otto Struve, past president of the American Astronomical Society, of the Astronomical Society of the Pacific, and of the International Astronomical Union, died on April 6, 1963. Struve's immense and illustrious services to astronomy have rarely been equaled; and few astronomers have received such exceptional and universal recognition.

"The *Astrophysical Journal* had particular cause to be grateful to Dr. Otto Struve: it was his faith which sustained the *Journal* during a most difficult period (which included the war years 1939–1945). In a letter written only a few months before he died he wrote that at the time (July 1, 1932) he received his appointment as the director of the Yerkes Observatory, 'Dean Henry G. Gale wanted to close the *Astrophysical Journal;* but I told him that in my opinion the continuation of the *Astrophysical Journal* was more important than the continuation of the Yerkes Observatory.' That was the measure of Struve's faith in the purposes of this *Journal;* but for that faith this *Journal* could hardly have survived and grown to its present firm base in the entire astronomy of this country.

"Struve's active editorship of this *Journal* continued unbroken from 1932 to 1947 (vols. 76–105); however, the files in the *Journal* office indicate that his period of active participation in the editing of the *Journal* dates from 1927. During the period of Struve's editorship, the *Journal* developed from a medium for the publication, principally, of the researches at the Mount Wilson and the Yerkes Observatories to its beginnings as a national journal. Struve had taken many of the initial steps toward the achievement of the national goal; but the goal was accomplished only in 1952 when the *Journal* became one of the official organs of the American Astronomical Society.

"It would be difficult even to begin listing the principal milestones in Struve's long and heroic career; suffice it, then, to say that in this *Journal* alone Struve published 220 papers and a total of 2,390 pages."

43

HAROLD CLAYTON UREY

1893–1981

CLYDE A. HUTCHISON JR.

DURING THE YEARS of the Second World War the University of Chicago, because of its group of distinguished physicists and chemists, became one of the principal centers for basic scientific research related to the development of the atomic bomb. During this period there was gathered together in the Metallurgical Laboratory, established at the University for this work, a group of the world's most outstanding scientists in various fields of physics, chemistry, and related sciences. In the spring of 1945 Arthur H. Compton, William H. Zachariasen, and other members of the faculties of physics and chemistry of the prewar years began a consideration of the possibility of keeping together as University faculty members some of these eminent scientists from elsewhere who were working in the Metallurgical Laboratory and in other laboratories associated with Chicago in the wartime work. The fruition of these ideas, with the formation of three research institutes at the University of Chicago in late 1945, brought into the faculty from other institutions a group of established world leaders in scientific fields and also a group of younger persons who had been affiliated with the wartime atomic bomb projects.

One of these institutes was the Institute for Nuclear Studies (now the Enrico Fermi Institute). Although the aims of the institute were quite explicitly and narrowly defined in the university catalogue for 1946–47 to be the provision of facilities for research in nuclear chemistry and nuclear physics, the institute developed immediately into an interdisciplinary department embracing a very broad spectrum of scientific interests and fields. In fact a list of permanent members of the institute published in June 1946 included the names of persons with the following stated fields of interest: statistical mechanics of gases and liquids, lattice energies of ionic crystals, electron affinities, properties of the inorganic hydrides, surface chemistry, crystal structure, the theory of diffraction, and the nature of cosmic rays, in addition to those whose fields of study lay close to the catalogue's stated aims. Among the younger members' interests were included the nature and origin of meteorites, radiochemistry, electronic computers, and magnetic properties of the heaviest elements.

· I ·

Of all the original members of the Institute for Nuclear Studies, none better represented this broad interdisciplinary character than did Harold Clayton Urey, who in 1945 came from Columbia University to become Distinguished Service Professor of Chemistry and later the Martin H. Ryerson Distinguished Service Professor of Chemistry in the institute and in the Department of Chemistry. In 1934 he had at age forty-one been awarded the Nobel Prize in chemistry for his discovery of the heavy isotope of hydrogen, which he named deuterium. During the war years, in view of the fact that he was at the time the world leader in the field of separation of isotopes, he had been selected to head the work on isotope separation the headquarters of which were at Columbia University where he had been a professor since 1929. He had broad responsibilities for separation of the fissionable uranium isotope, ^{235}U, from ordinary naturally occurring uranium by both diffusion and centrifugation processes. He also supervised other separation work, involving other methods and other isotopes related to the atomic bomb project.

Although in 1939 when the atomic bomb work began, Harold Urey was deeply involved in the theory and practice of isotope separation processes, he had by no means been working in that field of activity since the beginning of his scientific career, nor was he to remain in that field after the war. He had, after a relatively late entrance into graduate school at Berkeley in 1921 at the age of twenty eight, already by 1932 made seminal contributions in several fields of physics and chemistry.

As a graduate student in Berkeley he was the first to suggest and show that the rotational contributions to heat capacities and entropies of molecular gases can be predicted from optical spectroscopic data, and his calculations opened a field that spanned both physics and chemistry and provided methods used extensively by both himself and others in the following years. In the year following completion of his doctoral research he worked in the laboratory of Niels Bohr in Copenhagen. This resulted in several publications on the quantum mechanics of atoms. He next taught at

HAROLD CLAYTON UREY, 1955

The Johns Hopkins University and while continuing his interest in the application of molecular spectroscopy to chemistry was led to a study in the field of chemical reaction kinetics, producing publications in 1928 and the succeeding years on the mechanism of homogeneous gas reactions. In 1929 he left Hopkins to take up an appointment at Columbia University. There his interest in molecular spectroscopy and isotope effects in the band spectra of molecules led him to consideration of regularities in the building of the naturally occurring nuclei from the more fundamental particles, at that time believed to be electrons and protons. He posted on the wall of his laboratory a chart with number of electrons as abscissa and number of protons as ordinate and saw that the known nuclei of low atomic number fitted on straight line segments. From a study of this chart he predicted the natural occurrence of an isotope of hydrogen with mass two. Such observations, together with the discovery of the isotopes of oxygen which led to a disagreement between the mass-spectrometrically and chemically determined relative atomic weights of hydrogen and oxygen obtained at that time, led Urey to undertake a diligent search for this heavy hydrogen. He applied his knowledge of calculation of thermodynamic properties to a prediction of the relative vapor pressures of ordinary and heavy liquid hydrogen and predicted that he could concentrate the predicted naturally occurring heavy hydrogen by distillation of the liquid. Together with F. G. Brickwedde of the National Bureau of Standards and G. M. Murphy of Columbia University he distilled liquid hydrogen, and in 1931 the ^2H isotope was identified spectroscopically in the residue. It was this discovery for which he received the Nobel Prize of 1934. This remarkable accomplishment led quickly to far-reaching research developments in chemistry, physics, biology, astronomy, and many other scientific fields.

Urey then became intensely interested in the general problems of isotope separation and enrichment. His own immediately following experimental and theoretical work provided enriched isotopes of hydrogen, oxygen, nitrogen, and carbon for researchers in many laboratories of many different types throughout the world as well as for many applications in his own laboratory at Columbia University.

From the very beginning in 1921 it had been clear that he had an insatiable scientific curiosity and that he followed fearlessly into whatever new field it led him. He never recognized the classical boundaries between various fields of scientific endeavor. He never allowed himself to become tied to a particular experimental technique or methodology. Throughout his career his greatest interest was in the exploration of new fields and not in consolidating and tying up the loose ends of a field in which he had already made the pioneering advances. Cyril Smith has described him as an explorer in the realms of science and not interested in the establishing of colonies. Urey himself said, "I remember when I was a child in Indiana, I put my nose between the pickets, looked out, and wondered what was on the other side of the fence. That was the beginning. I've had my nose to the picket fence ever since, wondering what was on the other side."

Thus Harold Urey was the prototypical member of our Institute for Nuclear Studies. His influence as a founding member, his entry into an entirely new field of research on arriving here in late 1945, his continuing development of new fields of research interest, and his encouragement of the younger members as they entered research fields with the great diversity of subject matter described above, were a major stimulus for the form which this interdisciplinary research department of the University developed in those earliest days.

· II ·

A major influence on Urey's catholicity of scientific interests was undoubtedly his early experience as a graduate student at Berkeley. After his graduation from high school and three months at Earlham College in Indiana, Harold became a teacher in country schools, first in Indiana, then in Montana. Feeling dissatisfied with the prospect of spending the rest of his life as a schoolteacher, in 1914 at age twenty-one he entered, as an undergraduate, the University of Montana, where he decided to major in psychology. But soon his attention turned to zoology, and his very first research effort was a study of the protozoa in a backwater of the Missoula River. His interest in the origins of life, a field in which he was to make a major contribution much later at the University of Chicago, originated with that earliest research. He graduated from the University of Montana in 1917, and until the end of the First World War worked at the Barrett Chemical Company in Philadelphia. So it was that after returning at the end of the war to the University of Montana as instructor in chemistry for two years and realizing that for university teaching he would need a doctorate, he entered the University of California at Berkeley as a graduate student at the relatively advanced age of twenty-eight. There he was in the department of chemistry, whose chairman was professor Gilbert N. Lewis, a world leader in the field of physical chemistry. Urey often said that the particular influence of that department that stood out in his memory was the departmental colloquium presided over by Professor Lewis and attended by all of the professors and all of the graduate students. On Harold's seventieth birthday, in a volume of scientific papers that was written for the occasion by former students, colleagues, and associates, Professor Joel Hildebrand of Berkeley wrote as follows concerning those colloquia. "The staff sat about a long table, Lewis in 'the chair' at one end, near the blackboard. Graduate students sat in two rows surrounding those at the table. Lewis would say, 'Mr. Blank, will you tell us about your work?' Mr. Blank might be a member of the faculty or a graduate student; his research might be concerned with physical, inorganic, organic, analytical, or applied chemistry. No one could claim, as was often the case in Germany at the turn of the century, 'Das ist aber *mein* Gebiet'. Any hot problem was fair game. . . . There were very few graduate courses; the main reliance was upon research, upon seminars concerned with 'hot' subjects, and upon personal effort on the part of the student. No obligation was felt to pass on to students what was already available in the literature." Urey himself wrote, many years later, "Lewis had a very broad definition of what chemistry was. He said *anything* interesting was chemistry. Moreover he didn't believe that you learned things necessarily in courses. For example I never troubled to go down to the Registrar's office to find out what grades I got in my courses. I don't know to this day what they were."

· III ·

The Thursday afternoon seminars that Urey, Mayer, and Libby, the Berkeley chemistry alumni at the Institute, initiated in 1946 closely followed the pattern of the Berkeley colloquium described by Professor Hildebrand. However it was often the case that Lewis's counterpart, Joe Mayer, had no opportunity to call on anyone to talk because there were so many eager to tell us about their most recent interests. No speaker or program was announced beforehand. The discussion was entirely spontaneous and informal. The blackboard, not slides and transparencies, was used. Sometimes there were two or three at the blackboard commenting on each other's equations or graphs. During the years the topics discussed ranged from the latest results of work in theoretical and experimental nuclear physics to the theory of nitrogen intoxication during scuba diving. And as the early years passed, on many Thursday afternoons Harold arrived early so as to get a first chance to tell us about his recent thoughts on his measurements of the temperatures of the oceans in early geologic times, the early reducing atmosphere of the earth and its relation to the origin of life, the cosmic abundances of the elements and the chemical composition of the solar system, the composition of Mars, the origin of the planets, the origin of continents and mountains, the origin and age of meteorites, and the moon's surface features and internal structure. Questioning and critical discussion were engaged in by the members of the audience regardless of their personal fields of interest. I still remember well Fermi's active participation in Harold's discussion of mountain formation one Thursday afternoon, and I recall Harold's surprise and dismay at having his punch line stolen by Fermi's interjection of an estimate of the time required for the formation of the Rocky Mountains, based on what Harold had already said.

One memorable seminar discussion given by Harold occurred early in the history of Thursday afternoons at the time when he had devised a method for learning the temperatures of the oceans in early periods of the earth's history. He had shown in the middle 1930s, when he became interested in separation of the naturally occurring isotopes of the elements, that when two different oxygen-containing compounds are in chemical equilibrium with each other the relative abundances of ^{16}O and ^{18}O isotopes are different in the two and the size of the difference depends on the temperature at which they are in equilibrium. In fact he had been, with his student, David Rittenberg, shortly after the discovery of deuterium, the first to calculate such isotopic equilibria from spectroscopic data. Here at the University in 1946, for a time his interest in such problems returned and he published in 1947 his monumental paper in this field, "The thermodynamic properties of isotopic substances." In the course of this work it had occurred to him that inasmuch as calcium carbonate occurred in the shell structures of many marine organisms, if he recovered the oxygen of this calcite as carbon dioxide and determined the relative amounts of the oxygen isotopes in this gas, he would be able to tell the temperature of the sea at the time the calcium carbonate had appeared in the organism in equilibrium with the sea water. He felt he had good reason to believe that isotopic abundances in sea water had not changed appreciably since the Cambrian period and that the comparison of the calcite abundances with the present-day sea water abundances, together with the known changes in equilibrium abundances with temperature, would tell him the temperature of the sea in which the organism had grown. On the Thursday afternoon in question, he had just completed a most interesting study. Cyril Smith, then director of another of the three research institutes, the Institute for the Study of Metals (the third was the Institute for Radiobiology), had while visiting the Isle of Skye collected the fossil of a cephalopod of the Upper Cretaceous period and presented it to Harold. This organism, a belemnite, built a central rod-like support made of calcium carbonate in the form of massive single calcite crystals, very compact, and ideal for maintaining the temperature record of the sea in which the belemnite deposited the calcite. This central rod in circular cross section shows annual growth rings from center to outside surface. Harold and his students had successively sampled the calcite oxygen across the growth rings from birth to death and from the isotopic ratios could trace the summer-to-winter temperatures of the Upper Cretaceous sea in which the belemnite lived eighty million years ago. As he plotted on the blackboard the oxygen isotopic abundance ratio against distance of growth from the center, the life history of this creature appeared before us. Having started life in the spring of its first year, it lived and flourished through four summers but during its fourth and very cold winter had a difficult time and died two or three months before its fourth birthday anniversary. Shortly after this seminar, this belemnite's obituary was published by Urey, Lowenstam, Epstein, and McKinney in the *Bulletin* of the Geological Society of America.

The study of paleotemperatures was the first of a postwar succession of varying researches which engaged Harold Urey's attention until the end of his life. He seemed to have been flooded with new ideas and new interests during those early days of the Research Institutes. In 1949 there was offered a lecture course entitled "Chemistry in Nature" described by Professor Gerald Wasserberg as "a course on the origin of the solar system given by Professor Harrison S. Brown of the Institute for Nuclear Studies and starring Harold C. Urey." Harold wrote concerning that course, "My first lecture was to be on the heat balance of the earth; and when finally duty's insistent small voice became strident I turned to Louis B. Slichter's paper on this subject, with the idea of making a few routine notes that might fulfil the minimum requirements of a lecture on the matter. But the temperature of the earth appeared to be rising, not falling, which was a new idea to me. This led to a consideration of the curious fractionation of the elements which must have occurred during the formation of the earth. One fascinating subject after another came to my attention, and for two years I have thought about questions relating to the origin of the earth for an appreciable portion of my waking hours, and have found the subject one of the most interesting that has ever occupied me."

This line of thought led him on beyond the earth to the entire solar system. An interest in meteorites, first displayed in a publication of 1934, was reawakened at this time. His fascination with questions concerning chemical processes that had occurred during meteorite formation led him to engage with Hans Suess on the development of tables of the natural abundances of the elements in our solar system that were very influential for future theories of the origins of the elements. In the spring of 1951 his interests in these matters were summarized in his Silliman lectures at Yale University. In the preface of the book which was a publication of these lectures, and which was dedicated to his wife, Frieda, he wrote, "Perhaps it will surprise readers of this volume that a physical chemist should undertake to prepare a book on 'The Planets—Their Origin and Development.' And indeed it astonished me that I or anyone of similar training and experience should be able to say anything on the subject. As time has gone on my surprise has disappeared. . . . The chemical data must be understood in terms of physical facts and physical theory as well as in terms of geological and geophysical evidence, and all must fit into astronomical evidence and theory. However, as astronomers have had undisputed possession of the field since ancient times, except for some interference from religious leaders and religious writings, some discussion from other sciences may prove useful. In most scientific work it is necessary to have some acquaintance with neighboring scientific fields. In the case of the origin of planetary systems, the study of each new phase of the problem calls for learning another complete science." It was certainly the thought expressed in this last quoted sentence that appealed to and challenged Harold Urey to continue efforts along the lines we have just been discussing and has resulted in his being referred to as the founder of the field of cosmochemistry. Concerning his book, Cohen, Runcorn, Suess, and Thode, in the *Biographical Memoirs of the Royal Society of London,* have said, "its emphasis was not on explaining facts but on defining questions. The answers to his questions were often sketchy, perhaps inaccurate, but what Urey intended to do was to illustrate a new approach rather than present new and definitive conclusions."

One of the more important questions in his book concerned the nature of the early atmosphere of the earth. He concluded that whereas the present atmosphere is an oxidizing one consisting of oxygen and nitrogen, the early atmosphere had been reducing, being composed mainly of hydrogen, methane, ammonia, and water. In a seminar at which beginning graduate students were present, Urey suggested that under ultraviolet radiation from the sun and with electrically charged particles generated by lightning discharges in the atmosphere, the chemical processes that would have occurred would have produced the prebiotic molecules that would be necessary for, and lead to the development of, living organisms. After this talk, one of the students, Stanley Miller, went to Professor Urey with a request that he might study this problem for a doctoral dissertation. Within a short time Miller had shown that amino acids, essential constituents for living organisms and other organic compounds, were formed when, in the laboratory, he passed electrical discharges through mixtures of hydrogen, methane, ammonia, and water. This experiment opened an entirely new avenue of research into the evolution of life on this planet. This was the first time that conditions believed to be those of the ancient earth had been reproduced in the laboratory, and these conditions were shown to produce the chemicals that are required for the occurrence of life.

· IV ·

As the first decade of Urey's stay in Chicago drew to an end, his interests in the meteorites and the planets had led him to a topic that continued to be one of his favorites for the rest of his life, namely the surface and internal structure of the moon. Cyril Smith has stated, in his reminiscences concerning Urey, that at a social event in the Smith home Harold observed there a book on the moon, picked it up, became engrossed in reading it during the party, and that this probably started his particular interest in the moon. One book that he read early in the development of his interest in the earth's moon was *The Face of the Moon* by Ralph Baldwin. Urey gave Baldwin credit in many of his publications for the interest on his part that had been generated by Baldwin's argument that the craters of the moon were the result of meteoritic impact. He concluded that these craters were very old and represented the final stage of the accretion process of the kind that had formed all the planets. This was a main reason for the great interest in the moon. In describing his work in this field, his colleagues in La Jolla, Arnold, Miller, and Zimm, have spoken of "his love affair with the moon, as a Rosetta Stone for the solar system." He placed great emphasis on the known departure of the shape of the moon from an equilibrium hydrostatic form. He believed that the moon had formed cold and remained cold and that the shape could be explained as a statistical consequence of the accretion process and was not the result of tides in a molten moon as many had supposed. Any melting observed on the moon's surface he believed to be explainable as a result of the huge amounts of energy released upon meteoric impact.

Much later, after Urey had left Chicago, President Kennedy announced the goal of landing men on the moon. Urey was quick to point out the importance of having a serious scientific objective in this effort. He was invited to serve on a committee to consider the space program but he did not assume any leading administrative role in this project. He wrote, "I have carefully avoided any contact with administrative work since 1945." Very early in the development of national interest in space science, Urey's great ability through many contacts, in particular as a member of the Space Science Board, to stimulate the interest of the people in charge of the money for, and with the power to initiate, lunar exploration, played a major role in the inclusion of a strong lunar science component in the United States national space science program. Homer E. Newell of the National Aeronautics and Space Administration has written, "Urey felt that the Moon might well be a primitive body, formed in the early days of the solar system. If this were so, the record of its early history, preserved on the surface of the Moon, would provide invaluable clues to the origin and evolution of other bodies of the solar system as well. This was a powerful argument for including the Moon in the space science program. The persuasiveness of the argument carried the day at each stage within NASA, in the Administration, and finally in Congress, and in due course investigation of the Moon was formally and officially a part of the NASA space science program." Professors Arnold and Wasserburg and others who had been associated with him and strongly influenced by him here in Chicago and later in La Jolla contributed greatly to guiding the scientific space effort.

The first data from the moon showed that it had been subjected to melting and that the huge impact basins had been filled with lava from the melted interior. Harold was disappointed to learn that his ideas on this subject had been wrong, but he was quite capable of changing his mind and continuing with vigor his lunar studies. One contribution of note that he made at this time stemmed from his disagreement, while here, with Professor Kuiper's theory of the melting of the moon having been caused by radioactive decay of uranium, thorium, and potassium. Defending his cold-moon ideas, Urey correctly showed that Kuiper's theory could not be correct because the half-lives of these elements are too long. After the moon landing and after it was clear that there had been melting, Urey was puzzled but then suggested that decay of the aluminum nucleus, ^{26}Al, was the probable energy source. Evidence for this was subsequently obtained by Wasserburg, who had been closely associated with him in Chicago.

Harold Urey spent the 1956–57 academic year as Eastman Professor at Oxford University. There he lectured on the origins of the solar system and of living organisms on the earth. In 1958 he would become sixty-five years of age, at that time the retirement age at the University of Chicago. He and his wife, Frieda, began to think about making another change upon retirement. He said, "I guess we are rolling stones. Some people spend their whole life at one university. I have wandered many places, partly from necessity, but mostly by choice."

· V ·

In 1958 Urey became professor of chemistry-at-large at the University of California. Roger Revelle had earlier told Harold of the formation of a new University of California in San Diego to be associated with the Scripps Institution of Oceanography in La Jolla. Urey was very intrigued by this new venture and even more so when he learned that a number of present and former colleagues would be there, Joe and Maria Mayer of the Institute for Nuclear Studies, Hans Suess, with whom he had worked here on the abundances of the elements, and Harmon Craig, who had been involved closely with him in the paleotemperature work. As Charles Perrin of Scripps has said, La Jolla was not a "retirement home" chosen by Harold Urey. His work continued with unabated intensity and he published 105 scientific papers, 47 of them concerned with his study of the moon, in the twenty-three remaining years of his life after leaving Chicago.

Urey's scientific achievements were extraordinarily widely recognized and honored. He was awarded some thirty medals, awards, and prizes including the Nobel Prize, the Davy medal of the Royal Society of London, the gold medal of the Royal Astronomical Society of London, and in this country the Franklin, Priestley, and Willard Gibbs medals. He was the recipient of twenty-four honorary degrees, including those from Oxford, Athens, McGill, Princeton, Columbia, Yale, Berkeley and our own university. He was elected to foreign memberships in the Royal Society of London and the Royal Swedish Academy, and to membership in numerous learned societies and organizations both in this country and abroad.

Thus far we have been discussing Harold Urey, the scientist. We have recalled his scientific achievements on the way from country schoolteacher to becoming one of the world's most eminent scientists. But he is equally well remembered by all who knew him inside and outside the academic community as a person intensely interested in the well-being of his fellow man. This concern was displayed not only for his students, research associates, and faculty colleagues, but also with respect to social and political problems of national and international importance. He had an intense interest in such problems, some of them closely related to the wartime work in which he had been involved. He devoted the same concentrated effort and careful thought to their possible solutions as he did to the solving of the problems of his scientific research. Having concluded that certain actions were required, he then, with the same vigor and determination that were characteristic of his scientific work, would bend every effort toward furthering these actions.

He had while at Columbia University been chairman of the University Federation for Democracy and Intellectual Freedom and a champion of Loyalist Spain. As early in 1932 he espoused Clarence Streit's Atlantic Union plan for a world governmental federation. He became greatly disturbed by the rise of Hitler and the progress of Nazism. He became active in securing posts for refugee scientists and in extending his hospitality to them when they arrived in this country. In her book, *Atoms in the Family,* Laura Fermi recounts how Harold and his wife, Frieda, helped her and her husband, Enrico, become their neighbors in Leonia, New Jersey, when the Fermis arrived at Columbia University from Italy.

At the end of the war, by then at the University of Chicago, Urey became extremely concerned about the potential use of the atomic bombs in whose creation he had played such an important role. His interest in world government, begun at Columbia University, returned with renewed rigor. In an article entitled "The Atom and Humanity," written at the University of Chicago for *Science,* in November 1945, after a careful consideration of many suggested possibilities for control of atomic energy developments and avoidance of world conflict resulting from the availability of the bomb, he wrote, "We are inevitably led to the conclusion that a superior world government of some kind, possessing adequate power to maintain the peace and with the various divisions of the world relatively disarmed, is the only way out."

At this time Urey was very active in lecturing widely on the problems created by nuclear energy developments. He opposed the passage of the May-Johnson bill, which he feared would permit military control of peacetime activities in the field of nuclear energy. He strongly supported the eventual McMahon bill in its final form and was a leader in the fight for its passage.

His doubts concerning the justice of the executions of Ethel and Julius Rosenberg for atomic energy secrecy violations received national attention. His views on this matter were not ones that were popular with large sections of the American public. He was called before the House Un-American Activities Committee. He wrote, "I doubted seriously if justice had been done—I was only interested in one question. Had they indeed violated the laws of the United States and had justice been done? It is my firm conviction that justice was not done in that case."

It is remarkable that during all this "extracurricular" activity there was no abatement in his ever-expanding and changing scientific interests or any diminishing of his production of new and significant research developments.

Harold was greatly concerned with the welfare of his scientific colleagues, students, and research associates. He was always interested in his students' development of their own independent scientific careers. He was concerned that they be established in suitable posts upon completion of their researches in his laboratory and was active in locating suitable academic and other positions for them. He was diligent in seeing that they received appropriate credit for their work under his supervision. The first paper on the establishment of the Urey paleotemperature scale was published under the sole authorship of his student, John McCrea. Likewise, at Urey's insistence, the sole author of the first article on the Urey-Miller theory and experiment on the origin of terrestrial life was Stanley Miller, his student.

Harold Urey's intense devotion to, and enthusiasm for, his work, and his power of concentration on whatever task he might be engaged in at the moment, are legendary among his former students and postdoctoral research associates. This intensity and concentration were often mistaken for absentmindedness and sometimes for lack of appreciation of his colleagues' and students' efforts. Often in scientific conversation, in his office or in the laboratory, I would see that he had completely lost consciousness of my presence because something said had triggered a train of thought that was occupying his full attention. I would stop in mid-sentence. Silence would prevail for a period, sometimes a rather long one it seemed, and then, with the problem, whatever it was, solved, "Oh yes! You were saying?" All of his students have had this same experience on many occasions. His concentration on his research and his fantastic enthusiasm for the problems on which he was working were very contagious. As a result, many of his students have gone on to make notable contributions in scientific fields.

One day a few hours after he had left the University for the airport, while engaged in concentrated thought on a research problem of great current interest, my phone rang. It was Harold asking whether my key would admit me to his office. It did, and he told me he was at La Guardia airport, and a piece of paper on his desk, which he had forgotten to take with him, would say what he was to do next. I found who it was he was to meet, and where, and he thanked me with, "That's exactly what I needed to know."

On another occasion a European scientist arrived at Urey's office with samples of ice cores from deep in the Greenland ice cap which had required a considerable effort for their procurement. Harold had expressed great interest in the possibility of obtaining such water samples and had pointed out their importance at a time when he was very interested in paleotemperatures and in obtaining oxygen isotope abundance ratios in water samples from widely distributed places on the earth's surface. But the obtaining of these samples had required quite a period of time and by the time that task had been completed Urey's interests had shifted to a fascination with the moon. So the visitor found him seated in his office in front of the large photograph of the moon before which it was then his wont to sit for long hours in contemplation of its detailed surface features, lost in his thoughts concerning the origins of the craters and related problems. The visitor, who had clearly disturbed Harold's train of thought, had to remind him of the request for the Greenland samples, which had been totally forgotten. But then Harold in his customary pleasant and hospitable manner, thanked the visitor, asked his secretary to put the samples in the laboratory, seated the visitor beside him before the moon, and without further conversation, other than "I would like to point out this most interesting feature of the surface," delivered a fascinating discussion of the origin of that satellite.

Although this absolute absorption in his work sometimes affected adversely persons in situations such as that of the scientist just mentioned, it could on occasion also be a source of very pleasant interactions with others. I remember meeting Russell Meigs, a fellow of Balliol, on the Broad Street in Oxford not long after Urey had assumed his Eastman professorship in Balliol in 1956. I asked Meigs how the fellows were enjoying Harold's presence among them and he said, "He's just wonderful. It's so pleasant to have an American visitor who is so interested in the weather on Mars that he, unlike most of you who complain so much about it, takes no notice of the weather in England."

· VI ·

Harold was very fond of, and very proud of, his family. While at The Johns Hopkins University he had visited his mother, then living in Seattle. While on that visit he renewed his acquaintance with a friend from University of Montana days and she introduced him to her younger sister, Frieda Daum, who was working as a bacteriologist. As Roger Revelle of La Jolla has described it, "Harold Urey was never thought of as an outdoor man but he spent the next two weeks hiking in the Cascade Mountains with Frieda. Within a year they were married and their careers as mountaineers were ended. After that Harold's outdoor activity was confined to his garden." There were three daughters and a son in the family. At the time Harold was notified of the Nobel award, Frieda was expecting their third child. In order to be with Frieda he did not attend the December 10 ceremonies in Stockholm. Mary Alice was born on December 2. Frieda and Harold sailed to Stockholm the following February and attended a special award ceremony. In reminiscences presented by F. G. Brickwedde, who was, with G. M. Murphy, a coauthor of the original announcement of the deuterium discovery, he told how Urey had shared the prize money he received on that occasion with the other two authors.

The friendliness and hospitality of Harold and Frieda brought people together socially in a way that created a most pleasant academic atmosphere and added greatly to the enjoyment of life at the University by the families of the members of Harold's department and Institute. The evenings in their home on Forty-ninth Street on the occasions of the departmental potluck dinners, the parties to bid farewell and bon voyage to those colleagues departing for a sabbatical leave, and the celebrations of special events of many kinds have been remembered by many very nostalgically. This hospitality was also extended to postdoctoral fellows and graduate students. One particular Thanksgiving dinner will be well remembered by the postdoctoral fellows and their wives who were the guests. Harold had invited them the week before just as he became involved in an exciting research problem. As a result the guests learned from Frieda after their arrival that Harold had forgotten to notify her of his issuance of the invitation until a few hours before. But Frieda with her usual grace and most charming hospitality, and Harold's last-minute assistance, provided a wonderful feast.

Harold Urey was an educator in the undergraduate and graduate classroom, in the research laboratory, and on the public platform. He came to our University at a time when many, including himself, felt that this country had temporarily abandoned both basic research and the training of a new generation of scientists in the course of intensive war research. Soon after his arrival here, at a time when many were worried about how to keep the "secret" of the atomic bomb and how to prevent dominance of the Soviet Union, he wrote apropos of these problems. "The real problem that faces the country is a long term one. It is a problem of the proper education and inspiration of our youth." He approached with great zest the teaching of first-year undergraduate chemistry courses. Although he often assumed a broader knowledge and greater understanding than was warranted, his obvious and contagious enthusiasm for science inspired his young listeners. In a panel discussion on "Science in Higher Education," Joel Hildebrand said, "Survey courses about science given by logicians or historians are no substitute for the competence and contagious enthusiasm of an actively working scientist. It is important for young persons to be exposed to such men in their early, formative years. If I were a student today, and were permitted to listen to Harold Urey, I think I would want to start pell-mell for belemnites or the moon." Along with Enrico Fermi, Harold joined in the continuation of the Chicago tradition of undergraduate contact with the great leaders in their fields of study. His interest in "inspiration of our youth" even extended to the public grade schools. He had with his own hands constructed a globe showing the moon's surface and Frieda has written, "He enjoyed nothing so much as taking his moonglobe to a fifth grade class in the La Jolla schools and telling the students about the moon and planets".

· VII ·

The abolition of the boundaries between scientific disciplines was a basic tenet of Urey's philosophy. His own academic career, outlined above, was exemplary in this respect. Concerning his stay at Bohr's Institute for Theoretical Physics he said, "Bohr didn't know I was a chemist. He thought I was a physicist." He claimed he had learned most of his physics in Copenhagen restaurants while dining with H. A. Kramers. In 1933, Harold founded the interdisciplinary *Journal of Chemical Physics,* which provided an appropriate medium for the publication of the already large body of work that bridged the traditional fields of chemistry and physics. Harold became the first editor of that journal. Professor James Arnold of the University of California has written, "The first years's issues, under his editorship, possibly contained more epochal papers than have ever appeared in any other scientific journal in a single year." When Urey came to Chicago from Columbia University, Joseph E. Mayer, who was then editor of the journal, came at the same time from Columbia to the Institute for Nuclear Studies. The editorship has to this day remained in the hands of members of the University of Chicago.

Urey may be considered to have established at least four fields of scientific research: stable isotope chemistry, including isotope geochemistry, geochronology, and isotope separation; paleotemperature measurements; cosmochemistry; and origin of terrestrial life. Karl Cohen, world authority on isotope separation processes, has said, "Urey's pioneering work underlies every method of isotope separation successfully deployed on a large scale, for every element from hydrogen to uranium." Craig, Miller, and Wasserburg have written, "The measurement of the paleotemperatures of the ancient oceans stands as one of the great developments of the earth sciences; a truly remarkable scientific and intellectual achievement." Cohen, Runcorn, Suess, and Thode in their biographical memoir, speaking of Harold as "the founder of the field of cosmochemistry," wrote, "Urey, undoubtedly, was the first who rigorously defined this field by its problems and by asking precise questions." His ideas concerning the primordial atmosphere and the beginning of life on earth were experimentally demonstrated by his student, Stanley Miller, and opened up a completely new approach to the study of the origin of life on this planet. The last three of these epochal achievements were initiated and developed by him at our University during the thirteen years he was here, during a period of time and in an academic environment that he found most conducive to giving free rein to his wide-ranging interests and flow of new ideas. His vigorous and concentrated pursuit of these researches, and his enthusiastic interactions with those around him concerning his latest ideas, continued in La Jolla. In 1979, two years before his death at eighty-six, he published the article "The Origin of the Earth" in *Life: Origin and Evolution*. Some ten years after he retired from our University, he was asked by Professor Jim Arnold in La Jolla, "Harold, why do you put in so many hours at work?" Jim says he replied, "Well, you know I'm not on tenure anymore."

Harold Urey's decision to come to Chicago at the time of the formation of the new research institutes was indeed a fortunate one for us. His major role in the development of an atmosphere of interdisciplinary interaction unequaled at any other school; his inspiration of students at all levels, undergraduate, graduate, and postdoctoral, and on all academic colleagues; his intense, concentrated, and productive devotion to his scientific work; and his parallel involvement in considerations of, and efforts toward, possible solutions of social and political problems, have indeed left indelible marks on this University.

44

JACOB VINER

1 8 9 2 – 1 9 7 0

P A U L   A.   S A M U E L S O N

 JACOB VINER spent more than half of a long academic career at the University of Chicago. It was during this time that Lionel Robbins of the London School of Economics declared Viner to be the most learned living economist. Yet I doubt that very many of my five thousand fellow undergraduates of 1935 had even heard of him—a fact that tells you something about the chasm that prevailed in the Hutchins university between the graduate schools and the undergraduate student body.

At the frontier of economic science Jacob Viner was very well known, respected, and—let us acknowledge it—feared. He was regarded as a ferocious critic, who cleaned the Augean stables of error. And far from the Midway the legends of his ferocity in the seminar room were told and retold in senior common rooms wherever economists gathered. Mostly the good stories were true stories. Because of Chicago's quarter system, both Frank Knight and Viner would often offer advanced seminars in the summer, and postdoctoral economists from around the world would brave the Midwest heat to sit before their blackboards and absorb their radiated genius. It was the closest approach to the German custom in which scholars trooped from university to university sampling the cafeteria offerings of the *Gelehreten*. When an Evsey Domar or a Robert Triffin experienced the Vinerian Socratic method firsthand, the experience was indelible and got reported widely throughout the profession.

· I ·

Before I describe Viner the teacher, let me recall his career. He was born and went to school in Montreal before the First World War. Quebec was then a divided society: the English-speaking Establishment ruled the roost and the French-speaking majority were an underclass. Children of immigrant Jews were marginal in that bigoted universe. I have heard Viner say that in all his years in the Montreal public schools he was never taught a word of French. At McGill University Stephen Leacock was Viner's teacher. Yes, the humorist Leacock, who by his pupil's testimony was a stimulating lecturer on the politics of empire if not on economics. Fortunately J. C. Hemmeon, a dour Scot, did teach Viner some of the niceties of neoclassical economics. The McGill of Osler and Rutherford must have been at its high noon in those Edwardian years. It was still sending top students to the Harvard of my day in the 1930s. We used to joke that the best American economists were Canadians: Simon Newcomb, Jacob Viner, Frank D. Graham, John Kenneth Galbraith, William Vickrey, Lloyd Reynolds, and Harry Johnson to name just a few.

Viner's brilliance must have been recognized (and resented!) from the beginning. But as with Sherlock Holmes who had a more brilliant brother Mycroft, Jacob had a more brilliant older brother who became a distinguished Canadian physician. He used to tease his younger brother, saying: "The trouble with you, Jake, is that you have the sense of humor of Hemmeon and the economics of Leacock." Viner spent a couple of years in the Harvard Graduate School during a dry season there. He had a low opinion of his fellow graduate students. Frank Taussig, leading scholar in Ricardian theories of international trade and dean of American economists, spotted Viner's talent. For the rest of his life Viner was known as Taussig's favorite pupil and it was from him that Viner got his Socratic manner in the seminar room. Jacob may have been the Sheik's favorite but that did not get him a permanent appointment at the Harvard of President Lowell: many an Esau walked before him in the academic procession.

It says something for the post-Harper University of Chicago that Viner was called to a rung on the ladder in the economics department there. Indeed, a decade later, in the late 1920s when the economics department at Chicago was contemplating recruiting the budding econometrician Henry Schultz, Viner and Paul Douglas persisted even after being told that President Max Mason did not care for Jews. Quite aside from any ethnic impediments, Viner was not one to suffer mediocrities gladly and must have irritated the Bullocks, Carvers, and Gays who were Taussig's rivals. For it was as late as 1922, when Viner was already world-famous, had written a classic thesis on the Canadian balance of payments, and had returned to Cambridge to defend it orally and accept his doctorate, that Taussig had to cancel the elaborate dinner he had planned in celebration—because

JACOB VINER

Jacob Viner was flunked in his final orals! (When he was a visiting Taussig Research Professor at Harvard during his retirement years from Princeton, I heard him say: "I deserved to flunk." What cant. Only Allyn Young in that assembled conclave was fit to kiss the hem of Viner's crimson robe. This reminded me of the account I heard from Professor John Black's lips about the famous flunking of Harry Dexter White at his generals orals in the Harvard of the late 1920s: "Harry White dominated every seminar and economic discussion group. But every bully is a coward at heart. At his generals *we* were asking the questions, and we flunked him.")

While Viner was climbing the ladder at Chicago, he began what was to be a long and distinguished career as editor of the *Journal of Political Economy,* Chicago's journal that came to surpass in prestige and influence Taussig's *Quarterly Journal of Economics* and the official *American Economic Review.* Later, around 1927, Viner was one of those who worked hard to recruit Frank Knight. (Knight, reliable rumor relates, ignored Harvard's whistle to come replace Allyn Young: Knight disapproved of how Mr. Lowell had handled the Sacco-Vanzetti investigation!) Knight and Viner were long listed as co-editors of the *JPE:* it was a good team but Viner did most of the work, just as Harry Johnson did in later similar arrangements. (Work goes to those who don't lock the doors.)

· II ·

Now I enter on delicate ground. The University of Chicago economics department, like Gaul, was divided into parts. Knight and Viner were the theorist patriarchs and rivals. Paul Douglas was the more-than-token liberal. Henry Schultz represented the wave of the future in econometrics and mathematical economics. Henry Simons, critic of the regulated state and advocate of redistributive income taxation, was in Knight's camp. Although Aaron Director began in the Douglas workshop, his heart was with Knight. Indeed Frank Knight was the irresistible Pied Piper. For five years—from the time I was sixteen until I was twenty-one—I was bewitched by Knight. The cream of the graduate school—a Stigler, Friedman, Wallis, Homer Jones, or Hart—downplayed the Vinerian sagacity and erudition. Schultz, an earnest pioneer who lacked in self-confidence and brilliance, was, I fear, patronized by the arrogant youth of the day; that did not add to his serenity or sureness of judgment.

Internal rivalry and incivility is a scenario seen a hundred times in the universities of Europe. The picture it presents is never a pretty one. Out of diversity there usually does not arise scientific fruitfulness. Too often from dissension comes polarization and the waste heat of friction. As an undergraduate I lived through it all with, so to speak, a foot in four camps. Later as a friend and visitor, two or three times a year I watched the pot boiling. I have been the confidant of half-a-dozen generations of Chicago economists, with most of the traffic coming of course from those with oxen they deemed recently gored.

Let me merely report that Frank Knight was not the easiest chap to live with. He had no guile but was quite unaware of what his frankness entailed. Like Joan Robinson, he constantly exploded. To the two of them everything was absurdly simple or simply absurd. Even Henry Simons, Knight's ally and disciple, complained to me bitterly. Paul Douglas of course had reason to complain, something that Knight found astonishing. Being the father of a large brood, I am an expert on children's quarrels: it is absolutely pointless to try to determine who was first at fault. Let me only say that Jacob Viner, never known for his diplomacy or sweetness, was something of a saint in getting along with Knight. (Only in his eighth decade did Viner permit himself to say privately: "I always felt we should have treated Frank as if he were on the verge of a nervous breakdown in the 1930s. His financial problems and concerns about the disintegrating world economy and society were an important part of the picture.")

Although Jacob Viner had the reputation of a conservative economist who defended the orthodoxies of neoclassical and classical economics, he played a role of modest importance in Franklin Roosevelt's New Deal. Henry Morgenthau, Jr., secretary of the treasury, was no great intellect but he came to have respect for Jacob Viner. Through Viner, Harry Dexter White was called from Lawrence College in Wisconsin to begin his Napoleonic rise in the Treasury. Indeed not a few Chicago students of Viner, who were identified in the McCarthy hunts as communists or fellow travelers, were recommended by Viner. This occasioned some snickers among Chicagoans who were critical of Viner on fine points of doctrine, but who should have had reason and experience to know that Jacob Viner was a center to right-of-center thinker and actor. (If the probability was one-tenth that A. C. Pigou, Alfred Marshall's protégé at Cambridge and Keynes's post-1933 antagonist, was the Fifth Man in Britain's spy ring, it was epsilon that Viner was ever a radical of any sort. Viner agreed with the majority of economists who deplored Roosevelt's devaluation of the dollar. Today's majority sides with Roosevelt.)

Actually, Viner's heresies in 1931 were to advocate with his Chicago colleagues a deliberate program of deficit spending to temper the Great Depression; and, pragmatically, he espoused a version of the quantity theory of money and prices that gave interest rates and confidence roles to play in determining the velocity of circulation of money and that treated output as an endogenous unknown in the truism of exchange MV = PQ. Postwar workshops in money finally did catch up with the Vinerian platitudes.

This brings me, finally, to Jacob Viner's place in "the Chicago school." Yes, there is a Chicago school in economics despite occasional disclaimers that all reasonable scholars believe in the same truth. Indeed, the data require us to recognize two Chicago schools. The first Chicago school was that of Knight, Viner, and Simons. It advocated use of the market, but recommended redistributive taxes and transfers to mitigate the worst inequalities of the laissez-faire system. It pragmatically favored macroeconomic policies in the areas of credit and fiscal policies to attenuate the amplitude of cyclical fluctuations. It endorsed antitrust policies to improve competition and favored utility regulation where competition was severely compromised. If time is short, call it the Knightian Chicago school. Without question, Viner belonged to it even if he was more pragmatic and less dogmatic than some of his colleagues.

The second Chicago school ought properly to be associated with the names of Milton Friedman, George Stigler, Aaron Director, and Gary Becker. Call it the Friedman Chicago school for short. It has lost the Simonsian imperative to use the tax system to modify economic inequality and has reverted to Adam Smith's view that most attempts by government to improve on the effectiveness of competition will only make matters worse. Viner has not gone on record with his assents and dissents. As a third Chicago School is gestating in the workshops of Robert Lucas's rational expectationism, one can conjecture what Viner's discontents would be with strong hypotheses of quick convergence to neutral-money homeostasis.

· III ·

The New Palgrave: A Dictionary of Economics (1987, vol. 4, 812–14) contains a fine piece by Henry W. Spiegel on Viner's contributions to economics, and I refer the reader to it. Worth quoting from it is the account of a little-known Viner item of 1921 that essentially anticipated the Sraffa-Robinson-Chamberlin paradigm of imperfect competition.

Five years ahead of Sraffa, six years ahead of the publication of Joan Robinson's and Edward Chamberlin's books on the subject, Viner developed here, in a short paragraph, the outlines of the theory of monopolistic competition. He writes of inflexible prices, "differentiation" of products, advertising, non-price competition and other characteristics of markets that are neither fully competitive nor completely monopolistic. In such markets producers may succeed in creating a special demand for their products. They can then to some extent determine prices independently of the prices charged by their competitors and still maintain their sales.

Jacob Viner earned a top reputation as an economic theorist in the Marshallian tradition of neoclassical economics. Along with Bertil Ohlin of Sweden and Gottfried Haberler of Austria and Harvard, Viner played a key role in advancing theory of international trade a quantum jump beyond the Ricardo-Taussig paradigm of comparative labor advantage. An erudite historian of economic thought, Viner was without peers in the history of the theory of international trade. His *Studies in the Theory of International Trade,* published in 1937, is a masterpiece, both as history of the subject and as definitive synthesis of the subject at the threshold of the Lerner-Meade-Samuelson-McKenzie-Jones-Chipman-Mundell-Kemp era.

Viner's article on "Cost Curves and Supply Curves" of 1931 gained him earned and inadvertent fame. Marshall had neglected to relate closely the theory of the firm to the supply of the competitive industry. Viner did well what needed doing, as Joan Robinson and Edward Chamberlin did a couple of years later in connection with imperfect competition. The new Appendix, added by Viner when the 1931 item was anthologized, shows how around 1940 he and Joan Robinson were getting a glimpse of the general equilibrium that transcends Marshall's partial equilibrium. Viner's contretemps with his mathematician draftsman Y. K. Wong, over the long-run *envelope* to his descending U-shaped curves, brought the inadvertent fame that was in part bittersweet. Among the article's many gems is Viner's so-called Pure Ricardian case, where a good is produced by an industry that uses specialized land and transferable labor—the manageable case known today in the literature on international trade as the Haberler-Jones-Samuelson technology. (Incidentally, Viner here is in effect showing up the root fallacy in Piero Sraffa's 1926 classic article, which purported to prove that only constant-cost industries are compatible with the logic of Marshall's partial equilibrium; fortunately this fallacy that bewitched six decades of pedants is accompanied by Sraffa's correct vision of decreasing-cost firms kept in equilibrium by facing market demand curves such that they can sell more of their product only by accepting a lower net price for it. As mentioned already in *Palgrave,* Viner and Chicago colleagues such as J. M. Clark and Theodore Yntema were comfortable with such notions long before Robinson and Chamberlin wrote their classics.)

One can only sample Viner's fabulous learning. Friedrich Hayek, Eli

Heckscher, and possibly Lionel Robbins were the few contemporaries in his league. In 1972, William Baumol gave some flavor of Viner's erudition in his memoir on the Princeton years. Aaron Director and Lloyd Mints, if they found an old item in Harper Library that didn't show a checkout slip with Viner's name on it, would confront him with glee; almost always he would reply, "I read that in the stacks standing up." For years Viner bought rare books for Harper Library, in jovial competition with such collectors as Piero Sraffa, Edwin Cannan, and H. S. Foxwell, each of whom would kill for a newly discovered letter of Ricardo.

I lack competence to judge the material Viner worked on in his last twenty-five years at Princeton. What was put in publishable state was apparently only the tip of a weighty iceberg. From the beginning Viner was much of a perfectionist. Some of his great Chicago lectures he for some reason never chose to publish. (His recent editor, Dr. Douglas Irwin of the Federal Reserve research staff, has spoken of a paper that was revised in some degree without authority by the journal that published it. And for that reason Viner excluded it from his list of publications.) As he grew old, Viner seems to have succumbed to a scholarly disease more virulent than arthritis or osteoporosis—increased reluctance to publish material regarded as incomplete only by himself.

As an elder statesman Viner gave out sage judgment and advice. His human wisdom and his reputation for that is illustrated by the advice he gave when the London School of Economics authorities asked what should be done with the papers and correspondence of Edwin Cannan. Since that irascible Scot treated the great minds of the past like schoolchildren, rather untalented schoolchildren, one can guess the terms in which he recommended his own students. After sampling the trove, Viner advised: "Burn them."

Back in the 1950s, the great foundations sent economists like Viner, Haberler, and Robbins to lecture in Brazil and Argentina. They cast their pearls before small audiences, while in nearby halls, so to speak, such Marxists as Paul Baran and Paul Sweezy lectured to the plaudits of hundreds. Clio must smile at the spectacle of present-day South American governments that are trying to limit past economic damages by applying the Viner-type wisdoms to their developmental problems.

I should mention that Viner did original work on patterns of imperialism, documenting the naiveté of the fashionable view that business interests generally succeed in manipulating the powers of the state for their selfish interests. Eugene Staley, as Viner's student, showed how it was often the flag that manipulated trade rather than vice versa. While at Princeton Viner did do pathbreaking analysis of customs unions, going beyond his precocious 1923 classic on dumping.

Brevity requires that I sample Viner's originality as a theorist: with respect to his valid polemics in favor of an eclectic merger of utility and real-cost elements in value theory; and with respect to his foreign-trade innovations.

Knight, Haberler, and Robbins underplayed real-cost determinants of price in the Austrian manner of opportunity cost and derive utility. (For a time Knight seemed even to defend a Sraffian-like paradigm that left relative prices invariant to shifts in consumers' demand patterns.) As Edgeworth had done in the 1890s in rebutting Böhm-Bawerk, Viner took the general position of Marshall and Walras: when factor supplies are variable, and labor is not indifferent between working for an hour on food or on clothing, then the Austrian position is shown to be oversimple. Of course, Viner was sitting in the poker game with four aces and in the end his opponents gave way, grew silent, or copped a Stiglerian plea that they were 93 percent free of error.

Viner's eclecticism with respect to a modern theory of value contrasts with his longtime effort to defend Taussig's use in international economics of Ricardian technologies that involved labor as the only input of production. Tom Kuhn, the methodologist of revolutions in science, should savor the contrasting styles of Ohlin and Viner: along with Haberler they both arrived at essentially the same general equilibrium model; but Ohlin did so claiming great novelty for his own innovations, while Viner always played down the departures from the previous status quo. Both were right—and wrong. Baumol and Ellen Viner Seiler (Viner's daughter), in their biography of Viner in the *International Encyclopedia of the Social Sciences* in 1979, attribute Viner's being overshadowed by Haberler and Ohlin to his eschewing the oversimplifications of the opportunity-cost dogma. That does not quite hit the nail on the head. Viner did present in a lecture at the London School of Economics in January 1931 the canonical trade diagram involving indifference contours and a concave production-possibility frontier. But he did not publish it for half a dozen years, leaving to A. P. Lerner the garnering of fame that eclipsed both Ohlin and Haberler.

Like a glassblower or hand-weaver, Jacob Viner was a victim of technical obsolescence. He lacked training in the mathematics that was to sweep the realms of economic theory. Being sensitive, he well realized this and let it become something of a King Charles's head. That is why, I believe, after the age of forty-five he disengaged from competition at the frontier of mainstream economics. He had much company in the generation of my teachers: their presidential addresses to the American Economics Association bristle with complaints about the over-mathematization of economics.

· IV ·

It is proper to conclude with an account of Jacob Viner as the toreador of the graduate seminar room. When the *Journal of Political Economy* asked me to write an obituary of Viner's Chicago days, I was in a quandary. *Nihil nisi bonum* was not Viner's own credo, but rather *nisi verum*. And my sister-in-law Professor Anita Arrow Summers of Pennsylvania, who registered in one of his last courses at Chicago, insisted that posterity deserved an accurate testimony. But, on the other hand, I kept thinking of the surviving Frances Viner, and her natural sensibilities. In the end I tried to compromise between verisimilitude and affectionate memory. When I received no comment on the reprint sent to his guileless widow, I at first had misgivings that I had overshot the mean; but, as I later learned, Frances was in a terminal illness and the issue was moot. As I reread my words of almost two decades back I doubt that I can do better than paraphrase them here.

The problem resides in the fact that the Viner who was so stimulating was also the teacher who caused not only young maidens to burst into tears but also battle-hardened officers from two world wars. Here is an abridgement of the account which I wrote in 1972.

Viner was my teacher, I heard many lectures by Knight and had chances to talk to him. However, it was chance of the draw that the famous 301 graduate course in economic theory, which oscillated between Frank Knight and Jacob Viner, happened to be given by Viner in the winter quarter of 1935, my senior year and just after I had learned Marshallian economics from Paul Douglas. It was no easy matter to get into Viner's course (and, as we shall see, still harder to stay in it). For an undergraduate it was still harder, but Paul Douglas said he would write a letter on my behalf, reporting that I was somewhat "cantankerous" but a good bet.

Fortunately for me, Viner had just returned from his tour of duty in Morgenthau's Treasury and must have been in an indulgent mood. With about thirty-five other aspirants, who I recall included Martin Bronfenbrenner and Warren Scoville, we lined up around a huge seminar table on the ground floor of the then new Social Science

Research Building. Viner appeared, holding our names on index cards; and after a speedy inquisition, five of us were found wanting in previous preparation or motivation. But that was only the beginning.

My impression of Viner never changed from that first glimpse. He was short and intense, like a bantam cock. His upper lip, usually bedewed by a bead of moisture, curled in what seemed half a smile. In my imperfect memory his hair was then reddish, and his complexion matched. His suit coats were on the short side and his posture was not that of a West Point cadet. How I remember anything about his person I do not know, since every eye in the room was fastened upon the diabolical deck of index cards in his hands through which he shuffled nervelessly. To be scrupulously honest, subsequent legend has contaminated my account. I was too innocent to be nervous. In contrast to the graduate students present, I had nothing at stake. But from them their whole careers and professional futures were in jeopardy each time he riffled through the cards.

Viner was a student of Frank Taussig, the master of the Socratic method. Taussig played on his classes as Pablo Casals played on his cello. He knew which idiot would botch up Ricardo's trade-off between the profit rate and the real wage; he knew which showoff student had to be kept out of the classroom verbal interaction lest he short-circuit the dialogue.

Viner added one new ingredient: terror. Members of the seminar sat tensely around the table, and when the name of the victim was read off the cards, you could almost hear the sighs of relief and the slumping back into chairs of those who had won temporary respite. Indeed, the stakes were high. Three strikes and you were out, with no appeal possible to any higher court. And this was no joke. I remember an able graduate student who, having failed to give an acceptable answer on two previous occasions, was told by Viner: "Mr. ——, I am afraid you are not equal to yourself or this class." This man barely managed to retrieve his position at the final moment. When one victim alibied, "I am beyond my depth," Viner is supposed to have said, "Sir, you drown in shallow water." If a graduate student was refused admittance to 301, the basic course in theory, he had no choice but to drop out or to transfer to the slums of political science or sociology. (Years later when I discussed with Jack Viner the legend of his ferocity, he said that the department had given him the function of screening the candidates for higher degrees. It was not work for which he was ill-equipped.)

What shall I say about the course? By reputation it was considered the best course in economic theory being given in the America of those days. On reflection, I think it probably deserved that accolade [this in 1972]. To my regret, the notes that I took for Viner's course, if they still exist, are not in any location known to me. But that is perhaps just as well, for Viner was vehement in his belief that it was a sacrilege to take skimpy notes from a course and present it to the world as a fair sample of the course's quality. To his indignation, a student had done just that around 1930, and a mimeographed copy of the notes was on deposit in Harper Library. In 1935 the course that I took was somewhat better in scope and coverage from the version presented in 1930. To buttress his sensitivity on this point, Viner made reference to Wesley Mitchell's famous course at Columbia. Without authorization, a student circulated rather elaborate mimeographed notes (which, subsequent to my conversation with Viner, were published by Augustus Kelley). Viner had read these notes and reported that their content was extremely disappointing, a fact he blamed on the unauthorized paraphraser, not on the quality of Mitchell's thought. It was an uncharacteristically gentle verdict *I* thought.

Viner put considerable store on the historical development of the subject. Since this was my first graduate course, I did not know there was any other way to do it. Viner made clear at the beginning that he would not be covering the latest wrinkles in the theory of imperfect or monopolistic competition. However, since Viner himself, along with his student and colleague Theodore Yntema, had independently discovered the marginal cost-marginal revenue conditions for maximization of an imperfect competitor's profits, much of what was contained in the Chamberlin and Robinson treatises was adequately covered. Although I had the best undergraduate education in economics that opportunity could provide anywhere at that date, only once and there in Viner's graduate course was I exposed to the mysteries of indifference curves and the production-possibility frontier; this latter under the heading of Pareto's "production indifference" curve. In the first minute of the course Viner made clear that a proper prerequisite for it would be knowledge of the calculus. But that, since the instructor lacked the qualification, he would waive it for the rest of us. Jacob Viner was a respecter of mathematics, but also both critical and defensive about it. Let me make clear that Viner possessed in superlative degree what might be called *native* mathematical ability.

In writing these reminiscences of Viner as a teacher at Chicago I have consulted a number of eminent scholars who took his graduate courses both before and after the 1935 term I have spoken of. One view is that he mellowed over the years. A psychologist will be amused to learn that the Viner of 1946 at Princeton was "mellow" and the Viner of 1946 at Chicago was "unmellow." Saul must have become

Paul on the Pennsylvania Limited! The truth is that he used a teaching technique which to the best students was inordinately stimulating. I could quote testimony after testimony to this effect. I myself found his course enormously stimulating. Evsey Domar, who took it in 1940, tells me it was the best course he has even taken, and in part because of Viner's challenging manner. Martin Bronfenbrenner, who took many of Viner's Chicago courses, recalls that it was customary to sit in on the same course year after year because of the new insights to be gleaned.

After I left Chicago I learned that I was something of a teen-age legend myself in Viner's course of that year. Legends grow on legends. So let me set the record straight. The prosaic fact is that Viner had the custom of coming to class with complicated diagrams to be copied on the blackboard. Such transcriptions are notoriously subject to minor errors in which curves intersect on the wrong side of axes, and so forth. Fools rush in where angels fear to tread, and so it was left to the only undergraduate in the course to point out such occasional petty aberrations which detracted nothing from his evident erudition and keenness. Once Viner was a bit slow in providing a reference for Wicksteed's view of supply curve as a reserve demand curve. Always ready to do my boy scout's good deed of the day, I piped up: "Schultz's book on sugar demand deals with that." He threw his chalk down on the desk in annoyance I can now well understand.

Few of us like to be wrong. Jacob Viner, consummate scholar that he was, and meticulous in his knowledge of the literature, was no exception in this respect. Yet I would argue that it is the occasional errors of geniuses like Viner which make the reputations of mere mortals, and which also seminally advance the body of science. Who in economics would remember Dr. Wong if his memory had not been perpetuated by his correcting of Viner's long-run cost-curve envelope? Precisely because Viner was so Jovianly impervious to error, the economics profession got a modicum of *Schadenfreude* at his expense over the envelope incident. Certainly he had no need to be sensitive about it. Indeed I later identified what I called the deeper Viner-Wong envelope theorem in a 1929 Viner review of Cannon. By 1935 Viner reported to the class that Wong had been right in their dispute in 1931 and he, Viner, had been wrong, mathematically and economically. "But" he said to me privately, just as the hour chimes had rung, "although there seems to be some esoteric mathematical reason why the envelope cannot be drawn so that it passes smoothly through the declining bottoms of the U-shaped cost curves, nevertheless I can do it." "Yes," I replied impishly, "with a good thick pencil, you can do it."

Now for a few second thoughts in 1990 on these 1972 formulations.

1. By 1935, Viner's 301 was probably not the best that America could then offer. Schumpeter's unsystematic Harvard lectures that I heard in the fall of 1935 referred to the future of our subject, not its past.

2. The Socratic method of Taussig was a bad pattern for the twenty-one-year-old Viner to emulate. It was a slow, slow, very slow procedure —appropriate for a science in its degenerate stage when no fundamental problems are deemed to admit of a definitive answer. Also, I learned with surprise from Paul Douglas's autobiography that he found the sweet old Taussig I knew to have been a seminar bully around 1915 when Douglas took his famous Ec 11 as a visitor from Columbia. Alas, Viner learned more from Taussig than I had realized. Taussig's Socratic method was grossly overpraised in my Harvard times. My friends, Abram Bergson and Alice Bourneuf, from their own experience, told me not to believe all I heard. And, as I said in 1972, Taussig himself told me that his Ec 11 was overrated in his post-1919 years.

3. Screening out unpromising recruits to the graduate economics program, like dusting for athlete's foot, is I suppose a necessary activity. But how weak must be the statistical power of a procedure that uses as evidence against you your inability to respond quickly to vaguely defined questions, in an atmosphere of fright. That way one might lose a John Hicks and gain a J. R. McCulloch.

Some outsiders have looked at the University of Chicago as a jungle red in tooth and claw. That has always been an exaggeration. Yet when I used to wonder how Hutchins's university stayed so near the top after John D. Rockefeller had put it on its own, I decided that part of the story was that Chicago was a premature meritocracy. It was the kind of place where long-time teachers were finally refused permanent tenure; where, let it be said, colleagues occasionally fought over priorities and plagiarisms; and where a professor of economics or physics might receive five to eight times what some professors of classics would be paid. (When Hirofumi Uzawa left Chicago for Tokyo University, his yearly salary there barely matched his monthly salary on the Midway.)

History may be written by survivors but science is fabricated by over-achievers. One understands why Jacob Viner, at the peak of his prime, would reveal a preference for the green lawns of Princeton. His children lived in the East. Along with Knight and Harry Gideonse, Viner played an important and honorable role in opposing the Machiavellian Robert Hutchins, surely a tedious distraction for a creative scholar. Frances and

Jacob Viner were not entranced by the Chicago social circle or entrapped by collegial friendships. At Princeton they did live happily ever after. (Frances Viner was a much loved extrovert, as hinted at by the following anecdote. At Princeton's retirement dinner for Viner, Frances spoke about his alleged helplessness: "Why, if I broke my leg in the basement, two people would starve to death. I in the basement and Jack upstairs in his study." With quick wit, Viner replied: "I had a colleague who cut his leg chopping kindling wood in the basement. I told him: 'That's what you get for doing woman's work'.")

Jacob Viner departed from Chicago with honor and without rancor. He had paid his dues and helped to make economists remember his Midway as Camelot.

45

BERNARD WEINBERG

1 9 0 9 – 1 9 7 3

P E T E R   F.   D E M B O W S K I

 BERNARD WEINBERG died suddenly, of a heart attack followed by a pulmonary embolism, on February 13, 1973. At sixty-three, he was the Robert Maynard Hutchins Distinguished Service Professor in the department of Romance languages and literatures at the University of Chicago. He had just announced to his colleagues that the University had postponed his retirement until his sixty-eighth birthday. He was also a former chairman of the department and a *spiritus movens* of much of the division of the humanities. He was a popular figure at the University, always involved, formally or informally, in countless committees, advisory boards, and other academic enterprises. He was known and respected outside the University. In 1972 he was elected fellow of the American Academy of Arts and Science. Every scholar in French or Italian on this continent, every practitioner of what was then known as the "Chicago school" of criticism, knew him as "Bernie." His person and his works were known in Europe, particularly in Italy, where Bernie—sometimes Italianized to Berni—was a familiar figure and an admired colleague. If I refer to Bernard Weinberg henceforth as Bernie, it is not as a concession to the journalistic habit of familiarity in treating public figures, but rather as a simple admission of fact: he was known to all his colleagues as Bernie. To his students, however, he was Mr. Weinberg.

· I ·

Bernard Weinberg was essentially a Chicago man. His personal life as well as his activities as a student, teacher, and scholar were always centered on Chicago and, more specifically, on the University of Chicago. Both his parents, William Weinberg and Anna Goldstein, were American-born descendants of Central European Jewish immigrants who brought with them something which became Bernie's priceless possession: an abiding love of

BERNARD WEINBERG

learning and an uncompromising respect for knowledge. Although he never married, his extraordinary closeness to his parents, his brothers, and their families kept him very humane and interested in all aspects of daily existence. It certainly counterbalanced his decidedly intellectual outlook on life.

Bernie was born in Chicago on August 23, 1909. I have no doubt that he inherited his passion for learning and his love of language from his family. His father, William, who survived him by a year, was largely a self-taught man. He had to abandon normal learning after the first year of high school in order to earn his living as a distributor of electrical supplies. He passed onto his sons—Bernie had two brothers: Saul, now professor emeritus of classical archaeology at the University of Missouri, and Norman, who retired as director of data processing in Lyons Township—his great love of language. His father, like Bernie, was not only a careful and colorful speaker, but also a sophisticated and indefatigable punster.

All his life, Bernie was an excellent student. Learning had always come easily to him because he always considered it a pleasure. Many years after his own student days, he was very surprised, when one of his colleagues, in welcoming the new students in the department, emphasized the rules and regulations of the Ph.D. program. Visibly surprised and pained, he said: "You talked all the time about the obstacles to overcome and the pitfalls to avoid, but you never mentioned the fun of it all." This joy of learning manifested itself early in his life. He went to John Marshall High School on the city's west side. In those days, it was a solid and decidedly intellectual institution. Since it had a large Jewish student population, it obtained the right to teach Hebrew as a foreign language. Young Bernie soon became writer for the school's Hebrew magazine. The linguistic, editorial, and scholarly talents, which were his lifelong attributes, thus developed early both at home and in school. He graduated second in his high school class.

Strangely enough, this natural-born scholar and teacher did not plan at first to enter the academic profession, but rather wished to become a journalist. He sought admission to the Northwestern University School of Journalism. Here, goddess Fortuna smiled on him and on the University of Chicago: his admission was denied. As a result, he applied to the College of the University of Chicago, where he was accepted. Some forty years later, in 1965, when he was persuading me to come to Chicago as a teacher, he told me that his acceptance by the College was one of the most important, if not the most important thing, which ever happened to him. It decided the rest of his life, because, in a way, he never left the University.

In spite of some fainthearted, initial attempts at a practical (that is to say, business) education, Bernie devoted most of his undergraduate work to the study of literature. He studied English literature as well as French and Italian. He obtained his Ph.B. in 1930, which was the first year of the Hutchins presidency. All his life he was a faithful and energetic partisan of the "Hutchins College." He also remained an enthusiastic supporter of the reforms later introduced into the division of the humanities by Richard McKeon when he was dean. Bernie simply could not support anything without enthusiasm. It was this enthusiasm, controlled by an extraordinary intelligence and an enormous capacity for work, which made him not only a remarkable teacher and scholar, but also a very valuable full-time citizen of the University. Robert E. Streeter describes this side of Bernie's activity in his letter to me: "In my eleven years as a dean [of the division of the humanities] no member of the Policy Committee was more meticulous and fair-minded than Bernie in reviewing the work of our colleagues being considered for continuing appointment or advancement. During those busy autumn weeks when these decisions were being made, he spent many hours weighing the written evidence and then, in committee, helping the rest of us reach responsible judgments."

Bernie's astonishing capacity for work was enhanced by his rigorous graduate training at the University of Chicago. But first he received a fellowship for the 1930–31 academic year to study in France. He spent that year in Paris, where he greatly improved his French and where he also easily obtained a *Diplôme d'enseignement supérieur*. He had a truly unusual capacity for the acquisition of foreign languages. When I became well-acquainted with him in the early 1960s, I was immediately impressed by his capacity to lecture without notes in excellent and elegant French or Italian.

Bernie returned to Chicago in 1931 to work for his doctorate, which he was granted in 1936. His doctoral studies clearly indicated the path of his future development. His dissertation, for which he did the research at the Bibliothèque nationale in 1934–35, dealt with the history of French criticism in the middle of the nineteenth century. *French Realism: The Critical Reaction, 1830–1870* was published by the Modern Language Association in 1937, and established Bernie once and for all as an erudite historian of critical thought and practice.

· II ·

The history of criticism constituted one part of the "triad" of his intellectual life. The most important area of Bernie's scholarly production lies in the domain of intellectual history, and more precisely in the study and interpretation of literary criticism. *A History of Literary Criticism in the Italian Renaissance* (2 vols., 1961) was his magnum opus. It was dedicated to the leading critics of the "Chicago school" of criticism: Ronald Crane, Richard McKeon, and Elder Olson. This dedication shows that Bernie did not see any real opposition between historical considerations of literary criticism and literary criticism itself. I believe that it was only later that such oppositions became evident to a large number of literary scholars. One of the reasons that Bernie was an excellent teacher was his rejection of such critical and methodological dichotomies. He could understand and explain "both sides" of an issue, for he knew very well that there was always more than one side to any intellectual problem.

The second side of Bernie's intellectual "triad" was literary criticism, based in a large part on close reading, and in his case, more specifically, on the traditional French method of the *explication de texte*. Pierre Robert Vigneron had endorsed and taught the *explication de texte* at Chicago, and energetically propagated its use in the teaching of language and literature from the 1920s on. Bernie became one of the outstanding practitioners of this method. But he also became involved in the discussions of the larger area of the theory and practice of criticism. The department of English, particularly under the aegis of Ronald Crane, became the focal point of these discussions. In the 1940s, this group of critics was recognized as the "Chicago school," the "Chicago critics," or the "Chicago (Neo)Aristotelians." Their Aristotelianism permitted them to stress the accomplishments of an author in terms of responses and solutions that he brought to bear upon the artistic problems inherent in a given work. This approach influenced Bernie's critical outlook perhaps more profoundly than that of many of his contemporaries, because he was also conversant with other forms of criticism. He chose the philosophy and methods of the "Chicago school" with the full knowledge of what was involved.

Bernie, like other "Chicago critics," regarded the text as the main thing, and was skeptical of the materials brought in from the "outside" of the work. However, unlike other critics, Bernie never exaggerated his distance from traditional criticism, which he knew very well. His intellectual commitment to the "Chicago school" resulted in two influential studies—often quoted as outstanding examples of the practical application of the basic tenets of this school—*The Art of Jean Racine* (1963) and *The Limits of Symbolism: Studies in Five Modern French Poets* (1966). Bernie's involvement in the "Chicago school" was nourished by intellectual activity and sustained by personal ties to the various members of the group. His friendship with Elder Olson, who was his classmate in the College and himself became a well-known critic, professor in the department of English, and a good poet, had doubtless profoundly reinforced Bernie's intellectual commitment to the "Chicago school." Everything in him was always both intellectual and artistic. As an intellectual descendant of sixteenth-century humanists, he believed that friendship is a form of art. Elder Olson fondly recalls their friendship. "We met as freshmen . . . when he asked me to look at a poem he had written—some dozen heroic couplets called "The Grind." It was completely hopeless, and I told him so. We often met thereafter, took courses together, studied together, and become more truly brothers than most real brothers ever are. He taught me French and French literature, I taught him music and modern poetry. His family accepted me as a member."

The third side of Bernie's intellectual "triad" was also largely a product of his rigorous training at the University of Chicago. In the 1930s, the department was run and dominated by its head, William Nitze, professor of medieval French. Nitze was an excellent example of a German-trained philologist who was an accomplished and intelligent editor and commentator on Old French texts. Nitze set a team of graduate students to work on the commentary and notes to the edition of a difficult prose text of an Arthurian romance (*Perlesvaus*), which he co-edited with T. Atkinson Jenkins, another outstanding philologist of the University of Chicago at that time. The volume of commentaries came out in 1937, signed by Nitze and "collaborators," whose names were listed in the introduction. Bernie was, of course, a member of this team of collaborators. From the very beginning of his career, Bernie was exposed firsthand to the intricate art and science of textual philology and commentary; his first article dealt with the magic chessboard in *Perlesvaus*. This early training would stand him in good stead later in his great Italian edition of *Trattati di poetica e retorica del Cinquecento* published in four volumes between 1970 and 1974.

· III ·

Once he received the doctorate, Bernie spent his first year in Chicago as a research assistant to Nitze and began to look for a teaching position. It was at this moment that the following incident was alleged to have taken place. Nitze called Bernie to his office and told him that since he was a capable scholar he should have no difficulties in finding a teaching position at a good university, but in order to do so he should change his name. In his characteristically brusque manner, Nitze gave Bernie a couple of hours to think it over. After some time spent in the stacks of Harper Library, Bernie told Nitze that he would be willing to change his name to "MacWeinberg." This story was told to me by various contemporaries, I repeated it myself a few times, and I never heard Bernie deny it.

Despite the refusal of his advice, Nitze helped Bernie to gain an appointment at Washington University in St. Louis, where he remained until 1949, except for the years of service in the United States Army Air Corps as a ground-school instructor. Even during his military service, he continued to exercise two *métiers* of his vocation: teaching and textual work; he taught various courses to soldiers, including one on aircraft identification, and he also practiced the craft of editing. He edited various manuals for the Air Corps.

His attention to and control of the details of language were phenomenal. I asked him once, when he was typing the notes to the first volume of *Trattati,* how he kept the final text free from error. He smiled and said that he got it right in the first place. He explained to me that he always typed his own texts, and that he seldom had to retype them. The first draft of an article was very often the last. I did not believe him at first, but later, when I learned more about his work, I realized that he had been telling me the truth.

After the Second World War, Bernie returned to Washington University, but in 1949 he became associate professor and then professor of French at Northwestern University. In 1955, Bernie's "exile years," as he characteristically referred to his distinguished careers at Washington and Northwestern Universities, came to an end. He joined the University of Chicago faculty as a professor of Romance languages and literatures. This was, however, not an easy position for him to hold at first. By that time, the scholars with whom he had worked, principally Nitze, Jenkins, and Dargan, were gone. Bernie's appointment did not begin in the department, but in the dean's office. He was appointed to an unwilling department, which by then had lost much of its sense of direction. It was under the chairmanship of Vigneron, who knew Bernie from his student days. He taught him much of the technique of the *explication de texte* and regarded him as a brilliant scholar. Nonetheless, he disapproved of Bernie on both national and professional grounds. Vigneron considered the department an island of *la petite France* in an American sea. Bernie was for him the eternal foreigner, not to be really trusted with the civilization of the old continent. Vigneron was probably jealous of Bernie's ability to complete a large work; Vigneron himself had worked for years on Stendhal and on Proust's correspondence, work which he could never complete. Despite Vigneron's obvious hostility, I never heard Bernie utter any word against or, for that matter, about him.

In 1958, Vigneron retired and Bernie was appointed chairman of the department of Romance languages and literatures and began the long process of rebuilding it. He served three terms as chairman, retiring from that position in 1967, but remaining active in all departmental affairs as the moral leader, a situation which most members of the department freely accepted. Although it was thought by some that Bernie was too rigid in his adherence to the critical doctrines of the "Chicago school," the appointments that were made under his chairmanship or influence cannot possibly serve as a gauge of his ideological purity. Among those whom he appointed, Bruce Morrissette and myself in French, and Paolo Cherchi and Elissa Weaver in Italian, were not adherents of the "Chicago school"; only George Haley in Spanish had a decided, but far from orthodox, commitment to it.

Bernie was an outstanding teacher. One of his students, Dr. Barbara H. Lloyd, wrote to me: "I adored Professor Weinberg, and what struck me was his ability to convey so simply ideas and thoughts that were very complex. I remember one course on French literary criticism, taught in French, where he analyzed one work from each genre of literature (a play by Racine, *Mme Bovary*, "L'Après-midi d'une faune," etc.). Each one was a revelation of the style and the construction of the piece. He loved what he taught. . . . I still see his trim figure in those double-breasted suits as he jauntily made his way to the classroom. . . ." In a similar vein, John McClelland, professor of French at Victoria College, University of Toronto, describes Bernie's teaching: "He re-read texts every time before teaching them and lectured in flawless French, without notes and without stumbling or hesitating. What he communicated in his classes was an inordinate sense of how works were structured and how they functioned. Whether reading Montaigne or Rimbaud, he stripped away the veils of mystery and made everything seem clear. As a method, his teaching had the inestimable advantage of making the student look at the text and take nothing for granted. In the Chicago tradition, he believed in the 'Great Books' and taught us that what made them great was, in the first instance, their internal coherence. As students and later teachers it was our job to discover and to communicate this coherence to later generations."

· IV ·

Yet Bernie never believed that all approaches to criticism were equally correct. He was convinced that any intelligent and civilized reader or listener could come to his point of view. He believed that a good critic's views must be presented with patience, simplicity, and clarity in order to persuade the readers and to elicit, in turn, from them critical responses of their own. In all this there was, of course, a considerable tough-mindedness. Bernie always had a deep conviction that laxness and laziness are not to be confused with intellectual tolerance. This made him a formidable opponent, and, especially toward the end of his life, opened him to the accusation of intolerance. In these years he was becoming aware that various doctrinaire dichotomies were not only becoming more and more widely accepted, but he was also aware that the critical theory and practice of the "Chicago school" were, by its positive insistence on the study of literature in as purely a literary frame of reference as possible, and in terms of its search for inherent unity and sense of the work, to a certain point, responsible for these developments.

In the agitated days of the late 1960s and the early 1970s, literary criticism came to be affected by the ideological politics which became common among the students and some teachers. Bernie then found himself defending the intellectual and cultural traditions in which he had worked. He was offended by the rude criticism made by radicals, who, nevertheless, expected the usual courtesies and service from those whom they abused. He could not understand how a bright graduate student could have wished to have him as director of his doctoral dissertation and, at the same time, continued to lead a wing of organized dissent. When the student reported to the *Maroon* Bernie's refusal to direct his dissertation as an example of the oppressive "black listing" by the "establishment," Bernie's sorrow turned into a stony silence.

These rather sad developments in the last years of Bernie's life did not leave many traces in his scholarly production. He never engaged in controversial criticism. As a good philologist, he continued to work on the difficult task of editing the *Trattati,* and kept away from the debates concerning the theory and practice of criticism. He broke his silence, as far as I can remember, only once. One of his last public acts was the 341st Commencement Address delivered on September 1, 1972, and entitled "The Humanities as Humanities." The address was a testament of his own literary and critical principles. But the address was also sad to read, because it showed how profoundly discouraged Bernie was by the intellectual developments of those days.

The main theme, as the title indicates, is a plea for the humanities to remain humanities: "The arts of 'reading' are a central part of the discipline of the humanities. So are the arts of 'evaluation' and 'appreciation,' in which to the act of understanding is added the act of judgment—and the pleasure or approbation that follows upon favorable judgment." He was discouraged by what he saw as an invasion of the humanities by the two ideologies of Marxism and Freudianism. These ideologies were for him "fundamentally anti-humanistic." A real sense of catastrophe was to be seen in the closing words of this exhortation to the graduating class: "When you do use them [i.e. the humanities], see to it that you do not deform or corrupt them by combinations or conjunctions within incompatible procedures. Keep your distinctions up, look under the bed for the anti-intellectuals, and be sure that the latch is on the front door."

Bernie was overwhelmed by the events of the late 1960s and the early 1970s not only because he realized more than others what was at stake, but also, and above all, because he loved, perhaps more than others, his intellectual pursuits and because he loved his University.

Happily, there were parts of Bernie's life that remained seemingly untouched by the influence of what he called *i tempi difficili.* He continued his editorial work, and his time free from teaching was spent more and more either in his Lake Michigan cottage or in his apartment in Florence. His cottage and his apartment, Via Borgo Pinti, 55, were not only his refuge from the sound and fury raging in his university, but also the places where he practiced the graceful art of hospitality. Bernie loved company, and he was an inspired cook.

He was sustained also by music and art. He was a devoted and knowing opera- and concert-goer; he bequeathed his own collection of art to the Art Institute of Chicago. His special passion was book-collecting. It began modestly during his student years, and as his own research took shape his book collection matured, reflecting the acumen of a scholar and the taste of a collector. His collection spread over Italian and French literature. It began with an array of Renaissance texts on literary criticism, including important Renaissance editions of Greek and Latin works. When he completed his *A History of the Literary Criticism of the Italian Renaissance,* many of his rare books were given to the Regenstein Library, a great joy to him. The Bernard Weinberg Special Collection at the Regenstein Library numbers 516 rare books, while the Newberry Library, a residual legatee, received 47 volumes. He left his personal fortune to his department, where the William and Anna Weinberg Fund was established to support graduate students.

Bernie bequeathed to us an idea of what a tough-minded historian of criticism, meticulous textual philologist, perspicacious literary critic, and inspired teacher should be. The same qualities which made him an outstanding scholar made him also an inspired teacher. He was a warm, jovial, and generous human being.

46

QUINCY WRIGHT

1 8 9 0 – 1 9 7 0

J O H N   N .   H A Z A R D

 DURING QUINCY WRIGHT'S term as president of the American Society of International Law in the late 1950s a group of juniors amused themselves during an annual banquet by referring to him as a focal point of a discussion over the best education for a career in international law. Should it be a doctorate in political science or a doctorate in law? Wright had qualified in the first category at the University of Illinois in 1915, and he had gone on to become a member of the political science department at the University of Chicago in 1923.

To the juniors Wright personified the political science approach. In his *magnum opus,* entitled quite simply *A Study of War,* published while the Second World War was in progress, he had elaborated in two large volumes the history, causes, and future prospects of war. Clyde Eagleton, professor of international law at New York University and himself a political scientist, stated in his review in the *American Journal of International Law* of 1943 that only experts in many fields could evaluate the volumes. He cited the fields of anthropology, sociology, psychology, science, and mathematics as well as the military, political, and legal sciences. Wright had commissioned memoranda from colleagues in these fields and had synthesized the results. He had concluded with a mathematical formula for calculating the probability of war.

Wright was an encyclopedist in the best sense of the word. He had delved deeply into many disciplines, and he could write of them in his analysis without fear of contradiction. He was never arrogant, but preferred to be cautious. Eagleton said, "Professor Wright's study is a cautious

QUINCY WRIGHT

one, revealing what a complex thing is the institution of war. He didn't, however, hesitate to utter his beliefs."

· I ·

I had come to know Wright when, as a graduate student in law in the late 1930s, I was invited by Samuel N. Harper of the department of history to teach his popular course in "Soviet Political Institutions" during his sabbatical leave. I was working with Professor Max Rheinstein in comparative law after having completed three years as a foreign student in a Soviet law institute. As a junior lecturer I could sit in while Charles E. Merriam, the chairman of the department of political science, conducted staff meetings in his noted quizzical manner, sparked by his wry sense of humor. Wright demonstrated in those meetings that he had a point of view which he was prepared to express strongly. He believed in high standards of scholarship and that the department's role was to demand the best of its students.

Wright's students will remember how hard he pressed them. In oral examinations for the doctorate, which I attended as a member of the jury, I saw Wright in action. He knew his international law as few others knew it. He had a prodigious memory for facts. Without notes he could quote the points made in treaties and the dates of even minuscule events. I had seen some of this display of erudition when as a student in the early 1930s I had been permitted by Manley O. Hudson, of Harvard and later to become a judge of the Permanent Court of International Justice at The Hague, to sit as an observer at sessions of a committee preparing the *Harvard Research in International Law*.

Wright was a member of that committee. He seemed to be able to come to the rescue whenever a fact was needed. Hudson was a stickler for facts, and he was determined to have them to support or contradict the proposed black-letter law to be placed in the final product. Hudson gave the impression that although Wright was a political scientist, a nonlawyer, he belonged foursquare in the group of assembled specialists, the most illustrious of the period before the Second World War. Hudson clearly implied that an international lawyer trained in political science was not really up to snuff, but we students along the back wall felt that Wright held his own against criticism. He would not be cowed by Hudson, who was notorious for bellowing his opposition whenever thwarted in his effort to support his position. Wright just would not be downed, for he had his facts at his finger tips, and every member of this group of eminent scholars and lawyers knew that he was right.

· II ·

Eagleton identified Wright's vision of an acceptable world order in a few sentences of his book review. He wrote of Wright, "He leans toward a federal world organization; he favors international planning and regulation in the economic field, but thinks that a competitive world will work best, granted such regulation. . . . He is strongly in favor of recognition of the individual as a subject of international law and government, and over and over again asserts the success of international government will depend on its ability to reach beyond the sovereign state to the individual human being."

On the issue of the individual as a subject of international law, Wright and Philip C. Jessup of Columbia University, later to become a judge of the International Court of Justice, were in agreement. Wright had been compared with both Jessup and Hudson by the juniors during the banquet discussion because they were models of international lawyers trained in law schools.

Jessup had pioneered in the United States the view that individuals are subjects of international law in his monograph *Transnational Law,* a title invented by him as an alternative to the traditional title "international law" which was used by everyone else. Hudson had been traditional on the place of the individual, sensing that the world would continue to accept only states as subjects. His formula for peace was to tie states to obligations by an ever-expanding net of treaties, which he called "international legislation." He rejoiced when the great and near-great powers of the time signed the Kellogg-Briand Pact in 1924 outlawing war. Thereafter, he ceased to teach the law of war to his Harvard students on the ground that no one needed to know this since it had become anachronistic in a world which had outlawed war.

Wright was opposed to Hudson's position. His *magnum opus* was proof of his position. He had searched for the causes of war and drafted a formula for predicting wars. Perhaps he hoped that if wars could be predicted, they could be prevented, but he seemed to be confident that treaties alone would not prevent them. On the issue of the individual's role, Wright sided with Jessup, but not entirely. His attitude seemed to be that if individuals could be brought into the peace process, they might reduce the incidence of war. Eagleton saw this in Wright's work. In Eagleton's view Wright found wars an increasing problem as the world shrank, as history accelerated, as military interventions occurred, and as democracies replaced emperors, but Eagleton did not think that democracy alone would reduce the likelihood of war in Wright's mind, since Wright thought war the result of many causes. To Wright, cultures must be adjusted to changing world conditions before war could be avoided.

· III ·

Wright had been developing his ideas for decades. He had begun his teaching career as an instructor in international law in the department of political science at Harvard in 1916, alongside the eminent political scientist and authority on international law, George Grafton Wilson. He moved on to the University of Minnesota in 1919 to become assistant professor of political science. By 1922 he had advanced there to the rank of professor, from which he was called to Chicago in 1923 as professor of political science. In 1931 he stepped into the chair of international law, in which he was to remain until his retirement in 1956. Following his official retirement from the University of Chicago, he lectured at, taught in, or otherwise served the Carnegie Endowment for International Peace in New York in 1956–57, the School of International Studies in New Delhi in 1957–58, Columbia University in 1962–63, the Universities of Cairo, Ankara, and Makerere in 1964, Cornell and Syracuse Universities in 1965, Rice University in 1966–67. During those decades he began his writing.

Wright's bibliography lists as his first book his dissertation at the University of Illinois, *The Enforcement of International Law Through Municipal Law in the United States,* published in the Illinois series of dissertations in 1916. He went on to publish nineteen more books. One was a trial balloon for his major work, entitled *The Causes of War and Conditions of Peace,* published in 1935. For the University of Chicago, perhaps one of his greatest contributions was to arrange the annual Norman Waite Harris Foundation conference, which was one of the University's jewels at the time. Between 1924 and 1942 Wright edited the volume made up of the papers from each conference and wrote its introduction. Even after he ceased to edit the volumes, he occasionally wrote an introduction to them, until his retirement.

His publications in journals began with a paper in 1916 on "The Legal Nature of Treaties." Hundreds of articles followed, until the last, appearing just before his death in 1970. Its title indicated his new interest, "Legal Aspects of the Middle Eastern Situation," which was published in Duke University's *Law and Contemporary Problems* in 1968.

Wright enjoyed participation in popular activities as well as those of universities. From 1938 to 1955 his voice was heard on the air as a participant in the University of Chicago Round Table. He wrote the article on international law for the annual volume of the *Encyclopaedia Britannica* from 1948 through 1966. In 1954 he wrote the articles on "Casus Belli," "Hostage," "Successor State," and "Surrender" for the revised edition of the *Britannica.*

His *A Study of War* was revised to appear in a second edition in 1965; to it he added a supplemental commentary on wars after 1942. Because its weight was still too great to attract the casual reader, his wife, Louise Leonard Wright, abridged the two large volumes to a convenient paperback of 451 pages in 1965.

No account of Wright's life would be adequate if it were to omit Louise. She was a notable helpmate after their marriage in 1922. She was the perfect choice to abridge the volume, for she was a scholar and promoter of studies of international relations in her own right. As the impresario of the influential Chicago Council on Foreign Relations for decades, she brought together for luncheon meetings in the Loop considerable numbers of highly educated business leaders of the city, many of them graduates of the University. Louise Wright's speakers were drawn from around the world, and it was the rare man or woman who aspired to prominence in Chicago who did not attend the luncheons. Louise had a commanding presence which contributed greatly to her husband's career. She made their home a haven not only for visiting scholars on the South Side but to great numbers of graduate students and younger teachers invited to meet the visitors. She accompanied Quincy as he traveled the world following formal retirement from the University.

During the Second World War Wright served as consultant to the United States Foreign Economic Administration in 1943 and 1944. After the war he served as technical adviser to the American judge in the trial of German leaders on the International Military Tribunal sitting in Nuremberg in 1945. Later, in 1949, he became a consultant to UNESCO in Paris, from which he went on to become consultant to the United States High Commissioner for Germany, returning thereafter to his chair in Chicago.

· IV ·

The juniors at the American Society's banquet in the late 1950s had reason to think of Quincy Wright as a political scientist as well as a specialist in law. Not only was he presiding over the lawyers on the dais above them, but he had presided over the American Political Science Association in

1949, becoming one of the few scholars honored by both the lawyers and the political scientists with high office in their respective professional societies. His honors were many: member of the American Academy of Arts and Sciences, member of the American Philosophical Society, recipient of the award of the American Council of Learned Societies, and finally president of the International Political Science Association in 1950 and member of the Institut de Droit International, than which there is no higher honor for an international lawyer.

Perhaps Wright epitomized in his writing, his teaching, and in his life as a whole the political approach to international law. He found law being used often by foreign offices as an instrument of state politics. Wright was a realist. He knew that statesmen often had no sense of loyalty to principles but manipulated legal principles to give the appearance of support, so as to attract peoples craving peace and thinking that peace would be enhanced if law were to be respected in the conduct of international relations. Even though skeptical of law's enduring influence on statesmen, Wright expressed confidence in treaties and customary law as weaving a web which could hamper those pressing their own national cause. He looked beyond the technique of the law, beyond the infinite detail which lawyers know and which he knew.

Wright raised his eyes to the East where the professedly "socialist" powers were coming to the fore after the victories of the Second World War. He phrased his thinking of "socialism" in terms of the great depression of the 1930s, through which his generation had lived. He hoped for the best, but he never permitted himself to reside in the clouds. He was not a wishful thinker. Eagleton summed up Wright's position, for he thought revealing Wright's conclusion: "Capitalism has been historically peaceful—while socialism tends toward war. The subordination of capitalism to nationalism and its failure to solve depressions suggest that what is needed is a reform of capitalism rather than a substitution of a new form of economy."

If Wright's conclusion can be interpreted in the light of decades that have passed since it was written, Wright seemed to have expected that Soviet leaders would fail in their effort to remake the world's economies in their Marxist-Leninist image, but he thought also that the Western system of private enterprise would not win the loyalty of the masses unless it reformed its structures to avoid depressions. It was those depressions which threw the discontented into the arms of the Marxist-Leninists.

Wright expressed his views more fully in the Harris Memorial Foundation lecture in 1946 which he focused on a discussion of foreign policy in light of the emergence of the Soviet Union as a preponderant force in politics. He invited me to participate with John Wilson, William T. R. Fox of the University of Chicago, and others from outside the University. My task was to write a paper on the emergence of the Soviet Union as a world power. As Wright wrote in his introduction to the volume eventually printed as a record of the event, times had changed with the creation of the United Nations, with the presence of the atomic bomb, and, most important, with the increased importance of the Soviet Union in the formulation of American foreign policy.

Wright noted the remarkable increase in attention given to the Soviet Union over the years, as evidenced by Harris Foundation records: In 1924 the annual event had not referred to the Soviet Union at all; in 1930, the only reference was by a British participant who referred to the Soviet Union "as the outermost ring of 'world diplomacy'." Wright noted that the balance had been somewhat rectified later when the University of Chicago's historian of Russia, Professor Samuel N. Harper, had led a round table on "The Soviet Union and World Problems," but the topic seemed to Wright to have been presented as rather marginal to United States concerns. Wright told me to explore motivations of Soviet leaders because he thought motivations a key to the problem of keeping the peace.

In the discussion that followed my paper Wright said nothing until we reached the issue of prospective balance of power. Then he pointed to the enormous change to be expected with the emergence of but two great powers, "the only great powers in the world." He drew upon his broad knowledge of history to make a generalization: "During the last generation there has been an extraordinary reduction in the number of great powers. I think that it is a proposition in world politics as it is in physics, that the smaller the number of forces in relation to one another, the less stable the equilibrium. A bipolar equilibrium is in its nature an unstable equilibrium because there are no weights which can be shifted from one side to another to rectify disturbances. If one side in such an equilibrium believes that time is weakening its relative position, it is under a strong compulsion to go to war."

Wright then listed the factors which affected the balance of power in 1946: apprehension under conditions of power politics, Marxian ideology "which adds to mutual suspicion between the Soviet Union and the West," the peasant mentality of the Russian people that makes negotiation difficult, and the influence of world public opinion "which under the influence of the United Nations may accept some common interests and some common fears, as of the atomic bomb." He suggested that world public opinion might in time make it possible to substitute a rule of law for power politics as a means of state security, but for the time being he thought that "we must assume . . . that states will follow the normal pattern of power politics."

Wright concluded that the world might be ripe for the "universal state" formed by conquest, but he seemed to side with the World Federalists, who would probably say that if there were to be a "universal state," it would be a good deal better to make it by some system of federation than to drift into universal conquest. He noted that it would be necessary to "crack sovereignty" to succeed in such a process of federation. He drew comfort from the fact that the United Nations commissions on human rights and the atomic bomb were at work in cracking sovereignty.

· V ·

More than forty years after Wright wrote his lines, he can be praised for analyzing correctly the forces influencing contemporary world politics in the late 1980s. I can recall his conversations at the round table in the dining room of the Quadrangle Club as he sat with Samuel Harper, Harry Gideonse, and others. He was ready to talk and to listen. He brought to the discussion his vast knowledge of history, and even his peers were reluctant to challenge him.

Time seems to be vindicating Wright's vision. Eastern Europe is mending its once-sacred Marxist structures because its peoples, and even some of its leaders, have noted the failure of Stalinist-type structures to satisfy needs. On the other side of the barrier long existing between East and West, not all leaders are satisfied with results. Wright suggested that the West would need to mend its own structures so as to avoid depressions like that of the 1930s, and writers on financial pages of Western papers still reflect worry that serious setbacks can occur in currently prosperous economies. Further, Wright's expectation that interdependence would make itself felt in the minds of men and women is being realized widely as nationalism is being subordinated to peaceful order in some former hotbeds of war, notably Western Europe. Even capitalism is being reformed not only in the European "welfare states" but also in North America. Most important, in judging Wright's vision, international law is appearing as a politically acceptable alternative to violence in the conduct of foreign relations, although pockets of resistance remain.

It is not too much to say, twenty years after his death, that in a sense

Quincy Wright epitomized the spirit of the University of Chicago in performing an educational mission to a public which included not only his students but the people beyond the campus. He became a world figure, moving in and stimulating circles having broad influence upon the formulation of policies to accept international law.

47

SEWALL WRIGHT

1 8 8 9 – 1 9 8 8

H E W S O N   S W I F T

SEWALL WRIGHT was professor of zoology at the University of Chicago from 1926 to 1954. After retirement from Chicago he became the Leon J. Cole Professor of Genetics at the University of Wisconsin. Following his second retirement in 1960, he continued work in Madison for another twenty-eight years, finally finding time to write his long-planned treatise on *Evolution and the Genetics of Populations* in four volumes. His long career began when genetics was largely the concern of animal and plant breeders and involved the often philosophical questions of Darwinian evolution, when geneticists were still trying to understand the basic tenets of heredity. It extended almost to the present time, when genetics has grown to provide an essential underpinning for every aspect of biological thought. Wright published his first scientific contribution at the age of twenty-three and his last when he was ninety-nine. Throughout his life he was always interested in the quantitative aspects of genetics, less as a mathematician than as a biologist seeking precise formulation of biological phenomena. There were two not unrelated foci to his research interests. His laboratory research at Chicago was spent on a detailed investigation of coat color and hair growth patterns in guinea pigs, used as a model system for understanding the nature of gene action and interaction. But increasingly his interests turned to the theoretical formulation of gene frequencies in natural populations, in attempts to model the fundamental patterns of evolution. He made important contributions in both areas, but it was as an evolutionary biologist that he is widely considered to be among the greatest contributors to genetic theory in the century.

SEWALL WRIGHT

· I ·

I became an instructor in the department of zoology in 1949. Sewall Wright was a colleague until his retirement from Chicago in 1955, although he returned to Chicago many times from his later home in Madison. My laboratory was down the hall from his. Our discussions, some lengthy, were typically held with him standing in the doorway to his laboratory. He was always very cordial, completely unassuming, but seemed shy and somewhat ill at ease on such occasions, shifting his weight from one foot to the other, always having more and more things to say, as if he found it hard to terminate the conversation. Nowadays any well-trained geneticist knows much about probability theory and statistical analyses, as well as the importance of phrasing genetic problems, where possible, in mathematical terms. Half a century ago many biologists were mathematically naive. Wright was far ahead of his time in his ability in mathematical conceptualization, and consequently he had many requests for opinions and advice. He took such requests very seriously. On one occasion, probably typical, he showed me a manuscript on fly populations he had been given by a journal editor to review. He determined that the mathematical treatment by the author was incorrect, and it had taken him almost a month of solid work to develop a proper formulation. At that point the grateful author, easily recognizing that the supposedly anonymous reviewer was Sewall Wright, asked him to collaborate as a co-author, which Wright did not wish to do. A great deal of time must have been devoted to these sometimes anonymous attempts at educating his colleagues. In fact, Wright had few collaborators. Most of his papers had a single author, the one most important exception being the five papers he published jointly with Dobzhansky between 1941 and 1947, prompted by insistent demands from that vigorous and intuitive geneticist for assistance in the planning and analysis of data collected from natural populations of *Drosophila.*

Wright's lectures tended to be scholarly but lengthy; they were well prepared, and were apt to be delivered in a formal fashion even to small classes. They did not appeal to undergraduates, and in later years his lectures in the College were dropped. Graduate courses in fundamental genetics (with a drosophila laboratory), physiological genetics, evolution, and biometry continued. They were delivered in the small, drab lecture room on the third floor of the Zoology Building, and were usually well attended, both by students and auditors from various laboratories on campus. Most of his courses, particularly the last two, typically maintained an emphasis on quantitation and the expression of genetic concepts in mathematical terms. Wright lectured from a pack of 3" × 5" cards, which he shuffled through when they got out of order. He tended to write down equations with great rapidity and to lecture to the blackboard as much as to the class. Students copied equations feverishly, and often complained that material was erased too soon.

The small cage of guinea pigs for demonstration was a frequent prop for the course in physiological genetics. The much reproduced photograph of 1954 shows Wright holding a guinea pig in typical fashion, with equations written on the board behind him. The story is often told that once in his preoccupation he erased the blackboard with the guinea pig instead of the eraser; it seems quite plausible. To this story I have heard him reply, "Well, it could have happened, but it didn't." Among the characters of guinea pigs studied by Wright were genes affecting dorsal hair growth patterns of length and direction. Students taking the "guinea pig course" have pointed out, more with affection than malice, that some of the animals he demonstrated bore an interesting resemblance to the lecturer himself, who parted his hair near the middle, had wavy forelocks, and quick jerky movements.

The lectures were up-to-date. Wright always made conscious attempts to integrate the latest findings into his lectures. I was personally surprised when he incorporated some of my research findings from very recent papers into one of his lectures. I remembered being frustrated, however, when he failed to state my final conclusions, having misplaced the appropriate card. Because the lectures attempted to be contemporary, Wright was usually behind in the lecture outline. On one occasion we met in the hallway. It was near the end of the quarter and he was on the way to class. He told me "So far I've covered half the course. I'm giving them the second half today." This is a phenomenon any professor can understand. On another occasion Wright prepared a final examination for one of his courses, and was upset when none of the usual roomful of students showed up. When he went to the department office to check, he found that his class had consisted entirely of auditors; no one was officially registered. Students tended to sit in on his lectures again and again, partly because they were apt to be so condensed it was hard to absorb all the contents at one sitting, but also because the lectures were continually changed to keep up with new research and new concepts.

There were two centers of activity for Wright's research. The guinea pig colony and record room were in the Whitman Laboratory while the fly laboratory and center for most graduate student research were located in the Zoology Building two blocks away. In later years Wright was seldom at Whitman, and the door was always locked. Across the hall was another research laboratory, for a time occupied by a former student of Wright's, Benson Ginsburg, for his research on the genetics of noise-induced seizures in mice. On one occasion a mouse escaped from the Ginsburg laboratory and ran across the hall under the door of the guinea pig room, pursued by a young and usually timid graduate student. As told by her, since she was mad at the loss and unable to follow she banged on the door and cursed the escaped animal, only to be confronted by Wright, who promptly opened the door to provide what must have been one of her more embarrassing moments. I expect they together searched the room, which was usually almost bare except for files and a table for measuring animals.

In the biographical notes that follow I have relied heavily on the extensive biography by William B. Provine: *Sewall Wright and Evolutionary Biology,* University of Chicago Press, 1986, which includes a complete bibliography of all Wright's publications. Also helpful has been the paper by Horatio Hackett Newman: "History of the Department of Zoology in the University of Chicago," *Bios* 19:215–39, 1948, and an as yet unpublished memoir by Thomas Park, "Sewall Wright: The Chicago Years," prepared for delivery at the American Academy of Arts and Sciences meeting in April 1990, to commemorate the 100th anniversary of Wright's birth, a copy of which was kindly provided by the author. Park's personal recollections of Wright have helped to reinforce my own impressions. The Sewall Wright Papers, about 15,000 pages of letters and manuscripts, and also including 55 audiocassettes of oral history interviews with Provine, have been donated by Provine to the Library of the American Philosophical Society in Philadelphia (*Amer. Philos. Soc. News* 4:4, 1989).

· II ·

Sewall Wright was born in Medford, Massachusetts, in 1889, the oldest of three sons. Brother Quincy became a distinguished professor of international relations at the University of Chicago. Youngest brother Ted became vice-president at Curtiss-Wright, was chairman of the Aircraft Resources Board in the Second World War and then vice-president for research at Cornell University. Their father, with a master's degree from Harvard in economics, worked at the New England Mutual Life Insurance Company at the time of Sewall's birth, but left Massachusetts in 1891 to teach at Lombard College in Galesburg, Illinois. That college then had about 100 students, and Wright senior taught small classes in economics, mathematics, astronomy, and English. He also wrote poetry and was director of the gymnasium. As a boy Sewall roamed the northwestern Illinois countryside, early developing an interest in natural history with collections of butterflies, moths, and birds' eggs. He entered Lombard College in 1907, majoring in chemistry, and taking mathematics courses from his father, the only formal training in mathematics he ever received. He later recalled that, as students, he and his brother ran the school printing press where he helped to set type for a first book of poems by another Lombard student, Carl Sandburg. In the summer of his junior year he worked as surveyor with the Milwaukee Railroad in South Dakota. His first exercise in mathematical application was computing the volumes of dirt needed for cuts and fills, the dimensions estimated by his controlled "standard step." He stayed on for a year but came home in 1910 with a lung infection and diagnosis of possible tuberculosis, declining the offer of a permanent position with the railroad. Once at home, he rapidly recovered and went back to college, obtaining his bachelor of science degree from Lombard in 1911.

During his senior year Wright's interests turned from chemistry and engineering to biology, through contact with a young professor, Wilhelmine Entemann Key, appointed to the college teaching staff the year before. Mrs. Key received her doctorate from Chicago in 1901, one of the first women to receive a doctorate from the University of Chicago. She was a student of the geneticist Charles Benedict Davenport, a pioneer in biostatistics and variation in animals, but she also studied with the first chairman of the department of zoology, Charles Otis Whitman, who was famous for his research on heredity in pigeons. In a seminar with Mrs. Key, Sewall Wright read the classical articles on heredity and evolution by Darwin, Galton, and Wallace, but was particularly impressed with an article by Punnett on Mendelism in the *Encyclopaedia Britannica* of 1911. The remarkable paper by Gregor Mendel on "Experiments in Plant Hybridization," unappreciated at the time it was published in 1866, had been rediscovered in 1900 by three geneticists, Correns, De Vries, and Tschermak, and its impact was spreading among biologists. Much controversy involved whether the patterns of segregation of characters discovered by Mendel were applicable to all organisms, and if so, what was the nature of their implications for the Darwinian conception of evolution.

One can be sure these questions were much discussed at the Cold Spring Harbor Station for Experimental Evolution of the Carnegie Institution of Washington on Long Island, where Wright spent the summer of 1911, sent by Mrs. Key. Davenport became director of the station in 1904, and Mrs. Key wanted her stellar student to have contact with her former adviser. By then Davenport had shifted his interests from animal variation to eugenics, a subject Wright never found particularly appealing. He chose to take a course in invertebrate zoology with Henry S. Pratt, author of the standard text on the systematics of invertebrates. In the fall, Wright continued his study of invertebrates at the University of Illinois in Urbana, but this work was abruptly terminated the following spring, after Wright attended a seminar given by a visitor from Harvard. The talk was by William Ernest Castle, another student of Davenport's, on the genetics of hooded rats. Castle showed that the black and white hooded pattern could be shifted among progeny to all black or almost all white by selective breeding. Wright was fascinated by the implications of these studies, and immediately applied to Castle to continue his graduate work at Harvard. His research at Urbana was completed for a master's degree, on the anatomy of a flatworm (trematode), under the direction of Henry B. Ward.

Next summer (1912) was again spent at Cold Spring Harbor, where Wright studied the estuarine ecology of fresh-water and salt-water snails and then left for Harvard in the fall. He was given the position of caretaker of Castle's guinea pig colony, which was housed at the Bussey Institution. Two important genetic problems concerned the Castle laboratory at that time, the effects of inbreeding (for which Castle pioneered in the first use of *Drosophila* for genetic studies), and whether the "determinants" of Mendel, which we now know as genes, retained their characteristics even when their genetic background was experimentally altered. Behind both problems was the attempt to understand the nature of genes and gene action, and the role of mutation and selection in the evolutionary process. The followers of Hugo De Vries, the influential Dutch plant physiologist, believed that new species could arise by single mutations, which they thought of as sudden major changes in the structure of organisms, based on the classic De Vriesan studies on evening primroses. Others felt that most change occurred gradually through the accumulation of numerous small events in the repeated selection of many genes each with small effects. Over the next three years, Wright made and analyzed several hundred guinea pig crosses. In his doctoral dissertation, entitled "An Intensive Study of the Inheritance of Color and Other Coat Characters in Guinea Pigs," several genetic problems, puzzling to workers in Castle's laboratory, were explored. This "intensive study" indicated that many of the baffling segregation patterns could be explained by the phenomenon of incomplete or partial dominance, the presence of one or more modifying genes, and by the occurrence of allelic series (i.e., alternative forms or alleles of a particular gene). These are now all well-recognized phenomena, but in 1915 their application to mammalian genetics was pioneering. This work, possibly more than any other from the Castle laboratory at that time, demonstrated that the effects of genetic characters could be modified when placed against new backgrounds but could, with proper crosses, be readily recovered and shown to be basically unchanged. Thus genes were specific entities not altered by changes in their genetic context. Wright also showed that apparent continuous variation in coat color and texture—what the non-Mendelians considered to demonstrate blending inheritance—were attributable to the relatively small effects of modifiers and to the presence of multiple alleles, but the genetic units themselves were nevertheless discrete and stable. Many problems of guinea pig inheritance had not yet been readily explained, but from the success of his doctoral research, the theory of the importance of sudden large mutations was refuted, and the optimistic attitude prevailed that many presently inexplicable mysteries of heredity and evolution could be readily dispelled by application of Mendelian principles.

Wright's first position following his receipt of the Ph.D. was with the United States Department of Agriculture. He left Harvard in September 1915 for Bethesda, Maryland, to work at the Animal Husbandry Division in the analysis of their extensive records on guinea pigs, thirty-five lines of which had been inbred since 1906. The studies had been developed to obtain data of relevance for cattle breeding, but the carefully kept records had largely gone unanalyzed. The next ten years at Bethesda were highly productive, resulting in some forty papers which established Wright's reputation as an accomplished mammalian geneticist. Among the papers were a basic series on hair color inheritance in nine different mammals, including guinea pigs and humans, analysis of hair pigmentation in physiological terms, the effects of inbreeding on guinea pigs and cattle, development of a statistical method for the analysis of single factors against a multiple factor background (path coefficients), and the first of many theoretical papers on the evolution of gene frequencies in natural populations. During a summer period again spent at Cold Spring Harbor in 1920, Wright met Louise Williams, a young instructor in genetics from Smith College. They were married in September.

· III ·

In November 1924, Castle wrote to tell Wright that the University of Chicago was looking for a geneticist. At the time the chairman of the department of zoology was the embryologist Frank R. Lillie, later dean of the division of biological sciences, director of the Marine Biological Laboratory at Woods Hole, and president of the National Academy of Sciences. Also in the department were Benjamin H. Willier in embryology, Charles Manning Child in embryology and regeneration, Carl R. Moore in endocrinology, Horatio Hackett Newman in genetics, and Warder Clyde Allee in ecology and behavior in animal communities. Wright expressed reluctance to leave the extensive animal colony at Bethesda, but was encouraged by Lillie to bring some of his guinea pigs with him to Chicago. New space and new pens for the animals were provided in the Guinea Pig House, a one-room building beside the Whitman Laboratory attached by a breezeway to disperse animal odors in the days before air conditioning. Wright accepted the invitation in March 1925, and looked forward to the association with his distinguished new colleagues. The department, with Lillie, Willier, and Child, was strong in embryology. Wright early expressed an interest in the role of genetic mechanisms in development, but except for the descriptive research of a graduate student, and his early work on different strengths of alleles in the production of gradations of coat colors, which he correctly postulated indicated genetic control of the pigments producing enzymes, he did no further research on the subject. The current explosion of basic understanding in the field of developmental genetics happened only recently, too late to engage Wright's research interests. In the 1920s and 1930s the chemical nature of the gene was not understood, and its role in development was scarcely glimpsed. Both Child and Lillie were busy postulating gradients and morphogenetic fields in development, for which there were as yet no chemical guideposts. Child never accepted the concept that chromosomes were associated with heredity or development, as indicated by his vigorous—and quite erroneous—defense of amitosis, the supposedly unregulated separation of one interphase nucleus into two during cell division in the process of tissue regeneration. Although Wright, Child, and Willier took weekend excursions together to the dune country, and Wright always had good friends among his colleagues, he must have been disappointed in their lack of appreciation of his research interests. Newman taught genetics, but he was a student of Lillie in embryology, did no research in genetics, and was largely concerned with undergraduate teaching. He later became known for his studies on the characteristics of identical twins, as indicators of which human traits were under genetic control.

With the optimism provided by the success of his research at the Department of Agriculture, and in anticipation of the pleasures of academic life, Wright came with his wife, Louise, and their two young boys to Chicago in January 1926. The assignment to teach six courses a year in general zoology and genetics was somewhat daunting, since Wright had never met formal classes. His research on guinea pigs, with their slow development and large chromosome number, was scarcely appropriate to laboratory exercises for students. Wright obtained *Drosophila* stocks from the Columbia University Laboratory of T. H. Morgan, and prepared laboratory sessions with them for the class. Since fruit fly males may become sterilized by the summer heat, water tables were prepared, as at Columbia, so bottoms of the bottles could be cooled in running tap water, a mechanism long since abandoned in favor of cold rooms and air conditioning. In 1928 the Wright family moved into a modest frame house on the 5700 block of Harper Avenue, with an enormous cottonwood tree in the back yard. Their third child, Betty, was born in 1929. Brother Quincy and the Williers lived nearby. The house was to serve the Wrights throughout their stay in Chicago.

Wright had eighteen graduate students and five postdoctoral students during his twenty-nine years in Chicago. Most students worked on problems of mammalian physiological genetics, including eight on guinea pig hair color and patterning, three on mice, and five on problems of *Drosophila*. Only one student worked on population genetics, the area on which Wright's later reputation was based. At Chicago, Wright considered himself as a physiological geneticist. The theoretical studies on population structure he kept largely for himself, but these increasingly occupied his attention.

It is possible in a small space to provide only the barest outlines of Wright's scientific contributions to both laboratory experimentation and genetic theory. It is also necessary to consider the contributions in the context of the history of his science, since genetics, like most other fields, changed fundamentally both in experimental approach and in theory during the period of Wright's scientific career.

Guinea pig genetics proved to be exceedingly complex, and beyond the initial findings from Harvard and the Department of Agriculture, the studies in Chicago largely provided ever finer consideration of the intricacies of gene interaction. Extensive allelic series were described that affected spotting patterns and hair texture and direction of growth. Effects of the same allele were shown to differ markedly under the influence of different modifying genes. With carefully controlled matings, the seemingly endless variety of phenotype (the physical appearance of an individual) could be attributed to the specific interaction of a finite series of alleles. Although the extent of gene interaction was frequently unpredictable, the crosses where the genetic background was controlled were very reproducible. Effects of multiple genes were cumulative. With appropriate selection procedures, major changes in progeny could result by the concerted action of numerous small changes. These fundamental aspects of genetic systems were important not only in making animal breeding into a science; they also provided valuable clues to the way genes act in evolution.

The inbreeding experiments, carried on for many generations, resulted in a striking demonstration of the wide number of characteristics that are under genetic control. As summarized by Wright in 1977 (*J. Animal Science* 46:1192–1200), animals from one inbred line had long legs and walked well off the ground. In another the legs were so short the animals glided along on their stomachs, "like oversize planarians." Some strains had rounded noses and bent ears, in others the noses were pointed and the ears erect. Some had protruding eyes, while in others the eyes were sunken. Litter size and general vigor, number of stillborn, characteristic color pattern, size and shape of internal organs (thyroid, adrenal, spleen) showed striking differences. There were also striking differences in temperament—some strains could be picked up like sacks of meal while others struggled violently. Strains were also later shown to be markedly different in susceptibility to tuberculosis. Such patterns have since been demonstrated with even more striking variety in mouse strains developed by Wright's students, Elizabeth Russell at the Jackson Laboratory in Bar Harbor, Maine, an institution that supplies purebred mice to research workers around the world, and also by William L. Russell, who helped to develop the enormous mouse-breeding facilities at the Oak Ridge National Laboratory in Tennessee. Later work on the inbred guinea pig lines in Chicago included the detailed study of otocephaly, where jaw structures become congenitally deformed, and the presence of extra digits (polydactyly). Both conditions were shown to be affected in their incidence by multiple genetic factors but also strongly influenced by nongenetic factors, such as maternal age.

Can evolutionary processes be explained by our knowledge of the nature of the gene and gene action? Wright started work on a genetic modeling of evolution in the early 1920s, basing his theories on guinea pig crosses and his analysis of records of cattle breeding for the Department of Agriculture. His ideas were stimulated by the early papers of British statistician R. A. Fisher, particularly in the Fisherian concept of the evolution of dominance, and also by the British physiologist and geneticist J. B. S.

Haldane. Both Fisher and Haldane, like Wright, were attempting to predict the distribution of genes in natural populations of sexually reproducing organisms in accordance with Mendelian segregation patterns. Fisher's first papers on population genetics concerned his theory of the origins of dominant genes through selection, with which Wright disagreed. Their correspondence in 1922 was polite and circumspect, but the interaction in print became more contentious in the years ahead. All three considered that the major factors influencing the genetic composition of natural populations were population size, rates of mutation, selection pressures, number of alleles present at one location, and rates of migration. The basic concepts in the models of Wright, Fisher, and Haldane were often similar, but disagreement, sometimes heated, lay in the relative importance attached to particular variables, especially population size.

Wright's most influential paper, "Evolution in Mendelian Populations," was published in 1931, after five years of preparation and more than a year in press. (*Genetics,* 16:97–159, 1931). It was followed by "The Roles of Mutation, Inbreeding, Crossbreeding and Selection in Evolution," presented to the Sixth International Congress of Genetics in Ithaca, New York, in 1932 (*Proceedings of the Sixth International Congress of Genetics,* 1: 356–66). The papers attracted wide and immediate attention, although from contemporary comments it is clear they were held somewhat in awe by geneticists who often embraced the conclusion but found the statistical treatment difficult to understand. The nature of the theory in Wright's own summary, made in 1932, is as follows;

> I have attempted to form a judgment as to the conditions for evolution based on the statistical consequences of Mendelian heredity. The most general conclusion is that evolution depends on a certain balance among its factors. There must be gene mutation, but an excessive rate gives any array of freaks, not evolution; there must be selection, but too severe a process destroys the field of variability, and thus the basis for further advance; prevalence of local inbreeding within a species has extremely important evolutionary consequences, but too close inbreeding leads merely to extinction. A certain amount of crossbreeding is favorable but not too much. In this dependence on balance the species is like a living organism. At all levels of organization life depends on the maintenance of a certain balance among its factors.

The theory is novel and important in several respects. It emphasizes the balance of factors that Wright postulated were continuously active in a bisexually interbreeding population, "like a living organism." It also demonstrated that the size of the population, which controlled the frequency of inbreeding, was an essential factor. In very small populations particular alleles may be lost or reach complete fixation, because each offspring of necessity contains only half the gene pool of the two parents. A small population "is extremely uniform. Only very rarely is an old gene replaced by a new one. Even severe selection has little effect, and the fixation process, being random, is in general injurious. The end can only be extinction for a group, permanently reduced below a certain size of population (in relation to other evolutionary factors)." On the other hand, in very large populations "random variation of gene frequencies is a negligible factor. . . . Although the variability of the population may be great . . . the average condition remains the same as long as conditions are constant." Wright concluded: "Neither a small nor a large freely interbreeding population offers an adequate basis for a continuing evolutionary process" (1931, *Journal of the American Statistical Association* 26 [Suppl.]: 201–2). The optimal conditions for evolutionary change are considered to be a large population, broken up by geographical terrain or other isolating factors, into a number of small, partially but not completely, isolated subpopulations. This would permit the random events of gene fixation or loss to occur, but if the subpopulation still maintained occasional crossbreeding contact with neighboring populations, novel and occasionally successful new gene combinations could result. Thus the small, partially isolated population would escape the dire fate of gene loss or fixation, and on rare but significant occasions could launch out in new directions. Such innovative populations could then grow and develop under new patterns of selection. Eventually by migration and crossbreeding they could favorably affect surrounding populations, and their influence would spread. Wright thus postulated that the essentially random processes which control gene frequencies in small populations produce "genetic drift" which can help the small, partially isolated population to override the pressures of selection. Large homogeneous populations, on the other hand, may become well adapted to their environment through processes of mutation and selection, but the population goes nowhere in evolution, unless selection pressure somehow changes, for example, by a shift in environmental pressures.

The concept of "genetic drift" acting on small, partially isolated populations, many evolutionary geneticists found particularly attractive. The theory also caused great controversy. R. A. Fisher and others unfairly accused

Wright of replacing the concept of Darwinian selection with the concept of "genetic drift," which Fisher and E. B. Ford, in 1950 (*Heredity* 4:117–19), named the "Sewall Wright effect." Although Wright somewhat softened the emphasis placed on random processes in later versions of his theory, he staunchly maintained that genetic drift always worked in conjunction with selection but was never a substitute for it. On the other hand, Fisher never acknowledged that "genetic drift" had anything to do with evolutionary processes, which he considered always took place in large populations. The controversy, at first with polite letters and later with increasingly acerbic printed commentary, continued unabated until Fisher's death in 1962.

At the International Congress of Genetics in 1932, Wright was asked to explain his theory to his colleagues in a plenary address, where statistical equations seemed inappropriate. For this talk he devised his famous evolutionary landscape, where his multifactorial space was considered in three dimensions, as a terrain with peaks and valleys. One could imagine populations of organisms occupying the peaks of the landscape, where the heights represented degrees of evolutionary fitness. Large populations were considered to be trapped on peaks, unable to explore new gene arrangements because of their size. The very small populations again were subject to loss and fixation of genes, and faced extinction. The large population, broken up into subpopulations, however, could explore new combinations, through random events, and on rare occasions they crossed valleys to develop new peaks of fitness. To illustrate his theory, Wright drew a series of diagrams of his "field of gene combinations," figures that graphically illustrated his concept of gene balance in evolution. The diagrams have been widely reproduced. Even though the statistical analysis of factors in evolution was scarcely comprehended by many geneticists, the diagrams helped them to obtain an intuitive glimpse of the theory.

Over the rest of his career Wright published almost sixty papers on the statistical distribution of gene frequencies in the evolutionary process, including the monumental *Evolution and the Genetics of Populations,* which was published by the University of Chicago Press between 1968 and 1978. His papers of 1931 and 1932, however, laid the foundations for much of his later work in evolutionary genetics, which concerned the development of mathematical statements of greater simplicity and generality. He also considered the application of his theories to special cases such as polyploid speciation and the influence of genes for self-sterility.

On two occasions he collaborated with geneticists who were attempting to apply his theoretical concepts to actual gene frequencies obtained in the field and laboratory. The five papers with Dobzhansky in *Genetics* between 1941 and 1947 were in part an effort to find and to quantitate genetic drift, but although they provided much important information on species polymorphism, the populations of *Drosophila pseudoobscura* in the high Sierras proved to be much too large. The three papers published in collaboration with the Brazilian bee geneticist, Warwick E. Kerr in *Evolution,* in 1954 when he was on sabbatical leave in Madison, on the other hand, involved very small laboratory populations of *Drosophila melanogaster,* and the postulated and obtained drift in gene frequencies were in complete agreement.

In 1980 the Field Museum in Chicago held a Conference on Macroevolution, stimulated by the "punctuated equilibrium" theory of paleontologists Niles Eldredge and Stephen Gould. Paleontologists have frequently noted that new species seem to appear abruptly in the fossil record, and that intergrades with older related forms are rare. If morphological changes in evolution occurred gradually over time, blending one form into another, as classical concepts of evolution would postulate, then the fossil record should show these intergrades. Intergrades do occur within some lineages, but, as noted by Darwin, they tend to be very scarce. Assuming the record presents a true picture of the rates of structural change in evolution, this distribution of fossils suggests that species undergo long periods of morphologic stability punctuated on rare occasions by the rapid development of new forms. Eldredge and Gould suggest that these periods of rapid speciation occur in the peripheral regions of species distribution (allopatric speciation). Whether or not these periods of rapid speciation are attributable to genetic drift alone (i.e., the "Sewall Wright effect") or involve some as yet ill-defined evolutionary mechanism has been much discussed, although an early resolution of the question seems unlikely. In 1980 Wright, at the age of ninety, presented a paper at the Macroevolution Conference, entitled "Character Change, Speciation, and the Higher Taxa," published in *Evolution* (1982, 36:427–43). The diagrams of the field of gene combinations were again presented. Wright told Provine that he had more reprint requests for this paper then for any other he ever published. This is evidence of the surprising amount of interest the theory of punctuated equilibrium has engendered. The theory, as commented on by the evolutionary geneticist John Maynard Smith in *Did Darwin Get It Right?* (Chapman and Hall, New York, 1989, p. 11), is "reminiscent of those of Hugo De Vries and early Mendelians, but rest[s] on a misunderstanding of the fossil record rather than of mutation."

The importance of Wright's papers on evolutionary theory and the creativity of his approach were widely recognized around the world. Among his numerous honors were nine honorary degrees, including those from Yale in 1949 and Harvard in 1951. He mentioned, on his return from Harvard, that no one at that University had offered to pay his travel expenses to Cambridge, so in typical fashion, he paid them himself, and I doubt if he ever mentioned the oversight to his hosts. Wright became president of the Genetics Society of America in 1934, the American Society of Zoologists in 1944, the American Society of Naturalists in 1952 and the Society for the Study of Evolution in 1955. He also received the Daniel Giraud Elliot Award from the National Academy of Sciences, the Weldon Memorial Medal from Oxford University, and the Lewis Prize from the American Philosophical Society. He also gave the Hitchcock lectures at the University of California, Berkeley, in 1943.

At one time Wright agreed to write a monograph on statistical genetics, in collaboration with Alexander Weinstein, geneticist at Johns Hopkins University. The project was repeatedly delayed and then put off for the retirement years. At Chicago the teaching load, heavy by contemporary standards, the conscientious fulfilling of his obligations to the community of geneticists through correspondence and manuscript reviews, the graduate students, and the guinea pigs took a tremendous portion of his time.

A sabbatical leave was arranged in 1954 which Sewall and Louise spent in Edinburgh. He had hopes that he could spend a quiet year in Scotland working on his monograph. But upon his arrival in Edinburgh, Wright found that a course of lectures had been planned by the department of genetics, and there were also numerous requests for seminars around the country. Wright also told how he had rented a car, and was proud of the way he had mastered left-hand driving and a strange gear shift, although his first encounter with the newly rented vehicle on the car rental lot was to drive it violently backwards with almost, but not quite, disastrous results. He said the rental agent followed his departure from the lot with a worried look. To anyone who had ridden in a car driven by Wright, this was scarcely surprising, since his mind often seemed to dwell on intellectual matters and not on the immediate environment. Also the car was apt to acquire something of the quick and jerky movements characteristic of the driver.

· IV ·

Wright was asked to stay on at the University of Chicago past the age of sixty-five, and to continue with his research program. He chose instead to accept the offer of a professorship at the University of Wisconsin, and for the first years there to teach a graduate seminar. He closed his guinea pig colony before he left Chicago, but took enough unpublished data with him to produce seven more papers on guinea pig genetics. For most of the time, however, he concentrated on his theoretical studies on evolutionary genetics. Provine attributed his leaving Chicago to his concern about the deterioration of the campus neighborhood, but a more important factor probably was the lateness of the offer that came from the University of Chicago to remain. Carl Moore was chairman of the department of zoology from 1934 until his death in 1955. He was ill for many months, suffering from a terminal blood disorder, and near the end of his life attended to departmental duties only with great personal effort. By the time the delayed offer from Chicago was made, Wright had already accepted the bid from James Crow in Madison. The Chicago neighborhood has changed somewhat, but has not deteriorated. The block of frame houses on Harper Avenue is much the same today.

The Madison period in Wright's life was remarkably productive. He had the opportunity for rewarding interaction with old friends, particularly Malcolm R. Irwin, R. A. Brink, and James F. Crow. The students and postdoctoral fellows of the Crow laboratory, particularly Motoo Kimura from Japan, were also a great stimulus. The Wrights lived less than three miles from the campus in Madison, and on most occasions over the years Wright walked to work.

Clearly one of the most remarkable accomplishments in Wright's life was his four-volume treatise on *Evolution and the Genetics of Populations,* written over a ten-year period from 1968 to 1978. This gave him the opportunity to rework many of his lifelong attempts to characterize in quantitative terms the genetic factors that shape the process of evolution and also to place his shifting-balance theory in the context of later concepts of evolutionary biology. Volume I, *Genetic and Biometric Foundations,* reviews theories of evolution and discusses the nature of genetic systems, including allelic series, gene interaction, and their analysis by path coefficients. Volume 2, The *Theory of Gene Frequencies,* discusses the mathematical treatment of gene frequencies in populations. Volume 3, *Experimental Results and Evolutionary Deductions,* presents the shifting-balance theory in the light of experimental studies on laboratory populations and animal breeding. Volume 4, *Variability within and among Natural Populations,* discusses the data obtained from field studies and their interpretation.

When Kimura came to Madison in 1955 to work with Crow, he confronted Wright with his concept of neutral mutations in evolution. Molecular studies on proteins and DNA demonstrate that a tremendous amount of variability exists among the individuals within a single population. The classical concept that most mutations are deleterious and rapidly selected against can no longer be accepted in the context of all this genetic variation. It must follow that most mutations are selectively neutral or nearly so. Kimura concluded that mutation frequency had been grossly underestimated. It is interesting to note Wright's reaction. In a letter to Kimura he states that his (Wright's) theory "applies only to mutations that have some conspicuous physiological effect, and has nothing to do with nucleotide replacements or amino acid replacements that have no physiological consequences." Again in Volume 3 of *Evolution and the Genetics of Populations* Wright discusses briefly some of the more striking contemporary molecular analyses of gene structure, e.g., the small amount of DNA that actually codes for structural genes, the large amounts of DNA sequences too simple in base sequence structure to code for proteins, and the evidence for multiple gene families. These and other findings, which have had a tremendous impact upon our concept of evolution obviously greatly interested Wright, but he did not find them destructive to his shifting-balance theory, provided that alleles are considered to be "those that could . . . be separated by breeding tests."

The great power and robustness of Wright's theories of the evolutionary process derive from their comprehensive and fundamental qualities, aspects that cannot be subverted by the complexities of molecular biology. They are also why a basic theory proposed in 1931, highly significant to the history of population genetics, can be refurbished and reworked in 1977 and still be required learning for the students of today. It has been a tremendous stimulus over the past sixty years to all students of evolutionary biology. But an inherent difficulty lies in its intestability. Richard Lewontin, for a period Wright's successor in population genetics in Chicago, voiced his despair that the role of chance processes in evolution could ever be evaluated. "The most that such a theory can do is to tell us not to be surprised at anything we see and to caution us against supposing that only one hypothesis will explain our observations" (*The Genetic Basis of Evolutionary Change,* Columbia University Press, 1974, p. 269). Concerning the famous controversy between Wright and Fisher, the contemporary comments of John Maynard Smith (1989, ibid., pp. 13–14) are of interest. "There are, however, two points of view, which one could almost call the 'English' view, deriving from Fisher, and the "American' view, deriving from Wright. To oversimplify matters somewhat, Fisher thought that each substitution of one gene for another in evolution occurred because it was beneficial, on its own, and that the role of chance events (other than mutation) was slight. Wright thinks that, often, several gene substitutions would be beneficial if they occurred simultaneously, but that each by itself would be harmful. If so, the only way the change can take place is by chance in a small local population. In effect, the English think that evolution is a hill-climbing process, and the Americans that it also involves jumping across valleys. As a student of Haldane's, I take an impartial view." A leading evolutionary geneticist, almost sixty years after the first salvos of the battle, still cannot name the victor.

What cannot be demonstrated in a popular discussion is anything concerning the artistry and creativity of Wright's mathematical approach to problems of great intellectual complexity. Wright was largely a self-taught mathematician. He often derived his own detours around difficult obstacles in routes that others might not take. He also tackled problems others considered insoluble, and reworked his equations again and again to bring to them greater simplicity and power. The intellectual accomplishments of the Madison period surely constitute one of the milestones in the history of genetics. In 1979 Wright returned to Chicago to receive the Laing Prize, awarded by the University of Chicago Press to the author of their most notable book of the year, for volume 3 of *Evolution and the Genetics of Populations*. Again, in December of the same year, he was invited back to Chicago for a symposium in his honor. On that occasion we had the privilege of celebrating his ninetieth birthday.

CONTRIBUTORS

Gabriel A. Almond is professor emeritus of political science at Stanford University.

Edward C. Banfield is the George Markham Professor of Government Emeritus at Harvard University.

Gary S. Becker is University Professor of Economics and Sociology and re-search associate at the Economics Research Center of the National Opinion Research Center at the University of Chicago.

Martin J. Beckmann is professor emeritus of economics at Brown University and of applied mathematics and statistics at the Technische Universität, Munich.

R. Stephen Berry is the James Franck Distinguished Service Professor in the department of chemistry at the University of Chicago.

Vincent Blasi is the Corliss Lamont Professor of Civil Liberties at Columbia University Law School.

Robert H. Bork is the John M. Olin Scholar in Legal Studies at the American Enterprise Institute.

Felix Browder is vice-president for research at Rutgers University.

James M. Buchanan is the Holbert L. Harris University Professor of Economics at George Mason University. In 1986 he was awarded the Nobel Prize in economics.

Gerhard Casper is provost and William B. Graham Distinguished Service Professor of Law at the University of Chicago.

Subrahmanyan Chandrasekhar is the Morton D. Hull Distinguished Service Professor Emeritus in the departments of astronomy and astrophysics, and of physics, at the University of Chicago. In 1983 he was awarded the Nobel Prize in physics.

Ronald Coase is senior fellow in law and economics and Clifton R. Musser Professor Emeritus of Economics in the Law School at the University of Chicago.

Peter F. Dembowski is Distinguished Service Professor of Romance Languages and Literatures and a member of the Committee on Medieval Studies at the University of Chicago.

Fred Eggan was the Harold H. Swift Distinguished Service Professor Emeritus of Anthropology and director of the Philippine Studies Program at the University of Chicago.

Hans G. Güterbock is the Tiffany and Margaret Blake Distinguished Service Professor Emeritus of the Oriental Institute and the departments of Near Eastern languages and civilizations and linguistics at the University of Chicago.

John N. Hazard is the Nash Professor Emeritus of Law at Columbia University.

Alfred Heller is professor in the department of pharmacological and physiological sciences at the University of Chicago.

Richard Hellie is professor of Russian history in the department of history and is chairman of the Russian Civilization Program in the College at the University of Chicago.

Paul Hodges is professor emeritus of radiology at the University of Chicago.

Philip C. Hoffmann is professor in the department of pharmacological sciences at the University of Chicago.

Charles Huggins is the William B. Ogden Distinguished Service Professor Emeritus in the Ben May Institute and the department of surgery at the

University of Chicago. In 1966 he was awarded the Nobel Prize in medicine and physiology.

Clyde A. Hutchison Jr. is the Carl William Eisendrath Distinguished Service Professor Emeritus in the department of chemistry at the University of Chicago.

Leon O. Jacobson is the Joseph Regenstein Professor Emeritus the Biological and Medical Sciences at the University of Chicago.

Abraham Kaplan is professor emeritus of philosophy and chairman of the department of philosophy and dean of the faculty of social sciences at Haifa University, Israel.

Richard L. Landau is emeritus professor of medicine at the University of Chicago, Pritzker School of Medicine.

Louise H. Marshall is associate director of the neuroscience history program, Brain Research Institute, University of California at Los Angeles.

Elder Olson is Distinguished Service Professor Emeritus of English at the University of Chicago.

Triloki N. Pandey is professor of anthropology and a fellow of Crown College at the University of California, Santa Cruz.

Erica Reiner is the John A. Wilson Distinguished Service Professor of the Oriental Institute and the departments of Near Eastern languages and civilizations and linguistics.

Leo Rosten is an author residing in New York City.

Donald A. Rowley is professor in the departments of pediatrics and pathology at the University of Chicago.

Robert G. Sachs is professor emeritus in the department of physics and the Enrico Fermi Institute at the University of Chicago.

Paul A. Samuelson is Institute Professor Emeritus at the Massachusetts Institute of Technology. He was awarded the Nobel Prize in economics in 1970.

Sidney Schulman is the Ellen C. Manning Professor of Neurology in the division of the biological sciences at the University of Chicago.

Edward Shils is Distinguished Service Professor in the Committee on Social Thought and the department of sociology at the University of Chicago, and Honorary Fellow of Peterhouse, Cambridge. In 1983 he was awarded the International Balzan Prize for sociology.

Lee S. Shulman is the Charles E. Ducommun Professor of Education and professor of psychology at Leland Stanford University.

John A. Simpson is the Arthur Holly Compton Distinguished Service Professor Emeritus in the department of physics and the Enrico Fermi Institute at the University of Chicago.

Milton Singer is professor emeritus of anthropology and the Paul Klapper Professor Emeritus of the Social Sciences in the College at the University of Chicago.

Hewson Swift is the George Wells Beadle Distinguished Service Professor Emeritus of molecular genetics, cell biology and pathology at the University of Chicago.

Paul Talalay is the John Jacob Abel Distinguished Service Professor in the department of pharmacology and molecular sciences at the Johns Hopkins University School of Medicine.

V. L. Telegdi is visiting professor at the Charles C. Lauritsen Laboratory of High Energy Physics of the California Institute of Technology.

Edward Teller is director emeritus of the Lawrence National Laboratory and senior research fellow at the Hoover Institution on War, Revolution, and Peace.

Kameshwar C. Wali is professor of physics at Syracuse University.

W. Allen Wallis is resident scholar at the American Enterprise Institute in Washington, D.C.

James Whitman is assistant professor of law at Leland Stanford University.

PHOTO CREDITS

ERNEST W. BURGESS, about 1950. Photo by Stephen Deutch. Courtesy of the University of Chicago Archives.

PAUL R. CANNON. John Kaspar Studio. Courtesy of the University of Chicago Archives.

RUDOLF CARNAP. Courtesy of the University of Chicago Archives.

SUBRAHMANYAN CHANDRASEKHAR, 1984. Photo by K. G. Somsekhar.

LOWELL T. COGGESHALL. Courtesy of the University of Chicago News and Publications.

ARTHUR HOLLY COMPTON, about 1940. Courtesy of the University of Chicago Archives.

R. S. CRANE. Courtesy of the University of Chicago Archives.

FRED EGGAN. Photo by Joan Eggan. Courtesy of Joan Eggan.

ENRICO FERMI. Courtesy of the University of Chicago Archives.

ENRICO FERMI (Portrait). Courtesy of the University of Chicago News and Publications.

JAMES FRANCK. Town and Country Photographers. Courtesy of the University of Chicago Archives.

MILTON FRIEDMAN. Courtesy of the University of Chicago Archives.

E. M. K. GEILING. Wide World Photos, Inc. Courtesy of the University of Chicago Archives.

CHARLES JUDSON HERRICK, around 1955. Courtesy of Louise H. Marshall.

CHARLES BRENTON HUGGINS, 1987. © Copyright David Teplica MD, MFA; courtesy of the Catherine Edelman Gallery, Chicago.

ROBERT MAYNARD HUTCHINS. Photo by Myron Davis, Life Magazine © Copyright Time Warner Inc.

HARRY G. JOHNSON, about 1975. Courtesy of the University of Chicago News and Publications.

ARCADIUS KAHAN. Photo by Mark Hankin.

HARRY KALVEN. Courtesy of the University of Chicago Archives.

HEINRICH KLÜVER. Courtesy of the University of Chicago Archives.

FRANK H. KNIGHT. Courtesy of the University of Chicago Archives.

TJALLING C. KOOPMANS, 1975. Courtesy of the University of Chicago Archives.

BENNO LANDSBERGER, 1965. Photo by Ursula Schneider. Courtesy of The Oriental Institute of The University of Chicago.

HAROLD D. LASSWELL. Courtesy of the University of Chicago News and Publications.

EDWARD LEVI. Courtesy of the University of Chicago Archives.

RICHARD MCKEON. Courtesy of the University of Chicago Archives.

FRANKLIN CHAMBERS MCLEAN. Photo by Karsh, Ottawa. Courtesy of the University of Chicago Archives.

MARIA GOEPPERT MAYER. Courtesy of the University of Chicago Archives.

CHARLES EDWARD MERRIAM, 1911. Courtesy of the University of Chicago Archives.

ARNALDO MOMIGLIANO. Courtesy of the University of Chicago Archives.

ROBERT SANDERSON MULLIKEN, 1984. Courtesy of the University of Chicago News and Publications.

A. LEO OPPENHEIM. Courtesy of the University of Chicago News and Publications.

ROBERT E. PARK. Courtesy of the University of Chicago Archives.

DALLAS B. PHEMISTER. Courtesy of the University of Chicago Archives.

A. R. RADCLIFFE-BROWN. Courtesy of Milton Singer.

ROBERT REDFIELD, 1951. Photo by Stephen Lewellyn. Courtesy of the University of Chicago Archives.

MAX RHEINSTEIN. Courtesy of the University of Chicago Archives.

LEONARD JIMMIE SAVAGE. Courtesy of the Department of Statistics, University of Chicago.

JOSEPH JACKSON SCHWAB. Courtesy of the University of Chicago News and Publications.

GEORGE J. STIGLER, about 1960. Photo by Charles Reynolds.

MARSHALL STONE, 1952. Photo by Stephen Lewellyn. Courtesy of the University of Chicago Archives.

LEO STRAUSS. Courtesy of the University of Chicago Archives.

OTTO STRUVE. Courtesy of the University of Chicago Archives.

HAROLD CLAYTON UREY, 1955. Photo by Frank P. Fritz. Courtesy of the University of Chicago Archives. Reprinted from Popular Mechanics, April 1955. © Copyright The Hearst Corporation. All Rights Reserved.

JACOB VINER. Courtesy of the *Journal of Political Economy.*

BERNARD WEINBERG. Courtesy of the University of Chicago Archives.

QUINCY WRIGHT. Courtesy of the University of Chicago Archives.

SEWALL WRIGHT. Photo by Ernest Martin. Courtesy of the University of Chicago Archives.